Operations Research

NITA H. SHAH
Professor, Department of Mathematics
Gujarat University, Ahmedabad

RAVI M. GOR
Associate Professor
Department of Mathematics
Gujarat University, Ahmedabad

HARDIK SONI
Professor
Chimanbhai Patel Institute of Computer Applications
Gujarat University, Ahmedabad

PHI Learning Private Limited
Delhi-110092
2018

₹ 350.00

OPERATIONS RESEARCH

Nita H. Shah, Ravi M. Gor, and Hardik Soni

ISBN-978-81-203-3128-0

The export rights of this book are vested solely with the publisher.

Seventh Printing ... ... December, 2017

Published by Asoke K. Ghosh, PHI Learning Private Limited, Rimjhim House, 111, Patparganj Industrial Estate, Delhi-110092 and Printed by Mudrak, 30-A, Patparganj, Delhi-110092.

Contents

Preface

Operations Research is a scientific approach to problem solving. It requires the formulation of mathematical, economical and statistical models for decision and control problem, to deal with the situations arising out of risk and uncertainty. In the process of various sub-systems of the organization, various decisions are involved, viz. strategic decisions, tactical decisions and operational decisions. Decision makers have to apply scientific techniques to analyze the firm's ongoing activities like production scheduling, inventory control, maintenance, replacement, etc. Thus, operations research may be defined as the application of scientific tools to decision making problems arising from operations involving integrated systems of people, machines and materials. The aim of operations research is to find the best possible course of action of a decision making problem with or without constraints.

For over 50 years, hundreds of thousands of students globally have been exposed to operations research in various disciplines. The implications of the various topics of operations research motivated us to come out with a book that meets the demands of forthcoming generations of students. The book caters to the needs of students of various disciplines where the subject is taught. However, we feel that the essential theory of operations research can best be understood and appreciated if it is presented from a mathematical viewpoint.

In this text, an attempt is made to provide the theoretical aspects of the subject with practical applications. It covers the following topics: linear programming, integer programming, goal programming, non-linear programming, geometric programming, transportation problems, assignment problems, decision analysis, inventory models, queuing theory, replacement models, network analysis, project management, sequencing problems, simulation and game theory.

The optimization of linear programming problem (LPP) by graphical method, simplex method and dual simplex method is presented. Sensitivity analysis is also carried out. Mathematical methods and solved examples are given in transportation and assignment problems. In LPP, the property of the continuity of the variable may lead to some practical difficulties, for example units cannot be produced in fractions, and rounding off the solution of LPP to the nearest integer may not conclude to optimal solution. Hence, the concept of integer programming is introduced, followed by the cutting-plane algorithm, branch-and-bound algorithm, and zero-one implicit enumeration technique. The concept of achieving different goals in the order of priority to optimize the objective function is discussed in goal programming. Non-linear programming problem techniques are given to illustrate the Lagrangian method, Kuhn–Tucker conditions and quadratic programming. The various criteria of decision making under certainty, uncertainty and risk are discussed in decision analysis. These criteria, when extended to competitive situations among two opponents, lead to the theory of games.

Four types of basic inventory models are explained to study different inventory strategies. The concept of queuing system and its various disciplines are derived. The most crucial decision of replacing part of a machine or the machine as a whole is discussed in replacement models. Dynamic programming is then demonstrated in the context of inventory and queues. Under project management, different techniques of analyzing the time involved in completing a project and the related costs are presented after defining the prerequisites of networks. These tools are the key components for effective scheduling of activities which, in turn, reduce the project completion time and result in smooth resource allocation and resource levelling. The practical situations involving the knowledge of an optimum order of doing jobs are discussed in sequencing problems. In some of the complex problems, mathematical techniques could not be searched out. Therefore, simulation approach for tackling such problems is discussed.

In this book easy-to-use algorithms are presented, illustrating different techniques of operations research. Each chapter contains several fully worked-out problems and ends with exercises to give the students an opportunity to hone their understanding of the important concepts involved.

This book is designed for the students of MBA/PGDBM, MCA, MA/MSc (Mathematics, Statistics, Operations Research), MIT, MSc (IT), M.Com., CA, ICWA. It may be of great help to the students who are preparing for competitive examinations like Civil Services and UGC-NET. The concepts and results explained here can be applied to real-life industrial, business problems with some changes as per the requirements.

We are thankful to our students whose queries helped us in making the various concepts of operations research techniques more clear. We are also grateful to the editorial and production team of Prentice-Hall of India for their cooperation and sincerity.

Finally, we are very thankful to our family members for their constant support and encouragement, particularly during the prepartion of the manuscript. Dr. Ravi Gor conveys special thanks to his kids Tosha and Mandaar, who have missed him very much during the preparation of this book. Hardik Soni is thankful to D.M. Sikh, Director of Sardar Vallabhbhai Patel Education Trust, for his cooperation.

Suggestions and constructive comments from the readers for improvement of the book are most welcome.

NITA H. SHAH
RAVI M. GOR
HARDIK SONI

1 Why Operations Research?

1.1 INTRODUCTION

Operations Research (OR) is a scientific approach to analyzing problems and making decisions. OR professionals aim to provide rational bases for decision-making by seeking to understand and structure complex situations, and to use this understanding to predict system behaviour and improve system performance. Much of this work is done using analytical and numerical techniques to develop and manipulate mathematical and computer models of organizational systems composed of people, machines, and procedures.

Operations Research is a branch of mathematics used to provide a scientific base for management to take timely and effective decisions. It possibly avoids the dangers arising from decisions based on guesswork. The concept of management has basically two characteristics:

- *Multidimensional:* Because managerial problems and their probable solutions have repercussions in several fields such as human, economic, social and political fields.
- *Dynamic:* A manager will never remain static while prevailing in the business.

Hence, any manager, while taking decisions, considers all aspects in addition to economic aspect, to make his solution useful in every respect. The general approach is to analyze the problem in every aspect and implement the solution only if it does not violate human, social and political constraints.

Management problems can also be solved using quantitative approach. This approach requires the problem to be properly defined and thoroughly analyzed. This includes collecting data, facts, and information and then solving the problem in a rational and systematic way, based on analysis rather on mere guesswork, or using trial and error methods. Operations research is primarily concerned with helping managers and executives to arrive at better decisions.

Nowadays, managers are working in a dynamic environment. They require common sense, experience and commitment in making decisions as they have to deal with systems with complex interrelationship of various factors among them, as well as equally complicated dependence of the criterion of effective performance of the system on these factors. The science of operations research helps them take value–based decisions in such a dynamic environment.

The scope of quantitative methods is very broad. They are applied in defining the problems and getting solutions of various organizations dealing with finance, manufacturing, services, etc.

1.2 ORIGIN OF OPERATIONS RESEARCH

Operations research is a *war baby* as its idea first germinated during the Second World War. The first problem to have been attempted in a systematic way was concerned with how to set the time fuse bomb to be dropped from an aircraft onto a submarine.

At the time of the Second World War, the military management in England invited a team of experts to analyze the problems related to the defense of the country. At that time, the resources available with England were limited and they targeted to win the war with these resources. Therefore, it was necessary to decide the most effective utilization of the available resources including the military resources. The experts were given the problem of resource utilization and asked to come out with a feasible solution. After much deliberation, these specialists came out with a method for solving the problem. They termed the method "Linear Programming". This method worked out well in solving the war problem. As the name indicates, the word *Operations* is used to refer to the problems of military, and the word *Research* is used for inventing a new method. After the Second World War, there was a scarcity of industrial material and industrial productivity reached its nadir. Industrial recession was there and to solve the industrial problem, the method *linear programming* was used to get the optimal solution. From then onwards, a lot of work has been done in the field, and today OR has numerous methods for solving different types of problems.

After the success of the British military, the United States military management started applying the techniques to various activities to solve military, civil and industrial problems. Some called it Operational Analysis, while some others called it Operations Evaluation, Operations Research, System Analysis, System Evaluation, Systems Research, Quantitative methods, and so on. But the most commonly used one is Operations Research. In the industrial world, the most important problem for which these techniques are used is how to optimize the profit or how to reduce the costs.

1.3 DEFINITIONS OF OPERATIONS RESEARCH

Here we give a few definitions to explain what exactly Operations Research is.

> *Operations research applies scientific methods to deal with the problems of a system where men, material and other resources are involved and the system under study may be industry, defense or business, etc.*

It also says that the manager has to build a scientific model to study the system which must be provided with the facility to measure the outcomes of various alternatives under various degrees of risk, which helps the managers to take optimal decisions.

> *Operational Research can be described as a scientific approach to the solution of problems in the management of complex systems.*

In a rapidly changing environment, an understanding is sought which will facilitate the choice of more effective solutions which, typically, may involve complicated interaction among people, materials, and money.

Operational Research in practice is a team effort, requiring the close cooperation among the decision-makers, the skilled OR analysts, and the people who will be affected by management action.

Because of wide scope and numerous applications of operations research, different mathematicians and researchers ended up giving different definitions. Although giving a precise definition of operations research is not possible, here we discuss some of them.

Operations Research is the art of winning wars without actually fighting.

—Aurther Clarke

This definition is oriented towards warfare. It means that the directions and guidance come from the minister or the king, according to which the war is fought and won.

Operations Research is the art of giving bad answers to problems where otherwise worse answers are given.

—T.L. Satty

This definition covers one aspect of decision making, i.e. choosing the best among the available alternatives. If the decisions are made on guesses, we may face the worse situation. But if the decisions are made on a scientific basis, it will help us to make better decisions. Hence, this definition deals with one aspect of decision-making and not clearly tells what operations research is.

Operations Research is Research into Operations.

—J. Steinhardt

This definition does not state anything in clear terms about the subject of Operations Research and simply says that it is a research into operations. Operations may here be referred as military activities or simply the operations that an executive performs in his organization while taking decisions. Research means finding a new approach. That is, when an executive is involved in performing his operations for taking decisions, he has to go for newer ways so that he can make a better decision for the benefit of his organization.

Operations Research is defined as scientific method for providing executive department quantitative basis for decisions regarding the operations under their control.

—P.M. Morse and G.E. Kimball

This definition suggests that Operations Research provides scientific methods to an executive to make optimal decisions. But it does not give any information about various models or methods. This suggests that executives can use scientific methods for decision-making.

Operations Research is the application of scientific methods, techniques and tools to the operation of a system with optimum solution to the problem.

—Churchman, Ackoff and Arnoff

This definition clearly states that the Operations Research applies scientific methods to find an optimum solution to the problem of a system. A system may be a production system or information system or any system, which involves men, machine and other resources.

Operations Research is the application of the theories of Probability, Statistics, Queuing, Games, Linear Programming etc., to the problems of war, Government and Industry.

This definition gives a list of various techniques used in Operations Research by various managers to solve the problems. A manager has to study the problem, formulate the problem, identify the variables and formulate a model and select an appropriate technique to get optimal solution. We can say that Operations Research is a bunch of mathematical techniques to solve the problems of a system.

> *Operations Research is applied decision theory. It uses any scientific, mathematical or logical means to attempt to cope with problems that confront the executive, when he tries to achieve a thorough going rationally in dealing with his decision problem.*
>
> **—D.W. Miller and M.K. Starr**

This definition also explains that Operations Research uses scientific methods or logical means for getting solutions to the executive problems. It, too, does not give the characteristics of Operations Research.

Besides these definitions, there are numerous definitions which explain what Operations Research is. But many of them are not satisfactory because of the following reasons.

(a) Operations Research is not a well-defined science like Physics, Chemistry, etc. Hence none of the definitions given above defines operations research precisely.

(b) In operations research, decisions are made by brain storming of people from various walks of life. This indicates that operations research approach is an *interdisciplinary* one, which is an important characteristic of operations research. This aspect is not included in many of the definitions. Hence they are not satisfactory.

(c) These definitions are given by various people at different times and stages of development of operations research. As such, they have considered the field in which they are involved. Hence each definition is concentrating on one or two aspects. No definition is having a universal approach.

1.4 CHARACTERISTICS OF OPERATIONS RESEARCH

After considering the definitions of Operations Research, let us now deal with the characteristics of OR.

It is an interdisciplinary team approach: The problems an operations research analyst faces are heterogeneous in nature, involving the number of variables and constraints, which are beyond the analytical ability of one person. So, a number of people from various disciplines are required to understand the problem. They apply their specialized knowledge and experience to get a better understanding and solution to the problem on hand.

It helps in increasing the creative ability of the decision makers: Operations Research provides the managers mathematical tools, techniques and models to analyze the problem on hand and to evaluate the result of all alternatives and make an optimal choice, thereby helping him in making faster and better decisions.

A manager, without the knowledge of these techniques, just takes decisions by guessing or by trial and error method, which can give troublesome result. Hence, a manager who uses Operations Research techniques will have a better creative ability than a manager who does not use these techniques.

It is a systems approach: Any organization, be it a business or government or a defense organization, can be considered as a system having various sub-systems. The decision made by any sub-system will have its effect on other sub-systems. Say, for example, a decision taken by department A will have its effect on department B. When dealing with Operations Research problems, the system should be treated as a whole so that the interrelationship between sub-systems and the effect of the problem on the entire system are kept in mind. Hence, Operations Research is a systems approach.

The additional characteristics of operations research can be listed as follows:

- OR approaches problem solving and decision making from the total system perspective.
- OR not only necessarily uses interdisciplinary teams, but it is also interdisciplinary; it draws on techniques from sciences like biology, physics, chemistry, mathematics and economics and applies the appropriate techniques from each field to the system being studied.
- OR does not experiment with the system itself but constructs a model of the system for conducting experiments.
- Model building and mathematical manipulation provide the methodology that has perhaps been the key contribution to OR.
- The primary focus is on decision-making.
- Computers are used extensively.

1.5 MODELS IN OPERATIONS RESEARCH

Dealing with reality is complex, dynamic, and multifaceted. It is neither possible nor desirable to consider each and every element of reality before deciding the courses of action. This is an opportunity for managers because of the time available to decide the courses of action and the resources, which are limited in nature. Moreover, in many cases, it will be impossible to conduct experiment in real environment. For example, if an engineer wants to measure the inflow of water into a reservoir through a canal, he cannot sit on the banks of the canal and conduct experiment to measure the flow. He constructs a similar model in a laboratory and studies the problem and decides the inflow of water. Hence, for many practical problems, a model is necessary.

An operations research model is a mathematical abstraction or simplification of reality. The degree of simplification is a function of data availability, time and resources available to develop the model and the situational issues and decisions that the model is designed to address. With a mathematical model in hand, the operations researcher can work with managers and decision makers to evaluate decision alternatives or system redesign. This analysis is typically carried out in a computer implementation of the model that enables the decision makers and managers to explore changes in the mathematical representation without changing the actual system.

1.5.1 What are Models?

We can define an operations research model as some sort of mathematical or theoretical description of variables of a system representing some aspects of a problem on some subject of interest.

> *An approximation or abstraction of real world including its essential elements, which is constructed by establishing relationships among various variables of the system, is called a model.*

The model allows carrying out a number of experiments involving manipulations to find some optimum solution to the problem on hand. Models do not attempt to duplicate the reality in every aspect. This explains the exact use of a model. In military, the military officer explains to his soldiers various aspects of the warfront by drawing neat sketches pictorially. This makes them easy to understand the scenario in which they will be put in when they come across the real warfront. Hence, a model allows explaining the aspect of the problem.

1.5.2 Classifications of Models

Models are also categorized depending on the structure, purpose, nature of environment, behaviour, by method of solution and by use of digital computers.

1.5.2.1 Classification by structure

1. *Iconic models:* These models are a scaled version of the actual object. For example, a toy of a car is an iconic model of a real car. The iconic models explain all the features of the actual object. A globe is a very good example of iconic model of the earth. These models may be of enlarged version or reduced version. Big objects are scaled down (reduced version) and small objects, when we want to show the features, are scaled up to a bigger version. In fact, it is a descriptive model giving the description of various aspects of the real object.

   The advantages of these models are:
   - It is easy to work with an iconic model as these are easy to construct.
   - These are useful in describing static or dynamic phenomenon at some definite time.

   The limitations are:
   - It is difficult to study the changes in the operation of the system.
   - The model building is very costly for some type of systems.
   - Many times it is difficult to perform experiments on these models.
2. *Analogue models:* In these models, a set of properties are used to represent another set of properties. For example, the green colour generally represents the grass. Whenever we want to show ground on a map, it is represented in the green colour. These are also not much used in operations research. The best examples are warehousing problem and layout problems.
3. *Symbolic models or mathematical models:* In these models, the variables of a problem are represented by mathematical symbols, letters, etc. To show the relationships between variables and constraints, we use mathematical symbols. Hence these are known as *symbolic models* or *mathematical models*. These models are used very much in operations research. Examples of such models are resource allocation model, transportation model, etc.

1.5.2.2 Classification by utility

Depending on the use of the model or purpose of the model, the models are classified as descriptive, predictive and prescriptive.

1. *Descriptive models:* The descriptive models explain and predict facts and relationships among the various activities of the problem. These do not have an objective function, the system being modeled to evaluate decision alternative. Hence in a descriptive model, it is possible to get information as to how one or more factors change as a result of changes in other factors.

2. *Predictive models:* These models are based on the data collected. It predicts the possible outcomes of the situation under question. For example, based on your performance in the examination and the discussions and verification with your friends after the examination, you can predict your results. This is one type of predictive model.
3. *Prescriptive models:* The predictive models predict the approximate results. But if the predictions of these models are successful, then it can be used conveniently to prescribe the courses of actions to be taken. In such cases, it is termed as *prescriptive model*. Prescriptive models prescribe the courses of action to be taken by the manager to achieve the desired goal.

1.5.2.3 Classification by nature of environment

Depending on the environment in which the problem exists and the decisions are made, and depending on the conditions of variables, the models may be categorized as deterministic models and probabilistic models.

1. *Deterministic models:* These models are used when all the parameters, constants, values of the variables, the available resources and relationship among those resources are complete or known with certainty and when it is expected that they do not change during the planning horizon. Linear programming models are deterministic models as they assume certainty regarding the values of variables and constraints.
2. *Probabilistic or stochastic models:* These models are used when the values of variables cannot be predicted accurately because of existence of probability. It takes into account certain elements of risk. The degree of certainty varies from situation to situation. A good example of this is the sale of insurance policies by Life Insurance Companies to its customers. Here the failure of life is highly probabilistic in nature. The models in which the pattern of events has been compiled in the form of probability distributions are known as *probabilistic* or *stochastic models*.

1.5.2.4 Classification depending on the behaviour of the problem variables

Depending on the behaviour of the variables and constraints of the problem, they may be classified as static models or dynamic models.

1. *Static models:* These models assume that no changes occur in the values of variables given in the problem for the given planning horizon due to any change in the environment or conditions of the system. All the values given are independent of the time.
2. *Dynamic models:* In these models the values of given variables keep on changing with many factors. The factors may include change in time or environment or the conditions of the given system. Generally, in the dynamic models, there is a series of interdependent decisions during the planning period.

1.5.2.5 Classification depending on the method of getting the solution

We may use different methods for getting the solution of a given model. Depending on these methods, the models are classified as analytical models and simulation models.

1. *Analytical models:* These models have a well-defined mathematical structure and can be solved only by applying some mathematical techniques. The models like Resource allocation

model, Transportation model, Assignment model, Sequencing model etc. have well defined mathematical structure and can be solved by different mathematical techniques. For example, Resource allocation model can be solved by Graphical method or by Simplex method depending on the number of variables involved in the problem.

2. *Simulation models:* To simulate is to duplicate the features of the problem in a working model, which is then solved using well-known OR techniques. The results, hence, obtained are tested for sensitivity analysis, after which these are applied to the original problem. These models have a mathematical structure but cannot be solved by using mathematical techniques. It needs certain experimental analysis.

1.5.3 Characteristics of a Good Model

1. A large number of parameters should be avoided in a model for better understanding of the problem.
2. A good model should be flexible to accommodate any necessary information during the stages of model building.
3. A model must take less time to construct.

1.5.4 Steps in Constructing a Model

The following steps should be followed in the model building process.

1. Formulate the model, which consists of real-world managerial situations, abstract them into formulation, and then develop the mathematical terms of a symbolic model.
2. Analyze the model to generate results.
3. Interpret and validate model results, making sure that the available information obtained from the analysis is understood in the context of the original real-world situation.
4. Implement the validated knowledge gained from the interpretation of the model results, in real-world decision-making.

1.5.5 Points to Remember while Building a Model

1. When we can solve the situation with a simple model, do not try to build a complicated model.
2. Build a model that can be easily fit in the techniques available. Do not try to search for a technique, which suits your model.
3. In order to avoid complications while solving the problem, the formulation stage of modeling must be conducted rigorously.
4. Before implementing the model, it should be validated/tested properly.
5. Use the model for the purpose for which it is deduced. Do not use the model for the purpose for which it is not meant.
6. Without having a clear idea for which the model is built, do not use it.
7. Models cannot replace decision makers. It can guide them but it cannot make decisions.
8. Do not be under the impression that a model solves every type of problem.
9. The model should be as accurate as possible.

1.5.6 Advantages of a Good Model

1. A model provides logical and systematic approach to the problem.
2. It provides the analyst a base for understanding the problem and think of methods of solving.
3. A model will avoid the duplication work in solving the problem.
4. A model helps the analyst to find newer ways of solving the problem.
5. A model saves resources like money, time, mankind, etc.
6. A model helps the analyst to make the complexities of a real environment simple.
7. Risk of tampering the real object is reduced, when a model of the real system is subjected to experimental analysis.
8. Models provide distilled economic descriptions and explanations of the operation of the system they represent.

1.5.7 Limitations of a Model

1. A model is constructed only to understand the problem and attempt to solve the problem; they are not to be considered as the real problem or system.
2. The validity of any model can be verified by conducting the experimental analysis and with relevant data characteristics.

1.5.8 Quantitative Methods in Practice

1.5.8.1 Allocation models

The resources—whether natural or man-made—are scarce and how to utilize them properly is a very important decision. Allocation models are concerned only with the problem of optimal allocating of these precious and scarce resources for optimizing the given objective function, subject to the limiting factors prevailing at that point of time or the constraints within which a firm has to operate. Linear programming models are good examples of such models. At this point, it is important to differentiate between a linear and a non-linear programming model.

The nature of the objective function along with its constraints separates a linear programming problem from a non-linear one. Organizational problems, where both the objective and the constraints functions are capable of being represented as a linear function, are solved with the help of linear programming. Even the assignment and transportation problems can be viewed essentially as a linear programming problem, though of a special type requiring procedures devised specially for them. On the other hand, if the decision-parameters could be restricted to either integer value or zero-one values in a linear programming problem, these are known as integer programming and zero one programming, respectively. Linear goal programming models are concerned with those types of special problems, which have conflicting, multiple objective functions in relation to their linear constraints.

1.5.8.2 Sequencing model

Sequencing model deals with the selection of the most appropriate or the optimal sequence in which a series of jobs can be performed on different machines so as to maximize the operational efficiency of the system, e.g. consider a job shop, where jobs are required to be processed on Y machines.

Different jobs require different amounts of time on different machines and each job must be processed on all the machines. In what order should the jobs be processed on all the machines so as to minimize the total processing time of completing all the job. There are several variations of the same problem, which can be evaluated by sequencing models with the different kinds of optimization criterion. Hence, sequencing is primarily concerned with those problems in which the efficiency of operations depends solely upon the sequence of performing a series of jobs.

1.5.8.3 Waiting line model or Queueing model

Any problem that involves waiting before the required service could be provided is termed as a *queuing* or *waiting line problem*. These models seek to ascertain the various important characteristics of queuing systems such as:

- Average time spent in the line by a customer
- Average length of the queue, etc.

The waiting line models find very wide applicability across virtually every organization and in our daily life. Examples of queuing or waiting-line models are waiting for service in a bank, waiting at a doctor's clinic, etc. These models aim at minimizing the cost of providing the services. Most of the realistic waiting line problems are extremely complex and often, simulation is used to analyze such situations.

1.5.8.4 Replacement model

These models are concerned with determining the optimal time required to replace equipment or machinery that deteriorates or fails. Hence it seeks to formulate the optimal replacement policy of an organization. For example, when to replace an old machine with a newer one in the factory, or at what interval should an old car be replaced with a newer one? In all such cases, there exists an economic trade-off between the increasing and the decreasing cost functions.

1.5.8.5 Inventory models

The inventory models primarily deal with the determination of how much to order at a point of time. Inventory problems are also concerned with the determination of optimum levels of different inventory items and ordering policies, optimizing a pre-specified standard of effectiveness. It is concerned with the factors such as demand per unit time, cost of placing orders, costs incurred while keeping the goods in inventory, stock-out costs and costs of lost sales.

If a customer demands a certain quantity of a product, which is not available, then it results in a lost sale. Similarly, in the case of raw materials, shortage of even a very small item may cause bottlenecks in the production and the entire assembly line may block. These models can be of two types:

- Deterministic inventory models and
- Probabilistic inventory models.

1.5.8.6 Network models

Networking models are extensively used in planning, scheduling and controlling large-scale projects, which can be represented in the form of a network of various activities and sub-activities. Two commonly used networking models are:

- Critical Path Method (CPM) and
- Program Evaluation and Review Technique (PERT).

PERT is extensively applied for finding the time requirements of a given project, and the allocation of scarce resources to complete the project as scheduled within the stipulated time and with minimum cost. CPM is a technique widely used in the construction and maintenance of a project in which duration of start and completion of each phase is known with certainty. It establishes the trade-off between scheduled time and the cost of the project.

1.5.8.7 Routing and trans-shipment models

These problems involve finding out the optimal route from the starting point to the destination or termination point, where a finite number of possible routes are available. For example: travelling salesman problems, finding the shortest path and transport dispatching problems could be solved by the routing and trans-shipment models.

1.6 OPERATIONS RESEARCH—AN APPROACH TO DECISION-MAKING

Many times we speak of the word *décision* as if we know much about it. But do we know what exactly decision is? What does it consist of? What are its characteristics?

Let us have a brief discussion about the word decision. A *decision* is the conclusion of a process designed to weigh the relative uses or utilities of a set of alternatives on hand, so that the decision maker selects the alternative which is best for his problem or situation and implement it. *Decision making* involves all activities and thinking that are necessary to identify the most optimal or preferred choice among the available alternatives.

The basic requirements of decision-making are:

- A set of goals or objectives
- Methods of evaluating alternatives in an objective manner
- A system of choice criteria and a method of projecting the repercussions of alternative choices or courses of action.

The process of decision-making consists of two phases.

- Formulation of goals and objectives, enumeration of environmental constraints, identification and evaluation of alternatives
- Selection of optimal course of action for a given set of constraints

Decisions may be classified in different ways, depending upon the criterion or the purpose of classification. Some of them are shown below:

- Decision depending on the purpose
- Decision depending on the nature
- Decision depending on the persons involved
- Decision depending on the sphere of interest
- Decision depending on the time horizon

Decisions may also be classified depending on the future situations. Some of them are shown below:

- Decision making under certainty
- Decision making under uncertainty
- Decision making under risk

The first two are the two extremes and the third one falls between these two with certain probability distribution.

1.7 ROLE OF OPERATIONS RESEARCH IN DECISION-MAKING

Operations Research has been used intensively in business, industry, and government. Many new analytical methods have evolved, such as mathematical programming, simulation, game theory, queuing theory, networks, decision analysis, multicriteria analysis, which have powerful application to practical problems with the appropriate logical structure. An easy approach to solve such problems is to model them and then try to find a possible solution to it. The mathematical model in decision-making should take care of the following points:

- Make objectives explicit
- Identify decisions that influence objectives
- Clarify trade-offs among decisions and objectives
- Require identification and definition of quantifiable variables
- Explore the interaction between variables
- Help to identify critical data elements and their role as model inputs
- Assist in recognizing and clarifying constraints on decisions and operations
- Facilitate communication.

1.8 METHODS OF SOLVING OPERATIONS RESEARCH PROBLEMS

There are three methods of solving an operations research problem. They are:

1. Analytical method
2. Iterative method
3. Monte-Carlo method.

Analytical method: When we use mathematical techniques such as differential calculus, probability theory, etc. to find the solution of a given operations research model, the method of solving is known as *analytical method* and the solution is known as *analytical solution*. Examples are problems of inventory models. This method evaluates alternative policies efficiently.

Iterative method: This is a numerical method. When we have a large number of variables, and we cannot use analytical methods successfully, we use iterative process. First, we set a trial solution and then go on changing the solution under a given set of conditions, until no more modification is possible. The characteristic of this method is that the trial and error method used is laborious, tedious, time-consuming and costly. The solution we get may not be an accurate one and is an approximate one. Many a time, we find that after certain number of iterations, the solution cannot be improved and we have to accept it as the optimal solution.

Monte-Carlo method: This method is based on the random sampling of the values of the variables from a distribution of the random variable. This uses sampling technique. A table of random numbers must be generated to solve the problems. In fact, it is a simulation process.

1.9 PHASES IN SOLVING OPERATIONS RESEARCH PROBLEMS

Any Operations Research analyst has to follow certain sequential steps to solve the problem on hand. The following figure (Figure 1.1) shows the various steps to be followed:

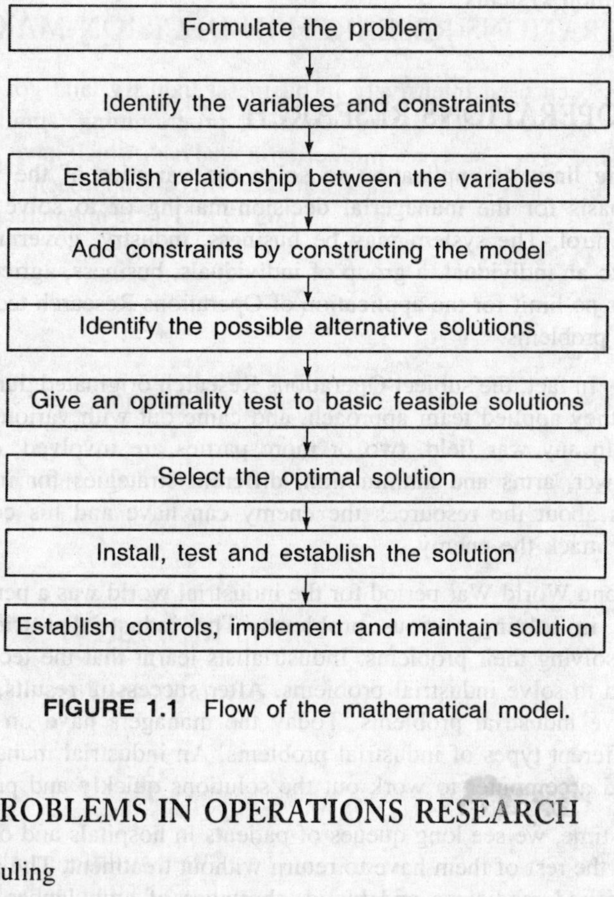

FIGURE 1.1 Flow of the mathematical model.

1.10 TYPICAL PROBLEMS IN OPERATIONS RESEARCH

- Aircraft scheduling
- Architectural layout planning
- Computer systems design
- Congressional district borders
- Drug design optimization
- Emergency vehicle location
- Fuel blending

- Hospital staff scheduling
- Inventory management
- Investment portfolio selection
- Medical diagnosis and prognosis
- Optimal energy distribution
- Scheduling in manufacturing systems
- Scheduling courses in schools
- Telecommunication systems
- Vehicle routing

1.11 SCOPE OF OPERATIONS RESEARCH

The scope indicates the limit of application to solve the varieties of the problems. Operations Research provides a basis for the managerial decision-making or to solve the problems of the systems under their control. The system may be business, industry, government or defense. The problems may pertain to an individual, a group of individuals, business, agriculture, government or defense. Hence, there is no limit for the application of Operations Research techniques; they may be applied to any type of problems.

In defense operations: In fact, the subject Operations Research originated during World War II. To war-related problems, they applied team approach, and came out with various approaches to solve the problem in hand. In any war field, two or more parties are involved; each having different resources likes manpower, arms and ammunition, different strategies for implementation. Every opponent has to guess about the resources the enemy can have and his courses of action, and accordingly, he has to attack the enemy.

In industry: Post Second World War period for the industrial world was a period of depression and the industry indulged in solving various problems. The industrialist tried the contemporary successful models for solving their problems. Industrialists learnt that the techniques of operations research can be applied to solve industrial problems. After successful results, various models have been developed to solve industrial problems. Today the managers have on their hand numerous techniques to solve different types of industrial problems. An industrial manager has these various models in his hand and a computer to work out the solutions quickly and precisely.

In hospitals: Many a time, we see long queues of patients in hospitals and only a few of them get treatments on time and the rest of them have to return without treatment. The additional reasons can be unavailability of desired medicines and blood, shortages of ambulances and beds, etc. These problems can be conveniently solved by the application of operations research techniques.

In planning for economic growth: In India, we have five-year planning for a steady economic growth. Every state government prepares plans for the balanced growth of the state. Various people from various departments coordinate and plan for steady economic growth. For all these activities, departments can use Operations Research techniques. The questions like how many engineers, doctors, software specialists, etc. are required in future and what should be their quality to face the problems, etc. can be easily solved.

In agriculture: The population of India is exploding day by day and hence the demand for food products. And this is also a fact that the land available for agriculture is limited. So newer methods are required for increasing agriculture yield. For the same reason, the selection of land area for agriculture for sowing seeds of food grains must be cautiously done, so that it could result into dual advantage: one to the farmer and the other to the users. The farmers should not experience losses and the people should get their grains on right time and at right cost.

1.12 WHY TO STUDY OPERATIONS RESEARCH?

OR is distinguished by its broad applicability and by the wide variety of career opportunities and work styles it embraces. OR specialists may be theoreticians or practitioners. They may work in academia, in industry, or in public service, teaching, doing research, consulting or implementing OR models. OR professionals may participate in just one phase of an OR study, such as modelling, analysis, or implementation, or they may participate in all portions of a project. Within the field, some OR professionals remain generalists while others specialize in particular tools or problem domains. Some OR professionals move from technical positions to managerial functions. Because the concepts and methods of OR are pervasive, it offers very flexible career paths.

Operations Research is concerned with optimal decision making in, and modeling of, deterministic and probabilistic systems that originate from real life. These applications, which occur in government, business, engineering, economics, and the natural and social sciences, are characterized largely by the need to allocate limited resources. In these situations, considerable insight can be obtained from the scientific analysis such as that provided by operations research. The contribution from the operations research approach stems primarily from:

- Structuring the real-life situation into a mathematical model, abstracting the essential elements so that a solution relevant to the decision maker's objectives can be sought. This involves looking at the problem in the context of the entire system.
- Exploring the structure of such solutions and developing systematic procedures for obtaining them.
- Developing a solution, including the mathematical theory, if necessary, that yields an optimal value of the system measure of desirability or possibly comparing alternative courses of action by evaluating their measure of desirability.

Most operations research studies involve the construction of a mathematical model. The model is a collection of logical and mathematical relationships that represents the aspects of the situation under study. Models describe important relationships between variables; include an objective function with which alternative solutions are evaluated, and constraints that restrict solutions to feasible values.

To summarize, Operations Research is to provide a scientific basis to the decision-makers for solving the problems involving the interaction of various components of an organization by employing a team of scientists from various disciplines, all working together for finding a solution which is in the best interest of the organization as a whole. The best solution thus obtained is known as *optimal decision.*

REVIEW EXERCISES

1. Trace the origin of operations research.
2. Discuss the objectives of operations research.
3. "Operations research is an interdisciplinary approach". Comment.
4. What are operations research models? Discuss the advantages and limitations of operations research models.
5. Discuss the operations research models.
6. What do you mean by decision-making? How operations research helps managers in decision-making?
7. Briefly explain the characteristics of operations research.
8. Discuss the various steps used in solving operations research problems.

2 Prerequisite for Operations Research

2.1 INTRODUCTION

The purpose of this chapter is to furnish the elementary concepts required in understanding Operations Research. It covers some important topics on *matrices* and *determinants*, *vectors* and *linear algebra*, *convex sets*, etc.

2.2 MATRICES AND DETERMINANTS

2.2.1 Definitions

Matrix: A *matrix* is a rectangular arrangement of the system of mn real or complex numbers into m rows and n columns.

The matrix is represented by a bracket [ ] or ( ). The following are some examples of matrices:

$$\begin{bmatrix} 1 & 5 \\ 9 & 3 \end{bmatrix} \qquad \begin{pmatrix} 0 & 2 & 3 \\ 1 & 5 & 6 \end{pmatrix} \qquad \begin{bmatrix} 1 & 2 & 3 \\ 5 & 9 & 7 \\ 3 & 4 & 6 \end{bmatrix}$$

Usually, a matrix is denoted by a capital letter such as A, B, C, etc. *Matrix A* is denoted by

$$A = \begin{bmatrix} a_{11} & a_{12} & \cdots & a_{1n} \\ a_{21} & a_{22} & \cdots & a_{2n} \\ \vdots & \vdots & \vdots & \vdots \\ a_{m1} & a_{m2} & \cdots & a_{mn} \end{bmatrix}$$

Row 'k' of $[A]$ has n elements and is $[a_{k1} \quad a_{k2} \quad \ldots \quad a_{kn}]$ and column 'j' has m elements and is

$$\begin{bmatrix} a_{j1} \\ a_{j2} \\ \vdots \\ a_{jm} \end{bmatrix}$$

The number of rows and columns defines the size of the matrix. If a *matrix A* has 'm' rows and 'n' columns, then the *size of the matrix* is denoted by $m \times n$. In the above examples, the size of the matrix is 2×2, 2×3 and 3×3, respectively.

The matrix is also denoted as $A = [a_{kj}]_{m \times n}$ to indicate that A is matrix with 'm' rows and 'n' columns. A matrix makes the presentation of numbers clearer and is simply used to convey information in a concise manner that makes calculation easier.

Diagonal entries (or elements) of a matrix: The entries a_{kj} of a matrix $A = [a_{kj}]$ for which $k = j$ are called *diagonal entries* (or elements) of A.

Sometimes the diagonal of the matrix is also called *principal* or *main* of the matrix.

Equality of two matrices: Two matrices $A = [a_{kj}]_{m \times n}$ and $B = [b_{kj}]_{r \times s}$ are said to be *equal* if $m = r$, $n = s$, and $a_{kj} = b_{kj}$ for all k and j.

Transpose of a matrix: Let $A = [a_{kj}]$ be an $m \times n$ matrix. Then *transpose* of A is a matrix $B = [b_{kj}]$ with $b_{kj} = a_{jk}$ for all k and j. That is, the k-th row and the j-th column element of A is the j-th row and k-th column element of B. Thus, transpose of a *matrix A* is obtained by interchanging the rows and columns of A. The transpose of A is denoted by A^T or A', i.e. $B = A^T$. Note that B would be an $n \times m$ matrix.

Row matrix: A matrix having only a single row is called a *row matrix* (or row vector). The size of the row matrix is $1 \times n$.

Matrix $A = [1 \quad 5 \quad 7 \quad 9]$ is an example of row matrix of size 1×4.

Column matrix: A matrix having only a single column is called a *column matrix* (or column vector). The size of the row matrix is $m \times 1$.

Matrix $A = [1 \quad 5 \quad 7 \quad 9]^T$ is an example of column matrix of size 4×1.

Square matrix: A matrix in which number of rows (m) is the same as number of columns (n), i.e. $m = n$, is called a *square matrix*. In this case, matrix A is said to be of order n.

Null matrix: A matrix $A = [a_{kj}]$ in which $a_{kj} = 0$ for all k and j, is called a *null matrix*. A null matrix is denoted by O.

Symmetric matrix: A square matrix A with real entries in which $a_{kj} = a_{jk}$ for all $k = j = 1, 2, \ldots, n$ is called a *symmetric* matrix. Equivalently, if $A = A^T$, then A is a symmetric matrix.

Skew-symmetric matrix: A square matrix A with real entries in which $a_{kj} = -a_{jk}$ for all $k = j = 1, 2, \ldots, n$ is called a *skew-symmetric* matrix. Equivalently, if $A = -A^T$, then A is a skew-symmetric matrix.

Identity (or Unit) matrix: A square matrix of size 'n', whose all main diagonal elements are 1, and off-diagonal elements are zero, that is, $[a_{kj}]$, where $a_{kj} = 1$, $k = j$; and $a_{kj} = 0$, $k \neq j$ is called *identity* (or unit) matrix of order n, and is denoted by I_n.

2.2.2 Algebra of Matrices

2.2.2.1 *Addition and subtraction of matrices*

The sum of two matrices $A = [a_{kj}]$ and $B = [b_{kj}]$ of the same size is a matrix $C = [c_{kj}]$ where $c_{kj} = a_{kj} + b_{kj}$ for each k and j.

Similarly, the subtraction of two matrices is defined as a matrix $C = [c_{kj}]$ where $c_{kj} = a_{kj} - b_{kj}$ for each k and j.

2.2.2.2 *Scalar product*

Let $A = [a_{kj}]$ be an $m \times n$ matrix and α be any scalar (real number). Then scalar product of α and A is another matrix $B = [b_{kj}]$, where $b_{kj} = \alpha a_{kj}$ for all k and j.

For any three matrices A, B and C of the same size and scalar α, β, the following properties hold:

(a) Addition of matrices is commutative.

$$A + B = B + A$$

(b) Addition of matrices is associative.

$$A + (B + C) = (A + B) + C$$

(c) $A + O = O + A = A$, that is, O is the *additive identity* for addition.

(d) If $A + B = O = B + A$ then $B = (-A)$. Matrix B is called *negative* of A.

(e) Addition is distributed over scalar multiplication.

$$\alpha (A + B) = \alpha A + \alpha B$$

(f) $(\alpha + \beta)A = \alpha A + \beta A$

2.2.2.3 *Product of matrices*

Two matrices A and B can be multiplied only if the number of columns in A is same as the number of rows in B.

Let $A = [a_{kj}]$ be a $p \times q$ matrix and $B = [b_{jl}]$ be a $q \times r$ matrix. The product of matrices A and B, denoted by AB, is the matrix $C = [c_{il}]$ of size $p \times r$, where

$$c_{il} = \sum_{j=1}^{q} a_{kj} b_{jl} = a_{k1}b_{1l} + a_{k2}b_{2l} + \cdots + a_{kq}b_{ql} \quad \text{for each } k = 1, 2, \ldots, p \text{ and } l = 1, 2, \ldots, r.$$

2.2.2.4 *Properties of matrix multiplication*

(a) *Associative property:* If A, B and C are $p \times q$, $q \times r$ and $r \times s$ size matrices, respectively, then $A(BC) = (AB)C$ and the size of the resulting matrix on both sides is $p \times r$.

(b) *Distributive property:* If A and C are matrices of size $p \times q$ and B and D are matrices of size $q \times r$, then

(i) $A(B + D) = AB + AD$
(ii) $(A + C)B = AB + CB$

and the size of the resulting matrix on both sides is $p \times r$.

(c) $\alpha(AB) = (\alpha A)B = A(\alpha B)$ for any scalar α.

(d) $IA = A = AI$, that is, I is the *multiplicative identity* for matrix multiplication.

Note that matrix multiplication, in general, is not commutative, that is, $AB \neq BA$.

For example, consider the following matrices:

$$A = \begin{bmatrix} 1 & 5 & 7 \\ 3 & 0 & -2 \end{bmatrix} \text{ and } B = \begin{bmatrix} 0 & 1 \\ -5 & 3 \\ 4 & -2 \end{bmatrix}$$

Then
$$AB = \begin{bmatrix} 3 & 2 \\ -8 & 7 \end{bmatrix} \text{ and } BA = \begin{bmatrix} 3 & 0 & -2 \\ 4 & -25 & -41 \\ -4 & 20 & 32 \end{bmatrix}$$

2.2.3 Determinant of Square Matrix

A *determinant* of a square matrix A, denoted by $|A|$ or det (A), is a single unique real number corresponding to a matrix.

For 2×2 matrix,

$$A = \begin{bmatrix} a_{11} & a_{12} \\ a_{21} & a_{22} \end{bmatrix} \Rightarrow |A| = a_{11}a_{22} - a_{12}a_{21}.$$

Let $A = [a_{kj}]$ be matrix of order n. The *minor* of element a_{kj} is defined as the determinant of the sub-matrix of A of size $(n - 1) \times (n - 1)$, where the sub-matrix is obtained by removing the k-th row and j-th column of the matrix A. It is denoted by M_{kj}. The determinant is then given by

$$|A| = \sum_{k=1}^{n} (-1)^{k+j} a_{kj} M_{kj} \qquad \text{for } j = 1, 2, \ldots, n$$

The number $(-1)^{k+j} M_{kj}$ is known as *cofactor* of entry a_{kj} and it is denoted by C_{kj}.
For example, consider the following matrix.

$$A = \begin{bmatrix} 1 & 2 & 1 \\ 4 & 5 & 8 \\ 6 & 3 & 4 \end{bmatrix}$$

To determine the matrix of cofactors C, suppose

$$C = \begin{bmatrix} C_{11} & C_{12} & C_{13} \\ C_{21} & C_{22} & C_{23} \\ C_{31} & C_{32} & C_{33} \end{bmatrix}$$

Cofactors C_{11}, C_{12}, C_{13}, etc. can be computed as follows:

$$C_{11} = (-1)^{1+1}\begin{vmatrix} 5 & 8 \\ 3 & 4 \end{vmatrix}, \text{ (by deleting the first row and first column)}$$

$$= +(20 - 24) = -4$$

$$C_{12} = (-1)^{1+2}\begin{vmatrix} 4 & 8 \\ 6 & 4 \end{vmatrix}, \text{ (by deleting the first row and second column)}$$

$$= -(16 - 48) = 32$$

$$C_{13} = (-1)^{1+3}\begin{vmatrix} 4 & 5 \\ 6 & 3 \end{vmatrix}, \text{ (by deleting the first row and third column)}$$

$$= +(12 - 30) = -18$$

Proceeding in the same manner, we can determine other cofactors. Therefore, the cofactor matrix is:

$$C = \begin{bmatrix} -4 & 32 & -18 \\ -5 & -2 & 9 \\ 11 & -4 & -3 \end{bmatrix}$$

2.2.4 Adjoint of Matrix

The transpose of cofactor matrix is called *adjoint* of a matrix A. Adjoint of A is denoted by adj. A. That is, if C is cofactor matrix of matrix A, then adj. $A = C^T$.

The adjoint of a matrix defined in the above example is:

$$\text{adj. } A = \begin{bmatrix} -4 & -5 & 11 \\ 32 & -2 & -4 \\ -18 & 9 & -3 \end{bmatrix}$$

We now state, without proof, one result which shows the relationship between A and adj. A.

Theorem 2.1 *A (adj. A) = $|A|\, I$ = (adj. A) A, I being identity matrix.*

Corollary 2.1: If $|A| \neq 0$ then $A\left(\dfrac{\text{adj. } A}{|A|}\right) = I = \left(\dfrac{\text{adj. } A}{|A|}\right)A$.

2.2.5 Inverse of Matrix

If A is a square matrix, and if matrix B can be found such that $AB = BA = I$; I being unit matrix, then B is called the *inverse* of A and A is said to be *invertible* (or *non-singular*). The inverse of matrix A is denoted by A^{-1}.

It follows from the above corollary that the inverse of A exists if $|A| \neq 0$, and is given by adj. $A/|A|$. Thus, A^{-1} = adj. $A/|A|$.

Note that non-square matrices cannot possess inverses.

A square matrix A is said to be *singular* (or *non-invertible*) if $|A| = 0$.

2.2.6 Rank of Matrix

First, let us introduce some convenient terminology.

(a) A row or column that contains at least one non-zero entry is called *non-zero row* or *column*.

(b) A left most non-zero entry of row (or column) is called *leading entry*.

(c) A matrix A is said to be equivalent to matrix B if B can be obtained from A by performing the following operations called elementary row (column) operations:

- (Scaling) Multiply all entries in a row (column) by non-zero constant.
- (Interchange) Interchange two rows (columns).
- (Replacement) Replace one row (column) by the sum of itself and multiple of another row (column).

(d) An $n \times m$ matrix is in *echelon form* (or *row echelon form*) if it satisfies the following conditions:

- Any row of all zeros occur below every non-zero rows.
- Each column of a matrix containing leading entry of row has all entries zero below it.
- Each leading entry of a row is in a column to the right of the leading entry of its preceding row.

In addition, if a matrix in echelon form satisfies the following properties, then it is in reduced row echelon form, abbreviated as RREF.

- The leading entry in each non-zero row is 1.
- Each leading 1 is the only non-zero entry in its column.

The matrices

$$\text{(i) } A = \begin{bmatrix} 0 & -1 & 3 & 0 & 7 \\ 0 & 0 & 0 & 2 & \frac{2}{5} \\ 0 & 0 & 0 & 0 & 0 \end{bmatrix} \text{ is an echelon matrix.}$$

$$\text{(ii) } A = \begin{bmatrix} 1 & 0 & 0 & 35 \\ 0 & 1 & 0 & 4 \\ 0 & 0 & 1 & 8 \end{bmatrix} \text{ is in reduced echelon form.}$$

$$\text{(iii) } A = \begin{bmatrix} 1 & 0 & 0 & 5 \\ 0 & 1 & 3 & 4 \\ 0 & 0 & -1 & 9 \end{bmatrix} \text{ is not an echelon form.}$$

Now, we are in a position to define rank of a matrix.

The number of non-zero rows of an echelon matrix is the *rank of the matrix*. The rank of the matrix A is denoted by $\rho(A)$.

The following matrix A has rank 2.

$$\begin{bmatrix} 1 & 2 & 1 \\ 2 & 4 & 3 \\ 3 & 6 & 5 \end{bmatrix} \xrightarrow[R_3 - 3R_1]{R_2 - 2R_1} \begin{bmatrix} 1 & 2 & 1 \\ 0 & 0 & 1 \\ 0 & 0 & 2 \end{bmatrix} \xrightarrow{R_3 - 2R_2} \begin{bmatrix} 1 & 2 & 1 \\ 0 & 0 & 1 \\ 0 & 0 & 0 \end{bmatrix}$$

Note: The rank of a matrix is equal to the number of linearly independent rows/columns of a matrix.

2.3 SYSTEM OF LINEAR EQUATIONS AND CONSISTENCY

Many problems in linear algebra are equivalent to studying a system of linear equations. Here, we shall discuss how to find the solutions of a system of 'm' linear equations in 'n' variables or unknowns.

Consider system of 'm' linear equations in 'n' unknowns namely $x_1, x_2, \ldots, x_n$:

$$\begin{aligned} a_{11}x_1 + a_{12}x_2 + \cdots + a_{1n}x_n &= d_1 \\ a_{21}x_1 + a_{22}x_2 + \cdots + a_{2n}x_n &= d_2 \\ \cdots\cdots\cdots\cdots\cdots\cdots\cdots\cdots & \\ a_{m1}x_1 + a_{m2}x_2 + \cdots + a_{mn}x_n &= d_m \end{aligned} \tag{2.1}$$

where all a_{kj}'s and d_j's are real or complex numbers.

The system in Eq. (2.1) can be rewritten in a matrix form as

$$\begin{bmatrix} a_{11} & a_{12} & \cdots & a_{1n} \\ a_{21} & a_{22} & \cdots & a_{2n} \\ \vdots & \vdots & & \vdots \\ a_{m1} & a_{m2} & \cdots & a_{mn} \end{bmatrix} \begin{bmatrix} x_1 \\ x_2 \\ \vdots \\ x_n \end{bmatrix} = \begin{bmatrix} d_1 \\ d_2 \\ \vdots \\ d_m \end{bmatrix}$$

Designate the matrices by A, X and D, the system of equations is

$$AX = D \tag{2.2}$$

where A is called coefficient matrix, X is called column matrix of unknowns, and D is column matrix of constants.

The system in Eq. (2.1) is said to be *homogeneous* if the constants $d_1, d_2, \ldots, d_n$ are all 0. That is, $D = 0$ (null matrix).

A set of values $x_1, x_2, \ldots, x_n$ which satisfy the system of equations, is called a *solution*. If the system has one or more solutions, the system is called *consistent* and *inconsistent* otherwise.

The homogeneous system always has a solution, namely $x_1 = x_2 = \cdots = x_n = 0$. This solution is known as *trivial* solution. Any other solution, if it exists, is called *non-trivial* solution.

The matrix obtained by adjoining constant column matrix to coefficient matrix is known as *augmented matrix*. That is,

$$[A|D] = \left[\begin{array}{cccc|c} a_{11} & a_{12} & \cdots & a_{1n} & d_1 \\ a_{21} & a_{22} & \cdots & a_{2n} & d_2 \\ \vdots & \vdots & & \vdots & \vdots \\ a_{m1} & a_{m2} & \cdots & a_{mn} & d_m \end{array}\right]$$

We now state, without proof, two important results which are often used.

1. A system $AX = D$ of m linear equations in n unknowns is consistent if and only if the coefficient matrix A and the augmented matrix $[A|D]$ have same rank.
2. If $\rho(A) = \rho([A|D]) = r = n$; the number of unknowns, then the system possesses unique solution; and if $\rho(A) = \rho([A|D]) = r < n$, then the infinite solution exists.

2.4 VECTORS AND CONVEXITY

Vector quantities have both a magnitude and a direction associated with them. That is, when we speak about velocity, we are not just talking about speed. Velocity is speed in a certain direction. So, the magnitude of the velocity vector might be 50 miles per hour and the direction of the velocity vector might be due north. Vectors are denoted by boldface letters for example, **u** denotes a vector. When a bold typeface is not available, an arrow is drawn over a normal letter to let it denote a vector for example, $\vec{u}$ denotes a vector.

2.4.1 Definitions

A *scalar* is a real number. Scalars are denoted by normal letters.

An *n-vector* **u** is an ordered sequence of real numbers. For example, $\mathbf{u} = (x_1, x_2, x_3,\ldots, x_n)$ is a vector of an ordered n-tuple of real numbers. The real numbers $x_1, x_2, x_3, \ldots, x_n$ are called the *components* of **u**.

An *n-dimensional Euclidean space* is defined as the collection of n-vectors. The n-dimensional Euclidean space will be denoted by $\mathbf{E}^n$. We shall confine our study to $\mathbf{E}^n$.

For example, 3-dimensional vector $\mathbf{u} = (x_1, x_2, x_3)$ is an ordered triplet of real numbers. The *length* or *magnitude* of a vector $\mathbf{u} = (x_1, x_2, x_3, \ldots, x_n)$ in $\mathbf{E}^n$ is given by

$$\|\mathbf{u}\| = \sqrt{x_1^2 + x_2^2 + \cdots + x_n^2}$$

Note that, the magnitude of a vector is scalar. Vertical bars surrounding a boldface letter denote the magnitude of a vector. Since the magnitude is a scalar, it can also be denoted by a normal letter; $u = \|\mathbf{u}\|$ denotes the magnitude of a vector.

Suppose that c is a scalar and $\mathbf{u} = (x_1, x_2, x_3, \ldots, x_n)$ is a vector. Then *scalar multiplication* is defined by $c\mathbf{u} = c(x_1, x_2, x_3, \ldots, x_n) = (cx_1, cx_2, cx_3, \ldots, cx_n)$. Each component of the vector is multiplied by the scalar. The magnitude of the vector $c\mathbf{u}$ is c times the magnitude of **u**.

Two vectors with the same dimension can be added to each other or subtracted from each other. The result is another vector.

The *sum* of two vectors $\mathbf{u} = (x_1, x_2, x_3, \ldots, x_n)$ and $\mathbf{v} = (y_1, y_2, y_3, \ldots, y_n)$ is defined to be the vector

$$\mathbf{u} + \mathbf{v} = (x_1 + y_1, x_2 + y_2, x_3 + y_3, \ldots, x_n + y_n)$$

Subtracting $\mathbf{v}$ from $\mathbf{u}$ yields

$$\mathbf{u} - \mathbf{v} = (x_1 - y_1, x_2 - y_2, x_3 - y_3, \ldots, x_n - y_n).$$

Unit vector is a vector whose magnitude is 1. The standard unit vector in $\mathbf{E}^n$ is denoted by e_i in which 1 occurs at i-th place and 0 elsewhere. That is, $e_i = (0, 0, \ldots, 1, \ldots, 0, 0)$.

Let $\mathbf{u} = (x_1, x_2, x_3, \ldots, x_n)$ and $\mathbf{v} = (y_1, y_2, y_3, \ldots, y_n)$. Then $\mathbf{u}$ is said to be *greater than or equal to* $\mathbf{v}$ if $x_k \geq y_k$ for $k = 1, 2, \ldots, n$. This is denoted by writing $\mathbf{u} \geq \mathbf{v}$.

Note that, two vectors with same dimension can be order comparable.

Suppose we are given two vectors $\mathbf{u}_1$ and $\mathbf{u}_2$. The expressions like $u_1 + u_2$, $u_1 - u_2$, $5u_1 + 7u_2$, $2u_1 - 3u_2$, etc. can be obtained by performing the operations of addition and scalar multiplication. Such vectors are called linear combination of vectors $\mathbf{u}_1$ and $\mathbf{u}_2$. More specifically, the vector $\mathbf{v} = \theta_1\mathbf{u}_1 + \theta_2\mathbf{u}_2$ is a *linear combination* of $\mathbf{u}_1$ and $\mathbf{u}_2$.

Thus, if $\{u_1, u_2, \ldots, u_p\}$ is a set of $\mathbf{p}$ vectors in $\mathbf{E}^n$ and $\{\theta_1, \theta_2, \ldots, \theta_p\}$ is a set of p scalars, then the vector $\mathbf{v} = \theta_1\mathbf{u}_1 + \theta_2\mathbf{u}_2 + \cdots + \theta_p\mathbf{u}_p$ is a *linear combination* of the given set of vectors $u_1, u_2, \ldots, u_p$.

The notion of linear combination provides us the following definitions.

Let u_1 and u_2 be two points in $\mathbf{E}^n$. The set $L = \{v/v = \theta u_1 + (1 - \theta)u_2\}$, $(\theta \in \mathbb{R})$ is defined as a *line* in $\mathbf{E}^n$ passing through $\mathbf{u}_1$ and $\mathbf{u}_2$.

In E^2, with usual notation $\mathbf{v} = (x, y)$ and $\mathbf{u}_1 = (x_1, y_1)$ and $\mathbf{u}_2 = (x_2, y_2)$, the definition gives $x = \theta x_1 + (1 - \theta)x_2$, $y = \theta y_1 + (1 - \theta)y_2$, when rewrite in the form

$$\frac{x - x_2}{x_1 - x_2} = \frac{y - y_2}{y_1 - y_2} = \theta$$

which is a standard form of the equation of the line passing through two points (x_1, y_1) and (x_2, y_2). By restricting θ between 0 and 1 (both inclusive), we get the set of points lying on the *line segment* between $\mathbf{u}_1$ and $\mathbf{u}_2$. That is, the set $L = \{v/v = \theta u_1 + (1 - \theta)u_2\}(0 \leq \theta \leq 1)$ is called *line segment* joining two points $\mathbf{u}_1$ and $\mathbf{u}_2$. When $\theta = 0$, we are at $\mathbf{u}_1$, when $\theta = 1$, we are at $\mathbf{u}_2$, and when $\theta = 1/2$, we are at the mid-point of the line segment.

2.4.2 Convex Sets

Convexity is really a simple property to describe. A special class of sets of points in E^n, known as *convex sets*, plays an important role in optimization theory. Now onwards, unless otherwise stated, a set of vectors or points is always a subset of Euclidean space $\mathbf{E}^n$.

Convex set: A set $S \subseteq \mathbf{E}^n$ is said to be *convex* if S contains the line segment between any two points in the set. That is, a set $S \subseteq \mathbf{E}^n$ is said to be convex if

$$u_1, u_2 \in S \Rightarrow \theta u_1 + (1 - \theta)u_2 \in S; \quad (0 \leq \theta \leq 1)$$

The above definition can be restated as: A set S is *convex* if for any two points u_1 and u_2 belonging to S there are no points on the line between $\mathbf{u}_1$ and $\mathbf{u}_2$ those are not members of S. Equivalently, a set S is convex if there are no points $\mathbf{u}_1$ and $\mathbf{u}_2$ in S such that there is a point on the line between

u_1 and u_2 that does not belong to *S*. The point of this equivalent definition is to include the empty set within the definition of convexity. The definition also includes singleton sets where $\mathbf{u}_1$ and $\mathbf{u}_2$ have to be the same point and thus the line between $\mathbf{u}_1$ and $\mathbf{u}_2$ is the same point.

The set *S* in Figure 2.1 is convex, while the set *T* is not.

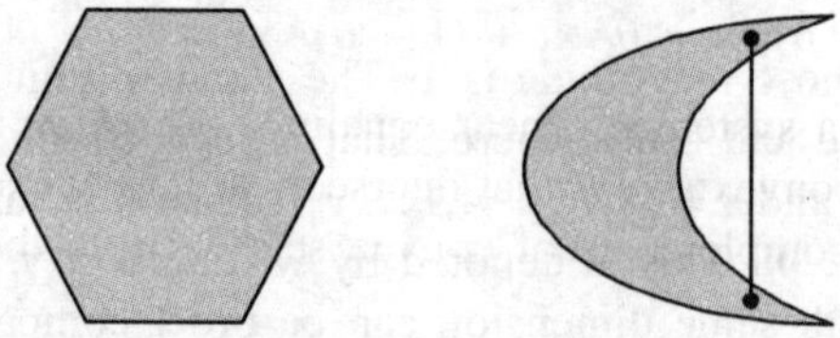

Figure 2.1 Convex and non-convex sets.

EXAMPLE 2.1: The unit ball in $\mathbf{E}^n$ is convex. The ball is the set $B = \{\mathbf{u} \in \mathbf{E}^n\colon \|\mathbf{u}\| \le 1\}$.
Suppose that **u** and **v** are in *B*. Then

$$\|\theta\mathbf{u} + (1-\theta)\,\mathbf{v}\| \le |\theta|\,\|\mathbf{u}\| + |1-\theta|\,\|\mathbf{v}\|$$
$$\le |\theta| + |1-\theta| = 1$$

Thus $\theta\mathbf{u} + (1-\theta)\mathbf{v} \in B$, and so *B* is convex.

EXAMPLE 2.2: The set $\mathbf{E}^n$ is convex. But if we remove any point from $\mathbf{E}^n$, then the resulting set is no longer convex.

EXAMPLE 2.3: The set $\mathbf{E}^n$ is convex; so is the empty set and a one-point set.

EXAMPLE 2.4: Consider the set $S = \{\mathbf{u} \in \mathbf{E}^n\colon \|\mathbf{u}\| = 1\}$.
Suppose that **u** and **v** be two different points in *S*. Then
$\|\theta\mathbf{u} + (1-\theta)\mathbf{v}\| \le |\theta|\,\|\mathbf{u}\| + |1-\theta|\,\|\mathbf{v}\|$, $0 < \theta < 1$, with equality possible if and only if either (i) $\mathbf{u} = \mathbf{0}$ or (ii) $\mathbf{v} = \mathbf{0}$ or (iii) $\theta\mathbf{u} = t(1-\theta)\mathbf{v}$, $t > 0$.

Since $\|\mathbf{u}\| = \|\mathbf{v}\| = 1$, neither (i) nor (ii) is true. If (iii) is satisfied, then it is necessary that $\|\theta\mathbf{u}\| = \|t(1-\theta)\mathbf{v}\| \Rightarrow \theta\|\mathbf{u}\| = t(1-\theta)\|\mathbf{v}\| \Rightarrow \mathbf{u} = \mathbf{v}$, which contradict the fact that **u** and **v** are distinct. Hence, (iii) is not true.

Therefore, $\|\theta\mathbf{u} + (1-\theta)\mathbf{v}\| < 1$. So, *S* is not convex.

In particular, for $n = 2$, $\mathbf{u} = (1, 0)$, $\mathbf{v} = (0, 1)$ and $\theta = \dfrac{1}{2}$;

$$\|\theta\mathbf{u} + (1-\theta)\,\mathbf{v}\| = \sqrt{\frac{1}{2}} \ne 1$$

EXAMPLE 2.5: Any (connected) interval $[a, b]$, (a, b), $[a, b)$, or $(a, b]$ in **R** is convex, as the reader can easily verify, where *a* and *b* can be finite or infinite. In fact, the finite interval $[a, b]$ is just the ball of radius $(b - a)/2$ about $(a + b)/2$, which is convex as we saw in Example 2.1. However, if we remove a point from the interior of one of these intervals, the remaining set is no longer convex. In fact, if we remove a point from the interior of any convex set, the resulting set is no longer convex.

For example, $\mathbf{E}^n/\{0\}$ is not convex. The points (1, 0, ..., 0) and (–1, 0, ..., 0) are in the set, but the midpoint of the line segment joining these points is not in the set.

EXAMPLE 2.6: The solution set S of a system of linear equalities $\mathbf{Ax} = \mathbf{b}$ is convex. For if $\mathbf{x}_1$ and $\mathbf{x}_2$ are in S, then

$$\mathbf{A}(\theta\mathbf{x}_1 + (1 - \theta)\mathbf{x}_2) = \theta\mathbf{A}\mathbf{x}_1 + (1 - \theta)\mathbf{A}\mathbf{x}_2 = \theta\mathbf{b} + (1 - \theta)\mathbf{b} = \mathbf{b}$$

Sets described as solutions to a system of linear equalities are *affine sets.*

An important property of convex sets is that intersection of convex sets is convex. As the reader can easily verify, unions and complements of convex sets need not be convex.

Theorem 2.2: *Let* $\{S_\alpha\}_{\alpha\in I}$ *be a (possibly infinite) collection of convex sets. Then* $\bigcap_{\alpha\in I} S_\alpha$ *is convex.*

Proof: Let $\mathbf{u}$ and $\mathbf{v}$ be points in $\bigcap_{\alpha\in I} S_\alpha$, and choose θ between 0 and 1.

Since $\mathbf{u}$ and $\mathbf{v}$ are in each S_α, so $\theta\mathbf{u} + (1 - \theta)\mathbf{v} \in S_\alpha$ for each α.

Hence, $\theta\mathbf{u} + (1 - \theta)\,\mathbf{v} \in \bigcap_{\alpha\in I} S_\alpha$.

2.4.3 Constructing a Convex Set

The defining property of convex sets is that such sets contain the line segment connecting any two points in the set. More generally, choose any finite number, say P, of points in a convex set S. Then, the polygon,· which has these P points as vertices, is contained in S. The following figure (Figure 2.2) illustrates this for a convex set in the plane when $P = 3$ and $P = 4$.

Figure 2.2 Examples of convex sets.

Convex linear combination: Let $\mathbf{u}_1$, $\mathbf{u}_2$, ..., $\mathbf{u}_m$ be m points in $\mathbf{E}^n$ and let θ_1, θ_2, ..., θ_m be non-negative real numbers such that $\sum_{j=1}^{m} \theta_j = 1$. Then

$$\mathbf{v} = \theta_1\mathbf{u}_1 + \theta_2\mathbf{u}_2 + \cdots + \theta_m\mathbf{u}_m$$

is called the *convex linear combination* of points $\mathbf{u}_j$, $j = 1, 2, \ldots, m$.

For $m = 2$ this reduce to the definition of convex set. The definition of a convex set is that the convex combination of any *two* points in the set is contained in the set. In fact, a convex set is closed under all ***finite*** *convex combinations.* We have following theorem in this context.

Theorem 2.3: *A necessary and sufficient condition for a set S to be convex is that every convex linear combination of points in S belongs to S.*

Proof: Without loss of generality, we assume that S consists m points say $\mathbf{u}_1, \mathbf{u}_2, \ldots, \mathbf{u}_m$. Suppose that any convex combination of $\mathbf{u}_1, \mathbf{u}_2, \ldots, \mathbf{u}_m$ is also in S. This implies, any convex combination of two points in S belongs to S. Hence, S is convex. The proof of converse is done by induction on m, the number of elements in convex combination. Let S be a convex and $v = \sum_{j=1}^{m} \theta_j u_j$. The Theorem is true for $m = 1$ by default and for $m = 2$ by the definition of convexity. We need only prove the theorem for $m = k + 1$, under the inductive hypothesis that it is true for $m = k$.

Suppose that it is true for $m = k$.

Now consider $v = \sum_{j=1}^{k+1} \theta_j u_j$, $\sum_{j=1}^{k+1} \theta_j = 1$, $\theta_j \geq 0$, $j = 1, 2, \ldots, k + 1$

Two cases arise: (i) $\theta_{k+1} = 0$, (ii) $\theta_{k+1} > 0$

Case (i): $\theta_{k+1} = 0 \Rightarrow v = \sum_{j=1}^{k+1} \theta_j u_j = \sum_{j=1}^{k} \theta_j u_j \in S$, by hypothesis.

Case (ii): $\theta_{k+1} > 0 \Rightarrow v = \sum_{j=1}^{k+1} \theta_j u_j = (1 - \theta_{k+1}) \sum_{j=1}^{k} \dfrac{\theta_j}{(1 - \theta_{k+1})} u_j + \theta_{k+1} u_{k+1}$

Since
$$\sum_{j=1}^{k+1} \theta_j = 1 \Rightarrow \sum_{j=1}^{k} \theta_j = 1 - \theta_{k+1}$$

and so
$$\sum_{j=1}^{k} \frac{\theta_j}{(1 - \theta_{k+1})} = 1$$

So the vector
$$z = \sum_{j=1}^{k} \frac{\theta_j}{(1 - \theta_{k+1})} u_j$$

is a convex combination of the k vectors $\mathbf{u}_1, \mathbf{u}_2, \ldots, \mathbf{u}_k$. By the induction hypothesis, z is in S. By the definition of convexity

$$v = (1 - \theta_{k+1})z + \theta_{k+1} u_{k+1}$$

is in S.

As we have just seen, a convex set contains all convex combinations of vectors in the set. Similarly, given any collection of vectors, we can identify the convex set that they generate.

Convex hull: Let S be a set of vectors in $\mathbf{E}^n$. The set of all convex combinations of every finite subset of S is called the ***convex hull*** of S and is often written as $[S]$.

For example, in Figure 2.3

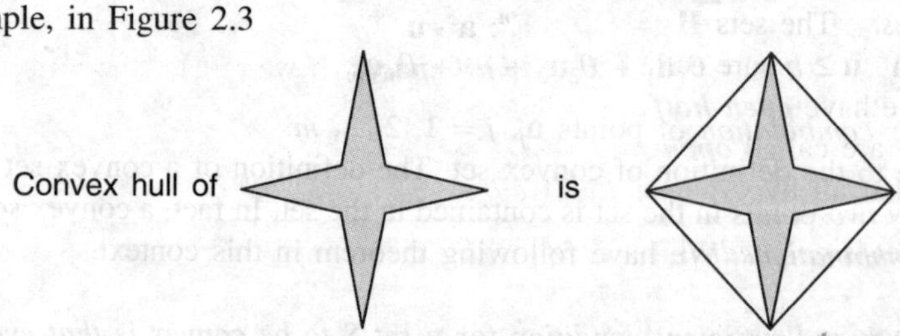

Figure 2.3

Clearly, S itself is always contained in $[S]$. By Theorem 2.1, it follows that if S is convex, then $S = [S]$. Theorem 2.3 also implies that if S is any set and if T is a convex set containing S, then

$$S \subseteq [S] \subseteq T.$$

This implies that $[S]$ is the smallest convex set containing S; equivalently to say $[S]$ is the "Convex set generated by S". This leads to an alternative definition of $[S]$: The ***convex hull*** of a set S is the intersection of all convex sets containing S.

EXAMPLE 2.7: $S = \{\mathbf{u} \in \mathbf{E}^n: \|\mathbf{u}\| = 1\} \Rightarrow [S] = \{\mathbf{u} \in \mathbf{E}^n: \|\mathbf{u}\| \leq 1\}$.

EXAMPLE 2.8: Let S be a set consisting of only two points. Then $[S]$ is the line segment joining given points.

EXAMPLE 2.9: For three points, the convex hull would be a triangle with internal points and the convex hull of the set having four points is either any quadrilateral or convex triangle (see Figure 2.4) with interior part.

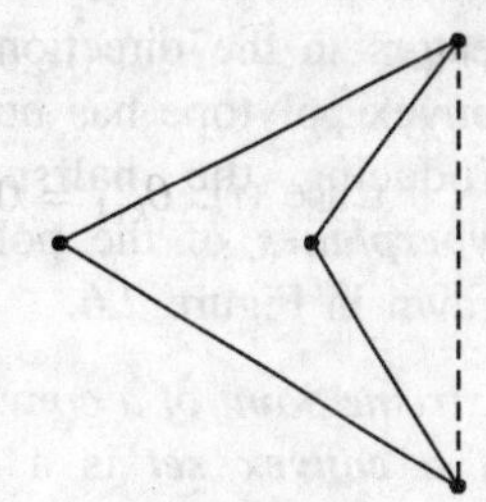

Figure 2.4

Theorem 2.4: *If $S \in \mathbf{E}^n$, each vector in $[S]$ can be written as the convex combination of at most $n + 1$ vectors in S.*

We omit the proof of this theorem.

2.4.4 Hyperplanes

Hyperplane: Choose a vector $\mathbf{a} = (a_1, a_2, a_3, \ldots, a_n) \neq \mathbf{0}$ in $\mathbf{E}^n$ and a scalar b. The set of the points $\mathbf{u} = (x_1, x_2, x_3, \ldots, x_n)$ satisfying $a_1x_1 + a_2x_2 + \cdots + a_nx_n = b$

i.e.

$$\mathbf{H} = \{\mathbf{u} \in \mathbf{E}^n: \mathbf{a} \cdot \mathbf{u} = b\}$$

is called ***hyperplane*** in $\mathbf{E}^n$.

In E^2, hyperplanes are straight lines. In E^3, hyperplanes are planes.

For any $\mathbf{n}$, a hyperplane in $\mathbf{E}^n$ divides $\mathbf{E}^n$ into two ***half-spaces***, as pictured in Figure 2.5.

Note: If $b = 0$, then the hyperplane is said to pass through the origin and its equation is then written as $a_1x_1 + a_2x_2 + \cdots + a_nx_n = 0$.

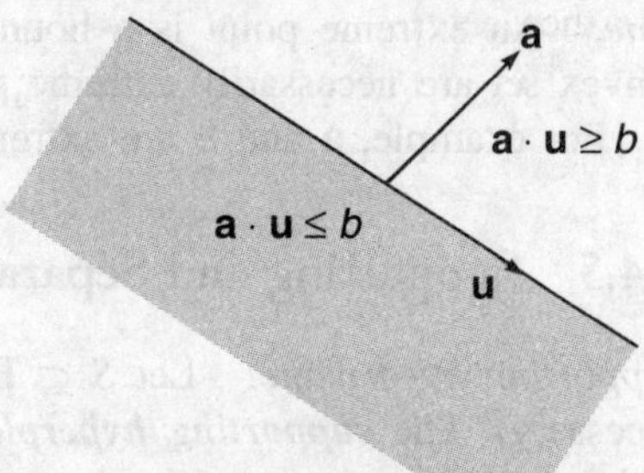

Figure 2.5

Closed (Open) half-spaces: The sets $\mathbf{H}_- = \{\mathbf{u} \in \mathbf{E}^n: \mathbf{a} \cdot \mathbf{u} \leq b\}$ and $\mathbf{H}_+ = \{\mathbf{u} \in \mathbf{E}^n: \mathbf{a} \cdot \mathbf{u} \geq b\}$ are called ***closed half-spaces***. If we replace the weak inequalities with strict inequalities, we have ***open half-spaces***. That is, the sets defined by $\{\mathbf{u} \in \mathbf{E}^n: \mathbf{a} \cdot \mathbf{u} < b\}$ and $\{\mathbf{u} \in \mathbf{E}^n: \mathbf{a} \cdot \mathbf{u} > b\}$ are called ***open half-spaces***.

It is easy to verify that all hyperplanes, open and closed half-spaces, are convex.

Polyhedral: A convex set is *polyhedral* if it is a solution set of finitely many linear inequalities and equalities.

Let $\mathbf{a}_1, \mathbf{a}_2, \ldots, \mathbf{a}_m$ denote m vectors in $\mathbf{E}^n$, and let $b_1, b_2, \ldots, b_m$ denote the corresponding scalars.

Let $\mathbf{H}_j = \{\mathbf{u}_j \in \mathbf{E}^n: \mathbf{a}_j \cdot \mathbf{u}_j \le b_j\}$. Each $\mathbf{H}_j$ is half-space. The set $S = \bigcap_{j=1}^{m} \mathbf{H}_j$ is a ***polyhedral convex set***. The set S is a set of solution to the system of inequalities:

$$a_{11}x_1 + a_{12}x_2 + \cdots + a_{1n}x_n \le b_1$$
$$a_{21}x_1 + a_{22}x_2 + \cdots + a_{2n}x_n \le b_2$$
$$\cdots\cdots\cdots\cdots\cdots\cdots\cdots\cdots$$
$$a_{m1}x_1 + a_{m2}x_2 + \cdots + a_{mn}x_n \le b_m$$

Bounded convex polyhedra are called convex polytopes. The direction vectors of an unbounded convex polyhedron are vectors in the direction of its bounding rays. Note that a convex polytope has no direction vectors. The hyperplanes producing the halfspaces are called the ***generating hyperplanes*** of the polytope. A polyhedral convex set is drawn in Figure 2.6.

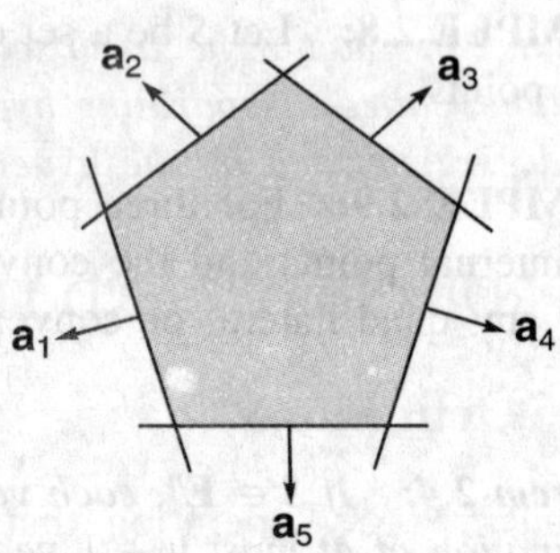

Figure 2.6 A polyhedra convex set.

Extreme point of a convex set: An ***extreme point or vertex of a convex set*** is a corner point of polyhedron. More formally, an extreme point is a point which cannot be expressed as a convex combination of other points in the polyhedron.

Thus, a point $\mathbf{u}$ of a convex set S is an extreme point of the set, if there does not exist any pair of points $\mathbf{u}_1$, $\mathbf{u}_2$ in S, such that

$$\mathbf{u} = \theta\mathbf{u}_1 + (1 - \theta)\mathbf{u}_2 \qquad 0 < \theta < 1$$

Note: An extreme point is a boundary point of the set; however, not all boundary points of a convex set are necessarily extreme points.

For example, **a** and **b** are extreme points in the following figure.

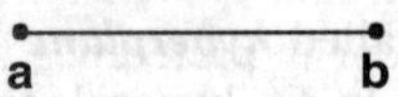

2.4.5 Supporting and Separating Hyperplane

Supporting hyperplane: Let $S \subseteq \mathbf{E}^n$ be any non empty set (not necessary). The ***supporting hyperplane*** to S at boundary point $\mathbf{z}$ is the set $\{\mathbf{u}: \mathbf{a} \cdot \mathbf{u} = \mathbf{a} \cdot \mathbf{z}\}$ where $\mathbf{a} \ne \mathbf{0}$ and $\mathbf{a} \cdot \mathbf{u} \le \mathbf{a} \cdot \mathbf{z}$ for all $\mathbf{u} \in S$. See Figure 2.7.

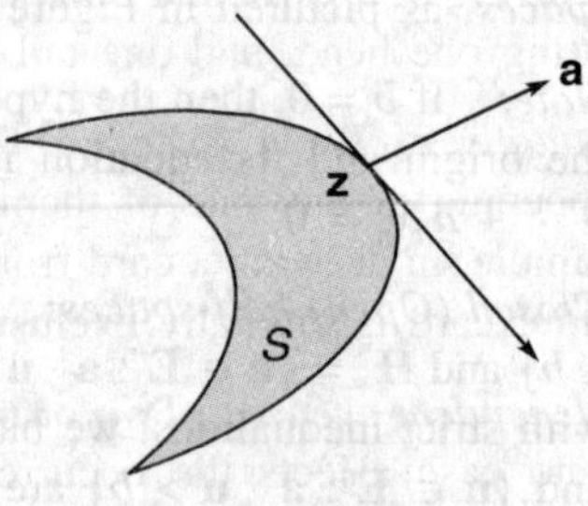

Figure 2.7 Supporting hyperplane.

Theorem 2.5: (*Supporting hyperplane theorem*): *If S is closed and convex, then there exists a supporting hyperplane at every boundary point of S.*

We omit the proof of this theorem.

Note: Through any boundary point $\mathbf{x}$ of a convex set S, there passes a hyperplane $\mathbf{H}$ with S entirely on one side of it.

An extremely useful fact about convex sets is illustrated in Figure 2.8. If C is a closed convex set in $\mathbf{E}^n$ and $\mathbf{x}$ is a point not in S, then there exists a hyperplane $\mathbf{H}$ in $\mathbf{E}^n$ such that C lies on one side of $\mathbf{H}$ and $\mathbf{x}$ lies on the other. We say that the hyper plane $\mathbf{H}$ separates $\mathbf{x}$ from S or that $\mathbf{H}$ is a *separating hyperplane.* Theorems which give conditions under which a point or set of points can be separated from S are called *separation theorems*.

Here we present the statement of separation theorem without proof.

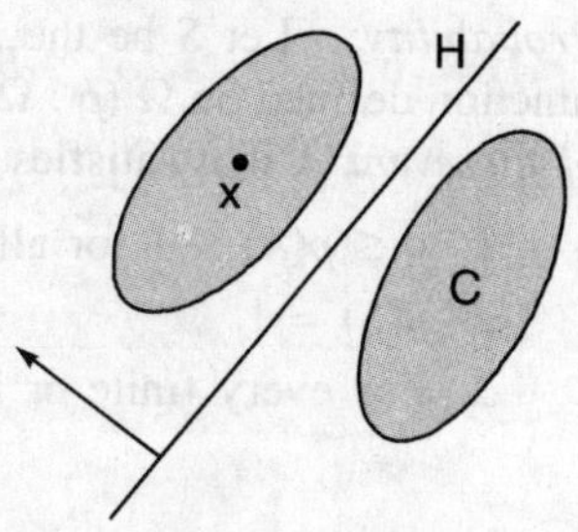

Figure 2.8

Theorem 2.6: *Let S be a closed convex set and* $\mathbf{x}$ *be a point not in S. Then there exists a hyperplane, called a separating hyperplane, which contains* $\mathbf{x}$ *such that S is contained in one of the half-spaces generated by the hyperplane.*

2.5 PROBABILITY AND ITS FUNDAMENTALS

2.5.1 Definitions

Experiment: Any operation that results in two or more outcomes is called an experiment. For example, tossing a coin results in heads or tails; drawing a card from a well-shuffled pack of cards, etc.

Possible outcomes: The results of a random experiment are called a ***possible outcome***.

Sample space: The set of all possible outcomes is called ***sample space***. It is denoted by S.

Collectively exhaustive outcomes: The total number of possible outcomes of a random experiment is called the ***collectively exhaustive outcomes*** of the experiment.

Equally likely outcomes: The outcomes are said to be ***equally likely*** if none of them is expected to occur in preference to other. For example, tossing a dice, all outcomes 1, 2, 3, 4, 5, 6 are equally likely to occur.

Favourable outcomes: The number of outcomes of a random experiment which result in the occurring of a particular outcome is known as ***favourable outcomes***. For example, tossing two coins getting one head, and one tail or getting two tails or two heads are favourable outcomes.

Mutually exclusive events: Two or more events are said to be ***mutually exhaustive events*** if happening of any one of them excludes the happening of all other events in the experiment. For example, in drawing a card from a well-shuffled pack of 52 cards, getting a red colour card or black colour card is mutually exclusive events.

Independent events: Two or more events are said to be ***independent*** if the occurrence of one event in no case affects the occurrence of the other. When the experiments are consecutive and not simultaneous, the independence of events makes more sense. In tossing a coin, a consecutive trial is not affected by what occurred in the previous trial and so trials are independent.

Dependent events: If two events A and B are so related that the occurrence of B is affected by the occurrence of A, then the two events are said to be ***dependent events***.

Probability: Let S be the sample space. Let Ω be the class of events and let p be a real-valued function defined on Ω ($p : \Omega \to R$). p is called *probability measure* and $p(A)$ is called the *probability of the event A* if p satisfies the following axioms:

1. $0 \le p(A) \le 1$ for all $A \in \Omega$.
2. $p(S) = 1$.
3. For every finite or infinite sequence of disjoint events $A_1, A_2, \ldots$

$$p\left(\bigcup_{k=1}^{\infty} A_k\right) = p(A_1) + p(A_2) + \cdots$$

Note: For finite sequence $p_1 + p_2 + \cdots + p_n = 1$.

Addition rule:

1. When A and B are mutually exclusive events,

$$p(A \cup B) = p(A) + p(B)$$

2. When A and B are not mutually exclusive events,

$$p(A \cup B) = p(A) + p(B) - p(A \cap B)$$

Multiplication rule:

1. When A and B are independent events,

$$p(A \cap B) = p(A) * p(B)$$

2. When A and B are dependent events, the probability of event B depending on the occurrence of event A is called *conditional probability* and is written as $p(B\backslash A)$ to be read as the probability of B given A.

$$p(A \cap B) = p(A) * p(B\backslash A)$$

Baye's theorem: If an event B occurs in conjunction with one of the n-mutually exclusive and exhaustive events $A_1, A_2, \ldots, A_n$ the probability of A_k, $k = 1, 2, \ldots, n$ given B is

$$P(A_k\backslash B) = \frac{p(A_k \cap B)}{p(B)}, \quad k = 1, 2, \ldots, n$$

and $p(B) = p(A_1 \cap B) + p(A_2 \cap B) + \ldots + p(A_n \cap B)$.

EXAMPLE 2.10 A company has two plants to manufacture cars. Plant I manufactures 80% of the car and plant II manufactures 20%. At plant I, 85% of the cars are rated standard quality and that from plant II is 65%. What is the probability that the car selected at random from plant I is of standard quality? What is the probability that the car selected at random from plant II is of standard quality?

Solution: Let A be the event of drawing a car from plant I,

B be the event of drawing a car from plant II, and

C be the event of drawing a standard quality car from plant I or from plant II.

Then $p(A) = 0.80$, $p(B) = 0.20$, $p(A \cap C) = 0.85$ and $p(B \cap C) = 0.65$.

Now $p(C) = p(A) * p(A \cap C) + p(B) * p(B \cap C) = 0.80 * 0.85 + 0.20 * 0.65 = 0.81$.

So, $p(A\backslash C) = p(A) * p(A \cap C)/p(C) = 68/81$ and

$p(B\backslash C) = p(B) * p(B \cap C)/p(C) = 13/81$.

We will use these concepts and results throughout the book.

3

Linear Programming

3.1 INTRODUCTION

A typical mathematical program consists of a single objective function, representing either profits to be maximized or costs to be minimized, and a set of constraints that circumscribe the decision variables. In the case of a linear program (LP), the objective function and constraints are all linear functions of the decision variables. At first glance these restrictions would seem to limit the scope of the LP model, but this is hardly the case. Because of its simplicity, softwares are capable of solving problems containing millions of variables and tens of thousands of constraints have been developed. Countless real-world applications have been successfully modelled and solved using linear programming techniques.

Linear programming is a widely used model type that can solve decision problems with thousands of variables. Generally, the feasible values of the decision variables are limited by a set of constraints that are described by mathematical functions of the decision variables. The feasible decisions are compared using an objective function that depends on the decision variables. For a linear program, the objective function and constraints are required to be linearly related to the variables of the problem.

The examples in the forthcoming section illustrate that linear programming can be used in a wide variety of practical situations. We illustrate how a situation can be translated into a mathematical model, and how the model can be solved to find the optimum solution.

A *linear programming problem (LPP)* is a special case of a mathematical programming problem. From an analytical perspective, a mathematical program tries to identify an *extreme* (i.e. minimum or maximum) point of a function $f(x_1, x_2, \ldots, x_n)$, which furthermore satisfies a set of constraints, e.g. $g(x_1, x_2, \ldots, x_n) \geq b$. Linear programming is the specialization of mathematical programming to the case where both function f, to be called the ***objective function***, and the problem constraints are *linear*.

From an applications perspective, mathematical (and therefore, linear) programming is an *optimization* tool, which allows the rationalization of many managerial and/or technological decisions required by contemporary techno-socio-economic applications. An important factor for the applicability of the mathematical programming methodology in various application contexts is the computational tractability of the resulting analytical models. After the advent of modern computing technology, this tractability requirement translates to the existence of effective and efficient algorithmic procedures able to provide a systematic and fast solution to these models. For linear programming problems, the *Simplex* algorithm, discussed later in the text, provides a powerful computational tool, and is able to provide fast solutions to very large-scale applications, sometimes including hundreds of thousands of variables (i.e. decision factors). In fact, the Simplex algorithm was one of the first mathematical programming algorithms to be developed (George Dantzig, 1947), and its subsequent successful implementation in a series of applications significantly contributed to the acceptance of the broader field of *Operations Research* as a scientific approach to decision making.

As it happens, however, with every modeling effort, the effective application of linear programming requires a good understanding of the underlying modeling assumptions, and a pertinent interpretation of the obtained analytical solutions. Therefore, in this section we discuss the details of the LP modeling and its underlying assumptions.

3.1.1 Model Components

A model consists of linear relationships representing a firm's objectives and resource constraints.

- *Decision variables:* Mathematical symbols representing levels of activity of an operation.
- *Objective function:* A linear mathematical relationship describing an objective of the firm, in terms of decision variables, that is maximized or minimized.
- *Constraints:* Restrictions placed on the firm by the operating environment stated in linear relationships of the decision variables.
- *Parameters/cost coefficients:* Numerical coefficients and constants used in the objective function and constraint equations.

3.1.2 Properties of Linear Programming Models

- *Proportionality:* The rate of change (slope) of the objective function and the constraint equations with respect to the particular decision variable is constant.
- *Additivity:* Terms in the objective function and constraint equations must be additive.
- *Divisability:* Decision variables can take on any fractional value and are therefore continuous as opposed to integer in nature.
- *Certainty:* Values of all the model parameters are assumed to be known with certainty (non-probabilistic).

In the next section, let us see the steps of mathematical formulation of the problem.

3.2 STEPS OF FORMULATING LINEAR PROGRAMMING PROBLEM (LPP)

The following steps are involved in the formulation of linear programming problem (LPP).

Step 1: Identify the decision variables of the problem.

Step 2: Construct the objective function as a linear combination of the decision variables.

Step 3: Identify the constraints of the problem such as resources, limitations, inter-relation between variables, etc. Formulate these constraints as linear equations or inequations in terms of the non-negative decision variables.

Thus, LPP is a collection of the objective function, the set of constraints and the set of the non-negative constraints.

Let us study some examples.

EXAMPLE 3.1 *(Production allocation problem):* A manufacturer produces two types of models *M* and *N*. Each *M* model requires 4 hours of grinding and 2 hours of polishing, whereas each *N* model requires 2 hours of grinding and 5 hours of polishing. The manufacturer has 2 grinders and 3 polishers. Each grinder works for 40 hours a week and each polisher works for 60 hours a week. Profit on model *M* is Rs. 3 and model *N* is Rs. 4. Whatever is produced in a week is sold in the market. How should the manufacturer allocate his production capacity to the two types of models so that he may make the maximum profit in a week?

Solution: Let x_1 be the number of model *M* to be produced and x_2 be the number of model *N* to be produced.

Clearly $$x_1, x_2 \geq 0.$$

The manufacturer gets profit of Rs. 3 for model *M* and Rs. 4 for model *N*. So, the objective function is to maximize profit.

$$P = 3x_1 + 4x_2$$

It is given that each model *M* requires 4 hours and each model *N* requires 2 hours for grinding. The maximum available time for grinding is 40 hours and there are two grinders. So we have the constraint on the availability of the hours of grinding,

$$4x_1 + 2x_2 \leq 80$$

Again model *M* requires 2 hours of polishing and model *N* requires 5 hours of polishing. The maximum available time for polishing is 60 hours and there are three polishers. Thus, the constraint for the hours available for polishing is,

$$2x_1 + 5x_2 \leq 180$$

Thus, the manufacturer's allocation problem is to

Maximize $$P = 3x_1 + 4x_2$$

subject to the constraints:

$$4x_1 + 2x_2 \leq 80$$
$$2x_1 + 5x_2 \leq 180$$

and $x_1, x_2 \geq 0$.

EXAMPLE 3.2 (*Inspection problem*): A company has two grades of inspector 1 and 2, who are to be assigned for a quality control inspection. It is required that at least 2,000 pieces be inspected per 8-hour day. Grade 1 inspector can check pieces at the rate of 40 pieces per hour with an accuracy of 97%. Grade 2 inspector checks at the rate of 30 pieces per hour with an accuracy of 95%. The wage rate of a Grade 1 inspector is Rs. 5 per hour while that of a Grade 2 inspector is Rs. 4 per hour. An error made by an inspector costs Rs. 3 to the company. There are only nine Grade 1 inspectors and eleven Grade 2 inspectors available in the company. The company wishes to assign work to the available inspectors so as to minimize the daily inspection cost.

Solution: Let x_1 and x_2 be the number of Grade 1 and Grade 2 inspectors doing inspections in a company, respectively. Clearly $x_1, x_2 \geq 0$.

One hour cost of inspection incurred by the company while employing an inspector = cost paid to the inspector + cost of errors made during inspection. Thus, costs for

Inspector Grade 1 = 5 + 3 * 40 * (1 – 0.97) = Rs. 8.60

Inspector Grade 2 = 4 + 3 * 30 * (1 – 0.95) = Rs. 8.50

The inspectors of both the grade work for 8 hours a day. So the objective function (to minimize daily inspection cost) is

Minimize $$C = 8(8.60x_1 + 8.50x_2) = 68.80x_1 + 68.00x_2$$

Now the constraint of the inspection capacity of the inspectors for 8-hours is

$$8 * 40x_1 + 8 * 30x_2 \geq 2000$$

Also, the company has only nine Grade 1 inspectors and eleven Grade 2 inspectors. So we have $x_1 \leq 9$ and $x_2 \leq 11$.

Thus, LPP is

Minimize $$C = 68.80x_1 + 68.00x_2$$

subject to the constraints:

$$320x_1 + 240x_2 \geq 2000$$

$$x_1 \leq 9$$

$$x_2 \leq 11$$

and $x_1, x_2 \geq 0$.

EXAMPLE 3.3: A pharmaceutical company produces two products: *A* and *B*. Production of both products requires the same process, I and II. The production of *B* results also in a by-product *C* at no extra cost. The product *A* can be sold at a profit of Rs. 3 per unit and *B* at a profit of Rs. 8 per unit. Some of this by-product can be sold at a unit profit of Rs. 2, the remainder has to be destroyed and the destruction cost is Rs. 1 per unit. Forecasts show that only up to 5 units of *C* can be sold. The company gets 3 units of *C* for each unit of *B* produced. The manufacturing times are 3 hours per unit for *A* on process I and II, respectively, and 4 hours and 5 hours per unit for *B* on process I and II, respectively. Because the product *C* results from producing *B*, no time is used in producing *C*. The available times are 18 and 21 hours of process I and II, respectively. Formulate this problem as an LP model to determine the quantity of *A* and *B* which should be produced, keeping *C* in mind, to make the highest total profit to the company.

Solution: Let x_1 units of product *A* be produced and x_2 units of product *B* be produced. Let x_3 and x_4 units of product *C* be produced and destroyed respectively.

It is given that the company gets a profit of Rs. 3 per unit of product *A*, Rs. 8 per unit of product *B*, Rs. 2 per unit of product *C* and looses Re. 1 for destroying one unit of the product *C*. So the objective function is

Maximize profit $$P = 3x_1 + 8x_2 + 2x_3 - x_4$$

Manufacturing constraints for products *A* and *B* are

$$3x_1 + 4x_2 \leq 18$$

$$3x_1 + 5x_2 \leq 21$$

Manufacturing constraints for by-product *C* are

$$x_3 \leq 5$$

$$-3x_2 + x_3 + x_4 = 0$$

and $x_1, x_2, x_3, x_4 \geq 0$.

EXAMPLE 3.4 A company, engaged in producing tinned food, has 300 trained employees on the rolls, each of whom can produce one can of food in a week. Due to the developing taste of the public for this kind of food, the company plans to add to the existing labour force by employing 150 people, in a phased manner, over the next five weeks. The newcomers would have to undergo a two-week training programme before being put to the work. The training is to be given by employees from among the existing ones and it is known that one employee can train three trainees. Assume that there would be no production from the trainers and the trainees during the training period as the training is off-the-job. However, the trainees would be remunerated at the rate of Rs. 300 per week, same rate as for the trainers.

The company has booked the following orders to supply during the next five weeks:

Week :	1	2	3	4	5
No. of cans :	280	298	305	360	400

Assume that the production in any week would not be more than the number of cans ordered for, so that every delivery of the food would be 'fresh'.

Formulate this problem as an LP model to develop a training schedule that minimizes the labour cost over the five-week period.

Solution: Let x_1, x_2, x_3, x_4 and x_5 be the number of trainees appointed in the beginning of the week 1, 2, 3, 4 and 5, respectively. The objective is to minimize the total labour force, i.e.

Minimize $$Z = 5x_1 + 4x_2 + 3x_3 + 2x_4 + x_5$$

subject to the capacity constraints:

$$300 - (x_1/3) \geq 280; \qquad 300 - (x_1/3) - (x_2/3) \geq 298$$

$$300 + x_1 - (x_2/3) - (x_3/30) \geq 305; \qquad 300 + x_1 + x_2 - (x_3/3) - (x_4/3) \geq 360$$

$$300 + x_1 + x_2 + x_3 - (x_4/3) - (x_5/3) \geq 400$$

New recruitment constraint:

$$x_1 + x_2 + x_3 + x_4 + x_5 = 150$$

and $x_1, x_2, x_3, x_4, x_5 \geq 0$.

EXAMPLE 3.5: A manufacturer of biscuits is considering four types of gift packs containing three types of biscuits: Orange cream (OC), Chocolate cream (CC) and wafers (W). A market research study conducted recently to assess the preference of the consumers shows the following types of assortments to be in good demand:

Assortments	*Contents*	*Selling price per kg* (Rs.)
A	Not less than 40% of OC Not more than 20% of CC Any quantity of W	20
B	Not less than 20% of OC Not more than 40% of CC Any quantity of W	25
C	Not less than 50% of OC Not more than 10% of CC Any quantity of W	22
D	No restrictions	12

For the biscuits, the manufacturing capacity and costs are given below:

Type of biscuits	*Plant capacity* (kg/day)	*Manufacturing cost* (Rs./kg)
OC	200	8
CC	200	9
W	150	7

Formulate this problem as an LP to find the production scheduling which maximizes the profit assuming that there are no market restrictions.

Solution: Let for gift pack A,

$x(A, OC)$ be the number of kg of OC in A

$x(A, CC)$ be the number of kg of CC in A

$x(A, W)$ be the number of kg of W in A

For gift pack B,

$x(B, OC)$ be the number of kg of OC in B

$x(B, CC)$ be the number of kg of CC in B

$x(B, W)$ be the number of kg of W in B

For gift pack C,

$x(C, OC)$ be the number of kg of OC in C
$x(C, CC)$ be the number of kg of CC in C
$x(C, W)$ be the number of kg of W in C

For gift pack D,

$x(D, OC)$ be the number of kg of OC in D
$x(D, CC)$ be the number of kg of CC in D
$x(D, W)$ be the number of kg of W in D

The objective function is

$$\begin{aligned}\text{Maximize} \quad P = {} & 20\,(x(A, OC) + x(A, CC) + x(A, W)) \\ & + 25\,(x(B, OC) + x(B, CC) + x(B, W)) \\ & + 22\,(x(C, OC) + x(C, CC) + x(C, W)) \\ & + 12\,(x(D, OC) + x(D, CC) + x(D, W)) \\ & - 8\,(x(A, OC) + x(B, OC) + x(C, OC) + x(D, OC)) \\ & - 9\,(x(A, CC) + x(B, CC) + x(C, CC) + x(D, CC)) \\ & - 7\,(x(A, W) + x(B, W) + x(C, W) + x(D, W))\end{aligned}$$

subject to the plant capacity constraints:

$$x(A, OC) + x(B, OC) + x(C, OC) + x(D, OC) \le 200$$

$$x(A, CC) + x(B, CC) + x(C, CC) + x(D, CC) \le 200$$

$$x(A, W) + x(B, W) + x(C, W) + x(D, W) \le 100$$

Specifications constraints:

For gift A,

$$x(A, OC) \ge 0.40\,(x(A, OC) + x(A, CC) + x(A, W))$$

$$x(A, CC) \le 0.20\,(x(A, OC) + x(A, CC) + x(A, W))$$

For gift B,

$$x(B, OC) \ge 0.20\,(x(B, OC) + x(B, CC) + x(B, W))$$

$$x(B, CC) \le 0.40\,(x(A, OC) + x(B, CC) + x(B, W))$$

For gift C,

$$x(C, OC) \ge 0.50\,(x(C, OC) + x(C, CC) + x(C, W))$$

$$x(C, CC) \le 0.10\,(x(C, OC) + x(C, CC) + x(C, W))$$

EXAMPLE 3.6: A businessman is opening a new restaurant and has budgeted Rs. 8,00,000 for advertisement in the coming month. He is considering four types of advertising:

(a) 30 second television commercials
(b) 30 second radio commercials
(c) Half-page advertisement in a newspaper
(d) Full-page advertisement in a weekly magazine which will appear four times during the coming month.

The owner wishes to reach families with income both over and under Rs. 50,000. The amount of exposure to families of each type and the cost of each of the media is shown below:

Media	*Cost of advertisement (Rs.)*	*Exposure to families with annual income over Rs. 50,000*	*Exposure to families with annual income under Rs. 50,000*
Television	40,000	2,00,000	3,00,000
Radio	20,000	5,00,000	7,00,000
Newspaper	15,000	3,00,000	1,50,000
Magazine	5,000	1,00,000	1,00,000

To have a balanced campaign, the owner has determined the following restrictions:

(a) No more than four television advertisements
(b) No more than four advertisements in the magazine
(c) No more than 60% of all the advertisements in newspaper and magazine
(d) There must be at least 45,00,000 exposures to families with incomes under Rs. 50,000.

Formulate this problem as an LP model to determine the number of each type of advertisement to pursue so as to maximize the total number of exposures.

Solution: Let x_1, x_2, x_3 and x_4 be the number of television, radio, newspaper and magazine advertisements to pursue, respectively. x_1, x_2, x_3 and $x_4 \geq 0$. The objective is to maximize the total number of exposures, i.e.

Maximize
$$E = (2{,}00{,}000 + 3{,}00{,}000)x_1 + (5{,}00{,}000 + 7{,}00{,}000)x_2$$
$$+ (3{,}00{,}000 + 1{,}50{,}000)x_3 + (1{,}00{,}000 + 1{,}00{,}000)x_4$$
$$= 5{,}00{,}000x_1 + 12{,}00{,}000x_2 + 4{,}50{,}000x_3 + 2{,}00{,}000x_4$$

subject to the constraint:
available budget
$$40{,}000x_1 + 20{,}000x_2 + 15{,}000x_3 + 5{,}000x_4 \leq 8{,}00{,}000$$

Maximum television advertisement
$$x_1 \leq 4$$

Maximum magazine advertisement
$$x_4 \leq 4$$

Maximum newspaper and magazine advertisement
$$\frac{x_3 + x_4}{x_1 + x_2 + x_3 + x_4} \leq 0.06, \quad \text{i.e.} -0.6x_1 - 0.6x_2 + 0.4x_3 + 0.4x_4 \leq 0$$

Exposure to families with income under Rs. 50,000
$$2{,}00{,}000x_1 + 5{,}00{,}000x_2 + 3{,}00{,}000x_3 + 1{,}00{,}000x_4 \geq 45{,}00{,}000$$

EXAMPLE 3.7: XYZ is an investment company. To aid in its investment decision, the company has developed the investment alternatives for a 10-year period, as given in the following table. The return on investment is expressed as an annual rate of return on the invested capital. The risk coefficient and growth potential are subjective estimates made by the portfolio manager of the company. The term investment is the average length of time period required to realize the return on investment as indicated.

Investment alternative	*Length of investment*	*Annual rate of return (year)*	*Risk coefficient*	*Growth potential Return (%)*
A	4	3	1	0
B	7	12	5	18
C	8	9	4	10
D	6	20	8	32
E	10	15	6	20
F	3	6	3	7
Cash	0	0	0	0

The objective of the company is to maximize the return on its investments. The guidelines for selecting the portfolio are:

(a) The average length of the investment for the portfolio should not exceed 7 years.

(b) The average risk for the portfolio should not exceed 5.

(c) The average growth potential for the portfolio should be at least 10%.

(d) At least 10% of all available funds must be retained in the form of cash at all times.

Formulate this problem as an LP model to maximize total return.

Solution: Let x_k be the proportion of funds to be invested in the k-th alternative ($k = 1, 2, \ldots, 7$). The objective function is

$$\text{Maximize (total return) } R = 0.03x_1 + 0.12x_2 + 0.09x_3 + 0.20x_4 + 0.15x_5 + 0.06x_6 + 0.00x_7$$

subject to the constraint

(a) $4x_1 + 7x_2 + 8x_3 + 6x_4 + 10x_5 + 3x_6 + 0x_7 \le 7$

(b) $x_1 + 5x_2 + 4x_3 + 8x_4 + 6x_5 + 3x_6 + 0x_7 \le 5$

(c) $0x_1 + 0.18x_2 + 0.10x_3 + 0.32x_4 + 0.20x_5 + 0.07x_6 + 0.00x_7 \ge 0.10$

(d) $x_7 \ge 0.10$

(e) Proportion of funds

$$x_1 + x_2 + x_3 + x_4 + x_5 + x_6 + x_7 = 1$$

and $x_1, x_2, x_3, x_4, x_5, x_6, x_7 \ge 0$.

EXAMPLE 3.8 An agriculturist has a farm with 126 acres. He produces radish, pea and potato. Whatever he raises is fully sold in the market. He gets Rs. 5 for radish per kg, Rs. 4 for pea per kg and Rs. 5 for potato per kg. The average yield is 1,500 kg of radish per acre, 1,800 kg of pea per acre and 1,200 kg of potato per acre. To produce each 100 kg of radish and pea and to produce each 80 kg of potato, a sum of Rs. 12.50 has to be used for manure. Labour required for each acre to raise the crop is 6-man-days for radish and potato each and 5-man-days for pea. A total of 500 man-days of labour at a rate of Rs. 40 per man-day are available. Formulate this problem as an LP model to maximize the agriculturist's total profit.

Solution: Let x_1, x_2, x_3 be the number of acres allocated for radish, pea and potato, respectively. $x_1, x_2, x_3 \geq 0$.

	Radish	*Pea*	*Potato*
Selling price	5 * 1500 = 7500	4 * 1800 = 7200	5 * 1200 = 6000
Manure cost	12.50 * 15 = 187.50	12.50 * 18 = 225	12.50 * 15 = 187.50
Labour cost	40 * 6 = 240	40 * 5 = 200	40 * 6 = 240
Profit	7500 – 427.50 = 7072.50	7200 – 425 = 6775	6000 – 427.50 = 5572.50

Thus LPP is

Maximize $$P = 7072.50x_1 + 6775x_2 + 5572.50x_3$$

subject to

Land constraint: $x_1 + x_2 + x_3 \leq 125$

Labour constraint: $6x_1 + 5x_2 + 6x_3 \leq 500$

and $x_1, x_2, x_3 \geq 0$.

EXAMPLE 3.9: A Mutual Fund company has Rs. 20 lakhs available for investment in government bonds, blue chip stocks, speculative stocks and short-term bank deposits. The annual expected return and risk factor are given below:

Type of investment	*Annual expected return (%)*	*Risk factor* (0 to 100)
Government bonds	14	12
Blue chip stocks	19	24
Speculative stocks	23	48
Short-term bank deposits	12	6

Mutual fund is required to keep at least Rs. 2 lakhs in short-term deposits and not to exceed an average risk factor of 42. Speculative stocks must be at most 20 % of the total amount invested. How should mutual fund invest the funds so as to maximize its expected annual return? Formulate this problem as an LPP so as to optimize return on the investment.

Solution: Let x_1, x_2, x_3 and x_4 be the amount of funds to be invested in government bonds, blue chip stocks, speculative stocks and short-term bank deposits, respectively. $x_1, x_2, x_3, x_4 \geq 0$. The objective is to maximize annual return, i.e.

Maximize $$R = 0.14x_1 + 0.19x_2 + 0.23x_3 + 0.12x_4$$

subject to

Total fund constraint: $x_1 + x_2 + x_3 + x_4 \leq 20{,}00{,}000$

Liquidity constraint: $x_4 \geq 2{,}00{,}000$

Average risk factor constraint:

Investment in speculative stock constraint: $x_3 \leq 0.2(x_1 + x_2 + x_3 + x_4)$ i.e.

$$-0.2x_1 - 0.2x_2 + 0.8x_3 - 0.2x_4 \leq 0$$

and $x_1, x_2, x_3, x_4 \geq 0$.

EXAMPLE 3.10 Two alloys A and B are made from four different metals I, II, III and IV according to the following specifications:

A: at most 80 % of I	B: between 40 % and 60 % of II
at most 30 % of II	at least 30 % of III
at most 50 % of III	at most 70 % of IV

The four metals are extracted from different ores whose constituents % of these metals, maximum available quantity, and cost per tonne are given below:

Ore	*Maximum quantity* (tonnes)	*Constituents* (%) I	II	III	IV	*Other price*	Rs/Tonne
1	1,000	20	10	30	30	10	30
2	2,000	10	20	30	30	10	40
3	3,000	5	5	70	20	0	50

Assuming the selling prices of alloys A and B are Rs. 200 and Rs. 300 per tonne respectively, formulate this problem as an LP model, selecting appropriate objective and constraints.

Solution: Given that two alloys, A and B, are to be manufactured. Let $x(1, A)$, $x(2, A)$, ..., be used for producing A or B from I, II, III or IV as shown in the given data table.

Maximize

$$P = 200A + 300B - \{30(x(1, A) + x(1, B)) + 40(x(2, A) + x(2, B)) + 50(x(3, A) + x(3, B))\}$$

subject to

Alloy specification for A

$$0.2x(1, A) + 0.1x(2, A) + 0.5x(3, A) \le 0.8A$$

$$0.1x(1, A) + 0.2x(2, A) + 0.05x(3, A) \le 0.3A$$

$$0.3x(1, A) + 0.3x(2, A) + 0.2x(3, A) \le 0.5A$$

Material balance for A

$$0.6x(1, A) + 0.6x(2, A) + 0.3x(3, A) = A$$

Alloy specification for B

$$0.1x(2, B) + 0.2x(3, B) + 0.05x(4, B) \le 0.4B$$

$$0.1x(2, B) + 0.2x(3, B) + 0.05x(4, B) \le 0.6B$$

$$0.3x(2, B) + 0.3x(3, B) + 0.07x(4, B) \ge 0.3B$$

$$0.3x(2, B) + 0.3x(3, B) + 0.2x(4, B) \le 0.7B$$

Material balance for B

$$0.7x(2, B) + 0.8x(3, B) + 0.95x(4, B) = B$$

$$x(1, A) + x(2, B) \le 1000$$

$$x(2, A) + x(3, B) \le 2000$$

$$x(3, A) + x(4, B) \le 3000$$

EXAMPLE 3.11: Suppose a media specialist has to decide on the allocation of advertising in three media vehicles. Let x_k be the number of messages carried in the media, $k = 1, 2, 3$. The unit costs of message in the three media are Rs. 1000, Rs. 750 and Rs. 500. The total budget available is

Rs. 2,00,000 for the campaign period of one year. The first media is a monthly magazine and it is desired to advertise not more than one insertion in one issue. At least six messages should appear in second media. The number of messages in the third media should strictly lie between 4 and 8. The expected effective audience for unit message in the media vehicles is shown below:

Vehicle	*Expected effective audience*
1	80,000
2	60,000
3	45,000

Formulate this problem as an LP model to determine the optimum allocation that would maximize total effective audience.

Solution: Let x_1, x_2 and x_3 be the number of messages carried in media 1, 2 and 3, respectively. $x_1, x_2, x_3 \geq 0$.

Maximize $$E = 80{,}000x_1 + 60{,}000x_2 + 45{,}000x_3$$

subject to the constraints:

$$1{,}000x_1 + 750x_2 + 500x_3 \leq 2{,}00{,}000$$

$$x_1 \leq 12;\ x_2 \geq 6;\ 4 \leq x_3 \leq 8$$

EXAMPLE 3.12: A wine maker has a stock of three different wines with the following characteristics:

Wine	*Proofs*	*Acid (%)*	*Specific gravity*	*Stock* (Gallons)
A	27	0.32	1.07	20
B	33	0.20	1.08	34
C	32	0.30	1.04	22

A good dry table wine should be between 30 and 31 degree proof, it should contain 25% acid and should have a specific gravity at least 1.06. The wine maker wishes to blend the three types of wine to produce as large a quantity as possible of a satisfactory dry table wine. However, his stock of wine *A* must be completely used in the blend because further storage would cause it to deteriorate. What quantities of wines *B* and *C* should be used in the blend? Formulate this problem as an LP model.

Solution: Let x_1 and x_2 the number of gallons of wine *B* and *C* to be blended respectively.

Maximize $$Z = 20 + x_1 + x_2$$

subject to

Resultant degrees proof of blend: $$30 \leq \frac{(20 \times 27) + 33x_1 + 32x_2}{20 + x_1 + x_2} \leq 31$$

Acidity constraint: $$\frac{(20 \times 0.32) + 0.2x_1 + 0.3x_2}{20 + x_1 + x_2} \geq 0.25$$

Specific gravity constraint: $\dfrac{(20 \times 1.07) + 1.08x_1 + 1.04x_2}{20 + x_1 + x_2} \geq 0.25$

Quality constraint: $x_1 \geq 34$

and $x_1, x_2 \geq 0$.

EXAMPLE 3.13 A paint manufacturing company manufactures paints at two plants. Firm orders have been received from three large contractors. The firm has determined that the following shipping cost data is appropriate for these contractors with respect to its two plants:

Contractor	*Order size* (gallon)	*Shipping cost*/Gallon (Rs.)	
		From Plant 1	*From Plant 2*
A	750	1.80	2.00
B	1,500	2.60	2.20
C	1,700	2.10	2.25

Each gallon of paint must be blended and tinted. The company's costs with two operations at each of the two plants are as follows:

Plant	*Operation*	*Hours required*/gallon	*Cost/hour* (Rs.)	*Hours available*
1	Blending	0.10	3.80	300
	Tinting	0.25	3.20	360
2	Blending	0.15	4.00	600
	Tinting	0.20	3.10	720

Formulate this problem as an LP model.

Solution: Try yourself.

Now, we have got sufficient insight into how to formulate LPP. The next step is to solve them. First, let us try to understand the general form of LPP.

3.3 GENERAL FORM OF LPP

The general LPP can be described as follows:

Given a set of *m*-linear inequalities or equalities in *n*-variables, we want to find non-negative values of these variables which will satisfy the constraints and optimize (maximize or minimize) linear function of these variables (objective function). Mathematically, we have *m*-linear inequalities or equalities in *n*-variables (*m* can be greater than, less than or equal to *n*) of the form

$$a_{k1}x_1 + ak_2x_2 + \cdots + a_{kn}x_n \; \{\geq, =, \leq\} \; b_k, \; k = 1, 2, \ldots, m \tag{3.1}$$

where for each constraint, one and only one of the signs $\geq, =, \leq$ holds, but the sign may vary from one constraint to another. The aim is to find the values of the variables x_j satisfying (3.1) and $x_j \geq 0$, $j = 1, 2, \ldots, n$, which maximize or minimize a linear function:

$$Z = c_1x_1 + c_2x_2 + \cdots + c_nx_n \tag{3.2}$$

The a_{kj}, b_k and c_j are assumed to be known constants. It is assumed that the variable x_j can take any non-negative values allowed by Eqs. (3.1) and (3.2). These non-negative values can be any real number. If the additional restriction is imposed that the variables must be integer, then linear programming problem is regarded as integer programming problem. We will discuss about integer programming problem in Chapter 4.

Thus, LPP is

Optimize $$Z = c_1x_1 + c_2x_2 + \cdots + c_nx_n \tag{3.3}$$

subject to the constraints

$$a_{k1}x_1 + a_{k2}x_2 + \cdots + a_{kn}x_n\{\geq, =, \leq\}b_k, \; k = 1, 2, \ldots, m \tag{3.4}$$

and $$x_j \geq 0, \; j = 1, 2, \ldots, n \tag{3.5}$$

3.3.1 LPP in Canonical Form

In general, ≤ constraints will be associated with maximization LPP and ≥ constraints with minimization LPP. Let us write canonical form of maximization problem

Maximize $$Z = c_1x_1 + c_2x_2 + \cdots + c_nx_n$$

subject to the constraints

$$a_{k1}x_1 + a_{k2}x_2 + \cdots + a_{kn}x_n \leq b_k, \; k = 1, 2, \ldots, m$$

and $x_j \geq 0$, $j = 1, 2, \ldots, n$

The canonical form of minimization problem is

Minimize $$z = c_1x_1 + c_2x_2 + \cdots + c_nx_n$$

subject to the constraints

$$a_{k1}x_1 + a_{k2}x_2 + \cdots + a_{kn}x_n \geq b_k, \; k = 1, 2, \ldots, m$$

and $x_j \geq 0$, $j = 1, 2, \ldots, n$

Note: Different constraints may have different signs.

Note: When nothing is mentioned about the non-negativity of the variables, they are said to be unrestricted in sign. To convert them in order that they can be set according to the format of LPP, we write the unrestricted variable x_j as a difference of two non-negative variables x_j' and x_j'', i.e. $x_j = x_j' - x_j''$; $x_j', x_j'' \geq 0$.

Note: The theoretical discussion is based on n-decision variables and m-constraints ($n \geq m$).

For solving any LPP by algebraic or analytic method, it is necessary to convert inequalities (inequations) into equality (equations). This can be done by introducing the so-called slack and surplus variables.

Consider an inequality of the form $a_{k1}x_1 + a_{k2}x_2 + \cdots + a_{kn}x_n \leq b_k$. Introduce a variable $s_{n+k} = b_k - \sum_{j=1}^{n} a_{kj}x_j \geq 0$. So that $\sum_{j=1}^{n} a_{kj}x_j + s_{n+k} = b_k$. Such a variable s_{n+k} is known as a ***slack variable***. Similarly, consider an inequality of the form $a_{k1}x_1 + a_{k2}x_2 + \cdots + a_{kn}x_n \geq b_k$. Introduce a variable $s_{n+k} = -b_k + \sum_{j=1}^{n} a_{kj}x_j \geq 0$. So that $\sum_{j=1}^{n} a_{kj}x_j - s_{n+k} = b_k$. Such a variable s_{n+k} is known as a ***surplus variable***. To each slack and/or surplus variable, assign a cost coefficient of zero in the objective function.

Note: Original variables and slack/surplus variables are known as legitimate variables associated with given LPP.

After introducing slack/surplus variables, any given LPP can be expressed as under:

Maximize $$Z = c_1x_1 + c_2x_2 + \cdots + c_nx_n$$

subject to the constraints

$$a_{k1}x_1 + a_{k2}x_2 + \cdots + a_{kn}x_n + s_{n+k} = b_k,\ k = 1, 2, \ldots, m$$

and $x_j \geq 0,\ j = 1, 2, \ldots, n + k$

Note: Bold face represents vector with a proper dimension.

Using matrix notations, above LPP in canonical form as well as standard form can be expressed as follows:

Canonical form: Maximize (Minimize) $Z = \mathbf{c}^T\mathbf{x}$ subject to $\mathbf{Ax} \leq (\geq)\ \mathbf{b},\ \mathbf{x} \geq 0$.

Standard form: Maximize (Minimize) $Z = \mathbf{c}^T\mathbf{x}$ subject to $\mathbf{Ax} = \mathbf{b},\ \mathbf{x} \geq 0$.

where $\mathbf{c}, \mathbf{x} \in \mathbf{R}^n$, $\mathbf{b} \in \mathbf{R}^m$ and $A = (a_{ij})_{m\times n}$ is a real valued matrix with rank equal to $m \leq n$. Thus, A will have m-linearly independent columns.

Let us introduce some definitions for our standard LPP:

Solution: Any $\mathbf{x} \in \mathbf{R}^n$ which satisfies $\mathbf{Ax} = \mathbf{b}$ is a solution.

Feasible solution: Any $\mathbf{x} \in \mathbf{R}^n$ which satisfies $\mathbf{Ax} = \mathbf{b}$, $\mathbf{x} \geq 0$ is called a feasible solution to the given LPP.

The set $S_F = \{\mathbf{x} \in \mathbf{R}^n\text{: } \mathbf{Ax} = \mathbf{b},\ \mathbf{x} \geq 0\}$ is known as the set of all feasible solutions.

Basic solution: Any solution $\mathbf{x}$ in which at most m-variables are non-zero is called a basic solution.

Basic feasible solution: Any feasible solution $\mathbf{x} \in \mathbf{R}^n$ in which k ($\leq m$) variables have positive values and the rest $(n - k)$ have zero values is called a basic feasible solution. If $k = m$, the basic feasible solution is called *non-degenerate*. If $k < m$, the basic feasible solution is called *degenerate*.

Our aim is to obtain a basic feasible solution to given LPP which optimizes the objective function.

Optimum solution: Any feasible solution, $\mathbf{x} \in \mathbf{R}^n$ which optimizes the objective function $Z = \mathbf{c}^T\mathbf{x}$ is known as the optimum solution to the given LPP.

Optimum basic feasible solution: A basic feasible solution is said to be optimum if it optimizes the objective function.

Unbounded solution: If the value of the objective function can be increased or decreased infinitely without violating the constraints, then the solution is known as unbounded solution.

Let us discuss some of the fundamental results.

Consider LPP:

Maximize (Minimize) $\quad Z = \mathbf{c}^T\mathbf{x}$ subject to $\mathbf{Ax} = \mathbf{b},\ \mathbf{x} \geq 0$

Let $S_F = \{\mathbf{x} \in \mathbf{R}^n\text{: } \mathbf{Ax} = \mathbf{b},\ \mathbf{x} \geq 0\}$ denote the set of all feasible solutions.

Theorem 3.1: *S_F is a convex set.*

Proof: Let $\mathbf{x}_1, \mathbf{x}_2 \in S_F$ and $\lambda \in [0, 1]$ be any scalar. Then $\mathbf{Ax}_1 = \mathbf{b}$ and $\mathbf{Ax}_2 = \mathbf{b}$, $\mathbf{x}_1 \geq 0$, $\mathbf{x}_2 \geq 0$. Consider a convex combination of $\mathbf{x}_1$ and $\mathbf{x}_2$ (say) $\mathbf{x}_\lambda$. Then $\mathbf{x}_\lambda = \lambda\mathbf{x}_1 + (1 - \lambda)\mathbf{x}_2$. Obviously, $\mathbf{x}_\lambda \geq 0$.

Further $\mathbf{Ax}_\lambda = \mathbf{A}(\lambda\mathbf{x}_1 + (1 - \lambda)\,\mathbf{x}_2) = \lambda\mathbf{Ax}_1 + (1 - \lambda)\mathbf{Ax}_2 = \lambda\mathbf{b} + (1 - \lambda)\mathbf{b} = \mathbf{b}$, implying $\mathbf{x}_\lambda \in S_F$. Hence, S_F is a convex set.

Note 1: If S_F is a null set, then there is no solution to given LPP.

Note 2: If S_F is a closed bounded convex set, i.e. a convex polyhedron, given LPP will have an optimum solution assigning finite value to the objective function.

Note 3: If S_F is a convex set unbounded in some direction of $\mathbf{R}^n$, then LPP will have a solution but the optimum value of the objective function may be finite or infinite.

Theorem 3.2: *Suppose the set S_F of feasible solutions to the given LPP is non-empty, then the basic feasible solution to the LPP (if it exists) lies at the vertex of a convex polygon.*

Proof: Suppose S_F has *p*-vertices (say) $\mathbf{x}_1, \mathbf{x}_2, \ldots, \mathbf{x}_p$. Let $\mathbf{x}_0$ be the basic feasible solution to given LPP. Two cases may arise:

Case (i): $\mathbf{x}_0$ is vertex of convex polygon. Then, the result is obvious.

Case (ii): Let $\mathbf{x}_0$ be interior point of vertex of S_F. Then $\mathbf{x}_0$ can be expressed as convex combination of its vertices. That is there exists scalars $\lambda_1, \lambda_2, \ldots, \lambda_p$ with $0 \leq \lambda_j \leq 1$, $1 \leq j \leq p$ and

$$\sum_{j=1}^{p} \lambda_j = 1 \text{ such that } \mathbf{x}_0 = \sum_{j=1}^{p} \lambda_j \mathbf{x}_j \tag{3.6}$$

Since $\mathbf{x}_0$ is optimum, we have

$$\mathbf{c}^T\mathbf{x}_0 \geq \mathbf{c}^T\mathbf{x}_j \text{ for all } 1 \leq j \leq p \tag{3.7}$$

In particular, let $\mathbf{x}_0$ be such that

$$\mathbf{c}^T\mathbf{x}_m \geq \mathbf{c}^T\mathbf{x}_j \text{ for all } 1 \leq j \leq p \tag{3.8}$$

From Eqs. (3.7) and (3.8), $\mathbf{c}^T\mathbf{x}_0 \geq \mathbf{c}^T\mathbf{x}_m$ (3.9)

Again, $\mathbf{c}^T\mathbf{x}_m \geq \mathbf{c}^T\mathbf{x}_j$ for all $1 \leq j \leq p$ then $\lambda_j\mathbf{c}^T\mathbf{x}_m \geq \lambda_j\mathbf{c}^T\mathbf{x}_j$ for all $1 \leq j \leq p$.

$$\lambda_j\,\mathbf{c}^T\mathbf{x}_m \geq \sum_{j=1}^{p} \lambda_j\mathbf{c}^T\mathbf{x}_j \text{ implies } \mathbf{c}^T\mathbf{x}_m \sum_{j=1}^{p} \lambda_j \geq \mathbf{c}^T \sum_{j=1}^{p} \lambda_j\mathbf{x}_j$$

i.e

$$\mathbf{c}^T\mathbf{x}_m \geq \mathbf{c}^T\mathbf{x}_0 \tag{3.10}$$

From Eqs. (3.9) and (3.10), it follows that $\mathbf{c}^T\mathbf{x}_0 = \mathbf{c}^T\mathbf{x}_m$.

Thus, there always exists a vertex $\mathbf{x}_m \in S_F$ such that $\mathbf{c}^T\mathbf{x}_m$ is optimum value. Thus, if a basic feasible solution to a given LPP exists then one of the vertex will give optimum value to the objective function.

Theorem 3.3: *The set of optimal solutions to the LPP is convex.*

Proof: Let S_{F0} denotes the set of optimal solutions. If S_{F0} is empty or singleton, then it is convex. Let S_{F0} contain more than one solution (say) $\mathbf{x}_{10}, \mathbf{x}_{20} \in S_{F0}$. Then $\mathbf{c}^T\mathbf{x}_{10} = \mathbf{c}^T\mathbf{x}_{20} = \max Z$. Consider convex combination of $\mathbf{x}_{10}$ and $\mathbf{x}_{20}$ as $\mathbf{w}_0 = \lambda\mathbf{x}_1 + (1 - \lambda)\mathbf{x}_2$, $0 \leq \lambda \leq 1$. Then $\mathbf{c}^T\mathbf{w}_0 = \mathbf{c}^T\{\lambda\mathbf{x}_{10} + (1 - \lambda)\,\mathbf{x}_{20}\} = \lambda\mathbf{c}^T\mathbf{x}_{10} + (1 - \lambda)\,\mathbf{c}^T\mathbf{x}_{20} = \lambda \max Z + (1 - \lambda) \max Z = \max Z$. Thus, $\mathbf{w}_0 \in S_{F0}$. S_{F0} is convex.

Theorem 3.4: *If the convex set of the feasible solution of* $\mathbf{Ax} = \mathbf{b}$, $\mathbf{x} \geq 0$ *is a convex polyhedron, then at least one of the extreme points gives a basic feasible solution.*

If the basic feasible solution occurs at more than one extreme point, the value of the objective function will be same for all convex combinations of these extreme points.

Proof: Let $\mathbf{x}_1, \mathbf{x}_2, \ldots, \mathbf{x}_k$ be the extreme points of the feasible region F of the LPP defined in Eqs. (3.3)–(3.5). Suppose $\mathbf{x}_m$ is the extreme point among $\mathbf{x}_1, \mathbf{x}_2, \ldots, \mathbf{x}_k$ at which the value of the objective function is maximum (say Z^*). Then

$$Z^* = \mathbf{c}^T\mathbf{x}_m \tag{3.11}$$

Now, consider a point $\mathbf{x}_0 \in S_F$, which is not an extreme point and let Z_0 be the corresponding value of the objective function. Then,

$$Z_0 = \mathbf{c}^T\mathbf{x}_0 \tag{3.12}$$

Since $\mathbf{x}_0$ is not an extreme point, it can be expressed as a convex combination of the extreme points $\mathbf{x}_1, \mathbf{x}_2, \ldots, \mathbf{x}_k$ of the feasible region F where F is assumed to be a closed and bounded set. Then there exists scalars $\lambda_1, \lambda_2, \ldots, \lambda_k$ with $\sum_{j=1}^{k} \lambda_j = 1$, $0 \leq \lambda_j \leq 1$, $1 \leq j \leq k$ such that $\mathbf{x}_0 = \lambda_1\mathbf{x}_1 + \lambda_2\mathbf{x}_2 + \cdots + \lambda_k\mathbf{x}_k$. Therefore Eq. (3.12) becomes

$Z_0 = \mathbf{c}^T\{\lambda_1\mathbf{x}_1 + \lambda_2\mathbf{x}_2 + \cdots + \lambda_k\mathbf{x}_k\} = \lambda_1\mathbf{c}^T\mathbf{x}_1 + \lambda_2\mathbf{c}^T\mathbf{x}_2 + \cdots + \lambda_k\mathbf{c}^T\mathbf{x}_k \leq \mathbf{c}^T\mathbf{x}_m$, i.e. $Z_0 \leq Z^*$ (from Eq. (3.11)) which implies that an optimum solution, the extreme point solution is better than any feasible solution in F.

Second part of the Theorem: Let $\mathbf{x}_1, \mathbf{x}_2, \ldots, \mathbf{x}_r$ $(r \leq k)$ be the extreme points of the feasible region F at which the objective function assumes the same optimum value. This means $Z^* = \mathbf{c}^T\mathbf{x}_1 = \mathbf{c}^T\mathbf{x}_2 = \ldots = \mathbf{c}^T\mathbf{x}_r$.

Further, let $\mathbf{x} = \lambda_1\mathbf{x}_1 + \lambda_2\mathbf{x}_2 + \cdots + \lambda_r\mathbf{x}_r$, $\sum_{j=1}^{r} \lambda_j = 1$, $0 \leq \lambda_j \leq 1$, $1 \leq j \leq r$ be the convex combination of $\mathbf{x}_1, \mathbf{x}_2, \ldots, \mathbf{x}_r$. Then,

$$\begin{aligned}\mathbf{c}^T\mathbf{x} &= \mathbf{c}^T\{\lambda_1\mathbf{x}_1 + \lambda_2\mathbf{x}_2 + \cdots + \lambda_r\mathbf{x}_r\} = \lambda_1\mathbf{c}^T\mathbf{x}_1 + \lambda_2\mathbf{c}^T\mathbf{x}_2 + \cdots + \lambda_r\mathbf{c}^T\mathbf{x}_r \\ &= \lambda_1\mathbf{Z}^* + \lambda_2\mathbf{Z}^* + \cdots + \lambda_r\mathbf{Z}^* = \mathbf{Z}^*\sum_{j=1}^{r}\lambda_j = \mathbf{Z}^*\end{aligned}$$

which completes the proof.

Theorem 3.5 *If there exists a feasible solution to the LPP, then there exists a basic feasible solution to a given LPP.*

Proof: Consider Maximize $Z = c_1x_1 + c_2x_2 + \cdots + c_nx_n$.
subject to the constraints

$\mathbf{a}_1\mathbf{x}_1 + \mathbf{a}_2\mathbf{x}_2 + \cdots + \mathbf{a}_n\mathbf{x}_n = \mathbf{b}$ where $a_j^T = (a_{j1}, a_{j2}, \ldots, a_{jn})$ is j-th column of A.

Suppose that there exists a feasible solution to above LPP in which $k > m$ variables have positive values. WLOG, we assume that first k-variates have positive values. Then $\mathbf{a}_1\mathbf{x}_1 + \mathbf{a}_2\mathbf{x}_2 + \cdots + \mathbf{a}_n\mathbf{x}_n = \mathbf{b}$. For each $\mathbf{a}_j \in \mathbf{R}^m$, $\{\mathbf{a}_1, \mathbf{a}_2, \ldots, \mathbf{a}_k\}$ forms a dependent set. Assume that $\mathbf{x}_r \neq 0$ and $\mathbf{a}_r$ is linear combination of the remaining vectors of the set. So there exists scalars $\alpha_1, \alpha_2, \ldots, \alpha_{r-1}, \alpha_{r+1}, \ldots, \alpha_k$ such that $\sum_{j=1}^{k} \alpha_j a_j = 0$ implies

$$\sum_{\substack{j=1\\j\neq r}}^{k} \alpha_j a_j + \alpha_r a_r = 0 \quad \text{i.e.} \quad a_r = \sum_{\substack{j=1\\j\neq r}}^{k} \left(-\frac{\alpha_j}{\alpha_r}\right) a_j$$

We have $$\mathbf{a}_r\mathbf{x}_r + \sum_{\substack{j=1\\j\neq r}}^{k} \mathbf{a}_j\mathbf{x}_j = \mathbf{b} \quad \text{i.e.} \quad \mathbf{a}_r\mathbf{x}_r + \mathbf{x}_r \sum_{\substack{j=1\\j\neq r}}^{k} \left(-\frac{\alpha_j}{\alpha_r}\right) a_j = \mathbf{b}$$

i.e. $$\sum_{\substack{j=1\\j\neq r}}^{k} \left[x_j + \left(-\frac{\alpha_j}{\alpha_r}\right) \mathbf{x}_r \right] a_j = \mathbf{b}$$

Put $$x'_j = x_j + \left(-\frac{\alpha_j}{\alpha_r}\right) \mathbf{x}_r$$

Then $$\sum_{\substack{j=1\\j\neq r}}^{k} x'_j a_j = \mathbf{b}$$

Thus, $\mathbf{x}'_j$ gives a new solution to given LPP which depends on $(k - 1)$—variables. In order that the new solution is feasible, we require $\mathbf{x}'_j \geq 0$.

Clearly, $$x_j + \left(-\frac{\alpha_j}{\alpha_r}\right) \mathbf{x}_r \geq 0, \quad j = 1, 2, \ldots, k$$

So $$x_j \geq \left(\frac{\alpha_j}{\alpha_r}\right) \mathbf{x}_r \quad \text{or} \quad \frac{x_r}{\alpha_r} \leq \frac{x_j}{\alpha_j}, \; a_j \neq 0.$$

Thus, if we choose $\mathbf{a}_r$ such that $\dfrac{x_r}{\alpha_r} = \min\limits_{j} \left\{ \dfrac{x_j}{\alpha_j}, \alpha_j \neq 0 \right\}$ then the solution will also be feasible.

Thus, we get a new feasible solution in which $(k - 1)$— variables have positive values. This process can be continued till we get a feasible solution in which m— variables have positive values.

Now let us discuss methods of solving LPP.

3.4 GRAPHICAL METHOD

LPP involving two decision variables can be solved graphically. Using results proved in Section 3.3, the optimal solution to LPP can be found by evaluating the value of the objective function at each vertex of the feasible region. Theorem 3.2 also states that an optimal solution to LPP will only occur at one of the extreme points. The algorithm to solve LPP using graphical method is described below.

3.4.1 Extreme Point Approach

Step 1: Formulate LPP as discussed in Section 3.2.

Step 2: Plot all constraints on the graph paper and shade the feasible region.

Step 3: List all extreme points of the feasible region. Evaluate the values of the objective function at each extreme point, and the extreme point of the feasible region that optimizes (maximize or minimize) the objective function value is the required basic feasible solution.

3.4.2 Iso-profit (cost) Function Line Approach

Follow step 1 and step 2 as stated in Section 3.4.1.

Step 3: Draw an Iso-profit (iso-cost) line for small value of the objective function without violating any of the constraints of the given LPP.

Step 4: Move iso-profit (iso-cost) lines parallel in the direction of increasing (or decreasing) objective function.

Step 5: The feasible extreme point for which the value of iso-profit (iso-cost) is maximum (minimum) is the optimal solution. This means that while moving the iso-profit line in the required direction, the last point after which we move out of the feasible region is the required optimal solution.

EXAMPLE 3.14: Solve graphically the LPP:

Maximize $$z = 45x_1 + 80x_2$$

Subject to the constraints:

$$5x_1 + 20x_2 \leq 400$$

$$10x_1 + 15x_2 \leq 450$$

and $x_1, x_2 \geq 0$.

Solution: From Figure 3.1, the vertices of the shaded region are (0,0), (0, 20), (45, 0) and (24, 14). The values of the objective function z at these extreme points are 0, 1600, 2025 and 2200, respectively. The maximum value of $z = 2200$ occurs at $x_1 = 24$ and $x_2 = 14$.

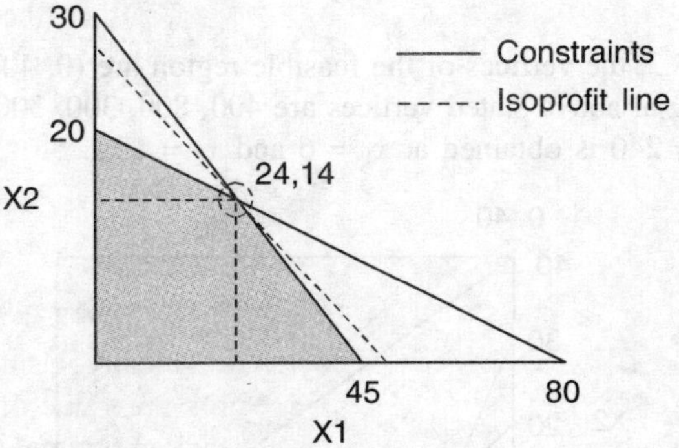

Figure 3.1

EXAMPLE 3.15: Solve graphically the LPP:

Maximize $$z = 7x_1 + 3x_2$$

Subject to the constraints:

$$x_1 + 2x_2 \geq 3$$

$$x_1 + x_2 \leq 4$$
$$0 \leq x_1 \leq 5/2$$
$$0 \leq x_2 \leq 3/2$$

and $x_1, x_2 \geq 0$.

Solution: The vertices of the convex polygon in Figure 3.2 are (0, 1.5), (2.5, 0.25), (2.5, 1.5). The values of the objective function z are 4.5, 18.25, 22, respectively of which maximum is 22, obtained at (2.5, 1.5).

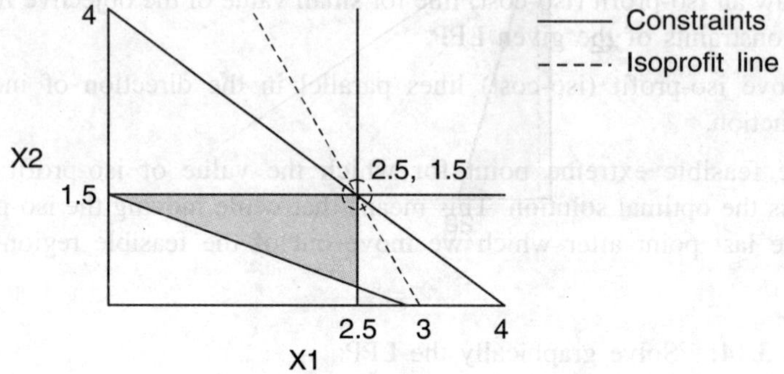

Figure 3.2

EXAMPLE 3.16: Solve graphically the LPP.

Minimize $$z = 20x_1 + 10x_2$$

Subject to the constraints:

$$3x_1 + x_2 \geq 30$$
$$x_1 + x_2 \leq 40$$
$$4x_1 + 3x_2 \geq 60$$

and $x_1, x_2 \geq 0$.

Solution: In Figure 3.3, the vertices of the feasible region are (0, 40), (40, 0), (0, 30), (15, 0) and (6, 12). The values of z at above stated vertices are 400, 800, 300, 300, 240, respectively. Thus, the minimum value of z = 240 is obtained at x_1 = 6 and x_2 = 12.

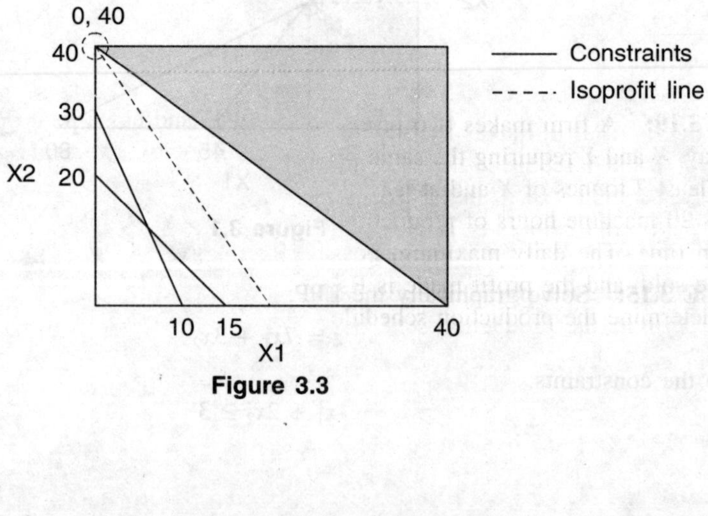

Figure 3.3

EXAMPLE 3.17: Solve Example 3.1 graphically.

Solution: The vertices of the shaded region in Figure 3.4 are (0, 0), (20, 0), (0, 36) and (2.5, 35). The values of z are 0, 60, 144 and 147.5. Thus, maximum z = 147.5 is obtained at x_1 = 2.5 and x_2 = 35.

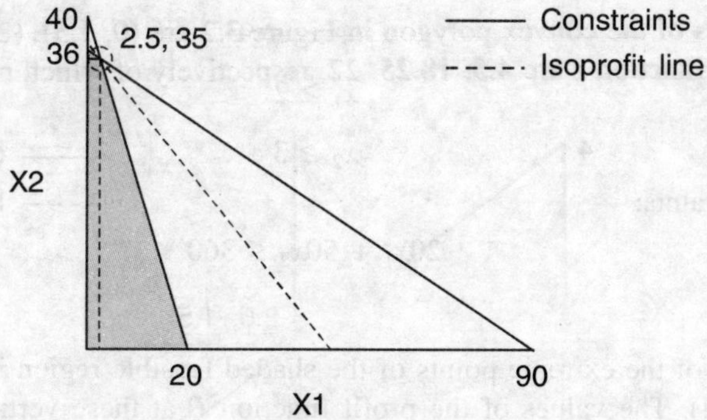

Figure 3.4

EXAMPLE 3.18: Solve Example 3.2 graphically.

Solution: In Figure 3.5, the vertices of unbounded feasible region are (0, 8.3), (6.25, 0), (9, 0), (0, 10) and (9, 10). The inspection costs at these vertices are 566.67, 430, 619.20, 680 and 1299.20, of which minimum cost is 430 for x_1 = 6.25 and x_2 = 0.

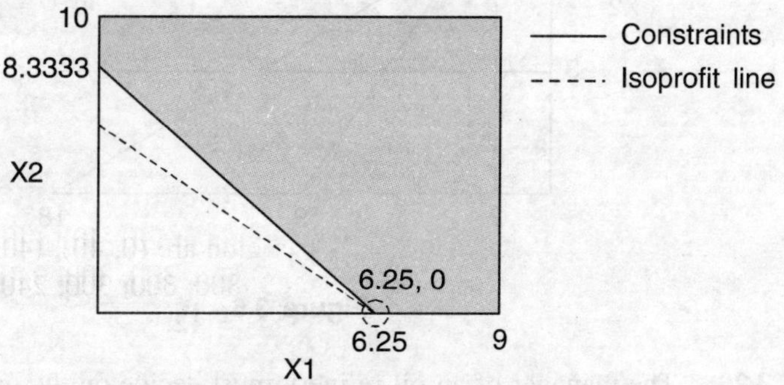

Figure 3.5

EXAMPLE 3.19: A firm makes two products X and Y, and has a total production capacity of 9 tonnes per day, X and Y requiring the same production capacity. The firm has a permanent contract to supply at least 2 tonnes of X and at least 3 tonnes of Y per day to another company. Each tonne of X requires 20 machine hours of production time and each tonne of Y requires 50 machine hours of production time. The daily maximum possible number of machine hour is 360. All the firm's output can be sold, and the profit made is Rs. 80 per tonne of X and Rs. 120 per tonne of Y. It is required to determine the production schedule for maximum profit and to calculate this profit.

Solution: Let x_1 and x_2 be the number of units (in tonnes) of product *X* and *Y* to be manufactured. Using steps of formulation of LP as discussed in Section 3.2, the LPP is

Maximize $$P = 80x_1 + 120x_2$$

subject to the production constraints:

$$x_1 + x_2 \leq 9$$

$$x_1 \geq 2$$

$$x_2 \geq 3$$

Machine hour constraints:

$$20x_1 + 50x_2 \leq 360$$

and $x_1, x_2 \geq 0$.

The coordinates of the extreme points of the shaded feasible region in Figure 3.6 are (2, 3), (6, 3), (3, 6) and (2, 6.4). The values of the profit function *P* at these vertices are 520, 840, 960 and 928, respectively. The maximum profit of Rs. 960 occurs at (3, 6). Hence, the company should produce three tonnes of product *X* and six tonnes of product *Y* in order to get maximum profit of Rs. 960.

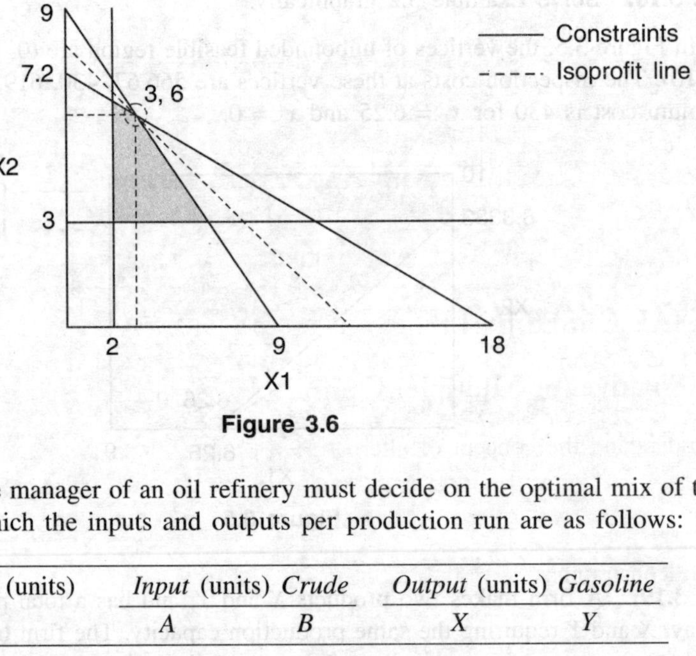

Figure 3.6

EXAMPLE 3.20: The manager of an oil refinery must decide on the optimal mix of two possible blending process, of which the inputs and outputs per production run are as follows:

Process (units)	*Input* (units) *Crude*		*Output* (units) *Gasoline*	
	A	*B*	*X*	*Y*
1	5	3	5	8
2	4	5	4	4

The maximum amounts available for crudes *A* and *B* are 200 units and 150 units, respectively. Market requirements show that at least 100 units of gasoline *X* and 80 units of gasoline *Y* must be produced. The profits per production run for process 1 and process 2 are Rs. 300 and Rs. 400, respectively. Solve the LPP by the graphical method.

Solution: Let x_1 and x_2 be the number of production runs for process 1 and process 2, respectively. We need to solve the LPP

Maximize $$P = 300x_1 + 400x_2$$

subject to the

(i) Input constraints: $5x_1 + 4x_2 \leq 200$ and $3x_1 + 5x_2 \leq 150$

(ii) Output constraints: $5x_1 + 4x_2 \geq 100$ and $8x_1 + 4x_2 \geq 80$

and $x_1, x_2 \geq 0$.

The feasible region in Figure 3.7 is the shaded region with vertices (20, 0), (40, 0), (30.77, 11.54), (0, 30) and (0, 25). The corresponding values of the profit is 6000, 12000, 13846.15, 12000 and 10000, respectively. The profit of Rs. 13846.15 is maximum if the manager of the oil refinery produces 30.77 units under process 1 and 11.54 units under process 2.

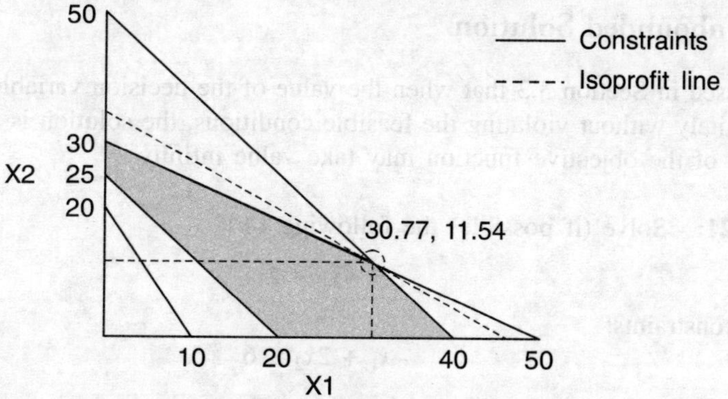

Figure 3.7

3.5 SPECIAL CASES IN LP

3.5.1 Alternative (or Multiple) Optimal Solution

We try to understand the concept of alternative or multiple solution by considering the following example.

Maximize $$P = 4x_1 + 4x_2$$

subject to the constraints:

$$x_1 + 2x_2 \leq 10$$
$$6x_1 + 6x_2 \leq 36$$
$$x_1 \leq 6$$

and $x_1, x_2 \geq 0$.

It can be observed in Figure 3.8 that the iso-profit line coincides with the edge of the convex feasible region. Thus there will be infinitely many points at which the objective function is maximum. Hence, any point on the iso-profit line will give optimum solutions and these solutions will yield the same maximum value of the objective function.

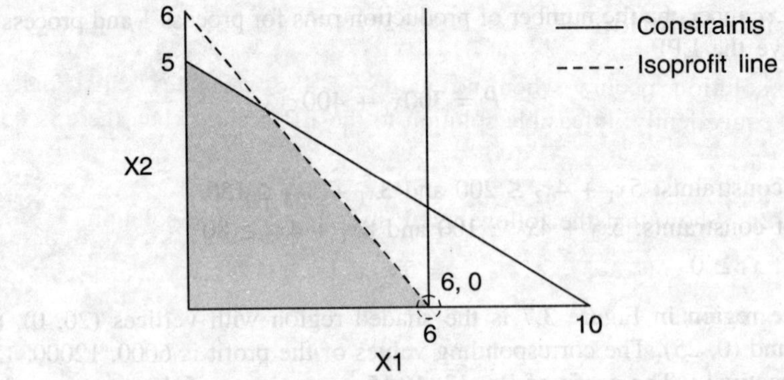

Figure 3.8

3.5.2 An Unbounded Solution

We have discussed in Section 3.3 that when the value of the decision variables in LP is allowed to increase indefinitely without violating the feasible conditions, the solution is said to be unbounded. Here, the value of the objective function may take value infinity.

EXAMPLE 3.21: Solve (if possible) the following LPP.

Maximize $$z = 4x_1 + 2x_2$$

subject to the constraints:

$$-x_1 + 2x_2 \leq 6$$

$$-x_1 + x_2 \leq 2$$

and $x_1, x_2 \geq 0$.

Solution: The feasible region in Figure 3.9 suggests that the given LP has an unbounded solution.

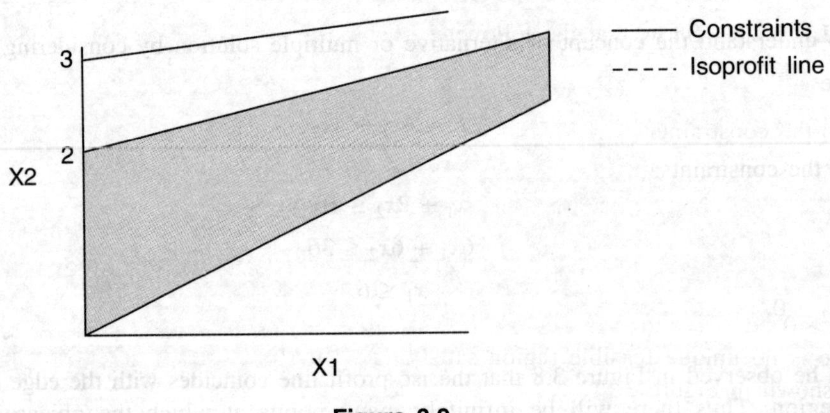

Figure 3.9

3.5.3 Infeasible Solution

The infeasible solution occurs when no value of the variables satisfy all the constraints simultaneously; equivalently, infeasible solution to the LP occurs when there is no unique feasible region.

EXAMPLE 3.22: Show that the following LP has an infeasible solution.

Maximize $$z = 5x_1 + 3x_2$$

subject to the constraints:

$$4x_1 + 2x_2 \leq 8$$

$$x_1 \geq 3$$

$$x_2 \geq 7$$

and x_1, $x_2 \geq 0$.

Solution: The given LP has an infeasible solution (See Figure 3.10).

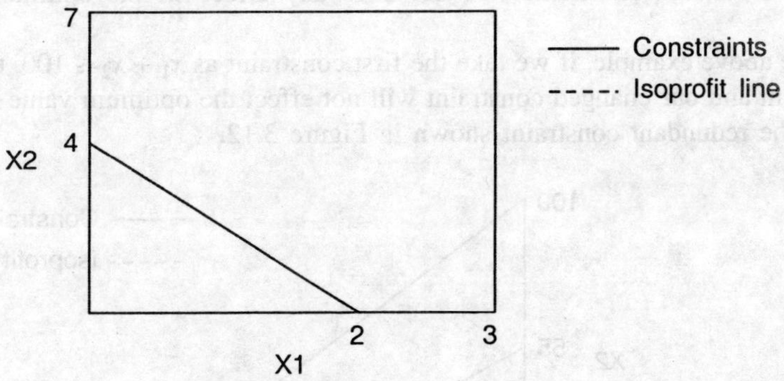

Figure 3.10

EXAMPLE 3.23: Show that the following LP has an infeasible solution.

Maximize $$z = 3x_1 + 5x_2$$

subject to the constraints:

$$x_1 + x_2 \geq 100$$

$$5x_1 + 10x_2 \leq 400$$

$$6x_1 + 8x_2 \leq 440$$

and x_1, $x_2 \geq 0$.

There is no unique feasible region satisfying all the constraints, and so LP has an infeasible solution shown in Figure 3.11.

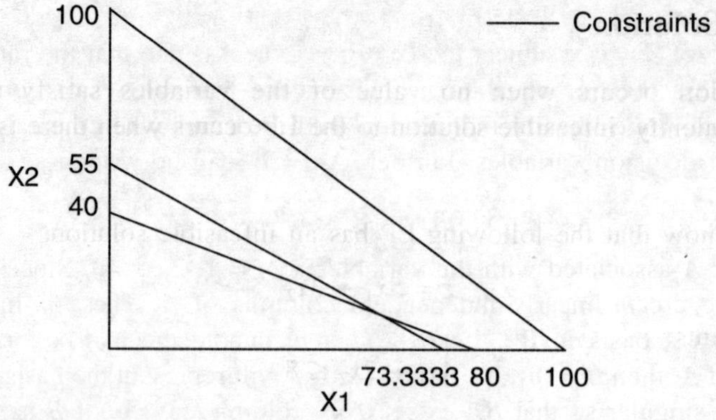

Figure 3.11

3.5.4 Redundant Constraint

A constraint which does not affect the feasibility of the region is said to be the *redundant constraint*. Thus, the redundant constraint will not have any effect on the optimum value of the objective function.

In the above example, if we take the first constraint as $x_1 + x_2 \leq 100$, then we get a solution for the problem and our changed constraint will not effect the optimum value of the objective function. So, it is the redundant constraint shown in Figure 3.12.

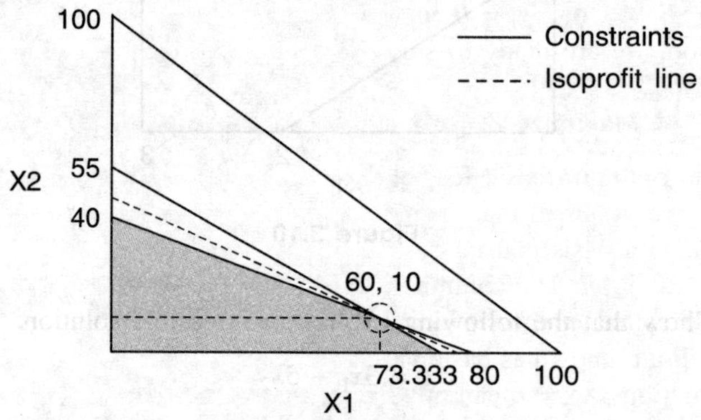

Figure 3.12

3.6 SIMPLEX METHOD

In general, any system may not be restricted to only two decision variables. In this section, we try to explore an algebraic technique to solve LPP iteratively in finite number of steps. This method is known as *simplex method*. In this method, we start with one of the vertex or extreme point of S_F and at each step or iteration move to an adjacent vertex in such a way that the value of the objective for iteration improves at each iteration. This method either gives an optimum solution (if it exists) or gives an indication that the given LPP has an unbounded solution.

Consider LPP:

Maximize (Minimize) $Z = \mathbf{c}^T\mathbf{x}$ subject to $\mathbf{Ax} = \mathbf{b}$, $\mathbf{x} \geq 0$. Assume that the rank of $(A, \mathbf{b})$ = rank of A equal to m but less than or equal to n. This means that the set of constraint equation is consistent, all m-rows of A are linearly independent and the number of constraints are less than or equal to the number of decision variables. Further, $\mathbf{Ax} = \mathbf{b}$, can be written as

$$x_1\mathbf{a}_1 + x_2\mathbf{a}_2 + \cdots + x_n\mathbf{a}_n = \mathbf{b}$$

i.e. $\mathbf{a}_j$ is the column of A associated with the variables x_j, $j = 1, 2, \ldots, n$. Since rank of A is equal to m less than n, there are m-linearly independent columns of A. These m-linearly independent columns of A will form a basis in $\mathbf{R}^m$. Let $B : m \times m$ denote the matrix formed by m-linearly independent columns of A, then $B = (\mathbf{b}_1, \mathbf{b}_2, \ldots, \mathbf{b}_j, \ldots, \mathbf{b}_m)$ will represent the basis matrix. Obviously, $B : m \times m$ will be non-singular so that B^{-1} exists. Any column (say) $\mathbf{b}_i$ of B is some column (say) $\mathbf{a}_j$ of A. Note that it is not necessary that the arrangement of column in B should be in accordance with those of A.

Any vector $\mathbf{a}_j \in A$ can be expressed as a linear combination of columns of B, i.e. for any $\mathbf{a}_j \in A$, there exists scalars $y_{1j}, y_{2j}, \ldots, y_{mj}$ such that

$$\mathbf{a}_j = \sum_{j=1}^{m} y_{ij} b_i \quad \text{or} \quad \mathbf{a}_j = B\mathbf{y}_j,\ j = 1, 2, \ldots, n$$

where $\qquad \mathbf{y}_j = (y_{1j}, y_{2j}, \ldots, y_{mj})$

Thus,

$$A = (\mathbf{a}_1, \mathbf{a}_2, \ldots, \mathbf{a}_j, \ldots, \mathbf{a}_n) = (By_1, By_2, \ldots, By_j, \ldots, By_n) = B(y_1, y_2, \ldots, y_j, \ldots, y_n)$$

i.e $A = B\mathbf{y}$ implies $y = B^{-1}A$ or $\mathbf{y}_j = B^{-1}\mathbf{a}_j$, $j = 1, 2, \ldots, n$.

With this discussion, we are ready to study the Simplex method.

Consider the LPP :

$$\text{Maximize } Z = \mathbf{c}^T\mathbf{x} \text{ subject to } \mathbf{Ax} = \mathbf{b},\ \mathbf{x} \geq 0.$$

The aim is to obtain an optimum basic feasible solution for given LPP. Since the simplex method is an iterative method, we assumed that an initial basic feasible solution is available.

Let $B : m \times m$ denote a basis matrix (say) $B = (\mathbf{b}_1, \mathbf{b}_2, \ldots, \mathbf{b}_j, \ldots, \mathbf{b}_m)$. Each $\mathbf{b}_i$ is some $\mathbf{a}_j$ of A, $i = 1, 2, \ldots, m$ and $j = 1, 2, \ldots, n$. The columns of A included in B are called *basic vectors* and those which are not in B are called *non-basic vectors*. The variables vector $\mathbf{x}$ chosen corresponding to vectors in basis matrix B are known as basic variables and the rest are known as non-basic variables. Then the constraint equations $\mathbf{Ax} = \mathbf{b}$ can now be written as $B\mathbf{x}_B + P\mathbf{x}_R = \mathbf{b}$ where $B : m \times m$ is the basis matrix and $R : m \times (n - m)$ is the non-basis matrix formed by the non-basic vectors of A. $\mathbf{x}_B : m \times 1$ is the vector corresponding to basic variables and $\mathbf{x}_R : (n - m) \times 1$ is the vector corresponding to non-basic variables. Taking $\mathbf{x}_R = 0$, we get $B\mathbf{x}_B = \mathbf{b}$ or $\mathbf{x}_B = B^{-1}\mathbf{b}$.

The basis matrix $B : m \times m$ is chosen in such a way that $\mathbf{x}_B = B^{-1}\mathbf{b} \geq 0$. Then we have basic feasible solution to the given LPP.

Let $C_B : m \times 1$ denote the cost vector corresponding to the variables in $\mathbf{x}_B$. Then the value of the objective function for this solution is

$$Z_B = \mathbf{c}_B^T\mathbf{x}_B + \mathbf{c}_R^T\mathbf{x}_R = \mathbf{c}_B^T\mathbf{x}_B = \mathbf{c}_B^T B^{-1}\mathbf{b}$$

Further, corresponding to the above basis matrix we define a new quantity

$$Z_j = \mathbf{c}_B^T\mathbf{y}_j = \sum_{i=1}^{m} \mathbf{c}_{Bi}^T \mathbf{y}_{ij} = \mathbf{c}_B^T B^{-1}\mathbf{b}$$

Further, corresponding to the above basis matrix we define a new quantity

$$c_j = \mathbf{c}_B^T\mathbf{y}_j = \sum_{i=1}^{m} \mathbf{c}_{Bi}^T \mathbf{y}_{ij}\ \mathbf{c}_B^T B^{-1}\mathbf{a}_j,\ j = 1, 2, \ldots, n$$

The quantity $\mathbf{z}_j - c_j$ (or $c_j - z_j$), $j = 1, 2, \ldots, n$ is known as net evaluations. After obtaining a basic feasible solution, check the following:

1. Whether the basic feasible solution is optimum or not and
2. If not, to obtain a new improved basic feasible solution. This can be done by removing one of the basic vectors from the matrix $B = (\mathbf{b}_1, \mathbf{b}_2, \ldots, \mathbf{b}_r, \ldots, \mathbf{b}_m)$ and inserting a non-basic vectors of $A = (\mathbf{a}_1, \mathbf{a}_2, \ldots, \mathbf{a}_j, \ldots, \mathbf{a}_n)$ in its place.

The problem is, "Which basic variable should be removed from B and which of the non-basic variable should be introduced in its place ?"

Suppose we remove a basic vector $\mathbf{b}_r$ from B and introduce a non-basic vector $\mathbf{a}_j \in A$ in its place. Let B^* denote the non-basic matrix obtained by replacing $\mathbf{a}_j$ in place of $\mathbf{b}_r$ then

$$\begin{aligned} B^* &= (\mathbf{b}_1, \mathbf{b}_2, \ldots, \mathbf{b}_{r-1}, \mathbf{a}_j, \mathbf{b}_{r+1}, \ldots, \mathbf{b}_m) \\ &= (\mathbf{b}_1, \mathbf{b}_2, \ldots, \mathbf{b}_{r-1}, \mathbf{b}_r + \mathbf{a}_j - \mathbf{b}_r, \mathbf{b}_{r+1}, \ldots, \mathbf{b}_m) \\ &= (\mathbf{b}_1, \mathbf{b}_2, \ldots, \mathbf{b}_{r-1}, \mathbf{b}_r, \mathbf{b}_{r+1}, \ldots, \mathbf{b}_m) + (0, 0, \ldots, 0, \mathbf{a}_j - \mathbf{b}_r, 0, \ldots, 0) \end{aligned}$$

Therefore, $B^* = B + (\mathbf{a}_j - \mathbf{b}_r)\, e_r^T$ where $e_r^T \in \mathbf{R}^m$ is the r-th unit vector in $\mathbf{R}^m$. This gives

$$B^{*-1} = B^{-1} - \frac{B^{-1}(a_j - b_r)\, e_r^T B^{-1}}{1 + e_r^T B^{-1}(a_j - b_r)} = B^{-1} - \frac{B^{-1}(a_j - b_r)\, e_r^T B^{-1}}{y_{rj}} = B^{-1} - \frac{(y_j - e_r)\, e_r^T B^{-1}}{y_{rj}}$$

In order that B^{*-1} can be obtained, the necessary condition is $y_{rj} \neq 0$. Thus, $\mathbf{a}_j$ can replace $\mathbf{b}_r$ if and only if $y_{rj} \neq 0$. The new solution is then

$$\begin{aligned} x_B^* = B^{-1}\mathbf{b} &= \left[B^{-1} - \frac{(y_j - e_r)\, e_r^T B^{-1}}{y_{rj}}\right]\mathbf{b} = B^{-1}\mathbf{b} - \frac{(y_j - e_r)\, e_r^T B^{-1}}{y_{rj}}\mathbf{b} = \mathbf{x}_B - \frac{(y_j - e_r)\, e_r^T}{y_{rj}}\mathbf{x}_B \\ &= \mathbf{x}_B - \frac{(y_j - e_r)\, e_r^T}{y_{rj}}\mathbf{x}_{Br} \end{aligned}$$

Therefore, $$\mathbf{x}_B^* = \mathbf{x}_B - \frac{x_{Br}}{y_{rj}}(\mathbf{y}_j - \mathbf{e}_r).$$

Hence, the new solution is

$$\mathbf{x}_{Bi}^* = \mathbf{x}_{Bi} - \frac{x_{Br}}{y_{rj}}(\mathbf{y}_j - 0),\ i = 1, 2, \ldots, m,\ i \neq r$$

because in $\mathbf{e}_r$, i-th element is zero. So

$$\mathbf{x}_{Bi}^* = \mathbf{x}_{Bi} - \frac{x_{Br}}{y_{rj}}\mathbf{y}_{ij} \quad \text{or} \quad \mathbf{x}_{Br}^* = \mathbf{x}_{Br} - \frac{x_{Br}}{y_{rj}}(\mathbf{y}_{rj} - 1) = \frac{x_{Br}}{y_{rj}}$$

We thus have a new basic solution. In order that the new solution is feasible, we require

$$\mathbf{x}^*_{Bi} \geq 0,\ i = 1, 2,\ldots, m, \quad \text{i.e. } \mathbf{x}^*_{Br} = \frac{x_{Br}}{y_{rj}} > 0,\ i = 1, 2,\ldots, m,\ i \neq r$$

Since $\quad x_{Br} \geq 0,\ \mathbf{x}^*_{Br} = \dfrac{x_{Br}}{y_{rj}} > 0 \text{ if } \mathbf{y}_{rj} > 0$

Thus, we require that $\mathbf{y}_{rj} > 0$. Further, $\mathbf{x}_{Bi} - \dfrac{x_{Br}}{y_{rj}}\mathbf{y}_{ij} \geq 0$ implies $\dfrac{x_{Br}}{y_{rj}} \leq \dfrac{x_{Bi}}{y_{ij}}$, $i = 1, 2, \ldots, m$. Hence,

$$\frac{x_{Br}}{y_{rj}} = \min_i \left\{ \frac{x_{Bi}}{y_{ij}},\ \mathbf{y}_{ij} > 0 \right\} \tag{3.6}$$

Thus, the vector $\mathbf{b}_r$ to be removed from B should be chosen in accordance with Eq. (3.6). Let $\mathbf{c}^*_B$ denote the new cost vector corresponding to the new solution then

$$\mathbf{c}^*_B = (c_{B1}, c_{B2},\ldots, c_{Br-1}, c_{Bj}, c_{Br+1},\ldots, c_{Bm})^T$$
$$= (c_{B1}, c_{B2},\ldots, c_{Br-1}, c_{Br} + c_j - c_{Br}, c_{Br+1},\ldots, c_{Bm})^T$$

and the new value of the objective function is

$$Z^* = \mathbf{c}^{T*}_B\mathbf{x}^*_B = [\mathbf{c}^T_B + (c_j - c_{Br})\,\mathbf{e}^T_r]\left[\mathbf{x}_B - \frac{x_{Br}}{y_{rj}}(\mathbf{y}_j - \mathbf{e}_r)\right].\ \text{Put } \frac{x_{Br}}{y_{rj}} = \theta$$

$$= \mathbf{c}^{T*}_B\mathbf{x}^*_B = [\mathbf{c}^T_B + (c_j - c_{Br})\,\mathbf{e}^T_r][\mathbf{x}_B - \theta\,(\mathbf{y}_j - \mathbf{e}_r)]$$
$$= Z - \theta(\mathbf{z}_j - c_j) \tag{3.7}$$

Our aim is to maximize Z, and so we require $Z^* > Z$ equivalently $\mathbf{z}_j - c_j$ (or $c_j - z_j$) > 0 (< 0). Therefore, the vector $\mathbf{a}_j \in A$ to be introduced into the basis matrix B must be such that $\mathbf{z}_j - c_j > 0$ (or $c_j - z_j < 0$). Note that determination of $\mathbf{a}_j$ does not require information about $\mathbf{b}_r$. However, determination of vector $\mathbf{b}_r$ to be removed from the basis requires information about both r and j.

We should first determine the vector $\mathbf{a}_j$ to be introduced into new basis and then using Eq. (3.6) determine the vector $\mathbf{b}_r$ to be removed from B. Continuing in this way for finite number of steps, we can ultimately obtain optimum solution. The new y-matrix is

$$y^* = B^{*-1}\,A = \left[B^{-1} - \frac{(y_j - e_r)\,e_r^T B^{-1}}{y_{rj}}\right]A = B^{-1}A - \frac{(y_j - e_r)\,e_r^T B^{-1}}{y_{rj}}A$$

$$= y - \frac{1}{y_{rj}}(\mathbf{y}_j - \mathbf{e}_r)\,\mathbf{e}_r^T\,y$$

$$= y - \frac{1}{y_{rj}}(\mathbf{y}_j - \mathbf{e}_r)\,(y_{r1}, y_{r2},\ldots, y_{ij},\ldots, y_{rn})$$

Comparing the elements on both sides, we get $y^*_{ik} = y_{ik} - \dfrac{1}{y_{rj}}y_{ij}\,y_{rk}$

So $\quad y^*_{ij} = y_{ij} - \dfrac{1}{y_{rj}}(y_{ij}\,y_{rj} - 0),\ i = 1, 2,\ldots, m,\ i \neq r,\ j = 1, 2,\ldots, n,\ k \neq j$

and
$$y^*_{rj} = y_{rj} - \frac{1}{y_{rj}}(y_{rj}y_{rj} - y_{rj}) = 1$$

Note:

1. While discussing the simplex method, we have assumed an initial basic feasible solution with a basis matrix B. If $B = I$ then $B^{-1} = I$, then initial solution $\mathbf{x}_B = B^{-1}\mathbf{b} = \mathbf{b}$ and y matrix is $y = B^{-1}A = A$. Net evaluations, $\mathbf{z}_j - c_j = -\mathbf{c}_j + \mathbf{c}_B^T B^{-1}\mathbf{a}_j = -\mathbf{c}_j + \mathbf{c}_B^T\mathbf{a}_j$, $j = 1, 2, \ldots, n$ and value of the objective function $Z = \mathbf{c}_B^T\mathbf{x}_B = \mathbf{c}_B^T\mathbf{b}$. Thus, we observe that if initial basis matrix is a unit matrix, then it is easy to obtain initial solution and related parameters. Hence, in order to obtain initial basic feasible solution, we shall assume that a unit matrix is present as a sub-matrix of the coefficient matrix A.
2. For choosing incoming vector $\mathbf{a}_j$ in the next basis, choose that $\mathbf{z}_j - c_j$ (or $c_j - z_j$) which is most negative (positive). If two or more $\mathbf{z}_j - c_j$ (or $c_j - z_j$) have the same most negative (positive) value, choose any one of the corresponding vector to enter into the basis.
3. After choosing the incoming vector, choose the outgoing vector which satisfies Eq. (3.6). If this minimum value is assumed for more than two vectors, choose any one of the corresponding basis vector from B.

The following two theorems are stated without proof.

Theorem 3.6: *Every basic feasible solution to an LPP corresponds to a vertex of the set of feasible solution.*

Theorem 3.7: *For the LPP: Maximize $Z = \mathbf{c}^T\mathbf{x}$ subject to $\mathbf{Ax} = \mathbf{b}$, $\mathbf{x} \geq 0$. A necessary and sufficient condition for a basic feasible solution $\mathbf{x}_B = B^{-1}\mathbf{b}$ corresponding to a basis matrix $B : m \times m$ to be optimum is that $\mathbf{z}_j - c_j \geq 0$ (or $c_j - z_j \leq 0$) for all $j = 1, 2, \ldots, n$.*

To find an optimum basic feasible solution to a standard LPP (maximization case, all constraints $\leq$, all b_j values positive), perform the following steps.

Step 1: Select an initial basic feasible solution to initiate the solution.

Step 2: Test for the optimality as discussed in Section 3.6. That is, if all $\mathbf{z}_j - \mathbf{c}_j \geq 0$ (or $\mathbf{c}_j - \mathbf{z}_j \leq 0$), then the basic feasible solution is optimal. If at least for one of the coefficient matrix $\mathbf{z}_j - \mathbf{c}_j < 0$ (or $\mathbf{c}_j - \mathbf{z}_j > 0$) and elements in that columns are negative (positive), then there exists an unbounded solution to the given problem. If at least one $\mathbf{z}_j - \mathbf{c}_j < 0$ (or $\mathbf{c}_j - \mathbf{z}_j > 0$) and each of these has at least one positive (negative) element for some row then solution can be improved.

Step 3: For selecting the variable entering into the basis, select a variable that has the most negative $\mathbf{z}_j - \mathbf{c}_j$ value (or most positive $\mathbf{c}_j - \mathbf{z}_j$). The column to be entered is called *key column*.

Step 4: After selecting the key column, the next step is to decide the outgoing variable using Eq. (3.6). This ratio is called *replacement ratio* (RR). The replacement ratio restricts the number of units of incoming variables that can be obtained from the exchange. The row selected in this manner is called *key row*. The element at the intersection of key row and key column is called *key element*.

Note that division by negative or zero element in the key column is not allowed. Denote these cases by –.

Step 5: Now we want to find a new solution. If the key element is 1, then do not change the row in the next simplex table. If the key element is other than 1, then divide the element in that key row by that element including the element in $\mathbf{x}_B$—column and formulate the new row. The new values of the elements in the remaining rows for the next iteration can be evaluated by performing elementary operations on all rows, so that all elements except the key element in the key column are zero. If the new solution so obtained satisfies step 2 then terminate the process, otherwise perform step 4 and step 5.

Repeat the steps for finite number of steps to obtain the basic feasible solution, i.e. no further improvement is possible.

EXAMPLE 3.24: Use the simplex method to maximize $z = 5x_1 + 4x_2$ subject to the constraints:

$$4x_1 + 5x_2 \leq 10,\ 3x_1 + 2x_2 \leq 9,\ 8x_1 + 3x_2 \leq 12 \text{ and } x_1, x_2 \geq 0$$

Solution: Writing the given LPP in the standard form, we need to add slack variables s_1, s_2 and s_3 in the constraints. Thus, LPP is

Maximize $\quad z = 5x_1 + 4x_2 + 0s_1 + 0s_2 + 0s_3$

subject to the constraints:

$$4x_1 + 5x_2 + s_1 = 10$$

$$3x_1 + 2x_2 + s_2 = 9$$

$$8x_1 + 3x_2 + s_3 = 12$$

and $x_1, x_2, s_1, s_2, s_3 \geq 0$.

Putting $x_1 = x_2 = 0$, we get the first iteration as given below.

		c_j	5	4	0	0	0	*RR*
c_B	*B*	x_B	x_1	x_2	s_1	s_2	s_3	
0	s_1	10	4	5	1	0	0	10/4
0	s_2	9	3	2	0	1	0	9/3
0	s_3	12	8	3	0	0	1	12/8→
z	0	$z_j - c_j$	–5 ↑	–4	0	0	0	

Clearly, most negative $z_j - c_j$ corresponds to x_1. So x_1 will enter into the basis. The minimum replacement ratio corresponds to s_3, so s_3 will leave the basis. So, the key column corresponds to x_1 and the key row corresponds to s_3. The leading (key) element is 8 which is other than 1, so divide all elements of the key row by 8 and use elementary row transformations so that in the key column entries of the first and second rows are zero. The new iteration table is as given below.

		c_j	5	4	0	0	0	*RR*
c_B	*B*	x_B	x_1	x_2	s_1	s_2	s_3	
0	s_1	4	0	7/2	1	0	–1/2	8/7→
0	s_2	9/2	0	7/8	0	1	–3/8	36/7
5	x_1	3/2	1	3/18	0	0	1/8	9
z	15/2	$z_j - c_j$	0	–17/8 ↑	0	0	5/8	

Clearly, most negative $z_j - c_j$ corresponds to x_2, so x_2 will enter into the basis. The minimum replacement ratio corresponds to s_1, so s_1 will leave the basis. So, the key column corresponds to x_2 and key row corresponds to s_1. The leading (key) element is 7/2 which is other than 1, so divide all elements of the key row by 2/7 and use elementary row transformations so that in the key column entries of the second and third rows are zero. The new iteration table is as given below.

		c_j	5	4	0	0	0
c_B	B	x_B	x_1	x_2	s_1	s_2	s_3
4	x_2	8/7	0	1	1	0	–1/7
0	s_2	7/2	0	0	0	1	–2/8
5	x_1	15/14	1	0	0	0	5/28
z	139/14	$z_j - c_j$	0	0	17/28	0	9/28

Since all $z_j - c_j \geq 0$, the solution $x_1 = 15/14$, $x_2 = 8/7$ maximizes $z = 139/14$.

EXAMPLE 3.25: Use the simplex method to maximize $z = 10x_1 + x_2 + 2x_3$ subject to the constraints:

$$x_1 + x_2 - 2x_3 \leq 10,\ 4x_1 + x_2 + x_3 \leq 20 \text{ and } x_1, x_2, x_3 \geq 0$$

Solution: Writing the given LPP in the standard form, we need to add slack variables s_1 and s_2 in the constraints. Thus, LPP is

$$\text{Maximize } z = 10x_1 + x_2 + 2x_3 + 0s_1 + 0s_2$$

subject to the constraints:

$$x_1 + x_2 - 2x_3 + s_1 = 10$$

$$4x_1 + x_2 + x_3 + s_2 = 20$$

and $x_1, x_2, x_3, s_1, s_2 \geq 0$.

Putting $x_1 = x_2 = x_3 = 0$, we get the first iteration as given below.

		c_j	10	1	2	0	0	*RR*
c_B	B	x_B	x_1	x_2	x_3	s_1	s_2	
0	s_1	10	1	1	–2	1	0	10
0	s_2	20	4	1	1	0	1	5→
z	0	$z_j - c_j$	–10	–1	–2	0	0	
			↑					

Clearly, most negative $z_j - c_j$ corresponds to x_1. So x_1 will enter into the basis. The minimum replacement ratio corresponds to s_2, so s_2 will leave the basis. So, the key column corresponds to x_1 and the key row corresponds to s_3. The leading (key) element is 4 which is other than 1, so divide all elements of the key row by 4 and use elementary row transformations so that in the key column entries of the first row are zero. The new iteration table is as given below.

		c_j	10	1	2	0	0
c_B	B	x_B	x_1	x_2	x_3	s_1	s_2
0	s_1	5	0	3/4	−9/4	1	−1/4
10	x_1	5	1	1/4	1/4	0	1/4
z	50	$z_j - c_j$	0	3/2	1/2	0	5/2

Since all $c_j - z_j \geq 0$, the solution $x_1 = 10$, $x_2 = 0 = x_3$ maximizes $z = 50$.

EXAMPLE 3.26: Use the simplex method to maximize $z = 2x_1 + 4x_2 + x_3 + x_4$ subject to the constraints:

$$x_1 + 3x_2 + x_4 \leq 4,\ 2x_1 + x_2 \leq 3,\ x_2 + 4x_3 + x_4 \leq 3 \text{ and } x_1, x_2, x_3, x_4 \geq 0$$

Solution: Writing the given LPP in the standard form, we need to add slack variables s_1, s_2 and s_3 in the constraints. Thus, LPP is

Maximize $$z = 2x_1 + 4x_2 + x_3 + x_4 + 0s_1 + 0s_2 + 0s_3 + 0s_4$$

subject to the constraints:

$$x_1 + 3x_2 + x_4 + s_1 = 4$$
$$2x_1 + x_2 + s_2 = 3$$
$$x_2 + 4x_3 + x_4 + s_3 = 3$$

and $x_1, x_2, x_3, x_4, s_1, s_2, s_3 \geq 0$.

Putting $x_1 = x_2 = x_3 = x_4 = 0$, we get the first iteration as given below.

		c_j	2	4	1	1	0	0	0	RR
c_B	B	x_B	x_1	x_2	x_3	x_4	s_1	s_2	s_3	
0	s_1	4	1	3	0	1	1	0	0	4/3→
0	s_2	3	2	1	0	0	0	1	0	3
0	s_3	3	0	1	4	1	0	0	1	3
z	0	$z_j - c_j$	−2	−4	−1	−1	0	0	0	
				↑						

x_2 will enter into the basis and s_1 will leave the basis. The new iterative table is as given below.

		c_j	2	4	1	1	0	0	0	RR
c_B	B	x_B	x_1	x_2	x_3	x_4	s_1	s_2	s_3	
4	x_2	4/3	1/3	1	0	1/3	1/3	0	0	–
0	s_2	5/3	5/3	0	0	−1/3	−1/3	1	0	–
0	s_3	5/3	−1/3	0	4	2/3	−1/3	0	1	5/12→
z	16/3	$z_j - c_j$	−2/3	0	−1	1/3	4/3	0	0	
					↑					

x_3 will enter into the basis and s_3 will leave the basis. The new iterative table is as given below.

		c_j	2	4	1	1	0	0	0	RR
c_B	B	x_B	x_1	x_2	x_3	x_4	s_1	s_2	s_3	
4	x_2	4/3	1/3	1	0	1/3	1/3	0	0	4
0	s_2	5/3	5/3	0	0	–1/3	–1/3	1	0	1→
1	x_3	5/12	–1/12	0	1	1/6	–1/12	0	1/4	–
z	23/4	$z_j - c_j$	–3/4 ↑	0	0	1/2	5/4	0	1/4	

x_1 will enter into the basis and s_2 will leave the basis. The new iterative table is as given below.

		c_j	2	4	1	1	0	0	0
c_B	B	x_B	x_1	x_2	x_3	x_4	s_1	s_2	s_3
4	x_2	1	0	1	0	2/5	2/5	–1/5	0
2	x_1	1	1	0	0	–1/5	–1/5	3/5	0
1	x_3	1/2	0	0	1	3/20	–1/10	1/20	1/4
z	13/2	$z_j - c_j$	0	0	0	7/20	11/10	9/20	1/4

Since all $z_j - c_j \geq 0$, the optimal basic feasible solution is $x_1 = 1, x_2 = 1, x_3 = 1/2, x_4 = 0$ and maximum $z = 13/2$.

EXAMPLE 3.27: Use the simplex method to maximize $z = 4x_1 + x_2 + 3x_3 + 5x_4$ subject to the constraints:

$$4x_1 - 6x_2 - 5x_3 - 4x_4 \geq -20$$
$$3x_1 - 2x_2 + 4x_3 + x_4 \leq 10$$
$$8x_1 - 3x_2 + 3x_3 + 2x_4 \leq 20$$

and $x_1, x_2, x_3, x_4 \geq 0$.

Solution: We have seen that in maximization case all constraints should be of the form $\leq$. So we need to multiply first constraint by –1. Then writing the given LPP in the standard form, we need to add slack variables s_1, s_2 and s_3 in the constraints. Thus, LPP is

Maximize $$z = 4x_1 + x_2 + 3x_3 + 5x_4 + 0s_1 + 0s_2 + 0s_3$$

subject to the constraints:

$$-4x_1 + 6x_2 + 5x_3 + 4x_4 + s_1 = 20$$
$$3x_1 - 2x_2 + 4x_3 + x_4 + s_2 = 10$$
$$8x_1 - 3x_2 + 3x_3 + 2x_4 + s_3 = 20$$

and $x_1, x_2, x_3, x_4, s_1, s_2, s_3 \geq 0$.

Putting $x_1 = x_2 = x_3 = x_4 = 0$, we get the first iteration as given below.

		c_j	4	1	3	5	0	0	0	RR
c_B	B	x_B	x_1	x_2	x_3	x_4	s_1	s_2	s_3	
0	s_1	20	4	6	5	–4	1	0	0	–
0	s_2	10	3	–2	4	1	0	1	0	10 →
0	s_3	10	8	–3	3	2	0	0	1	10
z	0	$z_j - c_j$	–4	–1	–3	–5	0	0	0	
						↑				

x_4 enters into the basis and s_2 leaves the basis. The new iterative table is as given below.

		c_j	4	1	3	5	0	0	0	RR
c_B	B	x_B	x_1	x_2	x_3	x_4	s_1	s_2	s_3	
0	s_1	60	8	2	21	0	1	4	0	30
5	x_4	10	3	–2	4	1	0	1	0	–
0	s_3	0	2	1	–5	0	0	–2	1	0 →
z	50	$z_j - c_j$	11	–11	17	0	0	5	0	
				↑						

x_2 enters into the basis and s_3 leaves the basis. The new iterative table is as given below.

		c_j	4	1	3	5	0	0	0	RR
c_B	B	x_B	x_1	x_2	x_3	x_4	s_1	s_2	s_3	
0	s_1	60	12	0	11	0	1	0	2	60/11→
5	x_4	10	7	0	–6	1	0	–3	2	–
1	x_2	0	2	1	–5	0	0	–2	1	–
z	50	$z_j - c_j$	33	0	–38	0	0	–17	11	
					↑					

x_3 enters into the basis and s_1 leaves the basis. The new iterative table is given below.

		c_j	4	1	3	5	0	0	0
c_B	B	x_B	x_1	x_2	x_3	x_4	s_1	s_2	s_3
3	x_3	60/11	12/11	0	1	0	1/11	0	2/11
5	x_4	470/11	149/11	0	0	1	6/11	–3	34/11
1	x_2	300/11	82/11	1	0	0	5/11	–2	21/11
z	2827/11	$z_j - c_j$	> 0	0	0	0	> 0	< 0	> 0

Here $z_j - c_j < 0$ for s_2 but coefficients in that column are negative or zero, so the given LPP has an unbounded solution.

EXAMPLE 3.28: A farmer has 1,000 acres of land on which he can grow corn, wheat or soyabeans. Each acre of corn costs Rs. 100 for preparation, requires 7 man-days of work and yields a profit of Rs. 30. An acre of wheat costs Rs. 120 to prepare, requires 10 man-days of work and yields a profit of Rs. 40. An acre of soyabeans costs Rs. 70 to prepare, requires 8 man-days of work and yields a profit of Rs. 20. If the farmer has Rs. 1,00,000 for preparation and can count on 8,000 man-days of work, how many should be allocated to each crop to maximize profits?

Solution: Let x_1, x_2 and x_3 be acres of land to be used for corn, wheat and soyabeans, respectively.

Maximize $$z = 30x_1 + 40x_2 + 20x_3$$

subject to the constraints:

$$100x_1 + 120x_2 + 70x_3 \leq 1,00,000$$

$$7x_1 + 10x_2 + 8x_3 \leq 8,000$$

$$x_1 + x_2 + x_3 \leq 1,000$$

Writing the given LPP in the standard form, we need to add slack variables s_1, s_2 and s_3 in the constraints. Thus, LPP is

Maximize $$z = 30x_1 + 40x_2 + 20x_3 + 0s_1 + 0s_2 + 0s_3$$

subject to the constraints:

$$10x_1 + 12x_2 + 7x_3 + s_1 = 10,000$$

$$7x_1 + 10x_2 + 8x_3 + s_2 = 8,000$$

$$x_1 + x_2 + x_3 + s_3 = 10,000$$

and $x_1, x_2, x_3, s_1, s_2, s_3 \geq 0$.

Putting $x_1 = x_2 = x_3 = 0$, we get the first iteration as given below.

		c_j	30	40	20	0	0	0	*RR*
c_B	B	x_B	x_1	x_2	x_3	s_1	s_2	s_3	
0	s_1	10,000	10	12	7	1	0	0	10,000/12
0	s_2	8,000	7	10	8	0	1	0	8000/10→
0	s_3	1,000	1	1	1	0	0	1	1000
z	0	$z_j - c_j$	–30	–40	–20	0	0	0	
				↑					

x_2 enters into the basis and s_2 leaves the basis. The new iterative table is as follows.

		c_j	30	40	20	0	0	0	*RR*
c_B	B	x_B	x_1	x_2	x_3	s_1	s_2	s_3	
0	s_1	400	16/10	0	–26/10	1	–12/10	0	4000/16→
40	x_2	800	7/10	1	8/10	0	1/10	0	8000/7
0	s_3	200	3/10	0	2/10	0	–1/10	1	2000/3
z	32,000	$z_j - c_j$	–2 ↑	0	12	0	4	0	

x_1 enters into the basis and s_1 leaves the basis. The new iterative table is as given below.

		c_j	30	40	20	0	0	0
c_B	B	x_B	x_1	x_2	x_3	s_1	s_2	s_3
30	x_1	250	1	0	–26/16	10/16	–12/16	0
40	x_2	625	0	1	31/16	–7/6	10/16	0
0	s_3	125	0	0	11/16	–3/6	1/8	1
z	32,500	$z_j - c_j$	0	0	35/4	5/4	5/2	0

Thus, $x_1 = 250$, $x_2 = 625$, $x_3 = 0$ maximizes the profit z = Rs. 32,500.

EXAMPLE 3.29: Use the simplex method to maximize $z = 2x_1 + 3x_2$ subject to the constraints:

$$-x_1 + 2x_2 \le 4$$

$$x_1 + x_2 \le 6$$

$$x_1 + 3x_2 \le 9$$

and x_1, x_2 unrestricted.

Solution: s_1, s_2, s_3 are slack variables introduced in the given three constraints. Since x_1 and x_2 are unrestricted, we introduce the non-negative variables $x_1' \ge 0$, $x_1'' \ge 0$ and $x_2' \ge 0$, $x_{22}'' \ge 0$ so that

$$x_1 = x_1' - x_1'' \quad \text{and} \quad x_2 = x_2' - x_2''$$

Putting $x_1' = x_1'' = x_2' = x_2'' = 0$, we get initial solution as follows.

		c_j	2	–2	3	–3	0	0	0	*RR*
c_B	B	x_B	x_1'	x_1''	x_2'	x_2''	s_1	s_2	s_3	
0	s_1	4	–1	1	2	–2	1	0	0	2→
0	s_2	6	1	–1	1	–1	0	1	0	6
0	s_3	9	1	–1	3	–3	0	0	1	3
z	0	$z_j - c_j$	–2	2	–3 ↑	3	0	0	0	

x'_2 enters into the basis and s_1 leaves the basis. The iterative table is as follows.

		c_j	2	−2	3	−3	0	0	0	RR
c_B	B	x_B	x'_1	x''_1	x'_2	x''_2	s_1	s_2	s_3	
3	x'_2	2	−1/2	1/2	1	−1	1/2	0	0	–
0	s_2	4	3/2	−3/2	0	0	−1/2	1	0	8/3
0	s_3	3	5/2	−5/2	0	0	−3/2	0	1	6/5→
z	6	$z_j - c_j$	−7/2	7/2	0	0	3/2	0	0	
			↑							

x'_1 enters into the basis and s_3 leaves the basis. The iterative table is as follows.

		c_j	2	−2	3	−3	0	0	0	RR
c_B	B	x_B	x'_1	x''_1	x'_2	x''_2	s_1	s_2	s_3	
3	x'_2	13/5	0	0	1	−1	1/5	0	1/5	65/5
0	s_2	11/5	0	0	0	0	2/5	1	−3/5	55/10→
2	x'_1	9/5	1	−1	0	0	−3/5	0	2/5	–
z	51/5	$z_j - c_j$	0	0	0	0	−3/5	0	7/5	
							↑			

s_1 enters into the basis and s_2 leaves the basis. The iterative table is as follows.

		c_j	2	−2	3	−3	0	0	0
c_B	B	x_B	x'_1	x''_1	x'_2	x''_2	s_1	s_2	s_3
3	x'_2	3/2	0	0	1	−1	0	−1/2	1/2
0	s_1	11/2	0	0	0	0	1	5/2	−3/2
2	x'_1	9/2	1	−1	0	0	0	3/2	−1/2
z	27/2	$z_j - c_j$	0	0	0	0	0	3/2	1/2

Since $z_j - c_j$ are all non-negative, the optimum solution $x'_1 = 9/2$ and $x'_2 = 3/2$ with maximum $z = 27/2$ is obtained. Therefore, $x_1 = 9/2 - 0 = 9/2$ and $x_2 = 3/2 - 0 = 3/2$ is the required basic feasible solution.

3.7 MINIMIZATION CASE

Consider LPP

Minimize $$Z = \sum_{i=1}^{m} c_i x_i$$

subject to the constraints $$\sum_{j=1}^{n} a_{ij} x_j \ge b_i,\ x_j \ge 0$$

The inequality of ≥ (or =)—type should be transformed in equality by subtracting surplus variables, i.e.

$$\sum_{j=1}^{n} a_{ij} x_j - s_i = b_i,\ x_j,\ s_i \ge 0$$

By putting $x_j = 0$, $j = 1, 2, \ldots, n$, we get an initial solution $s_i = -b_i$, which violates non-negativity criteria of surplus variables. In this, to preserve the non-negativity of surplus variables, we add artificial variables (say) A_i, $i = 1, 2, \ldots, m$ to get initial basic feasible solution. Thus, we have constraint equations as

$$\sum_{j=1}^{n} a_{ij} x_j - s_i + A_i = b_i,\ x_j,\ s_i,\ A_i \ge 0$$

Now, the resultant LPP has n decision variables, m artificial variables and m surplus variables. An initial basic feasible solution of the resultant LPP can be obtained by putting $(n + m)$ variables equal to zero; i.e. the iteration starts with $A_i = b_i$, $i = 1, 2, \ldots, m$ which does not contribute any value to the optimal solution but are added to retain the feasibility condition of LPP. We will discuss the following two methods to remove artificial variables first from the optimal solution.

1. Two-phase method
2. Big-M method (penalty method)

Note: For constraints with equality, we will add only the artificial variable.

3.7.1 Two-Phase Method

In phase I of this method, we will try to minimize the sum of the artificial variables subjected to the constraints of the given LPP. Phase II minimizes the original objective function with initial iteration as the final iteration of phase I. Let us study steps to be performed in solving LPP by two-phase method.

Step 1: Check the non-negativity of the b_i (constant terms). If some of them are negative, make them positive by multiplying those constraints by –1.

Step 2: Subtract surplus variables and add artificial variables to reformulate inequality constraints into equations.

Step 3: Initialize iterative step by taking $A_i = b_i$.

Step 4: Assign a cost '–1' to each artificial variables for a maximization problem ('1' for minimization) and a cost '0' to all other variables (surplus and decision variables) of LPP in the objective function; thus, objective function for phase I will be

Maximize $$z^* = -A_1 - A_2 - \cdots - A_p \ (p \le m)$$

Step 5: Solve the problem written in step 4 until either of the following three cases does arise:

1. If all $z_j - c_j \ge 0$ and at least one artificial variable occurs in the optimum basis and hence max $z^* < 0$, then LPP has infeasible solution.
2. If all $z_j - c_j \ge 0$, max $z^* = 0$ and at least one artificial variable occurs in the optimum basis, then go to phase II.
3. If all $z_j - c_j \ge 0$ and no artificial variable appears in the optimum basis.

If cases 2 or 3 occur, then go to phase II.

Step 6: Use the optimum basic feasible solution of phase I as an initial solution for the given LPP. Assign actual costs to the original variables and '0' to other variables in the objective function. Use the simplex method to improve the solution.

Note: Maximize $z = -$ Minimize $(-z)$

EXAMPLE 3.30: Use the two-phase method to minimize $z = x_1 + x_2$ subject to the constraints: $2x_1 + x_2 \ge 4$, $x_1 + 7x_2 \ge 7$, and $x_1, x_2 \ge 0$.

Solution: In order to get constraints equations, introduce surplus variables $s_1, s_2 \ge 0$; and artificial variables $A_1, A_2, \ge 0$. Then LPP converted to the maximization form is

Maximize $$z = -x_1 - x_2 + 0s_1 + 0s_2 - A_1 - A_2$$

subject to the constraints:

$$2x_1 + x_2 - s_1 + A_1 = 4$$

$$x_1 + 7x_2 - s_2 + A_2 = 7$$

and $x_1, x_2, s_1, s_2, A_1, A_2 \ge 0$.

Phase I: Here the objective function is Maximize $z^* = 0x_1 + 0x_2 + 0s_1 + 0s_2 - A_1 - A_2$ subject to the above constraints. Initialize the solution by putting $x_1 = x_2 = s_1 = s_2 = 0$ then $A_1 = 4$ and $A_2 = 7$. The simplex table is as follows.

	c_j		0	0	0	0	–1	–1	*RR*
c_B	*B*	x_B	x_1	x_2	s_1	s_2	A_1	A_2	
–1	A_1	4	2	1	–1	0	1	0	4
–1	A_2	7	1	7	0	–1	0	1	1→
z^*	–11	$z_j - c_j$	–3	–8 ↑	1	1	0	0	

x_2 enters into the basis and A_2 leaves the basis. The new iterative table is as shown below.

		c_j	0	0	0	0	–1	–1	*RR*
c_B	B	x_B	x_1	x_2	s_1	s_2	A_1	A_2	
–1	A_1	3	13/7	0	–1	1/7	1	–1/7	21/13→
0	x_2	1	1/7	1	0	–1/7	0	1/7	7
z^*	–3	$z_j - c_j$	–13/7	0	1	–1/7	0	8/7	
			↑						

x_1 enters into the basis and A_1 leaves the basis. The new iterative table is as shown below.

		c_j	0	0	0	0	–1	–1
c_B	B	x_B	x_1	x_2	s_1	s_2	A_1	A_2
0	x_1	21/13	1	0	–7/13	1/13	7/13	–1/13
0	x_2	10/13	0	1	1/13	–2/13	–1/13	2/13
z^*	0	$z_j - c_j$	0	0	0	0	1	1

Since $z_j - c_j$ are all non-negative and no artificial variable appears in the basis, the optimum basic feasible solution to the objective function of phase I is obtained and go to phase II.

Phase II: Consider the objective function with the original cost associated to the decision variables, i.e. Maximize $z = -x_1 - x_2 + 0s_1 + 0s_2$. Here we will initialize the solution with the last table of phase I.

		c_j	–1	–1	0	0
c_B	B	x_B	x_1	x_2	s_1	s_2
–1	x_1	21/13	1	0	–7/13	1/13
–1	x_2	10/13	0	1	1/13	–2/13
z	–31/13	$z_j - c_j$	0	0	6/13	1/13

Since $z_j - c_j$ are all non-negative, the optimum basic feasible solution is $x_1 = 21/13$, $x_2 = 10/13$ and minimum $z = 31/13$ is obtained.

EXAMPLE 3.31: Use the two-phase method to minimize $z = x_1 - 2x_2 - 3x_3$ subject to the constraints:

$$-2x_1 + x_2 + 3x_3 = 2,\ 2x_1 + 3x_2 + 4x_3 = 1, \text{ and } x_1, x_2, x_3 \geq 0$$

Solution: In order to get constraints equations, introduce artificial variables A_1, A_2, ≥ 0. Then LPP is

Maximize $$z = -x_1 + 2x_2 + 3x_3 - A_1 - A_2$$

subject to the constraints:

$$-2x_1 + x_2 + 3x_3 + A_1 = 2$$

$$2x_1 + 3x_2 + 4x_3 + A_2 = 1$$

and $x_1, x_2, A_1, A_2 \geq 0$.

Phase I: Here the objective function is Maximize $z^* = 0x_1 + 0x_2 + 0x_3 - A_1 - A_2$ subject to the above constraints. Initialize the solution by putting $x_1 = x_2 = 0$, then $A_1 = 2$ and $A_2 = 1$. The simplex table is as follows.

		c_j	0	0	0	−1	−1	*RR*
c_B	*B*	x_B	x_1	x_2	x_3	A_1	A_2	
−1	A_1	2	−2	1	3	1	0	2/3
−1	A_2	1	2	3	4	0	1	1/4→
z^*	−3	$z_j - c_j$	0	−4	−7	0	0	
					↑			

x_3 enters into the basis and A_2 leaves the basis. The new iterative table is as follows.

		c_j	0	0	0	−1	−1
c_B	*B*	x_B	x_1	x_2	x_3	A_1	A_2
−1	A_1	5/4	−7/2	−5/4	0	1	−3/4
0	x_3	1/4	1/2	3/4	1	0	1/4
z^*	−5/4	$z_j - c_j$	7/2	5/4	0	0	3/4

Since $z_j - c_j$ are all non-negative, an optimum basic feasible solution to the reduced problem is attained, but, at the same time, artificial variable A_1 appears in the basis at a positive level, so given LPP does not possess any feasible solution.

EXAMPLE 3.32: Show that there does not exist any feasible solution to the following LPP:

Maximize $$z = 2x_1 + 3x_2 + 5x_3$$

subject to the constraints:

$$3x_1 + 10x_2 + 5x_3 \leq 15$$

$$33x_1 - 10x_2 + 9x_3 \leq 33$$

$$x_1 + 2x_2 + x_3 \geq 4$$

and $x_1, x_2, x_3 \geq 0$.

Solution: Writing the given LPP in the standard form, we need to add slack variables s_1 and s_2 in the first two constraints, surplus variable s_3 and artificial variable A_1 in the third constraint. The initialization of iteration is with $s_1 = 15$, $s_2 = 33$ and $A_1 = 4$.

Phase I: Assigning a cost –1 to the artificial variable and '0' to the remaining variables, we get the iterative table as shown below.

		c_j	0	0	0	0	0	–1	–1	RR
c_B	B	x_B	x_1	x_2	x_3	s_1	s_2	s_3	A_1	
0	s_1	15	3	10	5	1	0	0	0	15/10→
0	s_2	33	33	–10	9	0	0	0	0	–
–1	A_1	4	1	2	1	0	1	–1	1	2
z^*	–4	$z_j - c_j$	–1	–2	–1	0	0	1	0	
				↑						

x_2 enters into the basis and s_1 leaves the basis. The new iterative table is as given below.

		c_j	0	0	0	0	0	–1	–1	RR
c_B	B	x_B	x_1	x_2	x_3	s_1	s_2	s_3	A_1	
0	x_2	3/2	3/10	1	1/2	1/10	0	0	0	5
0	s_2	48	36	0	14	1	1	0	0	4/3→
–1	A_1	1	2/5	0	0	–1/5	0	–1	1	5/2
z^*	–1	$z_j - c_j$	–2/5	0	0	1/5	0	1	0	
			↑							

x_1 enters into the basis and s_2 leaves the basis. The new iterative table is as follows.

		c_j	0	0	0	0	0	–1	–1
c_B	B	x_B	x_1	x_2	x_3	s_1	s_2	s_3	A_1
0	x_2	11/10	0	1	23/60	11/120	–1/120	0	0
0	x_1	4/3	1	0	7/18	1/36	1/36	0	0
–1	A_1	7/15	0	0	–7/45	–2/9	–2/9	–1	1
z^*	–7/15	$z_j - c_j$	0	0	7/45	95/18	5/18	1	0

Since $z_j - c_j$ are all non-negative, an optimum basic feasible solution to the reduced problem is attained, but at the same time max $z^* < 0$ and artificial variable A_1 appear in the basis at a positive level, so the given LPP does not possess any feasible solution.

EXAMPLE 3.33: Use the two-phase method to

Minimize $z = x_1 + x_2 + x_3$

subject to the constraints:

$$x_1 - 3x_2 + 4x_3 = 5$$
$$x_1 - 2x_2 \le 3$$
$$2x_2 - x_3 \ge 4$$

and $x_1, x_2 \ge 0$, x_3 is unrestricted.

Solution: Since x_3 is unrestricted, put $x_3 = x_3' - x_3''$ where x_3' and $x_3'' \ge 0$. Introduce slack variable s_1 in the second constraint, surplus variable s_2 in the third constraint and the artificial variables A_1 and A_2 in the first and third constraints. The resultant LPP is

Maximize $z^* = -x_1 - x_2 - x_3 + 0s_1 + 0s_2 - A_1 - A_2$

Subject to the constraints:

$$x_1 - 3x_2 + 4(x_3' - x_3'') + A_1 = 5$$
$$x_1 - 2x_2 + s_1 = 3$$
$$2x_2 - (x_3' - x_3'') - s_2 + A_2 = 4$$

and $x_1, x_2, x_3', x_3'', s_1, s_2, A_1, A_2 \ge 0$.

Phase I: Assigning a cost –1 to artificial variables and zero to the rest of the variables, we get $s_1 = 3$, $A_1 = 5$ and $A_2 = 4$. The iterative table is given below.

	c_j		0	0	0	0	0	0	–1	–1	*RR*
c_B	B	x_B	x_1	x_2	x_3'	x_3''	s_1	s_2	A_1	A_2	
–1	A_1	5	1	–3	4	–4	0	0	1	0	5/4→
0	s_1	3	1	–2	0	0	1	0	0	0	–
–1	A_2	4	0	2	–1	1	0	–1	0	1	–
z^*	–9	$z_j - c_j$	–1	1	–3 ↑	3	1	0	0	0	

x_3' enters into the basis and A_1 leaves the basis. The new iterative table is as follows.

	c_j		0	0	0	0	0	0	–1	–1	*RR*
c_B	B	x_B	x_1	x_2	x_3'	x_3''	s_1	s_2	A_1	A_2	
0	x_3'	5/4	1/4	–3/4	1	–1	0	0	1/4	0	–
0	s_1	3	1	–2	0	0	1	0	0	0	–
–1	A_2	21/4	1/4	5/4	0	0	0	–1	–1/4	1	21/5→
z^*	–21/4	$z_j - c_j$	–1/4	–5/4 ↑	0	0	0	1	–1/4	0	

x_2 enters into the basis and A_2 leaves the basis. The new iterative table is given below.

	c_j		0	0	0	0	0	0	−1	−1
c_B	B	x_B	x_1	x_2	x_3'	x_3''	s_1	s_2	A_1	A_2
0	x_3'	22/5	2/5	0	1	−1	0	−3/5	2/5	3/5
0	s_1	57/5	7/5	0	0	0	1	−8/5	2/5	8/5
0	x_2	21/5	1/5	1	0	0	0	−4/5	1/5	4/5
z^*	0	$z_j - c_j$	0	0	0	0	0	0	0	0

Since $z_j - c_j$ are all non-negative, an optimum basic feasible solution to the reduced problem is attained. Move to the next phase.

Phase II: Consider LPP with original cost coefficients associated with each variable and start with the last table as the initial iteration.

	c_j		−1	−1	−1	1	0	0
c_B	B	x_B	x_1	x_2	x_3'	x_3''	s_1	s_2
−1	x_3'	22/5	2/5	0	1	−1	0	−3/5
0	s_1	57/5	7/5	0	0	0	1	−8/5
−1	x_2	21/5	1/5	1	0	0	0	−4/5
z^*	−43/5	$z_j - c_j$	2/5	0	0	0	0	7/5

Thus, the optimal solution is $x_1 = 0$, $x_2 = 21/5$, $x_3 = 22/5 - 0 = 22/5$ and minimum $z = 43/5$.

EXAMPLE 3.34: Use the simplex method to solve the following system of linear equations:

$$x_1 - x_3 + 4x_4 = 3,\ 2x_1 - x_2 = 3,\ 3x_1 - 2x_2 - x_4 = 1;\ x_1, x_2, x_3, x_4 \geq 0$$

Solution: Since the objective function for the above mentioned constraints is not given, we introduce a dummy objective function $z = 0x_1 + 0x_2 + 0x_3 + 0x_4$. Add artificial variables A_1, A_2 and A_3 (≥ 0) in the above constraints and putting $x_1 = x_2 = x_3 = x_4 = 0$, we get initial solution $A_1 = 3$, $A_2 = 3$ and $A_3 = 1$. Assign cost −1 to artificial variables and zero to the remaining, we get the initial iterative table as given below.

	c_j		0	0	0	0	−1	−1	−1	*RR*
c_B	B	x_B	x_1	x_2	x_3	x_4	A_1	A_2	A_3	
−1	A_1	3	1	0	−1	4	1	0	0	3
−1	A_2	3	2	−1	0	0	0	1	0	3/2
−1	A_3	1	3	−2	0	−1	0	0	1	1/3→
z^*	−7	$z_j - c_j$	−6 ↑	3	1	−3	0	0	0	

x_1 enters into the basis and A_3 leaves the basis. The new iterative table is as given below.

		c_j	0	0	0	0	−1	−1	RR
c_B	B	x_B	x_1	x_2	x_3	x_4	A_1	A_2	
−1	A_1	8/5	0	2/3	−1	13/3	1	0	12/5→
−1	A_2	7/3	0	1/3	0	2/3	0	1	7
0	x_1	1/3	1	−2/3	0	−1/3	0	0	–
z^*	−5	$z_j - c_j$	0	−1	1	−5 ↑	0	0	

x_4 enters into the basis and A_1 leaves the basis. The new iterative table is shown below.

		c_j	0	0	0	0	−1	RR
c_B	B	x_B	x_1	x_2	x_3	x_4	A_2	
0	x_4	8/13	0	2/13	−3/13	1	0	4→
−1	A_2	25/13	0	3/13	2/13	0	1	25/3
0	x_1	7/13	1	−8/13	−1/13	0	0	–
z^*	−25/13	$z_j - c_j$	0	−3/13 ↑	−2/13	0	0	

x_2 enters into the basis and x_4 leaves the basis. The new iterative table is as follows.

		c_j	0	0	0	0	−1	RR
c_B	B	x_B	x_1	x_2	x_3	x_4	A_2	
0	x_2	4	0	1	−3/2	13/2	0	–
−1	A_2	1	0	0	1/2	−3/2	1	2→
0	x_1	3	1	0	−1	4	0	–
z^*	−1	$z_j - c_j$	0	0	−1/2 ↑	3/2	0	

x_3 enters into the basis and A_2 leaves the basis. The new iterative table is given below.

		c_j	0	0	0	0
c_B	B	x_B	x_1	x_2	x_3	x_4
0	x_2	7	0	1	0	2
0	x_3	2	0	0	1	−3
0	x_1	5	1	0	0	1
z^*	−1	$z_j - c_j$	0	0	0	0

Since $z_j - c_j$ are zero, the optimal solution is $x_1 = 5$, $x_2 = 7$, $x_3 = 2$ and $x_4 = 0$.

3.7.2 Big-M Method

To solve the LPP involving ≥ or = – to type, another method is Big-M method in which a high penalty cost is associated to the artificial variables. The computational algorithm is as follows.

Step 1: Write the given LPP in the standard form maximization. Add slack, surplus and artificial variables in the constraints as stated in previous two sections but assign a very high value '– M' as a coefficient of the artificial variable.

Step 2: Proceed according to the simplex method. At any iteration of the simplex method, there can be any one of the following three cases:

1. Net evaluations $z_j - c_j$ $(j = 1, 2, \ldots, n)$ are non-negative and the artificial variables are not to be present in the basis.
2. Net evaluations $z_j - c_j$ $(j = 1, 2, \ldots, n)$ are non-negative and there is at least one artificial variable in the basis and the objective function value z contains M. Then the LPP has no solution, i.e. infeasible solution.
3. At least one net evaluation $z_j - c_j$ $(j = 1, 2, \ldots, n)$ is negative indicating that some variable is trying to enter the basis, but if all RR-entries are negative or undefined then the problem has an unbounded solution.

EXAMPLE 3.35: Use Big-M method to maximize $z = 3x_1 - x_2$
subject to the constraints:

$$2x_1 + x_2 \geq 2$$

$$x_1 + 3x_2 \leq 3$$

$$x_2 \leq 4$$

and $x_1, x_2 \geq 0$.

Solution: Introduce surplus variable s_1 and artificial variable A_1 in the first constraint and slack variables s_2 and s_3 in the second and third constraints. The modified LPP is

Maximize $$z = 3x_1 - x_2 + 0s_1 + 0s_2 + 0s_3 - MA_1$$

subject to the constraints:

$$2x_1 + x_2 - s_1 + A_1 = 2$$

$$x_1 + 3x_2 + s_2 = 3$$

$$x_2 + s_3 = 4$$

and $x_1, x_2, s_1, s_2, s_3, A_1 \geq 0$.

Putting $x_1 = x_2 = s_1 = 0$ gives the initial iterate as $A_1 = 2$, $s_2 = 3$ and $s_3 = 4$. The iterative table is as follows.

		c_j	3	−1	0	0	0	−M	RR
c_B	B	x_B	x_1	x_2	s_1	s_2	s_3	A_1	
−M	A_1	2	2	1	−1	0	0	1	1→
0	s_2	3	1	3	0	1	0	0	9
0	s_3	4	0	1	0	0	1	0	−
z	−2M	$z_j - c_j$	−2M − 3 ↑	−M + 1	M	0	0	0	

x_1 enters into the basis and A_1 leaves the basis. The new iterative table is shown below.

		c_j	3	−1	0	0	0	RR
c_B	B	x_B	x_1	x_2	s_1	s_2	s_3	
3	x_1	1	1	1/2	−1/2	0	0	−
0	s_2	2	0	5/2	1/2	1	0	4→
0	s_3	4	0	1	0	0	1	−
z	3	$z_j - c_j$	0	5/2	−3/2 ↑	0	0	

s_1 will enter into the basis and s_2 will exit in the next iteration.

		c_j	3	−1	0	0
c_B	B	x_B	x_1	x_2	s_1	s_3
3	x_1	3	1	3	0	0
0	s_1	4	0	5	1	0
0	s_3	4	0	1	0	1
z	3	$z_j - c_j$	0	10	0	0

The optimum basic feasible solution is $x_1 = 3$, $x_2 = 0$ and maximum $z = 9$.

EXAMPLE 3.36: Use Big-M method to maximize $z = 3x_1 + 2x_2$
subject to the constraints:

$$2x_1 + x_2 \leq 2$$
$$3x_1 + 4x_2 \geq 12$$

and $x_1, x_2 \geq 0$.

Solution: Introduce slack variable s_1 in the first constraint and surplus variable s_2 and artificial variable A_1 in the second constraint. The reformatted LPP is

Maximize $$z = 3x_1 + 2x_2 + 0s_1 + 0s_2 - MA_1$$

subject to the constraints:

$$2x_1 + x_2 + s_1 = 2$$

$$3x_1 + 4x_2 - s_2 + A_1 = 12$$

and $x_1, x_2, s_1, s_2, A_1 \geq 0$.

Putting $x_1 = x_2 = s_2 = 0$ gives the initial iterate as $A_1 = 12$ and $s_1 = 2$. The iterative table is shown below.

		c_j	3	2	0	0	$-M$	RR
c_B	B	x_B	x_1	x_2	s_1	s_2	A_1	
0	s_1	2	2	1	1	0	0	$2 \rightarrow$
$-M$	A_1	12	3	4	0	-1	1	3
z	$-12M$	$z_j - c_j$	$-3M - 2$	$-4M$ ↑	0	M	0	

Thus, x_2 enters and s_1 exits in the next iteration.

		c_j	3	2	0	0	$-M$
c_B	B	x_B	x_1	x_2	s_1	s_2	A_1
2	x_2	2	2	1	1	0	0
$-M$	A_1	4	-5	0	-4	-1	1
z	$-4M + 4$	$z_j - c_j$	$5M + 1$	0	$4M + 2$	M	0

Here the coefficients of M in each $z_j - c_j$ are non-negative and the artificial variable appears at the zero level. Thus, the LPP has an infeasible solution.

EXAMPLE 3.37: Use Big-M method to maximize $z = 6x_1 + 4x_2$
subject to the constraints:

$$2x_1 + 3x_2 \leq 30$$

$$3x_1 + 2x_2 \leq 24$$

$$x_1 + x_2 \geq 3$$

and $x_1, x_2 \geq 0$.

Solution: Introduce slack variables s_1 and s_2 in the first and second constraints and surplus variable s_3 and artificial variable A_1 in the third constraint. The modified LPP is

Maximize $$z = 6x_1 + 4x_2 + 0s_1 + 0s_2 + 0s_3 - MA_1$$

subject to the constraints :

$$2x_1 + 3x_2 + s_1 = 30$$

$$3x_1 + 2x_2 + s_2 = 24$$

$$x_1 + x_2 - s_3 + A_1 = 4$$

and $x_1, x_2, s_1, s_2, s_3, A_1 \geq 0$.

Putting $x_1 = x_2 = s_3 = 0$ gives initial iterate as $s_1 = 30$, $s_2 = 24$ and $A_1 = 4$. The iterative table is as follows.

		c_j	6	4	0	0	0	$-M$	RR
c_B	B	x_B	x_1	x_2	s_1	s_2	s_3	A_1	
0	s_1	30	2	3	1	0	0	0	15
0	s_2	24	3	2	0	1	0	0	8
$-M$	A_1	3	1	1	0	0	-1	1	3→
z	$-3M$	$z_j - c_j$	$-M - 6$ ↑	$-M + 4$	0	0	M	0	

x_1 enters into the basis and A_1 leaves the basis. The new iterative table is given below.

		c_j	6	4	0	0	0	RR
c_B	B	x_B	x_1	x_2	s_1	s_2	s_3	
0	s_1	24	0	1	1	0	2	–
0	s_2	15	0	-1	0	1	3	5→
6	x_1	3	1	1	0	0	-1	–
z	18	$z_j - c_j$	0	2	0	0	-6 ↑	

s_3 enters into the basis and s_2 leaves the basis. The new iterative table is shown below.

		c_j	6	4	0	0	0
c_B	B	x_B	x_1	x_2	s_1	s_2	s_3
0	s_1	14	0	5/3	1	$-2/3$	0
0	s_3	5	0	$-1/3$	0	1/3	1
6	x_1	8	1	2/3	0	1/3	0
z	48	$z_j - c_j$	0	0	0	2	0

Since all $z_j - c_j \geq 0$, the optimum solution $x_1 = 8$ and $x_2 = 0$ is attained with maximum $z = 48$.

It is observed from the table that the net evaluation corresponding to non-basic variable x_2 is zero, which indicates that there is an alternative solution to the LPP. Enter x_2 into the basis instead of s_1 or s_3. The alternative solution will be as follows.

	c_j		6	4	0	0	0
c_B	B	x_B	x_1	x_2	s_1	s_2	s_3
4	x_2	42/5	0	1	3/5	–2/5	0
0	s_3	39/5	0	0	1/5	1/5	1
6	x_1	12/5	1	0	–2/5	3/5	0
z	48	$z_j - c_j$	0	0	0	2	0

Here the optimum solution is $x_1 = 12/5$ and $x_2 = 42/5$ with maximum $z = 48$.

EXAMPLE 3.38: Use the Big-M method to maximize $z = 2x_1 + x_2 + 3x_2$ subject to the constraints:

$$x_1 + x_2 + 2x_3 \leq 5$$

$$2x_1 + 3x_2 + 4x_3 = 12$$

and $x_1, x_2, x_3 \geq 0$.

Solution: Introduce slack variable s_1 in the first constraint and surplus variable s_2 and artificial variable A_1 in the second constraint. We start simplex table with initial basic feasible solution $s_1 = 5$ and $A_1 = 12$. The iterative table is given below.

	c_j		1	1	3	0	$-M$	RR
c_B	B	x_B	x_1	x_2	x_3	s_1	A_1	
0	s_1	5	1	1	2	1	0	5/2 →
$-M$	A_1	12	2	3	4	0	1	3
z	$-12M$	$z_j - c_j$	$-2M - 2$	$-3M - 1$	$-4M - 3$	0	0	
					↑			

x_3 enters into the basis and s_1 leaves the basis. The new iterative table is shown below.

	c_j		1	1	3	0	$-M$	RR
c_B	B	x_B	x_1	x_2	x_3	s_1	A_1	
3	x_3	5/2	1/2	1/2	1	1/2	0	5
$-M$	A_1	2	0	1	0	–2	1	2 →
z	$-2M + 15/2$	$z_j - c_j$	–1/2	$-M + 1/2$	0	$2M + 3/2$	0	
				↑				

x_2 enters into the basis and A_1 leaves the basis. The new iterative table is shown below.

		c_j	1	1	3	0	RR
c_B	B	x_B	x_1	x_2	x_3	s_1	
3	x_3	3/2	1/2	0	1	3/2	3→
1	x_2	2	0	1	0	–2	–
z	13/2	$z_j - c_j$	–1/2	0	0	5/2	
			↑				

x_1 enters into the basis and x_3 leaves the basis. The new iterative table is given below.

		c_j	1	1	3	0
c_B	B	x_B	x_1	x_2	x_3	s_1
2	x_1	3	1	0	2	3
1	x_2	2	0	1	0	–2
z	8	$z_j - c_j$	0	0	1	4

All $z_j - c_j$ are non-negative, so the optimum solution is $x_1 = 2$, $x_2 = 1$, $x_3 = 0$ and maximum $z = 8$.

EXAMPLE 3.39: Use the Big-M method to maximize $z = 3x_1 + 2x_2 + x_3$ subject to the constraints:

$$2x_1 + 5x_2 + x_3 = 12$$

$$3x_1 + 4x_2 = 11$$

and $x_2, x_3 \geq = 0$, x_1 unrestricted.

Solution: Introducing artificial variable $A \geq 0$, the initial basic feasible solution is $x_3 = 12$ and $A = 11$. Now since x_1 is unrestricted, we write $x_1 = x_1' - x_1''$, where x_1' and $x_1'' \geq 0$

		c_j	3	–3	2	1	–M	RR
c_B	B	x_B	x_1'	x_1''	x_2	x_3	A	
1	x_3	12	2	–2	5	1	0	12/5→
–M	A	11	3	–3	4	0	1	11/4
z	$-11M + 12$	$z_j - c_j$	$-3M - 1$	$3M + 1$	$-4M + 3$	0	0	
					↑			

x_2 enters into the basis and x_3 leaves the basis. The new iterative table is shown below.

		c_j	3	−3	2	1	−M	RR
c_B	B	x_B	x_1'	x_1''	x_2	x_3	A	
2	x_2	12/5	2/5	−2/5	1	1/5	0	6
−M	A	7/5	7/5	−7/5	0	−4/5	1	1→
z	−7M/5 + 24/5	$z_j - c_j$	−3M − 1	3M + 1	−4M + 3	0	0	
			↑					

x_1' enters into the basis and A leaves the basis. The new iterative table is shown below.

		c_j	3	−3	2	1	RR
c_B	B	x_B	x_1'	x_1''	x_2	x_3	
2	x_2	2	0	0	1	3/7	14/3→
3	x_1'	1	1	−1	0	−4/7	–
z	7	$z_j - c_j$	0	0	0	−13/7	
						↑	

x_3 enters into the basis and x_2 leaves the basis. The new iterative table is as follows.

		c_j	3	−3	2	1
c_B	B	x_B	x_1'	x_1''	x_2	x_3
1	x_3	14/3	0	0	7/3	1
3	x_1'	8/3	1	−1	4/3	0
z	47/3	$z_j - c_j$	0	0	13/3	0

Since all $z_j - c_j \geq 0$, the optimum basic feasible solution is $x_1' = 8/3$, $x_2 = 0$ and $x_3 = 14/3$, i.e. $x_1 = 8/3$, $x_2 = 0$, $x_3 = 14/3$ and maximum $z = 47/3$.

3.8 DEGENERACY IN LP

Sometimes we come across one of two situations: (i) at least one basic variable is zero in the initial iteration or (ii) at subsequent iteration of simplex method more than one vector leaves the basis. The solution so obtained is called *degenerate solution*. In this case, we do not improve value of the objective function in the next iteration. This results in *cycling*.

Let us see in the following algorithm how to avoid cycling at any stage.

Algorithm to rule out cycling

Step 1: Let x_r enter the basis and $\min_i \left\{ \frac{x_{Bi}}{x_{ir}} : x_{ir} > 0 \right\}$ is not unique.

Step 2: Rearrange the column vector of A so that the initial basis can be chosen by the first m-column vectors of A. Then $x_j = B^{-1}a_j = e_j\,(j = 1, 2, \ldots, m)$.

Step 3: Compute the non-negative ratios $\min_i \left\{ \frac{x_{Bi}}{x_{ir}} : x_{ir} > 0 \right\}$ for those values of i for which $\min_i \left\{ \frac{x_{Bi}}{x_{ir}} : x_{ir} > 0 \right\}$ have a tie. If this minimum is unique for $i = k$, then the vector x_k leaves the basis. Otherwise go to step 4.

Step 4: Continue step 3 until a unique minimum non-negative ratio is obtained.

Note: Any artificial variable (if exists) should not be removed from the basis at any stage.

EXAMPLE 3.40: Solve the following

$$\text{Maximize } z = 3x_1 + 9x_2$$

subject to the constraints: $x_1 + 4x_2 \leq 8$, $x_1 + 2x_2 \leq 4$ and $x_1, x_2 \geq 0$.

Solution: We need to add slack variables s_1 and s_2 in the constraints.

Putting $x_1 = x_2 = 0$, we get first iteration as shown below.

		c_j	3	9	0	0	RR
c_B	B	x_B	x_1	x_2	s_1	s_2	
0	s_1	8	1	4	1	0	2
0	s_2	4	1	2	0	1	2
z	0	$z_j - c_j$	–3	–9	0	0	

Clearly, most negative $z_2 - c_2$ corresponds to x_2. So x_2 will enter into the basis. The minimum ratio 2 occurs for both s_1 and s_2, and so both tend to leave the basis. So we have degeneracy. Let us rearrange columns corresponding to x_1, x_2, s_1 and s_2 in such a way that the initial identity matrix appears first.

		c_j	0	0	3	9	RR
c_B	B	x_B	s_1	s_2	x_1	x_2	
			1	2	3	4	
0	s_1	8	1	0	1	4	4
0	s_2	4	0	1	1	2	2→
z	0	$z_j - c_j$	0	0	–3	–9↑	

Using algorithm, $\min\left\{\frac{x_{11}}{x_{14}}, \frac{x_{21}}{x_{24}}\right\} = \min\left\{\frac{1}{4}, \frac{0}{2}\right\} = 0$ which corresponds to s_2. Hence, s_2 will leave the basis. So the new iteration table is as follows.

		c_j	0	0	3	9
c_B	B	x_B	s_1	s_2	x_1	x_2
			1	2	3	4
0	s_1	0	1	–2	–1	0
9	x_2	2	0	1/2	1/2	1
z	18	$z_j - c_j$	0	9/2	3/2	0

Since all $z_j - c_j \geq 0$, an optimal solution is $x_1 = 0$ and $x_2 = 9$ with maximum $z = 18$.

EXAMPLE 3.41: Solve the following

Maximize
$$z = 5x_1 - 2x_2 + 3x_3$$
subject to the constraints:
$$2x_1 + 2x_2 - x_3 \geq 2$$
$$3x_1 - 4x_2 \leq 3$$
$$x_2 + 3x_3 \leq 5$$
and $x_1, x_2, x_3 \geq 0$.

Solution: We need to add surplus variable s_1 and artificial variable A_1 in the first constraint and slack variables s_2 and s_3 in the next two constraints. Then initial basic feasible solution is $x_2 = 2$, $s_1 = 3$ and $s_2 = 5$, so we get first iteration as shown below.

	c_j		5	–2	3	0	0	0	–M	RR
c_B	B	x_B	x_1	x_2	x_3	s_1	s_2	s_3	A_1	
–M	A_1	2	2	2	–1	–1	0	0	1	1→
0	s_2	3	3	–4	0	0	1	0	0	1
0	s_3	5	0	1	3	0	0	1	0	–
z	–2M	$z_j - c_j$	–2M – 5 ↑	–2M + 2	M – 3	M	0	0	0	

Most negative $z_1 - c_1$ corresponds to x_1. So x_1 will enter into the basis. The minimum ratio 1 occurs for both A_1 and s_2, and so both tend to leave the basis. So, we have degeneracy. But since A_1 is an artificial variable, we first allow it to exist. The new iteration table is given below.

		c_j	5	−2	3	0	0	0
c_B	B	x_B	x_1	x_2	x_3	s_1	s_2	s_3
5	x_1	1	1	1	−1/2	−1/2	0	0
0	s_2	0	0	−7	3/2	3/2	1	0
0	s_3	5	0	1	3	0	0	1
z	5	$z_j - c_j$	0	7	−11/2	−5/2	0	0
					↑			

Following standard steps of the simplex table, we have the following iterations.

		c_j	5	−2	3	0	0	0	RR
c_B	B	x_B	x_1	x_2	x_3	s_1	s_2	s_3	
5	x_1	1	1	−4/3	0	0	1/3	0	–
3	x_3	0	0	−14/3	1	1	2/3	0	–
0	s_3	5	0	15	0	−3	−2	1	3→
z	5	$z_j - c_j$	0	−56/3	0	3	11/3	0	
				↑					

		c_j	5	−2	3	0	0	0	RR
c_B	B	x_B	x_1	x_2	x_3	s_1	s_2	s_3	
5	x_1	13/9	1	0	0	-4/15	7/45	4/45	–
3	x_3	14/9	0	0	1	1/15	2/45	14/45	1/14→
−2	x_2	1/3	0	1	0	−1/5	−2/15	1/15	–
z	101/9	$z_j - c_j$	0	0	0	−11/15	53/45	56/45	
						↑			

		c_j	5	−2	3	0	0	0
c_B	B	x_B	x_1	x_2	x_3	s_1	s_2	s_3
5	x_1	23/3	1	0	4	0	1/3	4/3
0	s_1	70/3	0	0	15	1	2/3	14/3
−2	x_2	5	0	1	3	0	0	1
z	85/3	$z_j - c_j$	0	0	11	0	5/3	14/3

Since all $z_j - c_j \geq 0$, an optimal solution is $x_1 = 23/3$ and $x_2 = -2$ and $x_3 = 0$ with maximum $z = 85/3$.

3.9 DUALITY IN LPP

From both the theoretical and practical points of view, the theory of duality is one of the most important and interesting concepts in linear programming. The basic idea behind the duality theory is that every linear programming problem has an associated linear program called its *dual* such that a solution to the original linear program also gives the solution to its dual. Thus, whenever a linear program is solved by the simplex method, we are actually getting solutions for two linear programming problems. The original problem is called the *primal* problem.

Although the idea of duality is essentially mathematical, we shall see that duality has important interpretations which can help managers to answer questions about alternative courses of action and their relative values.

Let us understand the concepts and the managerial significance of duality with the help of the following example.

ABC Company makes three products, T, C and B, which must be processed through the Assembly, Finishing and the Packaging departments. The three departments have maximum 60, 40 and 80 hours available. The profit on one unit of each of the products is Rs. 2 per T, Rs. 4 per C and Rs. 3 per B. The other data is given below.

	Hours required for 1 unit of product		
	T	C	B
Assembly	3	4	2
Finishing	2	1	2
Packaging	1	3	2

The problem can be formulated as:

Maximize: $$2T + 4C + 3B$$

subject to the constraints:

$$3T + 4C + 2B \leq 60$$
$$2T + 1C + 2B \leq 40$$
$$1T + 3C + 2B \leq 80$$

and T, C and $B \geq 0$.

Let the slack variables S_A, S_F and S_P be the unused hours in the three departments. So the above LP becomes

Maximize: $$2T + 4C + 3B + 0S_A + 0S_F + 0S_P$$

subject to the constraints:

$$3T + 4C + 2B + S_A = 60$$
$$2T + 1C + 2B + S_F = 40$$
$$1T + 3C + 2B + S_P = 80$$

and T, C and $B \geq 0$.

The following table gives the simplex solution to the above problem.

c_B	B	c_j / x_B	2 / T	4 / C	3 / B	0 / S_A	0 / S_F	0 / S_P	RR
0	S_A	60	3	4	2	1	0	0	15→
0	S_F	40	2	1	2	0	1	0	40
0	S_P	80	1	3	2	0	0	1	80/3
z	0	$c_j - z_j$	2	4 ↑	3	0	0	0	
4	C	15	3/4	1	1/2	1/4	0	0	30
0	S_F	25	5/4	0	3/2	–1/4	1	0	50/3→
0	S_P	35	5/4	0	1/2	–3/4	0	1	70
z	60	$c_j - z_j$	–1	0	1 ↑	–1	0	0	
4	C	20/3	1/3	1	0	1/3	–1/3	0	
3	B	50/3	5/6	0	1	–1/6	2/3	0	
0	S_P	80/3	–5/3	0	0	–2/3	–1/3	1	
z	228/3	$c_j - z_j$	–11/6	0	0	–5/6	–2/3	0	

This being a maximization problem, the optimality criteria is satisfied as all net evaluation entries, that is all $c_j - z_j$ entries are ≤ 0.

Recall that

(a) Each positive number in the $c_j - z_j$ row represents the net profit obtainable if 1 unit of the variable heading that column were added to the solution.

(b) Each negative number (a net loss) in the $c_j - z_j$ row indicates the decrease in the total profit if 1 unit of the variable heading that column were added to the product mix. A negative number in the $c_j - z_j$ row under one of the columns representing time has another interpretation also. A negative number here represents the amount of increase in total profit if the number of hours available in that department could be increased by 1.

We see from the table that the optimal solution is to produce 20/3 units of C, 50/3 units of B and no unit of T. The total contribution for this product mix is about Rs. 76.67. The values under the S_A, S_F and S_P columns in the $c_j - z_j$ row indicate that removing 1 productive hour from each of the three departments would reduce the total contribution respectively, by Rs. 5/6, 2/3 and 0. This can be taken to mean also that if additional capital were available to expand productive time in these departments, the value of increased production to ABC Company of 1 more hour in each of these departments would be Rs. 5/6, 2/3 and 0, i.e. adding another hour of Assembly time will increase profit by Rs. 5/6, adding another hour of Finishing will increase profit by Rs. 2/3, and adding another hour of packaging time will leave profit unchanged. These three values 5/6, 2/3 and 0 are called *dual prices*, *shadow prices*, or simply *unit worth of a resource*. To be more specific, if adding another hour to each department costs the same, we would add the time to the Assembly department, for there it is worth Rs. 5/6, which is more than 2/3 or 0.

This *primal* was concerned with maximizing the contribution from the three products; the *dual* will be concerned with evaluating the time used in the three departments to produce T, C and B.

The production manager of the ABC Company recognizes that the productive capacity of the three departments is a valuable resource to the firm; he wonders whether it would be possible to place a monetary value on its worth. He soon comes to think in terms of how much he would receive from another manufacturer, a renter who wants to rent all the capacity in ABC Company's three departments. He reasons along the following lines.

Suppose the rental charges were Rs. A per hour of Assembly time, Rs. F per hour of Finishing and Rs. P per hour of Packaging time, then the cost to the renter of all the time would be

$$\text{Total rent paid} = 60A + 40F + 80P$$

and of course the renter would want to set the rental prices in such a way as to minimize the total rent he would have to pay; so the *objective of the dual* is

Minimize: $60A + 40F + 80P$

The production manager of ABC Company will not rent out his time unless the rent offered enables him to net as much as he would if he used the time to produce products T, C and B for ABC Company. This observation leads to the *constraints of the dual.*

To make one unit of T requires 3 Assembly hours, 2 Finishing hours and 1 packaging hour. The time that goes into making one unit of T would be rented out for Rs. $3A + 2F + 1P$. If the manager used all that time to make T, he would earn Rs. 2 in contribution to profit, and so he will not rent out the time unless

$$3A + 2F + 1P \geq 2$$

and this gives the first constraint in the dual. A similar reasoning with respect to C and B gives the other two dual constraints:

$$4A + 1F + 3P \geq 4$$

$$2A + 2F + 2P \geq 3$$

So the entire dual problem which determines for the manager of the ABC Company, the value of the productive resources of the company (its plant hours) is:

Minimize $60A + 40F + 80P$

subject to the constraints:

$$3A + 2F + 1P \geq 2$$

$$4A + 1F + 3P \geq 4$$

$$2A + 2F + 2P \geq 3$$

and A, F, and $P \geq 0$

We add appropriate surplus and artificial variables as follows and then solve the dual problem. Only the initial and the final tables are shown below.

Minimize: $60A + 40F + 80P$

subject to the constraints:

$$3A + 2F + 1P - S_1 + A_1 = 2$$

$$4A + 1F + 3P - S_2 + A_2 = 4$$

$$2A + 2F + 2P - S_3 + A_3 = 3$$

with A, F, and $P \geq 0$.

	c_j		60	40	80	0	0	0	M	M	M	
c_B	B	x_B	A	F	P	S_1	S_2	S_3	A_1	A_2	A_3	RR
M	A_1	2	3	2	1	−1	0	0	1	0	0	2/3→
M	A_2	4	4	1	3	0	−1	0	0	1	0	1
M	A_3	3	2	2	2	0	0	−1	0	0	1	3/2
z	$9M$	$c_j - z_j$	$60-9M$	$40-5M$	$80-6M$	M	M	M	0	0	0	
			↑									
⋮	⋮	⋮	⋮	⋮	⋮	⋮	⋮	⋮	⋮	⋮	⋮	
60	A	5/6	1	0	2/3	0	−1/3	1/6	0	1/3	−1/6	
0	S_1	11/6	0	0	5/3	1	−1/3	−5/6	−1	1/3	5/6	
40	F	2/3	0	1	1/3	0	1/3	−2/3	0	−1/3	2/3	
z	228/3	$c_j - z_j$	0	0	80/3	0	20/3	50/3	M	$M-20/3$	$M-50/3$	

This being a minimization problem, the optimality criteria is satisfied as all net evaluation entries, that is, all $c_j - z_j$ row entries are ≥ 0.

The optimum solution to the dual problem indicates that the worth to ABC Company of 1 productive hour in Assembly department is Rs. 5/6 (A = 5/6 in the final table), in Finishing department is Rs. 2/3, and in Packaging department is Rs. 0 (T is not in the basis).

Of course, these are the same values we got by looking at the $c_j - z_j$ row in the final table of the primal problem. Thus, when we solved the primal, we also got the solution to the dual. Does solving the dual also give us the solution to the primal? Yes, if we look at the values contained under the S_1, S_2 and S_3 columns in the $c_j - z_j$ row in the final table of solution of the dual, we find 0, 20/3 and 50/3, which are the optimal values for T, C and B in the primal.

Now look at the two problem formulations again.

Primal problem	*Dual problem*
Maximize: $2T + 4C + 3B$	Minimize: $60A + 40F + 80P$
Subject to:	Subject to:
$3T + 4C + 2B \leq 60$	$3A + 2F + 1P \geq 2$
$2T + 1C + 2B \leq 40$	$4A + 1F + 3P \geq 4$
$1T + 3C + 2B \leq 80$	$2A + 2F + 2P \geq 3$
and T, C and $B \geq 0$	and A, F, and $P \geq 0$.

Some direct observations from the table above are given below.

1. The objective function coefficients of the primal problem have become the right-hand side constants of the dual. Similarly, the right-hand side constants of the primal have become the objective function coefficients of the dual.
2. The inequalities have been reversed in the constraints.
3. The objective is changed from maximization in primal to minimization in dual.
4. Each column in primal corresponds to a constraint (row) in a dual. Thus, the number of dual constraints is equal to the number of primal variables.
5. Each constraint (row) in the primal corresponds to a column in the dual. Hence, there is one dual variable for every primal constraint.
6. The transpose of the technological (input-output) coefficient matrix of the primal becomes the technological (input-output) coefficient matrix of the dual.

Further economic interpretations of duality:

1. Suppose T, C, B is a feasible solution to the primal (a level of output that can be achieved with the current resources) and A, F, P is a feasible solution of the dual (a set of rents which would induce the manager to rent out the plant rather than to use it himself). Then,
$$2T + 4C + 3B \leq 60A + 40F + 80P$$
2. The optimal values are the same in both problems. It means that the value to ABC Company of all its productive resources is precisely equal to the profit the firm can make if it employs these resources in the best possible way. In this way, the profit made on the firm's output is used to derive the imputed values of the inputs to produce that output.
3. In the above problem, the dual variable P was equal to 0 and not all the packaging time was used. This is entirely reasonable, since if the company already has excess packaging time, additional packaging time cannot be profitably used and so it is worthless. This is half of what is called the *principle of complimentary slackness*.
4. $A = 5/6$, $F = 2/3$ and $P = 0$, $3A + 2F + 1P = 23/6$. This shows us that the value of the time needed to produce one unit of T is Rs. 23/6. But one unit of T contributes a profit of Rs. 2. Since the time needed to produce T is worth more than the return on it, the optimal solution to the primal does not produce any T. This is the other half of the *principle of complimentary slackness*.

Now we look at the concept of duality by introducing mathematical rigour.

To every LPP, there is an associated LPP called dual of the given LPP. The given problem is called *primal problem*, i.e. every LPP when expressed in its standard form has associated unique LPP based on the same data. These primal-dual pairs are interrelated and the variables of this pair have interesting implications in econometrics, production engineering, etc. Let us define dual of

Primal: Maximize $z = \mathbf{c}^T\mathbf{x},\ x \in \mathbf{R}^n$

subject to the constraints: $\mathbf{Ax} \leq \mathbf{b}$, $\mathbf{x} \geq 0$, $\mathbf{b} \in \mathbf{R}^m$, A is $m \times n$ – matrix.

Dual: Minimize $z^* = \mathbf{b}^T\mathbf{w},\ \mathbf{w} \in \mathbf{R}^m$

subject to the constraints: $A^T\mathbf{w} \geq \mathbf{c},\ \mathbf{w} \geq 0$

Note: In order to convert any problem into its dual, the primal LPP must be expressed in the maximization form with all constraints in ≤ type or = type. Thus, primal – dual pairs are as follows:

Primal problem	*Dual problem*
1. Maximize $z = \mathbf{c}^T\mathbf{x}$ subject to the constraints: $\mathbf{Ax} \le \mathbf{b}, \mathbf{x} \ge 0$	Minimize $z^* = \mathbf{b}^T\mathbf{w}$ subject to the constraints: $A^T\mathbf{w} \ge \mathbf{c}, \mathbf{w} \ge 0$
2. Maximize $z = \mathbf{c}^T\mathbf{x}$ subject to the constraints: $\mathbf{Ax} = \mathbf{b}, \mathbf{x} \ge 0$	Minimize $z^* = \mathbf{b}^T\mathbf{w}$ subject to the constraints: $A^T\mathbf{w} \ge \mathbf{c}$, **w** is unrestricted
3. Minimize $z = \mathbf{c}^T\mathbf{x}$ subject to the constraints: $\mathbf{Ax} = \mathbf{b}, \mathbf{x} \ge 0$	Maximize $z^* = \mathbf{b}^T\mathbf{w}$ subject to the constraints: $A^T\mathbf{w} \le \mathbf{c}$, **w** is unrestricted
4. Minimize (maximize) $z = \mathbf{c}^T\mathbf{x}$ subject to the constraints: $\mathbf{Ax} = \mathbf{b}$, **x** is unrestricted	Maximize (minimize) $z^* = \mathbf{b}^T\mathbf{w}$ subject to the constraints: $A^T\mathbf{w} = \mathbf{c}$, **w** is unrestricted

Given an LPP, it can be directly converted into its dual using the following table:

Primal problem	*Dual problem*
1. Maximization with constraints ≤ or =	Minimization with constraints ≥ or =
2. No. of constraints	No. of variables
3. Coefficients of the objective function	RHS of constraints
4. Input-output matrix A	Input-output matrix A^T
5. j-th constraint of = type	j-th variable unrestricted in sign
6. k-th variable unrestricted in sign	k-th constraint of = type

EXAMPLE 3.42: Write dual of LPP:

Maximize
$$z = 8x_1 + 6x_2$$
subject to the constraints: $x_1 - x_2 \le \frac{3}{5},\ x_1 - x_2 \ge 2,\ x_1, x_2 \ge 0$

Solution: To write the given LPP in maximization form with all constraints ≤-type. So the primal is

Maximize
$$z = 8x_1 + 6x_2$$
subject to the constraints:
$$x_1 - x_2 \le \frac{3}{5}$$
$$-x_1 + x_2 \le -2$$
and $x_1, x_2 \ge 0$.

Let w_1 and w_2 be dual variables. Then dual problem is

Minimize $$z^* = \frac{3}{5}w_1 - 2w_2$$

subject to the constraints:

$$w_1 - w_2 \geq 8$$
$$-w_1 + w_2 \geq 6$$

and $w_1, w_2 \geq 0$.

EXAMPLE 3.43: Write dual of LPP:

Minimize $$z = 4x_1 + 6x_2 + 18x_3$$

subject to the constraints:

$$x_1 + 3x_2 \geq 3$$
$$x_2 + 2x_3 \geq 5$$

and $x_1, x_2, x_3 \geq 0$.

Solution: Primal is

Minimize $$z = 4x_1 + 6x_2 + 18x_3$$

subject to the constraints:

$$x_1 + 3x_2 + 0x_3 \geq 3$$
$$0x_1 + x_2 + 2x_3 \geq 5$$

and $x_1, x_2, x_3 \geq 0$.

Let w_1 and w_2 be dual variables corresponding to each of the primal constraint. Then dual problem is

Maximize $$z^* = 3w_1 + 5w_2$$

subject to the constraints:

$$w_1 + 0w_2 \leq 4$$
$$3w_1 + w_2 \leq 6$$

and $$0w_1 + 2w_2 \leq 18.$$

Rewriting the dual problem as

Maximize $$z^* = 3w_1 + 5w_2$$

subject to the constraints:

$$w_1 \leq 4$$
$$3w_1 + w_2 \leq 6$$
$$2w_2 \leq 18$$

and $w_1, w_2 \geq 0$.

EXAMPLE 3.44: Write dual of LPP:

Minimize $$z = 7x_1 + 3x_2 + 8x_3$$

subject to the constraints:

$$8x_1 + 2x_2 + x_3 \geq 3$$
$$3x_1 + 6x_2 + 4x_3 \geq 4$$
$$4x_1 + x_2 + 5x_3 \geq 1$$
$$x_1 + 5x_2 + 2x_3 \geq 7$$

and $x_1, x_2, x_3 \geq 0$.

Solution: Primal is

Minimize $$z = 7x_1 + 3x_2 + 8x_3$$

subject to the constraints:

$$8x_1 + 2x_2 + x_3 \geq 3$$
$$3x_1 + 6x_2 + 4x_3 \geq 4,$$
$$4x_1 + x_2 + 5x_3 \geq 1$$
$$x_1 + 5x_2 + 2x_3 \geq 7$$

and $x_1, x_2, x_3 \geq 0$.

Let w_1, w_2, w_3 and w_4 be dual variables corresponding to each of the primal constraint. Then dual problem is

Maximize $$z = 3w_1 + 4w_2 + w_3 + 7w_4$$

subject to the constraints:

$$8w_1 + 3w_2 + 4w_3 + w_4 \leq 7$$
$$2w_1 + 6w_2 + w_3 + 5w_4 \leq 3$$
$$w_1 + 4w_2 + 5w_3 + 2w_4 \leq 8$$

and $w_1, w_2, w_3, w_4 \geq 0$.

EXAMPLE 3.45: Write dual of LPP:

Maximize $$z = 3x_1 + x_2 + x_3 - x_4$$

subject to the constraints:

$$x_1 + 5x_2 + 3x_3 + 4x_4 \leq 4$$
$$x_1 + x_2 = -1$$
$$x_3 - x_4 \leq -5$$

and $x_1, x_2, x_3, x_4 \geq 0$

Solution: Primal is

Maximize $$z = 3x_1 + x_2 + x_3 - x_4$$

subject to the constraints:

$$x_1 + 5x_2 + 3x_3 + 4x_4 \leq 4$$
$$-x_1 - x_2 = 1$$
$$x_3 - x_4 \leq -5$$

and $x_1, x_2, x_3, x_4 \geq 0$.

Let w_1, w_2, and w_3 be dual variables corresponding to each of the primal constraint. Then dual problem is

Minimize $z^* = 4w_1 + w_2 - 5w_3$

subject to the constraints:

$$w_1 - w_2 \geq 3$$
$$5w_1 - w_2 \geq 1$$
$$3w_1 + w_3 \geq 1$$
$$4w_1 - w_2 \geq -1$$

and w_1, $w_3 \geq 0$, and w_2 unrestricted.

EXAMPLE 3.46: Write dual of LPP:

Minimize $z = x_1 - 3x_2 - 2x_3$

subject to the constraints:

$$3x_1 - x_2 + 2x_3 \leq 7$$
$$2x_1 - 4x_2 \geq 12$$
$$-4x_1 + 3x_2 + 8x_3 = 10$$

and x_1, $x_2 \geq 0$ and x_3 is unrestricted.

Solution: Putting $x_3 = x'_3 - x''_3$, we have primal as

Minimize $z = x_1 - 3x_2 - 2(x'_3 - x''_3)$

subject to the constraints:

$$-3x_1 + x_2 - 2(x'_3 - x''_3) \geq -7$$
$$2x_1 - 4x_2 \geq 12$$
$$-4x_1 + 3x_2 + 8(x'_3 - x''_3) = 10$$

and x_1, x_2, x'_3, $x''_3 \geq 0$.

Also, as the third constraint is an equality, we convert it into inequalities as follows:

$$-4x_1 + 3x_2 + 8(x'_3 - x''_3) \leq 10 \quad \text{and} \quad -4x_1 + 3x_2 + 8(x'_3 - x''_3) \geq 10$$

Rewriting primal problem as minimization problem with all constraints ≥ – type:

Minimize $z = x_1 - 3x_2 - 2(x'_3 - x''_3)$

subject to the constraints:

$$-3x_1 + x_2 - 2(x'_3 - x''_3) \geq -7$$
$$2x_1 - 4x_2 \geq 12$$
$$4x_1 - 3x_2 - 8(x'_3 - x''_3) \geq -10$$
$$-4x_1 + 3x_2 + 8(x'_3 - x''_3) \geq 10$$

and x_1, x_2, x'_3, $x''_3 \geq 0$.

Let w_1, w_2, w_3 and w_4 be dual variables corresponding to each of the primal constraint. Then dual problem is

Maximize $$z^* = -7w_1 + 12w_2 - 10w_3 + 10w_4$$

subject to the constraints:

$$-3w_1 + 2w_2 + 4w_3 - 4w_4 \le 1$$
$$w_1 - 4w_2 - 3w_3 + 3w_4 \le -3$$
$$-2w_1 - 8w_3 + 8w_4 \le -2$$
$$2w_1 + 8w_3 - 8w_4 \le 2$$

and $w_1, w_2, w_3, w_4 \ge 0$.

The third and the fourth constraints can be written as $2w_1 + 8w_3 - 8w_4 = 2$. From the objective function and the constraints, w_3 and w_4 can be put together by writing $w = w_3 - w_4$. So w becomes unrestricted in sign. Rewriting the dual problem as

Maximize $$z^* = -7w_1 + 12w_2 - 10w$$

subject to the constraints:

$$-3w_1 + 2w_2 + 4w \le 1$$
$$w_1 - 4w_2 - 3w \le -3$$
$$2w_1 + 8w = 2$$

$w_1 \ge 0$, $w_2 \ge 0$ and w is unrestricted.

Instead of working out the dual in the above manner, the following way can also be applied by using the table given below.

Primal (minimize with ≥)	*Dual*
Minimize $z = x_1 - 3x_2 - 2x_3$	Maximize $z^* = -7w_1 + 12w_2 - 10w$
subject to the constraints:	subject to the constraints:
$-3x_1 + x_2 - 2x_3 \ge -7$	$-3w_1 + 2w_2 + 4w \le 1$
$2x_1 - 4x_2 \ge 12$	$Tw_1 - 4w_2 - 3w \le -3$
$4x_1 - 3x_2 - 8x_3 = -10$	$-2w_1 - 8w = -2$
$x_1, x_2 \ge 0$ and x_3 is unrestricted.	$w_1 \ge 0$, $w_2 \ge 0$ and w is unrestricted

3.9.1 Duality Theorems

Theorem 3.8: *The dual of dual is the primal.*

Proof: Consider the standard LPP:

Primal: To find, $\mathbf{x} \in \mathbf{R}^n$ which maximize $z = \mathbf{c}^T\mathbf{x}$, $\mathbf{x} \in \mathbf{R}^n$

subject to the constraints:

$$\mathbf{Ax} \le \mathbf{b},\ \mathbf{x} \ge 0,\ \mathbf{b} \in \mathbf{R}^m,\ A \text{ is } m \times n - \text{matrix} \tag{3.13}$$

Then dual of Eq. (3.13) is to find $w \in \mathbf{R}^m$ which minimize $z^* = \mathbf{b}^T\mathbf{w}$, $\mathbf{w} \in \mathbf{R}^m$

subject to the constraints: $$A^T\mathbf{w} \ge \mathbf{c}, \quad \mathbf{w} \ge 0 \tag{3.14}$$

Equation (3.14) can be written as find $\mathbf{w} \in \mathbf{R}^m$ which maximize $z^* = -\mathbf{b}^T\mathbf{w}, \mathbf{w} \in \mathbf{R}^m$

subject to the constraints: $\quad -A^T\mathbf{w} \le -\mathbf{c}, \quad \mathbf{w} \ge 0 \quad (3.15)$

Now dual of Eq. (3.15) is find, $\mathbf{x} \in \mathbf{R}^n$ which minimize $z^{**} = (-\mathbf{c})^T\mathbf{x}, \quad \mathbf{x} \in \mathbf{R}^n$

subject to the constraints: $\quad -(A^T)^T\mathbf{x} \le \mathbf{b}, \quad \mathbf{x} \ge 0, \quad \mathbf{b} \in \mathbf{R}^m \quad (3.16)$

Rewriting Eq. (3.16), we get Eq. (3.13), i.e. the dual of dual is the primal.

Theorem 3.9: *If $\mathbf{x}_0$ is a feasible solution of the primal Eq. (3.13) and $\mathbf{w}_0$ is a feasible solution of the dual problem Eq. (3.14) then $\mathbf{c}^T\mathbf{x}_0 \le \mathbf{b}^T\mathbf{w}_0$.*

Proof: Since $\mathbf{x}_0$ is a feasible solution of the primal Eq. (3.13), $A\mathbf{x}_0 \le \mathbf{b}$. Pre-multiply by $\mathbf{w}_0^T$. Then

$$\mathbf{w}_0^T A\mathbf{x}_0 \le \mathbf{w}_0^T \mathbf{b} \quad \text{or} \quad \mathbf{w}_0^T A\mathbf{x}_0 \le \mathbf{b}\mathbf{w}_0^T \tag{3.17}$$

(because both are 1×1 size matrices of real numbers). Now $\mathbf{w}_0$ is a feasible solution of the dual problem Eq. (3.14), so $A^T\mathbf{w}_0 \ge \mathbf{c}$. Taking transpose, we get $\mathbf{w}_0^T A \ge \mathbf{c}^T$ or

$$\mathbf{w}_0^T A\mathbf{x}_0 \ge \mathbf{c}^T\mathbf{x}_0 \tag{3.18}$$

From Eqs. (3.17) and (3.18), we have the result.

Theorem 3.10: *The value of the objective function z for any feasible solution of the primal is not less than the value of the objective function z^* for any feasible solution of the dual.*

Proof: Consider the primal problem Eq. (3.13) to find $\mathbf{x} \in \mathbf{R}^n$ which maximize $z = \mathbf{c}^T\mathbf{x}, \mathbf{x} \in \mathbf{R}^n$ subject to the constraints:

$$A\mathbf{x} \le \mathbf{b}, \mathbf{x} \ge 0, \mathbf{b} \in \mathbf{R}^m, A \text{ is } m \times n - \text{matrix}$$

Then dual Eq. (3.14) is to find $\mathbf{w} \in \mathbf{R}^m$ which minimize $z^* = \mathbf{b}^T\mathbf{w}, \mathbf{w} \in \mathbf{R}^m$

subject to the constraints: $\quad A^T\mathbf{w} \ge \mathbf{c}, \mathbf{w} \ge 0$

Introducing the necessary slack variables in constraints of Eqs. (3.13) and (3.14), we get

Primal

Maximize $\quad z = c_1x_1 + c_2x_2 + \cdots + c_nx_n$

subject to the constraints:

$$a_{11}x_1 + a_{12}x_2 + \cdots + a_{1n}x_n + x_{n+1} = b_1;$$
$$a_{21}x_1 + a_{22}x_2 + \cdots + a_{2n}x_n + x_{n+2} = b_2;$$
$$\vdots$$
$$\vdots$$
$$a_{m1}x_1 + a_{m2}x_2 + \cdots + a_{mn}x_n + x_{m+n} = b_m;$$

and $\quad x_1, x_2, \ldots, x_{n+m} \ge 0;$

and its dual is

Maximize $\quad z^* = b_1w_1 + b_2w_2 + \cdots + b_nw_n$

Subject to the constraints:

$$a_{11}w_1 + a_{21}w_2 + \cdots + a_{m1}w_m + w_{m+1} = c_1;$$
$$a_{12}w_1 + a_{22}w_2 + \cdots + a_{m2}w_m + w_{m+2} = c_2;$$
$$\vdots$$
$$\vdots$$
$$a_{1n}w_1 + a_{2n}w_2 + \cdots + a_{mn}w_m + w_{m+n} = b_m;$$

and $w_1, w_2, \ldots, w_{m+n} \geq 0$.

Let $x_1, x_2, \ldots, x_{n+m}$ and $w_1, w_2, \ldots, w_{m+n}$ be any feasible solutions of Eqs. (3.13) and (3.14) respectively. Multiply primal constraints by $w_1, w_2, \ldots, w_m$ and add. Similarly, multiply dual constraints by $x_1, x_2, \ldots, x_n$ and add. Subtracting the resultant equations, we get

$$z - z^* = x_1w_{m+1} + \cdots + x_nw_{m+n} + w_1x_{n+1} + \cdots + w_mx_{n+m}$$

Clearly, RHS is non-negative, so $z - z^* \geq 0$.

Theorem 3.11: *The value of the objective function z for any feasible solution of the primal (if it exists) is equal to the value of the objective function z^* for any feasible solution of the dual.*

Proof: It is left for the reader as an exercise.

3.9.2 Advantages of Duality

1. It is advantageous to solve the dual of the primal having fewer number of constraints which needs fewer number of iterations to solve the problem.
2. In economics, duality plays an important role in the formulation of input-output system.
3. The economic interpretation of the dual is found useful in the long-term planning.
4. Sensitivity analysis which facilitates strategic decision making, may be carried out with the help of the dual for more details, see Section 3.10.

3.9.3 Dual Simplex Method

Solving LPP, we come across the situation where some of the variables are negative, contradicting the non-negative constraints. In such a situation, for getting feasible solution, the dual simplex method can be used. This method guarantees that all variables will be non-negative in the final solution provided that the corresponding row has at least one negative entry.

Note: The final solution may not give maximum value of *z*.

The dual simplex algorithm follows the following steps.

Step 1: Express the given LPP in maximization form with all constraints less than or equal to – type. There must be a negative entry in the RHS constants.

Step 2: The most negative value of the variable in $\mathbf{x}_B$ is considered to be an outgoing variable (including zero).

Step 3: The incoming variable is decided by the replacement ratio (RR) max $\{(z_j - c_j)/a_{ij}: j = 1, 2, \ldots, n)\}$ is taken and the corresponding variable is an incoming variable. (Negative values are to be ignored).

Note:

1. If either the primal or the dual problem has a finite optimal solution, then the other problem also has a finite optimal solution. Also, the optimal values are same (by Theorem 3.11).
2. If either problem has an unbounded optimal solution then the other problem has an infeasible solution.
3. Both the problems may have infeasible solution.

EXAMPLE 3.47: Use the dual simplex method to solve the following LPP:

Maximize $z = -3x_1 - x_2$

subject to the constraints:

$$x_1 + x_2 \geq 1$$

$$2x_1 + 3x_2 \geq 2$$

and $x_1, x_2 \geq 0$.

Solution: Converting constraints in ≤ – type, we get

Maximize $z = -3x_1 - x_2$

subject to the constraints:

$$-x_1 - x_2 \leq -1$$

$$-2x_1 - 3x_2 \leq -2$$

and $x_1, x_2 \geq 0$.

Introducing slack variables s_1 and s_2 in the constraints and putting $x_1 = x_2 = 0$, we get initial basic infeasible solution $s_1 = -1$ and $s_2 = -2$. The initial iterative table is as follows.

		c_j	–3	–1	0	0	*RR*
c_B	B	x_B	x_1	x_2	s_1	s_2	
0	s_1	–1	–1	–1	1	0	–1
0	s_2	–2	–2	–3	0	1	–2→
z	0	$z_j - c_j$	3	1	0	0	
		$(z_j - c_j)/x_{2j} : x_{2j} < 0$	3/–2	1/–3 ↑	–		

Thus, x_2 will enter into the basis and s_2 will leave the basis in the next iteration.

		c_j	–3	–1	0	0	*RR*
c_B	B	x_B	x_1	x_2	s_1	s_2	
0	s_1	–1/3	–1/3	0	1	–1/3	–1/3→
–1	x_2	2/3	2/3	1	0	–1/3	–1/3
z	2/3	$z_j - c_j$	7/3	0	0	1/3	
		$(z_j - c_j)/x_{2j} : x_{2j} < 0$	(7/3)/(–1/3)	–	–	(1/3)/(1/–3) ↑	

Thus, s_2 will enter into the basis and s_1 will leave the basis in the next iteration.

		c_j	−3	−1	0	0
c_B	B	x_B	x_1	x_2	s_1	s_2
0	s_2	1	1	0	−3	1
−1	x_2	1	1	1	−1	0
z	−1	$z_j - c_j$	2	0	1	0

Since $z_j - c_j$ are non-negative for all j, the optimum solution is $x_1 = 0$, $x_2 = 1$ and maximum $z = -1$.

EXAMPLE 3.48: Use the dual simplex method to solve the following LPP:

Maximize
$$z = -3x_1 - 2x_2$$
subject to the constraints:
$$x_1 + x_2 \geq 1$$
$$x_1 + x_2 \leq 7$$
$$x_1 + 2x_2 \geq 10$$
$$x_2 \leq 3$$
and $x_1, x_2 \geq 0$.

Solution: Converting constraints in ≤ – type, we get

Maximize
$$z = -3x_1 - 2x_2$$
subject to the constraints:
$$-x_1 - x_2 \leq -1$$
$$x_1 + x_2 \leq 7$$
$$-x_1 - 2x_2 \leq -10$$
$$x_2 \leq 3$$
and $x_1, x_2 \geq 0$.

Introducing slack variables s_1, s_2, s_3 and s_4 in the constraints and putting $x_1 = x_2 = 0$, we get initial basic infeasible solution $s_1 = -1$, $s_2 = 7$, $s_3 = -10$ and $s_4 = 3$. The initial iterative table is shown below.

		c_j	−3	−2	0	0	0	0	RR
c_B	B	x_B	x_1	x_2	s_1	s_2	s_3	s_4	
0	s_1	−1	−1	−1	1	0	0	0	
0	s_2	7	1	1	0	1	0	0	
0	s_3	−10	−1	−2	0	0	1	0	→
0	s_4	3	0	0	0	0	0	1	
z	0	$z_j - c_j$	3	2	0	0	0	0	
		$(z_j - c_j)/x_{2j} : x_{2j} < 0$	3/−1	2/−2 ↑	–	–	–	–	–

Drop s_3 and enter x_2 in the next iteration.

		c_j	–3	–2	0	0	0	0	RR
c_B	B	x_B	x_1	x_2	s_1	s_2	s_3	s_4	
0	s_1	4	–1/2	0	1	0	–1/2	0	
0	s_2	2	1/2	0	0	1	1/2	0	
–2	x_2	5	1/2	1	0	0	–1/2	0	
0	s_4	–2	–1/2	0	0	0	1/2	1	→
z	–10	$z_j - c_j$	2	0	0	0	1	0	
		$(z_j - c_j)/x_{1j} : x_{1j} < 0$	2/(–1/2) ↑	–	–	–	–	–	–

Drop s_4 and enter x_1 in the next iteration.

		c_j	–3	–2	0	0	0	0
c_B	B	x_B	x_1	x_2	s_1	s_2	s_3	s_4
0	s_1	6	0	0	1	0	–1	–1
0	s_2	0	0	0	0	1	1	1
–2	x_2	3	0	1	0	0	0	1
–3	x_1	4	1	0	0	0	–1	–2
z	–18	$z_j - c_j$	0	0	0	0	3	4

Since $z_j - c_j$ are non-negative for all j, the optimum solution is $x_1 = 4$, $x_2 = 3$ and maximum $z = -18$.

EXAMPLE 3.49: Use the dual simplex method to solve the following LPP:

Maximize
$$z = -2x_1 - 2x_2 - 4x_3$$

subject to the constraints:
$$2x_1 + 3x_2 + 5x_3 \geq 2$$
$$3x_1 + x_2 + 7x_3 \leq 3$$
$$x_1 + 4x_2 + 6x_3 \leq 5$$

and $x_1, x_2, x_3 \geq 0$

Solution: Converting constraints in ≤ – type and adding slack variables s_1, s_2 and s_3 in the constraints and putting $x_1 = x_2 = x_3 = 0$, we get initial basic infeasible solution $s_1 = -2$, $s_2 = 3$, $s_3 = 5$. The initial iterative table is given as follows.

		c_j	−2	−2	−4	0	0	0	RR
c_B	B	x_B	x_1	x_2	x_3	s_1	s_2	s_3	
0	s_1	−2	2	−3	−5	1	0	0	→
0	s_2	3	3	1	7	0	1	0	
0	s_3	5	1	4	6	0	0	1	
z	0	$z_j - c_j$	2	2	4	0	0	0	
		$(z_j - c_j)/x_{2j} : x_{2j} < 0$	–	2/–3 ↑	–	–	–	–	

Drop s_1 and enter x_2 in the next iteration.

		c_j	−2	−2	−4	0	0	0
c_B	B	x_B	x_1	x_2	x_3	s_1	s_2	s_3
−2	x_2	2/3	2/3	1	5/3	−1/3	0	0
0	s_2	7/3	7/3	0	16/3	1/3	1	0
0	s_3	7/3	−5/3	0	−2/3	4/3	0	1
z	−4/3	$z_j - c_j$	2/3	0	2/3	2/3	0	0

Since $z_j - c_j$ are non-negative for all j, the optimum solution is $x_1 = 0$, $x_2 = 2/3$, $x_3 = 0$ and maximum $z = -4/3$.

EXAMPLE 3.50: Use the dual simplex method to solve the following LPP:

Minimize $$z = 2x_1 + x_2 + x_3$$

subject to the constraints:

$$4x_1 + 6x_2 + 3x_3 \leq 8$$

$$x_1 - 9x_2 + x_3 \leq -3$$

$$-2x_1 - 3x_2 + 5x_3 \leq -4$$

and $x_1, x_2, x_3 \geq 0$.

Solution: Adding slack variables s_1, s_2 and s_3 in the constraints and putting $x_1 = x_2 = x_2 = 0$, we get the initial basic infeasible solution $s_1 = 8$, $s_2 = -3$, $s_3 = -4$. The initial iterative table is as follows.

		c_j	2	1	1	0	0	0	RR
c_B	B	x_B	x_1	x_2	x_3	s_1	s_2	s_3	
0	s_1	8	4	6	3	1	0	0	
0	s_2	–3	1	–9	1	0	1	0	
0	s_3	–4	2	–3	5	0	0	1	→
z	0	$z_j - c_j$	2	1	1	0	0	0	
		$(z_j - c_j)/x_{2j} : x_{2j} < 0$	–	1/–3	–	–	–	–	
				↑					

s_3 leaves the basis and enter x_2 in the next iteration.

		c_j	2	1	1	0	0	0
c_B	B	x_B	x_1	x_2	x_3	s_1	s_2	s_3
0	s_1	0	0	0	13	1	0	2
0	s_2	0	7	0	–14	0	1	–3
1	x_2	4/3	2/3	1	–5/3	0	0	–1/3
z	–4/3	$z_j - c_j$	4/3	0	8/3	0	0	1/3

Since $z_j - c_j$ are non-negative for all j, the optimum solution is $x_1 = 0$, $x_2 = 4/3$, $x_3 = 0$ and minimum $z = -(-4/3) = 4/3$.

EXAMPLE 3.51: Use the dual simplex method to solve the following LPP:

$$\text{Minimize} \quad z = 2x_1 + 9x_2 + 24x_3 + 8x_4 + 5x_5$$

subject to the constraints: $x_1 + x_2 + 2x_3 - x_5 - x_6 = 1$, $-2x_1 + x_3 + x_4 + x_5 - x_7 = 2$; $x_j \geq 0$, $j = 1, 2, \ldots, 7$.

Solution: Multiplying the constraints equations by (–1) on both sides, we get the initial basic infeasible solution $x_6 = -1$, $x_7 = -2$. The initial iterative table is given below.

		c_j	2	9	24	8	5	0	0	RR
c_B	B	x_B	x_1	x_2	x_3	x_4	x_5	x_6	x_7	
0	x_6	–1	–1	–1	–2	0	1	1	0	
0	x_7	–2	2	0	–1	–1	–1	0	1	→
z	0	$z_j - c_j$	2	9	24	8	5	0	0	
		$(z_j - c_j)/x_{5j} : x_{5j} < 0$	–	–	24/–1	–	5/–1	–	–	
							↑			

x_7 leaves the basis and enter x_5 in the next iteration.

		c_j	2	9	24	8	5	0	0	RR
c_B	B	x_B	x_1	x_2	x_3	x_4	x_5	x_6	x_7	
0	x_6	−3	1	−1	−3	−1	0	1	1	→
−5	x_5	2	−2	0	1	1	1	0	−1	
z	−10	$z_j - c_j$	12	9	19	3	0	0	5	
		$(z_j - c_j)/x_{4j} : x_{4j} < 0$	–	–	19/–3	3/–1 ↑	–	–	–	

x_6 leaves the basis and enter x_4 in the next iteration.

		c_j	2	9	24	8	5	0	0	RR
c_B	B	x_B	x_1	x_2	x_3	x_4	x_5	x_6	x_7	
−8	x_4	3	−1	1	3	1	0	−1	−1	
−5	x_5	−1	−1	−1	−2	0	1	1	0	→
z	−19	$z_j - c_j$	15	6	10	0	0	3	5	
		$(z_j - c_j)/x_{3j} : x_{3j} < 0$	–	6/–1	10/–2 ↑	–	–	–	–	

x_5 leaves the basis and enter x_3 in the next iteration.

		c_j	2	9	24	8	5	0	0
c_B	B	x_B	x_1	x_2	x_3	x_4	x_5	x_6	x_7
−8	x_4	3/2	−5/2	−1/2	0	1	3/2	1/2	−1
−24	x_3	1/2	1/2	1/2	1	0	−1/2	−1/2	0
z	−24	$z_j - c_j$	10	1	0	0	5	8	8

Since $z_j - c_j$ are non-negative for all j, the optimum solution is $x_1 = 0$, $x_2 = 0$, $x_3 = 1/2$, $x_4 = 3/2$, $x_5 = 0$, $x_6 = 0$, $x_7 = 0$ and minimum $z = -(-24) = 24$.

3.10 REVISED SIMPLEX METHOD

The revised simplex method is the procedure of upgrading the simplex table to compute values of x_B and z. Thus, we need to know only about the coefficients of non-basic variables in the objective function and the coefficient of variable to be entered into the basis at each iteration. In fact, this is more suitable for the computer and not on paper. Let us discuss the following two standard forms.

3.10.1 Standard Form I

It is assumed here that an identity matrix is available after introducing slack and/or surplus variables in the constraints of the given LPP. The steps of algorithm are as follows:

Step 1: Write the given LPP in the maximization form.

Step 2: Obtain an initial basic feasible solution with an initial basis $B = I_m$. Form the auxiliary basis matrix as $B^* = \begin{pmatrix} B & 0 \\ -c_B^T & I \end{pmatrix}$. Then $B^{*-1} = \begin{pmatrix} B^{-1} & 0 \\ c_B^T B^{-1} & I \end{pmatrix}$

Step 3: Write the objective function $z = \mathbf{c}^T\mathbf{x}$ as an additional constraint and form A^* and b^* as $A^* = \begin{pmatrix} A \\ -c^T \end{pmatrix}$ and $b^* = \begin{pmatrix} b \\ 0 \end{pmatrix}$.

Step 4: Compute the net evaluations $z_j - c_j$, $j = 1, 2, \ldots, n$ by using the formula

$$z_j - c_j = (c_B B^{-1} \; I)\begin{pmatrix} A \\ -c^T \end{pmatrix}$$

If all $z_j - c_j$ are non-negative, then the current basic solution is the optimum solution.

If at least one $z_j - c_j$ is negative, determine the most negative of them, say $(z_k - c_k)$, then the corresponding variable y_k enters the basis. Go to step 5.

If there is a tie for the most negative $z_j - c_j$, resolve the tie by methods explained in the Section 3.5. Go to step 5.

Step 5: Compute $\overset{*}{y_k} = B^{*-1} \overset{*}{a_k}$. If all $y_{ik} \le 0$, there exists an unbounded solution to the given LPP. If at least one $y_{ik} > 0$, then consider the current x_B and find the leaving variable. Go to step 6.

Step 6: Write down the results obtained in step 2 through step 5 in a tabular form known as revised simplex table.

Step 7: Reduce the leading element to unity and all other elements of the entering column to zero by elementary row operations and improve the current basic feasible solution.

Step 8: Go to step 4 and repeat the process until an optimum basic feasible solution is obtained, or there is an indication of an unbounded solution.

EXAMPLE 3.52: Use the revised simplex method to

Maximize $$z = 3x_1 + 5x_2$$

subject to the constraints: $x_1 \le 4, \quad x_2 \le 6, \quad 3x_1 + 2x_2 \le 18; \quad x_1, x_2 \ge 0.$

Solution: Introducing slack variables s_1, s_2, and s_3 in the constraints, the given LPP can be written as

Maximize $$z = \mathbf{c}^T\mathbf{x}$$

subject to the constraints:

$$\mathbf{Ax} = \mathbf{b} \text{ where } \mathbf{A} = \begin{pmatrix} 1 & 0 & 1 & 0 & 0 \\ 0 & 1 & 0 & 1 & 0 \\ 3 & 2 & 0 & 0 & 1 \end{pmatrix}, \mathbf{b} = \begin{pmatrix} 4 \\ 6 \\ 18 \end{pmatrix}$$

and $c = (3, 5, 0, 0, 0)$. The initial solution is $s_1 = 4$, $s_2 = 6$, $s_3 = 18$, with I_3 as the initial basic matrix. Now

$$A^* = \begin{pmatrix} A \\ -c^T \end{pmatrix} = \begin{pmatrix} 1 & 0 & 1 & 0 & 0 \\ 0 & 1 & 0 & 1 & 0 \\ 3 & 2 & 0 & 0 & 1 \\ . & . & . & . & . \\ -3 & -5 & 0 & 0 & 0 \end{pmatrix}, \; B^{*-1} = \begin{pmatrix} B^{-1} & 0 \\ c_B^T B^{-1} & I \end{pmatrix} = \begin{pmatrix} 1 & 0 & 0 & 0 \\ 0 & 1 & 0 & 0 \\ 0 & 0 & 1 & 0 \\ . & . & . & . \\ 0 & 0 & 0 & 1 \end{pmatrix}$$

and $c_B^T = (0, 0, 0)$. Then, net evaluation corresponding to x_2^* is most negative, so x_2^* will enter into the basis. Now $y_2^* = B^{*-1} a_2^* = [0, x_2 = 1, 2 : z_2 - c_2 = -5]$ and

$$x_B^* = B^{*-1} [\mathbf{b}^T, 0] = [4, s_3 = 6, 18 : z = 0] \text{ and } \min_i \left\{ \frac{x_{Bi}}{x_{i2}} : x_{i2} > 0 \right\} = \min_i \left\{ \frac{6}{1}, \frac{18}{2} \right\} = 6$$

Then the initial revised simplex table is as shown below.

y_B^*	x_B^*	B^{*-1}				y_2^*
s_1	4	1	0	0	0	0
s_2	6	0	1	0	0	1→
s_3	18	0	0	1	0	2
z	0	0	0	1	−5	0
					↑	

So y_2^* enters and s_2 leaves the basis in the next iteration. We have

$$B^{*-1} = \begin{pmatrix} 1 & 0 & 0 & 0 \\ 0 & 1 & 0 & 0 \\ 0 & -2 & 1 & 0 \\ . & . & . & . \\ 0 & 5 & 0 & 1 \end{pmatrix}$$

and therefore, $z_j - c_j = (0, 5, 0, 1)\, a_j^* = (-3, 0, 0, 5, 0)$, i.e. So y_1^* will enter into the basis. The iteration table is as follows.

y_B^*	x_B^*	B^{*-1}				y_1^*
s_1	4	1	0	0	0	0
y_2^*	6	0	1	0	0	1
s_3	6	0	0	0	0	2→
z	30	0	5	0	1	–3
						↑

After introducing y_1^* and removing s_3, we get

$$B^{*-1} = \begin{pmatrix} 1 & 2/3 & -1/3 & 0 \\ 0 & 1 & 0 & 0 \\ 0 & -2/3 & 1/3 & 0 \\ \cdot & \cdot & \cdot & \cdot \\ 0 & 3 & 1 & 1 \end{pmatrix}$$

and therefore, $z_j - c_j = (0, 3, 1, 1)\ a_j^* = (0, 0, 0, 3, 1)$ all are non-negative, so we get optimal basic feasible solution $x_1 = 2$, $x_2 = 6$ and maximum $z = 36$.

3.10.2 Standard Form II

In order to handle artificial variables required to get an identity, we formulate steps to be used for using *two-phase method.*

In phase 1, we try to maximize $z^* = -$ (sum of the artificial variables). Two cases may arise:

1. max $z^* < 0$. In this case if there is at least one artificial variable in the optimum solution, then LPP has infeasible solution.
2. max $z^* = 0$. Go to phase 2.

In phase 2, the objective is to maximize z. Apply the revised simplex method of standard form I.

EXAMPLE 3.53: Use the revised simplex method to solve the LPP:

Maximize $$z = x_1 + 2x_2$$

subject to the constraints: $3x_1 + 2x_2 \geq 6$, $x_1 + 6x_2 \geq 3$; and $x_1, x_2 \geq 0$.

Solution: Writing standard form of LPP by introducing surplus variables s_1 and s_2 and artificial variables A_1 and A_2 respectively in the constraints, we have

Maximize $$z = \mathbf{c}^T\mathbf{x}$$

subject to the constraints:

$$\mathbf{Ax} = \mathbf{b} \text{ where } \mathbf{A} = \begin{pmatrix} 3 & 2 & -1 & 0 & 1 & 0 \\ 1 & 6 & 0 & -1 & 0 & 1 \end{pmatrix},\ \mathbf{b} = [6\ \ 3]^T$$

and $\mathbf{c}^T = [1, 2, 0, 0, -M, -M]$. The initial basic feasible solution is $A_1 = 6$ and $A_2 = 3$ with $B = I_2$ as initial basis. Now

$$A^* = \begin{pmatrix} A \\ -c^T \end{pmatrix} = \begin{pmatrix} 3 & 2 & -1 & 0 & 1 & 0 \\ 1 & 6 & 0 & -1 & 0 & 1 \\ \cdot & \cdot & \cdot & \cdot & \cdot & \cdot \\ -1 & -2 & 0 & 0 & M & M \end{pmatrix}, \quad B^{*-1} = \begin{pmatrix} B^{-1} & 0 \\ c_B^T B^{-1} & I \end{pmatrix} = \begin{pmatrix} 1 & 0 & 0 \\ 0 & 1 & 0 \\ \cdot & \cdot & \cdot \\ -M & -M & 1 \end{pmatrix} \text{ and}$$

$c_B^T = (-M, -M)$. Then net evaluations for non-basic variables are

$$z_j - c_j = [-M, -M, 1]$$

$$a_j^* = [-4M - 1, -8M - 2, M, M]$$

Clearly $z_2 - c_2$ is the most negative,

so $$y_2^* = B^{-1}\, a_2^* = [2, 6 : -8M - 2]$$

will enter into the basis and

$$x_B^* = B^{-1}[b^T, 0] = [6, 3 : -9M]$$

The iterative table is given below

y_B^*	x_B^*	B^{*-1}			y_2^*
A_1	6	1	0	0	2
A_2	3	0	1	0	6→
z	$-9M$	$-M$	$-M$	1	$-8M - 2$
					↑

By introducing y_2^* and deleting A_2 from the basis, we get

$$B^{*-1} = \begin{pmatrix} 1 & -1/3 & 0 \\ 0 & 1/6 & 0 \\ \cdot & \cdot & \cdot \\ -M & M/3 + 1/3 & 1 \end{pmatrix} \text{ and}$$

$z_j - c_j = [-M, M/3 + 1/3, 1]$ $a_j^* = [(-8M - 2)/3, M, -(M + 1)/3]$. Clearly $z_1 - c_1$ is the most negative, so y_1^* will enter into the basis. The iterative table is as follows.

y_B^*	x_B^*	B^{*-1}			y_1^*
A_2	5	1	$-1/3$	0	8/3→
y_2^*	1/2	0	1/6	0	1/6
z	$-M + 1$	$-M$	$(M + 1)/3$	1	$-8M - 2$
					↑

After introducing y_1^* and removing A_1, the new

$$B^{*-1} = \begin{pmatrix} 3/8 & -1/8 & 0 \\ -1/16 & 3/16 & 0 \\ \cdot & \cdot & \cdot \\ 1/4 & 1/4 & 1 \end{pmatrix}$$

and $z_j - c_j = [1/4,\ 1/4,\ 1]\ a_j^* = [-1/4, -1/4]$. Since both $z_3 - c_3$ and $z_4 - c_4$ are equal and negative, any of the non-basis variable s_1 and s_2 enters the basis. Let s_2 enter in the basis. The revised iterative table is as given below.

y_B^*	x_B^*	B^{*-1}			s_2
s_2	15/8	3/8	−1/8	0	1/8
y_2^*	3/16	−1/16	3/16	0	−1/16
z	9/4	1/4	1/4	1	−1/4

Now

$$B^{*-1} = \begin{pmatrix} 3 & -1 & 0 \\ 1/2 & 0 & 0 \\ 1 & 0 & 1 \\ \cdot & \cdot & \cdot \\ 1 & 0 & 1 \end{pmatrix}$$

and therefore $z_j - c_j = [1,\ 0\ ,\ 1]\ a_j^* = [2, -1]$ which indicates that s_1 enters into the basis.

$s_1 = B^{*-1}\ a_3^* = [-3, -1/2 : -1]$. As both the entries of s_1 are negative, the given LPP has an unbounded solution.

EXAMPLE 3.54: Use the revised simplex method to solve the LPP:

Minimize $$z = 4x_1 + 2x_2 + 3x_3$$

subject to the constraints:

$$2x_1 + 4x_3 \geq 5$$

$$2x_1 + 3x_2 + x_3 \geq 4$$

and $x_1, x_2, x_3 \geq 0$.

Solution: Writing standard form of LPP by introducing surplus variables s_1 and s_2 and artificial variables A_1 and A_2 respectively in the constraints, we have initial basic feasible solution as $A_1 = 5$ and $A_2 = 4$ with $B = I_2$ as initial basis.

Phase 1: The redundant equation is

$$z^* - \{(2x_1 + 2x_1) + 3x_2 + (4x_3 + x_3) - x_4 - x_5\} = (-5) + (-4)$$

i.e. $$-4x_1 - 3x_2 - 5x_3 + x_4 + x_5 + z^* = -9$$

$$\text{Thus} \qquad A^* = \begin{pmatrix} 2 & 0 & 4 & -1 & 0 & 1 & 0 & 0 & 0 \\ 2 & 3 & 1 & 0 & -1 & 0 & 1 & 0 & 0 \\ . & . & . & . & . & . & . & . & . \\ 4 & 2 & 3 & 0 & 0 & 0 & 0 & 1 & 0 \\ -4 & -3 & -5 & 1 & 1 & 0 & 0 & 0 & 1 \end{pmatrix}$$

and $B^* = I_4 = B^{*-1}$. The net evaluations $z_j - c_j = [-4 \quad -3 \quad -5 \quad 1 \quad 1]$ which shows that y_3^* enters the basis and $y_3^* = B^{*-1}\, a_3^* = [4 \quad 1 \quad 3 \quad -5]$, $x_B^* = B^{*-1}\, b^* = [5 \quad 4 \quad 0 \quad -9]$. Thus, the initial revised simplex table is

y_B^*	x_B^*	B^{*-1}				y_3^*
A_1	5	1	0	0	0	4
A_2	4	0	1	0	0	1
	0	0	0	1	0	3
z^*	–9	0	0	0	1	–5

The updated

$$B^{*-1} = \begin{pmatrix} 1/4 & 0 & 0 & 0 \\ -1/4 & 1 & 0 & 0 \\ -3/4 & 0 & 1 & 0 \\ . & & . & . \\ 5/4 & 0 & 0 & 1 \end{pmatrix}$$

and $z_j - c_j = [5/4 \quad 0 \quad 0 \quad 1]\,[a_1^* \quad a_2^* \quad a_3^* \quad a_4^*] = [-3/2 \quad -3 \quad -1/4 \quad 1]$. This shows that y_2^* enters the basis and the iterative table is as follows.

y_B^*	x_B^*	B^{*-1}				y_2^*
y_2^*	5/4	1/4	0	0	0	0
A_2	11/4	–1/4	1	0	0	3
	–15/14	–3/4	0	1	0	2
z^*	–11/4	5/4	0	0	1	–3

Again

$$B^{*-1} = \begin{pmatrix} 1/4 & 0 & 0 & 0 \\ -1/12 & 1/3 & 0 & 0 \\ -7/12 & -2/3 & 1 & 0 \\ . & . & . & . \\ 1 & 1 & 0 & 1 \end{pmatrix}$$

and $z_j - c_j = [1\ 1\ 0\ 1]\ a_j^* = [0\ 0\ 0\ 0\ 0]$ are zero, so the current solution $x_1 = 0$, $x_2 = 11/12$, $x_3 = 5/4$ and maximum z^* is an optimum solution for phase 1. Since there is no artificial variable present, go to phase 2.

Phase 2: From $B^{*-1} = \begin{pmatrix} 1/4 & 0 & 0 \\ -1/12 & 1/3 & 0 \\ -7/12 & -2/3 & 1 \end{pmatrix}$.

The net evaluations are $z_j - c_j = [-7/12\ -2/3\ 1]\ [a_1^*\ a_4^*\ a_5^*] = [3/2\ 7/12\ 2/3]$ are all non-negative, the optimum solution is $x_1 = 0$, $x_2 = 11/12$, $x_3 = 5/4$ and minimum $z = 67/12$.

3.11 POST OPTIMALITY ANALYSIS

Now let us study the effect of changes in the components of cost coefficients (c) of the objective function or in column matrix b, on the optimum solution of the LP. This is known as *post optimality analysis*.

3.11.1 Variations in b

If $\mathbf{x}_B$ is the optimal basic feasible solution of the standard LPP with B as the required basis, then $\mathbf{x}_B = B^{-1}\mathbf{b}$. Let the component b_k of the vector $\mathbf{b}$ be changed to $b_k + \Delta b_k$. Denote new requirement vector by $\mathbf{b}^*$. Then $\mathbf{b}^* = [b_1, b_2, \ldots, b_{k-1}, b_k + \Delta b_k, b_{k+1}, \ldots, b_m]$. The new basic feasible solution is $\mathbf{x}_B^* = B^{-1}\mathbf{b}^* = \mathbf{x}_B + \sum_{k=1}^{m} b_k\,\Delta b_k$. If $\mathbf{x}_B^* \geq 0$ then $x_{Bi} + b_{ik}\Delta b_k \geq 0$. Thus range of Δb_k, for optimal feasible solution is

$$\max_{b_{ik}>0}\left\{\frac{-x_{Bi}}{b_{ik}}\right\} \leq \Delta b_k \leq \min_{b_{ik}<0}\left\{\frac{-x_{Bi}}{b_{ik}}\right\}$$

EXAMPLE 3.55: Discuss the effect on the optimal solution of the changes in the requirement vector for the following LPP:

Maximize $z = 2x_1 + x_2$

subject to the constraints:

$$3x_1 + 5x_2 \leq 15$$

$$6x_1 + 2x_2 \leq 24$$

and $x_1, x_2 \geq 0$.

Solution: It is left for the students to check that the following solution is the optimum solution.

c_B	B	x_B	x_1	x_2	s_1	s_2
1	x_2	3/4	0	1	1/4	−1/8
2	x_1	15/4	1	0	−1/12	5/24
	z	33/4	0	0	1/3	7/24

Thus $x_1 = 15/4$, $x_2 = 3/4$ and $B^{-1} = \begin{pmatrix} 1/4 & -1/8 \\ -1/12 & 5/24 \end{pmatrix}$. Then individual changes in b_1 and b_2 are

$$\max_{b_{11}>0}\left\{\frac{-2/4}{1/4}\right\} \le \Delta b_1 \le \min_{b_{12}<0}\left\{\frac{-15/4}{-1/12}\right\} \quad \text{i.e. } -3 \le \Delta b_1 \le 45$$

and $$\max_{b_{22}>0}\left\{\frac{-15/4}{5/24}\right\} \le \Delta b_2 \le \min_{b_{21}<0}\left\{\frac{-3/4}{-1/8}\right\} \quad \text{i.e. } -18 \le \Delta b_2 \le 6$$

Now, since given $b_1 = 15$ and $b_2 = 24$, the required range of variation is $15 - 3 \le b_1 \le 15 + 45$ and $24 - 18 \le b_2 \le 24 + 6$ or $12 \le b_1 \le 60$ and $6 \le b_2 \le 30$.

EXAMPLE 3.56: Given LPP:

Maximize $$z = -x_1 + 2x_2 - x_3$$

subject to the constraints:

$$3x_1 + x_2 - x_3 \le 10$$
$$-x_1 + 4x_2 + x_3 \ge 6$$
$$x_2 + x_3 \le 4$$

and $x_1, x_2, x_3 \ge 0$.

Solution: It is left for the students to check that the following solution is the optimum solution. (Note that s_1 and s_3 are slack variables, s_2 is surplus variable and A_1 is artificial variable.)

c_B	B	x_B	x_1	x_2	x_3	s_1	s_2	s_3	A_1
0	s_1	6	3	0	−2	1	0	−1	0
2	x_2	4	0	1	1	0	0	1	0
0	s_2	10	1	0	0	0	1	4	−1
z	8	$z_j - c_j$	1	0	0	0	0	2	M

Thus, $x_1 = 0$, $x_2 = 4$, $x_3 = 0$, $s_1 = 4$ and $s_2 = 10$. We want to find changes in b_2 and b_3. It is given by

$$\Delta b_2 \le \left\{\frac{-10}{-1}\right\} \quad \text{i.e. } \Delta b_2 \le 10$$

and $$\max\left\{\frac{-4}{1}, -\frac{10}{4}\right\} \le \Delta b_3 \le \left\{\frac{-6}{-1}\right\} \quad \text{i.e. } -5/2 \le \Delta b_3 \le 6$$

Now, since given $b_2 = 6$ and $b_3 = 4$, the required range of variation is $b_2 \le 10 + 6$ and $4 - 5/2 \le b_2 \le 4 + 6$ or $b_2 \le 16$ and $3/2 \le b_3 \le 10$.

3.11.2 Variations in c

Let the component c_k of the cost vector **c** be changed to $c_k + \Delta c_k$. Since the condition for optimality requires $z_j - c_j \geq 0$, it may violate the condition of optimality depending on whether $c_k \notin c_B$ or $c_k \in c_B$.

In case (i) $z_k^* - c_k^* = z_k - (c_k + \Delta c_k)$. Then the current solution will remain optimal if $z_k - (c_k + \Delta c_k) \geq 0$, i.e. $\Delta c_k \leq z_k - c_k$ for all $c_k \notin c_B$.

In case (ii) $z_j^* - c_j^* = (z_j - c_j) + \Delta c_k y_{kj}$. The current solution will remain optimal if $z_j^* - c_j^* \geq 0$, i.e. the range of Δc_k is $\max\limits_{y_{kj}>0}\left\{\dfrac{-(z_j - c_j)}{y_{kj}}\right\} \leq \Delta c_k \leq \min\limits_{y_{kj}<0}\left\{\dfrac{-(z_j - c_j)}{y_{kj}}\right\}$ to have an optimum solution.

EXAMPLE 3.57: Find the optimal solution of the following LPP:

Maximize $$z = 15x_1 + 45x_2$$

subject to the constraints:

$$x_1 + 16x_2 \leq 240$$

$$5x_1 + 2x_2 \leq 162$$

$$x_2 \leq 50$$

and $x_1, x_2 \geq 0$.

If c_2 is kept fixed, determine how much can c_1 be changed without affecting optimal solution.

Solution: It is left for the students to check that the following solution is the optimum solution.

c_B	B	x_B	x_1	x_2	s_1	s_2	s_3
45	x_2	173/13	0	1	5/78	−1/78	0
15	x_1	352/13	1	0	−1/39	8/39	0
0	s_3	477/13	0	0	−5/78	1/78	1
	z	1005	0	0	5/2	5/2	0

Note: s_1, s_2 and s_3 are slack variables added in the given three constraints.
We have $c_1 \in c_B$. Therefore, feasibility of the optimal solution is maintained if

$\max\left\{\dfrac{-5/2}{8/39}\right\} \leq \Delta c_1 \leq \min\left\{\dfrac{-5/2}{-1/39}\right\}$ or $-195/16 \leq \Delta c_1 \leq 195/2$. Therefore, the range of c_1 is

$15 - 195/16 \leq c_1 \leq 15 + 195/2$ or $45/16 \leq c_1 \leq 225/2$.

EXAMPLE 3.58: Find the optimal solution of the following LPP:

Maximize $$z = 3x_1 + 5x_2$$

subject to the constraints:

$$x_1 \leq 4,\ x_2 \leq 6$$

$$3x_1 + 2x_2 \leq 18$$

and $x_1, x_2 \geq 0$.

Discuss the effect on the optimality of the solution when the objective function is changed to $3x_1 + x_2$.

Solution: It is left for the students to check that the following solution is the optimum solution.

c_B	B	x_B	x_1	x_2	s_1	s_2	s_3
0	s_1	2	0	0	1	2/3	–1/3
5	x_2	6	0	1	0	1	0
3	x_1	2	1	0	0	–2/3	1/3
	z	36	0	0	0	3	1

Note: s_1, s_2 and s_3 are slack variables added in the given three constraints.

Since the objective function is changed to $3x_1 + x_2$; c_2 has been changed to 1 keeping c_1 fixed. Clearly, $c_2 \in c_B$. Therefore, feasibility of the optimal solution is maintained if

$$\max\left\{\frac{-3}{1}\right\} \le \Delta c_2 \le \infty \quad \text{or} \quad -3 \le \Delta c_2 \le \infty$$

Therefore, the range of c_2 is $5 - 3 \le c_2 \le \infty$ or $2 \le c_2 \le \infty$. This indicates that if c_2 is changed, optimality does not hold. Then the aim is to find the new optimal solution. It is left for the reader to work out the following table.

c_B	B	x_B	x_1	x_2	s_1	s_2	s_3
0	s_2	3	0	0	3/2	1	–1/2
1	x_2	3	0	1	–3/2	0	1/2
3	x_1	4	1	0	1	0	0
	z	15	0	0	3/2	0	1/2

Then optimal solution is $x_1 = 3$, $x_2 = 1$ and maximum $z = 15$.

EXAMPLE 3.59: Find the optimal solution of the following LPP:

Maximize
$$z = 3x_1 + 5x_2 + 4x_3$$

subject to the constraints:

$$2x_1 + 3x_2 \le 8$$
$$2x_2 + 5x_3 \le 10$$
$$3x_1 + 2x_2 + 4x_3 \le 15$$

and $x_1, x_2, x_3 \ge 0$.

Find the ranges over which c_3 and c_4 and b_2 can be changed maintaining the optimality of the solution.

Solution: It is left for the students to check that the following solution is the optimum solution.

c_B	B	x_B	x_1	x_2	x_3	s_1	s_2	s_3
5	x_2	50/41	0	1	0	15/41	8/41	–10/41
4	x_3	62/41	0	0	1	–6/41	5/41	4/41
3	x_1	89/41	1	0	0	–2/41	–12/41	15/41
	z	765/41	0	0	0	45/41	24/41	11/41

Note: s_1, s_2 and s_3 are slack variables added in the given three constraints.

From the above table, $c_3 \in c_B$ and $c_4 \notin c_B$. The range of variations in Δc_3 is given by

$$\max\left\{\frac{-24/41}{5/41}, \frac{-11/41}{4/41}\right\} \le \Delta c_3 \le \min\left\{\frac{-45/41}{-6/41}\right\} \quad \text{or} \quad -11/4 \le \Delta c_3 \le 15/2$$

So the range of c_3 is

$$4 - \frac{11}{4} \le c_3 \le 4 + \frac{15}{2} \quad \text{or} \quad \frac{5}{4} \le c_3 \le \frac{23}{2}$$

For the range of variations in $c_4 \notin c_B$, we have $\Delta c_4 \le 45/41$ and so the range of c_4 is $c_4 \le 45/41$.

The range of variations in Δb_2 is given by

$$\max\left\{\frac{-50/41}{8/41}, \frac{62/41}{5/41}\right\} \le \Delta b_2 \le \min\left\{\frac{-89/41}{-12/41}\right\} \quad \text{or} \quad \frac{25}{4} \le \Delta b_2 \le \frac{89}{12}$$

So the range of b_2 is

$$10 - \frac{25}{4} \le b_2 \le 10 + \frac{89}{12} \quad \text{or} \quad \frac{15}{4} \le b_2 \le \frac{209}{12}$$

REVIEW EXERCISES

1. Solve graphically:

(a) Maximize $z = 90x_1 + 60x_2$

subject to:

$$5x_1 + 8x_2 \le 2000$$
$$x_1 \le 175$$
$$x_2 \le 225$$
$$7x_1 + 4x_2 \le 1400$$
$$x_1, x_2 \ge 0$$

[**Ans.** $x_1 = 800/9$, $x_2 = 1750/9$, max $z = 59{,}000/3$]

(b) Maximize $z = 60x_1 + 40x_2$

subject to:

$$x_1 \le 25$$
$$x_2 \le 35$$
$$2x_1 + x_2 = 60$$
$$x_1, x_2 \ge 0$$

[**Ans.** $x_1 = 25$, $x_2 = 10$, max $z = 1900$]

(c) Maximize $z = 30x_1 + 40x_2$

subject to:

$$4x_1 + 6x_2 \le 180$$
$$x_1 \le 20$$
$$x_2 \ge 10$$
$$x_1 + x_2 \le 40$$
$$x_1, x_2 \ge 0$$

[**Ans.** $x_1 = 16$, $x_2 = 16.66667$, max $z = 1266.67$]

(d) Minimize $z = 4x_1 + 3x_2$

subject to: $x_1 + 3x_2 \geq 9$

$2x_1 + 3x_2 \geq 12$

$x_1 + x_2 \geq 5$

$x_1, x_2 \geq 0$

[**Ans.** $x_1 = 0, x_2 = 5$, min $z = 15$]

(e) Maximize $z = x_1 + 3x_2$

subject to: $x_1 + 2x_2 \leq 9$

$x_1 - x_2 \geq 2$

$x_1 + 4x_2 \leq 11$

$x_1, x_2 \geq 0$

[**Ans.** $x_1 = 7, x_2 = 1$, max $z = 10$]

(f) Maximize $z = 10x_1 + 8x_2$

subject to: $2x_1 + x_2 \leq 20$

$x_1 + 3x_2 \leq 30$

$x_1 - 2x_2 \geq -15$

$x_1, x_2 \geq 0$

[**Ans.** $x_1 = 6, x_2 = 8$, max $z = 124$]

2. The Sue All Law Firm handles two types of lawsuits: medical malpractice suits against unscrupulous heart surgeons for performing unnecessary surgery, and suits against hard-working math professors for failing students who do not deserve to pass. Math professor lawsuits each require 6 person-months of preparation and the hiring of 5 expert witnesses, whereas medical lawsuits each require 10 person-months of preparation and the hiring of 3 expert witnesses. The firm has a total of 30 person-months to work with and it feels that it cannot afford to hire more than 15 expert witnesses. It makes an average profit of $1 million per math professor sued and $5 million per heart surgeon sued. How many of each type of lawsuit should it initiate in order to maximize its expected profits? Solve graphically.

[**Ans.** Initiate 3 medical malpractice suits and no math professor suits for a profit of $15 million]

3. A diet conscious housewife wishes to ensure certain minimum intake of vitamins A, B and C for the family. The minimum daily (quantity) needs of the vitamins A, B and C for the family are 30, 20 and 16 units respectively. For the supply of these minimum requirements, the housewife relies on two fresh foods. The first one provides 7, 5, 2 units of the three vitamins per gram respectively and the second one provides 2, 4, 8 units of the same three vitamins per gram of the foodstuff respectively. The first foodstuff costs Rs. 3 per gram and the second Rs. 2 per gram. How many grams of each foodstuff should the housewife buy every day to keep her food bill as low as possible? Solve graphically.

[**Ans.** $x_1 = 10, x_2 = 0$, min $z = 30$]

4. O'Hagan Bookworm Booksellers buys books from two publishers. Duffin House offers a package of 5 mysteries and 5 romance novels for $50, and Gorman Press offers a package of 5 mysteries and 10 romance novels for $150. O'Hagan wants to buy at least 2,500 mysteries and 3,500 romance novels, and he has promised Gorman (who has influence on the Senate Textbook Committee) that at least 25% of the total number of packages he purchases will come from Gorman Press. How many packages should O'Hagan order from each publisher in order to minimize his cost and satisfy Gorman? What will the novels cost him? Solve graphically.

[**Ans.** Buy 420 packages from Duffin House and 140 from Gorman Press for a total cost of $42,000]

5. In addition to the best selection of novels in South Park Mall, O'Hagan Booksellers also specializes in fantasy novels and art books. The manager at O'Hagan Booksellers, S. Shady, is considering a sales promotion of a new collection of fantasy novels and art books, and he plans to price the books so low as to actually take a loss: O'Hagan will lose $3 on every fantasy novel and $2 on every art book sold in the promotion. Since the store will only offer the art books to those who purchase two or more fantasy novels, the store will sell at least twice as many fantasy novels as art books, and also plans to sell at least 210 items in all. On the other hand, the store can spare up to 900 units of display space for the sale. S. Shady calculates that fantasy novels each require 3 units of display space, while art books require 2 units. Given these constraints, how many fantasy novels and art books should O'Hagan Booksellers order to lose the least amount of money in the sales promotion? Solve graphically.

[**Ans.** Order 140 fantasy novels and 70 art books]

6. A local travel agent is planning a charter trip to a major sea resort. The eight day/seven-night package includes the fare for round-trip travel surface transportation, board and loading and selected tour options. The charter trip is restricted to 200 persons and the past experience indicates that there will not be any problem for getting 200 persons. The problem for the travel agent is to determine the number of Deluxe, Standard, and Economy tour packages to offer for this charter. These three plans each differ according to seating and service for the flight, quality of accommodations, meal plans, and tour options. The following summarizes the estimated prices for the three packages and corresponding expenses for the travel agent. The travel agent has hired an aircraft for the flat fee of Rs. 2,00,000 for the entire trip.

Prices and costs for tour packages per person

Tour plan	*Price* (Rs.)	*Hotel costs* (Rs.)	*Meals & other expenses* (Rs.)
Deluxe	10,000	3,000	4,750
Standard	7,000	2,200	2,500
Economy	6,500	1,900	2,200

In planning trip, the following considerations must be taken into account:

(i) At least 10 per cent of the package must be of the deluxe type.

(ii) At least 35 per cent but not more than 70 per cent must be of the standard type.

(iii) At least 30 per cent must be of the economy type.

(iv) The maximum number of deluxe package available in any aircraft is restricted to 60.
(v) The hotel desires that at least 120 of the tourists should be on the deluxe and standard packages together.

The travel agent wishes to determine the number of packages to offer in each type so as to maximize the total profit.

(a) Formulate the above as a linear programming problem.
(b) Restate the above linear programming problem in terms of two decision variables, taking advantage of the fact those 200 packages will be sold.
(c) Find the optimum solution using the graphical method for the restated linear programming problem and interpret your results.

[**Ans.** maximize $z = 150x_1 - 100x_2 + 2{,}80{,}000$, $x_1 = 20$, $x_2 = 100$, max $z = 2{,}67{,}000$]

7. (a) Maximize $z = 40x_1 + 30x_2$
subject to: $x_1 + 2x_2 \le 40$; $4x_1 + 3x_2 \le 120$; $x_1, x_2 \ge 0$

[**Ans.** $x_1 = 30$, $x_2 = 0$, max $z = 1200$ or $x_1 = 24$, $x_2 = 8$, max $z = 1200$]

(b) Maximize $z = 3x_1 - x_2$
subject to: $15x_1 - 5x_2 \le 30$; $10x_1 + 30x_2 \le 120$; $x_1, x_2 \ge 0$

[**Ans.** $x_1 = 2$, $x_2 = 0$, max $z = 6$ or $x_1 = 3$, $x_2 = 3$, max $z = 6$]

8. (a) Maximize $z = 5x_1 + 3x_2$
subject to: $4x_1 + 2x_2 \le 8$; $x_1 \ge 4$; $x_2 \ge 6$; $x_1, x_2 \ge 0$

(b) Maximize $z = 6x_1 - 4x_2$
subject to: $2x_1 + 4x_2 \le 4$, $4x_1 + 8x_2 \ge 16$; $x_1, x_2 \ge 0$

[**Ans.** Infeasible solution]

9. (a) Maximize $z = 4x_1 + 2x_2$
subject to: $x_1 \ge 4$, $x_2 \le 2$; $x_1, x_2 \ge 0$

(b) Maximize $z = -x_1 + x_2$
subject to: $-x_1 + 4x_2 \le 10$, $-3x_1 + 2x_2 \le 2$; $x_1, x_2 \ge 0$

[**Ans.** Unbounded solution]

10. Find the maximum value of $p = x + 2y + 3z$
subject to: $7x + z \le 6$, $x + 2y \le 20$, $3y + 4z \le 0$; $x \ge 0$, $y \ge 0$, $z \ge 0$

[**Ans.** $x = 0.8571$, $y = 0$, $z = 0$, max $p = 0.8571$]

11. Find the maximum value of $p = 2x - 3y + 5z$
subject to: $2x + y \le 16$, $y + z \le 10$, $x + y + z \le 20$; $x \ge 0$, $y \ge 0$, $z \ge 0$

[**Ans.** $x = 8$, $y = 0$, $z = 10$, max $p = 66$]

12. Find the minimum value of $z = x_1 - 3x_2 + 2x_3$
subject to: $3x_1 - x_2 + 2x_3 \le 7$, $-2x_1 + 4x_2 \le 12$, $-4x_1 + 3x_2 + 8x_3 \le 10$; x_1, x_2 and $x_3 \ge 0$.

[**Ans.** $x_1 = 4$, $x_2 = 5$, min $z = -11$]

13. Find the maximum value of $p = 2x + 4y + z + w$
subject to: $x + 3y + w \le 4$, $2x + y \le 3$, $y + 4z + w \le 3$; $x, y, z, w \ge 0$.

[**Ans.** $x = 1$, $y = 1$, $z = 0.5$, $w = 0$, max $p = 13/2$]

14. Find the maximum value of $p = 107x + y + 2z$
subject to: $14x + y - 6z + 3w = 7$, $16x + 0.5y - 6z \le 5$, $3x - y - z \le 0$; $x, y, z, w \ge 0$.
[*Hint:* Divide the first equation by 3 (coefficient of w) and then treat w as the slack variable]

[**Ans.** Unbounded solution]

15. Find the maximum value of $p = 7x + y + 2z$
subject to: $x + y - 2z \le 10$, $4x + y + z \le 20$; $x, y, z \ge 0$.

[**Ans.** $x = y = 0$, $z = 20$, max $p = 40$]

16. Find the maximum value of $p = 2x + 4y + 3z$
subject to: $3x + 4y + 2z \le 60$, $x + 3y + 2z \le 80$, $2x + y + 2z \le 40$; $x, y, z \ge 0$.

[**Ans.** $x = 0$, $y = 20/3$, $z = 50/3$, max $p = 250/3$]

17. Find the maximum value of $p = 4x + 3y + 4z + 6w$
subject to: $2x + 2z + w \le 60$, $x + 2y + 2z + 4w \le 80$, $3x + 3y + z + w \le 80$; $x, y, z, w \ge 0$.

[**Ans.** $x = 280/13$, $y = 0$, $z = 20/13$, $w = 180/13$, max $p = 2{,}280/13$]

18. Find the maximum value of $p = 4x + 5y + 9z + 11w$
subject to: $7x + 5y + 3z + 2w \le 120$, $x + y + z + w \le 15$, $3x + 5y + 10z + 15w \le 100$; $x, y, z, w \ge 0$.

[**Ans.** $x = 50/7$, $y = 0$, $z = 55/7$, $w = 0$, max $p = 695/7$]

19. Find the maximum value of $p = 2x + 4y + z + w$
subject to: $2x + y + 2z + 3w \le 12$, $2x + y + 4z \le 16$, $3x + 2z + 2w \le 20$; $x, y, z, w \ge 0$.

[**Ans.** $x = 0$, $y = 12$, $z = 0$, $w = 0$, max $p = 48$]

20. Solve the following LP problems using Big-M method.

(a) Find the minimum value of $p = 4x + 8y + 3z$
subject to: $3x + 2y + z \le 3$, $2x + y + 2z \ge 3$; $x, y, z \ge 0$.

[**Ans.** $x = 3/4$, $y = 0$, $z = 3/4$, min $p = 3$]

(b) Find the maximum value of $p = 2x + y + 3z$
subject to: $2x + 3y + 4z = 12$, $x + y + 2z \le 5$; $x, y, z \ge 0$.

[**Ans.** $x = 3$, $y = 2$, $z = 0$, max $p = 10$]

(c) Find the maximum value of $p = 300x + 400y$
subject to: $5x + 4y \le 200$, $3x + 5y \le 150$, $5x + 4y \ge 100$, $8x + 4y \ge 80$; $x, y \ge 0$.

[**Ans.** $x = 30.7692$, $y = 11.5385$, max $p = 13{,}846.15$]

(d) Find the minimum value of $p = 5x + 2y + 10z$
subject to: $x - z \le 10$, $y + z \ge 10$; $x, y, z \ge 0$.

[**Ans.** $x = 0$, $y = 10$, $z = 0$, min $p = 20$]

(e) A transistor radio company manufactures four models A, B, C and D, which have profit contribution of Rs. 8, 12, and 22 on model A, B and C respectively and a loss of Re. 1 on model D. Each type of radio requires a certain amount of time for the manufacturing of components for assembling and for packing. Specially, a dozen units of model A require one hour of manufacturing, two hours for assembling and one hour for packing. The corresponding figures for a dozen units of model B are 2, 1 and 2 and for a dozen units of C are 3, 5 and 1, while a dozen units of model D require 1 hour of packing only. During the forthcoming week, the company will be able to make available 15 hours of manufacturing, 20 hours of assembling and 10 hours of packing time. Obtain the optimal production schedule for the company.

[*Hint:* max $p = 8x + 12y + 22z - w$ subject to: $x + 2y + 3z = 15$, $2x + y + 5z = 20$, $x + 2y + z + w = 10$; $x, y, z, w \geq 0$.

Solve the LP problem to show that these have alternative optimal solutions.

[Ans. $x = y = z = 2.5$, $w = 0$, max $p = 105$]

(f) Find the minimum value of $p = 2x + 8y$
subject to: $2x + 2y \geq 14$, $5x + y \geq 10$, $x + 4y \geq 12$; $x, y \geq 0$.

[Ans. (i) $x = 12$, $y = 0$, min $p = 24$. (ii) $x = 16/3$, $y = 5/3$, min $p = 24$]

(g) Find the maximum value of $p = x + 2y + 3z - w$
subject to: $x + 2y + 3z = 15$, $x + 2y + z + w \geq 10$, $2x + y + 5z \geq 20$; $x, y, z, w \geq 0$.

[Ans. (i) $x = y = z = 2.5$, $w = 0$, max $p = 15$ or $x = 0$, $y = 15/7$, $z = 25/7$, $w = 0$, max $p = 15$]

21. Solve the following LP problem to show that these have unbounded solutions.

(a) Find the minimum value of $p = x + 2y + 3z$
subject to: $x + y + z \geq 500$, $x + 2y + 3z \geq 700$, $-y + 3z \leq 0$; $x, y, z \geq 0$

[Ans. The solution is unbounded]

(b) Find the minimum value of $p = 50x + 150y + 100z$
subject to: $5x + 5y + 5z \geq 2{,}500$, $5x + 10y + 15z \geq 3{,}500$, $3x - y + 3z \leq 0$; $x, y, z \geq 0$

[Ans. The solution is unbounded]

22. Solve the following LP problem to show that these have no feasible solutions.

(a) Find the minimum value of $p = x - 2y - 3z$
subject to: $-2x + y + 2z = 2$, $2x + 3y + 2z = 1$; $x, y, z \geq 0$.

[Ans. There is no feasible solution]

(b) Find the maximum value of $p = x + 3y$
subject to: $x - y \geq 1$, $3x - y \leq -3$; $x, y \geq 0$.

[Ans. There is no feasible solution]

23. Senator Porkbarrel overdraws his accounts at the following banks: the Congressional Integrity Bank, Citizens' Trust, and "Checks R Us." There are no penalties for these withdrawals since the overdrafts are subsidized by the taxpayer. The Senate Ethics Committee tends to let slide irregular banking activities of this sort, provided they are not flagrant. At the moment (due to Congress' preoccupation with impeachment hearings) a total overdraft of up to $10,000 will be overlooked. Porkbarrel's underlying sense of guilt makes him feel funny about writing overdrafts for banks whose names include expressions like "integrity" and "citizens' trust." The effect of this is that his bad check writing for the first two banks combined amounts to no more than one-quarter of the total. On the other hand, the financial officers at Integrity Bank are eager to please Senator Porkbarrel due to his influential position on the Senate Banking Committee, so they would like him to overdraw his account by as much as possible. Find the amount he should draw from each bank in order to avoid investigation by the Ethics Committee and overdraw his account at Integrity by as much as his sense of guilt will allow.

[**Ans.** $2,500 from Congressional Integrity Bank, $0 from Citizens' Trust, $7,500 from Checks R Us]

24. Your software company has launched the latest version of its web browser, "Java Cruise 4.0." As the sales manager, you are planning to promote Java Cruise 4.0 by sending sales forces to software conventions running concurrently in Saint Louis and Detroit. You have 6 representatives available at each of your Little Rock, Ark. and Urbana, Ill. branches, and you would like to send at least 5 to the Saint Louis convention and at least 4 to the Detroit convention. The Saint Louis convention will last for three days, while the Detroit convention will last for two days. Air fares (per person) and hotel accommodation costs (per person) are shown in the following figure.

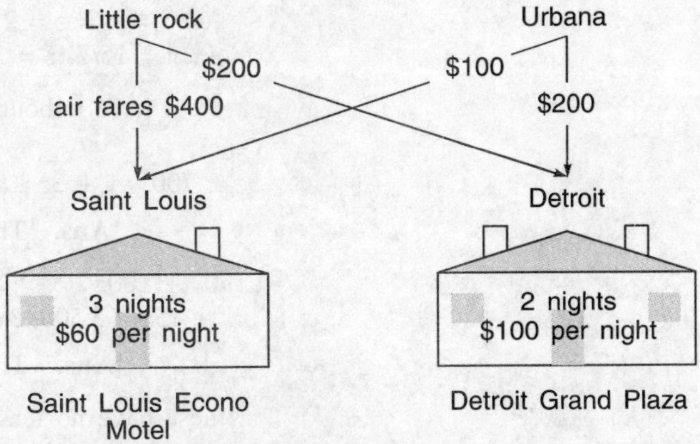

How many representatives should you send from each branch to each convention in order to minimize the total (air travel and accommodation) cost? What will the total cost amount to?

Let

x = the number of representatives sent from Little Rock to St. Louis

y = the number of representatives sent from Little Rock to Detroit

z = the number of representatives sent from Urbana to St. Louis

w = the number of representatives sent from Urbana to Detroit.

Minimize $C = 580x + 400y + 280z + 400w$

subject to: $x + y \leq 6$, $z + w \leq 6$, $x + z \geq 5$, $y + w \geq 4$, $x \geq 0$, $y \geq 0$, $z \geq 0$, $w \geq 0$

[**Ans.** x = 0, y = 4, z = 5, w = 0; C = 3,000
Thus, you should send 4 representatives from Little Rock to Detroit, and 5 from Urbana to St. Louis, for a total cost of $3,000]

25. Use the dual simplex method to solve LPP:

Minimize $p = 2x + 2y + 4z$

subject to: $2x + 3y + 5z \geq 2$, $3x + y + 7z \leq 3$, $x + 4y + 6z \leq 5$; $x, y, z \geq 0$.

[**Ans.** $x = z = 0$, $y = 2/3$ and min $p = 4/3$]

26. Use the dual simplex method to solve LPP:

Maximize $p = -2x - z$

subject to: $x + y - z \geq 5$, $x - 2y + 4z \geq 8$; $x, y, z \geq 0$.

[**Ans.** $x = 0$, $y = 14$, $z = 9$ and max $p = -9$]

4 Integer Programming

4.1 INTRODUCTION

In the previous chapter, we have studied that in LPP, each of the decision variables as well as slack and/or surplus variables is allowed to take non-negative real value. However, while solving for number of machines or mankind, real value like 2.3 or 4.8 is meaningless. Thus, in practice, we come across certain practical problems where integer values are desired. The next question arises: Can not we round off the solution obtained by the methods stated in previous chapter? The answer is: It may be beneficial in terms of efforts or time but may not be an optimal solution and some of the constraints may not remain valid.

Consider the following LPP:

Maximize $$z = 3x_1 + 4x_2$$

subject to the constraints:

$$2x_1 + 4x_2 \leq 13$$
$$-2x_1 + x_2 \leq 2$$
$$2x_1 + 2x_2 \geq 1$$
$$6x_1 - 4x_2 \leq 15$$

and $x_1, x_2 \geq 0$ are integers.

If we neglect the integer constraints then by the graphical solution (Figure 4.1), the optimum value is obtained at the point (3.5, 1.5) and $z = 16.5$. But since the variables have to be integers, we try to round off (3.5, 1.5) and get point as (3, 2), (4, 1), (4, 2) and (3, 1). But the first three points are out of the feasible region. So, if we consider that after rounding off the solution would be (3, 1), then we would be mistaken because $z = 13$ at (3,1) but (2, 2) gives $z = 14$, which is a better solution than (3, 1) and in this case optimal. So, there is a need to devise more sophisticated methods than merely rounding off. Let us discuss the following two methods to solve LPP in integer requirement.

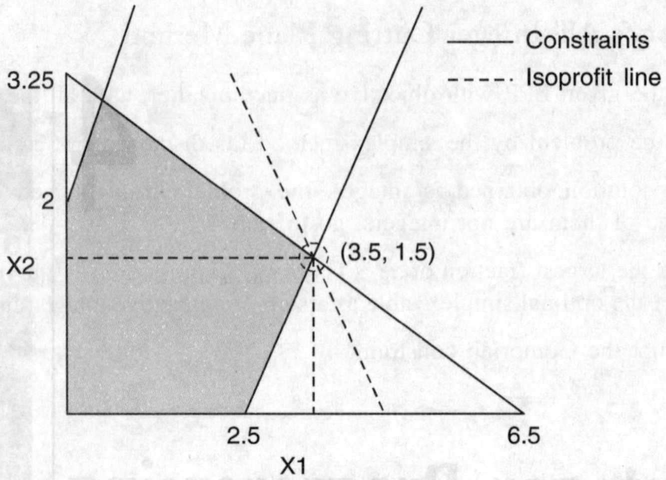

Figure 4.1

4.2 FORMS OF INTEGER PROGRAMMING PROBLEMS (IPP)

The LP can be classified into three forms:

1. Pure (all) integer programming problem in which all decision variables are required to have integer values. The standard form of IPP is:

   Maximize $z = \mathbf{c}^T\mathbf{x}$

   subject to the constraints:

   $$\mathbf{Ax} \le \mathbf{b},\ \mathbf{x} \ge 0 \text{ are integers where } \mathbf{x}, \mathbf{c} \in \mathbf{R}^n,\ \mathbf{A} : m \times n,\ \mathbf{b} \in \mathbf{R}^m.$$

2. Mixed integer programming problem in which some (but not all) of the decision variables are required to have integer values. The general form of IPP is:

   Maximize $z = \mathbf{c}^T\mathbf{x}$

   subject to the constraints:

   $$\mathbf{Ax} \le \mathbf{b},\ \mathbf{x} \ge 0,\ x_k,\ k = 1, 2, \ldots, r,\ r < n,$$

   are integers where $\mathbf{x}, \mathbf{c} \in \mathbf{R}^n,\ A : m \times n,\ \mathbf{b} \in \mathbf{R}^m$

3. Zero — One programming problem in which all decision variables take either ‘0’ or ‘1’.

   In this chapter, we discuss two methods: Gomory’s cutting plane method, and Branch and Bound (B&B) method for solving IPP.

4.3 GOMORY’S CUTTING PLANE

In 1956, R.E. Gomory developed this method to solve IPP using dual simplex method. He generated a sequence of linear inequalities called *cuts* which reduce a part of the feasible region of the corresponding LPP to obtain integer solution. The method of cutting the feasible region of an LPP is called the *cutting plane method*.

4.3.1 Gomory's All–Integer Cutting Plane Method

Step 1: Write the given LPP with objective as maximization with all the constraints as ≤ – type.

Step 2: Solve the problem by the simplex method (as discussed in Section 3.6).

Step 3: If the solution obtained is integer, the problem has obtained optimal solution. If all $x_{Bi} \geq 0$, but some of them are not integers, go to step 4.

Step 4: Choose the largest fraction of x_{Bi}'s (say) x_{Bk}. Express each of the negative fraction (if any) in the k-th row of the optimal simplex table as a sum of a negative integer and non-negative fraction.

Step 5: Construct the Gomorian constraint:

$$\sum_{j=1}^{n} f_{kj}x_j \geq f_k \quad \text{i.e.} \quad g_1 = -f_k + \sum_{j=1}^{n} f_{kj}x_j$$

where g_1 is called the Gomorian slack variable and all $f_{kj} \geq 0$.

Step 6: Add the cutting plane generated in step 5 at the bottom of the optimum simplex table obtained in step 2. Find the new optimum solution using the dual simplex method.

Step 7: Repeat steps 3 to 6 until all integral solution is obtained.

EXAMPLE 4.1: Find the optimum integer solution of LPP:

Maximize
$$z = 4x_1 + 3x_2$$
subject to the constraints:
$$x_1 + 2x_2 \leq 4$$
$$2x_1 + x_2 \leq 6$$
and $x_1, x_2 \geq 0$ are integers.

Solution: Using the simplex method, the optimum solution of the LPP without integer requirements is given below.

c_B	B	x_B	x_1	x_2	s_1	s_2
3	x_2	2/3	0	1	2/3	–1/3
4	x_1	8/3	1	0	–1/3	2/3
z	38/3	$z_j - c_j$	0	0	2/3	5/3

The fractional part for both x_1 and x_2 is 2/3. So, anyone can be selected. Consider the first row for constructing a cut. We have

$$\frac{2}{3} \leq x_2 + \frac{2}{3}s_1 - \frac{1}{3}s_2 \leq x_2 + \frac{2}{3}s_1 + \left(-1 + \frac{2}{3}\right)s_2$$

Taking all the integral parts on one side, the corresponding fractional cut is given by

$$g_1 = -\frac{2}{3} + \frac{2}{3}s_1 + \frac{2}{3}s_2$$

g_1 is called the Gomorian slack variable. Insert this constraint at the bottom of the previous optimal table.

c_B	B	x_B	x_1	x_2	s_1	s_2	g_1
3	x_2	2/3	0	1	2/3	−1/3	0
4	x_1	8/3	1	0	−1/3	2/3	0
0	g_1	−2/3	0	0	−2/3	−2/3	1 →
z	38/3	$z_j - c_j$	0	0	2/3	5/3	0
		RR	—	—	−1↑	−5/2	0

Using the dual simplex method, g_1 leaves the basis and s_1 enters.

c_B	B	x_B	x_1	x_2	s_1	s_2	g_1
3	x_2	0	0	1	0	−1	1
4	x_1	3	1	0	0	1	−1/2
0	s_1	1	0	0	1	1	−3/2
z	12	$z_j - c_j$	0	0	0	1	1

This gives an optimum integer solution $x_1 = 3$, $x_2 = 0$ and maximum $z = 12$.

EXAMPLE 4.2: Find the optimum integer solution of LPP:

Maximize
$$z = 2x_1 + 2x_2$$

subject to the constraints:
$$5x_1 + 3x_2 \le 8$$
$$x_1 + 2x_2 \ge 4$$

$x_1, x_2 \ge 0$ are integers.

Solution: Using the simplex method, the optimum solution of the LPP without integer requirements is as follows.

c_B	B	x_B	x_1	x_2	s_1	s_2
2	x_1	4/7	1	0	5/7	−3/14
2	x_2	12/7	0	1	−1/7	5/14
z	32/7	$z_j - c_j$	0	0	8/7	2/7

The fractional parts for x_1 and x_2 are 4/7 and 5/7. We select the largest fractional part which corresponds to the second row for constructing a Gomorian cut. Hence, we have

$$\frac{5}{7} = x_2 + \left(-1 + \frac{6}{7}\right)s_1 + \frac{5}{14}s_2$$

Therefore, the corresponding Gomorian slack variable is

$$g_1 = -\frac{5}{7} - \frac{6}{7}s_1 - \frac{5}{14}s_2$$

and adding this constraint at the bottom of the previous optimal table, we get

c_B	B	x_B	x_1	x_2	s_1	s_2	g_1
2	x_1	4/7	1	0	5/7	−3/14	0
2	x_2	12/7	0	1	−1/7	5/14	0
0	g_1	−5/7	0	0	−6/7	−5/14	1 →
z	32/7	$z_j - c_j$	0	0	8/7	2/7 ↑	0
	RR		—	—	4/3	4/5	

Solving by the dual simplex method suggests that g_1 leaves the basis and s_2 enters into the basis. So, we get the iterative table as follows.

c_B	B	x_B	x_1	x_2	s_1	s_2	g_1
2	x_1	1	1	0	61/35	0	−3/5
2	x_2	1	0	1	−1	0	1
0	s_2	2	0	0	12/5	1	−14/5
z	4	$z_j - c_j$	0	0	16/35	0	4/5

This gives an optimum integer solution as $x_1 = 1$, $x_2 = 1$ and maximum $z = 4$.

EXAMPLE 4.3: A manufacturer of baby-dolls makes two types of dolls: Doll X and doll Y. Processing of these two dolls is done on two machines, A and B. Doll X requires two hours of machine A and six hours on machine B. Doll Y requires five hours on machine A and also five hours on machine B. There are sixteen hours of time per day available on machine A and thirty hours on machine B. The profit gained on both the dolls is same, i.e. one rupee per doll. What should be the daily production of each of the two dolls? Set up and solve the LPP. If the optimal solution is not integer-valued, use the Gomory cutting plane method to find integer-valued solution.

Solution: The mathematical formulation is

Maximize $\quad z = x + y$

subject to the constraints: $\quad 2x + 3y \le 16$

$\quad 6x + 5y \le 30$

and $x, y \ge 0$ and are integers.

Using the simplex method, the optimum solution is

c_B	B	x_B	x	y	s_1	s_2
1	y	9/5	0	1	3/10	–1/10
1	x	7/2	1	0	–1/4	1/4
	z	53/10	$z_j - c_j$	0	0	1/20	3/20

$x = 7/2$ and $y = 9/5$ is not the integer-valued. A fractional cut is formatted with the first row as

$$1 + \frac{4}{5} = y + \frac{3}{10}s_1 + \left(-1 + \frac{9}{10}\right)s_2$$

The corresponding Gomorian slack variable is

$$g_1 = -\frac{4}{5} + \frac{3}{10}s_1 + \frac{9}{10}s_2$$

Solving the following table, using the dual simplex method suggests that

c_B	B	x_B	x	y	s_1	s_2	g_1
1	y	9/5	0	1	3/10	–1/10	0
1	x	7/2	1	0	–1/4	1/4	0
0	g_1	–4/5	0	0	–3/10	–9/10	1 →
z	53/10	$z_j - c_j$	0	0	1/20	3/20	0
		RR	–	–	–1/3	–1/6 ↑	

g_1 departs and s_2 enters. Thus, the new iterative table is as follows.

c_B	B	x_B	x	y	s_1	s_2	g_1
1	y	17/9	0	1	1/3	0	–1/9
1	x	59/8	1	0	–1/3	0	5/18
0	s_2	8/9	0	0	1/3	1	–10/9
z	31/6	$z_j - c_j$	0	0	0	0	1/6

Still the solution is not integral-valued. Insert the fractional cut from the third row as

$$\frac{8}{9} = \frac{1}{3}s_1 + s_2 + \left(-2 + \frac{8}{9}\right)g_1$$

The Gomorian slack variable is

$$g_2 = -\frac{8}{9} + \frac{1}{3}s_1 + \frac{8}{9}g_1$$

Adding the Gomorian slack variable in the previous table, we get

c_B	B	x_B	x	y	s_1	s_2	g_1	g_2
1	y	17/9	0	1	1/3	0	–1/9	0
1	x	59/8	1	0	–1/3	0	5/18	0
0	s_2	8/9	0	0	1/3	1	–10/9	0
0	g_2	–8/9	0	0	–1/3	0	–8/9	1 →
z	31/6	$z_j - c_j$	0	0	0 ↑	0	1/6	0

Solving the above table by the dual simplex method suggests that g_2 leaves and s_1 enters. So, we get

c_B	B	x_B	x	y	s_1	s_2	g_1	g_2
1	y	1	0	1	0	0	–1	1
1	x	25/6	1	0	0	0	7/6	–1
0	s_2	0	0	0	0	1	–2	1
0	s_1	8/3	0	0	1	0	8/3	–3
z	31/6	$z_j - c_j$	0	0	0	0	1/6	0

As x is not an integer, we need one more fractional cut from the fourth row.

$$2 + \frac{1}{3} = s_1 + \left(2 + \frac{2}{3}\right) g_1 + (-3 + 0)\, g_2$$

The corresponding Gomorian slack variable is

$$g_3 = -\frac{2}{3} + \frac{2}{3} g_1$$

Add this slack variable at the bottom of the previous table and solve by the dual simplex table. We observe that

c_B	B	x_B	x	y	s_1	s_2	g_1	g_2	g_3
1	y	1	0	1	0	0	–1	1	0
1	x	25/6	1	0	0	0	7/6	–1	0
0	s_2	0	0	0	0	1	–2	1	0
0	s_1	8/3	0	0	1	0	8/3	–3	0
0	g_3	–2/3	0	0	0	0	–2/3	0	1 →
z	31/6	$z_j - c_j$	0	0	0	0	1/6 ↑	0	0

g_3 leaves the basis and g_1 enters.

c_B	B	x_B	x	y	s_1	s_2	g_1	g_2	g_3
1	y	2	0	1	0	0	0	1	–3/2
1	x	3	1	0	0	0	0	–1	7/4
0	s_2	2	0	0	0	1	0	1	–3
0	s_1	0	0	0	1	0	0	–3	4
0	g_1	1	0	0	0	0	1	0	–3/2
z	5	$z_j - c_j$	0	0	0	0	0	0	1/4

This gives an optimum integer solution $x = 3$, $y = 2$ and maximum $z = 5$.

EXAMPLE 4.4: Solve the following IPP:

Maximize $$z = 2x_1 + 20x_2 - 10x_3$$

subject to the constraints:

$$2x_1 + 20x_2 + 4x_3 \leq 15$$

$$6x_1 + 20x_2 + 4x_3 = 20$$

and $x_1, x_2, x_3 \geq 0$ and are integers.

Solution: Introducing the slack variable s_1 in the first constraint and the artificial variable A in the second constraints and ignoring integer-valued requirement, the optimal solution is given by the simplex table.

c_B	B	x_B	x_1	x_2	x_3	s_1
20	x_2	5/8	0	1	1/5	3/40
2	x_1	5/4	1	0	0	–1/4
z	15	$z_j - c_j$	0	0	14	1

Since the solution is non-integer, a fractional cut is constructed from the first row,

$$\frac{5}{8} = x_2 + \frac{1}{5}x_3 + \frac{3}{40}s_1$$

The corresponding Gomorian slack variable is

$$g_1 = -\frac{5}{8} + \frac{1}{5}x_3 + \frac{3}{40}s_1$$

Adding this slack variable in the previous optimal table, we get

c_B	B	x_B	x_1	x_2	x_3	s_1	g_1
20	x_2	5/8	0	1	1/5	3/40	0
2	x_1	5/4	1	0	0	–1/4	0
0	g_1	–5/8	0	0	–1/5	–3/40	1 →
z	15	$z_j - c_j$	0	0	14	1 ↑	0
		RR	–	–	–70	–40/3	0

Solving the above table by the dual simplex method suggests that g_1 exits and s_1 enters.

c_B	B	x_B	x_1	x_2	x_3	s_1	g_1
20	x_2	0	0	1	0	0	1
2	x_1	10/3	1	0	2/3	0	–10/3
0	s_1	25/3	0	0	8/3	1	–40/3
z	20/3	$z_j - c_j$	0	0	34/3	0	40/3

Since the solution is non-integer, a fractional cut is constructed from the third row,

$$8 + \frac{1}{3} = \left(2 + \frac{2}{3}\right)x_3 + s_1 + \left(-14 + \frac{2}{3}\right)g_1$$

The corresponding Gomorian slack variable is

$$g_2 = -\frac{1}{3} + \frac{2}{3}x_3 + \frac{2}{3}g_1$$

Adding this slack variable in the previous optimal table, we get

c_B	B	x_B	x_1	x_2	x_3	s_1	g_1	g_2
20	x_2	0	0	1	0	0	1	0
2	x_1	10/3	1	0	2/3	0	–10/3	0
0	s_1	25/3	0	0	8/3	1	–40/3	0
0	g_2	–1/3	0	0	–2/3	0	–2/3	1 →
z	20/3	$z_j - c_j$	0	0	34/3 ↑	0	40/3	0
		RR	–	–	–17	–	–20	0

Then the dual simplex method suggests that x_3 enters and g_2 leaves the basis.

c_B	B	x_B	x_1	x_2	x_3	s_1	g_1	g_2
20	x_2	0	0	1	0	0	1	0
2	x_1	3	1	0	0	0	–4	1
0	s_1	7	0	0	0	1	–16	4
–10	x_3	1/2	0	0	1	0	1	–3/2
z	1	$z_j - c_j$	0	0	0	0	2	17

Since the solution is not integer, a third fractional cut is required. From the last row, we have

$$\frac{1}{2} = x_3 + g_1 + \left(-2 + \frac{1}{2}\right) g_2$$

The corresponding Gomorian slack variable is

$$g_3 = \frac{1}{2} + \frac{1}{2} g_2$$

The new iteration is

c_B	B	x_B	x_1	x_2	x_3	s_1	g_1	g_2	g_3
20	x_2	0	0	1	0	0	1	0	0
2	x_1	3	1	0	0	0	–4	1	1
0	s_1	7	0	0	0	1	–16	4	4
–10	x_3	1/2	0	0	1	0	1	–3/2	–3/2
0	g_3	1/2	0	0	0	0	0	–1/2	1 →
z	1	$z_j - c_j$	0	0	0	0	2	17 ↑	0
		RR	–	–	–	–	–	–34	0

Then drop g_3 and enter g_2. The improved solution is

c_B	B	x_B	x_1	x_2	x_3	s_1	g_1	g_2	g_3
20	x_2	0	0	1	0	0	1	0	0
2	x_1	2	1	0	0	0	–4	0	2
0	s_1	3	0	0	0	1	–16	0	8
–10	x_3	2	0	0	1	0	1	0	–3
0	g_2	1	0	0	0	0	0	1	–2
z	–16	$z_j - c_j$	0	0	0	0	2	0	34

Thus, we get the optimum integer-valued solution as $x_1 = 2$, $x_2 = 0$, $x_3 = 2$ and maximum $z = -16$.

EXAMPLE 4.5: Solve the following IPP:

Maximize $$z = x_1 + 2x_2$$

subject to the constraints:

$$2x_2 \leq 7$$
$$x_1 + x_2 \leq 7$$
$$2x_1 \leq 11$$

$x_1, x_2 \geq 0$ are integers.

Solution: Students are advised to check that ignoring integer requirement gives $x_1 = 7/2$, $x_2 = 7/2$ and $z = 21/2$.

c_B	B	x_B	x_1	x_2	s_1	s_2	s_3
2	x_2	7/2	0	1	1/2	0	0
1	x_1	7/2	1	0	−1/2	1	0
0	s_3	4	0	0	1	−2	1
z	21/2	$z_j - c_j$	0	0	1/2	−1	0

We choose any of the variables x_1 or x_2 because both have the same fractional part. Let us select x_2. So

$$\frac{7}{2} = 1x_2 + \frac{1}{2}s_1$$

The corresponding Gomorian slack variable is

$$g_1 = -\frac{1}{2} - \frac{1}{2}s_1$$

Adding this variable at the bottom of the previous optimum table, we get

c_B	B	x_B	x_1	x_2	s_1	s_2	s_3	g_1
2	x_2	7/2	0	1	1/2	0	0	0
1	x_1	7/2	1	0	−1/2	1	0	0
0	s_3	4	0	0	1	−2	1	0
0	g_1	−1/2	0	0	−1/2	0	0	1
z	21/2	$z_j - c_j$	0	0	1/2	−1	0	0

Solving by the dual simplex, we have

c_B	B	x_B	x_1	x_2	s_1	s_2	s_3	g_1
2	x_2	7/2	0	1	1/2	0	0	0
1	x_1	7/2	1	0	−1/2	1	0	0
0	s_3	4	0	0	1	−2	1	0
0	g_1	−1/2	0	0	−1/2	0	0	1 →
z	21/2	$z_j - c_j$	0	0	1/2	−1	0	0
		RR	–	–	−1 ↑	–	–	0

s_1 enters and g_1 leaves the basis. The improved solution is

c_B	B	x_B	x_1	x_2	s_1	s_2	s_3	g_1
2	x_2	3	0	1	0	0	0	1
1	x_1	4	1	0	0	1	0	–1
0	s_3	3	0	0	0	–2	1	2
0	s_1	1	0	0	1	0	0	–2
z	10	$z_j - c_j$	0	0	0	1	0	2

Thus, the integral solution is $x_1 = 4$, $x_2 = 3$ and max. $z = 10$.

We have $-s_1 \le -1$. Now, s_1 from the first constraint of the problem is $s_1 = 7 - 2x_2$. Substituting this in $-s_1 \le -1$, we get $x_2 \le 3$. Let us plot a graph and see how the cut works (see Figure 4.2).

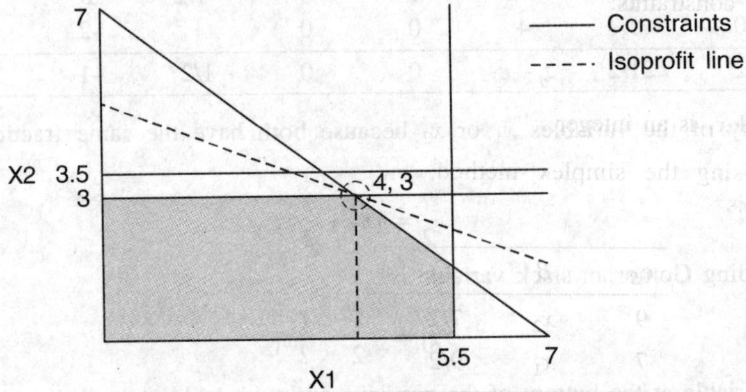

Figure 4.2

4.3.2 Gomory's Mixed—Integer Cutting Plane Method

The cutting plane obtained in Section 4.3.1 will fail (i.e. may not give feasible region) if decision variables are mix in nature, i.e. some take integer values and some can take real value. Thus, we need to develop a tool to solve mixed—integer programming problem.

The outline of the steps to be followed is as under:

Step 1: Write the given LPP into the standard maximization form and get optimum solution using the simplex method.

Step 2: If all $x_{Bi} \ge 0$ and are integers, the obtained solution is the optimal solution. If all $x_{Bi} \ge 0$ but integer restricted variables are not integers, then go to step 3.

Step 3: Pick up the k-th row having the largest fractional value corresponding to the basic variable x_{Bk}, among those variables which are supposed to take integer values and construct the Gomorian constraint (cutting plane) as

$$\sum_{j \in \mathbf{R}^+} a_{kj} x_j + \left(\frac{f_k}{f_k - 1}\right) \sum_{j \in \mathbf{R}^-} a_{kj} x_j \ge f_k$$

where $0 < f_k < 1$, $\mathbf{R}^+ = \{j : a_{kj} \geq 0\}$ and $\mathbf{R}^- = \{j : a_{kj} < 0\}$

i.e.
$$g_1 = -f_k + \sum_{j \in \mathbf{R}^+} a_{kj} x_j + \left(\frac{f_k}{f_k - 1}\right) \sum_{j \in \mathbf{R}^-} a_{kj} x_j$$

g_1 is called the Gomorian slack variable.

Step 4: Add the cutting plane generated in step 3 at the bottom of the optimum simplex table obtained in step 2. Obtain the improved solution using the dual simplex method.

Step 5: Repeat steps 3 and 4 until all $x_{Bi} \geq 0$ and all restricted variables are integers.

EXAMPLE 4.6: Find the optimum mixed – integer solution of LPP:

Maximize $z = 7x_1 + 9x_2$

subject to the constraints:

$$-x_1 + 3x_2 \leq 6$$
$$7x_1 + x_2 \leq 35$$

$x_1, x_2 \geq 0$ and x_1 is an integer.

Solution: Using the simplex method, the optimum solution of the LPP without integer requirements is

c_B	B	x_B	x_1	x_2	s_1	s_2
9	x_2	7/2	0	1	7/22	1/22
7	x_1	9/2	1	0	–1/22	3/22
z	63	$z_j - c_j$	0	0	28/11	15/11

In the optimal solution, x_1 is not an integer. Consider the second row for constructing a cut. We have

$$4 + \frac{1}{2} = x_1 - \frac{1}{22} s_1 + \frac{3}{22} s_2$$

The corresponding fractional cut is given by

$$g_1 = -\frac{1}{2} + \left[\frac{(1/2)}{(1/2) - 1}\right] s_1 + \frac{3}{22} s_2$$

g_1 is called the Gomorian slack variable. Insert this constraint at the bottom of the previous optimal table.

c_B	B	x_B	x_1	x_2	s_1	s_2	g_1
9	x_2	7/2	0	1	7/22	1/22	0
7	x_1	9/2	1	0	–1/22	3/22	0
0	g_1	–1/2	0	0	–1/22	–3/22	1 →
z	63	$z_j - c_j$	0	0	28/11	15/11 ↑	0

Using the dual simplex method, g_1 leaves the basis and s_2 enters.

c_B	B	x_B	x_1	x_2	s_1	s_2	g_1
9	x_2	10/3	0	1	10/33	0	1/3
7	x_1	4	1	0	–1/11	0	1
0	s_2	11/3	0	0	1/3	1	–22/3
z	58	$z_j - c_j$	0	0	23/11	0	10

The required optimum solution is $x_1 = 4$, $x_2 = 10/3$ and maximum $z = 58$.

EXAMPLE 4.7: Solve the following IPP:

Maximize
$$z = 4x_1 + 6x_2 + 2x_3$$

subject to the constraints:

$$4x_1 - 4x_2 \le 5$$
$$-x_1 + 6x_2 \le 5$$
$$-x_1 + x_2 + x_3 \le 5$$

$x_1, x_2, x_3 \ge 0$ and x_1 and x_3 are integers.

Solution: Introducing slack variables s_1, s_2, s_3 in the constraints and ignoring integer-valued requirement, the optimal solution is given by the simplex table.

c_B	B	x_B	x_1	x_2	x_3	s_1	s_2	s_3
4	x_1	5/2	1	0	0	3/10	1/5	0
6	x_2	5/4	0	1	0	1/20	1/5	0
2	x_3	25/4	0	0	1	1/4	0	1
z	30	$z_j - c_j$	0	0	0	2	2	2

Since the solution for x_1 and x_3 both is non-integer, a fractional cut is constructed from the first row,

$$2 + \frac{1}{2} = x_1 + \frac{3}{10}s_1 + \frac{1}{5}s_2$$

The corresponding Gomorian slack variable is

$$g_1 = -\frac{1}{2} + \frac{3}{10}s_1 + \frac{1}{5}s_2$$

Adding this slack variable in the previous optimal table, we get

c_B	B	x_B	x_1	x_2	x_3	s_1	s_2	s_3	g_1
4	x_1	5/2	1	0	0	3/10	1/5	0	0
6	x_2	5/4	0	1	0	1/20	1/5	0	0
2	x_3	25/4	0	0	1	1/4	0	1	0
0	g_1	–1/2	0	0	0	–3/10	–1/5	0	1 →
z	30	$z_j - c_j$	0	0	0	2 ↑	2	2	0

Solving the above table by the dual simplex method suggests that g_1 exits and s_1 enters.

c_B	B	x_B	x_1	x_2	x_3	s_1	s_2	s_3	g_1
4	x_1	2	1	0	0	0	0	0	1
6	x_2	7/6	0	1	0	0	1/6	0	1/6
2	x_3	35/6	0	0	1	0	–1/6	1	5/6
0	s_1	5/3	0	0	0	1	2/3	0	–10/3
z	80/3	$z_j - c_j$	0	0	0	0	2/3	2	20/3

Since x_3 is still not an integer, we write the third row,

$$\frac{+5}{6} = x_3 - \frac{1}{6}s_2 + s_3 + \frac{5}{6}g_1$$

The corresponding Gomorian slack variable is

$$g_2 = -\frac{5}{6} + \left[\frac{5/6}{(5/6) - 1}\right]\left(-\frac{1}{6}s_2\right) + \frac{5}{6}g_1 = -\frac{5}{6} + \frac{5}{6}s_2 + \frac{5}{6}g_1$$

Thus, the new iterative table is

c_B	B	x_B	x_1	x_2	x_3	s_1	s_2	s_3	g_1	g_2
4	x_1	2	1	0	0	0	0	0	1	0
6	x_2	7/6	0	1	0	0	1/6	0	1/6	0
2	x_3	35/6	0	0	1	0	–1/6	1	5/6	0
0	s_1	5/3	0	0	0	1	2/3	0	–10/3	0
0	g_2	–5/3	0	0	0	0	–5/6	0	–5/6	1 →
z	80/3	$z_j - c_j$	0	0	0	0	2/3 ↑	2	20/3	0

Solving by the dual simplex method suggests that drop g_2 and enter s_2.

c_B	B	x_B	x_1	x_2	x_3	s_1	s_2	s_3	g_1	g_2
4	x_1	2	1	0	0	0	0	0	1	0
6	x_2	1	0	1	0	0	0	0	0	1/5
2	x_3	6	0	0	1	0	0	1	1	–1/5
0	s_1	1	0	0	0	1	0	0	–4	4/5
0	s_2	1	0	0	0	0	1	0	1	–6/5
z	26	$z_j - c_j$	0	0	0	0	0	2	6	4/5

The optimum solution is $x_1 = 2$, $x_2 = 1$, $x_3 = 6$ and maximum $z = 26$.

4.4 BRANCH AND BOUND (B&B) METHOD

The Branch and Bound method divides the feasible region into smaller subprograms and examines each of the subprograms successively until a basic feasible solution is obtained. The iterative steps are as follows:

Step 1: Solve the given LPP ignoring integer requirements.

Step 2: If the solution obtained is integer then terminate the process, otherwise go to step 3.

Step 3: Calculate the value of the objective function and treat it as upper bound. Obtain the lower bound by rounding off to the integer values of the decision variables.

Step 4: Let x_j be not an integer value. Then sub-divide the given LPP into two subprograms.

Subprogram B: Add constraint $x_j \le [x_j]$ to the given LPP.

Subprogram C: Add constraint $x_j \ge [x_j] + 1$ to the given LPP.

where $[x_j]$ is the largest integer contained in x_j.

Step 5: Solve the subprograms obtained in step 4. There may arise three cases:

1. If the optimum solutions of the two subprograms are integral, then the required solution is one that gives larger value of the objective function.
2. If the optimum solution of one subprogram is integral and that of the other has no feasible solution, then the required solution is of that subprogram which satisfies integer requirement of the decision variables.
3. If the optimum solution of one subprogram is integral and that of the other is non-integral, then repeat steps 3 and 4 for the non-integer valued subprogram only.

Step 6: Repeat steps 3 to 5 until all-integer valued solution is obtained.

Step 7: Choose the solution amongst the obtained integer valued solutions that gives an optimal value of the objective function.

EXAMPLE 4.8: Find the optimum integer solution of LPP using B&B method:

Maximize $z = 6x_1 + 8x_2$

subject to the constraints:

$$4x_1 + 16x_2 \leq 32$$

$$14x_1 + 4x_2 \leq 6$$

$x_1, x_2 \geq 0$ are integers.

Solution: Ignoring the restriction of integers, the optimum solution is $x_1 = 20/13$, $x_2 = 21/13$ and maximum $z = 288/13$. The obtained solution is non-integral, the upper bound is $z = 288/13$ and the lower bound (obtained by rounding off values of $x_1 = 1$ and $x_2 = 1$ to nearest integer) is $z = 14$. Now maximum $\{20/13, 21/13\} = 21/13$ which corresponds to x_2 and hence, two new branches are $x_2 \leq 1$ (subprogram B) and $x_2 \geq 2$ (subprogram C) added in the original set of constraints. The optimum solution of subprogram B (see Figure 4.3) is

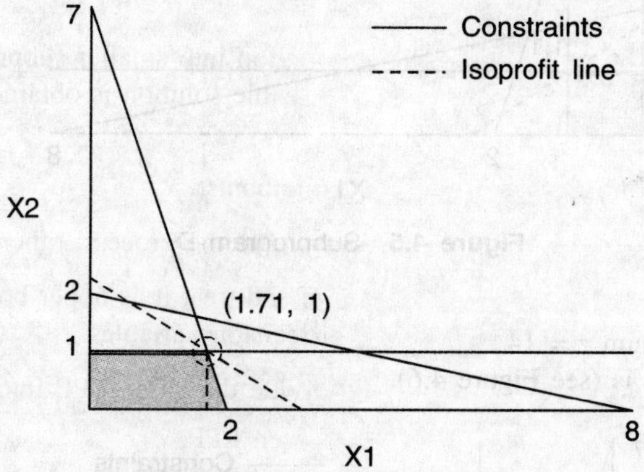

Figure 4.3 Subprogram B.

$x_1 = 12/7$, $x_2 = 1$ and maximum $z = 128/7$.

and that of subprogram C is (see Figure 4.4)

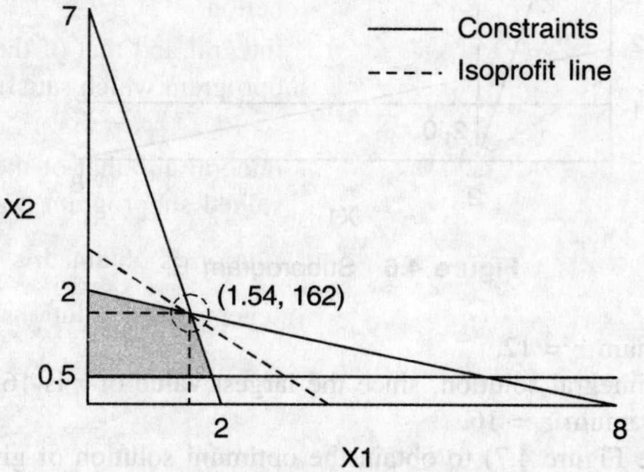

Figure 4.4 Subprogram C.

$x_1 = 0$, $x_2 = 2$ and maximum $z = 16$ satisfies integer requirement, and so no further branching is needed.

We need to have branching of subprogram B because $x_1 = 12/7$ is non-integer. We add two new branches $x_1 \le 1$ (subprogram D) and $x_2 \ge 2$ (subprogram E) in the original set of constraints. The optimum solution of subprogram D (see Figure 4.5) is

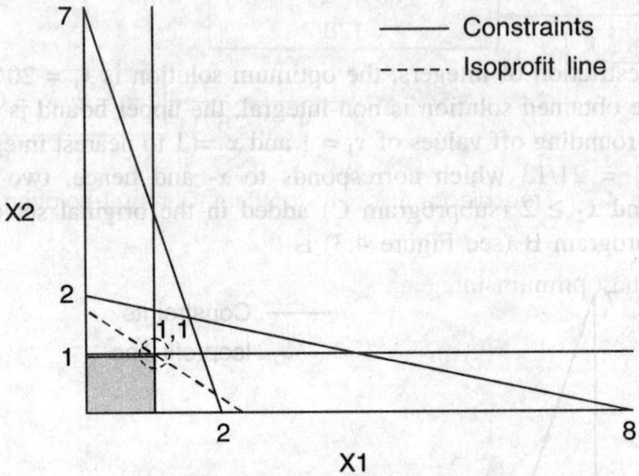

Figure 4.5 Subprogram D.

$x_1 = 1$, $x_2 = 1$ and maximum $z = 14$
and that of subprogram E is (see Figure 4.6)

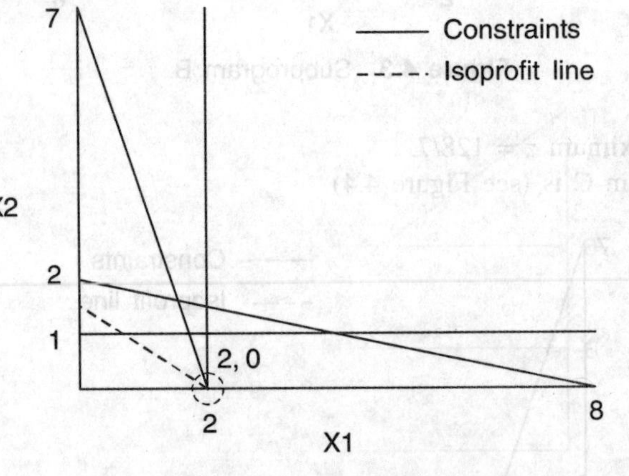

Figure 4.6 Subprogram E.

$x_1 = 2$, $x_2 = 0$ and maximum $z = 12$.

Among the obtained integral solution, since the largest value of z is 16, the optimum solution is $x_1 = 0$, $x_2 = 2$ and maximum $z = 16$.

The tree diagram (see Figure 4.7) to obtain the optimum solution of given LPP is as follows:

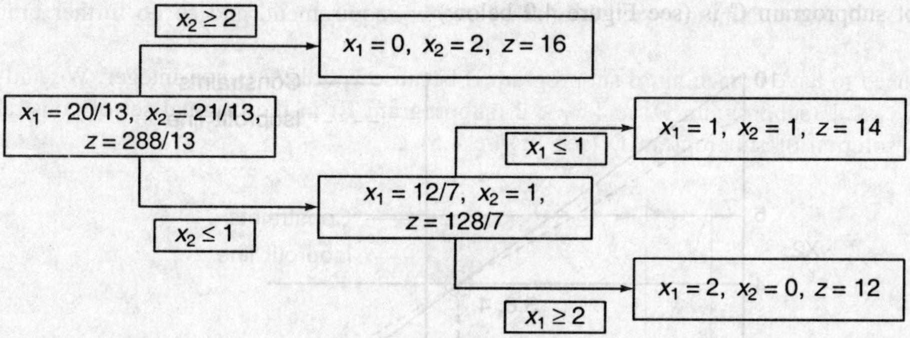

Figure 4.7 Tree diagram for the optimum integral solution.

EXAMPLE 4.9: Find the optimum integer solution of LPP using B&B method:

Minimize $$z = 4x_1 + 3x_2$$

subject to the constraints:

$$5x_1 + 3x_2 \geq 30$$
$$x_1 \leq 4$$
$$x_2 \leq 6$$

$x_1, x_2 \geq 0$ are integers.

Solution: Ignoring the restriction of integers, the optimum solution is $x_1 = 4$, $x_2 = 10/3$ and minimum $z = 26$. x_2 is non-integral and hence, two new branches are, $x_2 \leq 3$ (subprogram B) and $x_2 \geq 4$ (subprogram C), added in the original set of constraints. The optimum solution of subprogram B is infeasible (see Figure 4.8).

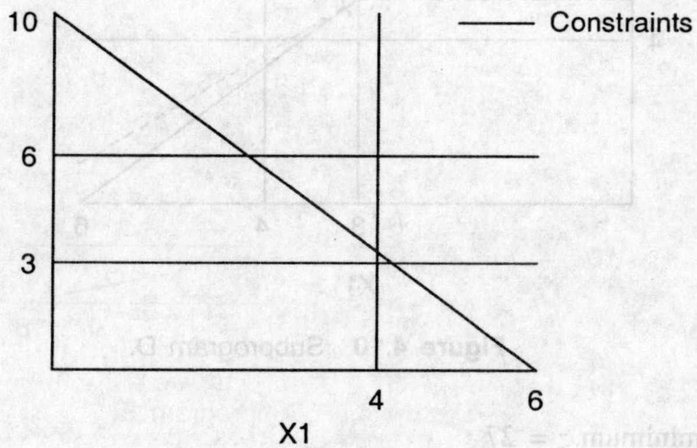

Figure 4.8 Subprogram B.

and that of subprogram C is (see Figure 4.9 below)

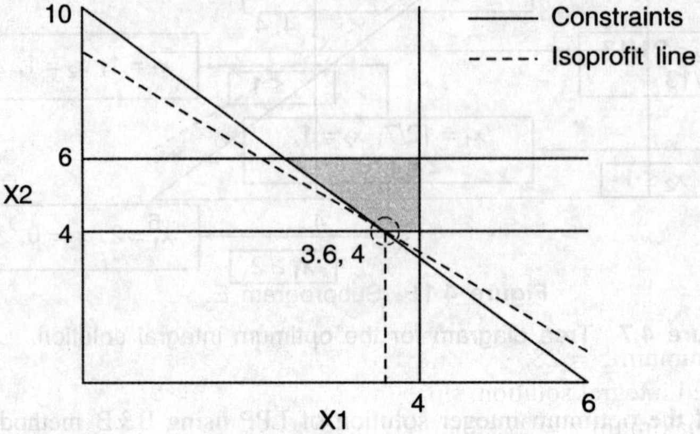

Figure 4.9 Subprogram C.

$x_1 = 18/5$, $x_2 = 4$ and minimum $z = 132/5$.

We need to have branching of subprogram C because $x_1 = 18/5$ is non-integer. We add two new branches, $x_1 \leq 3$ (subprogram D) and $x_1 \geq 4$ (subprogram E), in the original set of constraints. The optimum solution of subprogram D is (see Figure 4.10 below)

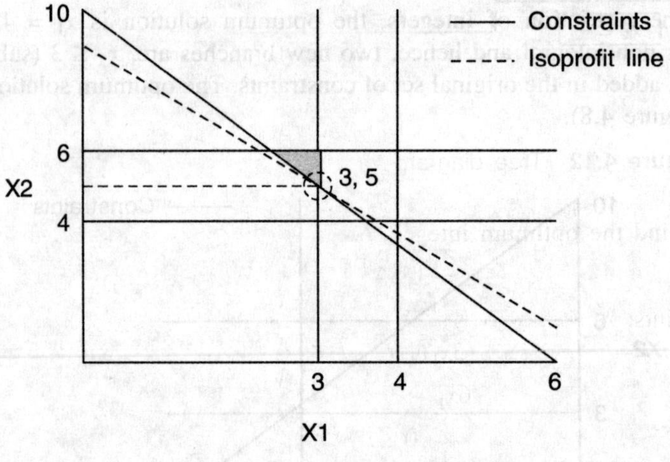

Figure 4.10 Subprogram D.

$x_1 = 3$, $x_2 = 5$ and minimum $z = 27$

and that of subprogram E is (see Figure 4.11)

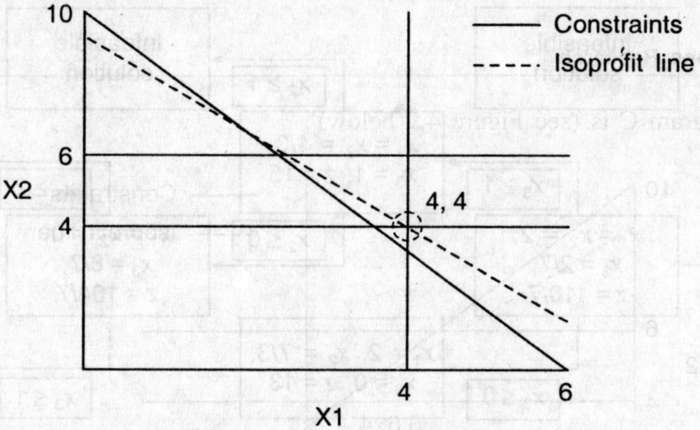

Figure 4.11 Subprogram E.

$x_1 = 4$, $x_2 = 4$ and minimum $z = 28$.

Among the obtained integral solution, since the minimum value of z is 27, the optimum solution is $x_1 = 3$, $x_2 = 5$ and maximum $z = 27$. The tree diagram for the optimal integral solution is given in Figure 4.12.

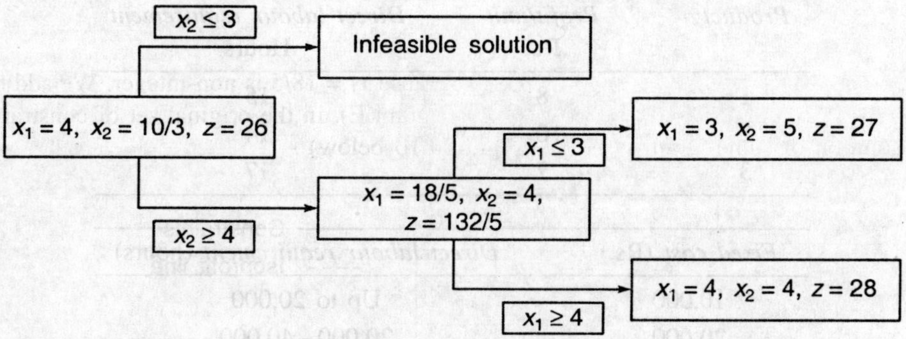

Figure 4.12 Tree diagram for the optimum integral solution.

EXAMPLE 4.10: Find the optimum integer solution of LPP using B&B method:

Maximize
$$z = 3x_1 + 3x_2 + 13x_3$$

subject to the constraints:
$$-3x_1 + 6x_2 + 7x_3 \le 8$$
$$6x_1 - 3x_2 + 7x_3 \le 8$$
$$0 \le x_j \le 5$$
$$j = 1, 2, 3$$

x_1, x_2, x_3 are integers.

Solution: Ignoring the restriction of integers, the optimum solution is $x_1 = x_2 = 8/3$, $x_3 = 0$ and maximum $z = 16$.

(Students are advised to check each subprogram shown in Figure 4.13 by the simplex method.)

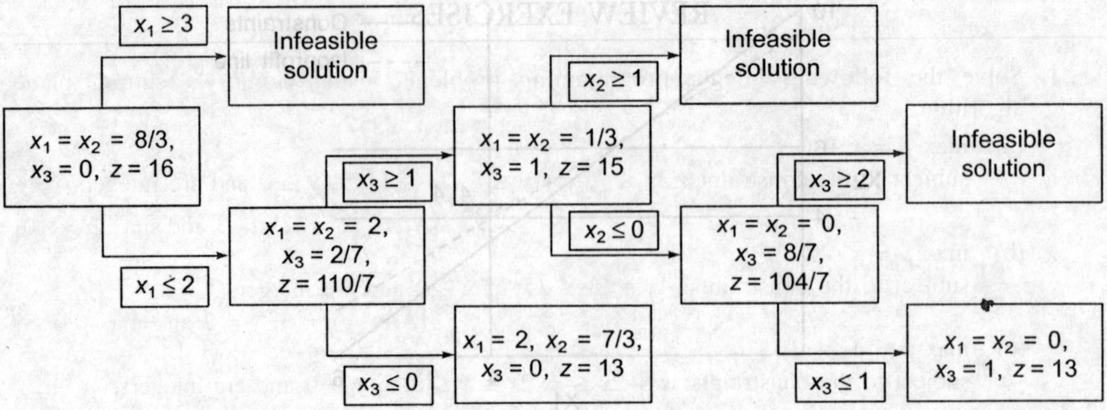

Figure 4.13 Tree diagram for the optimum integral solution.

The optimum integral solution is $x_1 = x_2 = 0$, $x_3 = 1$ and maximum $z = 13$.

EXAMPLE 4.11: Consider the following data:

Product	*Profit/unit* Rs.	*Direct labour requirement* Hours
1	8	15
2	10	14
3	7	17

Fixed cost (Rs.)	*Direct labour requirement* (hours)
10,000	Up to 20,000
20,000	20,000 – 40,000
30,000	40,000 – 70,000

Formulate an integer programming problem as 0 – 1 programming to determine the production scheduling so as to maximize the total net profit.

Solution: Let x_1, x_2, x_3 be the number of products 1, 2, 3 respectively and c_j, $j = 1, 2, 3$ be the fixed cost (in Rs.). Then

Maximize $$P = 8x_1 + 10x_2 + 7x_3 - 10{,}000c_1 - 20{,}000c_2 - 30{,}000c_3$$

subject to the constraints:

$$15x_1 + 14x_2 + 17x_3 \le 20{,}000c_1 + 40{,}000c_2 + 70{,}000c_3$$

$$c_1 + c_2 + c_3 = 1$$

and $x_j \ge 0$, $j = 1, 2, 3$.

REVIEW EXERCISES

1. Solve the following integer programming problems, using Gomory's cutting plane algorithm.

(a) max $p = x + y$
subject to the constraints: $2y \leq 7$, $x + y \leq 7$, $2x \leq 11$; $x, y \geq 0$ and are integers.
[**Ans.** $x = 4$, $y = 3$ and max $p = 10$]

(b) max $p = x - 2y$
subject to the constraints: $4x + 2y \leq 15$; $x, y \geq 0$ and are integers.
[**Ans.** $x = 3$, $y = 2$ and max $p = 5$]

(c) max $p = 4x + 3y$
subject to the constraints: $x + 2y \leq 4$, $2x + y \leq 6$; $x, y \geq 0$ and are integers.
[**Ans.** $x = 3$, $y = 0$ and max $p = 12$]

(d) max $p = 3x - 2y + 5z$
subject to the constraints: $5x + 2y + 7z \leq 28$, $4x + 5y + 5z \leq 30$; $x, y, z \geq 0$ and are integers.
[*Hint:* simplex method gives the integer solution]
[**Ans.** $x = 0$, $y = 0$, $z = 4$ and max $p = 20$]

(e) max $p = 3x + 5y$
subject to the constraints: $2x + 4y \leq 25$, $x \leq 8$, $2y \leq 10$; $x, y \geq 0$ and are integers.
[**Ans.** $x = 8$, $y = 2$, and max $p = 34$]

(f) max $p = 5x + 4y$
subject to the constraints: $x + y \geq 2$, $5x + 3y \leq 15$, $3x + 5y \leq 15$; $x, y \geq 0$ and are integers.
[**Ans.** $x = 3$, $y = 0$, and max $p = 15$]

(g) min $p = 3x + 2.5y$
subject to the constraints: $x + 2y \geq 20$, $3x + 2y \geq 50$; $x, y \geq 0$ and are integers.
[**Ans.** $x = 14$, $y = 4$, and max $p = 52$]

(h) max $p = -3x + y + 3z$
subject to the constraints: $-x + 2y + z \leq 4$, $x - 3y + 2z \leq 3$, $2x - 1.5z \leq 1$; $x, y \geq 0$ and z is non-negative integer.
[**Ans.** $x = 0$, $y = 8/7$, $z = 1$ and max $p = 29/7$]

(i) max $p = x + y$
subject to the constraints: $3x + 2y \leq 5$, $y \leq 2$; $x, y \geq 0$ and x is non-negative integer.
[**Ans.** $x = 0$, $y = 2$, and max $p = 2$]

(j) min $p = 4x + 3y + 5z$
subject to the constraints: $2x - 2y + 4z \geq 7$, $2x + 4y - 2z \geq 5$; $y \geq 0$, x and z are non-negative integers.
[**Ans.** $x = 4$, $y = 0$, $z = 0$ and max $p = 16$]

5

Goal Programming

5.1 INTRODUCTION

In the previous two chapters, we formulated linear programming problems and integer programming problems to optimize single objective function under a set of given constraints. However, in reality, decision-makers may not have to optimize single objective function. In fact, a decision-maker has to achieve objectives either economic or non-economic of any organization. He needs to attain a **satisfactory** level of achievement among different goals of an organization.

The programming used for solving a multi-objective optimization problem by setting equilibrium between conflicting goals is called *goal programming* (GP). The formulation of the problem in GP is similar to that of LP model except that in GP, we have multiple goals in a particular priority order. Ranking and weighing various goals establish a priority. The priority helps to deal with all goals, which cannot be attained completely and/or simultaneously. Here, the most important goals are satisfied first and least important goals later on.

Charnes and Cooper (1961) suggested the concept of goal programming for solving infeasible LP problems arising from various conflicting goals such as (i) to attain the best quality product at minimum production cost, (ii) to maximize profit and increase wages of the employee. Ijiri (1965) gave the concept of assigning different priority levels to incommensurable goals and different weights for the goals at the same priority. The main feature of GP is to achieve targets at a satisfactory level instead of optimizing a single goal.

In GP, instead of minimizing or maximizing objective function as in LP, the deviations from the established goals within the given set of constraints are minimized. In LP, these deviation variables are slack or surplus variables and they are used as dummy variables. In GP, these deviations play an important role to achieve a satisfactory level. These deviations can be positive deviation or negative deviation from each goal and sub-goal. The aim is to minimize a sum of these deviations bases on how they are to be achieved within the priority structure assigned to each deviation.

5.2 GOAL PROGRAMMING MODEL FORMULATION

5.2.1 Single Goal with Multiple Sub-goals

Let one unit of effort applied to activity x_j contribute amount a_{ij} towards the i-th goal. If the target level, b_i for the i-th goal is fully achieved, then we have

$$\sum_{j=1}^{n} a_{ij}x_j = b_i, \quad i = 1, 2, \ldots, m$$

However, the goal may be underachieved or overachieved within the given decision criteria. Let d_i^- represent under-achievement (similar to slack variable in LP) and is negative deviation from i-th goal and d_i^+ denotes over-achievement (similar to surplus variable in LP) and is positive deviation from i-th goal. Then we have

$$\sum_{j=1}^{n} a_{ij}x_j \le b_i, \; i = 1, 2, \ldots, m \text{ (under-achievement)}$$

$$\sum_{j=1}^{n} a_{ij}x_j \ge b_i, \; i = 1, 2, \ldots, m \text{ (over-achievement).}$$

Since both under- and over-achievement of a goal cannot be attained simultaneously, one or both of this negative or positive deviation must be zero in the solution. Equivalently, if one assumes a positive value then the other must be zero and vice-versa. The deviation variable d_i^+ is zero when over-achievement is acceptable and d_i^- is zero when under-achievement is acceptable. If utmost goal satisfaction is the requirement then both d_i^+ and d_i^- are to be considered in the objective function and according to their priority from the most important to the least important (see more details in Section 5.2.3).

EXAMPLE 5.1: A production unit produces the chair and the table. The unit profit per chair is Rs. 100 and that per table is Rs. 50. The goal of a production unit is to earn a total profit of exactly Rs. 700 during the sale season of a week. Formulate GP.

Solution: Let x_1 be the number of chairs produced and x_2 be the number of tables produced. We have a single goal of profit maximization $z = 100x_1 + 50x_2$.

Let us reformulate the above goal to allow for under-achievement (d_1^-) and over-achievement (d_1^+) as

$$100x_1 + 50x_2 + d_1^- - d_1^+ = 700$$

Now GP model is as follows:
Minimize $d_1^- + d_1^+$
subject to the constraints

$$100x_1 + 50x_2 + d_1^- - d_1^+ = 700$$

and $x_1, x_2, d_1^-, d_1^+ \ge 0$.

If the profit goal is below Rs. 700 then the slack in the profit goal will be expressed by negative deviational variable, d_1^- from the goal. On the other hand, if the profit is more than Rs. 700, the surplus in the profit will be given by positive deviational variable, d_1^+ from the goal. If the profit goal of exactly Rs. 700 is achieved, then both d_1^+ and d_1^- are zero.

Here, there are infinitely many solutions on the iso-profit line joining (70, 0) and (0, 14).

5.2.2 Multiple Goals with Equal Weightage

EXAMPLE 5.2: In example 5.1, the manager sets goals not only for profit maximization but also to achieve sales volume for product A (chair) and B (table) near to 5 and 4 respectively. Formulate this as a goal programming.

Solution: The mathematical formulation is

Maximum $$z = 100x_1 + 50x_2 = 700$$

subject to:

$$x_1 \le 5,\ x_2 \le 4 \quad \text{and} \quad x_1, x_2 \ge 0$$

The corresponding GP formulation is

Minimize $$d_1^- + d_1^+ + d_2^- + d_3^-$$

subject to the constraints

$$100x_1 + 50x_2 + d_1^- - d_1^+ = 700$$

$$x_1 + d_2^- = 5 \quad \text{and} \quad x_2 + d_3^- = 4$$

and $x_1, x_2, d_1^-, d_1^+, d_2^-, d_3^- \ge 0$. Here d_2^- and d_3^- denote under-achievement of sales volume for product A and B respectively.

Note: d_2^+ and d_3^+ are not included in the sales target constraints as the sales volume target is maximum.

Input table

	d^+	Prty (d^+)	d^-	Prty (d^-)	x_1	x_2		*RHS*
Constraint 1	1	1	1	1	100	50	=	700
Constraint 2	0	0	1	1	1	0	=	5
Constraint 3	0	0	1	1	0	1	=	4

Final table (Using the Simplex method)

	x_1	x_2	d_1^-	d_2^-	d_3^-	d_1^+	d_2^+	d_3^+	*RHS*
Constraint 1	0	1	0	0	1	0	0	−1	4
Constraint 2	1	0	0.01	0	−0.5	−0.01	0	0.5	5
Constraint 3	0	0	−0.01	1	0.5	0.01	−1	−0.5	0
Priority 1	0	0	−1.01	0	−0.5	−0.99	−1	−0.5	0

Thus, the solution is $x_1 = 5$ and $x_2 = 4$, i.e. all targets are achieved and hence $d_1^+ = d_1^- = d_2^- = d_3^- = 0$.

EXAMPLE 5.3: An office equipment manufacturer produces two kinds of products, chairs and lamps. The production of either a chair or a lamp requires 1 hour of production capacity in the plant. The plant has a maximum production capacity of 10 hours per week. Because of the limited sales capacity, the maximum numbers of chairs and lamps that can be sold are 6 and 8 per week respectively. The gross margin from the sales of a chair is Rs. 80 and Rs. 40 for that of a lamp.

The plant manager has a set of the following goals arranged in order of importance:

(i) He wants to avoid underutilization of production capacity.

(ii) He wants to sell as many as possible.

(iii) Overtime should not exceed 20% of the production time.

Formulate and solve this problem as a GP model so that the plant manager may achieve his goals as closely as possible.

Solution: Let x_1 be the number of chairs produced and x_2 be the number of lamps produced. The constraint of production capacity goal to be achieved in 10 hours per week can be stated as

$$x_1 + x_2 + d_1^- - d_1^+ = 10$$

where d_1^- is underutilization of production capacity and d_1^+ is overutilization of production capacity.

The constraints of maximum sales volume are

$$x_1 + d_2^- = 6$$

$$x_2 + d_3^- = 8$$

Clearly, $d_2^+ = d_3^+ = 0$ as over-achievement of sales goal is not allowed.

The goal corresponding to minimization of overtime can be formulated as

$$d_1^+ + d_4^- - d_4^+ = 0.2\,(10) = 2$$

where d_4^- = overtime less than 20 % of goal constraint

d_4^+ = overtime more than 20 % of goal constraint

d_1^+ = overtime beyond 10 hours per week.

The corresponding GP formulation is

Mini $$z = d_1^+ + d_2^- + d_3^- + d_4^+$$

subject to the constraints

$$x_1 + x_2 + d_1^+ - d_1^- = 10$$

$$x_1 + d_2^- = 6$$

$$x_2 + d_3^- = 8$$

$$d_1^+ + d_4^- - d_4^+ = 0.2\,(10) = 2$$

and $x_1, x_2, d_1^-, d_1^+, d_2^-, d_3^-, d_4^-, d_4^+ \geq 0$.

The input table is given below.

	wt (d^+)	*Prty* (d^+)	*wt* (d^-)	*Prty* (d^-)	x_1	x_2		*RHS*
Constraint 1	1	1	1	1	1	1	=	10
Constraint 2	0	0	1	1	1	0	=	6
Constraint 3	0	0	1	1	0	1	=	8
Constraint 4	1	1	1	1	0	0	=	2

Final table (Using simplex method)

	x_1	x_2	d_1^-	d_2^-	d_3^-	d_4^-	d_1^+	d_2^+	d_3^+	d_4^+	*RHS*
Constraint 1	0	1	1	–1	0	0	–1	1	0	0	4
Constraint 2	1	0	0	1	0	0	0	–1	0	0	6
Constraint 3	0	0	–1	1	1	0	1	–1	–1	0	4
Constraint 4	0	0	0	0	0	1	0	0	0	–1	2
Priority 1	0	0	–2	0	1	0	–1	–1	–1	–2	6

The constraint analysis is as follows :

Constraint No.	*RHS*	d^+ (row i)	d^- (row i)
1	10	0	0
2	6	0	0
3	8	0	4
4	2	0	2

So, $d_1^+ = d_2^+ = d_3^+ = d_4^+ = d_1^- = d_2^- = 0$ and $d_3^- = 4$, $d_4^- = 2$ and $x_1 = 6$, $x_2 = 4$, i.e. the company should produce 6 chairs and 4 lamps to achieve all goals.

5.2.3 Goal Programming with Weighted Goals

When priority levels are used in GP, any goal in the top priority level will be given the highest weightage. However, there may be times when one goal is more important compared to other goals. In that case, we use weighted goal programming. While using weighted GP, the coefficients in the objective function for the deviational variables are the weights assigned to the goals.

EXAMPLE 5.4: A company manufactures two products (say) *A* and *B*. Both the products require two-step production process involving wiring and assembly. It takes about 2 hours to wire *A* and 3 hours to wire *B*. Assembly times required by *A* and *B* are 6 and 5 hours respectively. The production capacity is such that only 12 hours of wiring and 13 hours of assembly time are available. The revenue generated by the manufacturer for product *A* is Rs. 7 per unit and for product B is Rs. 6 per unit.

The manager wants to achieve the following four goals:

(i) to produce as much profit above Rs. 30 as possible during the production period,

(ii) to fully utilize the available wiring department hours,

(iii) to avoid overtime in the assembly department,

(iv) to meet a contract requirement to produce at least seven units of product *B*.

He assigns priorities P_i's (i = 1, 2, 3, 4) to achieve the above goals by ranking $P_1 > P_2 > P_3 > P_4$. He takes $P_1 = 6$, $P_2 = 4$, $P_3 = 2$ and $P_4 = 1$.

Solve the problem using GP technique.

Solution: The goal programming formulation of the problem is

Minimum $$z = 6d_1^- + 4d_2^- + 2d_3^+ + d_4^-$$

subject to the constraints

$$7x_1 + 6x_2 + d_1^- - d_1^+ = 30 \quad \text{(Profit constraint)}$$

$$2x_1 + 3x_2 + d_2^- - d_2^+ = 12 \quad \text{(Wiring hour constraint)}$$

$$6x_1 + 5x_2 + d_3^- - d_3^+ = 12 \quad \text{(Assembly constraint)}$$

$$x_2 + d_4^- - d_4^+ = 30 \quad \text{(Product } B \text{ constraint)}$$

where

x_1 = number of product *A* produced

x_2 = number of product *A* produced

d_1^- = under-achievement of the profit target

d_1^+ = over-achievement of the profit target

d_2^- = underutilization in the wiring department

d_2^+ = overutilization in the wiring department

d_3^- = underutilization in the assembly department

d_3^+ = overutilization in the assembly department

d_4^- = under-achievement of the goal (iv)

d_4^+ = over-achievement of the goal (iv).

It is given that the manager is not in favour of over-achievement of the profit goal ($d_1^+ = 0$), overtime in the wiring department ($d_2^+ = 0$), underutilization in the assembly department ($d_3^- = 0$) and overachievement of goal, (iv) ($d_4^+ = 0$).

The input table is as follows:

	wt (d^+)	*Prty* (d^+)	*wt* (d^-)	*Prty* (d^-)	x_1	x_2		*RHS*
Constraint 1	0	0	1	1	7	6	=	30
Constraint 2	0	0	1	2	2	3	=	12
Constraint 3	1	3	0	0	6	5	=	30
Constraint 4	0	0	1	4	0	1	=	7

The readers are asked to verify the final table using Excel:

Final table

	x_1	x_2	d_1^-	d_2^-	d_3^-	d_4^-	d_1^+	d_2^+	d_3^+	d_4^+	*RHS*
Constraint 1	1.6	0	0	−1	0.6	0	0	1	−0.6	0	6
Constraint 2	1.2	1	0	0	0.2	0	0	0	−0.2	0	6
Constraint 3	0.2	0	−1	0	1.2	0	1	0	−1.2	0	6
Constraint 4	−1.2	0	0	0	−0.2	1	0	0	0.2	−1	1
Priority 4	−1.2	0	0	0	−0.2	0	0	0	0.2	−1	1
Priority 3	0	0	0	0	0	0	0	0	−1	0	0
Priority 2	0	0	0	−1	0	0	0	0	0	0	0
Priority 1	0	0	−1	0	0	0	0	0	0	0	0

We observe that $d_1^- = d_2^- = d_3^- = 0$ indicating complete achievement of the first three goals, while $d_4^- = 1$ depicts under-achievement of the goal (iv) by 1 – unit. Again $d_1^+ = d_2^+ = 6$ indicates over-achievement of the first two goals by 6–units each while $d_3^+ = d_4^+ = 0$ represents complete achievement of goals (iii) and (iv). The optimum solution is $x_1 = 0$ and $x_2 = 6$ with maximum profit of Rs. 36.00.

REVIEW EXERCISES

1. A firm manufactures two types of metal file cabinets. The demand for two-drawer model is up to 600 cabinets per week and that for three-drawer model is up to 400 per week. The firm has a weekly operating capacity of 1,300 hours, with the two-drawer cabinet taking 1 hour to produce and the three-drawer cabinet requiring 2 hours. Each two-drawer model sold yields a profit of Rs. 10 and profit for three-drawer model is Rs. 15. The manager sets the following goals in order of priority:

(i) to attain a profit as close to Rs. 11,000 as possible each week,
(ii) to avoid underutilization of the firm's production capacity,
(iii) to sell as many two- and three-drawer cabinets as the demand indicates.

Set this as a GP problem and solve it.

[**Ans.** 500 units of two-drawer and 400 units of three-drawer cabinet with underachievement of the third goal by 100 units]

2. A company produces motorcycle seats. The company has two production lines. The production rate for line 1 is 50 seats per hour and for line 2, it is 60 seats per hour. The company has a contract to supply 1,200 seats daily. The normal operation period for each line is 8 hours. The production manager of the company is trying to determine the best policy for daily operation hours for the two lines. He sets the priorities to achieve his goals as given below:

(i) to produce and deliver 1,200 seats daily,
(ii) to limit the daily overtime achievement operation hours of line 2 to be 3 hours,
(iii) to minimize underutilization of the regular daily operation hours of each line. Assign weights based on the relative productivity rate,
(iv) to minimize the daily overtime operation hours of each line as much as possible. Assign differential weights based on the relative cost of over time.

Solve the GP problem.

[**Ans.** $x_1 = 10.8$, $x_2 = 11$, $d_1^- = d_2^- = d_3^- = d_4^+ = 0$, $d_2^+ = 3.8$ and $d_3^+ = 3$]

3. A shoe manufacturer produces hiking boots and ski boots. The manufacturing process consists of sewing and stitching. It has available 60 hours per week for the sewing process and 80 hours per week for the stitching process at normal capacity. The firm realizes a profit of Rs. 150 per pair of hiking boots and Rs. 100 per pair on the ski boots. It requires 2 hours of sewing and 5 hours of stitching to produce one pair of hiking boots and 3 hours of sewing and 2 hours of stitching to produce one pair of ski boots. The manager of the company wishes to achieve the following goals listed in the order of their importance:

(i) to achieve the profit goal of Rs. 5,250 per week,
(ii) to limit the overtime operation of sewing department to 30 hours,
(iii) to meet the sales goal for each type of boot—25 hiking boots and 20 ski boots,
(iv) to avoid any underutilization of regular operation hours of the sewing centre.

Formulate and solve this as a GP problem.

4. The manager of the only record shop in a town has a decision problem that involves multiple goals. The record shop employs five full-time and four part-time salesmen. The normal working hours per month for a full-time salesman are 160 hours and for a part-time salesman 80 hours. According to the performance record of the salesman, the average sales have been five records per hour for the full-time salesman and two records for the part-time salesman. The average hourly wage rates are Rs. 3 for the full-time salesman and Rs. 2 for the part-time salesman. The average profit from the sales of a record is Rs. 1.50. In view of the past records, the manager feels that the sales goal for the next month should be 5,500 records. Since the shop is open for six days a week, overtime is often required of the salesman (not necessarily overtime but extra hours for a part-time salesman). The manager believes that a good employer–employee relationship is an essential factor of success in business. Therefore, he feels that a stable employment level with occasional overtime requirement is a better practice than an unstable employment level with no overtime. However, he feels that overtime of more than 100 hours among the full-time salesmen should be avoided because of the declining sales effectiveness caused by fatigue. The manager has set the following goals:

(i) to achieve a sales target of 5,500 records for the next month,
(ii) to limit overtime of full-time salesmen to 100 hours,
(iii) to provide job security to salesmen. The manager feels that full utilization of the employee's regular working hours (no layoffs) is an important factor for a good employer–employee relationship. However, he is twice as concerned with the full utilization of the full-time salesman as with that of the part-time salesman,
(iv) to minimize the sum of overtime for both full-time and part-time salesmen. The manager desires to assign different weights to the minimization of overtime according to the net marginal profit ratio between the full-time and part-time salesman.

Formulate and solve the given GP problem.

6 Non-linear Programming

6.1 INTRODUCTION

In studying linear programming we saw that all functional forms involved were linear in nature. While learning its solution techniques, there was a basic underlying structure which dictated that an optimal solution could be found by solving sets of linear equations. It was also known that the optimal solution would always be found at an extreme point of the feasible solution space, which will be convex.

However, in real-life problems the assumptions of linearity might be questionable. So the idea of non-linearity comes in. Problems involving non-linear functional forms are referred to as non-linear problems. They are characterized by terms or groups of terms that involve intrinsically non-linear functions like sinx, cosx, lnx, e^x or non-linearities arising as a result of interactions between two or more variables such as x_1x_2, $x_1\log x_2$, etc. When a programming problem contains non-linear constraints, it needs no longer to be true that the region of feasible solutions is convex. Also, while solvin~ such problems, an optimal solution might be found at an extreme point, a point interior to the feasible region, or at a point of discontinuity. It may be possible that when the set of feasible solutions is not convex, there can exist local optima different from the global optima even though the objective function is linear.

A major disadvantage in studying non-linear programming problems is the wide variety of techniques used to find its solution. Many algorithmic procedures have been suggested for solving non-linear programming problems. These techniques involve the solution of simultaneous linear equations, simultaneous non-linear equations, or both. In this chapter we will study the solution methodology of classical optimization problems and some basic techniques for solving non-linear programming problems. Our scope of studying the techniques of solving non-linear programming problems will be limited in nature and we will not consider advanced non-linear programming techniques. In general, this chapter will deal with what we call "well-behaved" functions; that is, those that do not have any discontinuities or singularity points such as outward pointing cusps. The remaining cases and methods will be left to further study from the rapidly expanding technical literature and texts on non-linear programming.

In order to gain an insight into the non-linear programming, we will study first the following very important prerequisite section.

Note: We shall assume that at each point in $\mathbf{E}^n$ where function f is defined, all n partial derivatives of f with respect to the variables x_j exist and are continuous. Hence in particular, the second partial derivatives of f exist and are continuous (we write this as $f \in \mathbf{C}^2$). When this happens, then we know that for all i and j

$$\frac{\partial^2 f}{\partial x_i \partial x_j} = \frac{\partial^2 f}{\partial x_j \partial x_i}$$

6.2 PREREQUISITES

6.2.1 Maxima and Minima of Functions and Their Solutions

Let us begin with the definition of the following terms.

Absolute (global) maximum: The function $f(x)$ defined over a closed set A is said to take on its absolute or the global maximum over A at the point x^* if $f(x) \le f(x^*)$ for every point x of A.

If the closed set is strictly bounded, then the global maximum of $f(x)$ over A will actually be taken on at one or more points in A, if one assumes that $f(x)$ is continuous over the set A.

If the set is not strictly bounded, then the global maximum may not be taken on at any point x with $|x|$ finite, but may instead be the limiting value of $f(x)$ as $|x| \to \infty$ in some specific way.

Strong relative (local) maximum: A function has a strong relative maximum at x^* if there exists an ε-neighbourhood of x^* such that for all x in this ε-neighbourhood different from x^*, $f(x)$ is strictly less than $f(x^*)$. If $f(x) \le f(x^*)$ then we say that x^* is a ***weak relative maxima***.

Frequently, we shall not need to distinguish between strong and weak local maxima. In such situations, we shall simply refer to as local maxima.

The definitions of the global minima and local minima are obtained from the corresponding definitions of maxima, by reversing the directions of the inequality signs.

Note that if $f(x)$ has a global maxima at x' and a local maxima at x^*, then $-f(x)$ has a global minima at x' and a local minima at x^*.

Points x_1 and x_7 represent the limit of the domain. The point x_2 is a global minimum and x_6 is the global maximum. Similarly, other points are seen from figure. It is clear from Figure 6.1 that the first derivatives (slope, gradient) of f vanish at all extrema. If a point with zero slope is not an extremum (minimum or maximum), then it is called a *point of inflexion* or a *saddle point*.

Consider a function of a *single* variable. A *necessary condition* for a particular solution,

$x = x^*$, to be either a minimum or a maximum is that $df(x)/dx = 0$ at $x = x^*$

For a function of a *single* variable *a sufficient condition* for a stationary point x^* to be an extremum is that $f''(x^*) < 0$ for maximum and $f''(x^*) > 0$ for minimum.

If the second order derivatives vanish, we need to check the higher order derivatives according to the following rule.

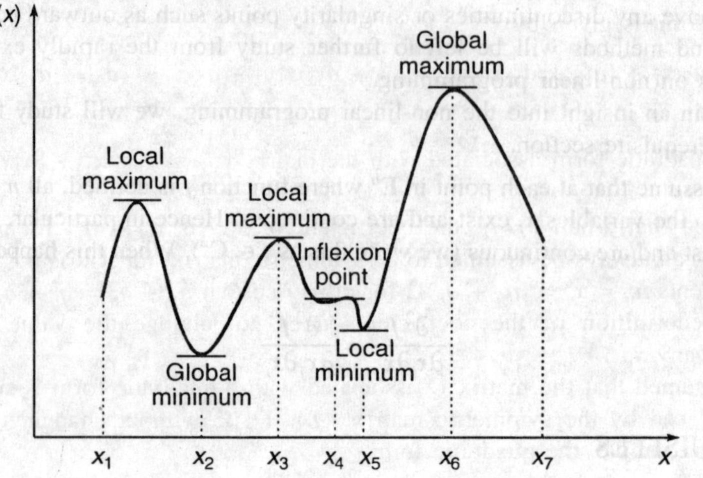

Figure 6.1

If at a stationary point x^* of $f(x)$, the first $n - 1$ derivatives vanish and $f^{(n)}(x^*) \neq 0$, then at $x = x^*$, $f(x)$ has (i) inflexion point if n is odd and (ii) an extreme point if n is even. This extreme point will be a maximum if $f^{(n)}(x^*) < 0$ and minimum if $f^{(n)}(x^*) > 0$.

For a function f of *n variables* $f(x_1, x_2, \ldots, x_n)$, the *necessary condition* is $\nabla f(x^*) = 0$.

For a function of *n variables*, a *sufficient condition* for a stationary point x^* to be an extremum is for the Hessian matrix H evaluated at x^* to be (i) positive definite when x^* is a minimum point, (ii) negative definite when x^* is a maximum point and (iii) indefinite when x^* is a point of inflexion. Now, we will discuss Hessian matrices.

Extreme points will be taken up after the discussion of convex and concave functions.

6.2.2 Quadratic Forms

A function of n variables $f(x_1, x_2,\ldots, x_n)$ is called a quadratic form (QF) if

$$f(x_1, x_2,\ldots, x_n) = \sum_{i=1}^{m} \sum_{j=1}^{n} q_{ij}x_i x_j = X^T QX$$

where $Q = (q_{ij})$ and $\mathbf{X} = (x_1, x_2, \ldots, x_n)^T$.

Let $x = (x_1, x_2)$ and $Q = (a_{ij})_{2\times2}$ i.e $Q = \begin{pmatrix} a_{11} & a_{12} \\ a_{21} & a_{22} \end{pmatrix}$

then the quadratic form is given by

$$f(x_1, x_2) = a_{11}x_1^2 + (a_{21} + a_{12})x_1x_2 + a_{22}x_2^2$$

Let $x = (x_1, x_2, x_3)$ and $Q = (a_{ij})_{3\times3}$ i.e $Q = \begin{pmatrix} a_{11} & a_{12} & a_{13} \\ a_{21} & a_{22} & a_{23} \\ a_{31} & a_{32} & a_{33} \end{pmatrix}$

then the quadratic form is given by

$$f(x_1, x_2, x_3) = a_{11}x_1^2 + (a_{21} + a_{12})x_1x_2 + (a_{13} + a_{31})x_1x_3 + a_{22}x_2^2 + (a_{23} + a_{32})x_2x_3 + a_{33}x_3^2$$

For example, the quadratic form associated with the matrix $\begin{pmatrix} 1 & 4 \\ 4 & 3 \end{pmatrix}$ is $x_1^2 + 8x_1x_2 + 3x_2^2$.

It will be noted that when $i \neq j$, the coefficient of x_ix_j is $q_{ij} + q_{ji}$. From this, it follows immediately that Q can always be assumed to be symmetric matrix, for if it is not, we can uniquely define new coefficients $a_{ij} = a_{ji} = (q_{ij} + q_{ji})/2$ for all i, j so that $a_{ij} + a_{ji} = q_{ij} + q_{ji}$ and $A = (a_{ij})$ is symmetric. This redefinition of the coefficients does not change the value of the function $f(x_1, x_2, \ldots, x_n)$ for any x_i.

It is always assumed that the matrix Q associated with a quadratic form is symmetric. If it is not, it may be replaced by the symmetric matrix $(Q + Q^T)/2$ without changing the value of the quadratic form. For example, the quadratic form

$$(x_1, x_2, x_3)\begin{pmatrix} 1 & 0 & 1 \\ 2 & 7 & 6 \\ 3 & 0 & 2 \end{pmatrix}\begin{pmatrix} x_1 \\ x_2 \\ x_3 \end{pmatrix}$$

is the same as the quadratic form

$$(x_1, x_2, x_3)\begin{pmatrix} 1 & 1 & 2 \\ 1 & 7 & 3 \\ 2 & 3 & 2 \end{pmatrix}\begin{pmatrix} x_1 \\ x_2 \\ x_3 \end{pmatrix}$$

Note that the matrix in the second case is symmetric.

The following definitions for a matrix (and also the quadratic form) are to be noted.

1. A matrix Q is positive definite ↔ the Quadratic form $X^TQX > 0$ for all $X \neq 0$.

   e.g., $\begin{pmatrix} 2 & -1 \\ -1 & 2 \end{pmatrix}$

   Note: "↔" denotes if and only if.

2. A matrix is positive semi definite ↔ the quadratic form $X^TQX \geq 0$ for all X and there exists an $X \neq 0$ such that $X^TQX = 0$.

   e.g., $\begin{pmatrix} 1 & -1 \\ -1 & 1 \end{pmatrix}$

3. A matrix Q is negative definite ↔ $-Q$ is positive definite, i.e. $X^TQX < 0$ for all $X \neq 0$

   e.g., $\begin{pmatrix} -2 & 1 \\ 1 & -3 \end{pmatrix}$

4. A matrix is negative semi definite $\leftrightarrow -Q$ is positive semi definite.

e.g., $\begin{pmatrix} -1 & 1 \\ 1 & -1 \end{pmatrix}$

5. A matrix Q is indefinite if X^TQX is positive for some X and negative for some other X.

e.g., $\begin{pmatrix} 1 & -1 \\ 1 & -2 \end{pmatrix}$

EXAMPLE

1. $z = x_1^2 + 2x_1x_2 + x_2^2 = (x_1 + x_2)^2$ is positive definite.
2. $z = x_1^2 - 2x_1x_2 + x_2^2 = (x_1 - x_2)^2$ is positive semi definite since it is never negative but is zero whenever $x_1 = x_2$. And in this case $-z$ is negative semi definite.
3. $z = x_1^2 - 2x_1x_2 - x_2^2$ is indefinite since $z > 0$ when $x_1 = 5$, $x_2 = 0$, and $z < 0$ when $x_1 = 0$, $x_2 = 5$.
4. $z = -x_1^2 + 3x_1x_2 - 4x_2^2 = -(x_1^2 - 3x_1x_2 + 4x_2^2)$ is negative definite when $x = (x_1, x_2) \neq 0$.

6.2.2.1 *Principal minor*

If Q is an $n \times n$ matrix, then the principal minor of order k is a sub matrix of size $k \times k$ obtained by deleting any $n - k$ rows and their corresponding columns from the matrix Q.
e.g.,

Let
$$Q = \begin{pmatrix} 1 & 2 & 3 \\ 4 & 5 & 6 \\ 7 & 8 & 9 \end{pmatrix}$$

Principal minors of order 1 are essentially the diagonal elements 1, 5, and 9. The principal minors of order 2 are the following 2×2 matrices.

$$\begin{pmatrix} 1 & 2 \\ 4 & 5 \end{pmatrix}, \begin{pmatrix} 1 & 3 \\ 7 & 9 \end{pmatrix} \text{ and } \begin{pmatrix} 5 & 6 \\ 8 & 9 \end{pmatrix}$$

The determinant of a principal minor is called the *principal determinant*. For an $n \times n$ square matrix, there are in all $2^n - 1$ principal determinants.

Leading principal minor of order k of an $n \times n$ square matrix is obtained by deleting the last $n - k$ rows and their corresponding columns. For the matrix Q in the above example, the leading principal minor of order 2 is $\begin{pmatrix} 1 & 2 \\ 4 & 5 \end{pmatrix}$, while that of order 3 is the matrix Q itself. The number of leading principal minor determinants of an $n \times n$ matrix is n.

There are some easier tests to determine whether a given matrix and the quadratic form is positive definite, negative definite, positive semi definite, negative semi definite or indefinite. All these tests are valid only when the matrix is symmetric. If the square matrix Q is not symmetric, change Q to $(Q + Q^T)/2$ and then apply the following tests.

Positive definite matrices	1. All diagonal elements must be positive 2. All the leading principal determinants must be positive
Positive semi definite matrices	1. All diagonal elements are non negative 2. All the principal determinants are non negative
Negative definite (semi definite) matrices	Test the negative of that matrix for positive definite (positive semi definite) OR The value of kth principal minor determinants of the matrix has the sign of $(-1)^k$, $k = 1, 2, \ldots, n$ for negative definite and is either zero or has the sign of $(-1)^k$, $k = 1, 2, \ldots, n$ for negative semi definite
Indefinite matrices	At least two of its diagonal elements are of opposite signs (sufficient test)

6.2.3 Convex and Concave Functions

A function of n variables $f(x_1, x_2, \ldots, x_n)$ is said to be a convex function if and only if for any two points $x^{(1)}$ and $x^{(2)}$ and $0 \le \lambda \le 1$,

$$f[\lambda x^{(1)} + (1 - \lambda)x^{(2)}] \le \lambda f(x^{(1)}) + (1 - \lambda)\, f(x^{(2)})$$

It is said to be strictly convex if $\le$ can be replaced by $<$.

A function $f(x_1, x_2, \ldots, x_n)$ is a concave function if and only if $-f(x_1, x_2, \ldots, x_n)$ is a convex function.

Geometrically it means that if a function is convex (concave) and if a line is drawn between any two points on the surface of the function, the line segment joining these two points will lie entirely above (below) that function or on that function. In other words, $f(x)$ is convex if it is always bending upwards. It is strictly convex if the line segment actually lies entirely above this graph except at the end points of the line segment.

For a function of a single variable, if $f(x)$ possesses a second derivative everywhere, then $f(x)$ is convex if and only if $d^2f(x)/dx^2 \ge 0$ for all values of x (for which $f(x)$ is defined). For strictness, we replace $\ge$ by $>$. Similarly, $f(x)$ is concave if and only if $d^2f(x)/dx^2 \le 0$.

Just as the second derivative can be used (when it exists everywhere) to check whether a function of a single variable is convex or not, so second partial derivatives can be used to check functions of several variables, although in a more complicated way.

For a function of two variables $f(x_1, x_2)$, f is convex if and only if the following three conditions hold for all possible values of (x_1, x_2), assuming that these partial derivatives exist everywhere. Again strictness can be viewed if $\ge$ can be replaced by $>$.

$$\frac{\partial^2 f(x_1, x_2)}{\partial x_1^2}\frac{\partial^2 f(x_1, x_2)}{\partial x_2^2} - \left[\frac{\partial^2 f(x_1, x_2)}{\partial x_1 \partial x_2}\right]^2 \ge 0$$

$$\frac{\partial^2 f(x_1, x_2)}{\partial x_1^2} \ge 0$$

$$\frac{\partial^2 f(x_1, x_2)}{\partial x_2^2} \geq 0$$

Note:

- The function would be concave if ≥ can be replaced by ≤ in the second and the third conditions.
- The definition of a convex (concave) function is not dependent on the definition of the function being continuous (discontinuous).
- A function can be concave over one region and convex over another.
- A linear function is both concave and convex.

The convexity and the concavity of the function of n variables is given with the help of the Hessian matrix.

The gradient of a function $f(x_1, x_2, \ldots, x_n)$ is given by

$$\nabla f(x_1, x_2, \ldots, x_n) = \left[\frac{\partial f}{\partial x_1}, \frac{\partial f}{\partial x_2}, \ldots, \frac{\partial f}{\partial x_n}\right]$$

The Hessian matrix of a function $f(x_1, x_2, \ldots, x_n)$ is an $n \times n$ symmetric matrix given by

$$H_f(x_1, x_2, \ldots, x_n) = \left[\frac{\partial^2 f}{\partial x_i x_j}\right]$$

The following table gives the test for the convexity or the concavity of the function $f(x_1, x_2, \ldots, x_n)$ based on the Hessian matrices.

f is convex	H_f is positive definite or positive semi definite for all values of $x_1, x_2, \ldots, x_n$
f is concave	H_f is negative definite or negative semi definite for all values of $x_1, x_2, \ldots, x_n$

e.g., For the function

$$f(x, y, z) = 3x^2 + 2y^2 + z^2 - 2xy - 2xz + 2yz - 6x - 4y - 2z$$

$$\nabla f(x, y, z) = \begin{pmatrix} 6x - 2y - 2z - 6 \\ 4y - 2x + 2z - 4 \\ 2z - 2x + 2y - 2 \end{pmatrix}$$

and

$$H_f(x, y, z) = \begin{pmatrix} 6 & -2 & -2 \\ -2 & 4 & 2 \\ -2 & 2 & 2 \end{pmatrix}$$

To show that f is a convex function, we test H for positive definite or positive semi definite property.

Note that

(i) H is symmetric.

(ii) All diagonal elements are positive.

(iii) The leading principal determinants are

$$|6| > 0, \begin{vmatrix} 6 & -2 \\ -2 & 4 \end{vmatrix} = 20 > 0, |H| = 16 > 0$$

Hence, H is a positive definite matrix, which implies that f is a convex function. When H_f is positive definite, f is said to be strictly convex with a unique minimum point.

So far in our discussion, convexity has been treated as a general property of a function. However, many non-convex functions do not satisfy the conditions for convexity over certain intervals for the respective variables. Therefore, it is meaningful to talk about a function being convex over a certain region. A function is said to be convex within a neighbourhood of a specified point if its second derivatives (or partial derivatives) satisfy the conditions for convexity at that point.

If a function f is convex then the function $-f$ is concave and vice versa. If f and g are two convex functions then $f + g$ is a convex function.

The concept of convex function leads to the related concept of a convex set. If $f(x_1, x_2, \ldots, x_n)$ is a convex function, then the collection of points that lie above or on the graph of f form a convex set. Similarly, the collection of points that lie below or on the graph of a concave function is also a convex set. Thus, convex sets may be viewed intuitively as a collection of points whose bottom boundary is a convex function and whose top boundary is a concave function. With this we can define a convex set as follows:

A convex set is a collection of points such that for each pair of points in the collection, the entire line segment joining these two points is also in the collection.

Thus, for non-convex sets, there may exist pairs of points such that the line segment joining them does not lie entirely within the set.

An extreme point of a convex set is a point in the set that does not lie on any line segment which joins two other points in the set.

Remarks

1. If a function is a convex function defined on a closed and bounded set then the local minimum of $f(x)$ is a global minimum of $f(x)$. If the function is concave and defined on a convex set then the local maximum is a global maximum.
2. If $f(x)$ is a concave function defined on a closed and bounded convex set then there exists a global minimum at an extreme point of that convex set.

6.3 NON-LINEAR PROGRAMMING PROBLEMS

The general programming problem can be formulated as follows:

It is desired to determine values for n non-negative variables $x_1, x_2, \ldots, x_n$ which satisfy the m inequalities or equations $g_i(x_1, x_2, \ldots, x_n)$ $(\leq, =, \geq)$ b_i, $i = 1, 2, \ldots, m$ and maximizes or minimizes the objective function $Z = f(x_1, x_2, \ldots, x_n)$.

If both the constraints and the objective function are linear, then the problem is of linear programming. If any of the objective function or the constraints contain non-linear functions, then we have a *non-linear programming problem* (NLPP).

So, the general *NLPP* can be stated mathematically as:

Find $x_1, x_2, \ldots, x_n$

so as to optimize $Z = f(x_1, x_2, \ldots, x_n)$

subject to $g_i(x_1, x_2, \ldots, x_n)\ (\le, =, \ge)\ b_i,\ i = 1, 2, \ldots, m$ and $m < n$

and $x_j \ge 0,\ j = 1, 2, \ldots, n$

where at least one of f and g_i's is non-linear.

Note:

1. In the above form, if both f and all g_i's are convex functions, then it is termed as convex programming.
2. In the above form, if $f(x)$ is a quadratic expression and all g_i's are linear, then it is termed as quadratic programming.

If no inequalities appear in the constraint set $g_i\ (\le, =, \ge)\ b_i$ in a NLPP and no non-negative conditions are imposed on the variables, then such a class of problems are called *classical optimization problems.* In such problems, it is assumed that the functions considered possess continuous first and second derivatives and partial derivatives everywhere.

A *classical optimization problem* looks like:

Find $x_1, x_2, \ldots, x_n$

so as to optimize $Z = f(x_1, x_2, \ldots, x_n)$

subject to $g_i(x_1, x_2, \ldots, x_n) = b_i,\ i = 1, 2, \ldots, m$ and $m < n$

Such problems can be solved by using calculus. The techniques of solving such problems are called *classical optimization methods.*

These classical optimization methods serve as a base in understanding the solution procedures of a general NLPP. Before starting our discussion on such methods, let us note some points regarding the position of the solution depending on the nature of a function.

Note 1: While dealing with bounded continuous functions, a maximum or minimum will always exist, either at a point interior to the boundaries of feasible solution variables or at the boundary itself. This is so because a bounded function must always possess a maximum or minimum value somewhere within the region of interest.

Note 2: If the function is continuous over the region of interest, stationary points can be located through the use of differential calculus, provided all derivatives can be found. A stationary point will exist in the interior or at a boundary if the partial derivatives of an *unconstrained* function vanish (become zero) at a particular solution vector.

Note 3: If there are finitely many discontinuities in the function, then one (or more) of these derivatives might fail to exist. These points would then need to be considered separately.

Note 4: An optimal solution might exist at a boundary point defined by the constraints on the problem. This is precisely the case in linear programming, which is a special case of non-linear programming.

Thus, in short, if we are to devise a procedure for solving non-linear programming problems, we need to examine the following three:

1. All points at which the continuous first derivatives are all zero.
2. All points interior to the region at which discontinuities exist for the first derivatives.
3. Points on the boundaries of the solution space.

Some of the cases arising while searching for the optimum if the function is concave/convex are:

1. *Maximum or Minimum—Unconstrained:* If the non-linear programming problem consists of only an objective function, $f(x)$, and if the objective function is convex (concave), then a unique (single) optimum solution will be found at a point (a) interior to the feasible region where all derivatives vanish, or (b) at a boundary point.
2. *Maximization—Constrained:* If the NLPP consists of both an objective function and constraints, the uniqueness of an optimal solution depends on the nature of both the objective function and the constraint set. If the objective function is concave, and the constraint set forms a convex region, there will be only one maximizing solution to the problem. Hence, any stationary point must be a global maximum solution.
3. *Minimization—Constrained:* If the non-linear programming problem consists of both an objective function and constraints, and if the objective function is convex and the constraint set also forms a convex region, then any stationary point will be a global minimizing solution.
4. *Minimizing (Maximizing) a concave (convex) function:* If a concave (convex) function is to be minimized (maximized), then the optimal solution will only be found at one of the extreme points of the constraint set.
5. *The linear function:* A linear function is both convex and concave. Thus, if the solution space is convex, then a solution will always be found at a boundary point. This observation is precisely what gave rise to the simplex algorithm of LPP.
6. *Non-convex regions:* If the constraint set forms a non-convex solution space, then any algorithmic procedure based on local properties of the NLPP might produce a local stationary point that may be neither globally maximum nor minimum. This is valid even if the objective function is linear.

6.4 UNCONSTRAINED OPTIMIZATION

6.4.1 Functions with Single Variables

Here we use the rules and conditions regarding derivatives and convexity and concavity to solve problems.

EXAMPLE 6.1: Consider the function $f(x) = x^3 - 3x + 6$. The necessary condition for a minimizing solution is that the first derivatives vanish.

Hence,
$$\frac{df(x)}{dx} = 3x^2 - 3 = 0$$

Hence, $x^* = 1$ or -1 are the stationary points.
Now we look for the value of the second derivative at these points.

$$\frac{d^2 f(x)}{dx^2} = 6x$$

At $x^* = 1$, $(d^2f(x)/dx^2)^* = 6 > 0$. Therefore, this solution is a minimizing secondary point or a local minima.

$x^* = -1$, $(d^2f(x)/dx^2)^* = -6 < 0$. Therefore, this solution is a local maxima.

EXAMPLE 6.2: Consider $f(x) = x_4$. Now, $f^{(1)}(x) = 4x^3 = 0$ implies $x^* = 0$ a stationary point. Also $f^{(1)}(0) = f^{(2)}(0) = f^{(3)}(0) = 0$. But $f^{(4)}(0) = 24 > 0$. Hence $x^* = 0$ is a minimum point. Here since the function is convex, it is a global minima.

EXAMPLE 6.3: For $f(x) = x^3$, $f^{(1)}(x) = 3x^2 = 0$ implies $x^* = 0$ a stationary point. Also $f^{(2)}(x) = 6x = 0$. But $f^{(3)}(0) \neq 0$ at $n = 3$ and n is odd. So 0 is an inflexion point.

6.4.2 Multi Variable Functions

Here we make use of the partial derivatives and the Hessian matrix fundamentals and tests given in Section 6.2.

EXAMPLE 6.4: Consider the function $f(x_1, x_2, x_3) = x_1 + 2x_3 + x_2x_3 - x_1^2 - x_2^2 - x_3^2$. The necessary condition for a stationary point is $\nabla f(x) = 0$. This gives $\partial f/\partial x_1 = 1 - 2x_1 = 0$ which gives $x_1 = 1/2$.

$$\frac{\partial f}{\partial x_2} = x_3 - 2x_2 = 0$$

$$\frac{\partial f}{\partial x_3} = 2 + x_2 - 2x_3 = 0$$

Solving them we get (1/2, 2/3, 4/3).
To check for the sufficiency, consider the Hessian matrix.

$$H_f(X) = \begin{pmatrix} \dfrac{\partial^2 f}{\partial x_1^2} & \dfrac{\partial^2 f}{\partial x_1 \partial x_2} & \dfrac{\partial^2 f}{\partial x_1 \partial x_3} \\ \dfrac{\partial^2 f}{\partial x_2 \partial x_1} & \dfrac{\partial^2 f}{\partial x_2^2} & \dfrac{\partial^2 f}{\partial x_2 \partial x_3} \\ \dfrac{\partial^2 f}{\partial x_3 \partial x_1} & \dfrac{\partial^2 f}{\partial x_3 \partial x_2} & \dfrac{\partial^2 f}{\partial x_3^2} \end{pmatrix} = \begin{pmatrix} -2 & 0 & 0 \\ 0 & -2 & 1 \\ 0 & 1 & -2 \end{pmatrix}$$

As the principal minor determinants of order 1×1, 2×2 and 3×3 have values as -2, 4, -6, respectively, H is negative definite and the solution (1/2, 2/3, 4/3) is a local maximum. Even by examining the minors of the Hessian matrix, we can test the solutions for local maxima or minima.

Test (1): We know that for the extreme point to be a local minimum, the Hessian matrix H must be positive definite. This can be concluded of all its leading principal minors if order 1×1 are positive. We again remind the reader that a principal minor of H is the determinant of a square sub matrix whose elements lie on the diagonal of H, whereas leading principal minor is one whose (1, 1) element is the (1, 1) element of H.

Test (2): H is negative definite, if the signs of all even leading principal minors is positive.

Test (3): If the signs of determinants do not meet the conditions in Test (1) and Test (2) above, then the extreme point may be either a maximum or minimum or neither. In this case, H is termed as semi-definite or indefinite.

To make this simpler, consider the following Hessian matrix of the second partial derivatives evaluated at the stationary point x^*.

$$H_f(X) = \begin{pmatrix} \dfrac{\partial^2 f}{\partial x_1^2} & \dfrac{\partial^2 f}{\partial x_1 \partial x_2} & \cdots & \dfrac{\partial^2 f}{\partial x_1 \partial x_n} \\ \dfrac{\partial^2 f}{\partial x_2 \partial x_1} & \dfrac{\partial^2 f}{\partial {x_2}^2} & & \dfrac{\partial^2 f}{\partial x_2 \partial x_n} \\ \cdots & \cdots & & \cdots \\ \dfrac{\partial^2 f}{\partial x_n \partial x_1} & \dfrac{\partial^2 f}{\partial x_n \partial x_2} & & \dfrac{\partial^2 f}{\partial {x_n}^2} \end{pmatrix}$$

For this matrix, there exists exactly n-determinants formed from the single element in the upper-left-hand corner, successively through the entire matrix moving from upper left to lower right. Designate these determinants by $D_1, D_2, \ldots, D_n$.

The following tests are valid:

- For a stationary point to be a minimum, it is sufficient that $D_1, D_2, \ldots, D_n$ be all positive.
- For a stationary point to be a maximum, it is sufficient that all even numbered determinants are positive and all odd determinants are negative.

EXAMPLE 6.5: Consider the function $f(x_1, x_2) = x_1 + 2x_2 + x_1x_2 - x_1^2 - x_2^2$. Solving it according to the lines of the above example, the solution is (4/3, 5/3), the Hessian matrix is obtained as

$$H_f(X) = \begin{pmatrix} -2 & 1 \\ 1 & -2 \end{pmatrix}$$

The principal minor determinants of H are –2 and 3. Since they are alternate in signs, the matrix is negative definite and the point obtained (4/3, 5/3) is a local maximum.

EXAMPLE 6.6: Consider the function $f(x_1, x_2) = 8x_1x_2 + 3x_2^2$. We obtain the stationary point as (0,0). The Hessian matrix is

$$H_f(X) = \begin{pmatrix} 0 & 8 \\ 8 & 6 \end{pmatrix}$$

which cannot be concluded for definiteness. But if we transform it by the process of diagonalization it becomes

$$H_f(X) = \begin{pmatrix} -32/3 & 0 \\ 0 & 6 \end{pmatrix}$$

It turns out that H is indefinite. Thus, the point (0, 0) is a saddle point.

For such two-dimensional functions, instead of checking the Hessian matrix, we can directly take the conditions for the minimum.

$$\frac{\partial^2 f(x_1, x_2)}{\partial x_1^2}\frac{\partial^2 f(x_1, x_2)}{\partial x_2^2} - \left[\frac{\partial^2 f(x_1, x_2)}{\partial x_1 \partial x_2}\right]^2 > 0$$

$$\frac{\partial^2 f(x_1, x_2)}{\partial x_1^2} > 0$$

For maximum, the above instances are replaced by < and for weaker instances for the minimizing and the maximizing values, by ≥ and ≤, respectively. They are sufficient because they guarantee that the function is convex over the solution space.

EXAMPLE 6.7: Consider the function $f(x_1, x_2) = -2x_1 + x_1x_2 + x_1^2 + x_2^2$. Verify that the stationary values obtained after setting the first partial derivatives equal to zero are $(x_1, x_2) = (4/3, -2/3)$ and the two conditions

$$\frac{\partial^2 f(x_1, x_2)}{\partial x_1^2}\frac{\partial^2 f(x_1, x_2)}{\partial x_2^2} - \left[\frac{\partial^2 f(x_1, x_2)}{\partial x_1 \partial x_2}\right]^2 > 0$$

$$\frac{\partial^2 f(x_1, x_2)}{\partial x_1^2} > 0$$

give 3 > 0 and 2 > 0 respectively. Therefore, the point (4/3, –2/3) is a global minimum.

6.5 CONSTRAINED OPTIMIZATION

6.5.1 Equality Constraints

Here in the classical optimization problem, we discuss instances when the constraints are equations.

6.5.1.1 Method 1: Method of substitution

Since the constraint set $g_i(x)$ is continuous and differentiable, any variable in the constraint set can be expressed in terms of the remaining variables. When substituted in the objective function, the constraint variables and the objective function can be optimized by unconstrained optimization methods.

6.5.1.2 *Method 2: Lagrange multiplier method*

We now consider the classical approach to solve classical optimization problem. We wish to find point x^* which will yield the absolute maximum or minimum of $z = f(x)$ for those x which satisfy $g_i(x) = b_i$, $i = 1, 2, \ldots, m$ and $m < n$. We shall assume that f, g_i and their first derivatives are continuous, i.e. $f, g_i \in \mathbf{C}^1$.

It will be convenient to begin by studying the case in which there are only two variables and a single constraint. In other words, we wish to find the necessary conditions which $x_0 = (x_1', x_2')$ must satisfy if $Z = f(x_1, x_2)$ takes on a maximum or minimum at x_0 subject to $g(x_1, x_2) = b$. As $f, g \in \mathbf{C}^1$, suppose that either $\partial g/\partial x_1$ or $\partial g/\partial x_2$ does not vanish at x_0. To be specific, suppose $\partial g(x_0)/\partial x_2 \neq 0$. Then, we can solve $g(x_1, x_2) - b = 0$ explicitly for x_2 to get $x_2 = \phi(x_1)$. Any point $[x_1, \phi(x_1)]$ then belongs to the set of points satisfying $g(x_1, x_2) = b$. Thus, we can eliminate x_2 in $f(x_1, x_2)$ to obtain $Z = h(x_1) = f(x_1, \phi(x_1))$. If it takes on a relative maximum at x_0 for x satisfying $g(x) = b$, then the function $h(x_1)$ has an unconstrained relative maximum at x_1'. Similarly, if f takes on a relative minimum at x_0 for x satisfying $g(x) = b$, then the function $h(x_1)$ has an unconstrained relative minimum at x_1'. Since $\phi(x_1)$ is differentiable in the neighbourhood of x_1', $h(x_1)$ must be differentiable in the neighbourhood of x_1'. Since $h(x_1)$ has an unconstrained relative maximum or minimum at x_0, $dh(x_1')/dx_1 = 0$.

Therefore,

$$\frac{dh}{dx_1} = \frac{\partial f}{\partial x_1} + \frac{\partial f}{\partial x_2}\frac{\partial \varphi}{\partial x_1} = \frac{\partial f}{\partial x_1} - \frac{\partial f}{\partial x_2}\frac{\partial g/\partial x_1}{\partial g/\partial x_2}$$

Since
$$\frac{d\phi}{dx_1} = -\frac{\partial g/\partial x_1}{\partial g/\partial x_2}$$

we have
$$\frac{\partial f(x_0)}{\partial x_1} - \frac{\partial f(x_0)}{\partial x_2}\frac{\partial g(x_0)/\partial x_1}{\partial g(x_0)/\partial x_2} = 0$$

Let $\lambda = \dfrac{\partial f(x_0)/\partial x_2}{\partial g(x_0)/\partial x_2}$ because $\dfrac{\partial g(x_0)}{\partial x_2} \neq 0$

Thus, it is necessary that the point x_0 satisfies the equations

$$\frac{\partial f(x_0)}{\partial x_1} - \lambda\frac{\partial g(x_0)}{\partial x_1} = 0\,; \quad \frac{\partial f(x_0)}{\partial x_2} - \lambda\frac{\partial g(x_0)}{\partial x_2} = 0\,; \quad g(x_0) = b$$

provided that both the partial derivatives of g do not vanish at x_0.

The necessary conditions obtained above can be easily obtained as follows:
Form the function

$$F(\mathbf{X}, \lambda) = f(\mathbf{X}) + \lambda[b - g(\mathbf{X})]$$

and set to zero the partial derivatives of $\mathbf{F}(\mathbf{X}, \lambda)$ with respect to x_1, x_2 and λ (in taking the partial derivatives, treat all variables as being independent).
Thus,

$$\frac{\partial F}{\partial x_j} = \frac{\partial f}{\partial x_j} - \lambda\frac{\partial g}{\partial x_j} = 0 \quad i, j = 1, 2, \ldots, n$$

$$\frac{\partial F}{\partial \lambda} = b - g(X) = 0$$

The function $F(\mathbf{X}, \lambda)$ is called the ***Lagrangian function*** and λ is called a ***Lagrangian multiplier***.

Note that the necessary conditions so obtained become sufficient conditions for a maximum if $f(x)$ is concave (for a minimum if $f(x)$ is convex) with equality constraints.

For a general classical optimization problem with n variables and m constraint equations with $m < n$, the *necessary* conditions for the function to have a local optimum are as follows. For $X = (x_1, x_2, \ldots, x_n)$

Lagrange function

$$F(\mathbf{X}, \lambda) = f(\mathbf{X}) - \sum_{i=1}^{m} \lambda_i g_i(\mathbf{X})$$

Thus,

$$\frac{\partial F}{\partial x_j} = \frac{\partial f}{\partial x_j} - \sum_{i=1}^{m} \lambda_i \frac{\partial g_i}{\partial x_j} = 0 \qquad j = 1, 2, \ldots, n$$

$$\frac{\partial F}{\partial \lambda_i} = b_i - g_i(\mathbf{X}) = 0 \qquad i = 1, 2, \ldots, m$$

For any solution, x_0 to the above two conditions and the Lagrange multipliers are uniquely determined if the matrix of partial derivatives $\partial g_i/\partial x_j$ has rank m at x_0.

The above $m + n$ necessary conditions also become sufficient conditions for a maximum of the function $f(x)$ if it is concave (for a minimum of the function $f(x)$ if it is convex) and the constraints are equalities.

For a general problem, the sufficient conditions for an extreme point x to be a local minimum (maximum) of $f(x)$ subject to $g_i(x) = b_i$, $i = 1, 2, \ldots, m$ and $m < n$ is that the determinant of the bordered Hessian Matrix $D = \begin{pmatrix} 0 & H \\ H^T & Q \end{pmatrix}$ [order $(m + n) \times (m + n)$] is positive (negative) where

$$Q = \left[\frac{\partial^2 F(X, \lambda)}{\partial x_i \partial x_j}\right] \text{ (order } n \times n\text{)} \quad \text{and} \quad H = \left[\frac{\partial g_i(X)}{\partial x_j}\right] \text{ (order } m \times n\text{)}$$

The sufficient condition for the maxima and minima is determined by the signs of the last $(n - m)$ principal minors of the above matrix D.

1. If starting with the principal minor of order $(2m + 1)$, the extreme point gives the maximum value of the objective function when the signs of the last $(n - m)$ principal minors alternate starting with $(-1)^{m+1}$ sign.
2. If starting with the principal minor of order $(2m + 1)$, the extreme point gives the minimum value of the objective function when all signs of last $(n - m)$ principal minors are the same and of $(-1)^m$ type.

6.5.1.3 *Interpretation of the Lagrange multipliers*

Suppose x^* is the point where the function $Z = f(x)$ in the classical optimization problem attains the global optimum.

We calculate the partial derivatives of $Z^* = f(x^*)$; the global optimum with respect to b_i. We get

$$\frac{\partial Z^*}{\partial b_i} = \sum_{j=1}^{n} \frac{\partial f}{\partial x_j^*} \frac{\partial x_j^*}{\partial b_i} \tag{i}$$

Using $g_k(x^*) = b_k$

$$\sum_{j=1}^{n} \frac{\partial g_k}{\partial x_j^*} \frac{\partial x_j^*}{\partial b_i} = \delta_{ik}$$

where δ_{ik} is the Kronecker delta.

i.e. $$\delta_{ik} - \sum_{j=1}^{n} \frac{\partial g_k}{\partial x_j^*} \frac{\partial x_j^*}{\partial b_i} = 0 \qquad i, k = 1, 2, \ldots, m \qquad \text{(ii)}$$

Multiply (ii) by λ_k^*, sum over k and add to (i).
We get

$$\frac{\partial Z^*}{\partial b_i} = \sum_{k=1}^{m} \lambda_k^* \delta_{ik} + \sum_{j=1}^{m} \left[\frac{\partial f}{\partial x_j^*} - \sum_{k=1}^{m} \lambda_k^* \frac{\partial g_k}{\partial x_j^*} \right] \frac{\partial x_j^*}{\partial b_i}$$

Since x^* and λ^* must satisfy $\dfrac{\partial f(x^*)}{\partial x_j} - \sum_{i=1}^{m} \lambda_i \dfrac{\partial g_i(x^*)}{\partial x_j} = 0$

we have $\dfrac{\partial Z^*}{\partial b_i} = \lambda_i^*$.

Thus, we see that the partial derivative of the global optimum with respect to b_i is simply equal to the Lagrange multiplier λ_i^* evaluated at b_i. Frequently, Z will be a profit or a cost, and b_i will be the number of physical units of some resource. In this case, the physical dimensions of λ_i^* are rupees per unit of resource i, and λ_i^* can be interpreted as a price or value per unit of resource i. The Lagrange multipliers are thus the shadow prices or the imputed values. They tell us how much the maximum profit or the minimum cost will be changed if the quantity of resource i available is increased by one unit.

From a practical computational viewpoint, the method of Lagrange multipliers is not a particularly powerful procedure. However, for certain types of small problems, this method can sometimes be used successfully.

6.5.2 Inequality Constraints

Find $$X = (x_1, x_2, \ldots, x_n)$$

so as to optimize $$Z = f(X)$$

subject to $$g_i(x_1, x_2, \ldots, x_n) \le 0, \; i = 1, 2, \ldots, m \text{ and } m < n$$

where at least one of f and g_i's is non-linear.

The non-negativity conditions, if any, are made a part of the constraint set by writing $-x_j \le 0$.

6.5.2.1 Kuhn–Tucker conditions (necessary)

Consider the problem of maximization.

Find $$X = (x_1, x_2, \ldots, x_n)$$

so as to maximize $$Z = f(X)$$

subject to $\quad g_i(x_1, x_2, \ldots, x_n) \le 0, \quad i = 1, 2, \ldots, m$ and $m < n$

where at least one of f and g_i's is non-linear.

The non-negativity conditions, if any, are made a part of the constraint set by writing $-x_j \le 0$.

We add slacks S_i^2 to the constraints to convert them to equalities. Squaring ensures non-negative values and avoids $S_i \ge 0$ as an additional constraint.

Lagrange function can be formed as

$$F(X, S, \lambda) = f(X) - \sum_{i=1}^{m} \lambda_i [g_i(X) + S_i^2]$$

where λ_i are the Lagrange multipliers.

The necessary conditions for the extreme point to be local maximum are obtained by

$$\frac{\partial F}{\partial x_j} = \frac{\partial f}{\partial x_j} - \sum_{i=1}^{m} \lambda_i \frac{\partial g_i}{\partial x_j} = 0 \quad j = 1, 2, \ldots, n$$

$$\frac{\partial F}{\partial \lambda_i} = -[g_i(X) + S_i^2] = 0 \quad i = 1, 2, \ldots, m$$

$$\frac{\partial F}{\partial S_i} = -2S_i\lambda_i = 0$$

which can be further simplified as the following set of conditions.

$$\frac{\partial F}{\partial x_j} = \frac{\partial f}{\partial x_j} - \sum_{i=1}^{m} \lambda_i \frac{\partial g_i}{\partial x_j} = 0$$

$$\lambda_i g_i(X) = 0$$

$$g_i(X) \le 0 \quad \text{where } j = 1, 2, \ldots, n \text{ and } i = 1, 2, \ldots, m$$

$$\lambda_i \ge 0$$

Note:

1. For minimization problems or if constraints are $g_i(X) \ge 0$, then $\lambda_i \le 0$
2. For maximization problems or if constraints are $g_i(X) \le 0$, then $\lambda_i \ge 0$

Consider the maximization case. Because λ measures the rate of variation of f with respect to g ($\lambda = \partial f/\partial \mathbf{g}$), as the right-hand side of the constraint $\mathbf{g} \le 0$ increases above zero, the solution space becomes less constrained and hence f cannot decrease. This means that $\lambda \ge 0$. Similarly, for minimization, as a resource increases, f cannot increase, which implies that $\lambda \le 0$. If the constraints are equalities, that is $\mathbf{g}(\mathbf{X}) = 0$, then λ becomes unrestricted in sign. The above set of conditions applies to minimization case as well with the exception that $\lambda \le 0$. In both maximization and minimization, the λ corresponding to the equality constraints are unrestricted in sign.

6.5.2.2 Kuhn–Tucker conditions (sufficient)

The Kuhn–Tucker necessary conditions are sufficient if $f(X)$ is concave and all $g_i(X)$ are convex functions of X.

Required condition		
	Objective function	*Set of the solution space*
Maximization	Concave	Convex
Minimization	Convex	Convex

The convexity of the solution space can be established by checking directly the convexity or the concavity of the constraint functions. To provide these conditions in summary, we define the generalized NLPP as

Maximize or Minimize $Z = f(X)$

subject to $g_i(X) \leq 0, \quad i = 1, 2, \ldots, r$

$$g_i(X) \geq 0, \quad i = r + 1, r + 2, \ldots, p$$

$$g_i(X) = 0, \quad i = p + 1, p + 2, \ldots, m$$

Lagrangian function is formulated as

$$F(X, S, \lambda) = f(X) - \sum_{i=1}^{r} \lambda_i [g_i(X) + S_i^2] - \sum_{i=r+1}^{p} \lambda_i [g_i(X) + S_i^2] - \sum_{i=p+1}^{m} \lambda_i [g_i(X) + S_i^2]$$

where λ_i is the Lagrange multiplier associated with the constraint i. The conditions for establishing the convexity of the solution space by directly checking the convexity or concavity of the constraint functions are given in the following table.

	$f(X)$	$g_i(X)$	λ_i	
Maximization	Concave	Convex	≥ 0	$1 \leq i \leq r$
		Concave	≤ 0	$r + 1 \leq i \leq p$
		Linear	Unrestricted	$p + 1 \leq i \leq m$
Minimization	Convex	Convex	≤ 0	$1 \leq i \leq r$
		Concave	≥ 0	$r + 1 \leq i \leq p$
		Linear	unrestricted	$p + 1 \leq i \leq m$

The given conditions yield a concave Lagrange function $F(X, S, \lambda)$ in case of maximization and a convex $F(X, S, \lambda)$ in case of minimization. This result can be verified by seeing that if $g_i(X)$ is convex, then $\lambda_i g_i(X)$ is convex if $\lambda_i \geq 0$, and $\lambda_i g_i(X)$ is concave if $\lambda_i \leq 0$. Similar interpretations can be established for all the remaining conditions. In both maximization and minimization, the Lagrange multipliers corresponding to the equality constraints must be unrestricted in sign.

No sufficiency conditions can be established for non-linear programming problems with inequality constraints. Unless the conditions given in the above two tables can be established in advance, there is no way of verifying whether a non-linear programming algorithm converges to a local or a global optimum.

These K-T conditions help in solving quadratic programming problems.

EXAMPLE 6.8: Solve the following NLPP.

Minimize $z = f(x_1, x_2) = 3x_1^2 + x_2^2 + 2x_1x_2 + 6x_1 + 2x_2$

subject to the constraints: $2x_1 - x_2 = 4$

Solution: The Lagrangian function is

$$F(x_1, x_2, \lambda) = 3x_1^2 + x_2^2 + 2x_1x_2 + 6x_1 + 2x_2 - \lambda(2x_1 - x_2 - 4)$$

The necessary conditions for the stationary point are

$$\frac{\partial F}{\partial x_1} = 6x_1 + 2x_2 + 6 - 2\lambda = 0$$

$$\frac{\partial F}{\partial x_2} = 4x_2 + 2x_1 + 2 + \lambda = 0$$

$$\frac{\partial F}{\partial \lambda} = -(2x_1 - x_2 - 4) = 0$$

The solution to these simultaneous equations gives $x_1 = 1$, $x_2 = -2$ and $\lambda = 4$.

Since

$$\Delta_3 = \begin{pmatrix} 0 & 2 & -1 \\ 2 & 6 & 2 \\ -1 & 2 & 4 \end{pmatrix} < 0$$

$$\Delta_2 = \begin{pmatrix} 0 & 2 \\ 2 & 6 \end{pmatrix} < 0$$

The given solution provides the minimum solution to the given NLPP.

Hence, $x_1 = 1$, $x_2 = -2$ with minimum $z = 5$

EXAMPLE 6.9: Solve the following NLPP.

Maximize $Z = f(x_1, x_2) = -x_1^2 - x_2^2 + 6x_1 + 8x_2$

subject to the constraints: $4x_1 + 3x_2 = 16$

$3x_1 + 5x_2 = 15$

Solution: The Lagrangian function is

$$F(x_1, x_2, \lambda_1, \lambda_2) = -x_1^2 - x_2^2 + 6x_1 + 8x_2 - \lambda_1(4x_1 + 3x_2 - 16) - \lambda_2(3x_1 + 5x_2 - 15)$$

The necessary conditions for the stationary point are

$$\frac{\partial F}{\partial x_1} = 6 - 2x_1 - 4\lambda_1 - 3\lambda_2 = 0$$

$$\frac{\partial F}{\partial x_2} = 8 - 2x_2 - 3\lambda_1 - 5\lambda_2 = 0$$

$$\frac{\partial F}{\partial \lambda_1} = -(4x_1 + 3x_2 - 16) = 0$$

$$\frac{\partial F}{\partial \lambda_2} = -(3x_1 + 5x_2 - 15) = 0$$

Solving them we get, $x_1 = 35/11$, $x_2 = 12/11$.

The bordered Hessian matrix is given by

$$H = \begin{bmatrix} 0 & 0 & \vdots & 4 & 3 \\ 0 & 0 & \vdots & 3 & 5 \\ \cdots & \cdots & \cdots & \cdots & \cdots \\ 4 & 3 & \vdots & -2 & 0 \\ 3 & 5 & \vdots & 0 & -2 \end{bmatrix}$$

Since, $|H| = 121 > 0$, the obtained point is minimum.

EXAMPLE 6.10: Solve the following NLPP.

Minimize $$z = f(x_1, x_2, x_3) = 4x_1^2 + 2x_2^2 + x_3^2 - 4x_1x_2$$

subject to the constraints: $$x_1 + x_2 + x_3 = 15$$

$$2x_1 - x_2 + 2x_3 = 20.$$

Solution: The Lagrangian function is

$$F(x_1, x_2, x_3, \lambda_1, \lambda_2) = 4x_1^2 + 2x_2^2 + x_3^2 - 4x_1x_2 - \lambda_1(x_1 + x_2 + x_3 - 15) - \lambda_2(2x_1 - x_2 + 2x_3 - 20)$$

The necessary conditions for the stationary point are

$$\frac{\partial F}{\partial x_1} = 8x_1 - 4x_2 - \lambda_1 - 2\lambda_2 = 0$$

$$\frac{\partial F}{\partial x_2} = 4x_2 - 4x_1 - \lambda_1 + \lambda_2 = 0$$

$$\frac{\partial F}{\partial x_3} = 2x_3 - \lambda_1 - 2\lambda_2 = 0$$

$$\frac{\partial F}{\partial \lambda_1} = -(x_1 + x_2 + x_3 - 15) = 0$$

$$\frac{\partial F}{\partial \lambda_2} = -(2x_1 - x_2 + 2x_3 - 20) = 0$$

The solution to these simultaneous equations gives

$$x_1 = \frac{33}{9},\ x_2 = \frac{10}{3},\ x_3 = 8,\ \lambda_1 = \frac{40}{9},\ \lambda_2 = \frac{52}{9}$$

The bordered Hessian matrix at this solution gives

$$H = \begin{bmatrix} 0 & 0 & \vdots & 1 & 1 & 1 \\ 0 & 0 & \vdots & 2 & -1 & 2 \\ \cdots & \cdots & \cdots & \cdots & \cdots & \cdots \\ 1 & 2 & \vdots & 8 & -4 & 0 \\ 1 & -1 & \vdots & -4 & 4 & 0 \\ 1 & 2 & \vdots & 0 & 0 & 2 \end{bmatrix}$$

Here, $n = 3$ and $m = 2$, therefore, $n - m = 1$, $2m + 1 = 5$. This means we need to check the determinant of H only and it must have the sign of $(-1)^2$.

Now, $|H| = 72 > 0$ and so the obtained point is minimum.

EXAMPLE 6.11: Use the Kuhn–Tucker conditions to solve the NLPP.

Maximize $$z = 2x_1^2 - 7x_2^2 + 12x_1x_2$$

subject to the constraints: $$2x_1 + 5x_2 \le 98$$

Solution: Here $f(X) = 2x_1^2 - 7x_2^2 + 12x_1x_2$ and $g(X) = 2x_1 + 5x_2 - 98$

We leave it for the reader to write the Lagrangian function in the proper form by introducing slacks s_i^2.

Following the K-T conditions, we get

$$\frac{\partial f(X)}{\partial x_1} - \lambda \frac{\partial g(X)}{\partial x_1} = 0 \Rightarrow 4x_1 + 12x_2 - 2\lambda = 0 \tag{i}$$

$$\frac{\partial f(X)}{\partial x_2} - \lambda \frac{\partial g(X)}{\partial x_2} = 0 \Rightarrow 12x_1 - 14x_2 - 5\lambda = 0 \tag{ii}$$

$$\lambda g(X) = 0 \Rightarrow \lambda(2x_1 + 5x_2 - 98) = 0 \tag{iii}$$

$$g(X) \le 0 \Rightarrow 2x_1 + 5x_2 - 98 \le 0 \tag{iv}$$

$$\lambda \ge 0 \tag{v}$$

From Eq. (iii), either $\lambda = 0$ or $2x_1 + 5x_2 - 98 = 0$. If $\lambda = 0$ then we have $x_1 = 0$ and $x_2 = 0$ which does not satisfy Eq. (iv). Thus the optimal solution cannot be obtained for $\lambda = 0$.

Let us then take $\lambda \ne 0$. From Eq. (iii), we get $x_2 = (98 - 2x_1)/5$. Using it in Eq. (i) and (ii) and solving we get $x_1 = 44$, $x_2 = 2$ and $\lambda = 100$.

This solution does not violate any of the K-T conditions and thus the optimum solution is $x_1 = 44$, $x_2 = 2$ and maximum $z = 4900$.

EXAMPLE 6.12: Use the Kuhn-Tucker conditions to solve the NLPP.

Minimize $$z = f(x_1, x_2) = -x_1^2 - 2x_2^2 + 2x_1 + 3x_2$$

subject to the conditions: $$x_1 + 3x_2 \le 6, \quad 5x_1 + 2x_2 \le 10$$

and $x_1, x_2 \ge 0$.

Solution: Here $$f(X) = -x_1^2 - 2x_2^2 + 2x_1 + 3x_2$$

$$g_1(X) = x_1 + 3x_2 - 6 \le 0,\ g_2(X) = 5x_1 + 2x_2 - 10 \le 0,\ g_3(X) = -x_1 \le 0 \text{ and } g_4(X) = -x_2 \le 0$$

This being a minimization problem, $\lambda \le 0$.

We write the Lagrangian function in the proper form by introducing slacks s_i^2

$$F(x_1, x_2, \lambda_1, \lambda_2, \lambda_3, \lambda_4) = -x_1^2 - 2x_2^2 + 2x_1 + 3x_2 - \lambda_1(x_1 + 3x_2 - 6 + s_1^2)$$
$$- \lambda_2(5x_1 + 2x_2 - 10 + s_2^2) - \lambda_3(-x_1 + s_1^2) - \lambda_4(-x_2 + s_1^2)$$

Following the K–T conditions, we get

$$\frac{\partial f(X)}{\partial x_j} - \sum_{i=1}^{4} \lambda_i \frac{\partial g_i(X)}{\partial x_j} = 0 \Rightarrow -2x_1 + 2 - \lambda_1 - 5\lambda_2 + \lambda_3 = 0 \quad \text{(i)}$$

$$-4x_2 + 3 - 3\lambda_1 - 2\lambda_2 + \lambda_4 = 0 \quad \text{(ii)}$$

$$\lambda_i g_i(X) = 0 \Rightarrow \lambda_1(x_1 + 3x_2 - 6) = 0 \quad \text{(iii)}$$

$$\lambda_2(5x_1 + 2x_2 - 10) = 0 \quad \text{(iv)}$$

$$\lambda_3(-x_1) = 0 \quad \text{(v)}$$

$$\lambda_4(-x_2) = 0 \quad \text{(vi)}$$

$$g_i(X) \le 0 \Rightarrow x_1 + 3x_2 \le 6 \quad \text{(vii)}$$

$$5x_1 + 2x_2 \le 10 \quad \text{(viii)}$$

$$-x_1 \le 0 \quad \text{(ix)}$$

$$-x_2 \le 0 \quad \text{(x)}$$

$$\lambda_i \le 0 \quad \text{(xi)}$$

Case (1): Let all $\lambda_i = 0$. Then substituting them in the above conditions (i) and (ii) we get, $x_1 = 1$, $x_2 = 3/4$. This solution satisfies all the above conditions. The reader can easily verify this. So the minimum value of the function at the point (1, 3/4) is obtained as 17/8.

EXAMPLE 6.13: Use the Kuhn–Tucker conditions to solve the NLPP.

Maximize $\quad z = f(x_1, x_2) = -x_1^2 + 2x_1 + x_2$

subject to the constraints: $\quad 2x_1 + 3x_2 \le 6,$

$$2x_1 + x_2 \le 4$$

and $\quad x_1, x_2 \ge 0$

Solution: Here $\quad f(X) = -x_1^2 + 2x_1 + x_2$

$g_1(X) = 2x_1 + 3x_2 - 6 \le 0$, $g_2(X) = 2x_1 + x_2 - 4 \le 0$, $g_3(X) = -x_1 \le 0$ and $g_4(X) = -x_2 \le 0$

As this is a maximization problem, $\lambda \ge 0$.

We write the Lagrangian function in the proper form by introducing slacks s_i^2

$$F(x_1, x_2, \lambda_1, \lambda_2, \lambda_3, \lambda_4) = -x_1^2 + 2x_1 + x_2 - \lambda_1(2x_1 + 3x_2 - 6 + s_1^2)$$
$$- \lambda_2(2x_1 + x_2 - 4 + s_2^2) - \lambda_3(-x_1 + s_1^2) - \lambda_4(-x_2 + s_1^2)$$

Then K–T conditions result in following:

$$\frac{\partial f(X)}{\partial x_j} - \sum_{i=1}^{4} \lambda_i \frac{\partial g_i(X)}{\partial x_j} = 0 \Rightarrow -2x_1 + 2 - 2\lambda_1 - 2\lambda_2 + \lambda_3 = 0 \quad \text{(i)}$$

$$1 - 3\lambda_1 - \lambda_2 + \lambda_4 = 0 \quad \text{(ii)}$$

$$\lambda_i g_i(X) = 0 \Rightarrow \lambda_1(2x_1 + 3x_2 - 6) = 0 \quad \text{(iii)}$$

$$\lambda_2(2x_1 + 3x_2 - 4) = 0 \quad \text{(iv)}$$

$$\lambda_3(-x_1) = 0 \quad \text{(v)}$$

$$\lambda_4(-x_2) = 0 \quad \text{(vi)}$$

$$g_i(X) \le 0 \;\Rightarrow\; 2x_1 + 3x_2 \le 6 \quad \text{(vii)}$$

$$2x_1 + x_2 \le 4 \quad \text{(viii)}$$

$$-x_1 \le 0 \quad \text{(ix)}$$

$$-x_2 \le 0 \quad \text{(x)}$$

$$\lambda_i \ge 0 \quad \text{(xi)}$$

Solving these equations, we get $x_1 = 2/3$, $x_2 = 14/9$, $\lambda_1 = 1/3$ and $\lambda_2 = 0$ which satisfies all the above conditions. The maximum value of z at the obtained point is 22/9.

EXAMPLE 6.14: Use the Kuhn–Tucker conditions to solve the NLPP.

Minimize $\quad z = f(x_1, x_2, x_3) = x_1^2 + x_2^2 + x_3^2$

subject to the constraints: $\quad 2x_1 + x_2 \le 5$

$$x_1 + x_3 \le 2$$

and $x_1 \ge 1$, $x_2 \ge 2$, $x_3 \ge 0$.

Because this is a minimization problem, $\lambda \le 0$.

Here $\quad f(X) = x_1^2 + x_2^2 + x_3^2$

$$g_1(X) = 2x_1 + x_2 - 5 \le 0, \quad g_2(X) = x_1 + x_3 - 2 \le 0, \quad g_3(X) = 1 - x_1 \le 0$$

and $\quad g_4(X) = 2 - x_2 \le 0, \quad g_5(X) = -x_3 \le 0$

This being a minimization problem, $\lambda \le 0$.

We leave it for the reader to write the Lagrangian function in the proper form by introducing slacks s_i^2.

The K–T conditions simplify to the following.

$$\frac{\partial f(X)}{\partial x_j} - \sum_{i=1}^{5} \lambda_i \frac{\partial g_i(X)}{\partial x_j} = 0 \;\Rightarrow\; -2x_1 - 2\lambda_1 - \lambda_2 + \lambda_3 = 0 \quad \text{(i)}$$

$$2x_2 - \lambda_1 + \lambda_4 = 0 \quad \text{(ii)}$$

$$2x_3 - \lambda_2 + \lambda_5 = 0 \quad \text{(iii)}$$

$$\lambda_i g_i(X) = 0 \;\Rightarrow\; \lambda_1(2x_1 + x_2 - 5) = 0 \quad \text{(iv)}$$

$$\lambda_2(x_1 + x_3 - 2) = 0 \quad \text{(v)}$$

$$\lambda_3(1 - x_1) = 0 \quad \text{(vi)}$$

$$\lambda_4(2 - x_2) = 0 \quad \text{(vii)}$$

$$\lambda_5(-x_3) = 0 \quad \text{(viii)}$$

$$g_i(X) \le 0 \;\Rightarrow\; 2x_1 + x_2 \le 5 \qquad \text{(ix)}$$

$$x_1 + x_3 \le 2 \qquad \text{(x)}$$

$$x_1 \ge 1,\ x_2 \ge 2,\ x_3 \ge 0 \qquad \text{(xi)}$$

$$\lambda_i \le 0 \qquad \text{(xii)}$$

It is left for the reader to solve the above conditions. The solution is $x_1 = 1$, $x_2 = 2$, $x_3 = 0$, $\lambda_1 = \lambda_2 = \lambda_5 = 0$, $\lambda_3 = -2$, $\lambda_4 = -4$.

Because both $f(X)$ and the solution space $g(X)$ are convex, the Lagrangian function $F(X, S, \lambda)$ must be convex and the resulting stationary point yields a global constrained minimum.

6.5.2.3 *Lagrangian function and the saddle point*

For the programming problem

Find $\qquad X = (x_1, x_2, \ldots, x_n)$

so as to Minimize $\qquad z = f(x_1, x_2, \ldots, x_n)$

subject to $\qquad g_i(x_1, x_2, \ldots, x_n)\ (\le, =, \ge)\ 0,\ i = 1, 2, \ldots, m$ and $m < n$

Lagrange function is

$$F(X, \lambda) = f(X) - \sum_{i=1}^{m} \lambda_i g_i(X)$$

The vector $\lambda = (\lambda_1, \lambda_2, \ldots, \lambda_m)$ will be termed as $Y = (y_1, y_2, \ldots, y_m)$.
Writing in matrix notation, we have

$$F(X, Y) = f(X) - Y^T G(X)$$

where $\qquad Y^T = (y_1 y_2, \ldots, y_m)$ and $G(X) = [g_1(X), g_2(X), \ldots, g_m(X)]^T$

The point (X_0, Y_0) is called the saddle point of $F(X, Y)$ if

$$F(X_0, Y) \le F(X_0, Y_0) \le F(X, Y_0)$$

6.6 QUADRATIC PROGRAMMING

The form of NLPP in which the highest order of the polynomial of the objective function is restricted to at most 2 is called a *Quadratic Programming Problem* (QPP).

The objective function looks like:

$$\text{Optimize } Z = c_1x_1 + c_2x_2 + \cdots + c_nx_n + c_{n+1}x_1^2 + \cdots + c_{n+n}x_n^2 + c_{2n+1}x_1x_2 + \cdots + c_{2n+\binom{n}{2}}x_{n-1}x_n$$

subject to the constraints: $\quad a_{i1}x_1 + a_{i2}x_2 + \cdots + a_{in}x_n \le b_i \quad i = 1, 2, 3, \ldots, m$

$$x_1, x_2, \ldots, x_n \ge 0$$

The problem can thus be written as

Optimize $$Z = \sum_{j=1}^{n} c_j x_j + \sum_{j=1}^{n} \sum_{k=1}^{n} x_j d_{jk} x_k$$

Subject to $$\sum_{j=1}^{n} a_{ij} x_j \le b_i \quad i = 1, 2, \ldots, m$$

and $x_j \ge 0 \quad j = 1, 2, \ldots, n$.

In matrix notation, we write it as

Optimize $$Z = \mathbf{CX} + \mathbf{X}^T\mathbf{DX}$$

subject to the constraints: $$\mathbf{AX} \le \mathbf{b} \text{ and } \mathbf{X} \ge 0$$

where $\mathbf{X} = (x_1, x_2, \ldots, x_n)^T$, $\mathbf{C} = (c_1, c_2, \ldots, c_n)$, $b = (b_1, b_2, \ldots, b_m)^T$.

$\mathbf{D} = [d_{jk}]$ is symmetric and (1) positive definite (i.e. the quadratic term $\mathbf{X}^T\mathbf{DX}$ in $\mathbf{X}$ is positive for all values of $\mathbf{X}$ except at $\mathbf{X} = 0$) for minimization problems, (2) negative definite (i.e. $\mathbf{X}^T\mathbf{DX} < 0$ for all $\mathbf{X}$ except $\mathbf{X} = 0$) for maximization problems.

In $\mathbf{D}$, d_{jj} represents the coefficients of term x_j^2 in the objective function and d_{ij} $(i \ne j)$ represents the coefficient of terms $x_i x_j$ in the objective function.

Linear constraints guarantee convex solution space.

The objective function of QPP is strictly convex in $\mathbf{X}$ for minimization and concave in $\mathbf{X}$ for maximization.

Note: If $\mathbf{D}$ is zero matrix, then the QPP reduces to LPP.

The solution is based on the K–T conditions.

Since Z is strictly convex (or concave) and the solution space is convex, these conditions are also sufficient for a global optimum.

Taking the problem as

Maximize $$Z = \mathbf{CX} + \mathbf{X}^T\mathbf{DX}$$

subject to $$G(X) = \begin{bmatrix} A \\ -I \end{bmatrix} X - \begin{bmatrix} b \\ 0 \end{bmatrix} \le 0$$

Let $\lambda = (\lambda_1, \lambda_2, \ldots, \lambda_m)^T$ and $\mu = (\mu_1, \mu_2, \ldots, \mu_n)^T$ be the two sets of Lagrangian multipliers corresponding to the two sets of constraints to $\mathbf{AX} \le b$ and $-\mathbf{X} \le 0$.

K-T conditions give

$$\lambda \ge 0$$

$$\mu \ge 0$$

$$\lambda_i \left(b_i - \sum_{j=1}^{n} a_{ij} x_j \right) = 0 \quad i = 1, 2, \ldots, m$$

$$\mu_j x_j = 0 \quad j = 1, 2, \ldots, n$$

$$\mathbf{AX} \le \mathbf{b}$$

$$-\mathbf{X} \le 0$$

Now, $$\nabla Z = C + 2X^T\mathbf{D}$$

$$\nabla G(X) = \begin{bmatrix} A \\ -I \end{bmatrix}$$

Let $S = \mathbf{b} - \mathbf{AX} \geq 0$ be the slack variables.
The conditions reduce to

$$-2\mathbf{X}^T\mathbf{D} - \lambda^T\mathbf{X} - \mu^T = C$$

$$\mathbf{AX} + S = \mathbf{b}$$

$$\mu_j x_j = 0 = \lambda_i s_i \text{ for all } i \text{ and } j$$

$$\mu, \lambda, \mathbf{X}, S \geq 0$$

As $\mathbf{D}^T = \mathbf{D}$, the transpose of the first set of equations give

$$-2\mathbf{DX} + A^T\lambda - \mu = C^T$$

Hence the necessary conditions are combined as

$$\begin{bmatrix} -2D & A^T & -I & 0 \\ A & 0 & 0 & I \end{bmatrix} \begin{bmatrix} X \\ \lambda \\ \mu \\ S \end{bmatrix} = \begin{bmatrix} C^T \\ b \end{bmatrix}$$

$\mu_j x_j = 0 = \lambda_i s_i$ for all i and j and $\mu, \lambda, X, S \geq 0$.

All equations except $\mu_j x_j = 0 = \lambda_i s_i$ are linear in μ, λ, X and S.

Thus we have to solve a set of linear equations while satisfying the conditions

$$\mu_j x_j = 0 = \lambda_i s_i$$

As Z is strictly concave (Maximization case), and the solution space is convex, the feasible region satisfying all these conditions give the unique optimum solution.

6.7 WOLFE'S METHOD

Wolfe has developed a method to solve the above system of constraints. The steps of the method are listed below.

Step 1: Form the system of constraints using K-T (necessary) conditions from the Lagrangian function.

Step 2. Add Aj as the artificial variable for the j-th constraint of the first n constraints, since each of these first n constraints has no basic variable in it.

Step 3. A minimization type objective function is then formed by summing the artificial variables irrespective of the type of the objective function in the original problem.

Step 4. Solve the model consisting of the above objective function and system of constraints using the two phase simplex method.

The only restriction is to satisfy the conditions $\mu_j x_j = 0 = \lambda_i s_i$. This means if λ_i is basic at a positive level, s_i cannot become basic at positive level. Similarly, μ_j and x_j cannot be positive simultaneously.

EXAMPLE 6.15: Solve the following QP – problem.

Maximize $$z = 4x_1 + 6x_2 - 2x_1^2 - 2x_1x_2 - 2x_2^2$$

subject to the constraints: $x_1 + 2x_2 \le 2$ and $x_1, x_2 \ge 0$

Solution: The standard form of QP – problem is

Maximize $$z = 4x_1 + 6x_2 - 2x_1^2 - 2x_1x_2 - 2x_2^2$$

subject to the constraints:

$$x_1 + 2x_2 + s_1^2 = 2$$

$$-x_1 + r_1^2 = 0$$

$$-x_2 + r_2^2 = 0$$

and $$x_1, x_2, s_1, r_1, r_2 \ge 0.$$

The Lagrangian function is $L(x_1, x_2, s_1, \lambda_1, \mu_1, \mu_2, r_1, r_2)$

$$= (4x_1 + 6x_2 - 2x_1^2 - 2x_1x_2 - 2x_2^2) - \lambda_1(x_1 + 2x_2 + s_1^2 - 2) - \mu_1(-x_1 + r_1^2) - \mu_2(-x_2 + r_2^2)$$

$$\frac{\partial L}{\partial x_1} = 4 - 4x_1 - 2x_2 - \lambda_1 + \mu_1 = 0 \qquad \frac{\partial L}{\partial x_2} = 6 - 2x_1 - 4x_2 - 2\lambda_1 + \mu_2 = 0$$

$$\frac{\partial L}{\partial \lambda_1} = x_1 + 2x_2 + s_1^2 - 2 = 0 \qquad \frac{\partial L}{\partial s_1} = 2\lambda_1 s_1 = 0$$

$$\frac{\partial L}{\partial \mu_1} = -x_1 + r_1^2 = 0 \qquad \frac{\partial L}{\partial \mu_2} = -x_2 + r_2^2 = 0$$

$$\frac{\partial L}{\partial r_1} = 2\mu_1 r_1 = 0 \qquad \frac{\partial L}{\partial r_2} = 2\mu_2 r_2 = 0$$

Therefore,

$$4x_1 + 2x_2 + \lambda_1 - \mu_1 = 4$$

$$2x_1 + 4x_2 + 2\lambda_1 - \mu_2 = 6$$

$$x_1 + 2x_2 + s_1^2 = 2$$

$$\lambda_1 s_1 = 0$$

$\mu_1 r_1 = 0 = \mu_2 r_2$ and $x_1, x_2, s_1, \lambda_1, \mu_1, \mu_2 \ge 0$.

Introduce artificial variables A_1 and A_2 in the first two constraints. Therefore, modified LP–problem is

Min $$z^* = A_1 + A_2$$

subject to the constraints:

$$4x_1 + 2x_2 + \lambda_1 - \mu_1 + A_1 = 4$$

$$2x_1 + 4x_2 + 2\lambda_1 - \mu_2 + A_2 = 6$$

$$x_1 + 2x_2 + s_1^2 = 2$$

and $x_1, x_2, s_1, \lambda_1, \mu_1, \mu_2, A_1, A_2 \ge 0$.

Table 1

		c_j	0	0	0	0	0	0	1	1
c_B	B	x_B	x_1	x_2	λ_1	μ_1	μ_2	s_1	A_1	A_2
1	A_1	4	4	2	1	–1	0	0	1	0
1	A_2	6	2	4	2	0	–1	0	0	1
0	s_1	2	1	2	0	0	0	1	0	0
Z^*	10	$c_j - z_j$	–6	–6	–3	1	1	0	0	0

In Table 1, the largest negative values among $c_j - z_j$ is –6 corresponding to x_1 and x_2 columns, i.e. either of these two variables can be entered into the basis. Since $\mu_1 = 0$ (not in the basis) x_1 is considered to enter into the basis. It will replace A_1 already in the basis. The new solution is in Table 2.

Table 2

		c_j	0	0	0	0	0	0	1
c_B	B	x_B	x_1	x_2	λ_1	μ_1	μ_2	s_1	A_2
0	x_1	1	1	1/2	1/4	–1/4	0	0	0
1	A_2	4	0	3	3/2	1/2	– 1	0	1
0	s_1	1	0	3/2	–1/4	1/4	0	1	0
Z^*	4	$c_j - z_j$	0	–3	–3/2	–1/2	1	0	0

In Table 2, $\mu_2 = 0$ (not in the basis), therefore x_2 can be introduced into the basis to replace s_1 already in the basis. The new solution is in Table 3.

Table 3

		c_j	0	0	0	0	0	0	1
c_B	B	x_B	x_1	x_2	λ_1	μ_1	μ_2	s_1	A_2
0	x_1	2/3	1	0	1/3	–1/3	0	–1/3	0
1	A_2	2	0	0	2	0	–1	–2	1
0	x_2	2/3	0	1	–1/6	1/6	0	2/3	0
Z^*	2	$c_j - z_j$	0	0	–2	0	1	1	0

In Table 3, $s_1 = 0$ (not in a basis), therefore λ_1 can be entered into the basis to replace $A2$. The new solution is in Table 4.

Table 4

		c_j	0	0	0	0	0	0
c_B	B	x_B	x_1	x_2	λ_1	μ_1	μ_2	s_1
0	x_1	1/3	1	0	0	–1/3	1/6	0
0	λ_1	1	0	0	1	0	–1/2	–1
0	x_2	5/6	0	1	0	1/6	–1/12	1/2
Z^*	0	$c_j - z_j$	0	0	0	0	0	0

Here in Table 4, all $c_j - z_j = 0$. The optimal solution is

$$x_1 = \frac{1}{3},\ x_2 = \frac{5}{6},\ \lambda_1 = 1,\ \mu_1 = \mu_2 = s_1 = 0 \text{ and } z = \frac{25}{6}$$

EXAMPLE 6.16: Using Wolfe's method to solve QP-problem,

Maximize $$z = 2x_1 + x_2 - x_1^2$$

subject to the constraints:

$$2x_1 + 3x_2 \le 6$$

$$2x_1 + x_2 \le 4$$

and $$x_1, x_2 \ge 0$$

Solution: The standard form of QP-problem is

Maximize $$z = 2x_1 + x_2 - x_1^2$$

subject to the constraints:

$$2x_1 + 3x_2 + s_1^2 = 6$$

$$2x_1 + x_2 + s_2^2 = 4$$

$$-x_1 + r_1^2 = 0$$

$$-x_2 + r_2^2 = 0$$

and $x_1, x_2, s_1, r_1, r_2 \ge 0$.

The Lagrangian function is $L(x_1, x_2, s_1, s_2, \lambda_1, \mu_1, \mu_2, r_1, r_2)$

$$= (2x_1 + x_2 - x_1^2) - \lambda_1(2x_1 + 3x_2 + s_1^2 - 6) - \lambda_2(2x_1 + x_2 + s_2^2 - 4) - \mu_1(-x_1 + r_1^2) - \mu_2(-x_2 + r_2^2)$$

$$\frac{\partial L}{\partial x_1} = 2 - 2x_1 - 2\lambda_1 - 2\lambda_2 + \mu_1 = 0 \qquad \frac{\partial L}{\partial x_2} = 1 - 3\lambda_1 - \lambda_2 + \mu_2 = 0$$

$$\frac{\partial L}{\partial \lambda_1} = 2x_1 + 3x_2 + s_1^2 - 6 = 0 \qquad \frac{\partial L}{\partial \lambda_2} = 2x_1 + x_2 + s_2^2 - 4 = 0$$

$$\frac{\partial L}{\partial s_1} = -2\lambda_1 s_1 = 0 \qquad \frac{\partial L}{\partial s_2} = -2\lambda_2 s_2 = 0$$

$$\frac{\partial L}{\partial \mu_1} = -x_1 + r_1^2 = 0 \qquad \frac{\partial L}{\partial \mu_2} = -x_2 + r_2^2 = 0$$

$$\frac{\partial L}{\partial r_1} = -2\mu_1 r_1 = 0 \qquad \frac{\partial L}{\partial r_2} = -2\mu_2 r_2 = 0$$

Therefore,

$$2x_1 + 2\lambda_1 + 2\lambda_2 - \mu_1 = 2$$

$$3\lambda_1 + \lambda_2 - \mu_2 = 1$$

$$2x_1 + 3x_2 + s_1^2 = 6$$

$$2x_1 + x_2 + s_2^2 = 4$$

$$\lambda_1 s_1 = 0 = \lambda_2 s_2$$

$$\mu_1 r_1 = 0 = \mu_2 r_2$$

and $x_1, x_2, \lambda_1, \lambda_2, s_1, s_2, \mu_1, \mu_2 \geq 0$.

Introduce artificial variables A_1 and A_2 in the first two constraints. Therefore, the modified LP-problem is

Min $\quad z^* = A_1 + A_2$

subject to

$$2x_1 + 2\lambda_1 + 2\lambda_2 - \mu_1 + A_1 = 2$$

$$3\lambda_1 + \lambda_2 - \mu_2 + A_2 = 1$$

$$2x_1 + 3x_2 + s_1^2 = 6$$

$$2x_1 + x_2 + s_2^2 = 4$$

$$\lambda_1 s_1 = 0 = \lambda_2 s_2$$

$$\mu_1 r_1 = 0 = \mu_2 r_2$$

and $x_1, x_2, \lambda_1, \lambda_2, s_1, s_2, \mu_1, \mu_2, A_1, A_2 \geq 0$.

Table 1

		c_j	0	0	0	0	0	0	0	0	1	1
c_B	B	x_B	x_1	x_2	λ_1	λ_2	μ_1	μ_2	s_1	s_2	A_1	A_2
1	A_1	2	2	0	2	2	–1	0	0	0	1	0
1	A_2	1	0	0	3	1	0	–1	0	0	0	1
0	s_1	6	2	3	0	0	0	0	1	0	0	0
0	s_2	4	2	1	0	0	0	0	0	1	0	0
z^*	3	$c_j - z_j$	–2	0	–5	–3	1	1	0	0	0	0

In Table 1, the largest negative values among $c_j - z_j$ is –5 but we cannot enter λ_1 and λ_2 in the basis because of complementary conditions $\lambda_1 s_1 = 0 = \lambda_2 s_2$. Since $\mu_1 = 0$, x_1 can enter into the basis, with A_1 as leaving variable. The new solution is in Table 2.

Table 2

		c_j	0	0	0	0	0	0	0	0	1
c_B	B	x_B	x_1	x_2	λ_1	λ_2	μ_1	μ_2	s_1	s_2	A_2
1	x_1	1	1	0	1	1	1/2	0	0	0	0
1	A_2	1	0	0	3	1	0	−1	0	0	1
0	s_1	4	0	3	−2	−2	1	0	1	0	0
0	s_2	2	0	1	−2	−2	1	0	0	1	0
z^*	1	$c_j - z_j$	0	0	−3	−1	0	1	0	0	0

Again we cannot enter λ_1, λ_2 and μ_1 in the basis because s_1, s_2 and x_1 are already in the basis. So enter x_2 into the basis with s_1 as the leaving variable.

Table 3

		c_j	0	0	0	0	0	0	0	0	1
c_B	B	x_B	x_1	x_2	λ_1	λ_2	μ_1	μ_2	s_1	s_2	A_2
1	x_1	1	1	0	1	1	−1/2	0	0	0	0
1	A_2	1	0	0	3	1	0	−1	0	0	1
0	x_2	4/3	0	1	−2/3	−2/3	1/3	0	1/3	0	0
0	s_2	2/3	0	1	−4/3	−4/3	2/3	0	−1/3	1	0
z^*	1	$c_j - z_j$	0	0	−3	−1	0	1	0	0	1

Since $s_1 = 0$, λ_1 can enter into the basis, with A_2 as the leaving variable. The new solution is given in Table 4.

Table 4

		c_j	0	0	0	0	0	0	0	0
c_B	B	x_B	x_1	x_2	λ_1	λ_2	μ_1	μ_2	s_1	s_2
0	x_1	2/3	1	0	0	2/3	−1/2	1/3	0	0
0	λ_1	1/3	0	0	1	1/3	0	−1/3	0	0
0	x_2	14/9	0	1	0	−4/9	1/3	−2/9	1/3	0
0	s_2	10/9	0	1	0	−8/9	2/3	−4/9	−1/3	1
z^*	0	$c_j - z_j$	0	0	0	0	0	0	0	0

Therefore, the optimal solution is $x_1 = 2/3$, $x_2 = 14/9$, $\lambda_1 = 1/3$, $\lambda_2 = 0$, $\mu_1 = 0$, $\mu_2 = 0$, $s_1 = 0$ and $s_2 = 10/9$, Max $z = 22/9$

REVIEW EXERCISES

1. Solve the following NLPP.

(i) Minimize $Z = f(x_1, x_2, x_3) = 2x_1^2 - 24x_1 + 2x_2^2 - 8x_2 + 2x_3^2 - 12x_3 + 200$
subject to the constraints: $x_1 + x_2 + x_3 = 11$

[**Ans.** $(x_1, x_2, x_3) = (6, 2, 3)$]

(ii) Minimize $Z = x_1^2 + x_2^2 + x_3^2$
subject to the constraints: $4x_1 + x_2^2 + 2x_3 = 14$

[**Ans.** $(x_1, x_2, x_3) = (2, 2, 1)$]

(iii) Maximize $Z = -x_1^2 - x_2^2 - x_3^2 + 4x_1 + 6x_2$
subject to the constraints: $x_1 + x_2 \leq 2$, $2x_1 + 3x_2 \leq 12$ and $x_1, x_2 \geq 0$

[**Ans.** $(x_1, x_2, x_3) = (1/2, 3/2, 0)$ and $\lambda_1 = 3$, $\lambda_2 = 0$ and Max $Z = 17/2$]

(iv) Minimize $Z = (x_1 + 1)^2 + (x_2 + 2)^2$
subject to the constraints: $0 \leq x_1 \leq 2$, $0 \leq x_2 \leq 1$

[**Ans.** $(x_1, x_2) = (2, 1)$ and $\lambda_1 = 6$, $\lambda_2 = 6$ and Max $Z = 18$]

(v) Maximize $Z = -x_1^2 - x_2^2 + 8x_1 + 10x_2$
subject to the constraints: $3x_1 + 2x_2 \leq 6$, and $x_1, x_2 \geq 0$

[**Ans.** $(x_1, x_2) = (4/13, 33/13)$ and Max $Z = 21.3$]

(vi) Maximize $Z = 7x_1^2 + 6x_1 + 5x_2$
subject to the constraints: $x_1 + 2x_2 \leq 10$, $x_1 - 3x_2 \leq 9$ and $x_1, x_2 \geq 0$

[**Ans.** $(x_1, x_2) = (48/5, 1/5)$ and Max $Z = 703.72$]

2. Use Wolfe's method in solving the following QPP:

(i) Maximize $Z = 6 - 6x_1 + 2x_1^2 - 6x_1x_2 + 2x_2^2$
subject to the constraints: $x_1 + x_2 \leq 2$; $x_1, x_2 \geq 0$

[**Ans.** $(x_1, x_2) = (3/2, 1/2)$ and Max $Z = 1/2$]

(ii) Minimize $Z = x_1^2 - x_1x_2 + 2x_2^2 - x_1 - x_2$
subject to the constraints: $2x_1 + x_2 \leq 1$; $x_1, x_2 \geq 0$

[**Ans.** $(x_1, x_2) = (4/11, 3/11)$ and $Z = -5/11$]

(iii) Maximize $Z = 2x_1 + x_2 - x_1^2$
subject to the constraints: $2x_1 + 3x_2 \leq 6$, $2x_1 + x_2 \leq 4$; $x_1, x_2 \geq 0$

[**Ans.** $(x_1, x_2) = (2/3, 14/9)$ and Max $Z = 22/9$]

(iv) Maximize $Z = -4x_1 + x_1^2 - 2x_1x_2 + 2x_2^2$
subject to the constraints: $2x_1 + x_2 \leq 6$, $x_1 - 4x_2 \leq 0$; $x_1, x_2 \geq 0$

[**Ans.** $(x_1, x_2) = (32/13, 14/13)$ and Min $Z = -88/13$]

7

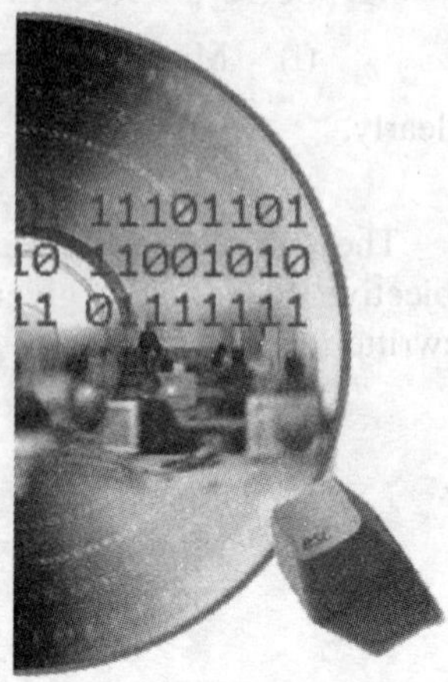

Geometric Programming

7.1 GEOMETRIC PROGRAMMING

Geometric programming is one type of non-linear programming. This technique was developed by R. Duttinear and C. Zener in 1964. It is based on the geometrical concept of orthogonality and arithmetic–geometric inequality. The special type of functions to be optimized are called *posynomials*.

General problem can be defined as

Minimize $$Z = f(X) = \sum_{j=1}^{N} U_j \tag{7.1}$$

where $$U_j = C_j \prod_{i=1}^{n} x_i^{\alpha_{ij}}, \quad j = 1, 2, \ldots, N \tag{7.2}$$

Here $C_j > 0$ and N is finite. The exponents α_{ij} are unrestricted in sign. The posynomial function $f(X)$ takes the form of a polynomial except that the exponents α_{ij} may be negative. The variables x_i are assumed to be strictly positive so that the region $x_i \leq 0$ represents an infeasible area. The necessary condition for function $f(x)$ to be minimum is, the partial derivatives of $f(x)$ vanish at a point. Thus,

$$\frac{\partial Z}{\partial x_k} = \sum_{j=1}^{N} \frac{\partial U_j}{\partial x_k} = \sum_{j=1}^{N} C_j \alpha_{kj} (x_{kj})^{\alpha_{kj-1}} \prod_{i \neq k} (x_i)^{\alpha_{ij}} = 0, \quad k = 1, 2, \ldots, n$$

Therefore, $$\frac{1}{x} \sum_{j=1}^{N} \alpha_{kj} U_j = 0, \quad k = 1, 2, \ldots, n \tag{7.3}$$

Let Z_0 be the minimum value of Z. Since Z is posynomial and each $(x_k)_0 > 0$, we have $Z_0 > 0$.

Define
$$y_j = \frac{U_{j0}}{Z_0} \tag{7.4}$$

Clearly,
$$y_j > 0 \quad \text{and} \quad \sum_{j=1}^{N} y_j = 1 \tag{7.5}$$

The value of y_j represents the contribution of the j-th term U_j to be the optimal value of the objective function Z_0 given in Eq. (7.1). Then necessary conditions given in Eq. (7.3) can be rewritten as

$$\sum_{j=1}^{N} \alpha_{kj} y_j = 0, \quad k = 1, 2, \ldots, n \tag{7.6}$$

$$\sum_{j=1}^{N} y_j = 1, \quad y_j > 0 \text{ for all } j \tag{7.7}$$

Equations (7.6) and (7.7) are called ***orthogonality*** and ***normality*** conditions respectively. If $n + 1 = N$, then a unique solution for y_j is obtained. The problem becomes complex when $N > (n + 1)$ because in that case, the values of y_j no longer remain unique. However, it is possible to determine y_j uniquely when the problem is minimization of an objective function given in Eq. (7.1).

Suppose that $(y_j)_0$ are the unique values obtained by solving Eq. (7.7). The next step is to determine Z_0 and $(x_i)_0$, $i = 1, 2, \ldots, n$ using $(y_j)_0$.

Consider

$$Z_0 = (Z_0)^{\sum_{i=1}^{N} (y_j)_0} \tag{7.8}$$

We have $Z_0 = U_{j0}/(y_j)_0$.

Therefore,
$$Z_0 = \left(\frac{U_{10}}{(y_1)_0}\right)^{(y_1)_0} \left(\frac{U_{20}}{(y_2)_0}\right)^{(y_2)_0} \cdots \left(\frac{U_{N0}}{(y_N)_0}\right)^{(y_N)_0}$$

$$= \left\{\prod_{j=1}^{N} \left(\frac{C_j}{(y_j)_0}\right)^{(y_j)_0}\right\} \left\{\prod_{j=1}^{N} \left(\prod_{i=1}^{N} (x_i)_0\right)^{(y_j)_0}\right\}$$

$$= \left\{\prod_{j=1}^{N} \left(\frac{C_j}{(y_j)_0}\right)^{(y_j)_0}\right\} \left\{\prod_{i=1}^{N} (x_i)_0^{\sum_{i=1}^{N} \alpha_{ij} (y_i)_0}\right\}$$

$$= \prod_{j=1}^{N} \left(\frac{C_j}{(y_j)_0}\right)^{(y_j)_0} \quad \because \sum_{i=1}^{N} \alpha_{ij} (y_i)_0 \tag{7.9}$$

Using values of $(y_j)_0$ and Z_0, $(U_j)_0 = (y_j)_0 Z_0$ can be found by Eq. (7.2) for $j = 1, 2, \ldots, n$. The procedure is actually the solution of a set of linear equations in y_j by transforming the original posynomial Z. The necessary condition said above also turns out to be sufficient condition. The proof is given in Beightler and Wilde [1979, p. 333].

The variables y_j actually define the dual variables associated with primal problem given by Eq. (7.1) with constraints given by Eq. (7.2). Let us study the relationship. Consider the primal problem

$$Z = \sum_{j=1}^{N} y_j \left(\frac{U_j}{y_j}\right) \tag{7.10}$$

Now define the function
$$w = \prod_{j=1}^{N} \left(\frac{U_j}{y_j}\right)^{y_j} \tag{7.11}$$

Using Cauchy's inequality, $\sum_{j=1}^{N} w_j z_j \geq \prod_{j=1}^{N} (Z_j)^{w_j}$ where $w_j > 0$ and $\sum_{j=1}^{N} w_j = 1$ (This is also known as arithmetic-geometric mean inequality), we have $w \leq Z$. The function w with its variables $y_1, y_2, \ldots, y_N$ defines the dual problem to Eqs. (7.1) to (7.2). Clearly, since w is the lower bound of Z, we have $w_0 = \max_{y_j} w = \min_{x_i} Z = Z_0$, i.e. the maximum value of $w = w_0$ over the values of y_j is equal to the minimum value of $Z = Z_0$ over the values of x_i.

EXAMPLE 7.1: Consider the problem

Minimize $\qquad Z = 7x_1x_2^{-1} + 3x_2x_3^{-2} + 5x_1^{-3}x_2x_3 + x_1x_2x_3$

Solution: Clearly $N = 4$ and $n = 3$. Then we have $N = n + 1$. So, the solution to the orthogonality and normality condition is unique. Rewrite the given problem as

Minimize $\qquad Z = 7x_1^1x_2^{-1}x_3^0 + 3x_1^0x_2^1x_3^{-2} + 5x_1^{-3}x_2^1x_3^1 + x_1^1x_2^1x_3^1$

Thus, $(C_1, C_2, C_3, C_4) = (7, 3, 5, 1)$

and
$$\begin{pmatrix} a_{11} & a_{12} & a_{13} & a_{14} \\ a_{21} & a_{22} & a_{23} & a_{24} \\ a_{31} & a_{32} & a_{33} & a_{34} \end{pmatrix} = \begin{pmatrix} 1 & 0 & -3 & 1 \\ -1 & 1 & 1 & 1 \\ 0 & -2 & 1 & 1 \end{pmatrix}$$

The orthogonality and normality conditions are given by

$$\begin{pmatrix} 1 & 0 & -3 & 1 \\ -1 & 1 & 1 & 1 \\ 0 & -2 & 1 & 1 \\ 1 & 1 & 1 & 1 \end{pmatrix} \begin{pmatrix} y_1 \\ y_2 \\ y_3 \\ y_4 \end{pmatrix} = \begin{pmatrix} 0 \\ 0 \\ 0 \\ 1 \end{pmatrix}$$

Then, $(y_1)_0 = 0.5$, $(y_2)_0 = 0.1667$, $(y_3)_0 = 0.2083$, $(y_4)_0 = 0.125$

Thus
$$Z_0 = \left(\frac{7}{0.5}\right)^{0.5} \left(\frac{3}{0.1667}\right)^{0.1667} \left(\frac{5}{0.2083}\right)^{0.2083} \left(\frac{1}{0.125}\right)^{0.125} = 15.23$$

Now using $U_{j0} = (y_j)_0 Z_0$ will give

$$7x_1x_2^{-1} = U_1 = 0.5\,(15.23) = 7.615$$

$$3x_2x_3^{-2} = U_2 = 0.1667\,(15.23) = 2.538$$

$$5x_1^{-3}x_2x_3 = U_3 = 0.2083\,(15.23) = 3.173$$

$$x_1x_2x_3 = U_4 = 0.125\,(15.23) = 1.904$$

Solving the above equations for x_1, x_2, x_3 gives $(x_1)_0 = 1.316$, $(x_2)_0 = 1.21$, $(x_3)_0 = 1.2$ as the optimal solution to minimize $Z = 15.23$.

EXAMPLE 7.2: Solve the problem

Minimize $$Z = 5x_1x_2^{-1} + 2x_1^{-1}x_2 + 5x_1 + x_2^{-1}, \quad x_1, x_2 > 0$$

Solution: We have $N = 4$ and $n = 2$. Then $N > n + 1$. Here $C = (5, 2, 5, 1)$
The orthogonality and normality conditions are given by

$$\begin{pmatrix} 1 & -1 & 1 & 0 \\ -1 & 1 & 0 & -1 \\ 1 & 1 & 1 & 1 \end{pmatrix}\begin{pmatrix} y_1 \\ y_2 \\ y_3 \end{pmatrix} = \begin{pmatrix} 0 \\ 0 \\ 1 \end{pmatrix}$$

Since $N > n + 1$, we try to get y_1, y_2, y_3 in terms of y_4.

$$\begin{pmatrix} 1 & -1 & 1 \\ -1 & 1 & 0 \\ 1 & 1 & 1 \end{pmatrix}\begin{pmatrix} y_1 \\ y_2 \\ y_3 \end{pmatrix} = \begin{pmatrix} 0 \\ y_4 \\ 1 - y_4 \end{pmatrix}$$

Therefore, $y_1 = 0.5\,(1 - 3y_4)$, $y_2 = 0.5\,(1 - y_4)$ and $y_3 = y_4$.
The corresponding dual problem is

Maximize $$w = \left(\frac{5}{0.5(1 - 3y_4)}\right)^{0.5(1 - 3y_4)} \left(\frac{2}{0.5(1 - y_4)}\right)^{0.5(1 - y_4)} \left(\frac{5}{y_4}\right)^{y_4} \left(\frac{1}{y_4}\right)^{y_4}$$

Therefore, $\ln w = 0.5(1 - 3y_4)\,[\ln 10 - \ln(1 - 3y_4)] + 0.5\,(1 - y_4)\,[\ln 4 - \ln(y_4)] + y_4\,(\ln 5 - 2\ln y_4)$
To find y_4, we differentiate $\ln w$ with respect to y_4 and equate to zero.

$$\frac{\partial(\ln w)}{\partial w} = -\frac{3}{2}\ln(10) - \frac{1}{2}\ln(4) + \ln(5) + \frac{3}{2}\ln(1 - 3y_4) + \frac{1}{2}\ln(1 - y_4) - 2\ln(y_4) = 0$$

Using properties of logarithm and simplifying, we get

$$-\ln\left(\frac{2 * 10^{3/2}}{5}\right) + \ln\left(\frac{(1 - 3y_4)^{3/2}(1 - y_4)^{1/2}}{y_4^2}\right) = 0$$

i.e. $$\frac{(1 - 3y_4)^{3/2}(1 - y_4)^{1/2}}{y_4^2} = 12.6$$

or $$\frac{(1-3y_4)^3(1-y_4)}{y_4^4} = 158.76$$

Solving for y_4 by suitable numerical method (Newton–Raphson's Method), we get $(y_4)_0 = 0.16$. Hence, $(y_1)_0 = 0.26$, $(y_2)_0 = 0.42$ and $(y_3)_0 = 0.16$

The value of $Z_0 = w_0 = \left(\frac{5}{0.26}\right)^{0.26}\left(\frac{2}{0.42}\right)^{0.42}\left(\frac{5}{0.16}\right)^{0.16} \approx 9.661$

Hence $5x_1 = U_3 = 0.16\ (9.661) = 1.546$

$$x_2^{-1} = U_4 = 0.16\,(9.661) = 0.1546.$$

Therefore, $(x_1)_0 = 0.309$, $(x_2)_0 = 0.647$ and $Z_0 \approx 9.661$ is the optimal solution.

7.2 PRIMAL GEOMETRIC PROGRAMMING WITH EQUALITY CONSTRAINTS

Consider the problem.

Minimize $$Z = f(X) \tag{7.12}$$

subject to the constraints

$$g_i(X) = \sum_{r=1}^{P(i)} C_{ir}U_{ir}(x), \quad i = 1, 2, \ldots, N \tag{7.13}$$

where $p(i)$ denotes the number of terms in the i-th constraint and

$$U_{ir} = \prod_{j=1}^{n}(x_i)^{\alpha_{ir}} \tag{7.14}$$

Construct Langrange function

$$L\,(X, \lambda) = f(X) + \sum_{i=1}^{N} \lambda_i\ [g_i\,(X) - 1] \tag{7.15}$$

Then orthogonality and normality conditions are

$$\frac{\partial L}{\partial x_k} = \frac{\partial f(X)}{\partial x_k} + \sum_{i=1}^{N} \lambda_i \frac{\partial g_i(X)}{\partial x_k} = 0, \qquad k = 1, 2, \ldots, n \tag{7.16}$$

and $$\frac{\partial L}{\partial \lambda_i} = g_i\,(X) - 1 = 0, \qquad i = 1, 2, \ldots, N \tag{7.17}$$

As far as the right-hand side in Eq. (7.17), $g_i\,(X) = 1$ (a positive number), the solution can be obtained by simple transformation. Note that $g_i\,(X) = 0$ is not permitted since we require $X > 0$.

Consider Eq. (7.16) again.

$$\frac{\partial L}{\partial x_k} = \sum_{j=1}^{N} \frac{C_j a_{kj} U_j(X)}{x_k} + \sum_{i=1}^{N} \lambda_i \left[\sum_{r=1}^{P(i)} \frac{C_{ir} a_{irk} U_{ir}(X)}{x_k}\right]$$

Introduce transformation $$y_j = \frac{C_j U_j}{f_0(X)}, \quad y_{ir} = \frac{\lambda_i C_{ir} U_{ir}}{f_0(X)}$$

Then the above equation becomes

$$\sum_{j=1}^{n} a_{kj} y_j + \sum_{i=1}^{N} \sum_{r=1}^{P(i)} a_{irk} y_{ir} = 0, \quad k = 1, 2, \ldots, n \tag{7.18}$$

is the required orthogonality condition and corresponding normality condition is

$$\sum_{j=1}^{n} y_j = 1 \tag{7.19}$$

Clearly, all y_j are positive though y_{ir} may be negative since we do not have any restriction on λ_i. To formulate a dual function, desirability is to have all $y_{ir} > 0$ and it can be obtained by reversing the sign of that term by writing $\lambda_q [1 - g_q(X)]$ in Lagrange's function. Hence, Eqs. (7.18) and (7.19) can be obtained as

$$\sum_{j=1}^{n} a_{kj} y_j + \sum_{i=1}^{N} \sum_{r=1}^{P(i)} a_{irk} y_{ir} = 0 \quad \text{(Orthogonality)}$$

and $$\sum_{j=1}^{N} y_j = 1 \quad \text{(Normality)}.$$

When these equations have a unique solution, the optimal solution of Eq. (7.12) subject to constraints Eq. (7.13) can be obtained by definitions of y_j, y_{ir} in terms of Z_0 and X. In case these equations have an infinite number of solutions, we tend to maximize the dual function given by

$$f(y) = \prod_{j=1}^{n} \left(\frac{C_j}{y_j}\right)^{y_j} \prod_{i=1}^{N} \left[\prod_{r=1}^{N} \left(\frac{C_{rj}}{y_{rj}}\right)^{y_{rj}}\right] \prod_{i=1}^{N} (v_i)^{v_i}$$

where $v_i = \sum_{r=1}^{P(i)} y_{ir}$

subject to orthogonality and normality conditions.

Note: In the above function, constraints are linear, and hence easy to obtain an optimal solution. Moreover, it is easy to work with the logarithm of the dual function, which is linear in the variable $\delta_j = \log y_j$ and $\delta_{ir} = \log y_{ir}$.

EXAMPLE 7.3: Solve the following NLP problem.

Minimize $$f(X) = Z = 2x_1 x_2^{-3} + 4x_1^{-1} x_2^{-1} + \frac{32}{3} x_1 x_2$$

subject to the constraint $10x_1^{-1} x_2^2 = 1$ and $x_1, x_2 \geq 0$.

Solution: The dual of the given NLP problem is

Maximize $$f(y) = \left(\frac{2}{y_1}\right)^{y_1} \left(\frac{4}{y_2}\right)^{y_2} \left(\frac{32}{3y_3}\right)^{y_3} \left(\frac{0.1}{y_4}\right)^{y_4}$$

subject to the constraints

$$y_1 + y_2 + y_3 = 1$$

$$y_1 - y_2 + y_3 - y_4 = 0$$

$$-3y_1 - 2y_2 + y_3 + 2y_4 = 0$$

Then $y_2 = 1 - \frac{4}{3}y_1,\ y_3 = \frac{1}{3}y_1,\ y_4 = \frac{8}{3}y_1 - 1.$

Hence the objective function becomes

$$\text{Maximize} \qquad f(y_1) = \left(\frac{2}{y_1}\right)\left(\frac{4}{1-(4/3)y_1}\right)^{1-(4/3)y_1}\left(\frac{32}{y_1}\right)^{y_1/3}(0.1)^{(8/3)y_1-1}$$

Taking log on both sides, we get

$$\ln f(y_1) = y_1 \ln\left(\frac{2}{y_1}\right) - \left\{1-\left(\frac{4}{3}\right)y_1\right\}\left\{\ln(4) - \ln\left[1-\left(\frac{4}{3}\right)y_1\right]\right\} + \frac{y_1}{3}[\ln(32) - \ln(y_1)] + \left(\frac{8}{3}y_1 - 1\right)\ln(0.1)$$

Differentiating with respect to y_1 and setting equal to 0 gives $y_1 = 0.662$. Hence $y_2 = 0.217$, $y_3 = 0.221$ and $y_4 = 0.766$.

Using relation $f_0(X) = C_jU_j/y_j$, we can compute the values of x_1, x_2 and $f_0(X)$ as given below:

$$y_1 = \frac{C_1U_1}{f_0(x)} = \frac{2x_1x_2^{-1}}{f_0(x)}; \quad y_2 = \frac{C_2U_2}{f_0(X)} = \frac{4x_1^{-1}x_2^{-2}}{f_0(X)}$$

$$y_3 = \frac{C_3U_3}{f_0(x)} = \frac{32x_1x_2}{3f_0(x)}; \quad y_4 = \frac{C_4}{f_0(X)} = \frac{10x_1^{-1}x_2^2}{f_0(X)}$$

A simple mathematical calculation gives $x_1 = 2.5$ and $x_2 = 0.5$.

REVIEW EXERCISES

1. Solve the following problems by geometric programming.

(i) Minimize $Z = 2x_1^2x_2^{-3} + 8x_1^{-3}x_2 + 3x_1x_2,\ x_1, x_2 > 0.$

[**Ans.** $x_1 = 1.39,\ x_2 = 1.13$]

(ii) Minimize $z = 5x_1x_2^{-1}x_3^2 + x_1^{-2}x_3^{-1} + 10x_2^3 + 2x_1^{-1}x_2x_3^{-3},\ x_1, x_2, x_3 > 0$

[**Ans.** $x_1 = 1.26,\ x_2 = 0.41,\ x_3 = 0.59,\ z = 10.28$]

(iii) Minimize $z = 2x_1^3x_2^{-3} + 4x_1^{-2}x_2 + x_1x_2 + 8x_1x_2^{-1},\ x_1, x_2 > 0$

[**Ans.** $x_1 = 1.26,\ x_2 = 1.887,\ z = 13.07$]

(iv) Minimize $z = 2x_1 + 4x_2 + 10x_1^{-1}x_2^{-1},\ x_1, x_2 > 0$

[**Ans.** $x_1 = 14.1,\ x_2 = 23,\ z = 112.9$]

(v) Minimize $z = 2x_1x_2^2x_3^{-1} + 4x_1^{-1}x_2^{-1} + 5x_1x_3$ subject to $x_1^{-1}x_2^{-1} = 5,\ x_1, x_2 > 0$

(vi) Minimize $z = -8x_1^2x_3 + 10x_2^{-1}x_3^2$ subject to $-2x_2^{-2}x_3^{-1} + 3x_1^{-1}x_2^{-1} = 1,\ x_1, x_2, x_3 > 0$

8 Transportation Problem

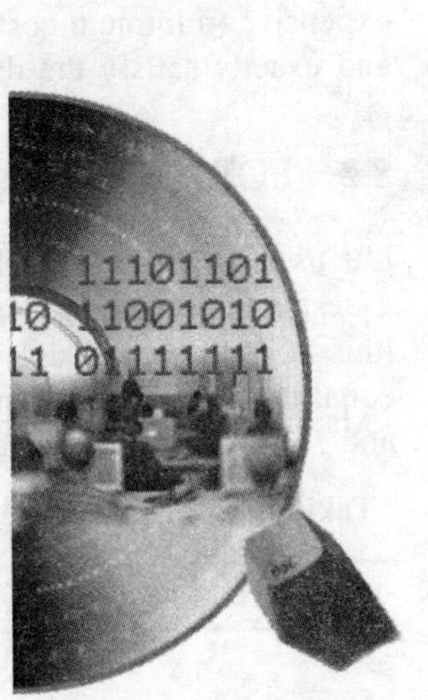

8.1 INTRODUCTION

The "transportation problem" refers to a special class of linear programming problems dealing with the distribution of single commodity from various sources of supply to various points of demand in such a manner that the total transportation costs are minimized. It was first studied by F.L. Hitchcock in 1941, then separately by T.C. Koopmans in 1947, and finally placed in the framework of linear programming and solved by simplex method by G.B. Dantzig in 1951. Since then, improved methods of solutions have been developed and the range of application has been steadily widened. It is now accepted as one of the important analytical and planning tools in business and industry.

Refer to the following table:

	M_1	M_2	Supplies (in tons)
W_1	5	8	15
W_2	4	10	5
Demand (in tons)	12	8	

We consider the shipment of steel from two warehouses W_1 and W_2 to two markets M_1 and M_2. The cost of shipping from warehouse W_i to market M_j is given in the ith-row and jth-column of the table. For example, the cost of shipping from W_2 to M_1 is c_{21}, i.e. Rs 4.00 per ton.

The supplies (a_i) at the warehouses are listed at the right of the table; thus the supply at W_1 is 15 tons. The demands (b_j) at the markets are listed at the bottom of the table; thus the demand at M_1 is 12 tons. Note that here the sum of the supplies equals the sum of the demands, i.e. $\sum a_i = \sum b_j$. Such problems are called *balanced transportation problems*. Let x_{ij} be the amount in tons to be shipped from warehouse W_i to market M_j. The problem is to ship the steel in least expensive (minimum cost) way, and, in doing so, completely exhaust the supplies at the warehouses and exactly satisfy the demands at the markets.

8.2 FORMULATION OF A GENERAL TRANSPORTATION PROBLEM

Let us assume in general that there are m sources $S_1, S_2, \ldots, S_m$ with capacities $a_1, a_2, \ldots, a_m$ and n-destinations (sinks) with requirements $b_1, b_2, \ldots, b_n$ respectively. The transportation cost from ith-source to the jth-sink is c_{ij} and the amount shipped is x_{ij}. If the total capacity of all sources is equal to the total requirement of all destinations, what must be the values of x_{ij} with $i = 1, 2, \ldots, m$ and $j = 1, 2, \ldots, n$ for the total transportation cost to be minimum?

Sinks (Destinations)

		D_1	D_2	D_3	$\cdots$	D_j	$\cdots$	D_n	*Availability*
Source	S_1	c_{11}	c_{12}	c_{13}	$\cdots$	c_{1j}	$\cdots$	c_{1n}	a_1
	S_2	c_{21}	c_{22}	c_{23}	$\cdots$	c_{2j}	$\cdots$	c_{2n}	a_2
	$\vdots$								$\vdots$
	S_i	c_{i1}	c_{i2}	c_{i3}	$\cdots$	c_{ij}	$\cdots$	c_{in}	a_i
	$\vdots$								$\vdots$
	S_m	c_{m1}	c_{m2}	c_{m3}	$\cdots$	c_{mj}	$\cdots$	c_{mn}	a_m
		b_1	b_2	b_3	$\cdots$	b_j	$\cdots$	b_n	$\sum a_i = \sum b_j$

Requirement

Upon examining the above statement of the problem, we realize that it has an objective function which is

$$f(x) = c_{11}x_{11} + \cdots + c_{21}x_{21} + \cdots + c_{2n}x_{2n} + \cdots + c_{m1}x_{m1} + \cdots + c_{mn}x_{mn}$$

$$= \sum_{i=1}^{m} \sum_{j=1}^{n} c_{ij}x_{ij}$$

Secondly, in view of the condition that the total capacity is equal to the total requirement, i.e. $\sum_{i=1}^{m} a_i = \sum_{j=1}^{n} b_j$, the individual capacity of each source must be fully utilized and the individual requirement of each destination must likewise be fully satisfied. Hence we have m capacity constraints and n requirements constraints. The capacity constraints impose on the solution the condition that the total shipments of all destinations from any source must be equal to the capacity of that source. Thus,

$$x_{i1} + x_{i2} + \cdots + x_{in} = a_i, \text{ where } i = 1, 2, \ldots, m$$

On the other hand, the requirement constraints require that the demand of every destination be fully satisfied by the total shipments from all sources. Thus,

$$x_{1j} + x_{2j} + \cdots + x_{mj} = b_j, \text{ where } j = 1, 2, \ldots, n$$

Thirdly, there are the usual non-negativity constraints, i.e. $x_{ij} \geq 0$ for all i and j. They are based on the practical aspect that either we shall send some positive quantity or no quantity from any source to any sink.

To sum up, we have the following mathematical formulation of the transportation problem:

Minimize
$$z = \sum_{i=1}^{m} \sum_{j=1}^{n} c_{ij} x_{ij} \quad (8.1)$$

subject to

$$\sum_{j=1}^{n} x_{ij} = a_i, \quad i = 1, 2, \ldots, m \quad (8.2)$$

$$\sum_{i=1}^{m} x_{ij} = b_j, \quad j = 1, 2, \ldots, n \quad (8.3)$$

and $x_{ij} \geq 0$ for all i and j. (8.4)

The above formulation looks like an LPP. This special LPP will be called a **Transportation Problem** (TP).

8.2.1 Matrix Form of a TP

We can write Eqs. (8.1) to (8.4) in a matrix form as

Minimize $z = \mathbf{cx},\ c,\ x^T \in \mathbf{R}^{mn}$

subject to $\mathbf{Ax} = \mathbf{b},\ x \geq 0,\ b^T \in \mathbf{R}^{m+n}$

where

$$x = [x_{11}, \ldots, x_{1n}x_{21}, \ldots, x_{2n}x_{m1}, \ldots, x_{mn}]$$
$$b = [a_1a_2, \ldots, a_mb_1b_2, \ldots, b_n]$$

and **A** is a $(m + n) \times (mn)$ real matrix containing the coefficients of constraints and **c** is the cost vector. The elements of **A** are either 0 or 1. Thus, an LPP can be reduced to a TP if:

1. the a_{ij}'s are restricted to the values 0 and 1,
2. The units among the constraints are homogeneous.

Remark: For a 2 × 3 – TP, A is given by

$$A = \begin{bmatrix} 1 & 1 & 1 & \vdots & 0 & 0 & 0 \\ 0 & 0 & 0 & \vdots & 1 & 1 & 1 \\ 1 & 0 & 0 & \vdots & 1 & 0 & 0 \\ 0 & 1 & 0 & \vdots & 0 & 1 & 0 \\ 0 & 0 & 1 & \vdots & 0 & 0 & 1 \end{bmatrix} = \begin{bmatrix} e_{mn}^1 & e_{mn}^2 \\ I_n & I_n \end{bmatrix}$$

In general, for a $m \times n$ TP, we have

$$A = \begin{bmatrix} e_{mn}^1 & e_{mn}^2 & \cdots & e_{mn}^m \\ I_n & I_n & \cdots & I_n \end{bmatrix}$$

where e^j_{mn} is a $m \times n$-matrix having the sum vector 1 as its jth-row and 0's elsewhere and I_n is the $n \times n$-identity matrix. If a_{ij} denotes the column vector of A associated with any variable x_{ij}, then

$$a_{ij} = e_i + e_{m+j} \quad \text{where } e_i,\ e_{m+j} \in \mathbf{R}^{m+n} \text{ are unit vectors.}$$

8.3 TYPES OF TRANSPORTATION PROBLEM

The TP can be classified into balanced TP or unbalanced TP. If the sum of the supplies of all the sources is equal to the sum of the demands of all the destinations, then the problem is termed as a balanced TP. Here

$$\sum_{i=1}^{m} a_i = \sum_{j=1}^{n} b_j$$

If the sum of the supplies of all the sources is not equal to the sum of the demands of all the destinations, then the problem is termed as an unbalanced TP. Here,

$$\sum_{i=1}^{m} a_i \neq \sum_{j=1}^{n} b_j$$

An unbalanced TP can be modified to a balanced one by introducing a dummy sink (destination) if $\sum_{i=1}^{m} a_i > \sum_{j=1}^{n} b_j$ and a dummy source if $\sum_{i=1}^{m} a_i < \sum_{j=1}^{n} b_j$. The inflow from the source to a dummy sink represents the surplus at the source. Similarly, the flow from the dummy source to a sink represents the unfilled demand at the sink. The costs of transporting a unit from a dummy source to a dummy sink are assumed to be zero. The resulting problem is now balanced and can be solved.

For example, consider the following problem:

Source \ Sink	D_1	D_2	D_3	Supply
O_1	30	50	15	300
O_2	35	70	20	200
O_3	20	45	60	500
Demand	300	200	400	900/1000

Here $\sum_{i=1}^{3} a_i = 1000$ and $\sum_{j=1}^{3} b_j = 900$. Thus it is an unbalanced TP. Here $\sum_{i=1}^{3} a_i > \sum_{j=1}^{3} b_j$. Thus, there is excess supply. So, we have to include a dummy sink to absorb this excess supply of 100 units $\left(\sum_{i=1}^{3} a_i - \sum_{j=1}^{3} b_j = 100\right)$. The cost coefficients in the dummy destination are assumed to be zeroes.

Modifying the given table yields a balanced TP as follows:

Source \ Sink	D_1	D_2	D_3	D_4	Supply
O_1	30	50	15	0	300
O_2	35	70	20	0	200
O_3	20	45	60	0	500
Demand	300	200	400	100	1000

Similarly, an unbalanced TP given in Table (8.1) can be converted to a balanced TP as in Table (8.2) by adding a dummy source.

Table 8.1

	Destination D_1	D_2	D_3	D_4	
O_1	5	12	6	10	300
O_2	7	8	10	3	400
O_3	9	4	9	2	300
	200	300	450	250	1200/1000

Table 8.2

	Destination D_1	D_2	D_3	D_4	
O_1	5	12	6	10	300
O_2	7	8	10	3	400
O_3	9	4	9	2	300
O_4	0	0	0	0	200
	200	300	450	250	1200

8.4 SOME THEOREMS

Theorem 8.1: *(Existence of a feasible solution):*
The necessary and sufficient condition for the existence of a feasible solution to the TP is $\sum_{i=1}^{m} a_i = \sum_{j=1}^{n} b_j$, *that is, the total capacity (supply) must equal total requirement (demand).*

Proof: (Necessary condition)
Let there exist a feasible solution to the TP given in Eqs. (8.1) to (8.4). Then

$$\sum_{i=1}^{m}\sum_{j=1}^{n} x_{ij} = \sum_{i=1}^{m} a_i$$

and
$$\sum_{j=1}^{n}\sum_{i=1}^{m} x_{ij} = \sum_{j=1}^{m} b_j$$

Therefore,
$$\sum_{i=1}^{m} a_i = \sum_{j=1}^{n} b_j$$

(Sufficient condition)
Let us assume that
$$\sum_{i=1}^{m} a_i = \sum_{j=1}^{n} b_j$$

We think of a working rule to distribute the supply at the ith-source in strict proportion to the requirements of all destinations, i.e. let $x_{ij} = \lambda_i b_j$, where λ_i is the proportionality factor for the ith-source.

Since this supply must be completely distributed,
$$\sum_{i=1}^{m} x_{ij} = \lambda_i \sum_{j=1}^{n} b_j = a_i$$

or
$$\lambda_i = \frac{a_i}{\sum_{j=1}^{m} b_j} = \frac{a_i}{\sum_{i=1}^{n} a_i} \quad \text{(by given)}$$

Thus
$$x_{ij} = \lambda_i b_j = \frac{a_i}{\sum_{j=1}^{m} b_j} b_j \tag{8.5}$$

Now
$$\sum_{j=1}^{n} x_{ij} = \sum_{j=1}^{n} \frac{a_i}{\sum_{j=1}^{m} b_j} b_j = \frac{a_i}{\sum_{j=1}^{m} b_j} \sum_{j=1}^{m} b_j = a_i$$

and
$$\sum_{i=1}^{m} x_{ij} = \sum_{i=1}^{m} \frac{a_i}{\sum_{j=1}^{m} b_j} b_j = \frac{b_i}{\sum_{i=1}^{m} a_i} \sum_{i=1}^{m} a_i = b_j$$

which shows that all the constraints of Eqs. (8.1) to (8.4) are satisfied. Furthermore, since all a_i and b_j are positive, x_{ij} determined from (8.5) must be all positive. Therefore, (8.5) yields a feasible solution.

Theorem 8.2: *The dimensions of the basis of a TP are $(m + n - 1)(m + n - 1)$. This means that a TP has only $(m + n - 1)$—independent structural constraints and its basic feasible solution has only $(m + n - 1)$—positive components.*

Proof: It can be seen from the mathematical model of a TP that there are m rows (capacity constraint equations) and n columns (requirement constraint equations). Thus there are total $(m + n)$ constraint equations. This is due to the condition that $\sum_{i=1}^{m} a_i = \sum_{j=1}^{n} b_j$.

For instance, suppose that we add together the m capacity constraints in Eq. (8.2),

$$\sum_{i=1}^{m}\sum_{j=1}^{n} x_{ij} = \sum_{i=1}^{m} a_i = \sum_{j=1}^{n} b_j \tag{8.6}$$

Now let us add the first $(n - 1)$—requirement constraints in (8.3),

$$\sum_{j=1}^{n-1}\sum_{i=1}^{m} x_{ij} = \sum_{j=1}^{n-1} b_j \tag{8.7}$$

Now subtract Eq. (8.7) from Eq. (8.6). Then $\sum_{i=1}^{m} x_{in} = b_n$ which is the last requirement constraint.

Hence, one of the $(m + n)$ constraints can always be derived from the remaining $(m + n - 1)$ constraints and the problem in effect has only $(m + n - 1)$ independent constraints.

Remarks:

1. This implies that from mn—variables of type x_{ij}, $(m + n - 1)$ are basic variables and remaining $mn - (m + n - 1)$ are non-basic variables. If at least one of these $(m + n - 1)$—variables takes up zero value then the solution is called degenerate solution.
2. The allocated cell in the transportation table will be called occupied cells (or basic cells) and the empty cells will be called non-occupied cells.

Theorem 8.3: *The values of the basic feasible solution are all differences between the partial sum of a_i and the partial sum of b_j,* i.e. $x_{ij} = \pm\sum_{i=1}^{m} r_i a_i \pm \sum_{j=1}^{n} s_j b_j$ *where r_i, s_j are either* 1 *or* 0.

Proof: Let us rewrite the model of TP given in Eqs. (8.1) to (8.4) as follows to reveal more clearly the structure of the coefficient matrix of TP.

Minimize $z = c_{11}x_{11} + \cdots + c_{1n}x_{1n} + c_{21}x_{21} + \cdots + c_{2n}x_{2n} + \cdots + c_{m1}x_{m1} + \cdots + c_{mn}x_{mn}$

subject to

$$\begin{aligned}
x_{11} + \cdots + x_{1n} &= a_1\\
x_{21} + \cdots + x_{2n} &= a_2\\
x_{m1} + \cdots + x_{mn} &= a_m\\
x_{11} + \cdots + x_{21} + x_{m1} &= b_1\\
x_{12} + \cdots + x_{m2} &= b_2\\
x_{1n} + \cdots + x_{2n} + x_{mn} &= b_n
\end{aligned}$$

and $x_{ij} \geq 0$, $i = 1, 2, \ldots, m$, $j = 1, 2, \ldots, n$.

As shown in the following figure, the matrix is characterized by staggered rows of 1's with slanted columns of 1's directly beneath and 0's elsewhere.

$x_{11}, \ldots, x_{1j}, \ldots, x_{1n}x_{21}, \ldots, x_{2j}, \ldots, x_{2n}, \ldots \ldots \ldots, x_{m1}, \ldots, x_{mj}, \ldots, x_{mn}$

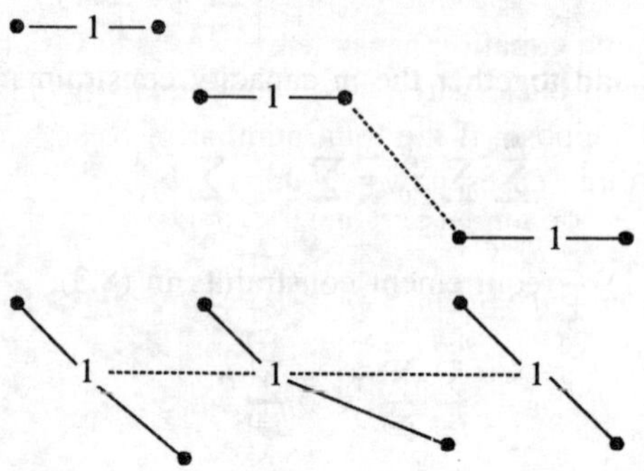

There are two important observations to be made. First, a basic variable (represented by a •) appears in two and only two of the constraints, i.e. one capacity constraint and one requirement constraint (• shows up in the vertical pairs).

Secondly, every constraint must be represented by at least one basis variable (one •), for otherwise that constraint will not be satisfied for $a_i \neq 0$ or $b_j \neq 0$. We recall from Theorem 8.2 that there are only $(m + n - 1)$ basic variables. Therefore, there are only $2(m + n - 1)$ • – dots in the system. However, they have to embrace $(m + n)$ constraints. Consequently, there must be at least two constraints which contain only one basis variable each. These two basis variables can be equated to the constants of the relevant constraints and determined immediately, i.e. $x_{ij} = a_i$ or b_j.

If $x_{ij} = a_i$, then the jth requirement constraint will have one less unknown and b_j must be adjusted to $b_j' = b_j - a_i$ to signify the reduced amount of unsatisfied demand. If $x_{ij} = b_j$, then the ith capacity constraint will have one less unknown and a_i must be adjusted to $a_i' = a_i - b_j$ to signify the reduced supply still available. In the meantime, the total number of undetermined basis variables is reduced to $(m + n - 3)$ and the number of unsolved constraints to $(m + n - 2)$.

Then by the same argument employed before, we reason that there must be two more constraints which contain one basis variable each. Furthermore, these two basis variables must be equal to either some other a_i, b_j or the adjusted a_i', b_j' obtained above. By repeated substitution of determined basis variables into unsolved constraints in this manner, all basis variables will be eventually determined and found equal to the differences between partial sums of a_i on the one hand, and partial sums of b_j on the other as stated in the statement of the theorem.

8.4.1 Triangular Basis

We know that the number of basic variables is equal to the number of constraints in linear programming. In the same way, when capacity and requirement constraints are expressed in terms of basic variables and all non-basic variables are given zero value, the matrix of coefficients of variables in the system of equations is triangular. This means that there is a row or a column in which there is only one basic variable. There is another row or column in which there are two basic variables, and so on.

Theorem 8.4: *The transportation problem has a triangular basis.*

Proof: Initially, we observe that there is no equation in which there is not at least one basic variable, i.e. every equation has a basic variable. Otherwise, the equation cannot be satisfied for $a_i \neq 0$ or $b_j \neq 0$.

Suppose, every row and column equation has at least two basic variables. Since there are m rows and n columns, the total number of basic variables in row equations and column equations will be at least $2m$ and $2n$ respectively. Suppose, if the total number of basic variables is B, then obviously $B \geq 2m$, $B \geq 2n$. There can be three cases now.

Case (i): $m > n$

$$m + m > m + n \Rightarrow 2m > m + n \Rightarrow B \geq 2m > m + n$$

Case (ii): $m < n$

$$m + n < n + n \Rightarrow m + n < 2n \Rightarrow B \geq 2n > m + n$$

Case (iii): $m = n$

$$m + m = m + n \Rightarrow 2m = m + n \Rightarrow B \geq 2m = m + n$$

Thus, in all cases $B \geq m + n$. But we know by Theorem 8.2 that the number of basic variables in TP is $(m + n - 1)$. Thus, we have a contradiction. So, our supposition that every equation has at least two basic variables is wrong. Therefore, there is at least one equation, either row or column, having only one basic variable.

Let the rth equation have only one basic variable and let x_{rs} be the only basic variable in the row r and column s, then $x_{rs} = a_r$. Eliminate rth row from the system of equation and substitute $x_{rs} = a_r$ in sth column equation and replace b_s by $b'_s = b_s - a_r$ (as explained in Theorem 8.3).

After eliminating the rth row, the system has $(m - 1)$ row equations and n column equations of which $(m + n - 2)$ are linearly independent. This implies that the number of basic variables is $(m + n - 2)$. Repeat the argument given earlier and conclude that in the reduced system of equations, there is an equation which has only one basic variable. But if this equation happens to be the sth column equation in the original system, then it will have two basic variables. This suggests that in our original system of equations, there is an equation which has at least two basic variables.

Continue the process to prove the theorem.

8.5 SOLVING THE TRANSPORTATION PROBLEM (FINDING INITIAL BASIC FEASIBLE SOLUTION)

The basic approach in solving the transportation problem is in fact the same as that employed by the simplex method. First, an initial basic feasible solution is obtained. Then a new and better feasible solution is determined by means of the substitution of a basis variable by a non-basis variable, which tends to improve the value of the objective function.

In the TP, a basis variable identifies a route (from specific source to specific sink) that is in use while a non-basis variable identifies a route that is not in use. The problem is a composite of the following three parts:

1. How can non-basis routes be evaluated for their effects on the transportation costs?
2. How can a favourable non-basis route be inserted into the basis to obtain a new basic feasible solution?
3. How can an optimal solution be recognized so that the iteration may be ended?

We now start by looking at methods to find out the initial basic feasible solution.

8.5.1 Why Using Simplex Method to Solve a TP is Unwise?

Consider the following TP.

EXAMPLE 8.1: The ABC car company has warehouses in Calcutta (W_1), Patna (W_2) and Bhavnagar (W_3) and markets in New Delhi (M_1), Dhanbad (M_2) and Calicut (M_3). At a particular time, the company has 61 cars in Calcutta, 49 in Patna and 90 in Bhavnagar. The company plans to transport 52 cars to New Delhi, 68 to Dhanbad and 80 to Calicut. The transportation costs per unit (in rupees) as well as the above data are given in the following table.

Markets

Warehouses	M_1	M_2	M_3	
W_1	26	23	10	61
W_2	14	13	21	49
W_3	16	17	29	90
	52	68	80	200

Formulating the above problem as an LPP, we obtain

Minimize $\quad 26x_{11} + 23x_{12} + 10x_{13} + 14x_{21} + 13x_{22} + 21x_{23} + 16x_{31} + 17x_{32} + 29x_{33}$

subject to

$$x_{11} + x_{12} + x_{13} = 61$$

$$x_{21} + x_{22} + x_{23} = 49$$

$$x_{31} + x_{32} + x_{33} = 90$$

$$x_{11} + x_{21} + x_{31} = 52$$

$$x_{12} + x_{22} + x_{32} = 68$$

$$x_{13} + x_{23} + x_{33} = 90$$

$x_{11}, x_{12}, x_{13}, x_{21}, x_{22}, x_{23}, x_{31}, x_{32}, x_{33} \geq 0.$

The problem has 6 constraints and 9 variables. It will be unwise, if not possible, to solve such a problem using the simplex method. This is why a special computational procedure is necessary to solve the transportation problem.

Now, we study the following three methods to find the initial basic feasible solution to a TP.

1. The North-West Corner Rule (NWCM)
2. Least Cost cell method (LCM)
3. Vogel's Approximation Method (VAM)

8.5.2 The North-West Corner Method (NWCM)

Algorithm

Step 1: Locate the cell (p, q) in the north-west (upper left) corner of the matrix of the data completely ignoring the transportation cost.

Step 2: Transport the minimum of the supply and demand values with respect to that cell and subtract this minimum from the supply and demand values. Thus, if x_{pq} is minimum of a_p and b_q, then give x_{pq} to the cell (p, q). Replace a_p by $a_p - x_{pq}$ and b_q by $b_q - x_{pq}$.

Step 3: Check whether exactly one of the row/column corresponding to the north-west corner cell has now zero supply/demand respectively. If yes, go to step 4; otherwise, go to step 5.

Step 4: Delete that row/column with respect to the north-west corner cell which has the zero supply/demand and go to step 6.

Step 5: Delete both the row and column with respect to the current north-west corner cell.

Step 6: Check whether exactly one row or column is left out. If yes, go to step 7; otherwise, go to step 1.

Step 7: Match the supply/demand of that row/column with the remaining demands/supplies of the undeleted columns/rows.

Step 8: The North-West Corner rule is over. Go to the next phase of solving the TP.

It is clear that as soon as a value of x_{ij} is determined, a row or a column is eliminated from further considerations. The last value of x_{ij} eliminates both a row and a column. Hence, a feasible solution computed by North-West Corner rule can have at most $(m + n - 1)$ positive x_{ij} if the TP has m origins and n destinations. Thus, the solution is a basic feasible solution.

EXAMPLE 8.2: Find the initial basic feasible solution for TP given in Example 8.1 by NWCM. Consider the TP given in Section 8.5.1.

Markets

Warehouses	M_1	M_2	M_3	
W_1	26	23	10	61
W_2	14	13	21	49
W_3	16	17	29	90
	52	68	80	200

As the problem is balanced, we move on to find the initial basic feasible solution by NWCM.

Step 1: The north-west corner cell is (1, 1)with a cost entry $c_{11} = 26$.

Step 2: Out of the supply value 61 and the demand value 52, minimum 52 is allocated to cell (1, 1) and that 52 is subtracted from the supply and demand values respectively.

	M_1	M_2	M_3	
W_1	52 26	23	10	9
W_2	14	13	21	49
W_3	16	17	29	90
	0	68	80	

Step 3: The first column now has demand zero. So we move to step 4.

Step 4: Deleting that column, we go to step 6.

Step 6: Still two columns are left. So we go to step 1.

Now the new data matrix is

	M_2	M_3	
W_1	23	10	9
W_2	13	21	49
W_3	17	29	90
	68	80	

(Rows: Warehouses)

Step 1: Gives us the new north-west cell as the cell corresponding to W_1 and M_2, i.e. with entry 23. We again allocate 9 (minimum of 9 and 68) to that cell and subtract 9 from the demand and supply values yielding after step 2 the following table.

	M_2	M_3	
W_1	9 23	10	0
W_2	13	21	49
W_3	17	29	90
	59	80	

Step 2: First row has supply zero. So we move to step 4.

Step 4: After deleting that row, we get

	M_2	M_3	
W_2	13	21	49
W_3	17	29	90
	59	80	

As still two rows and columns are left, we go to step 1 again and get the north-west corner cell as the cell with entry 13 and repeat the steps as above.

	M_2	M_3	
W_2	49 13	21	0
W_3	17	29	90
	10	80	

Now again the supply for second row is 0. Also according to step 6, we have only one row left at last.

	M_2	M_3	
W_3	17	29	90
	10	80	

So we give 10 to the cell with entry 17 and 80 to the cell with entry 29 and stop.

	M_2	M_3	
W_3	10 17	80 29	0
	0	0	

Thus, the full data table is now allocated as:

	M_1		M_2		M_3	
W_1	52	26	9	23	10	0
W_2		14	49	13	21	0
W_3		16	10	17	80	29	0
	0		0		0	

We read off the initial basic feasible solution from the allocated entries:

$$x_{11} = 52,\ x_{12} = 9,\ x_{22} = 49,\ x_{32} = 10,\ x_{33} = 80 \text{ and the other } x_{ij} = 0.$$

The cost associated with this basic feasible solution is computed as follows:

$$C = 26(52) + 23(9) + 13(49) + 17(10) + 29(80) = \text{Rs. } 4686.$$

The set B of $(m + n - 1)$ cells corresponding to the possible non-negative shipments (x_{ij}'s) of any basic feasible solution will be called the basis to the basic feasible solution. Thus, for this problem the basis is

$$B = \{(1, 1), (1, 2), (2, 2), (3, 2), (3, 3)\}.$$

Note: Instead of writing and drawing tables stepwise as shown above, the whole method can be performed on a single data matrix as shown in the following example.

EXAMPLE 8.3: Obtain the initial basic feasible solution for TP by North-West Corner rule.

Retail shops

Factory	R_1	R_2	R_3	R_4	R_5	Capacity
F_1	1	9	13	36	51	50
F_2	24	12	16	20	1	100
F_3	14	35	1	23	26	150
	100	70	50	40	40	300

Requirements

Solution: We first check whether the problem is balanced or not. It is, so we proceed with the North-West Corner cell (1, 1).

	R_1		R_2		R_3		R_4		R_5		
F_1	50	1		9		13		36		51	50/0
F_2	50	24	50	12		16		20		1	100/50/0
F_3		14	20	35	50	1	40	23	40	26	150/130/80/40/0
	100/50/0		70/20/0		50/0		40/0		40/0		

Since 50 < 100, we ship 50 by cell (1, 1); we slash the row 1 with a zero (/ 0) since b_1 has been reduced to zero. In addition, a_1 is reduced to 50. The remaining matrix (after neglecting first row), has the cell (2, 1) (corresponding to $F_2 - R_1$) as its north-West corner cell. Again $a_1 = 50 < b_2 = 100$. So we ship 50 by the cell (2, 1) and now $b_2 = 50$ and $a_1 = 0$. So we neglect column 1 and proceed. The cell (2, 2) is now the north-west corner cell for the new table and $b_2 = 50$, $a_2 = 70$ ($b_2 < a_2$). So we ship 50 by cell (2, 2) and now $a_2 = 20$, $b_2 = 0$. So we neglect row 2 and proceed.

Finally, the initial basic feasible solution is:

$$x_{11} = 50,\ x_{21} = 50,\ x_{22} = 50,\ x_{32} = 20,\ x_{33} = 50,\ x_{34} = 40,\ x_{35} = 40.$$

The corresponding transportation cost is given by

$$C = 50\ (1) + 50\ (24) + 50\ (12) + 20\ (35) + 50\ (1) + 40\ (23) + 40\ (26)$$
$$= \text{Rs. } 4560.$$

8.5.3 The Least-Cost (Matrix Minimum) Method (LCM)

Algorithm

Step 1: Find the minimum of the (undeleted) values in the cost matrix (i.e. find the matrix minimum).

Step 2: Find the minimum of the supply and demand values (X) with respect to the cell corresponding to the matrix minimum.

Step 3: Allocate X-units to that cell. Also subtract X-units from the supply and demand values of that cell.

Step 4: Check whether exactly one of the row/column corresponding to that cell has zero supply/ demand respectively. If yes, go to step 5; otherwise, go to step 6.

Step 5: Delete that row/column with respect to the cell with the matrix minimum which has zero supply/zero demand and go to step 7.

Step 6: Delete both the row and column with respect to the cell with the matrix minimum.

Step 7: Check whether exactly one row or column is left out. If yes, go to step 8; otherwise, go to step 1.

Step 8: Match the supply/demand of that row/column with the remaining demand supplies of the undeleted rows/columns.

Step 9: The least cost method is over. Go for the next phase of solving the TP.

Remark: In case the minimum cost cell is not unique, then select the cell where maximum allocation can be made.

The minimum transportation cost obtained by the matrix minimum method is much lower than the corresponding cost of the solution derived by using NWCR. This is to be expected as the matrix minimum method takes into account the unit transportation cost while choosing the values of basic variables.

EXAMPLE 8.4: Find the initial basic feasible solution for TP given in Example 8.1 by the least cost method.

Markets

Warehouses	M_1	M_2	M_3	
W_1	26	23	10	61
W_2	14	13	21	49
W_3	16	17	29	90
	52	68	80	200

Step 1: We identify the least cost cell as cell (1, 3) with cost 10.

Step 2: $a_1 = 61$, $b_3 = 80$, mini $\{61, 80\} = 61$.

Step 3: We allocate 61 in cell (1, 3) and new $a_1 = 0$, $b_3 = 80 - 61 = 19$. Thus, we get $x_{13} = 61$.

Step 4: As $a_1 = 0$, moving to step 5, we delete that row and obtain

	M_1	M_2	M_3	
W_2	14	13	21	49
W_3	16	17	29	90
	52	68	19	

As still two rows are left, we again identify the least cost cell in this new matrix. It is the cell with the entry 13. Proceed as above.

	M_1	M_2	M_3	
W_2	14	49 13	21	0
W_3	16	17	29	90
	52	19	19	

Again after deleting the second row of W_2, we have only one row left. Hence,

	M_1	M_2	M_3	
W_3	52 16	19 17	19 29	0
	0	0	0	

So, the final table looks like

Warehouses	M_1	M_2	M_3	
W_1	26	23	61 10	61/0
W_2	14	49 13	21	49/0
W_3	52 16	19 17	19 29	90/0
	52/0	68/19/0	80/19/0	

So the initial basic feasible solution is:

$$x_{13} = 61,\ x_{22} = 49,\ x_{31} = 52,\ x_{32} = 19,\ x_{33} = 19.$$

and the transportation cost is

$$C = 61\ (10) + 49\ (13) + 52\ (16) + 19\ (17) + 19\ (29) = \text{Rs. } 2953.$$

EXAMPLE 8.5: Find the initial basic feasible solution to the TP given in Example 8.3 by LCM.

Solution:

Retail shops

Factory	R_1	R_2	R_3	R_4	R_5	Capacity
F_1	1	9	13	36	51	50
F_2	24	12	16	20	1	100
F_3	14	35	1	23	26	150
Requirements	100	70	50	40	40	300

We select the cell (1, 1) with entry 1. Note that here there is a tie between cells (1, 1), (2, 5) and (3, 3) all having costs 1. But in cells (1, 1) and (3, 3), we can allocate 50 units and in cell (2, 5), 40 units. So we select cell (1, 1) to start. (You can also start with (3, 3)). Then we allocate in cell (3, 3) and at last to cell (2,5).

[50] 1	9	13	36	51	50
24	12	16	20	[40] 1	100/60
14	35	[50] 1	23	26	150/100
100/50	70	50/0	40	40/0	

As new $a_1 = 0$ and new $b_3 = b_5 = 0$, we neglect them and get reduced TP matrix as

24	12		20		60
14	35		23		100
50	70		40		

Proceeding, we start with cell (2, 3) and get

24	[60] 12		20		60/0
[50] 14	[10] 35		[40] 23		100/50/10/0
50/0	70/10/0		40/0		

This stops the method. The overall allocations can be viewed as

[50] 1	9	13	36	51
24	[60] 12	16	20	[40] 1
[50] 14	[10] 35	[50] 1	[40] 23	26

Thus, the initial basic feasible solution is:

$$x_{11} = 50,\ x_{22} = 60,\ x_{25} = 40,\ x_{31} = 50,\ x_{32} = 10,\ x_{33} = 50,\ x_{34} = 40.$$

and the initial minimum transportation cost is

$$C = 50\ (1) + 60\ (12) + 40\ (1) + 50\ (14) + 10\ (35) + 50\ (1) + 40\ (23) = 2830.$$

(Note that this cost is less compared to that in Example 8.3)

8.5.4 Vogel's Approximation Method (VAM)—Penalty Method

The core of Vogel's method is the idea that a penalty will be incurred if the best (lowest cost) route is not used for a source or a destination. Thus, for each source and destination, we compute a 'penalty' rating which is the difference in cost of the two cheapest routes for that source or destination. This penalty rating is recorded for all sources and destinations. Now, we choose that source or destination with the highest rating to attend first on the theory that it is more important to avoid the high penalty associated with a wrong assignment there. In this method, allocations are made so that the penalty cost is minimized. The advantage of this method is that it gives an initial solution which is nearer to an optimal solution than those obtained with NWCR and LCM.

Algorithm

Step 1: From the transportation table, we determine the penalty for each row and column. The penalties are calculated for each row (column) by subtracting the lowest cost element in that row (column) from the next lowest cost element in the same row (column). Write down the penalties below the rows (aside the columns) of the table.

Step 2: Select the row (column) with the highest penalty rating and allocate as much as possible from the supply and requirement values to the cell having the minimum cost. If there is a tie in the values of penalties, then select that cell where least cost cell occurs. If there is a tie in the least cost entries of a selected row/column, select that entry for which maximum allocations can be made.

Step 3: Adjust the supply and demand conditions for that cell. Eliminate those rows (columns) for which the supply and demand requirements are met.

Step 4: Repeat the above steps until the entire available capacity at various sources and requirements at various destinations are met.

Thus, we obtain an initial basic feasible solution.

EXAMPLE 8.6: Calculate the initial basic feasible solution for the TP in Example 8.1 by VAM.

Warehouses	M_1	M_2	M_3	
W_1	26	23	10	61
W_2	14	13	21	49
W_3	16	17	29	90
	52	68	80	200

Solution:

Step 1: First, we calculate the penalties for all sources and destinations. They are written below the table for the row differences and aside the table for the column differences.

				Penalty
26	23	10	61	13
14	13	21	49	1
16	17	29	90	1
52	68	80		
Penalty 2	4	11		

Step 2: We now select row 1 because it has the highest penalty rating 13. Now we look at the supply and demand values, corresponding to the cell with the least value in row 1. Here, it is the cell (1, 3) with entry 10 and $a_1 = 61$, $b_3 = 80$. So we allocate 61 to (1, 3).

Step 3: We also adjust the new supply and demand a_1 and b_3 as shown below:

				Penalty
26	23	61 10	61/0	13
14	13	21	49	1
16	17	29	90	1
52	68	80/19		
Penalty 2	4	11		

As the capacity for source 1 is satisfied, we neglect that row from further consideration.

				Penalty
14	13	21	49	1
16	17	29	90	1
52	68	19		
Penalty 2	4	8		

Here, we select the destination 3, i.e. at the 3rd column because it has the largest penalty and allocate the 19 units to the cell (2, 3) having the least cost 21.

14	13	19 21	30
16	17	29	90
52	68	0	

As the requirement constraint for the third destination is met, we neglect that from further consideration. Finding penalties for the new reduced matrix,

			Penalty
14	13	30	1
16	17	90	1
52	68		
Penalty 2	4		

Repeating the above procedure, we obtain

14	30 13	0
16	17	90
52	38	

Finally, we obtain

52 16	38 17	0
0	0	

The whole procedure can be done in a single table in the following way:

	M_1	M_2	M_3	*Capacity*	*Penalties*
W_1	26	23	61 10	61/0	13 – –
W_2	14	30 13	19 21	49/30/0	1 1 1
W_3	52 16	38 17	29	90/38/0	1 1 1
	52	68/38/0	80/19/0		
Penalties	2	4	11		
	2	4	8		
	2	4	–		

Thus, the initial basic feasible solution is:

$$x_{13} = 61,\ x_{22} = 30,\ x_{23} = 19,\ x_{31} = 52,\ x_{32} = 38$$

and the total transportation cost is computed as follows:

$$C = 61(10) + 30(13) + 19(21) + 52(16) + 38(17) = \text{Rs. } 2877.$$

Note: The same example when solved for the initial basic feasible solution by the three different methods gives

	Method used	*Transportation cost*
Ex 8.1	NWCM	4686
Ex 8.4	LCM	2953
Ex 8.6	VAM	2877

The reader can easily see that VAM gives a better initial solution in terms of less transportation cost.

EXAMPLE 8.7: Calculate the initial basic feasible solution for the TP given in Example 8.3 by VAM.

Solution: First, checking the penalties for the first round, we find it is 26 for column R_5. So, we allocate in its least cost cell with cost 1, the amount 40 of its requirements, leading to its new requirement being zero, thus neglecting the last column from future considerations.

	R_1	R_2	R_3	R_4	R_5	Capacity	Penalties		
F_1	[50] 1	9	13	36	51	50/0	8	8	
F_2	24	[60] 12	16	20	[40] 1	100/60/0	11	4	4
F_3	[50] 14	[10] 35	[50] 1	[40] 23	26	150/100	13	13*	13
Requirement	100/50/0	70/0	50/0	40/0	40/0	90/40/0			
Penalties	13	3	12	3	26				
	13*	3	12	3	–				
	10	21	15	3	–				

Now finding the penalties again for the new reduced matrix (i.e. after neglecting the last column), we find there is a tie between penalties of F_3 and R_1 (both are 13, marked with *). So, we select the least cost cell from both. In this case both have least cost cell as 1. So, we arbitrarily select the cell (1, 1), i.e. corresponding to $F_1 - R_1$. We allocate 50 capacity values thereby exhausting it and the new requirement value is $b_1 = 50$. Now we neglect the first row also from future consideration.

We proceed similarly and obtain the initial basic feasible solution as

$$x_{11} = 50,\ x_{22} = 60,\ x_{25} = 40,\ x_{31} = 50,\ x_{32} = 10,\ x_{33} = 50,\ x_{34} = 40$$

and the minimum transportation cost is

$$C = 50(1) + 60(12) + 40(1) + 50(14) + 10(35) + 50(1) + 40(23) = \text{Rs. } 2830.$$

Note that in this case this value is less than that obtained by NWCR for the same table in Example 8.3, but same as that of LCM in Example 8.5.

We have seen the first stage of solving a transportation problem, i.e. finding the initial basic feasible solution. We have also seen that VAM is more preferable to NWCR and LCM for finding the initial basic feasible solution. We now move ahead and see whether the initial basic feasible solution obtained is optimal or not. Thus, we have to check whether the set of allocations obtained in VAM are the best possible to reduce the total transportation costs, or do any other set of such allocations exist?

8.6 LOOPS IN A TRANSPORTATION METHOD

In a transportation table, an ordered set of four or more cells is said to form a loop if

1. any two adjacent cells in the ordered set lie either in the same row or in the same column, and
2. any three or more adjacent cells in the ordered set do not lie in the same row or the same column. The first cell of the set is considered to follow the last in the cell.

If we join the cells of a loop by horizontal and vertical segments, we get a closed path satisfying (1) and (2) above. Let us denote by (i, j), the (i, j)th cell of a transportation table, then it can be seen from the Figures 8.1(a)-(c) that the set

$L_1 = \{(2, 1), (4, 1), (4, 4), (1, 4), (1, 2), (2, 2)\}$ forms a loop, while

$L_2 = \{(3, 2), (3, 5), (2, 5), (2, 4), (2, 3), (1, 3), (1, 2)\}$ does not form a loop.

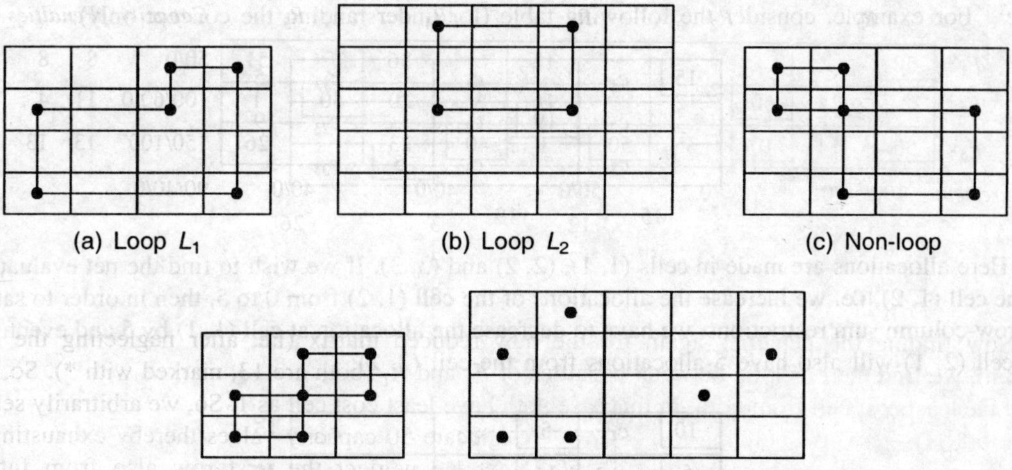

(a) Loop L_1 (b) Loop L_2 (c) Non-loop

(d) Loop (e)

Figure 8.1

The indication of independence of a set of individual positive allocations is that we cannot form a loop by joining positive allocations by horizontal and vertical lines only, for example see Figures 8.1(a)–(d). A closed loop is formed by joining the positive allocation cells by horizontal and vertical lines. But in Figure 8.1(e), we will not be able to form such a loop. Thus, allocations in Figure 8.1(a) and (d) are independent in position, while in Figure 8.1(e) are dependent in position.

Note that every loop will contain an even number of cells. Independent allocations have a property that it is impossible to increase or decrease any individual allocation without altering the positions of individual allocations or violating the row or column sum restrictions.

8.7 OPTIMALITY IN A TRANSPORTATION PROBLEM

After determining the initial basic feasible solution, the problem that arises is, how to recognize an optimum solution, i.e. whether or not the solution thus obtained minimizes the total transportation cost. For this we determine the value called net evaluation contributions (opportunity cost), corresponding to each empty cell (cell where no allocations are made) of the transportation matrix. If a unit is allocated in an unoccupied cell and the adjustments are made in the solution to maintain the row and column sums, then the net change in the total cost resulting from the adjustments is called the net evaluation contribution of that cell and is denoted by Δ_{ij}.

The unoccupied cell with the largest negative Δ_{ij} value is selected to include in the new set of allocations. It is an incoming variable. The outgoing variable in the current solution is the occupied cell (basic variable) in the unique close path (loop) whose allocation will become zero first as more units are allocated to the cell with largest negative Δ_{ij} value. Such an exchange reduces the total transportation cost. The process is continued until there is no negative Δ_{ij} value for all non allocated cells. That is, the current solution cannot be improved further. It is the optimal. We will discuss in detail as we move along.

Note: For example, consider the following table (for understanding the concept only).

15 c_{11}	c_{12}	c_{13}	15
c_{21}	19 c_{22}	c_{23}	19
c_{31}	c_{32}	5 c_{33}	5
15	19	5	

Here allocations are made in cells (1, 1), (2, 2) and (3, 3). If we wish to find the net evaluations of the cell (1, 2), i.e. we increase the allocations of the cell (1, 2) from 0 to 5, then in order to satisfy the row-column sum restrictions, we have to decrease the allocation at cell (1, 1) by 5 and eventually the cell (2, 1) will also have 5-allocations from the cell (2, 2).

10 c_{11}	5 c_{12}	c_{13}	15
5 c_{21}	14 c_{22}	c_{23}	19
c_{31}	c_{32}	5 c_{33}	5
15	19	5	

Note that the adjustments are done only on the positive allocations and except these four allocations, the other allocations remain unchanged, and so their transportation cost will also remain unchanged. The *net change* in the total transportation cost due to the allocations in cell (2, 1) is

$$5c_{21} - 5c_{11} + 5c_{12} - 5c_{22}$$

This is the relative cost coefficient of the variable x_{21}. Similarly, we can find such coefficients for all non-basic variables (empty cells).

8.7.1 Dual of a Transportation Problem

Consider the general transportation problem defined in Eqs. (8.1) to (8.4).

Minimize $$z = \sum_{i=1}^{m} \sum_{i=1}^{n} c_{ij} x_{ij}$$

subject to

$$\sum_{j=1}^{n} x_{ij} = a_i, \quad i = 1, 2, \ldots, m$$

$$\sum_{i=1}^{m} x_{ij} = b_j, \quad j = 1, 2, \ldots, n$$

and $x_{ij} \geq 0$ for all i and j.

Since all the constraints are equalities, we convert them into inequalities and reformulate the problem as

Minimize $$z = \sum_{i=1}^{m} \sum_{j=1}^{n} c_{ij} x_{ij}$$

subject to

$$\sum_{j=1}^{n} x_{ij} \geq a_i, \quad i = 1, 2, \ldots, m \tag{8.8}$$

$$\sum_{j=1}^{n} (-x_{ij}) \leq (-a_i), \quad i = 1, 2, \ldots, m \tag{8.9}$$

$$\sum_{i=1}^{m} x_{ij} \geq b_j, \quad j = 1, 2, \ldots, n \tag{8.10}$$

$$\sum_{i=1}^{m} (-x_{ij}) \leq (-b_j), \quad j = 1, 2, \ldots, n \tag{8.11}$$

and $x_{ij} \geq 0$ for all i and j.

Let u_i^+ and u_i^- be the dual variables one for each capacity constraint i in Eqs. (8.8) and (8.9) respectively. Let v_j^+ and v_j^- be the dual variables one for each requirement constraint j in Eqs. (8.10) and (8.11) respectively.

Dual of the above problem is

Maximize
$$z^* = \sum_{i=1}^{m} (u_i^+ - u_i^-)\, a_i + \sum_{j=1}^{n} (v_j^+ - v_j^-)\, b_j \tag{8.12}$$

subject to
$$(u_i^+ - u_i^-) + (v_j^+ - v_j^-) \leq c_{ij} \tag{8.13}$$

and u_i^+, u_i^-, v_j^+ and $v_j^- \geq 0$ for all i and j.

Let $u_i = u_i^+ - u_i^-$ and $v_j = v_j^+ - v_j^-$. Then u_i and v_j will be unrestricted in sign. Then problem in Eqs. (8.12) and (8.13) can now be rewritten as

Maximize
$$z^* = \sum_{i=1}^{m} u_i a_i + \sum_{j=1}^{n} v_j b_j \tag{8.14}$$

subject to
$$u_i + v_j \leq c_{ij} \quad \text{for all } (i, j) \tag{8.15}$$

and u_i, v_j unrestricted in sign for all i and j.

Remarks:

1. The variables u_i and v_j are the shadow prices for capacities and requirements respectively. They represent the implicit contribution (value) of an additional unit of capacity at source i and an additional unit transported to requirement j.
2. The variables x_{ij} form an optimal solution to the given transportation problem provided
   (a) solution x_{ij} is feasible for all (i, j) with respect to Eq. (8.4).
   (b) solution u_i and v_j is feasible for all (i, j) with respect to Eqs. (8.14)–(8.15).
   (c) $(c_{ij} - u_i - v_j)\, x_{ij} = 0$ for all i and j. This is the complementary slackness for a TP and indicate that
   → if $x_{ij} > 0$ and is feasible in Eqs. (8.1)–(8.4) then $c_{ij} - u_i - v_j = 0$ or $c_{ij} = u_i + v_j$ for each occupied cell.
   → if $x_{ij} = 0$ and $c_{ij} > u_i + v_j$ then it is not desirable to have $x_{ij} > 0$ in the basis because it would cost more to transport on a route (i, j).
   → if $c_{ij} < u_i + v_j$ for some $x_{ij} = 0$ then x_{ij} can be brought into the basis.

3. Recall from LPP that for any standard LPP with basis B and associated cost vector c_B, the associated solution to its dual is given by $u = c_B B^{-1}$. Thus, if a_j is the jth-column of the primal constraint matrix then an expression for evaluating the net evaluation is given by

$$c_j - z_j = c_j - c_B B^{-1} a_j = c_j - ua_j$$

In our present case of TP, the associated dual solution can be represented as $(u, v) = (u_1, u_2, \ldots, u_m, v_1, v_2, \ldots, v_n)$ and hence net evaluations are given by

$$\Delta_{ij} = c_{ij} - z_{ij} = c_{ij} - (u, v)\, a_{ij}$$

$$= c_{ij} - (u_1, u_2, \ldots, u_m, v_1, v_2, \ldots, v_n)(e_i + e_{m+j}) = c_{ij} - (u_i + v_j)$$

Here, it may be noted that $\Delta_{ij} = 0$ for occupied cells (basic variables). Except for the degeneracy case, there are $(m + n - 1)$ dual equations in $(m + n)$ dual unknowns, for the $(m + n - 1)$ basic cells. We can assign arbitrary value for one of these unknown u_i and v_j and solve uniquely for the remaining $(m + n - 1)$—variables. After an arbitrary assignment, say $u_1 = 0$, the rest of the values are obtained by simple addition and subtraction. (Here we will use a thumb rule that—that u_i or v_j should be taken as zero whose row/column has the maximum number of allocated cells.) Once all the u_i and v_j have been determined, the net evaluations for all the non-basic cells are obtained by using the relation $\Delta_{ij} = c_{ij} - (u_i + v_j)$.

Theorem 8.5: *If we have a non-degenerate basic feasible solution, i.e. a cell with exactly $(m + n - 1)$ independent positive allocations and a set of arbitrary numbers u_i and v_j, $i = 1, 2, \ldots, m$ and $j = 1, 2, \ldots, n$ such that $c_{rs} = u_r + v_s$ for all occupied cell (r, s) then the net evaluations are given by $\Delta_{ij} = c_{ij} - (u_i + v_j)$.*

Proof: The TP is to find $x_{ij} \geq 0$ so as to

Minimize
$$z = \sum_{i=1}^{m} \sum_{j=1}^{n} c_{ij} x_{ij} \tag{8.16}$$

subject to

$$a_i - \sum_{j=1}^{n} x_{ij} = 0, \quad i = 1, 2, \ldots, m \tag{8.17}$$

$$b_j - \sum_{i=1}^{m} x_{ij} = 0, \quad j = 1, 2, \ldots, n \tag{8.18}$$

Now adding u_i times (8.17) and v_j times (8.18) to the objective function (8.16), it becomes

$$z = \sum_{i=1}^{m} \sum_{j=1}^{n} c_{ij} x_{ij} + \sum_{i=1}^{m} u_i \left(a_i - \sum_{j=1}^{n} x_{ij} \right) + \sum_{j=1}^{n} v_j \left(b_j - \sum_{i=1}^{m} x_{ij} \right)$$

$$= \sum_{i=1}^{m} \sum_{j=1}^{n} [c_{ij} - (u_i + v_j)] x_{ij} + \sum_{i=1}^{m} u_i a_i + \sum_{j=1}^{n} v_j b_j \tag{8.19}$$

But given that for all occupied (basic cells), $c_{rs} = u_r + v_s$, all terms of positive allocations vanish from Eq. (8.19) as their coefficients become zero.

Therefore,

$$z = \sum_{i=1}^{m} u_i a_i + \sum_{j=1}^{n} v_j b_j \tag{8.20}$$

Suppose we want to determine the net evaluation for the cell (p, q). As we allocate one unit to cell (p, q), positive allocations become $(m + n)$ in number and hence dependent. So a loop can be formed as shown below:

$$\begin{array}{cccc} & (p, q) & (p, s) & \\ +1 & c_{pq} & c_{ps} & -1 \\ -1 & c_{rq} & c_{rs} & +1 \\ & (r, q) & (r, s) & \end{array}$$

Here all (p, s), (r, q), (r, s) are occupied cells, hence $c_{ps} = u_p + v_s$, $c_{rq} = u_r + v_q$, $c_{rs} = u_r + v_s$. Now to maintain row and column sums, we have to decrease the individual allocations at (p, s) and (r, q) cells and increase at cells (r, s) and (p, q) by 1 unit. Therefore, the value of the individual allocations in these occupied cells is changed but they contribute nothing in the objective function Eq. (8.19) as their coefficients are necessarily zero. Thus, the new values of the objective function corresponding to this new solution is given by

$$z^* = [c_{pq} - (u_p + v_q)] + \sum_{i=1}^{m} u_i a_i + \sum_{j=1}^{n} v_j b_j$$

Hence, the net evaluation is given by

$$\Delta_{pq} = z^* - z = [c_{pq} - (u_p + v_q)] \tag{8.21}$$

Thus, in general, $\Delta_{ij} = c_{ij} - (u_i + v_j)$.

8.8 TRANSPORTATION ALGORITHM: MODIFIED DISTRIBUTION (MODI) METHOD

Algorithm

Step 1: We find the initial basic feasible solution by applying VAM on a balanced transportation problem. Thereby we find the initial transportation cost.

Step 2: In order to check the optimality of the cost, we apply the optimality criteria: There must be $(m + n - 1)$ number of allocated cells (m—number of rows, n—number of columns). If the number of allocated cells is less than $(m + n - 1)$, then it is a degenerate TP.

For allocated cells, we break up the cost as $c_{ij} = u_i + v_j$. (That is u_i or v_j should be taken as zero, for which maximum number of allocations are made in its row/column).

Step 3: Now find the opportunity cost for non-allocated cells by $\Delta_{ij} = c_{ij} - (u_i + v_j)$.

Step 4: Examine the sign for each Δ_{ij}.

(i) If all $\Delta_{ij} \geq 0$, then the optimality criterion has been satisfied and the initial cost obtained is optimum. If some $\Delta_{ij} = 0$, then it is the case of the alternative optimal solution.

(ii) If some $\Delta_{ij} < 0$, then the cost obtained is not optimal. It has to be reduced by some technique (given in next step).

Step 5: In the cell having the most negative value of Δ_{ij}, we will make allocations. Rescheduling of allocations is done by the looping process.

Start the closed path with the selected unoccupied cell and mark (+) in this cell, trace a path along the rows (or columns) to an occupied cell with minimum allocations, mark (–) in this cell and continue down the column (or row) to an occupied cell and mark (+) and (–) signs alternatively. Close the path back to the selected unoccupied cell. All end points of the loop are allocated cells except the one which corresponds to the most negative Δ_{ij} entry. All (+) are acceptor cells and (–) are donor cells. (Hence a loop is always of an even number of cells and it is unique.

Step 6: Out of the donors, the one with the lowest allocation gives same number of allocated units to the most negative Δ_{ij} acceptor cell (+). Add that quantity to all other acceptor cells (+) and subtract it from the cells marked with (–) sign.

Step 7: Now find the new minimum cost by allocating units to the remaining non-allocated cells.

Step 8: Test the revised solution for optimality.

Note: Step 2 to step 8 above is known as *Modified Distribution* (MODI) method.

EXAMPLE 8.8: Check the optimality of the solution obtained by VAM for the TP in Example 8.6. If the solution is not optimal, modify it.

Solution: The initial basic feasible solution obtained in Example 8.6 is as follows:

	M_1	M_2	M_3
W_1	26	23	61 10
W_2	14	30 13	19 21
W_3	52 16	38 17	29

and the initial transportation cost is Rs. 2877.

Now, we apply the transportation algorithm (MODI Method) to check the optimality.

Step 1: We have already calculated.

Step 2: Here the allocated cells (basic cells) are the cells (1, 3), (2, 2), (2, 3), (3, 1), (3, 2), where the allocations 61, 30, 19, 52, 38 respectively are made and they are 5 in number. Also $m + n - 1 = 3 + 3 - 1 = 5$. Therefore, number of allocated cells are $5 = (m + n - 1)$.

Now we break up the cost for the basic cells as $c_{ij} = u_i + v_j$ with the thumb rule: That u_i or v_j should be taken as zero, for which the maximum number of allocations are made in its row/column.

		10	u_1
	13	21	$u_2 = 0$
16	17		u_3
v_1	v_2	v_3	

Let us take $u_2 = 0$.

As $u_2 + v_2 = 13 \Rightarrow v_2 = 13$

As $v_2 + u_3 = 17 \Rightarrow u_3 = 4$

As $u_3 + v_1 = 16 \Rightarrow v_1 = 12$

As $\quad u_2 + v_3 = 21 \quad \Rightarrow \quad v_3 = 21$

As $\quad u_1 + v_3 = 10 \quad \Rightarrow \quad u_1 = -11$

Thus, we get

		10	$u_1 = -11$
	13	21	$u_2 = 0$
16	17		$u_3 = 4$
$v_1 = 12$	$v_2 = 13$	$v_3 = 21$	

Step 3: We now find the opportunity cost for non-allocated cells (non-basic cells) by $\Delta_{ij} = c_{ij} - (u_i + v_j)$, i.e. we have u_i or v_j values from the previous step for all those cells, where allocations are not made, we will subtract $(u_i + v_j)$ from the initial cost given in the initial TP cost matrix.

26	23	
14		
		29

cost values given in the original matrix (for non-basic cells)

1	2		$u_1 = -11$
12			$u_2 = 0$
		25	$u_3 = 4$
$v_1 = 12$	$v_2 = 13$	$v_3 = 21$	

$(u_i + v_j)$ addition for non-basic cells from step 2.

Thus Δ_{ij} values are $c_{ij} - (u_i + v_j)$ as shown:

25	21	
2		
		4

Step 4: Examine the sign of each Δ_{ij}. As each $\Delta_{ij} > 0$, the optimality criterion is satisfied and the cost obtained is optimum.

Thus, here the initial cost obtained by applying VAM is optimum.

EXAMPLE 8.9: Check the optimality of the solution obtained by VAM for TP in Example 8.7. If the solution is not optimal, modify it.

Solution: The initial basic feasible solution obtained in Example 8.7 is:

50 1	9	13	36	51
24	60 12	16	20	40 1
50 14	10 35	50 1	40 23	26

and the initial transportation cost is Rs. 2830.

Step 1: Calculated.

Step 2: The number of allocated cells is $7 = (m + n - 1) = 3 + 5 - 1$. Thus, the number of allocated cells is equal to $(m + n - 1)$. Break up the cost for the basic cells as $c_{ij} = u_i + v_j$

1					$u_1 = -13$
	12			1	$u_2 = -23$
14	35	1	23		$u_3 = 0$
$v_1 = 14$	$v_2 = 35$	$v_3 = 1$	$v_4 = 23$	$v_5 = 24$	

As u_3 corresponds to a row which has the maximum allocations, we take $u_3 = 0$ and then $v_1 = 14$, $v_2 = 35$, $v_3 = 1$, $v_4 = 23$, $v_5 = 24$, $u_1 = -13$, $u_2 = -23$.

Step 3: We now find the opportunity cost for non-allocated cells by $\Delta_{ij} = c_{ij} - (u_i + v_j)$

	9	13	36	51
24		16	20	
				26

cost values given in the original matrix (for non-basic cells)

	22	−12	10	11
−9		−22	0	
				24

$(u_i + v_j)$ addition for non-basic cells

Thus, $\Delta_{ij} = c_{ij} - (u_i + v_j)$ are as shown below:

	−13	25	26	40
33		38	20	
				2

Hence the value of Δ_{ij} in the cell (1, 2) is −13, which is negative. This indicates that the initial basic feasible solution and hence the transportation cost obtained is not optimal.

Step 5: We have to make allocations in the cell where Δ_{ij} is most negative, i.e. in the cell (1, 2). We have to trace a closed path from this cell (non-basic) to the other cells which are basic cells. (In the above table, it is clear that those cells which are empty in Δ_{ij}-table are basic cells because we find Δ_{ij} only for non-basic cells.) Thus, a closed path can be easily identified. While making such a closed path we will also alternatively assign '+' and '–' sign indicating that all '+' are acceptor cells and '–' are donor cells. The traced path from the above table is identified as

+	+ −13	25	26	40
33		38	20	
+				2

We now make a new table indicating the basic cells and the cell with negative Δ_{ij} entry.

50	+			
33	60			40 1
50	10	50 1	40 23	

Now out of both the donors, cell (1, 1) and (3, 2), the one having lowest allocation gives 10 units to the cell (1, 2). Similarly, to balance this, the donor cell (1, 1) gives 10 units to the acceptor cell (3, 1). Thus, the new allocation table is

40 1	10 9			
	60 12			40 1
60 14		50 1	40 23	

and the new cost associated with it is

$$40\ (1) + 10\ (9) + 60\ (12) + 40\ (1) + 60\ (14) + 50\ (1) + 40\ (23) = \text{Rs. } 2700.$$

Therefore, the new feasible solution is

$$x_{11} = 40,\ x_{12} = 10,\ x_{22} = 60,\ x_{25} = 40,\ x_{31} = 60,\ x_{33} = 50,\ x_{34} = 40.$$

Now, again we need to check its optimality.

Number of allocated cells = 7 = $m + n - 1$.

Break up the cost for the basic cells as $c_{ij} = u_i + v_j$

1	9				$u_1 = -13$
	12			1	$u_2 = -10$
14		1	23		$u_3 = 0$
$v_1 = 14$	$v_2 = 22$	$v_3 = 1$	$v_4 = 23$	$v_5 = 11$	

Calculate the opportunity cost for non-allocated cells.

		13	36	51	
24		16	20		cost value given in the original matrix (for non-basic cells)
	35			26	

		−12	10	−2	
4		−9	13		$(u_i + v_j)$ addition for non-basic cells
	22			11	

Thus, $\Delta_{ij} = c_{ij} - (u_i + v_j)$ are as shown below:

		25	26	53
20		25	7	
	13			15

As all $\Delta_{ij} > 0$, the optimality criterion is satisfied and the solution is optimal, and the cost is minimum. Therefore, the optimal solution is $x_{11} = 40$, $x_{12} = 10$, $x_{22} = 60$, $x_{25} = 40$, $x_{31} = 60$, $x_{33} = 50$, $x_{34} = 40$ and the minimum transportation cost is Rs. 2700.

8.9 STEPPING STONE METHOD

The stepping stone method is another method for finding the optimum solution of the TP. The various steps necessary in the stepping stone method are given below.

Step 1: Find an initial basic feasible solution by any of the methods given in Section 8.5.

Step 2: Resolve the degeneracy if it occurs.

Step 3: Each empty (non-allocated) cell is examined for a possible decrease in the transportation cost. One unit is allocated to an empty cell. A number of adjacent cells are balanced so that the row and the column constraints are not violated. If the net result of such readjustment is a decrease in the transportation cost, we include as many units as possible in the selected empty cell and carry out the necessary readjustment with other cells.

Step 4: Step 3 is performed with all the empty cells till no further reduction in the transportation cost is possible. If there is another allocation with zero increase or decrease in the transportation cost, then the TP has multiple solutions.

EXAMPLE 8.10: Solve the following TP by using the stepping stone method to check optimality.

	D_1	D_2	D_3	D_4	
A	4	6	8	6	700
B	3	5	2	5	400
C	3	9	6	5	600
	400	450	350	500	

Solution: The initial basic feasible solution has been computed by using NWCR.

400 4	300 6	8	6	700
3	150 5	250 2	5	400
3	9	100 6	500 5	600
400	450	350	500	

There are 6 allocations $= m + n - 1$. The initial basic feasible solution is $x_{11} = 400$, $x_{12} = 300$, $x_{22} = 150$, $x_{23} = 250$, $x_{33} = 100$, $x_{34} = 500$ and the total cost = Rs. 7750.

Now we start with an empty cell (2, 1), i.e. cell BD_1. The result of allocating one unit along with the necessary adjustment in the adjacent cells is shown below:

	D_1	D_2	D_3	D_4	
A	399 4	301 6	8	6	700
B	1 3	149 5	250 2	5	400
C	3	9	100 6	500 5	600
	400	450	350	500	

The increase in the transportation cost per unit quantity of reallocation is

$$X + (1 \text{ unit in } BD_1) + (1 \text{ allocated in } AD_2) - (1 \text{ taken from } AD_1) - (1 \text{ taken from } BD_2)$$

$$= X + 3 + 6 - 4 - 5 = X$$

(where X is the initial cost), i.e. there is no change. This indicates that every unit allocated to route BD_1 will neither increase nor decrease the transportation cost. Thus, such a reallocation is unnecessary.

Now we again move to another empty cell (3, 1), i.e. CD_1. Allocate 1 unit to that cell.

	D_1	D_2	D_3	D_4	
A	399 6	301 6	8	6	700
B	3	149 5	251 2	5	400
C	1 3	9	99 6	500 5	600
	400	450	350	500	

The net increase in the transportation cost per unit quantity of reallocation is

$$X + 3 + 6 + 2 - 4 - 5 - 6 = X - 4.$$

Thus, the new route is beneficial. The minimum amount that can be allocated to that cell (3, 1) is 100. This will make the cell (3, 3), i.e. CD_3 empty.

	D_1	D_2	D_3	D_4	
A	300 4	400 6	8	6	700
B	3	50 5	350 2	5	400
C	100 3	9	6	500 5	600
	400	450	350	500	

The new improved solution is $x_{11} = 300$, $x_{12} = 400$, $x_{22} = 50$, $x_{23} = 350$, $x_{31} = 100$, $x_{34} = 500$ and the total cost = Rs. 7350.

This procedure is repeated with the remaining empty cells. The results are summarized as follows:

Unoccupied cells	*Net increase in the transportation cost*
CD_2, (3, 2)	$X + 9 + 4 - 6 - 3 = X + 4$
AD_3, (1, 3)	$X + 8 + 5 - 6 - 2 = X + 5$
CD_3, (3, 3)	$X + 6 - 2 + 5 - 6 + 4 = X + 4$
AD_4, (1, 4)	$X + 6 - 5 + 3 - 4 = X + 0$
BD_4, (2, 4)	$X + 5 - 5 + 6 - 4 + 3 - 5 = X + 0$

Since reallocation in any other unoccupied cell cannot decrease the transportation cost, the present solution is optimum. The minimum transportation cost is thus Rs. 7350 as obtained.

8.10 VARIATIONS OF A TRANSPORTATION PROBLEM

8.10.1 Maximization Transportation Problem

When, in a TP, the objective is to maximize the total value or benefit, instead of the unit cost c_{ij}, the unit profit or payoff p_{ij} associated with each route is given. The algorithm for solving such problem is same as discussed in Section 8.5, except the following two changes:

1. For finding the initial solution by VAM method, penalties will be computed as the difference between the largest and the second largest payoff in the row or column. Allocations are made in those cells where penalty is the largest in that row/column.
2. The optimality criteria is that—for all unoccupied cells $\Delta_{ij} \leq 0$.

Or, a maximization TP can be converted into the usual minimization TP by subtracting all the costs from the highest cost involved in the problem. Then our normal methods are applied.

8.10.2 Alternative Optimal Solutions

If an unoccupied cell in an optimal solution has opportunity cost Δ_{ij} equal to zero, then an alternative optimal solution can be formed with another set of allocations without increasing the total transportation cost.

In this case, if such a cell is entered into the basis, no change in the transportation cost would occur. We will form a loop for that cell and allocate it the maximum quantity available. After this change, the new solution is obtained and observed.

8.10.3 Infeasible Transportation Problem

When it is not possible to transport goods from certain sources to certain destinations, (say) from source i to sink j, we will assign a very large cost, (say) M, to the route (i, j). We try, then, to neglect that route from future consideration.

8.10.4 Degeneracy in a Transportation Problem

We have seen that a basic solution to an m origin, n destination transportation problem can have at most $(m + n - 1)$–positive (nonzero) basic variables. Whenever the number of basic cells is less than $(m + n - 1)$, the transportation problem is called a degenerate TP and the phenomenon of having a degenerate basic feasible solution is called degeneracy. Degeneracy can occur in two ways:

- While obtaining an initial solution, we have less than $(m + n - 1)$–allocations.
- While moving towards optimal solution, when two or more occupied cells with the same minimum allocation become unoccupied simultaneously.

To solve the degeneracy of case (1), we assign a very small quantity denoted by ε (epsilon) to an unoccupied cell so as to get $(m + n - 1)$–occupied cells. ε does not affect the total transportation cost of the allocation. Lastly, we remove ε from the transportation table.

Note: For the maximization case of TP, ε is allocated to unoccupied cells that have the highest transportation payoff.

To resolve the degeneracy of case (2), the quantity ε may be allocated to one or more cells which have become unoccupied recently to have $(m + n - 1)$—number of allocated cells in the new solution.

	D_1	D_2	D_3	D_4	D_5	
S_1	4	7	3	8	2	4
S_2	1	4	7	3	8	7
S_3	7	2	4	7	7	9
S_4	4	8	2	4	7	2
	8	3	7	2	2	

EXAMPLE 8.11: Solve the following transportation problem.

Solution: First of all, we observe that the TP is a balanced one. We now apply the MODI method.

Step 1: To find the initial basic feasible solution by VAM.

(Allocations shown in parentheses before the unit cost.)

						Penalties
(1) 4	7	(1) 3	8	(2) 2	4/2/1/0	1 1 1 1 1
(7) 1	4	7	3	8	7/0	2 2 – – –
7	(3) 2	(6) 4	7	7	9/6/0	2 2 2 3* –
4	8	2	(2) 4	7	2/0	2 2 2 2 2
8/1/0	3/0	7/1/0	2/0	2/0		

Penalties

3	2	1	1	5*
3*	2	1	1	–
0	5*	1	3	–
0	–	1	3*	–
0	–	1	4*	–

(*Note:* In case of 4th step of penalty, there is a tie at 3*, so we select the cell (3, 3) with cost 4 corresponding to the column penalty because there 6 allocations could be made at that stage, while at cell (4, 4), where again the cost is 4, only 2 allocations could be made at that stage.)

Thus, the initial basic feasible solution is $x_{11} = 1$, $x_{13} = 1$, $x_{15} = 2$, $x_{21} = 7$, $x_{32} = 3$, $x_{33} = 6$, $x_{44} = 2$ and the initial transportation cost is Rs. 56.

Step 2: We now see optimality criteria:

No. of allocated cells = 7 and $m + n - 1 = 4 + 5 - 1 = 8$.

Therefore, no. of allocated cells is $< m + n - 1$. Thus, it is a case of degeneracy at first iteration. Allocate a quantity ε ($\varepsilon \to 0$) to an independent least cost unoccupied cell to make the number of allocated cells equal to $m + n - 1$.

Here we allocate ε to cell (4, 3) having the cost least among other unoccupied cells.

(1) 4	7	(1) 3	8	(2) 2
(7) 1	4	7	3	8
7	(3) 2	(6) 4	7	7
4	8	(ε) 2	(2) 4	7

We now return back to MODI method and break up the cost for basic cells as $c_{ij} = u_i + v_j$. We start by taking $u_1 = 0$ (taking $v_4 = 0$ is also possible).

4		3		2	$u_1 = 0$
1					$u_2 = -3$
	2	4			$u_3 = 1$
		2	4		$u_4 = -1$
$v_1 = 4$	$v_2 = 1$	$v_3 = 3$	$v_4 = 5$	$v_5 = 2$	

Step 3: We now find the opportunity cost $\Delta_{ij} = c_{ij} - (u_i + v_j)$ for non-allocated cells.

	6		3	
	6	7	1	9
2			1	4
1	8			6

As all $\Delta_{ij} > 0$, the solution obtained is optimal. Hence, now we can neglect the allocation ε. So the final solution is $x_{11} = 1$, $x_{13} = 1$, $x_{15} = 2$, $x_{21} = 7$, $x_{32} = 3$, $x_{33} = 6$, $x_{44} = 2$ and the minimum transportation cost is Rs. 56.

EXAMPLE 8.12: A TP whose initial solution has been found out by some method is given below. Find its optimum solution.

			Supply
[2] 7	3	4	2
[2] 2	[1] 1	3	3
3	4	[5] 6	5
4	1	5	10

Solution: The initial solution is $x_{11} = 2$, $x_{21} = 2$, $x_{22} = 1$, $x_{33} = 5$ and the initial transportation cost is Rs. 49. Here, the number of allocated cells = 4 and $m + n - 1 = 3 + 3 - 1 = 5$.

Thus, as the number of allocated cells < $m + n - 1$, it is a degenerate transportation problem. To resolve degeneracy, we allocate a very small quantity ε to a least cost unoccupied cell. Here there is a tie in the least cost 3. So, we arbitrarily assign ε to cell (2, 3).

[2] 7	3	4
[2] 2	[1] 1	[ε] 3
3	4	[5] 6

We now break up the cost for basic cells as $c_{ij} = u_i + v_j$.

7			$u_1 = 5$
2	1	3	$u_2 = 0$
		6	$u_3 = 3$
$v_1 = 2$	$v_2 = 1$	$v_3 = 3$	

Now we find the opportunity cost $\Delta_{ij} = c_{ij} - (u_i + v_j)$ for non-allocated cells.

	−3	−4
−2	0	

As some Δ_{ij} are negative, the initial solution is not optimal. So we trace a loop from the cell with the most negative Δ_{ij} entry (−4) to other occupied cells.

(D) 2		(A)
(A) 2		ε (D)

The donor with min. $\{\varepsilon, 2\} = \varepsilon$ gives ε to cell (1, 3). To balance it, the donor at (1, 1) gives ε units to the acceptor at (2, 1).

2 7	3	ε 4
2 2	1 1	3
3	4	5 6

Thus, we can see that this solution is no different from the initial solution except that ε has shifted. We again break up the cost for basic cells as $c_{ij} = u_i + v_j$.

7		4	$u_1 = 0$
2	1		$u_2 = -5$
		6	$u_3 = 2$
$v_1 = 7$	$v_2 = 6$	$v_3 = 4$	

We now find the opportunity cost $\Delta_{ij} = c_{ij} - (u_i + v_j)$ for non-allocated cells. The most negative Δ_{ij} entry is (−6). Hence, a new loop is formed as

	−3	
		4
−6	−4	

So, new allocations, after the donor gives min. { 2, 5} = 2 to the cell (3, 1) and the donor at (3, 3)

−(D) 2		+(A) ε
+(A)		(D) 5

gives 2 out of its 5 to the acceptor at cell (1, 3), are as follows:

7	3	2 4
2 2	1 1	3
2 3	4	3 6

The new solution is $x_{13} = 2$, $x_{21} = 2$, $x_{22} = 1$, $x_{31} = 2$, $x_{33} = 3$ and the transportation cost is Rs. 37. We again check this solution for optimality. Break up cost for basic cells.

		4	$u_1 = -1$
2	1		$u_2 = 0$
3		6	$u_3 = 1$
$v_1 = 2$	$v_2 = 1$	$v_3 = 5$	

and the opportunity cost $\Delta_{ij} = c_{ij} - (u_i + v_j)$ for non-allocated cells are

6	3	
		−2
	2	

After the new looping process, the allocations look like

7	3	2 4
2	1 1	2 3
4 3	4	1 6

So the new solution is $x_{13} = 2$, $x_{22} = 1$, $x_{23} = 2$, $x_{31} = 4$, $x_{33} = 1$ and the transportation cost is Rs. 33. We again check this solution for optimality. Break up the cost for basic cells.

		4	$u_1 = 4$
	1	3	$u_2 = 3$
3		6	$u_3 = 6$
$v_1 = -3$	$v_2 = -2$	$v_3 = 0$	

and the opportunity cost $\Delta_{ij} = c_{ij} - (u_i + v_j)$ for non-allocated cells are

6	1	
2		
	0	

As all $\Delta_{ij} \geq 0$, the solution obtained is optimum. The 0 value of Δ_{ij} in cell (3, 2) indicates that there is also an alternative optimal solution possible. So, the final solution is $x_{13} = 2$, $x_{22} = 1$, $x_{23} = 2$, $x_{31} = 4$, $x_{33} = 1$ and the transportation cost is Rs. 33.

Remark: The reader can verify that for an alternative optimal solution, we need to start a loop from a cell where Δ_{ij} is zero and proceed to form a loop where other points are basic cells. Here

7	3	2 4
2	1 − 1	2 + 3
4 3	+ 4	1 − 6

The alternative optimal solution is

7	3	[2] 4	2
2	1	[3] 3	3
[4] 3	[1] 4	6	5
4	1	5	

$x_{13} = 2$, $x_{23} = 3$, $x_{31} = 4$, $x_{32} = 1$ and the total cost is Rs. 33.

EXAMPLE 8.13: A firm has three factories *A*, *B* and *C* and supplies goods to four dealers D_1, D_2, D_3 and D_4. The production capacities of these factories are 1000, 700 and 900 units per month. The net return per unit product varies for different combinations of dealers and factories which are given in the following table.

	D_1	D_2	D_3	D_4	
A	6	6	6	4	1000
B	4	2	4	5	700
C	5	6	7	8	900
	900	800	500	400	

Determine a suitable allocation to maximize the total net return.

Solution: This is maximization TP. In order to convert it into a minimization problem, we convert the entries by subtracting all entries from the highest entry 8 in the table. After doing that, we apply VAM and find the initial basic feasible solution as $x_{11} = 200$, $x_{12} = 800$, $x_{21} = 700$, $x_{33} = 500$, $x_{34} = 400$ and the total return (here we consider original matrix) = Rs. 15500.

Now we check this solution for optimality:

Number of allocated cells = $5 < m + n - 1 = 6$. Therefore, it is a degenerate TP. We allocate very small quantity ε to a least cost cell (say) (3, 2) with entry 2 as follows:

[200] 2	[800] 2	2	4
[700] 4	6	4	3
3	[ε] 2	[500] 1	[400] 0

Now we break up the cost for basic cells as $c_{ij} = u_i + v_j$.

2	2			$u_1 = 0$
4				$u_2 = 2$
	2	1	0	$u_3 = 0$
$v_1 = 2$	$v_2 = 2$	$v_3 = 1$	$v_4 = 0$	

and the opportunity cost $\Delta_{ij} = c_{ij} - (u_i + v_j)$ for non-allocated cells

		1	4
	2	1	1
1			

As all $\Delta_{ij} > 0$, the solution obtained is optimal.

8.11 TRANS-SHIPMENT PROBLEM

In a regular transportation model, the shipments are allowed only between a source and a destination. But see the following situations.

Take the example of a multi-plant firm which may find it necessary to send some goods from one plant to another in order to meet the substantial increase in the demand in the second market. The second plant here would act both as a source and a destination and there is no real distinction between the source and the destination.

Take another example of two plants P_1 and P_2 which are linked to three dealers D_1, D_2 and D_3 by way of two transit centres T_1 and T_2.

The trans-shipment model recognizes that in real life it may be cheaper to ship through intermediate or transient nodes before reaching the final destination. Instead of direct shipments to destinations, the commodity can be transported to a particular destination through one or more intermediate transient nodes. Each of these nodes in turn supplies to other nodes. Thus, the trans-shipment model allows for the shipment of goods both from one source to another, and from one destination to another. These transient nodes can be the sources and the destinations themselves, or can be different from the sources and destinations as we saw in the two situations given above.

In short, a transportation problem in which available commodity may be sent through one or more sources or destinations, before reaching its actual destination, is termed as a *trans-shipment problem*. The objective of the trans-shipment problem is to find the optimal shipping pattern such that the total cost of transportation is minimized. This section shows how a trans-shipment model can be converted into a regular transportation model using a slight modification and then solved by the regular transportation technique.

Two types of trans-shipment problems are discussed here:

1. Sources and destinations acting as transient nodes
2. Some transient nodes between sources and destinations

A transportation problem can be converted into a trans-shipment problem by relaxing the restrictions on receiving and sending the units on the origins and destinations respectively. An m-origin n-destination transportation problem, when expressed as a trans-shipment problem, shall become an enlarged problem with $(m + n)$—origins and $(m + n)$—destinations. With minor modifications, this problem can be solved using the transportation method.

8.11.1 Sources and Destinations Acting as Transient Nodes

To explain the method, consider a problem of converting a direct shipment transportation problem given below into a trans-shipment problem:

		Destination					a_i
		1	2			n	
Origin	1	c_{11}	c_{12}			c_{1n}	a_1
	2	c_{21}	c_{22}			c_{2n}	a_2
	⋮	⋮	⋮			⋮	⋮
	⋮	⋮	⋮			⋮	⋮
	m	c_{m1}	c_{m2}			c_{mn}	a_m
	Bj	b_1	b_2			b_n	

As in a trans-shipment problem, each given source and destination can act as a source and destination, we rename these sources from 1, 2, 3, …, m as points 1, 2, 3, …, m and these destinations from 1, 2, 3, …, n as points $m + 1, m + 2, \ldots, m + n$ respectively. If $c_{ij} \geq 0$ is the cost of transporting one unit from point i to j, then the new transportation array assumes the following form.

		Destination									Available
		1	2	…	…	m	$m+1$	…	…	$m+n$	
Origin	1	0									$a_1 + M$
	2		0								$a_2 + M$
	…										
	…										
	m					0					$a_m + M$
	$M+1$						0				M
	…										
	…										
	$M+n$									0	M
Required		M	M	…	…	m	$b_1 + M$			$b_n + M$	

Here note that $c_{ij} = c_{i(j-m)}$ if $i \leq m, j \leq m + 1$ and $c_{ii} = 0$, i.e., diagonal costs are zero necessarily. The remaining costs c_{ij}'s are obtained from the given problem. It is not necessary that $c_{ij} = c_{ji}$.

If we take the quantity available at each of $m + 1, m + 2, \ldots, m + n$ points to be zero and also requirement at each point from 1,2,…, m to be zero, then the new table also represents the same direct shipping transportation table. Therefore, to have a supply and demand from all the points, a fictitious supply and demand quantity, say M, termed as buffer stock, is assumed and added to both demand and supply of all the points. Generally, M is chosen equal to $\sum a_i$ or $\sum b_j$.

Thus, we have designed a trans-shipment model similar to the transportation problem and it can be solved by the usual transportation technique.

EXAMPLE 8.14: Following is a trans-shipment problem involving 4 sources and 2 destinations. The supply values at the sources A, B, C, and D are 100, 200, 150 and 350 units. The demand values of the destinations X and Y are 350 and 450 units. The shipping costs are given below.

		Destination					
		A	B	C	D	X	Y
Source	A	0	4	20	5	25	12
	B	10	0	6	10	5	20
	C	15	20	0	8	45	7
	D	20	25	10	0	30	6
	X	20	18	60	15	0	10
	Y	10	25	30	23	4	0

The total number of starting as well as ending nodes here becomes 6. We also have $M = \sum a_i = \sum b_j = 800$. The modified trans-shipment problem is now as follows.

		Destination						Supply
		A	B	C	D	X	Y	
Source	A	0	4	20	5	25	12	100 + 800 = 900
	B	10	0	6	10	5	20	200 + 800 = 1000
	C	15	20	0	8	45	7	150 + 800 = 950
	D	20	25	10	0	30	6	350 + 800 = 1150
	X	20	18	60	15	0	10	800
	Y	10	25	30	23	4	0	800
Demand		800	800	800	800	350 + 800 1150	450 + 800 1250	

This can be solved by the transportation technique.
The allocations on the main diagonal are to be ignored.

The solution is left as an exercise for the reader. The cost of transportation is Rs. 5250 and the allocations (diagonal entries ignored) are *A* – *B*: 100, *B* – *X*: 300, *C* – *Y*: 150, *D* – *Y*: 350, *Y* – *X*: 50.

8.11.2 Some Transient Nodes between Sources and Destinations

Here the situation is like the case of shipping items from different plants to different market places through some intermediate finished goods warehouses. To convert a problem in this format, add the transient nodes as additional sources as well as additional destinations and form a regular transportation table with necessary cost details. The supply as well as demand of each of the transient nodes is assumed as M where $M = \sum a_i = \sum b_j$. Assume a very large number, ∞, for the c_{ij} values between different sources and destinations. The shipping cost c_{ij} values for shipping from a transient node to itself is 0. Then solve the problem using regular transportation method.

The allocations on the main diagonal are to be ignored.

EXAMPLE 8.15: A multi-plant organization has three plants *A*, *B* and *C* and three market places *X*, *Y* and *Z*. The items from the plants are transported to the market places through two intermediate finished goods warehouses W_1 and W_2. The details on cost of transportation per unit for different combinations between the plants and warehouses, between warehouses and markets, between warehouses, supply values of the plants and demand values of the markets are summarized in the following table.

		Destination					
		X	*Y*	*Z*	W_1	W_2	*Supply*
Source	*A*	∞	∞	∞	25	40	400
	B	∞	∞	∞	38	20	500
	C	∞	∞	∞	40	25	600
	W_1	20	45	25	0	25	–
	W_2	30	20	40	40	0	–
Demand		300	700	500	–	–	

Here the number of plants = number of markets = 3 and the number of transient nodes in the form of the warehouses is 2. Therefore, the total number of sources and destinations is 3 + 2 = 5. Also $M = \sum a_i = \sum b_j = 1500$.

A revised format of the trans-shipment problem is shown below.

		Destination					
		X	*Y*	*Z*	W_1	W_2	*Supply*
Source	*A*	∞	∞	∞	25	40	400
	B	∞	∞	∞	38	20	500
	C	∞	∞	∞	40	25	600
	W_1	20	45	25	0	25	1500
	W_2	30	20	40	40	0	1500
Demand		300	700	500	1500	1500	

This can be solved by the transportation technique.

The allocations on the main diagonal are to be ignored.

The solution is left as an exercise for the reader. The cost of transportation is Rs. 72000 and the allocations (diagonal entries ignored) are $A - W_1$: 400, $B - W_2$: 500, $C - W_2$: 600, $W_1 - Z$: 400, $W_2 - X$: 300, $W_2 - Y$: 700, $W_2 - Z$: 100.

REVIEW EXERCISES

1. Solve the following transportation problems:

(i)

Sink

Source	1	2	3	
1	2	7	4	5
2	3	3	1	8
3	5	4	7	7
4	1	6	2	14
	7	9	8	

[**Ans.** $x_{11} = 5, x_{22} = 2, x_{23} = 6, x_{32} = 7, x_{41} = 2, x_{43} = 12$]

(ii)

Sink

Source	1	2	3	4	
1	10	7	3	6	3
2	1	6	8	3	5
3	7	4	5	3	7
	3	2	6	4	

[**Ans.** $x_{13} = 3, x_{21} = 3, x_{24} = 2, x_{32} = 2, x_{33} = 3, x_{34} = 2$]

(iii)

Sink

Source	1	2	3	4	
1	19	14	23	11	11
2	15	16	12	21	13
3	30	25	16	39	19
	6	10	12	15	

[**Ans.** $x_{14} = 11, x_{21} = 6, x_{22} = 3, x_{24} = 4, x_{32} = 7, x_{33} = 12, z = 796$]

(iv)

Sink

Source	1	2	3	4	
1	1	2	1	4	30
2	3	3	2	1	50
3	4	2	5	9	20
	20	40	30	10	

[**Ans.** $x_{11} = 20, x_{13} = 10, x_{22} = 20, x_{23} = 20, x_{24} = 10, x_{32} = 20$]

(v)

	A	B	C	
I	50	30	220	1
II	90	45	170	3
III	250	200	50	4
	4	2	2	

[**Ans.** $x_{11} = 1, x_{21} = 3, x_{31} = 0, x_{32} = 2, x_{33} = 2, z = 820$]

(vi)

	W_1	W_2	W_3	W_4	
F_1	19	30	50	10	7
F_2	70	30	40	60	9
F_3	40	8	70	20	18
	5	8	7	14	

[**Ans.** $x_{11} = 5, x_{14} = 2, x_{22} = 2, x_{23} = 7, x_{32} = 6, x_{34} = 12, z = 743$]

(vii)

	A	B	C	D	E	
I	4	1	3	4	4	60
II	2	3	2	2	3	35
III	3	5	2	4	4	40
	22	45	20	18	30	

[**Ans.** $x_{12} = 45, x_{15} = 15, x_{21} = 17, x_{24} = 18, x_{31} = 5, x_{33} = 20,$ $x_{35} = 15, z = 290$]

(viii)

	A	B	C	D	
I	15	10	17	18	2
II	16	13	12	13	6
III	12	17	20	11	7
	3	3	4	5	

[**Ans.** $x_{12} = 2, x_{22} = 1, x_{23} = 4, x_{24} = 1, x_{31} = 3, x_{34} = 4, z = 174$]

(ix)

	X	Y	Z	
A	8	7	3	60
B	3	8	9	70
C	11	3	5	80
	50	80	80	

[**Ans.** $x_{13} = 60, x_{21} = 50, x_{23} = 20, x_{32} = 80, z = 750$]

(x)

	1	2	3	4	
A	1	2	3	4	6
B	4	3	2	0	8
C	0	2	2	1	10
	4	6	8	6	

[**Ans.** $x_{12} = 6, x_{23} = 2, x_{24} = 6, x_{31} = 4, x_{33} = 6, z = 28$]

(xi)

	1	2	3	4	5	
A	5	8	6	6	3	800
B	4	7	7	6	6	500
C	8	4	6	6	3	900
	400	400	500	400	800	

[**Ans.** $x_{13} = 0, x_{15} = 800, x_{21} = 400, x_{24} = 100, x_{32} = 400,$
$x_{33} = 200, x_{34} = 300, x_{43} = 300, z = 9200$]

(xii)

	1	2	3	4	5	
A	4	7	3	8	2	4
B	1	4	7	3	8	7
C	7	2	4	7	7	9
D	4	8	2	4	7	2
	8	3	7	2	2	

[**Ans.** $x_{11} = 1, x_{13} = 1, x_{15} = 2, x_{21} = 7, x_{32} = 3, x_{33} = 6, x_{44} = 2, z = 56$]

(xiii)

	I	II	III	IV	V	VI	
A	9	12	9	6	9	10	5
B	7	3	7	7	5	5	6
C	6	5	9	11	3	11	2
D	6	8	11	2	2	10	9
	4	4	6	2	4	2	

[**Ans.** $x_{13} = 5, x_{22} = 4, x_{26} = 2, x_{31} = 1, x_{33} = 1, x_{41} = 3, x_{44} = 2, x_{45} = 4$
or $x_{13} = 5, x_{22} = 3, x_{23} = 1, x_{26} = 2, x_{31} = 1, x_{32} = 1, x_{41} = 3, x_{44} = 2, x_{45} = 4, z = 112$]

(xiv)

	M_1	M_2	M_3	M_4	
W_1	2	2	2	1	3
W_2	10	8	5	4	7
W_3	7	6	6	8	5
	4	3	4	4	

Find the initial basic feasible solution by (i) LCM and (ii) VAM. Start with the LCM allocations and get the optimal solution.

[**Ans.** $x_{11} = 3, x_{23} = 3, x_{24} = 4, x_{31} = 1, x_{32} = 3, x_{33} = 1, z = 68$]

2. A company has received a contract to supply gravel for three new construction projects located in towns *A*, *B* and *C*. Construction engineers have estimated the required amounts of gravel which will be needed at these construction projects as shown below:

Project location	*Weekly requirements* (truck loads)
A	72
B	102
C	41

The company has three gravel plants *X*, *Y* and *Z* located at three different towns. The gravel required by the construction projects can be supplied by these three plants. The amount of gravel which can be supplied by each plant is as follows:

Plant	*Amount available/week* (truck loads)
X	76
Y	62
Z	77

The company has computed the delivery cost from each plant to each project site. These costs (in rupees) are shown in the following table:

Cost per truck load

Plant	*A*	*B*	*C*
X	4	8	8
Y	16	24	16
Z	8	16	35

(a) Schedule the shipment so as to minimize the total transportation cost.

(b) Find the minimum cost.

(c) Is the solution unique? If not, find the alternative optimal solution?

[**Ans.** (a) $x_{12} = 76, x_{21} = 21, x_{23} = 41, x_{31} = 51, x_{32} = 56$, (b) $z = 2424$, (c) No, $x_{12} = 76, x_{22} = 21, x_{23} = 41, x_{31} = 72, x_{32} = 5$]

3. A company has plants A, B and C which have capacities to produce 300 kg, 200 kg, 500 kg respectively of a particular chemical per day. The production costs (per kg) in these plants are Rs. 70, Rs. 60 and Rs. 66 respectively. Four bulk consumers have placed orders for the product on the following basis:

Consumer	*Kg required/day*	*Price offered* (Rs./kg)
I	400	100
II	250	100
III	350	102
IV	150	103

Shipping costs (in rupees per kg) from plants to consumers are given in the following table:

	I	II	III	IV
A	3	5	4	6
B	8	11	9	12
C	4	6	2	8

Find the optimal schedule for the above situation.

[**Ans.** $x_{11} = 150, x_{14} = 150, x_{21} = 200, x_{31} = 50, x_{32} = 100, x_{33} = 350, x_{42} = 150$, profit = 30700]

4. Determine all optimal basic feasible solutions and the minimum total cost for the following TP.

30	27	14	60
18	17	25	50
20	21	29	90
52	68	80	

[**Ans.** $x_{13} = 60, x_{22} = 50, x_{31} = 52, x_{32} = 18, x_{33} = 20, z = 3688.$
or $x_{13} = 60, x_{22} = 30, x_{23} = 20, x_{31} = 52, x_{32} = 38, z = 3688$]

5. Determine the optimal solution and the minimum total cost.

22	17	15	30
20	25	19	50
22	26	24	10
50	30	10	

[**Ans.** $x_{12} = 30, x_{21} = 40, x_{23} = 10, x_{31} = 10, x_{32} = 0, z = 1720$]

9 Assignment Problem

9.1 INTRODUCTION

The assignment problem (AP) is a particular sub-class of the transportation problem. It can be stated in the general form as follows: Given n-facilities, n-jobs and the effectiveness of each facility for each job, the problem is to assign each facility to one and only one job in such a way that the measure of the effectiveness is optimized (maximized or minimized). Here the facilities represent the sources and the jobs represent the destinations or sinks in the transportation 'language'.

Associated to each assignment problem, there is a matrix called the *cost* or *effectiveness matrix* $[c_{ij}]$ where c_{ij} is the cost or measure of effectiveness of assigning ith job to the jth facility. An assignment plan is optimal if it also minimizes (optimizes) the total cost or effectiveness of doing all the jobs.

Facilities (Destinations)

Jobs	f_1	f_2	f_3	$\cdots$	f_m	a_i
J_1	c_{11}	c_{12}	c_{13}	$\cdots$	c_{1m}	1
J_2	c_{21}	c_{22}	c_{23}	$\cdots$	c_{2m}	1
.						
.						
J_m	c_{m1}	c_{m2}	c_{m3}	$\cdots$	c_{mm}	1
b_j	1	1	1	$\cdots$	1	

Distribute m-units (jobs) (one available at each of the origin $J_1, J_2, \ldots, J_m$) to the m-destination requiring only 1 unit (job) in a way which minimizes the total cost. We can see that the problem is similar to the transportation problem.

The only difference between the standard assignment and a transportation problem is that here the number of origins is always equal to the number of destinations and at each origin one unit is always available and one unit is always required at each destination. Here, the cost matrix is always square. Thus, each job can be assigned to only one facility.

9.2 MATHEMATICAL FORMULATION OF THE AP

Let
$$x_{ij} = \begin{cases} 1, & \text{if } i\text{-th jobs is assigned to } j\text{-th facility} \\ 0, & \text{if } i\text{-th jobs is not assigned to } j\text{-th facility} \end{cases}$$

Determine x_{ij}, $i, j = 1, 2, \ldots, m$ so as to

Minimize
$$z = \sum_{i=1}^{m} \sum_{j=1}^{m} c_{ij} x_{ij} \tag{9.1}$$

subject to
$$\sum_{i=1}^{m} x_{ij} = 1, \quad j = 1, 2, \ldots, m \tag{9.2}$$

$$\sum_{j=1}^{m} x_{ij} = 1, \quad i = 1, 2, \ldots, m \tag{9.3}$$

and
$$x_{ij} = 0 \text{ or } 1 \tag{9.4}$$

The condition Eq. (9.4) is similar to the condition Eq. (8.4) of a transportation problem which states that $x_{ij} \geq 0$. We can see that the assignment problem is thus a special case of a transportation problem where $m = n$ and $a_i = b_j = 1$. Due to this similarity with the transportation problem, we can handle AP by the transportation technique also.

It may however be easily observed that any basic feasible solution of an AP contains $(2m - 1)$—variables out of which $(m - 1)$—variables are zero. Due to this high degree of degeneracy, the computational techniques given in Chapter 8 of a TP become very inefficient. A separate computational method is required to solve AP.

The basic principles on which the solution of an AP is based can be stated as the following two theorems:

Theorem 9.1: *If a constant is added to every element of a row and/or column of the cost matrix of an AP, the resulting AP has the same optimal solution as the original problem and vice versa. Alternatively, if* $x_{ij} = x_{ij}^*$ *minimizes*

$$z = \sum_{i=1}^{m} \sum_{j=1}^{m} c_{ij}\, x_{ij} \text{ over all } x_{ij} \text{ such that } \sum_{i=1}^{m} x_{ij} = \sum_{j=1}^{m} x_{ij} = 1,\ x_{ij} \geq 0 \text{ then } x_{ij} = x_{ij}^* \text{ also minimizes}$$

$$z^* = \sum_{i=1}^{m} \sum_{j=1}^{m} c_{ij}^*\, x_{ij} \text{ where } c_{ij}^* = c_{ij} \pm u_i \pm v_j, \text{ for } i, j = 1, 2, \ldots, m \text{ and } u_i, v_j \text{ are real numbers.}$$

Proof:
$$z^* = \sum_{i=1}^{m}\sum_{j=1}^{m} c_{ij}^* x_{ij}$$
$$= \sum_{i=1}^{m}\sum_{j=1}^{m} (c_{ij} \pm u_i \pm v_j)\, x_{ij}$$
$$= \sum_{i=1}^{m}\sum_{j=1}^{m} c_{ij}\, x_{ij} \pm \sum_{i=1}^{m}\sum_{j=1}^{m} u_i\, x_{ij} \pm \sum_{i=1}^{m}\sum_{j=1}^{m} v_j\, x_{ij}$$
$$= z \pm \sum_{i=1}^{m} u_i \sum_{j=1}^{m} x_{ij} \pm \sum_{j=1}^{m} v_j \sum_{i=1}^{m} x_{ij}$$
$$= z \pm \sum_{i=1}^{m} u_i \pm \sum_{j=1}^{m} v_j \quad \text{as} \quad \sum_{j=1}^{m} x_{ij} = \sum_{i=1}^{m} x_{ij} = 1$$

Now $\sum_{i=1}^{m} u_i$ and $\sum_{j=1}^{m} v_j$ are added/subtracted from z to give z^* are independent of x_{ij}. Therefore, z^* is minimum when z is minimum. Hence, $x_{ij} = x_{ij}^*$ also minimizes z^*.

Theorem 9.2: *If all $c_{ij} \geq 0$ and we have obtained a solution with $x_{ij} = x_{ij}^*$ such that $\sum_{i=1}^{m}\sum_{j=1}^{m} c_{ij}^* x_{ij} = 0$, then the present solution is an optimal solution.*

Proof: **As neither of the c_{ij} is negative, the value of $z = \sum_{i=1}^{m}\sum_{j=1}^{m} c_{ij} x_{ij}$ cannot be negative. Hence its minimum value is zero which is attained at $x_{ij} = x_{ij}^*$. Hence, the present solution is optimal.**

9.3 SOLUTION METHODS OF AP

An assignment problem can be solved by the following four methods, out of which the Hungarian method is more suitable for solving the assignment problems.

- Enumeration method
- Simplex method
- Transportation problem
- Hungarian method.

9.3.1 Enumeration Method

It may be noted that with n-facilities and n-jobs there are $n!$ possible assignments. One way of finding an optimum assignment is to write all $n!$ possible arrangements, evaluate their total cost (in terms of the given measure of effectiveness), and select the assignment with the minimum cost. The method leads to a computational problem of formidable size even when the value of n is moderate. Even for n = 10, the possible number of arrangements is 3628800.

9.3.2 Simplex Method

An assignment problem can be solved by the simplex method after converting it into zero-one integer programming problem. But as there would be $n \times n$-decision variables and $2n$ (i.e. $n + n$)-equalities, it is again difficult to solve it manually.

9.3.3 Transportation Method

Section 9.2 clearly depicts why an assignment problem should not be solved by the transportation method.

9.3.4 The Hungarian Method

The Hungarian method was developed by H. Kuhn and is based upon the work of two Hungarian mathematicians—D. Konig and J. Egervary. For application of the algorithm, it is assumed that all of the c_{ij}'s of the starting cost matrix are non-negative integers and the assignment problem is of minimization case.

Algorithm for the Hungarian method

Step 1: Subtract the minimum of each row of the effectiveness matrix from all the elements of the respective rows.

Step 2: Further, modify the resulting matrix by subtracting the minimum element of each column from all the elements of the column.

Step 3: Draw the *minimum* number of horizontal and vertical lines to suppress all the zeros. Let the number of lines drawn be N.

(i) If $N = n$ (n = number of rows or columns), the optimal assignment can be made. Hence go to step 6.

(ii) If $N < n$, go to Step 4.

Step 4: Find the smallest uncovered element (that is not covered by the lines drawn). Subtract it from all uncovered entries. Add it to all entries on the intersection of the two lines.

Step 5: Repeat Step 3 and Step 4 until $N = n$.

Step 6: Find a row with exactly one 0 entry. Encircle it by □. Cancel that column and row showing that the zeroes in that column cannot be taken for further assignment. Continue this process until all rows are examined. Repeat it for columns also. This step is called **zero assigning**.

Step 7: Continue Step 6 until

(i) no unmarked zero is left.

(ii) there lies more than one of the unmarked zeroes in the column or row.

In case (i), the procedure terminates. In case (ii), mark □ one of the unmarked zeroes arbitrarily and cancel the remaining zeroes in its row and column. Repeat the process until no unmarked zero is left in the matrix.

Step 8: Exactly one marked □ zero in each row and each column is obtained. The assignment corresponding to these marked □ zeroes will give the optimum assignment.

This method is also known as *Flood's technique* or *Reduced Matrix Method.*

EXAMPLE 9.1: Suppose that there are three applicants for three jobs and that the cost incurred by the applicants to fill the jobs are given in the following table.

	J_1	J_2	J_3
A	26	23	27
B	23	22	24
C	24	20	23

Each applicant is assigned to only one job and each job is to be filled by one applicant only. Determine the assignment of applicants to jobs such that the total cost is minimized.

Solution: It is clear that we wish to minimize

$$z = 26\ x_{11} + 23\ x_{12} + 27\ x_{13} + 23\ x_{21} + 22\ x_{22} + 24\ x_{23} + 24\ x_{31} + 20\ x_{32} + 23\ x_{33}$$

where $x_{ij} = 0$ or 1.

Step 1: Applying Step 1 of the Hungarian algorithm, we subtract the minimum of each row from all the entries of the respective rows.

3	0	4
1	0	2
4	0	3

Step 2: We now subtract the minimum of each column from all entries of the respective columns.

2	0	2
0	0	0
3	0	1

Step 3: We now draw *minimum* number of horizontal or vertical lines to suppress all the zeroes.

2	0	2
0	0	0
3	0	1

Here, the number of lines drawn $N = 2 < n = 3$ (number of rows).

Step 4: The smallest uncovered entry is 1. We subtract it from all uncovered entries and add it to the entry on the intersection of the two lines.

1	0	1
0	1	0
2	0	0

Step 5: We now again draw minimum number of horizontal and vertical lines to suppress all the zeroes.

1	0	1
0	1	0
2	0	0

Here the number of lines drawn $N = 3 = n$ (number of rows).

Step 6. Zero assigning.

We first observe that row 1 has exactly 1 zero entry. Mark it with □. Cancel the first row and second column in which that entry lies.

1	0	1
0	1	0
2	0	0

Now we observe that the third row has exactly one zero entry which is uncovered. Mark it with □. Cancel that row and column.

1	0	1
0	1	0
2	0	0

It is clear that the first zero of row 2 should be now marked with □. Thus, the optimal assignment is

1	0	1
0	1	0
2	0	0

The final assignment is now viewed as

	J_1	J_2	J_3
A	26	23	27
B	23	22	24
C	24	20	23

i.e. persons A, B, and C are assigned jobs J_2, J_1 and J_3 respectively. Thus $x_{12} = 1$, $x_{21} = 1$ and $x_{33} = 1$ and the rest of all x_{ij}'s are zero. This assignment causes the total cost to be minimized at $c_{12} + c_{21} + c_{33} = 23 + 23 + 23 = 69$.

EXAMPLE 9.2: Consider the assignment problem shown below. In this problem, 5 different jobs are assigned to 5 different operators such that the total processing time is minimized. The matrix entries represent processing times in hours.

Job \ Operator	O_1	O_2	O_3	O_4	O_5
J_1	10	12	15	12	8
J_2	7	16	14	14	11
J_3	13	14	7	9	9
J_4	12	10	11	13	10
J_5	8	13	15	11	15

Solution: We want to find $x_{ij} = 0$ or 1 so as to minimize $z = \sum_{i=1}^{5} \sum_{j=1}^{5} c_{ij} x_{ij}$

Step 1: Row reduction

2	4	7	4	0
0	9	7	7	4
6	7	0	2	2
2	0	1	3	0
0	5	7	3	7

Step 2: Column reduction

2	4	7	2	0
0	9	7	5	4
6	7	0	0	2
2	0	1	1	0
0	5	7	1	7

Step 3: We now draw minimum number of horizontal or vertical lines to suppress all the zeroes.

2	4	7	2	0
0	9	7	5	4
6	7	0	0	2
2	0	1	1	0
0	5	7	1	7

Here, the number of lines drawn = 4 < number of rows (= 5).

Step 4: The smallest uncovered entry is 1. We subtract it from all uncovered entries and add it to entries on the intersection of the lines.

2	4	6	1	0
0	9	6	4	4
7	8	0	0	3
2	0	0	0	0
0	5	6	0	7

Step 5: We now draw minimum number of lines to suppress all the zeroes.

2	4	6	1	0
0	9	6	4	4
7	8	0	0	3
2	0	0	0	0
0	5	6	0	7

Here, the number of lines drawn = 5 = number of rows (= 5).

Step 6: Zero assigning

Row 1 and 2 have exactly 1 zero entry. Mark them with □. Cancel the respective rows and columns.

2	4	6	1	0
0	9	6	4	4
7	8	0	0	3
2	0	0	0	0
0	5	6	0	7

Now row 5 has exactly one uncovered zero entry. Mark it with □. Cancel the respective row and column.

2	4	6	1	0
0	9	6	4	4
7	8	0	0	3
2	0	0	0	0
0	5	6	0	7

It is clear that row 3 has only one uncovered zero entry. Mark it with □ and finally row 4 will have the zero entry in the cell (4, 2).

2	4	6	1	0
0	9	6	4	4
7	8	0	0	3
2	0	0	0	0
0	5	6	0	7

So the final solution will be $x_{15} = 1$, $x_{21} = 1$, $x_{33} = 1$, $x_{42} = 1$, $x_{54} = 1$ and the rest of x_{ij}'s are zero and the optimal assignment is

Job	*Operator*	*Time*
J_1	O_5	8
J_2	O_1	7
J_3	O_3	7
J_4	O_2	10
J_5	O_4	11
		43

The total processing time is 43 hours.

9.4 VARIATIONS OF THE ASSIGNMENT PROBLEM

9.4.1 Multiple Optimal Solutions

While making assignment in the reduced assignment matrix, it is possible to have two or more ways to strike off certain number of zeroes. Such a situation indicates multiple optimal solutions with the same optimal value of the objective function. In such cases, either of the solutions may be considered.

9.4.2 Unbalanced Assignment Problems

Whenever the cost matrix of an assignment problem is not a square matrix, that is, whenever the number of sources is not equal to the number of destinations, the assignment problem is called an **unbalanced assignment problem**. In such problems, dummy rows (or columns) are added in the matrix so as to complete it to form a square matrix. The dummy rows or columns will contain all costs elements as zeroes. Now, the Hungarian method may be used to solve the problem.

9.4.3 Problem with Infeasible (Restricted) Assignment

It is sometimes possible that a particular person is incapable of doing certain work or a specific job cannot be performed on a particular machine. The solution of the assignment problem should take into account these restrictions so that the infeasible assignment can be avoided. This can be achieved by assigning a very high cost (say ∞ or M) to the cells where assignments are prohibited, thereby restricting the entry of this pair of job-machine or resource-activity into the final solution.

9.4.4 Maximization Case in Assignment Problems

There are problems where certain facilities have to be assigned to a number of jobs so as to maximize the overall performance of the assignment. The problem can be converted into a minimization problem in the following two ways and then Hungarian method can be used for its solution.

Method 1: Select the greatest element of the given cost matrix and then subtract each element of the matrix from the greatest element to get the modified matrix.

Note that the new matrix will be $[c_{ij}^*]$ where $c_{ij}^* = c_{rk} - c_{ij}$ where c_{rk} is the greatest element and $[c_{ij}]$ is the original cost matrix.

Now (say) $x_{ij} = x_{ij}^*$ maximizes $z = \sum_{i=1}^{m}\sum_{j=1}^{m} c_{ij}x_{ij}$. Then

$$z^* = \sum_{i=1}^{m}\sum_{j=1}^{m} c_{ij}^* x_{ij}$$

$$= \sum_{i=1}^{m}\sum_{j=1}^{m} (c_{rk} - c_{ij})\, x_{ij}$$

$$= \sum_{i=1}^{m}\sum_{j=1}^{m} c_{rk}\, x_{ij} - \sum_{i=1}^{m}\sum_{j=1}^{m} c_{ij}x_{ij}$$

$$= \sum_{i=1}^{m}\sum_{j=1}^{m} c_{rk}\, x_{ij} - z$$

So if $x_{ij} = x_{ij}^*$ maximizes z, it also minimizes z^*.

Method 2: Multiply each element of the matrix by (–1) to get the modified matrix.

Note that in this case the new matrix is $[c_{ij}^*]$ where $c_{ij}^* = (-c_{ij})$. So if

$x_{ij} = x_{ij}^*$ maximizes $z = \sum_{i=1}^{m}\sum_{j=1}^{m} c_{ij}x_{ij}$. Then $z^* = \sum_{i=1}^{m}\sum_{j=1}^{m} (-c_{ij})\, x_{ij}$. Thus, $x_{ij} = x_{ij}^*$ minimizes z^*.

EXAMPLE 9.3: Five different machines can do any of the required five jobs with different profits resulting from each assignment as given below.

Job	Machine A	B	C	D	E
1	30	37	40	28	40
2	40	24	27	21	36
3	40	32	33	30	35
4	25	38	40	36	36
5	29	62	41	34	39

Find out the maximum profit possible through optimal assignment.

Solution: As this is an assignment problem of profit maximization type, we convert it into an assignment problem of cost minimization type by forming a new modified matrix, obtained by subtracting each entry of the matrix from the greatest entry 62 of the matrix. The resultant problem we will solve as the problem of minimization cost.

32	25	22	34	22
22	38	35	41	26
22	30	29	32	27
37	24	22	26	26
33	0	21	28	23

We now apply the Hungarian method to this problem.

Step 1: Row reduction

10	3	0	12	0
0	16	13	19	4
0	8	7	10	5
15	2	0	4	4
33	0	21	28	23

Step 2: Column reduction

10	3	0	8	0
0	16	13	15	4
0	8	7	6	5
15	2	0	0	4
33	0	21	24	23

Step 3: Drawing minimum number of lines to suppress the zeroes.

10	3	0	8	0
0	16	13	15	4
0	8	7	6	5
15	2	0	0	4
33	0	21	24	23

Here, the number of lines drawn $N = 4 <$ number of rows ($= 5$).

Step 4: The smallest uncovered entry is 4. Subtract 4 from all uncovered entries and add it to all entries on the intersection of the lines.

14	7	0	8	0
0	16	9	11	0
0	8	3	2	1
19	6	0	0	4
33	0	17	20	19

Step 5: Draw minimum number of lines to cover all the zeroes.

14	7	0	8	0
0	16	9	11	0
0	8	3	2	1
19	6	0	0	4
33	0	17	20	19

Here the number of lines drawn $N = 5$ = number of rows.

Step 6: Mark the zero entry with □ that occurs exactly once in a row and cancel that row or column.

14	7	0	8	0
0	16	9	11	0
[0]	8	3	2	1
19	6	0	0	4
33	[0]	17	20	19

After the above steps, row 2 has the last entry zero. Mark it with □. Now row 1 will have the third entry zero uncovered. Mark it with □. So row 4 will have only one entry in cell (4, 4) with zero. Therefore, the optimal assignment is done.

	A	*B*	*C*	*D*	*E*
1	14	7	[0]	8	0
2	0	16	9	11	[0]
3	[0]	8	3	2	1
4	19	6	0	[0]	4
5	33	[0]	17	20	19

Thus, $x_{13} = x_{25} = x_{31} = x_{44} = x_{52} = 1$ and the rest all $x_{ij} = 0$.
The optimal assignment is

Job	*Machine*	*Profit*
1	*C*	40
2	*E*	36
3	*A*	40
4	*D*	36
5	*B*	62
		214

Therefore, the maximum profit is 214.

EXAMPLE 9.4: Suppose that the cost matrix for assigning four workers to four jobs is as given in the following table. The three occurrences of M indicate that it is impossible to assign at that cell. Determine the optimal assignment and the corresponding minimum total cost.

Worker \ Job	J_1	J_2	J_3	J_4
W_1	M	30	23	25
W_2	34	M	16	24
W_3	22	19	21	M
W_4	21	23	14	20

Solution: We proceed by the Hungarian method.

Step 1: Row reduction

M-23	7	0	2
18	M-8	0	8
3	0	2	M-9
7	8	0	6

Step 2: Column reduction

M-26	7	0	0
15	M-16	0	6
0	0	2	M-21
4	8	0	4

Step 3: Minimum lines required to cover the zeroes = 3 < 4 (number of rows)

Step 4:

M-26	7	4	[0]
11	M-20	[0]	2
0	[0]	6	M-21
[0]	5	0	0

Step 5: As the number of lines required to cover all zeroes = 4 = (number of rows), the optimal assignment can be made (left for the reader to fill details).

Worker	*Job*	*Total cost*
W_1	J_4	25
W_2	J_3	16
W_3	J_2	19
W_4	J_1	21
		81

EXAMPLE 9.5: Suppose that there are six people applying for five jobs; and it is desired to fill each job with exactly one person. The costs for filling the jobs with six people are given in the following table.

	J_1	J_2	J_3	J_4	J_5
P_1	27	23	22	24	27
P_2	28	27	21	26	24
P_3	28	26	24	25	28
P_4	27	25	21	24	24
P_5	25	20	23	26	26
P_6	26	21	21	24	27

Determine the optimal assignment plan, i.e. the plan whereby the cost of assigning the people is minimized.

Solution: This is a case of unbalanced assignment problem. So we introduce a fictitious (dummy) job J_6 with all entries zero. After that, we apply the Hungarian method. Here we will not require to do row reduction because the last column J_6 contains all zeroes. So we will perform only column reduction.

Step 2 is left for the reader.

Step 3: Drawing minimum number of lines to cover the zeroes.

2	3	1	0	3	0
3	7	0	2	0	0
3	6	3	1	4	0
2	5	0	0	0	0
0	0	2	2	2	0
1	1	0	0	3	0

As the number of lines drawn $N = 5 < 6$ (number of rows), we go to step 4.

Step 4:

1	2	1	0	3	0
2	6	0	2	0	0
2	5	3	1	4	0
1	4	0	0	0	0
0	0	3	3	3	1
0	0	0	0	3	0

It is evident that the number of lines drawn = number of rows.

Step 6: Zero assigning shows that P_3 has to be assigned J_6 because there is exactly one zero entry. Again, canceling that row and column, P_1 is assigned to J_4. So the new solution is

1	2	1	0	3	0
2	6	0	2	0	0
2	5	3	1	4	0
1	4	0	0	0	0
0	0	3	3	3	1
0	0	0	0	3	0

Now both P_2 and P_4 have two choices of assignments:
If $P_2 \to J_3$ then $P_4 \to J_5$ or else $P_2 \to J_5$, $P_4 \to J_3$.
Again if $P_5 \to J_1$ then $P_6 \to J_2$ or else $P_5 \to J_2$, $P_5 \to J_1$.
So this is a case of alternative optimal solution.

Solution 1

Person	*Job*	*Cost*
P_1	J_4	24
P_2	J_3	21
P_3	J_6	0
P_4	J_5	24
P_5	J_1	25
P_6	J_2	21
		115

Solution 2

Person	*Job*	*Cost*
P_1	J_4	24
P_2	J_5	24
P_3	J_6	0
P_4	J_3	21
P_5	J_2	20
P_6	J_1	26
		115

Here, it may be noted that $P_3 \to J_6$ means P_3 is not assigned to any job J_1 to J_5.

REVIEW EXERCISES

1. Three jobs A, B, C are to be assigned to three machines X, Y, Z. The processing costs (Rs.) are given in the matrix below. Find the allocation that minimizes the overall processing cost.

	X	Y	Z
A	19	28	31
B	11	17	16
C	12	15	13

[**Ans.** $A \to X$, $B \to Y$, $C \to Z$, Mini. cost = Rs. 49]

2. Five men are available to do five different jobs. The time (in hours) that each man takes to do each job is known and is given below. Find the assignment that will minimize the total time taken.

		Jobs				
		1	2	3	4	5
	1	2	9	2	7	1
	2	6	8	7	6	1
Men	3	4	6	5	3	1
	4	4	2	7	3	1
	5	5	3	9	5	1

[**Ans.** Multiple assignments: $1 \to 3$, $2 \to 5$, $3 \to 1$, $4 \to 4$, $5 \to 2$
$1 \to 3$, $2 \to 5$, $3 \to 4$, $4 \to 2$, $5 \to 1$
$1 \to 3$, $2 \to 5$, $3 \to 4$, $4 \to 1$, $5 \to 2$
Minimum time = 13 hours]

3. Find the minimum cost solution for the 5 × 5-assignment problem whose cost coefficients are given below:

	1	2	3	4	5
1	–2	–4	–8	–6	–1
2	0	–9	–5	–5	–4
3	–3	–8	0	–2	–6
4	–4	–3	–1	0	–3
5	–9	–5	–8	–9	–5

[**Ans.** $1 \to 3$, $2 \to 2$, $3 \to 5$, $4 \to 1$, $5 \to 4$, Optimal cost = Rs. 36]

4. A company has five jobs to be done. The following matrix shows the return in rupees of assigning i-th machine ($i = 1, 2, \ldots, 5$) to the j-th job ($j = 1, 2, \ldots, 5$). Assign the five jobs to the five machines so as to maximize the total expected profit.

		Job				
		1	2	3	4	5
	1	5	11	10	12	4
	2	2	4	6	3	5
Machine	3	3	1	5	14	6
	4	6	14	4	11	7
	5	7	9	8	12	8

[**Ans.** $1 \to 3$, $2 \to 5$, $3 \to 4$, $4 \to 2$, $5 \to 1$, Maximum profit = Rs. 50]

5. Solve the assignment problem represented by the following matrix which gives the distances from the customers A, B, C, D, E to the depots a, b, c, d and e. Each depot has one car. How should the cars be assigned to the customers so as to minimize the distance travelled?

	a	*b*	*c*	*d*	*e*
A	160	130	175	190	200
B	135	120	130	160	175
C	140	110	125	170	185
D	50	50	80	80	110
E	55	35	80	80	105

[**Ans.** $A \to b$, $B \to e$, $C \to c$, $D \to a$, $E \to d$, 560 km]

6. Four engineers are available to design four projects. Engineer 2 is not competent to design the project B. Given the following time (in days) estimates needed by each engineer to design a given project, find how should the engineers be assigned to projects so as to minimize the total design time for four projects.

		Project			
		A	B	C	D
	1	12	10	10	8
	2	10	×	15	11
Engineer	3	6	10	16	4
	4	8	10	9	7

[**Ans.** $1 \to B$, $2 \to D$, $3 \to A$, $4 \to C$, Time = 36 days]

7. A department head has four tasks to be performed and three subordinates. The subordinates differ in efficiency. The estimate of the time, each subordinate would take to perform, is given below in the matrix. How should he allocate the tasks, one to each man, so as to minimize the total man-hours?

		Man		
		A	*B*	*C*
Task	I	9	26	15
	II	13	27	6
	III	35	20	15
	IV	18	30	20

[Ans. *I* → *A*, *II* → *C*, *III* → *B*, time 35 man-hours]

8. Solve the following minimal assignment problem.

		Man				
		I	II	III	IV	V
Job	*A*	1	3	2	3	6
	B	2	4	3	1	5
	C	5	6	3	4	6
	D	3	1	4	2	2
	E	1	5	6	5	4

[Ans. *A* → *I*, *B* → *IV*, *C* → *III*, *D* → *II*, *E* → *V*]

9. Solve the following minimal assignment problem.

		Man					
		1	2	3	4	5	6
Job	*A*	31	62	29	42	15	41
	B	12	19	39	55	71	40
	C	17	29	50	41	22	22
	D	35	40	38	42	27	33
	E	19	30	29	16	20	23
	F	72	30	30	50	41	20

[Ans. *A* → 5, *B* → 2, *C* → 1, *D* → 3, *E* → 4, *F* → 6]

10. A marketing manager has five salesmen and five sales districts. It is estimated that the sales per month (in hundred rupees) for each salesman in each district would be as follows. Find the assignment of the salesman to districts that will result in minimum sales.

		District				
		A	*B*	*C*	*D*	*E*
	1	32	38	40	28	40
	2	40	24	28	21	36
Salesman	3	41	27	33	30	37
	4	22	38	41	36	36
	5	29	33	40	35	39

[**Ans.** $1 \to B$, $2 \to A$, $3 \to E$, $4 \to C$, $5 \to D$, minimum sales = Rs. 19,100]

10 Decision Analysis

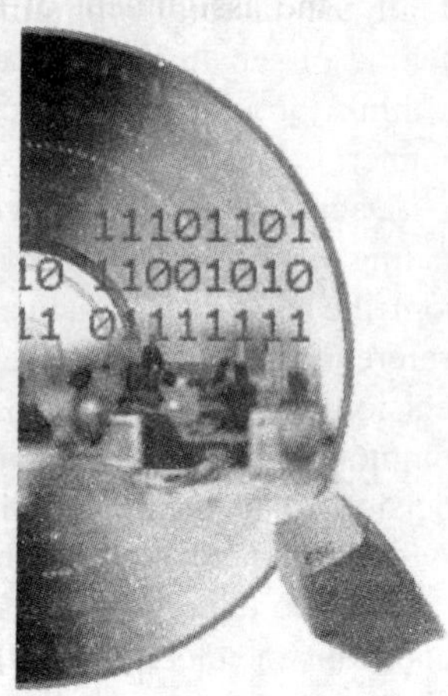

10.1 INTRODUCTION

In recent years, statisticians, engineers, economists and students of management have placed increasing emphasis on decision making under conditions of uncertainty. This area of study has been called *statistical decision theory*, *Bayesian decision theory*, *decision analysis*, and many other things. We shall henceforth use the term 'decision analysis' as a matter of expediency and as an anchor point in discussing this topic.

This chapter will deal with the problem of making decisions under conditions of uncertainty. Much of life, of course, involves making choices under uncertainty, that is, choosing from some set of alternative courses of action in situations where we are uncertain about the actual consequences that will occur for each course of action being considered. Often, however, we must make a choice and are naturally concerned about whether it is the best or optimal choice.

In today's fast-moving technological world, the need for sound, rational decision making by business, industry and government is vividly apparent. Consider, for example, the area of design and development of new and improved products and equipment. Typically, development from invention to commercialization is expensive and filled with uncertainty regarding both technical and commercial success. Product development problems related to research and development (R&D), production, finance and marketing activities, of both tactical and strategic nature, abound. In R&D, for example, decision makers might be faced with the problem of choosing whether to pursue a parallel versus a sequential strategy (i.e. pursuing two or more designs simultaneously versus developing the most promising design, and if it fails, going to the next most promising design, etc.). In production, they may have to decide on a production method or process for manufacture; or choose whether to lease, subcontract, or manufacture; or select a quality-control plan. In finance, they may have to decide whether to invest in a new plant, equipment, research programs, marketing facilities, even risky orders. In marketing, they may have to determine the pricing scheme, whether to do market research and what type and amount of it, the type of advertising campaign, and so on.

Each of these decision problems is characteristically complex and can have a significant impact on the health of a firm. It is almost impossible for any decision maker to intuitively take full account of all the factors impinging on a decision simultaneously. It thus becomes useful to find some method of separating such decision problems into parts in a way that would allow a decision maker to think through the implications of each set of factors, one at a time in a rational and consistent manner.

Decision analysis provides a rich set of concepts and techniques to aid the decision maker in dealing with complex decision problems under uncertainty. The decision analysis formulation differs from the classical statistical inference and decision procedures by considering explicitly both the preference structure of the individual decision maker and the uncertainties that characterize the decision situation. An exposure to the concepts of decision analysis rapidly makes one aware of the common shortcomings in more informal approaches, such as intuition. A particular benefit of the decision analysis approach is that it facilitates communication and analysis among individuals involved and affected by the decision problem.

Decision analysis is concerned with the making of rational, consistent decisions, notably under conditions of uncertainty. That is, it helps the decision maker to choose the best alternative in light of the information available (which normally is incomplete and unreliable). Decision analysis enables the decision maker to analyze a complex situation with many different alternatives, states and consequences. The major objective is to choose a course of action consistent with the basic values (tastes) and knowledge (beliefs) of the decision maker.

10.2 CHARACTERISTICS OF A DECISION PROBLEM

All decision problems have certain general characteristics. These characteristics constitute the formal description of the problems and provide the structure for solutions. The decision problem under study may be represented by a model in terms of the following elements.

1. *The decision maker.* The decision maker is responsible for making the decision. Viewed as an entity, the decision maker may be a single individual, committee, company, nation, or the like.
2. *Alternative courses of action.* An important part of the decision maker's task, over which the decision maker has control, is the specification and description of the alternatives. Given that the alternatives are specified, the decision involves a choice among the alternative courses of action. When the opportunity to acquire information is available, the decision maker's problem is to choose the best information source or sources and a best overall strategy. A *strategy* is a set of decision rules indicating which action should be taken contingent on a specific observation received from the chosen information source(s).
3. *Events.* *Events* are the scenarios or states of the environment, not under the control of the decision maker that may occur. Under conditions of uncertainty, the decision maker, when making the decision, does not know for certain which event will occur. The true event, indeed, may be a fact unknown to the decision maker.

   The events are defined to be mutually exclusive and collectively exhaustive. That is, one and only one of all possible events specified will occur. Events are also called *states of nature.*

Uncertainty is measured in terms of probabilities assigned to the events. One of the distinguishing characteristics of decision analysis is that these probabilities can be subjective (reflecting the decision maker's state of knowledge or beliefs) or objective (theoretically or empirically determined) or both. The decision maker must identify and specify the events as well as assess their probabilities of occurrence.

4. *Consequences.* The consequences, which must be assessed by the decision maker, are measures of the net benefit, or pay-off, received by the decision maker. The consequences that result from a decision depend not only on the decision but also on the event that occurs. Thus, there is a consequence (or vector of consequences) associated with each action-event pair. They can be conveniently summarized in a pay-off matrix, or decision matrix, which displays the consequences of all action-event combinations.

10.3 PAY-OFF TABLE

A pay-off table depicts the economies of the given problem. A pay-off is a conditional value—a conditional profit, loss or may be a conditional cost. It is conditional in the sense that, associated with each course of action is a certain profit/loss, given that certain event has occurred. Thus, the profit or loss resulting by the adoption of a certain strategy is dependent upon, and is therefore associated with, the particular event that may occur. A pay-off table thus represents the matrix of the conditional values associated with all the possible combinations of the acts and the events.

Our approach will be to structure the pay-off matrix as follows: The actions are listed on the left of the matrix along the rows, the states are listed at the top of the matrix along the columns, and the possible consequences are listed in the matrix cells, one consequence associated with each action-event pair.

10.4 THE DIFFERENT ENVIRONMENTS IN WHICH DECISIONS ARE MADE

Decision makers must function in three types of environments. In each of these environment, knowledge about the states of nature differs.

1. *Decision making under condition of certainty:* In this environment, only one state of nature exists; that is, there is complete certainty about the future. Although this environment sometimes exists, it is usually associated with very routine decisions involving fairly inconsequential issues; even here it is usually impossible to guarantee complete certainty about the future.
2. *Decision making under conditions of uncertainty:* Here more than one state of nature exists, but the decision maker has no knowledge about the various states, not even sufficient knowledge to permit the assignment of probabilities to the states of nature.
3. *Decision making under conditions of risk:* In this situation, more than one state of nature exists, but the decision maker has information which will support the assignment of probability values to each of the possible states.

We will discuss the various criteria of decision making with the help of an example.

EXAMPLE 10.1: A manufacturer of goods has only three options available for the existing plant: Expand the present plant, build a new plant, and subcontract out extra production to other manufacturers. The future events concern demand for the product. They are: high demand, moderate demand, low demand, and failure. The pay-off table, a table which shows the pay-offs which would result from each possible combination of decision alternative and state of nature, is given below.

Decision	*Future states of nature (Demand of the product)*			
alternatives	*High*	*Moderate*	*Low*	*Failure*
Expand	5,00,000	2,50,000	−2,50,000	−4,50,000
Build	7,00,000	3,00,000	−4,00,000	−8,00,000
Subcontract	3,00,000	1,50,000	−10,000	−1,00,000

Decision making under certainty

Under conditions of complete certainty, it is easy to analyze the situation and make good decisions. Since certainty involves only *one* state of nature, the decision maker simply picks up the best pay-off in that one column and chooses the alternative associated with that pay-off. In the above table, for example, if the manufacturer knew that the demand would be *moderate*, he would choose the alternative "build", since that yields him the highest alternative pay-off. Similarly, if he knew that the demand would be *low*, he would choose the alternative "subcontract," since even though that generates a loss, it is still his best alternative given that state of nature. Few of us ever enjoy the luxury of having complete information about the future, and thus decision making under conditions of certainty is not of consequential interest to us.

Linear programming models that we discussed in the earlier part of this book, provide an example of decision making under certainty. These models are suitable only for situations in which the decision alternatives can be interrelated by well-defined mathematical linear functions.

Decision making under uncertainty

In the case of making decisions under conditions of uncertainty, the decision maker knows which states of nature can happen, but he does not have the information which would allow him to specify the probability that these states will happen. In this situation, there are four criteria used to make decisions. We shall examine each of these.

1. *Maximax criteria:* The maximax criteria provide an **optimistic** criterion. For this, one selects the decision alternative which would maximize the maximum pay-off. We select the maximum pay-off possible for each decision alternative and then choose the alternative that provides us with the maximum pay-off within this group. For our Example 10.1, the optimal decision is to "build" a new plant with an associated pay-off of 7,00,000.

Decision making under uncertainty, as under risk, involves alternative actions whose pay-offs depend on the (random) *states of nature*. Specifically, the pay-off matrix of a decision problem with m alternative actions and n states of nature can be represented as

	s_1	s_2	...	s_n
a_1	$v(a_1, s_1)$	$v(a_1, s_2)$	...	$v(a_1, s_n)$
a_2	$v(a_2, s_1)$	$v(a_2, s_2)$	...	$v(a_2, s_n)$
...	...	...	...	...
...	...	...	...	...
...	...	...	...	...
a_m	$v(a_m, s_1)$	$v(a_m, s_2)$	...	$v(a_m, s_n)$

The element a_i-represents action i and the element s_j-represents state of nature j. The payoff or outcome associated with action a_i and state s_j is $v(a_j, s_j)$.

The difference between making decision under risk and under uncertainty is that in the case of uncertainty, the probability distribution associated with the states s_j, $j = 1, 2 \ldots, n$ is either unknown or cannot be determined.

2. *Maximin criteria:* The maximin criteria for decision making under conditions of uncertainty give a **pessimistic** decision. One tries to maximize one's minimum possible pay-offs. We begin by first listing the minimum pay-off that is possible for each decision alternative and then select the alternative within this group which results in maximum pay-off.

In our Example 10.1, the optimal decision based on maximin criteria is to "subcontract" with an associated pay-off of –1,00,000 (loss).

The maximin (minimax) criterion is based on the conservative attitude of making the best out of the worst possible conditions. If $v(a_i, s_j)$ is gain, then we select the action that corresponds to the *maximin* criterion.

$$\max_{a_i}\left\{\min_{s_j} v(a_i, s_j)\right\}$$

If $v(a_i, s_j)$ is loss, we use the *minimax* criterion given by

$$\min_{a_i}\left\{\max_{s_j} v(a_i, s_j)\right\}$$

Decision alternatives	*Future states of nature* High	Moderate	Low	Failure	*Maximum in row*	*Minimum in row*
Expand	5,00,000	2,50,000	–2,50,000	–4,50,000	5,00,000	–4,50,000
Build	7,00,000	3,00,000	–4,00,000	–8,00,000	**7,00,000**	–8,00,000
Subcontract	3,00,000	1,50,000	–10,000	–1,00,000	3,00,000	**–1,00,000**
					Maximax	**Maximin**

3. *The Laplace criteria:* The Laplace criterion is based on the *principle of insufficient reason.* Because the probability distributions of the state of nature, $P\{s_j\}$, are not known, there is no reason to believe that they are different. The alternatives are thus evaluated using the *optimistic* assumption that they are all equal—that is, $P\{s_1\} = P\{s_2\} = \cdots = P\{s_n\} = 1/n$

Given that pay-off $v(a_i, s_j)$ represents gain, the best alternative is the one that yields

$$\max_{a_i} \frac{1}{n}\left\{\sum_{j=1}^{n} v(a_i, s_j)\right\}$$

If $v(a_i, s_j)$ represents loss, then the "max" operator is replaced with the "min" operator. In our example, we compute the average of the pay-offs for each alternative

for Expand : {5,00,000 + 2,50,000 + (–2,50,000) + (–4,50,000)}/4 = 12,500

for Build : –50,000

for Subcontract : 85,000

According to the Laplace criterion the optimal decision is to "subcontract".

4. *The savage criterion (Regret criteria):* The savage criterion is based on the concept of regret and calls for selecting the course of action that minimizes the maximum regret. For our Example 10.1, suppose the decision maker earlier made a decision to subcontract production (based on the information he had at that time) and it turns out that the demand is high. The profit he will make from subcontracting with high demand is 3,00,000; but had he known that the demand was going to be high, he would not have subcontracted but would have chosen instead to build with a profit of 7,00,000. The difference between 7,00,000 (the optimal pay-off "had he known") and 3,00,000 (the pay-off he actually realized from subcontracting) is 4,00,000 and is known as the *regret* resulting from his decision. Let us look at the calculation of one more regret value. Suppose he had chosen alternative "build" and the demand turned out to be moderate. In this case there would be no regret because, as it turned out, the decision alternative "build" is optimum when the demand is moderate, and 3,00,000 is the maximum pay-off possible.

In the following table, we show the regret associated with all twelve combinations of decision alternatives and states of nature. These regret values are obtained by subtracting every entry in the original pay-off table for the problem from the largest entry in its column. Applying the minimax regret criterion requires the decision maker to indicate the maximum regret for each decision alternative (given in bold letters in the table for the three decision alternatives). Finally, he chooses the minimum of these three regret values (3,50,000, 7,00,000 and 4,00,000); in this case 3,50,000 is his minimum regret value, and this regret is associated with the decision alternative "expand".

Regret table

Decision	*Future states of nature*			
alternatives	*High*	*Moderate*	*Low*	*Failure*
Expand	2,00,000	50,000	2,40,000	**3,50,000**
Build	0	0	3,90,000	**7,00,000**
Subcontract	**4,00,000**	1,50,000	0	0

The savage regret criterion aims at moderating conservatism in the minimax (maximin) criterion by replacing the (gain or loss) pay-off matrix $v(a_i, s_j)$ with a loss (or regret) $r(a_i, s_j)$ matrix by using the following transformation:

$$r(a_i, s_j) = \begin{cases} \max\limits_{a_k}[v(a_k, s_j)] - v(a_i, s_j), & \text{if } v \text{ is gain} \\ v(a_i, s_j) - \min\limits_{a_k}[v(a_k, s_j)], & \text{if } v \text{ is loss} \end{cases}$$

5. *Hurwicz criterion (Criterion of realism):* This criterion for decision making under conditions of uncertainty is a middle ground criterion between maximax and maximin—that is, between optimism and pessimism. This compromise requires us to specify a coefficient, or index of optimism, symbolized α (the Greek letter alpha), where α is between 0 and 1 in value. When we assign α a value of 0, we are expressing pessimism about nature; an α equal to 1 indicates our optimism about nature. To apply this criterion, we first determine both the maximum pay-off and minimum pay-off for each decision alternative. Then for each decision alternative we compute this value:

$$\alpha\,(\text{maximum pay-off}) + (1 - \alpha)\ (\text{minimum pay-off})$$

We then select the decision alternative that gives the maximum value.

For example if we assign the value of 0.7 to α (being fairly optimistic), then the values we compute would be

For Expand : 0.7 (5,00,000) + 0.3 (–4,50,000) = 2,15,000

For Build : 0.7 (7,00,000) + 0.3 (–8,00,000) = 2,50,000

For Subcontract : 0.7 (3,00,000) + 0.3 (–1,00,000) = 1,80,000

The application of this criterion suggests that we choose the alternative "build".

The criterion is designed to reflect a range of decision-making attitudes from the most optimistic to the most pessimistic (or conservative). Define $0 \le \alpha \le 1$, and assume that $v(a_i, s_j)$ represents gain. Then the selected action must be associated with

$$\max_{a_i} \left\{ \alpha \max_{s_j} v(a_i, s_j) + (1 - \alpha) \min_{s_j} v(a_i, s_j) \right\}$$

The parameter α is known as the *index of optimism*. If $\alpha = 0$, the criterion is conservative because it is equivalent to applying the regular minimax criterion. If $\alpha = 1$, the criterion produces optimistic results because it is equivalent to applying the best of the best conditions. We can adjust the degree of optimism (or pessimism) through a proper selection of the value of α in the specified (0, 1) range. In the absence of strong feeling regarding optimism and pessimism, $\alpha = 0.5$ may be an appropriate choice.

If $v(a_i, s_j)$ represents loss, then the criterion must be changed to

$$\min_{a_i} \left\{ \alpha \min_{s_j} v(a_i, s_j) + (1 - \alpha) \max_{s_j} v(a_i, s_j) \right\}$$

10.5 CONSTRUCTING A REGRET TABLE FROM PROFIT TABLE

Regret or opportunity loss is defined as the difference between the actual pay-off and the pay-off one could have received if one knew which event was going to occur. We can convert the pay-off matrix (profit matrix) into a corresponding regret (opportunity loss) matrix as follows:

1. If the decision alternatives are in rows and future states of nature are in columns, subtract each entry in the pay-off matrix from the largest entry in the pay-off matrix from the largest entry in its column. The largest entry in a column will have zero regret.

   In the event that the original decision matrix was in terms of losses (costs), then we would select the smallest loss for each event and subtract it from each row entry. Each entry in the regret table is now the opportunity loss associated with an action-event combination. The cells where the smallest loss appeared before, now show zeros.

2. If the decision alternatives are in columns and future states of nature are in rows, subtract each entry in the pay-off matrix from the largest entry in its row. The largest entry in a row will have zero regret.

Before moving on to understand the expected value criterion for decision making under risk, let us see what is meant by expected value.

10.6 EXPECTED VALUE

To obtain the expected value of a discrete random variable, we multiply each value that the random variable can assume by the probability of occurrence of that value and then sum these products. The expected value weighs each possible outcome by the frequency with which it is expected to occur. Thus, more common occurrences are given more weight than are less common ones.

For a decision problem, which includes n states of nature and m alternatives, if P_j (>0) is the probability of occurrence for state of nature j and a_{ij} is the pay-off of alternative i given state of nature j ($i = 1, 2, \ldots, m$; $j = 1, 2, \ldots, n$) then the expected pay-off for alternative i is:

$$EV_i = a_{i1}P_1 + a_{i2}P_2 + \cdots + a_{in}P_n; \; i = 1, 2, \ldots, n$$

where, by definition $P_1 + P_2 + \cdots + P_n = 1$.

10.7 EXPECTED VALUE CRITERION FOR DECISION MAKING UNDER RISK

We explore the expected value criterion for decision making under risk by taking the following example.

EXAMPLE 10.2: A fruit vendor purchases fruits for Rs. 3 a box and sells them for Rs. 8 a box. The high mark-up reflects the perishability of the fruit and the great risk of stocking it, the product has no value after the first day it is offered for sale. The vendor faces the problem of how many boxes to order for tomorrow's business.

A 90-day observation of the past sales gives the following information.

Boxes sold during 90 days

Daily sales	*No. of days sold*	*Probability of each number being sold*
10	18	0.20
11	36	0.40
12	27	0.30
13	9	0.10
Total	90	1.00

If the buyer tomorrow calls for more boxes than the number in stock, the vendor's profits suffer by Rs. 5 per box, for the sale he cannot make. On the other hand, excess stock also reduces the profit per box by Rs. 3.

Expected value (EV) criterion

Preparing the conditional profit table: As observed sales magnitudes are given in Example 10.2, we have no reason to assume the vendor buying less than 10 and more than 13 boxes.

A conditional profit table shows the profit resulting from any possible combination of supply and demand. The profits can be either positive or negative and are conditional in that a certain profit results from taking a specific stocking action (ordering 10, 11, 12 or 13 boxes) and having sales of a specific number of boxes (10, 11, 12 or 13 boxes).

Conditional profit table

Future states of nature (Demand)	*Decision alternatives (Possible stock action)*			
	10 boxes	*11 boxes*	*12 boxes*	*13 boxes*
10 boxes	50	47	44	41
11 boxes	50	55	52	49
12 boxes	50	55	60	57
13 boxes	50	55	60	65

The table above reflects the losses which occur when the stock remains unsold at the end of a day. It does not reflect the profit denied because of an out-of-stock condition.

Notice that the stocking of 10 boxes each day will always result in a profit of Rs. 50. Even when buyers want 13 boxes on some days, he can sell only 10.

When he stocks 11 boxes, his profit will be Rs. 55 on days when buyers request 11, 12 or 13 boxes. But on days when he has 11 boxes in stock and buyers buy only 10 boxes, the profit drops to Rs. 47. The Rs. 50 profit on the 10 boxes sold must be reduced by Rs. 3, the cost of the unsold box.

A stock of 12 boxes will increase the daily profits to 60, but only on those days when buyers want 12 or 13 boxes . When buyers want only 10 boxes, the profit is reduced to Rs. 44, the Rs. 50 profit on the sale of 10 boxes is reduced by Rs. 6, the cost of two unsold boxes.

The stocking of 13 boxes will result in a profit of Rs. 65 when there is a market for 13 boxes. There will be Rs. 5 profit on each box sold, with no unsold boxes. When buyers buy fewer than 13 boxes, such a stock action results in a profit of less than Rs. 65. For example, with a stock of 13 boxes and sale of only 11 boxes, the profit is Rs. 49; the profit on 11 boxes, Rs. 55 is reduced by the cost of 2 unsold boxes, Rs. 6.

Such a conditional profit table does not tell the vendor how many boxes should he stock each day in order to maximize his profit. It only shows what the outcome will be if a specific number of boxes are stocked and a specific number of boxes are sold. Under conditions of risk, he does not know in advance the size of any day's market, but he must still decide which number of boxes, stocked consistently, will maximize profits over a long period of time.

Determining expected profits: The next step in determining the best number of boxes to stock is to assign probabilities to the possible outcomes or profits. It was stated earlier that we could compute the expected value of a random variable by weighting each possible value that the variable could take by the probability of its taking on each value. Using this procedure, we compute the expected daily profit from stocking 10 cases each day.

Expected profit from stocking 10 cases

Demand	*Conditional profit (a)*	*Probability of demand (b)*	*Expected profit = (a) × (b)*
10 boxes	50	0.20	10
11 boxes	50	0.40	20
12 boxes	50	0.30	15
13 boxes	50	0.10	5
Total		1.0	**50**

Likewise, we compute for all possible stocking options.

Expected profit from stocking

		10 boxes		*11 boxes*		*12 boxes*		*13 boxes*	
Demand	*Prob.*	*Cond. profit*	*Exp. profit*	*Cond. profit*	*Exp. profit*	*Cond. profit*	*Exp. profit*	*Cond. profit*	*Exp. profit*
10	0.20	50	10	47	9.40	44	8.80	41	8.20
11	0.40	50	20	55	22.00	52	20.80	49	19.60
12	0.30	50	15	55	16.50	60	18.00	57	17.10
13	0.10	50	5	55	5.50	60	6.00	65	6.50
Total			50		53.40		**53.60 Max.**		51.40

The optimum stock action is the one that results in the greatest expected profit. It is the action that will result in the largest daily average profits and thus the maximum total profit over a period of time. In this illustration, the proper number to stock each day is 12 cases, since this quantity will give the highest possible average daily profits under the conditions given.

We have not introduced certainty into the problem facing the vendor. Rather, we have used past experience to determine the best stock action open. He still does not know how many boxes will be requested on any given day. There is no guarantee that he will make a profit of Rs. 53.60 tomorrow. However, if he stocks 12 units each day under the conditions given, he will have average profits of Rs. 53.60 per day. This is the best he can do, because the choice of any one of the other three possible stock actions will result in a lower average daily profit.

Expected profit with perfect information: Now suppose for a moment that our vendor could remove all uncertainty from his problem by obtaining additional information. Complete and accurate information about the future, referred to as perfect information, would remove all uncertainty from the problem. This does not mean that sales would not vary from 10 to 13 boxes per day. Sales would still be 10 boxes per day 20 per cent of the time, 11 boxes 40 per cent of the time, 12 boxes 30 per cent of the time, and 13 boxes 10 per cent of the time. However, with perfect information the vendor would know in advance how many boxes were going to be demanded for each day.

Under these circumstances, he would stock today the exact number of boxes buyers will want tomorrow. For sales of 10 boxes, he would stock 10 boxes and realize a profit of Rs. 50. When sales were going to be 11 boxes, he would stock exactly 11 boxes, thus realizing a profit of Rs. 55.

The following table shows the conditional profit values that are applicable to the vendor's problem if he has perfect information. Given the size of the market in advance for a particular day, he chooses the stock action that will maximize his profits. This means he buys and stocks so as to avoid all losses from obsolete stock as well as all opportunity losses which reflect lost profits on unfilled requests for merchandise.

Conditional profit table under certainty

Market size, cases	*Possible stock actions*			
	10 cases	*11 cases*	*12 cases*	*13 cases*
10	50	–	–	–
11	–	55	–	–
12	–	–	60	–
13	–	–	–	65

We can now compute the *Expected Profit with Perfect Information* (EPPI). Here the conditional profit figures are the maximum profits possible for each sales volume.

For example, when buyers buy 12 boxes, the vendor will always make a profit of Rs. 60 under conditions of certainty because he will have stocked exactly 12 boxes.

Expected profit with perfect information

Market size cases	*Conditional profit under certainty*		*Probability of market size*		*EPPI*
10	50	×	0.20	=	10
11	55	×	0.40	=	22
12	60	×	0.30	=	18
13	56	×	0.10	=	6.50
			1.00		56.50 ← EPPI

With perfect information, he could count on making an average profit of Rs. 56.50 a day. This is the maximum profit possible.

An alternative approach: minimizing expected losses

We have just solved the problem by maximizing the expected daily profit. There is another approach to this same problem. We can compute the amounts by which the maximum profit possible (Rs. 56.50) will be reduced under various stocking actions; then we can choose that course of action which will minimize the expected value of these reductions or losses.

Two types of losses are involved: (i) *obsolescence losses* are those caused by stocking too many units; (ii) *opportunity losses* are those caused by being out of stock when buyers want to buy.

The following table is a table of conditional losses. Each value in the table is conditional on a specific number of boxes being stocked and a specific number being requested. The values include not only those losses from obsolete inventory when the number of boxes stocked exceeds the number the buyers desire, but also those opportunity losses resulting from lost sales when the market would have been more than the number stocked.

Conditional loss table

Future states of nature (Demand)	*Decision alternatives (Possible stock action)*			
	10 boxes	*11 boxes*	*12 boxes*	*13 boxes*
10 boxes	0	3	6	9
11 boxes	5	0	3	6
12 boxes	10	5	0	3
13 boxes	15	10	5	0

Neither of these losses is incurred when the number stocked on any day is the same as the number requested. This condition results in the diagonal row of zeros. Figures above any zero represent losses arising from obsolete inventory; in each case the number stocked is greater than the number sold. For example, if 13 boxes are stocked and only 10 boxes are sold, there is a Rs. 9 loss resulting from the cost of the 3 boxes unsold.

Values below the diagonal row of zeros represent opportunity losses resulting from requests that cannot be filled. For example, if only 10 boxes are stocked but 13 boxes are demanded, there is an opportunity loss of Rs. 15. This is represented by the loss of Rs. 5 per box on the 3 boxes requested but not available.

Just like we calculated expected profits, we now compute expected losses.

Expected loss from stocking

		10 boxes		*11 boxes*		*12 boxes*		*13 boxes*	
Demand	*Prob.*	*Cond. loss*	*Exp. loss*	*Cond. loss*	*Exp. loss*	*Cond. loss*	*Exp. loss*	*Cond. loss*	*Exp. loss*
10	0.20	0	0.00	3	0.60	6	1.20	9	1.80
11	0.40	5	2.00	0	0.00	3	1.20	6	2.40
12	0.30	10	3.00	5	1.50	0	0.00	3	0.90
13	0.10	15	1.50	10	1.00	5	0.50	0	0.00
Total			6.50		3.10		**2.90**	**Min**	5.10

The optimum stock action is the one which will minimize the expected losses.

We can approach the optimum stocking action from either point of view, maximizing expected profits or minimizing expected losses, both approaches lead to the same conclusion.

Expected value of perfect information (EVPI)

Assuming that the fruit vendor could obtain a perfect predictor of future demand, what would be the value of such a predictor to him? He would have to compare what such additional information would cost him with the additional profits he would realize as a result of having the information.

He can earn average daily profits of Rs. 56.50 if he has perfect information about the future. His best expected daily profit without the predictor is only Rs. 53.60. The difference of Rs. 2.90 is the maximum amount he would be willing to pay, per day, for a perfect predictor because that is the maximum amount by which he can increase his expected daily profit. This difference is the *Expected Value of Perfect Information* (EVPI). There is no sense in paying more than Rs. 2.90 for the predictor; to do so would lower the expected daily profit.

	Decision alternative (Stocking the boxes)			
	10 boxes	*11 boxes*	*12 boxes*	*13 boxes*
Expected profit	50.00	53.40	53.60	51.40
Expected loss	6.50	3.10	2.90	5.10
			Optimal decision	

Determining what additional information is worth in the decision-making process is a serious problem for managers. In our Example 10.2, we found that the vendor would pay Rs. 2.90 a day for a perfect predictor. Generalizing from this example, we can say that the expected value of perfect information is equal to the minimum expected loss.

EVPI = Minimum expected loss

To see intuitively why the minimum EOL equals the EVPI, consider what the EOL would be under perfect information; it would be equal to zero. That is, there would be no opportunity losses if the decision maker knew which event would occur and behaved rationally. Thus, under uncertainty the decision maker would do the best possible, that is, minimize the EOL. It can be proved mathematically that EVPI = EOL of the optimal act under uncertainty. Another term used for the EOL of the optimal act under uncertainty is cost of uncertainty. This term stresses the cost of making the best decision under uncertainty, a cost that would be eliminated if perfect information were available. Hence, the cost of uncertainty is also equal to the EVPI. In short, the EVPI, the EOL of the optimal action under uncertainty, and the cost of uncertainty are equivalent.

It is not often, however, that one is fortunate enough to be able to secure a perfect predictor. Thus in most decision-making situations, managers are really attempting to evaluate the worth of information which will enable them to make *better* rather than *perfect* decisions.

Criterion of maximum likelihood

If we want to use the criterion of maximum likelihood, we just select the state of nature that has the highest probability of occurrence. Then having assumed that this state will occur, we pick the decision alternative which will yield the highest pay-off.

In Example 10.2, from the table of conditional profit, we see that the demand for 11 boxes has the highest probability of occurrence 0.40.

Demand (boxes)	*Prob. of occurrence*	*Decision alternative (Stocking the boxes)*			
		10 boxes	*11 boxes*	*12 boxes*	*13 boxes*
10	0.20	50	47	44	41
11	**0.40**	**50**	**55**	**52**	**49**
12	0.30	50	55	60	57
13	0.10	50	55	60	65

So we select that row and then pick up the decision alternative of stocking that gives the maximum pay-off of Rs. 55. This decision is then to stock 11 boxes.

This decision criterion is rather widely used and will produce valid results when one state of nature is much more probable than any other, and when the conditional values are not extremely different; however, it is possible to make some serious errors if we use this criterion in a situation where a large number of states of nature exist and each of them has a small, nearly equal probability of occurrence.

10.8 METHOD OF MARGINAL PROBABILITIES

In many problems, the use of conditional profit tables and expected profit tables would be difficult because of the number of computations required. The marginal approach avoids this problem of excessive computational work. When an additional unit of an item is bought, two outcomes are possible, the unit will be sold or it will not be sold. The sum of the probabilities of these two events must be 1. If p denotes the probability of selling the additional unit, then $(1 - p)$ is the probability of not selling that unit. If the additional unit is sold, we shall realize an increase in our conditional profits as a result of the profit from the additional unit. We shall refer to this as *marginal profit* (**MP**). If the additional unit is not sold, it reduces our conditional profit. The amount of this reduction is referred to as the *marginal loss* (**ML**).

Now, the expected marginal profit from stocking and selling an additional unit is the marginal profit of the unit multiplied by the probability that the unit will be sold, i.e. $p \times \text{MP}$. Similarly, the expected marginal loss is $(1 - p) \times \text{ML}$.

It follows that the additional items will be stocked whilst the following relationship holds:

$$p \text{ (making additional sale)} \times \text{MP} > p \text{ (not making additional sale)} \times \text{ML}$$

We can generalize that the decision maker in this situation would stock up to the point where

$$p\,(\text{MP}) = (1 - p)(\text{ML})$$

$$p\,(\text{MP}) + p\,(\text{ML}) = \text{ML}$$

$$p\,(\text{MP} + \text{ML}) = \text{ML}$$

$$p = \text{ML}/(\text{MP} + \text{ML})$$

This equation represents the *minimum required probability* of selling at least an additional unit to justify the stocking of that additional unit. Additional units should be stocked so long as the probability of selling at least an additional unit is greater than p.

EXAMPLE 10.3: A distributor buys perishable articles for Rs. 2 per item and sells them at Rs. 5. Demand per day is uncertain and items unsold at the end of the day represent a write off because of perishability. If he understocks, he loses profit he could have made.

A 300-day record of past activity is as follows:

Daily demand (units)	*No. of days*	*p*
10	30	0.1
11	60	0.2
12	120	0.4
13	90	0.3
	300	1.0

What level of stock should be held from day to day to maximize profit?

Solution:

Conditional and expected profit table

Demand	*P*	*Stock Options*							
		10		11		12		13	
		CP	*EP*	*CP*	*EP*	*CP*	*EP*	*CP*	*EP*
10	0.1	30	3	28	2.8	26	2.6	24	2.4
11	0.2	30	6	33	6.6	31	6.2	29	5.8
12	0.4	30	12	33	13.2	36	14.4	34	13.6
13	0.3	30	9	33	9.9	36	10.8	39	11.7
	1.0		30		32.5		**34.0**		33.5

where (*CP*) stands for conditional profit and (*EP*) stands for expected profit.

The optimum stock position, for the given pattern of demand, is to stock *12 units per day.*

Solution by marginal probability formula: We work out the marginal profit, *MP*, i.e. the profit from selling one more unit, and the marginal loss, *ML*, i.e. the loss from not selling the marginal unit and to calculate the relationship between *MP* and *ML* in terms of probability.
Here,

$$MP = 3 \quad \text{and} \quad ML = 2$$

It follows those additional items will be stocked whilst the following relationship holds:

$$p \text{ (making additional sale)} \times \text{MP} > p \text{ (not making additional sale)} \times \text{ML}$$

From the above discussion, $p = \text{ML}/(\text{MP} + \text{ML})$
Inserting the data we obtain

$$p = 2/(3 + 2) = 0.4, \text{ i.e. the probability at break even point.}$$

This value of 0.4 means that in order to justify the stocking of an additional unit, we must have at least a 0.4 cumulative probability of selling that unit. The cumulative probability in the following table represents the probabilities that sales will reach or exceed each of the four sales levels. For example, 0.90 indicates that we are only 90 per cent sure of selling 11 or more units. This is obtained by summing up the probability values of the sales at level 11, 12 and 13 or by subtracting the probability of the sales higher than 11 from 1.

This probability is compared with the probability of demand at the various levels, the optimum position being the highest demand with a probability greater than *p*, i.e.

	Demand	*Probability*
Greater than 10 units	1.00	
Greater than 11 units	0.9	
Greater than 12 units	0.7	Break even probability = 0.4
Greater than 13 units	0.3	

12 items is the most profitable stock level.

10.9 DECISION TREES

Decisions that lend themselves to display in a decision table also lend themselves to display in a decision tree. We should analyze some decisions, however, using decision trees. It is convenient to use a decision table in problems having one set of decisions and one set of states of nature. Many problems, however, included *sequential* decisions and states of nature. When there are two or more sequential decisions and later decisions are based on the outcome of prior ones, the decision tree approach becomes appropriate. A decision tree is a graphical display of the decisions process that indicates decision alternatives, states of nature and their respective probabilities, and pay-offs for each combination of alternative and state of nature.

Although we may apply all previously discussed decision criteria, expected value (EV) is the most commonly used and usually the most appropriate criterion for the decision tree analysis. One of the first steps in the analysis is to graph the decision tree and to specify the monetary consequences of all contingencies or outcomes for a particular problem.

Analyzing problems with decision trees involves five steps:

1. Define the problem
2. Structure or draw the decision tree
3. Assign probabilities to the states of nature
4. Estimate pay-offs for each possible combination of alternatives and states of nature.
5. Solve the problems by computing expected values (EV) for each state of nature node. This is done by working *backward*, that is, starting at the right of the tree and working back to decision nodes on the left.

Symbols used in a decision tree:

(a) □ — a decision node from which one of several alternatives may be selected.

(b) ○ — a state of nature node out of which one state of nature will occur.

To present a manager's decision alternatives, we can develop decision trees and decision tables using the above symbols.

In constructing a decision tree, we must be sure that all alternatives and states of nature are in their correct and logical places and we include all possible alternatives and states of nature.

EXAMPLE 10.4: The Company is investigating the possibility of producing and marketing a new product. Undertaking this project would require the construction of either a large or a small manufacturing plant. The market for the product produced could be either favourable or unfavourable. The company, of course, has the option of not developing the new product line at all. A decision tree for this situation is presented in the following figure (Figure 10.1).

We construct a decision table including conditional values based on the following information. With a favourable market, a large facility would give a net profit of Rs. 2,00,000. If the market is unfavourable, a Rs. 1,80,000 net loss would occur. A small plant would result in a net profit of Rs. 1,00,000 in a favourable market, but a net loss of Rs. 20,000 would be encountered if the market was unfavourable.

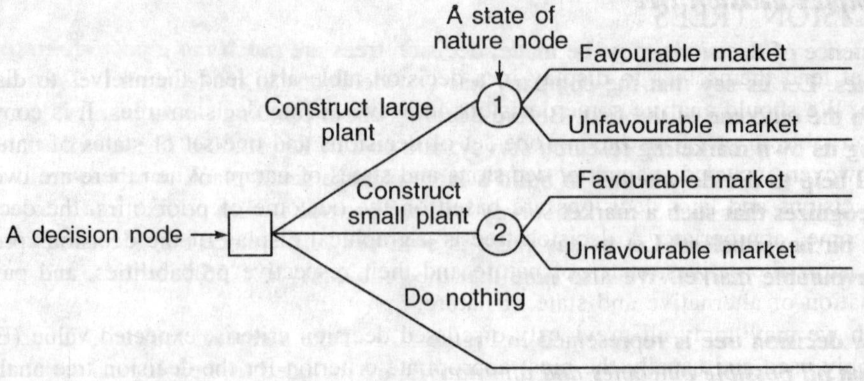

Figure 10.1

Decision table with conditional values

	States of nature	
Alternatives	*Favourable market*	*Unfavourable market*
Construct large plant	2,00,000	–1,80,000
Construct small plant	1,00,000	–20,000
Do nothing	0	0

Also, it is believed in this case, that the probability of a favorable market is exactly same as that of an unfavourable market, i.e. each state of nature has a 0.50 chance.

A completed and solved decision tree is presented in Figure 10.2. Note that the pay-offs are placed at the right-hand side of each of the tree's branches. The probabilities are placed in parentheses next to each state of nature. The expected monetary values of each state of nature node are then calculated and placed by their respective nodes. The EV of the first node is 10,000. This represents the branch from the decision node to construct a large plant. The EV for node 2, to construct a small plant, is 40,000. Building no plant or doing nothing has, of course, a pay-off of 0. The branch leaving the decision node leading to the state of nature node with the highest EV will be chosen. In the example (Figure 10.2) here, a small plant should be built.

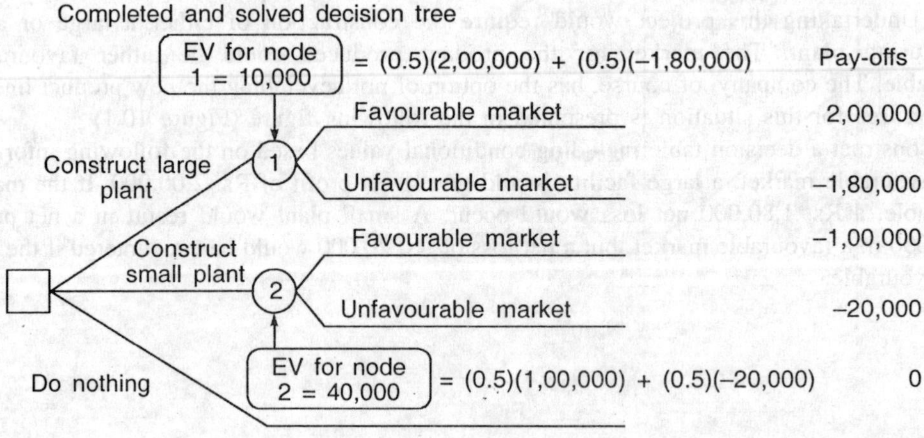

Figure 10.2

A more complex decision tree

When a sequence of decisions must be made, decision trees are much more powerful tools than are decision tables. Let us say that the company has two decisions to make, with the second decision dependent on the outcome of the first. Before deciding about building a new plant, it has the option of conducting its own marketing research survey, at a cost of Rs. 10,000. The information from this survey could help to decide whether to build a large plant, a small plant, or not to build at all. The company recognizes that such a market survey will not provide it with perfect information, but may help quite a bit nevertheless. Let us say there is a 45 per cent chance that the survey results will indicate a favourable market. We also note that the probability is 0.55 that the survey results will be negative.

The new decision tree is represented in Figure 10.3. Take a careful look at this more complex tree. Note that *all possible outcomes and alternatives* are included in their logical sequence. This is one of the strengths of using decision trees in making decisions. The manager is forced to examine all possible outcomes, including unfavourable ones. He or she is also forced to make decisions in a logical, sequential manner.

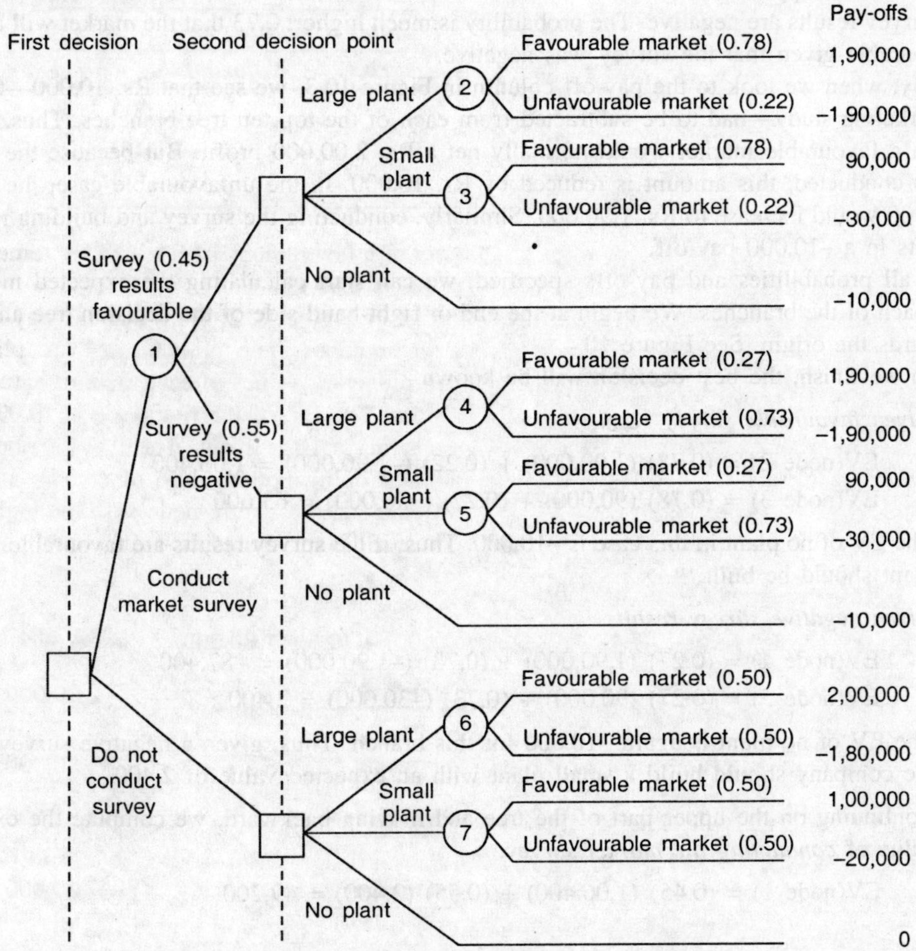

Figure 10.3

Examining the tree in the following figure, we see that the company's first decision point is whether to conduct the Rs. 10,000 market survey. If it chooses not to do the study (the lower part of the tree), it can either build a large plant, a small plant, or no plant. This is its second decision point. The market will either be favourable. (0.50 probability) or unfavourable (also 0.50 probability) if it builds. The pay-offs for each of the possible consequences are listed along the right-hand side. As a matter of fact, this lower portion of the company's tree is identical to the simpler decision tree shown in Figure 10.2.

The upper part of Figure 10.3 reflects the decision to conduct the market survey. State of nature node number 1 has two branches coming out of it.

The rest of the probabilities shown in parentheses are all conditional probabilities. For example, let us suppose that 0.78 is the probability of a favourable market for the product given that the research indicated that the market was good. Do not forget, though, there is a chance that Rs. 10,000 market survey did not result in perfect or even reliable information. Any market research study is subject to error. In this case, there is a 22 per cent chance that the market for the product will be unfavourable given that the survey results are positive.

Likewise, we suppose that there is a 27 per cent chance that the market will be favourable given that the survey results are negative. The probability is much higher, 0.73 that the market will actually be unfavourable given that the survey was negative.

Finally, when we look to the pay-off column in Figure 10.3, we see that Rs. 10,000—the cost of the marketing study—had to be subtracted from each of the top ten tree branches. Thus, a large plant with a favourable market would normally net a Rs. 2,00,000 profit. But because the market study was conducted, this amount is reduced by Rs. 10,000. In the unfavourable case, the loss of Rs. 1,80,000 would increase to Rs. 1,90,000. Similarly, conducting the survey and building no plant now results in a –10,000 pay-off.

With all probabilities and pay-offs specified, we can start calculating the expected monetary value of each of the branches. We begin at the end or right-hand side of the decision tree and work back towards the origin. See Figure 10.4.

When we finish, the best decision will be known.

1. *Given favourable survey results,*

   EV(node 2) = (0.78) (1,90,000) + (0.22) (–1,90,000) = 1,06,400

   EV(node 3) = (0.78) (90,000) + (0.22) (–30,000) = 63,600

   The EV of no plant in this case is –10,000. Thus, if the survey results are favourable, a large plant should be built.

2. *Given negative survey results,*

   EV(node 4) = (0.27) (1,90,000) + (0.73) (–1,90,000) = –87,400

   EV(node 5) = (0.27) (90,000) + (0.73) (–30,000) = 2,400

   The EV of no plant is again –10,000 for this branch. Thus, given a negative survey result, the company should build a small plant with an expected value of 2,400.

3. Continuing on the upper part of the tree and moving backward, we compute the expected value of *conducting the market survey.*

   EV(node 1) = (0.45) (1,06,400) + (0.55) (2,400) = 49,200

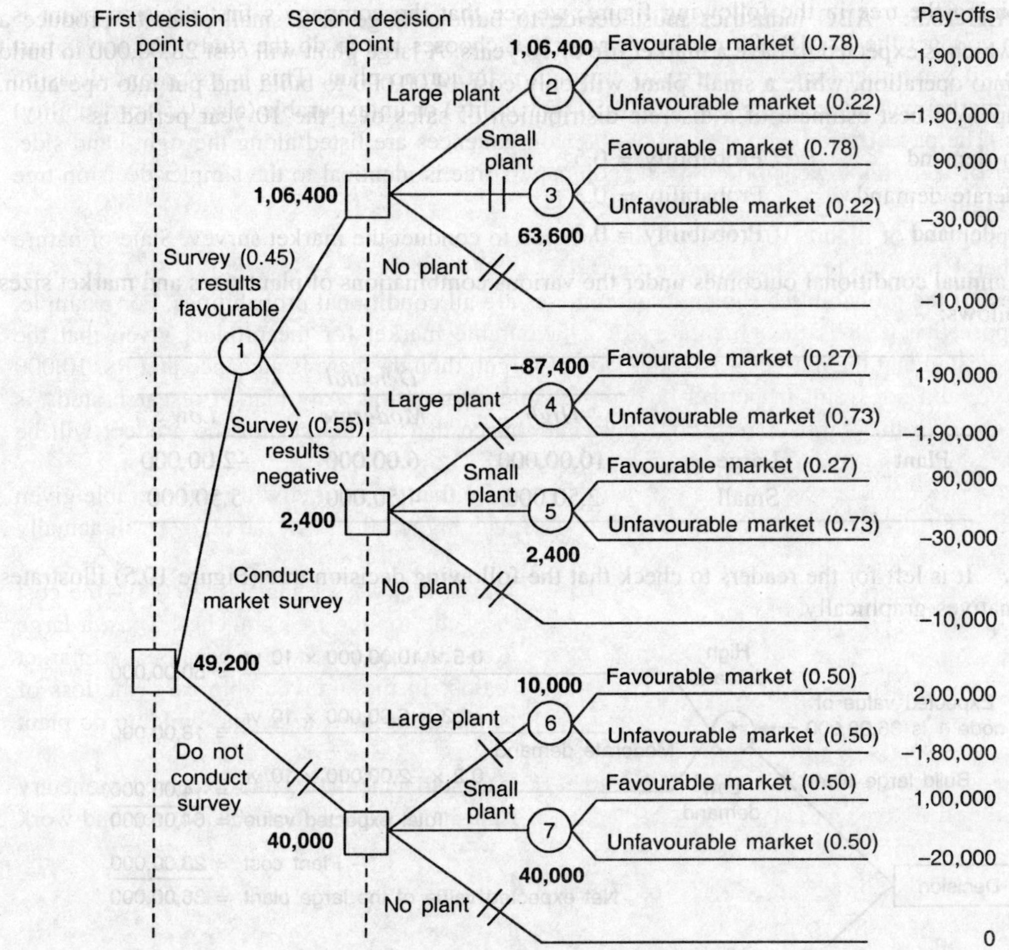

Figure 10.4

4. If the *market survey is not conducted,*

$$\text{EV(node 6)} = (0.50)\ (2{,}00{,}000) + (0.50)\ (-1{,}80{,}000) = 10{,}000$$

$$\text{EV(node 7)} = (0.50)\ (1{,}00{,}000) + (0.50)\ (-20{,}000) = 40{,}000$$

The EV of no plant is 0. Thus, building a small plant is the best choice, given that the marketing research is not performed.

5. Since the expected monetary value of conducting the survey is 49,200, versus an EV of 40,000 for not conducting the study—*the best choice is to seek marketing information*. If the survey results are favourable, the company should build the large plant; but if the research is negative, it should build the small plant.

EXAMPLE 10.5: ABC industries must decide to build a large or a small plant to produce a product which is expected to have a market life of 10 years. A large plant will cost 28,00,000 to build and put into operation, while a small plant will only cost 14,00,000 to build and put into operation. The company's best estimate of a discrete distribution of sales over the 10 year period is

High demand : Probability = 0.5
Moderate demand : Probability = 0.3
Low demand : Probability = 0.2

The annual conditional outcomes under the various combinations of plant sizes and market sizes are as follows:

		Demand		
		High	*Moderate*	*Low*
Plant	Large	10,00,000	6,00,000	–2,00,000
	Small	2,50,000	4,50,000	5,50,000

Solution: It is left for the readers to check that the following decision tree (Figure 10.5) illustrates the alternatives graphically.

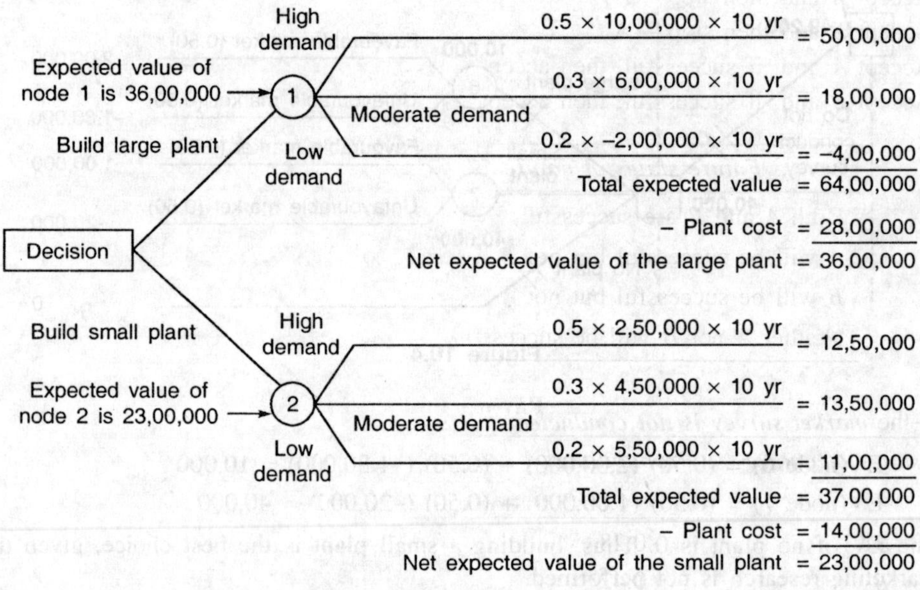

Figure 10.5

For each of the combinations of plant size and the market size, we have indicated

1. the probability that outcome will happen;
2. the conditional profit the company would receive if that outcome happened; and
3. the expected value of that outcome.

We work backward through the tree from right to left computing the expected value of each state-of-nature node. We then choose that particular branch leaving a decision node which leads to the state-of-nature node with the highest expected value.

From our decision tree-building, a large plant will produce 13,00,000 more profit over the next 10 years than the small plant. So building a large plant is the optimal decision.

EXAMPLE 10.6: A businessman has two independent investments A and B available to him, but he locks the capital to undertake both of them simultaneously. He can choose to take A first and then stop, or if A is successful then take B, or vice versa. The probability of success on A is 0.7, while for B it is 0.4. Both investments require an initial capital outlay of Rs. 2,000 and both return nothing if the venture is unsuccessful. Successful completion of A will return Rs. 3,000 (over cost), successful completion of B will return Rs. 5,000 (over cost).

1. Solve by preparing a pay-off table
2. Solve by preparing a decision tree.

Solution:

1. *Decision alternatives*

   Do nothing—A_1
   Accept A and then stop—A_2
   Accept B and then stop—A_3
   Accept A and, if successful, then accept B—A_4
   Accept B and, if successful, then accept A—A_5

Future states of nature		*Probabilities*
Both A and B are successful	B_1	$0.7 \times 0.4 = 0.28$
A will be successful but not B	B_2	$0.7 \times 0.6 = 0.42$
B will be successful but not A	B_3	$0.3 \times 0.4 = 0.12$
Neither A nor B will be successful	B_4	$0.3 \times 0.6 = 0.18$

Pay-off table

Future states of nature	*Probabilities*	*Decision alternatives*				
		A_1	A_2	A_3	A_4	A_5
$B1$	0.28	0	3,000	5,000	8,000	8,000
B_2	0.42	0	3,000	–2,000	1,000	–2,000
B_3	0.12	0	–2,000	5,000	–2,000	3,000
B_4	0.18	0	–2,000	–2,000	–2,000	–2,000
Expected pay-off		0	1,500	800	**2,060**	1,400

Since the expected pay-off is maximum for decision A_4 (i.e. accept A and, if successful, than accept B), it is the optimal decision.

2. The decision tree corresponding to the given information is shown in Figure 10.6.

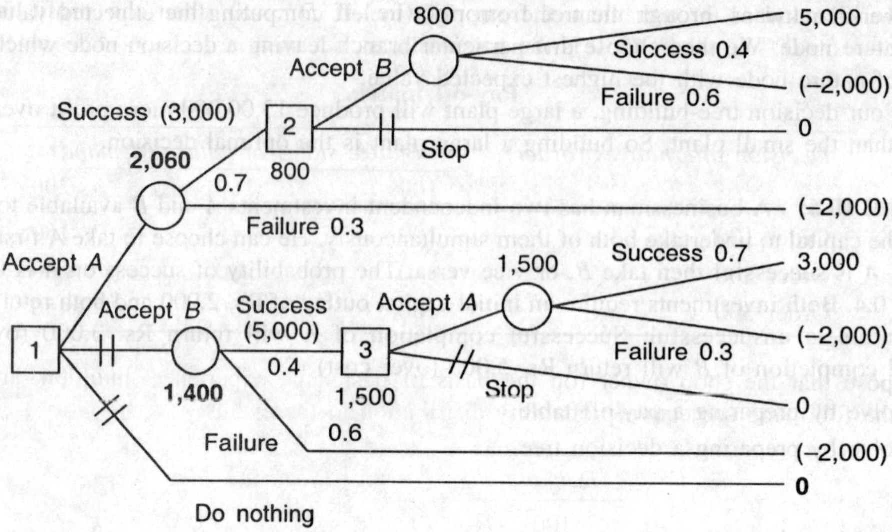

Figure 10.6

EXAMPLE 10.7: The owner of a shop must decide how many shirts to order for the summer season. For a particular type of shirt, he must order in batches of 100. If he orders 100 shirts, his cost is Rs. 10 per shirt; if he orders 200, the cost is Rs. 9 per shirt; and if he orders 300 or more shirts, his cost is Rs. 8.50 per shirt. The selling price is Rs. 12, but if any shirts are left unsold at the end of the summer, they will be sold for half the price. For simplicity, the owner believes that the demand for this shirt will be 100, 150 or 200. Of course, he cannot sell more shirts than he stocks. If, however, he understocks, there is a goodwill loss of Rs. 0.50 for each shirt a person wants to buy but cannot because it is out of stock. Furthermore, the owner must place the order now for the forthcoming summer season; he cannot wait to see how the demand is running for this shirt before he orders, nor can he place several orders.

In this problem:

1. The decision maker is the shop owner.
2. The alternative courses of actions are: order 100, order 200, and order 300.
3. The possible events are: demand is 100, demand is 150 and demand is 200.
4. There is one consequence associated with each of the nine action-event pairs (totalling nine possible consequences). For example, if the shop owner orders 100 shirts and the demand turns out to be 100, the consequence associated with this action-event pair is that the owner will make a profit of 200. The consequences for the other eight action-event pairs would be determined similarly.

Solution: The consequences for the problem are determined from the following consequence function. If the supply is greater than the demand (i.e. if $S > D$), then profit is equal to $D(R - C) - (C - 6)(S - D)$, where R is the per-unit revenue (selling price), C is the relevant unit cost, and the parameter 6 is the half price, end-of-summer selling price for unsold goods.

If the demand is greater than the supply (i.e. if $D > S$), then the profit is equal to $S(R - C) - 0.50(D - S)$, where 0.50 is the goodwill loss per shirt.

Pay-off matrix

Decision alternatives (order)	*Future states of nature (demand)*		
	100	**150**	**200**
Order 100	200	175	150
Order 200	0	300	600
Order 300	−150	150	450

Suppose that the shop owner (on the basis of past data, experience, intuition, and instinct) assigns the following subjective probability distribution to the events:

Demand	*Probability*
100	0.5
150	0.3
200	0.2
Total	1.0

Note that if the demand is 100, it cannot be 150 or 200 (i.e. events are mutually exclusive), and the probabilities sum to 1, as they should (i.e. events are collectively exhaustive).

The owner's expected profit for each act is shown below. Using the maximum expected value criterion, the owner should choose: order 200 shirts, with an expected profit of Rs. 210.

Calculating expected profits

Demand	*Probabilities*	*Decision alternatives*			
		Order 100		*Order 200*	
		Profit	*Exp. profit*	*Profit*	*Exp. profit*
100	0.5	200	100	0	0
150	0.3	175	52.5	300	90
200	0.2	150	30	600	120
Total	1		182.5		**210**

If the owner ordered 100 units and the demand was 150 units, then his regret would be Rs. 125, since he could have got 125 more by ordering 200 units had he known beforehand that the demand would actually be for 150 units. If, however, he had ordered 200 units and the demand was 150 units, his regret would be zero, since he could not have chosen a better action if he had known in advance that the demand would be 150 units.

Regret (opportunity loss matrix)

Decision alternatives (order)	*Future states of nature (demand)*		
	100	150	200
Order 100	0	125	450
Order 200	200	0	0

Now we calculate the expected loss.

Calculating expected opportunity losses

Demand	*Probabilities*	*Decision alternatives*			
		Order 100		*Order* 200	
		Opp. loss	*Exp. loss*	*Opp. loss*	*Exp. loss*
100	0.5	0	0	200	100
150	0.3	125	37.5	0	0
200	0.2	450	90	0	0
Total	1		127.5		**100**

Using the minimum expected value criterion, the owner should choose: order 200 shirts, with an expected opportunity loss of Rs. 100.

Suppose that in our problem, perfect information about the demand for the shirt in question is worth Rs. 100, and the survey, under consideration to find out what the demand will be, costs Rs. 200. In this case we would not have conducted the survey, since it would be irrational to pay Rs. 200 for information worth Rs. 100. To make such judgments, we need to determine the expected value of perfect information (EVPI). There are three ways EVPI can be calculated.

Method 1: We first calculate the expected value under certainty (i.e. having perfect information, EPPI) and subtract from this the expected value under uncertainty (the best action chosen using EV under the current information state).

First, we have said that under uncertainty we would take action: order 200 in our example, and obtain an EV of (0.5)(0) + (0.3)(300) + (0.2)(600) = Rs. 210. This is the expected value under uncertainty.

To obtain the expected value under certainty, we ask what our expected value is if we can choose our action after learning the true event (demand), that is, after obtaining perfect information.

Clearly, the availability of perfect information allows us to obtain a profit of Rs. 200 if the demand of 150 occurs, since we would choose to order 100 than to order 200. If the demand of 150 shirts occurs, then it allows us to obtain a profit of Rs. 300, since action: order 200 would be preferred to order 100. And, similarly, if we knew the demand will be 200, we would earn a profit of Rs. 600, since we would also choose the action: order 200 over order 100.

To understand and compute the expected value under certainty, it is necessary to adopt a long-run relative frequency point of view. That is, we must weigh each of these profits by the prior probabilities of each of these events occurring. In other words, from a relative frequency viewpoint, these probabilities are now interpreted as the proportion of times a perfect predictor would forecast that each of the given events would occur if the current situation were faced repeatedly. Each time the predictor makes a forecast, the decision maker chooses the optimal pay-off action. The calculation of the expected profit under certainty (i.e. with perfect information) is shown in the following table and is equal to Rs. 310.

Calculating expected profit under certainty

Decision alternatives (order)	*Future states of nature (demand)*		
	100 Prob = 0.5	150 Prob = 0.3	200 Prob = 0.2
Order 100	**200** (optimal for demand 100)	175	150
Order 200	0	**300** (optimal for demand 150)	**600** (optimal for demand 200)
Expected profit under certainty	= (200) (0.5) + (300) (0.3) + (600) (0.2) = **310**		

The EVPI is thus 310 – 210 = 100. This is the expected (average) profit that could be gained if the shop owner has perfect information about the future demand.

Method 2: Another way of computing the EVPI is by a sort of incremental analysis.

The shop owner's best act under uncertainty is to choose: order 200. Suppose that he knew that a demand of 100 would occur. Then, he would wish to choose, order 100 over order 200, his choice under uncertainty. The gain in profit by choosing order 100 over order 200 when the demand for 100 shirts occur is Rs. 200, but the demand of 100 would occur only 50 per cent of the time. Hence, on the average he would gain Rs. 100 if he chooses order 100 over order 200 when the demand of 100 was known to occur. However, if the demand of 150 or 200 occurred, the shop owner would still be content with ordering 200, the decision he made under uncertainty. Hence, his action would change only if the demand of 100 shirts was known to occur. His overall expected gain, then, under perfect information is Rs. 100, which is the EVPI.

Method 3: As discussed earlier, EVPI can also be determined by calculating the minimum EOL (Expected Opportunity Loss); that is, the minimum EOL is equal to the EVPI.

The EOL of choosing the optimal act under conditions of uncertainty in the shop owner's problem was shown earlier to be Rs. 100. That is, this amount represents the minimum value among the expected opportunity losses associated with each action. This value is equal to the EVPI. Note that all three methods yield an EVPI of Rs. 100.

It is interesting to note that the expected value plus the EOL is constant for all acts and is equal to Rs. 310 in our example, the expected value under certainty. Observe from the following table that the action of ordering 200 shirts has a maximum expected value and a minimum EOL.

Relationships among expected profit, expected opportunity loss, and expected profit under certainty

	Decision to order 100	*Decision to order 200*
Expected profit	182.5	210
Expected opportunity loss	127.5	100 (EVPI)
Total (Expected profit under certainty)	310	310

The decision tree for the problem is presented in Figure 10.7. Branch a_1 or branch a_2 are the choices: either to order 100 or 200 (ordering 300 was dominated and therefore eliminated from consideration). Chance forks determine whether the event that will occur is θ_1, θ_2, θ_3, i.e the demand is 100, 150 or 300.

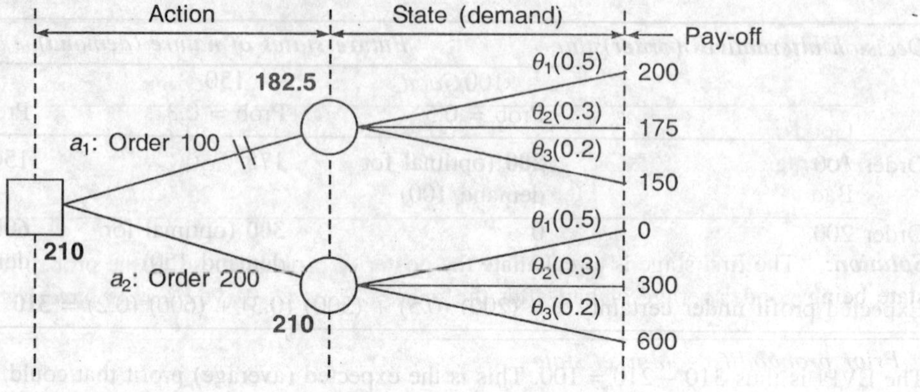

Figure 10.7

Since following path a_2 yields a higher expected pay-off than path a_1, we block off (prune) a_1 (using a double slash) as a non-optimal course of action. Hence a_2 is the optimal course of action, and it has the indicated expected pay-off of Rs. 210.

In practice, of course, the information is not perfect, yet may still be valuable. Organizations pay large sums for information which is reasonably accurate and which will enable them to improve their decision making. Market research opinion surveys, test marketing, and so on produce imperfect information, i.e. it is not perfectly accurate, yet it is still accurate enough to be relied upon. Under certain conditions it is possible to estimate the value of imperfect information.

10.10 VALUING IMPERFECT INFORMATION (USE OF BAYES' THEOREM)

Provided that there is some indication of how accurate the information is likely to be, it is possible to calculate the worth of imperfect information. For example, if a firm had used a market research agency on numerous occasions, it would be able to make an assessment of the accuracy of their information.

The method used to value imperfect information uses posterior probabilities based on Bayes' theorem and is demonstrated by the following example. (It is advised to the reader to clarify the concept of Bayes' theorem before moving ahead.)

EXAMPLE 10.8: ABC Limited is considering the launch of a new product, *XYZ*. Various prior estimates of outcome have been made as follows and the expected values calculated.

Market state	*Probability*	*Profit/(Loss)*	*Expected value*
Good	0.2	60,000	12,000
Bad	0.6	40,000	24,000
Average	0.2	–40,000	–8,000
			EV = Rs. 28,000

In order to have more information on which to base their decision, the management is considering whether to commission a market research survey at a cost of Rs. 1000. The agency concerned produces reasonably accurate, but not perfect, information and ABC's Trade Association provided the following information about the agency's performance.

Likely actual market state	*Market research agency survey findings*		
	Good	*Average*	*Bad*
Good	60%	30%	–
Average	40%	50%	10%
Bad	–	20%	90%

Solution: The first stage is to calculate the posterior probabilities, i.e. the probability of the market state being good, average or bad after the market research survey results have become available.

Prior probability	*Market state*	*Market research results*		*Posterior probability*
		State	*Probability*	
0.2	Good	Good	0.6	$GG = 0.12$*
		Average	0.4	$GA = 0.08$
0.6	Average	Good	0.3	$AG = 0.18$
		Average	0.5	$AA = 0.30$
		Bad	0.2	$AB = 0.12$
0.2	Bad	Average	0.1	$BA = 0.02$
		Bad	0.9	$BB = 0.18$
				1.00

* $GG = 0.12$ means that the probability of the market being good and the survey predicting a good state is $0.2 \times 0.6 = 0.12$

From the table, survey probabilities can be summarized thus:

p (survey will show 'good') $= GG + AG = 0.12 + 0.18 = 0.3$

p (survey will show 'average') $= GA + AA + BA = 0.08 + 0.30 + 0.02 = 0.4$

p (survey will show 'bad') $= AB + BB = 0.12 + 0.18 = 0.3$

Assuming that the product will be launched if the survey predicts a good or average market and not launched if the bad state is predicted, the following table can be prepared:

Survey results	*Decision*	*Actual market*	*Posterior probabilities*	*Profit (Loss)*	*EV of profits (Losses)*
Good	Launch	Good	0.12	60,000	7,200
		Average	0.18	40,000	7,200
Average	Launch	Good	0.08	60,000	4,800
		Average	0.30	40,000	12,000
		Bad	0.02	–40,000	–800
Bad	Do not launch		0.30	–	–
			1.00		30,400

∴ Value of imperfect information is 30,400 – 28,000 = 2,400
As the survey costs Rs. 1,000, it would appear to be worthwhile.

EXAMPLE 10.9: A company is considering whether to launch a new product or not. The success of the idea depends on the ability of a competitor to bring out a competing product (estimated at 60%) and the relationship of the competitor's price to the firm's price.

Table A shows the profits for each price range that could be set by the company related to the possible competing prices.

Table A

	Profits in '000s			
If the company's price is	*If the competitor's price is*			*Profit if no competitor*
	Low	*Medium*	*High*	
Low	30	42	45	50
Medium	34	45	49	70
High	10	30	53	90

The company must set its price first because its product will be on the market earlier so that the competitor will be able to react to the price. Estimates of the probability of a competitor's price are shown in Table B.

Table B

If the company's prices are	*Competitor's price expected to be*		
	Low	*Medium*	*High*
Low	0.8	0.15	0.05
Medium	0.2	0.70	0.10
High	0.05	0.35	0.60

(a) Draw a decision tree and analyze the problem.

(b) Recommend what the company should do.

Solution:

The first stage is to draw the tree, starting from the left, showing the various decision points and outcome nodes (*forward pass*).

In Figure 10.8, LP, MP and HP denote the company's prices and LPC, MPC and HPC denote the competitor's prices.

It will be seen that the tree is a mixture of decision points, D_1, D_2 and D_3 and outcome nodes, which reflect whether or not there will be competition and the prices the competition will set.

The next step is to fill in the outcome values and probabilities from Tables A and B in the problem.

The final stage uses the probabilities and outcome values and calculates the expected values at various points so that the correct decisions are highlighted (*backward pass*).

Figure 10.8 shows the expected values in the outcome modes (i.e. probability × values) and at D_2 and D_3 the highest expected values from the subsequent part of the tree indicating the best decisions.

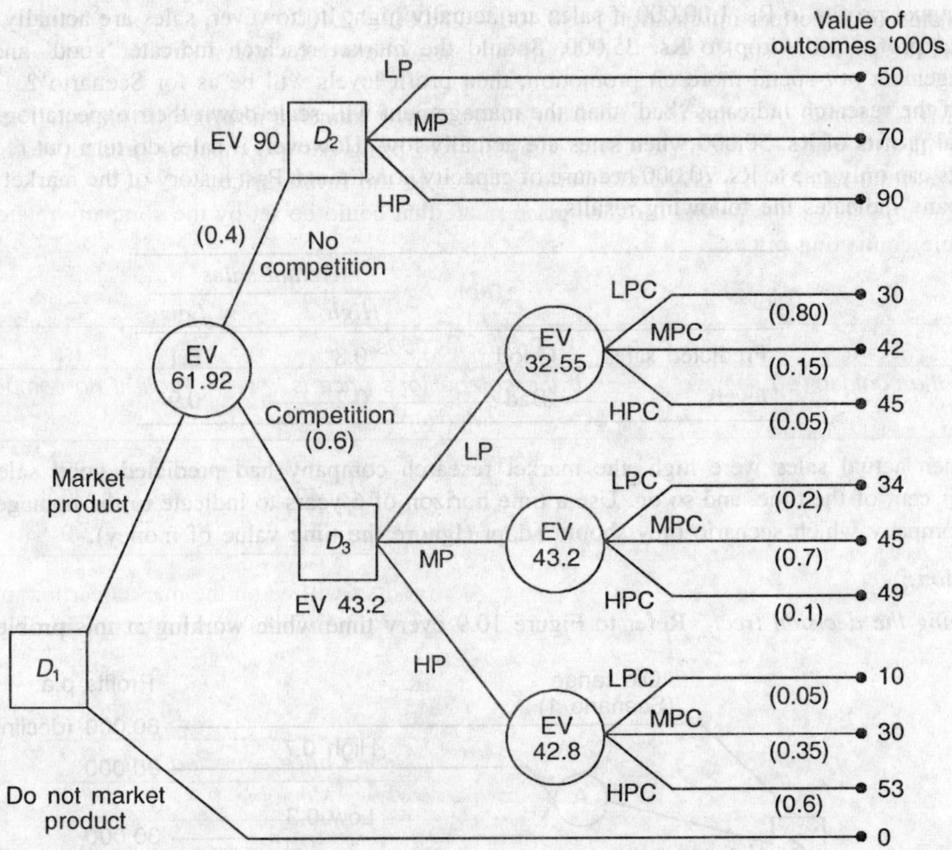

Figure 10.8

Interpretation and recommendation: Figure 10.8 shows that at D_1 the company should decide to market the product (EV 61.92). If there is no competition, D_2 decision should be to set a high price (EV 90). If there is competition, at D_3, the company should set a medium price as this gives the best EV, i.e. 43.2.

EXAMPLE 10.10: A company with an ageing product range is investigating the launch of a new range. Their business analysts have mapped out several possible scenarios which are given below.

Scenario 1: Continue with old range producing profits declining at 10 per cent per annum on a compounding basis. Last year's profits were Rs. 60,000 from this range.

Scenario 2: Introduce a new range *without* any prior market research. If the sales are *high*, the annual profit is put at Rs. 90,000, with a probability which from past data is put at 0.7. If the sales are *low*, the annual profit is put at Rs. 30,000, with a probability of 0.3.

Scenario 3: Introduce a new range with prior market research costing Rs. 30,000. The market research will indicate whether future sales are likely to be 'good' or 'bad'. If the research indicates 'good', then the management will spend Rs. 35,000 more on capital equipment and this will increase the annual profits to Rs. 1,00,000 if sales are actually high. If, however, sales are actually low, the annual profits will drop to Rs. 25,000. Should the market research indicate 'good' and should management *not* spend more on promotion, then profit levels will be as for Scenario 2.

If the research indicates 'bad' then the management will scale down their expectations to give annual profits of Rs. 50,000 when sales are actually low. However, if sales do turn out to be high, profits can only rise to Rs. 70,000 because of capacity constraints. Past history of the market research company indicates the following results.

		Actual sales	
		High	*Low*
Predicted sales	Good	*0.8	0.1
levels	Bad	0.2	0.9

* When actual sales were high, the market research company had predicted good sales levels 80 per cent of the time, and so on. Use a time horizon of 6 years to indicate to the management of the company which scenario they should adopt (Ignore the time value of money).

Solution:

Drawing the decision tree: Refer to Figure 10.9 every time while working at this problem.

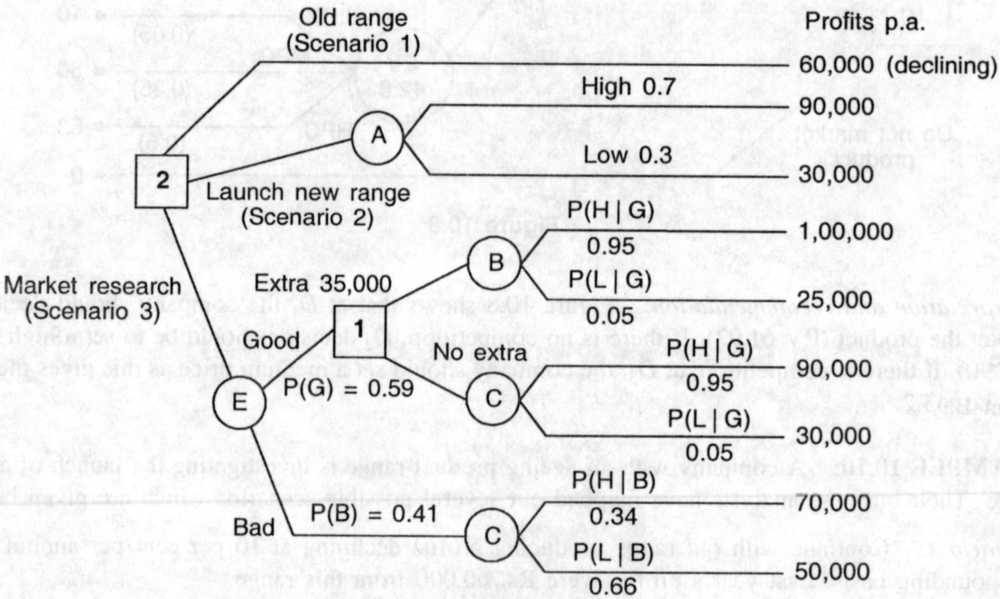

Figure 10.9

Calculating the probabilities: The decision tree reveals that the following probabilities must be calculated.

$$\left.\begin{array}{l} P(G) \\ P(B) \end{array}\right\} \text{ for market research}$$

$$\left.\begin{array}{l} P(H/G) \\ P(L/G) \\ P(H/B) \\ P(L/B) \end{array}\right\} \text{for sales outcomes}$$

From the data supplied, the following probabilities are available.

$$\left.\begin{array}{l} P(G/H)\ 0.8 \\ P(B/H)\ 0.2 \\ P(G/L)\ 0.1 \\ P(B/L)\ 0.9 \end{array}\right\} \text{These are prior probabilities}$$

The calculations are shown below:

Good	G&H = P(H) × P(G/H) 0.7 × 0.8 = 0.56	G&L = P(L) × (PG/L) 0.3 × 0.1 = 0.03
Bad	B&H = P(H) × P(B/H) 0.7 × 0.2 = 0.14	B&L = P(L) × P(B/L) 0.3 × 0.9 = 0.27
	High 0.7	Low 0.3

$$\begin{aligned} P(G) &= P(H) \times P(G/H) + P(L) \times P(G/L) \\ &= P(G\&H) + P(G\&L) \\ &= 0.56 + 0.03 \\ &= 0.59 \end{aligned}$$

$$\begin{aligned} P(B) &= P(H) \times P(B/H) + P(L) \times P(B/L) \\ &= P(B\&H) + P(B\&L) \\ &= 0.14 + 0.27 \\ &= 0.41 \end{aligned}$$

Note $\quad P(G) + P(B) = 0.59 + 0.41 = 1.00$

From Bayes' Rule,

$$P\left(\frac{H}{G}\right) = \frac{P(G/H) \times P(H)}{P(G)}$$

$$= \frac{0.56}{0.59} = 0.95$$

$$P\left(\frac{L}{G}\right) = \frac{P(G/L) \times P(L)}{P(G)}$$

$$= \frac{0.03}{0.59} = 0.05$$

$$P\left(\frac{H}{B}\right) = \frac{P(B/H) \times P(H)}{P(B)}$$

$$= \frac{0.14}{0.41} = 0.34$$

$$P\left(\frac{L}{B}\right) = \frac{P(B/L) \times P(L)}{P(B)}$$

$$= \frac{0.27}{0.41} = 0.66$$

These may be entered on the decision tree (see Figure 10.9).

Evaluating the financial outcome: It is now possible to evaluate the financial outcomes of the three scenarios using the information given in the question and the probabilities calculated above.

Scenario 1:

	Year	
Last year Rs. 60,000 profits	1	$60{,}000 \times 0.9 =$ 54,000
	2	$60{,}000 \times 0.9^2 =$ 48,600
	3	$60{,}000 \times 0.9^3 =$ 43,740
	4	$60{,}000 \times 0.9^4 =$ 39,366
	5	$60{,}000 \times 0.9^5 =$ 35,429.5
	6	$60{,}000 \times 0.9^6 =$ 31,886.5
		2,53,022.00

Scenario 2: Expected value of direct launch

Node (A): 0.7(90,000 × 6) + 0.3(30,000 × 6) = 3,78,000 + 54,000 = 4,32,000

Scenario 3: Expected value of market research

Node (B): 0.95(1,00,000 × 6) + 0.05(25,000 × 6) = 5,70,000 + 7,500 = 5,77,500

Deducted 35,000 for extensions = 5,42,500

Node (C): 0.95(90,000 × 6) + 0.05(30,000 × 6) = 5,13,000 + 9,000 = 5,22,000

Node [1]: Compare 5,42,500 and 5,22,000

∴ It is worth spending more.

Carrying 5,42,500 back to (E).

Node (D): 0.34(70,000 × 6) + 0.66 (50,000 × 6) 1,42,800 + 1,98,000 = 3,40,800

Node [2]: 3,40,800 or 0 from no launch.

Node (E): 0.59 × 5,42,500 + 0.41 × 3,40,800

3,20,075 + 1,39,728 = 4,59,803

Deducted market research expenditure

4,59,803 − 30,000 = 4,29,803

Node [2]: Final decision summary

Scenario 1 EV = 2,53,022

Scenario 2 EV = 4,32,000

Scenario 3 EV = 4,29,803

Therefore, choose Scenario 2 as this gives the greatest expected monetary value. However, Scenario 3 is close. Had the cash flows been discounted, the situation might have been different.

REVIEW EXERCISES

1. A major asset of a Motor Company is a franchise to sell automobiles of a major manufacturer. The general manager of the company is planning the staffing of the dealerships garage facilities. From the information provided by the manufacturer and from other nearby dealerships, he has estimated the number of annual mechanic hours that the garage will likely need.

Hours	10,000	12,000	14,000	16,000
Probability	0.2	0.3	0.4	0.1

The manager plans to pay each mechanic Rs. 9 per hour and to charge customers Rs. 16. Mechanics will work a 40-hour week and get an annual 2-week vacation.

(a) Determine how many mechanics the company should hire.

(b) How much should the company pay to get perfect information about the number of mechanics it needs?

[**Ans:** (a) 6 mechanics, (b) EVPI = 11,712 (assuming that the mechanics get paid vacations]

2. Suppose it is an overcast Sunday morning and you have 100 people coming for a party in the afternoon. You have a nice garden and your house is not too large; so weather permitting, you would like to set up the refreshments in the garden and have the party there (it would be pleasant, and your guests would be more comfortable). On the other hand, if you set up the party for the garden, and after all the guests arrive it begins to rain, the refreshments will be ruined, your guests will get wet, and you will surely wish you had decided to have the party in the house. Define the acts (decision alternatives), and events (future states of nature) and the consequences and represent the problem in a pay-off table.

3. A firm is considering the purchase of a complex piece of equipment from either of the two suppliers S_1 and S_2. The supplier S_1 is capable of supplying the equipment on time to meet a certain desired deadline. The price chargeable by S_1 is, however, considerably higher than that of S_2. It is felt by the management of the firm that S_2 may deliver the equipment, or may not be able to deliver on time. It is even suspected that the supplier S_2 may never be able to deliver the equipment to the specifications. However, the management believes that if it waits for some months, it may get better information on S_2's capabilities of supplying the equipment.

The management is considering three alternative courses of action.

A_1: Order from S_1. If later it is clear that S_2 can supply, the order from S_1 can be cancelled. Of course, a delay would be caused when the order is given to S_2.

A_2: Order from S_2. If it is known later on that S_2 cannot supply the equipment, the order may be switched to S_1.

A_3: Wait till the time information on S_2's capabilities are known. This would obviously cause delay.

The outcomes (profits) in the various possible situations are:

Event	*Course of action*		
	A_1	A_2	A_3
E_1	250	100	200
E_2	250	125	300
E_3	250	625	450

where

$E_1 = S_2$ fails to deliver, $E_2 = S_2$ delivers late, $E_3 = S_2$ delivers on time.

What would be the management's decision according to following criteria:

(a) Laplace, (b) Maximin, (c) Savage

[**Ans:** (a) A_3 (b) A_1 (c) A_2 or A_3]

4. A newsboy buys newspapers every day in bulk. The surplus at the end of the day has to be disposed of at a negligible price. Also, in case of his purchases falling short of the day's demand would result into regret in the sense discussed above. A newspaper costs him 70 paise. The distribution of the demand for papers for the last 50 days is as follows:

No. of papers demanded	:	24	25	26	27	28	29	30
No. of days	:	4	11	10	7	7	6	5

Assuming that the 50 days statistics adequately describe the probabilities, find the optimum number of papers the newsboy should buy each day. It is given that the paper sells for one rupee.

[**Ans:** Buy 25 or 26 copies. Expected profit = Rs. 7.42 per day]

5. For the past 200 days, the sales of bread from the bakery have been as follows:

Daily sales (loaves)	:	0	100	200	300	400
No. of days	:	10	60	60	50	20

(a) Determine the expected sales of bread.

(b) The bakery's production costs are Rs. 2 per loaf, sale price is Rs. 4 per loaf, and any bread unsold at the end of the day is contracted to a local vendor who pays Re. 1 per loaf. Draw up a pay-off table for each sales/production combination.

(c) Compute the expected profit arising from each level of production and determine the optimal policy.

6. The manager of the Gift Shop has to decide how many gift packs to buy for the forthcoming festive season. The gift packs have to be bought from a manufacturer in packs of 50. The profit per pack is Rs. 20. On the basis of trading conditions last festive season, the current economic conditions and competitive market factors, the manager's estimate of the sales of this gift pack this season is as follows:

Sales (packs)	:	5	10	15	20	25
Probability	:	0.20	0.20	0.30	0.20	0.10

Any unsatisfied demand does not affect the probability of future sales. Any unsold packs will be sold after the festive season at a loss of Rs. 10 per pack.

(a) Assuming that the quantity of stock is bought in units of 5 packs and ignoring storage costs, how many packs should the manager buy to maximize his expected profit?

(b) If the manager was completely uncertain about the likelihood of sales between 5 and 25 packs (inclusive), how many packs should he stock?

[**Ans:** (a) 15 packs, expected profit = Rs. 10,500, (b) 20 packs]

7. As a fund-raiser for a student organization, some students have decided to sell some products outside the union office. Each product will sell for Rs. 1.75 and cost the organization 77 paise. Historical sales indicated that between 55 and 60 dozen, products will be sold with the probability distribution given below:

Dozens of product	:	55	56	57	58	59	60
Probability	:	0.15	0.20	0.10	0.35	0.15	0.05

To maximize the profit contribution, how many products should be ordered? Assume that the products must be ordered by the dozen. What is the expected value of perfect information in this problem? What is the maximum amount the organization would be willing to pay for perfect information?

[**Ans:** 58 dozen, EVPI = Rs. 24.948]

8. The research department of a company has recommended to the marketing department to launch a product of three different types. The marketing manager has to decide one of the types of the product to be launched under the following estimated pay-offs for various level of sales:

Type of product	*Estimated level of sales (units)*		
	15,000	10,000	5,000
A	30	10	10
B	40	15	5
C	55	20	3

What will be the marketing manager's decision if (a) Maximin, (b) Maximax, (c) Laplace, and (d) regret criteria is applied?

[**Ans:** (a) *A*, (b) *C*, (c) *C*, (d) *C*]

9. The vice-president (VP) of a business consulting firm must decide how many MBAs to hire as full-time consultants for the next year. He knows from experience that the probability distribution on the number of consulting jobs his firm will get each year is as follows:

Consulting jobs	:	24	27	30	33
Probability	:	0.3	0.2	0.4	0.1

He also knows that each MBA hired will be able to handle exactly three consulting jobs per year. The salary of each MBA is Rs. 60,000. Each consulting job is worth Rs. 30,000 to the firm. Each consulting job that the firm is awarded but cannot complete costs the firm Rs. 10,000 in future business lost.

(a) How many MBAs should he hire?

(b) What is the expected value of perfect information to the VP?

10. The management is faced with the problem of choosing one of the products for manufacturing. The probability matrix after the market research for the two products is as follows:

Action	*State of nature*		
	Good	*Fair*	*Poor*
Product *A*	75%	15%	10%
Product *B*	60%	30%	10%

The profits that the management can make for different levels of market acceptability of the products are as follows:

Action	*Profit (in Rs.) if the market share is*		
	Good	*Fair*	*Poor*
Product *A*	35,000	15,000	5,000
Product *B*	50,000	20,000	–3,000

Calculate the expected value of the choice of the alternatives and advise the management.

11. A processor of frozen vegetables has to decide what crop to plant in a particular area. Suppose there are only two strategies: to plant cabbage and to plant cauliflower. Also, suppose that the states of nature can be summarized in three possibilities: perfect weather, variable weather, and bad weather. On the basis of weather records, it is determined that the probability of perfect weather is 0.25, of variable weather is 0.50, and that of bad weather is 0.25. The yields (in Rs.) of the two crops under these different conditions are known, and the utility of the company can be assessed to be measured by rupee amounts as shown in the following pay-off table.

Decision alternative	*Future state of nature (weather)*		
(plant)	*Perfect*	*Variable*	*Bad*
Cabbage	40,000	30,000	20,000
Cauliflower	70,000	20,000	0

What action should the processor select?

12. Consider the following pay-off matrix (in Rs.)

Decision alternative	*Future state of nature*		
	X	*Y*	*Z*
A	10	6	3
B	5	8	4
C	2	5	9

The prior probability distribution assessed by the decision maker is:

Future state of nature	X	Y	Z
Probability	0.25	0.50	0.25

(a) Specify the opportunity loss matrix.

(b) Compute EVPI in three different ways.

(c) If nearly perfect information about which event is going to occur could be bought for Rs. 2, would you buy it?

13. A farmer can plant either corn or soyabeans. The probabilities that the next harvest prices of these commodities will go up, stay the same, or go down are 0.25, 0.30 and 0.45, respectively. If the prices go up, the corn crop will give Rs. 30,000 and the soyabeans will give Rs. 10,000. If the prices remain unchanged, the farmer will barely break even. But if the prices go down, the corn and soyabeans crops will sustain losses of Rs. 35,000 and Rs. 5,000 respectively.

(a) Represent the farmer's problem as a decision tree.

(b) Which crop should he plant?

14. You have the chance to invest in three mutual funds: utility, aggressive growth, and global. The value of your investment will change depending on the market conditions. There is a 10 per cent chance that the market will go down, 50 per cent chance that it will remain moderate, and 40 per cent chance that it will go up. The following table provides the percentage change in the investment value under the three conditions:

Decision alternative	*% return on investment when the market is*		
	Down (%)	*Moderate (%)*	*Up (%)*
Utility	5	7	8
Aggressive growth	−10	5	30
Global	2	7	20

(a) Represent the problem as a decision tree.

(b) Which mutual fund should you select?

[**Ans:** EV(Utility) = 7.2%, EV(Aggressive growth) = 13.5%, EV(Global) = 11.7%]

15. You have been invited to play the Wheel of Fortune game. The wheel operates electronically with two buttons that produce hard (H) or soft (S) spin of the wheel. The wheel itself is divided into white (W) and red (R) half-circle regions. You have been told that the wheel is designed to stop with a probability of 0.3 in the white region and 0.7 in the red region. The pay-off you get for the game is

	W	R
H	800	200
S	−2,500	1,000

Draw the associated decision tree, and specify a course of action

[**Ans:** EV(H) = 380, EV(S) = −50]

16. A physician purchases a particular vaccine on Monday each week. The vaccine must be used within the week following, otherwise it becomes worthless. The vaccine costs Rs. 2 per dose and the physician charges Rs. 5 per dose. In the past 50 weeks, the physician has administered the vaccine in the following quantities:

Doses per week :	20	25	40	60
No. of weeks :	5	15	25	5

(a) Draw up a pay-off matrix.
(b) Obtain a regret matrix.
(c) Determine the optimum number of doses the physician should buy.
(d) The maximum amount the physician would be willing to pay per week for a perfect information about the number of doses expected to be demanded in a week.

17. A pharmaceutical company produces a compound which must be sold within a month it is produced, if the normal price of Rs. 100 per bottle is to be obtained. Anything unsold in that month is sold in a different market for Rs. 20 per bottle.
During the last three years, the monthly demand was recorded which showed the following frequencies:

Monthly demand (No. of bottles) :	2,000	3,000	6,000
Frequency (No. of months) :	8	16	12

(a) Prepare an appropriate pay-off table.
(b) Advise the production management on the number of bottles that should be produced next month.

18. Suppose you want to invest Rs. 10,000 in the stock market by buying shares in one of two companies: *A* and *B*. Shares in company *A* are risky but could yield a 50 per cent return on investment during the next year. If the stock market conditions are not favourable (Bear market), the stock may lose 20 per cent of its value. Company *B* provides safe investment with 15 per cent return in a favourable (Bull market) market and only 5 per cent in an unfavourable market. All the publications you have consulted are predicting a 60 per cent chance for a Bull market and 40 per cent for a Bear market. Where should you invest your money?

[**Ans:** EV(A) = 2,200, EV(B) = 1,100]

19. A man has the choice of running either a hot snack stall or an ice cream stall at a sea-side resort during the summer season. If it is a fairly cool summer, he should make Rs. 5,000 by running the hot snack stall, but if the summer is quite hot he can only expect to make Rs. 1,000. On the other hand, if he operates the ice cream stall, his profit is estimated at Rs. 6,500 if the summer is hot, but only Rs. 1,000 if it is cool. There is 40 per cent chance of the summer being hot. Should he opt for running the hot snack stall or the ice cream stall?

20. Find the best alternative in the following decision table using the expected value criterion and the criterion of expected regret. The entries in the matrix indicate profits associated with the different combinations of decisions and states of nature.

Future states of nature	*Probability*	*Decision 1*	*Decision 2*	*Decision 3*
A	0.6	0	3	–3
B	0.1	2	2	2
C	0.2	5	–1	3
D	0.1	–4	–3	1

21. Mukesh is considering three possible ways to invest the Rs. 2,00,000 he has just inherited.

Option 1: Some of his friends are considering financing a hotel. This venture is highly risky and could result in either a major loss or a substantial gain within a year. Mukesh estimates that with probability 0.6, he will lose all of his money. However, with probability 0.4, he will make a Rs. 2,00,000 profit.

Option 2: He can invest in some apartments. Within 1 year, that project will produce a profit of at least Rs. 10,000, but it might yield Rs. 15,000, Rs. 20,000, Rs. 25,000, or possibly even Rs. 30,000. Mukesh estimates the probabilities of these five returns at 0.20, 0.30, 0.25, 0.20, and 0.05, respectively.

Option 3: He can invest in some government securities that have a current yield of 8.25 per cent.

(a) Construct a decision tree to help Mukesh decide how to invest his money.

(b) Which investment will maximize his expected 1-year profit?

(c) How much would Mukesh be willing to pay for perfect information about the success of the hotel venture?

(d) How much would Mukesh be willing to pay for perfect information about the success of the apartment venture?

[**Ans:** (b) investment in apartments, (c) EVPI = 90,800 – 18,000 = 72,800
(d) EVPI = 19,750 – 18,000 = 1,750]

22. You have the chance to invest your money in either a 7.5 per cent bond that sells at a face value or an aggressive growth stock that pays only 1 per cent dividend. If inflation is feared, the interest rate will go up to 8 per cent, in which case the principal value of the bond will go down by 10 per cent, and the stock value will go down by 20 per cent. If recession is anticipated, the interest rate will go down to 6 per cent. Under this condition, the principal value of the bond is expected to go up by 5 per cent, and the stock value will increase by 20 per cent. If the economy remains unchanged, the stock value will go up by 8 per cent and the bond principal value remains the same. Economists estimate a 20 per cent chance that inflation will rise and 15 per cent that recession will set in. Assume that you are basing your investment decision on next year's economic conditions.

(a) Represent the problem as a decision tree.

(b) Would you invest in stocks or bonds?

11 Inventory Problems

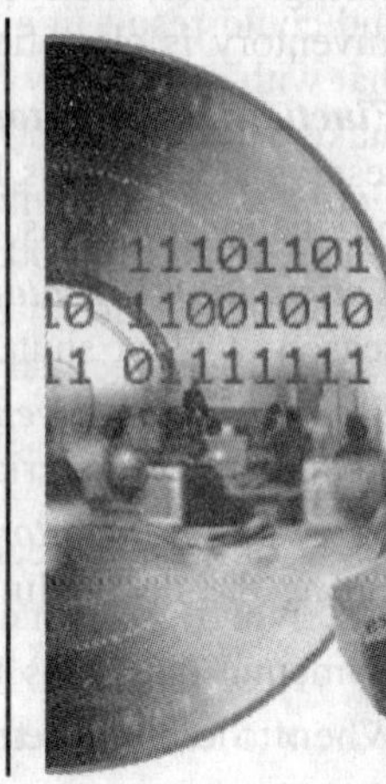

11.1 INTRODUCTION

The history of inventory problem has roots during World War II. ***Inventory*** may be defined as the physical stock of goods, units or economic resources that are stored or reserved for a smooth, efficient and effective functioning of business. Without inventory, customers would have to wait until their orders were filled from a source or were produced. In general, however, the customer will not like to wait for a long period of time. Another reason for maintaining inventory is the price fluctuation of some raw materials (maybe seasonal). It would be profitable for a buyer to procure a sufficient quantity of raw material at lower price and use it whenever needed. Levin et al. argued that maintaining inventories on display attracts more customers, resulting in increase in sale and profits. The study of controlling and management of such inventory is referred to as ***inventory management***.

11.2 TYPES OF INVENTORY

Inventory is divided into two categories—direct inventory and indirect inventory. Direct inventory is one that is used for manufacturing the product. It is further sub-divided into the following groups.

1. ***Raw material inventories*** are kept to enable changes in production, to provide production against delays in transportation, for seasonal fluctuations, etc.
2. ***Work-in-progress inventories*** provide to have economic-lot production even if sales vary to cater to the variety of products, etc.
3. ***Finished-goods inventory*** maintains delivery against order. It also allows stabilization of the production level. It aims at sales promotion.
4. ***Spare parts inventory*** for functioning of production units.

Indirect inventory does not play any role in finished goods product but it is required for manufacturing. Thus, indirect inventory acts as a catalyst which only speeds up/down the reaction. Indirect inventory is classified as follows:

1. ***Fluctuation inventory:*** This acts as an equilibrium between sales and production. The reserve stock that is kept to maintain fluctuations in the demand and lead-time affecting the production of items is called fluctuation inventory.
2. ***Anticipation inventory:*** This is programmed in advance for the seasonal large sales, slack season, a plant shut down period, etc.
3. ***Transportation inventory:*** The existence of transportation inventories is mainly due to the movement of materials from one place to another.
4. ***Decoupling inventory:*** These inventories are maintained for meeting out the demands during the decoupling period of manufacturing or purchasing.

Two fundamental questions that must be answered by a decision maker are

1. When to replenish the inventory and
2. How much to order for replenishment.

In this chapter, we will try to answer these questions under a variety of circumstances. Before we proceed to answer these questions, let us discuss about the costs involved in inventory decisions.

11.3 COSTS INVOLVED IN INVENTORY PROBLEMS

Costs play an important role in making a decision to maintain the inventory in the organization. These costs are as follows:

Purchase cost: The actual price paid for the procurement of items is called ***purchase cost***. It is denoted by C. It is independent of the size of the quantity ordered (or manufactured).

Inventory holding cost: The cost associated with holding the goods in stock is known as ***inventory holding cost***. It consists of interest charges over the capital investment, cost of labour, storage cost (may be in terms of rent of warehouse or depreciation, if own warehouse), taxes and insurance cost, etc. It is denoted by C_1 or h. Inventory holding cost is directly proportional to the size of the inventory as well as time for which the item is held in stock.

Shortage cost: This cost arises due to shortage of goods. It is denoted by C_2 or π per unit. If the unfilled demand for the goods can be satisfied on arrival of new stock, this cost varies directly both with the shortage quantity and the delay time. On the other hand, if the unfilled demand is lost, then the shortage cost is only proportional to short quantity.

Set-up cost: This is the fixed cost associated with placing of an order or setting up machinery before starting production. It includes costs of follow-up, receiving the goods, transportation cost, and loading-unloading cost. It is also known as *ordering cost* or *replenishment cost*. It is assumed to be independent of quantity order. It is denoted by C_3 or A.

Total inventory cost: If price discounts are available, then we should formulate total inventory cost by taking sum of purchase cost (PC), inventory holding cost (IHC), shortage cost (SC) and ordering cost (OC). Thus, the total inventory cost TC, is given by

$$TC = PC + IHC + SC + OC$$

When price discounts are not offered, then the total cost (TC) is given by

$$TC = IHC + SC + OC$$

Except costs, the other variables which play an important role in decision making are as follows:

Demand: The size of the demand is the number of units required in each period. It is not necessarily the amount sold because the demand may remain unfulfilled due to shortage or delays. The demand pattern of the items may be either deterministic or probabilistic. In the deterministic case, the demand over a period is known. This known demand may be fined or variable with time. Such demand is known as ***static*** and ***dynamic*** respectively. When the demand over a period is uncertain but can be predicted by a probability distribution, we say it a case of the probabilistic demand. A probabilistic demand may be stationary or non-stationary over time.

Lead-time: It is the time between placing an order and realization in stock. It can be deterministic or probabilistic. If both demand and lead-time are deterministic, one needs to order in advance by a time equal to lead-time. However, if lead-time is probabilistic, it is very difficult to answer when to order.

Cycle time: The cycle time is the time between placements of two orders. It is denoted by T. It can be determined in one of the two ways.

1. ***Continuous review:*** Here the number of units of an item on hand is known. In this case, an order of fixed size is placed every time the inventory level reaches a pre-specified level, called ***reorder level***. Many authors referred this as the ***two-bin systems*** or ***fixed order level system***.
2. ***Periodic review:*** Here the orders are placed at equal intervals of time and the size of the order depends on the inventory on hand and on order at the time of the review. This is also called the ***fixed order interval system***.

Planning horizon: The period over which a particular inventory level will be maintained is called ***planning horizon***. It may be finite or infinite. It is denoted by H.

11.4 NOTATIONS

We shall use the following notations for the discussion of models in the chapter.

C	:	Purchase or manufacturing cost of an item
A	:	The ordering cost per order
i	:	Inventory carrying charge fraction per unit per annum
H	:	Inventory holding cost of an item per unit per time unit
π	:	Shortage cost per unit short per time
R	:	Demand rate of an item
Q	:	Order quantity (a decision variable)
T	:	Cycle time (a decision variable)
ROL	:	Reorder level, i.e. the level of inventory at which an order is placed
L	:	Lead-time
N	:	Number of orders per time unit

T	:	Production time period
P	:	Production rate at which quantity is produced
PC	:	Total purchase cost
IHC	:	Total inventory holding cost per time unit
SC	:	Total shortage cost per time unit
OC	:	Ordering cost per order.
TC	:	Total inventory cost per time unit.
TVC	:	Total variable inventory cost per time unit

The parameters are defined with proper units.

11.5 ECONOMIC ORDER QUANTITY (EOQ) MODEL WITH CONSTANT RATE OF DEMAND

Economic order quantity is one of the oldest and most commonly known technique. This model was first developed by Ford Harris and R.Wilson independently in 1915. The objective is to determine economic order quantity, Q, which minimizes the total cost of an inventory system when the demand occurs at a constant rate. The model is developed under the following assumptions:

- The system deals with single item.
- The demand rate of R-units per time unit is known and constant.
- Shortages are not allowed. Lead-time is zero.
- Replenishment rate is infinite.
- Replenishment size, Q, is the decision variable.
- T is cycle time.
- The inventory holding cost, h per unit per time unit and ordering cost, A per order is known and constant during the period under review.

At each replenishment, Q-units are ordered and stocked in the system. Demand is occurring at the rate of R-units per time unit during cycle time T. So we have $Q = RT$. We analyze one cycle (Figure 11.1).

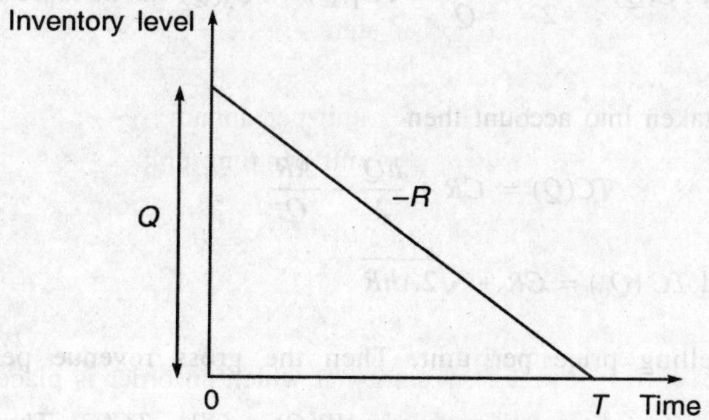

Figure 11.1

Let $Q(t)$ denote on-hand inventory at time t of a cycle. Then the differential equation that describes the instantaneous states of $Q(t)$, $0 \le t \le T$, is given by

$$\frac{dQ(t)}{dt} = -R, \; 0 \le t \le T \tag{11.1}$$

with initial condition $Q(0) = Q = RT$. Then the solution of Eq. (11.1) is given by

$$Q(T) = R\,(T - t), \quad 0 \le t \le T \tag{11.2}$$

Average inventory, $I_1(Q)$, in the system per time unit is

$$I_1(Q) = \frac{1}{T}\int_0^T Q(t)\,dt = RT = \frac{Q}{2} \tag{11.3}$$

Then the total cost, $TC(Q)$, of an inventory system per time unit is

$$TC(Q) = IHC + OC = \frac{hQ}{2} + \frac{AR}{Q} \tag{11.4}$$

Using the classical optimization technique, the optimum value of

$Q = Q_0$ can be obtained by setting $\dfrac{dTC(Q)}{dQ} = 0$. Hence

$$Q_0 = \sqrt{\frac{2AR}{h}} \tag{11.5}$$

and the total cost

$$TC\,(Q_0) = \sqrt{2AhR} \tag{11.6}$$

We have $\dfrac{d^2TC(Q)}{dQ_0^2} = \dfrac{2AR}{Q_0^3} > 0$ for all Q_o. So the total cost, $TC(Q_0)$, obtained in Eq. (11.6) is minimum. The optimum cycle time

$$T_0 = \frac{Q_0}{R} = \sqrt{\frac{2A}{hR}} \tag{11.7}$$

Graphically, the cost equation $TC(Q) = \dfrac{hQ}{2} + \dfrac{AR}{Q} = TC_1(Q) + TC_2(Q)$ can be represented as follows (Figure 11.2).

Note 1: If the unit cost is taken into account then

$$TC(Q) = CR + \frac{hQ}{2} + \frac{AR}{Q} \tag{11.8}$$

This gives $Q_0 = \sqrt{\dfrac{2AR}{h}}$ and $TC\,(Q_0) = CR + \sqrt{2AhR}$

Note 2: Let P be the selling price per unit. Then the gross revenue per time unit is $GR = (P - C)\,R$. Hence, the net profit per time unit is $NP(Q) = GR - TC(Q)$. Then $\dfrac{dNP(Q)}{dQ} = 0$ gives $Q_0 = \sqrt{\dfrac{2AR}{h}}$ and the maximum net profit per time unit is $NP(Q_0) = (P - C)\,R - \sqrt{2AhR}$.

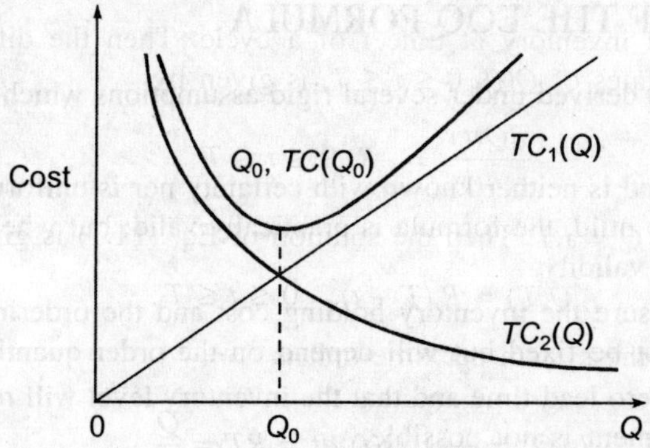

Figure 11.2 Order-quantity and cost representation.

When the lot-size Q is restricted to take discrete values, we cannot determine optimum lot-size $Q = Q_0$ by using the differential equation. In this case, we will use the difference equation approach.

Let the lot-size Q be restricted to take values u, $2u$, $3u$, ..., etc. Then the necessary condition for Q_0 to be optimum lot-size is

$$TC(Q_0) \leq TC(Q_0 + u) \tag{11.9}$$

and

$$TC(Q_0) \leq TC(Q_0 - u) \tag{11.10}$$

Equation (11.9) gives $\dfrac{hQ_0}{2} + \dfrac{AR}{Q_0} \leq \dfrac{h(Q_0 + u)}{2} + \dfrac{AR}{Q_0 + u}$

which on simplication is,

$$Q_0(Q_0 + u) \geq \frac{2AR}{h} \tag{11.11}$$

From Equations (11.10) and (11.11), the lot-size $Q = Q_0$ is optimum if

$$Q_0(Q_0 - u) \leq \frac{2AR}{h} \leq Q_0(Q_0 + u)$$

Sensitivity of lot-size model: For the lot-size model, we have total cost of an inventory system per time unit as

$$TC(Q) = \frac{hQ}{2} + \frac{AR}{Q} \quad \text{and} \quad Q_0 = \sqrt{\frac{2AR}{h}}$$

Now suppose that instead of ordering for Q_0-units (given above), we replenish another lot-size (say) Q^1. Such that $Q^1 = bQ_0$, $b > 0$ and let $TC^1\ (Q^1)$ be the corresponding total cost of an inventory system. The ratio $\dfrac{TC^1(Q^1)}{TC(Q_0)} = \dfrac{1 + b^2}{2b}$ is known as the ***measure of sensitivity*** of the lot-size model.

11.6 LIMITATIONS OF THE EOQ FORMULA

Note that the EOQ formula is derived under several rigid assumptions which give rise to limitations on its applicability.

- In practice, the demand is neither known with certainty nor is uniform over the time period. If the fluctuations are mild, the formula is practically valid; but when fluctuations are wild, the formula loses its validity.
- It is not easy to measure the inventory holding cost and the ordering cost accurately. The ordering cost may not be fixed but will depend on the order quantity Q.
- The assumptions of zero lead-time and that the inventory level will reach to zero at the time of the next replenishment is not possible.
- The stock depletion is rarely uniform and gradual.
- One may have to take into account the constraints of floor-space, capital investment, etc. in stocking the items in the inventory system.

EXAMPLE 11.1: Using the formula information, obtain the EOQ and the total variable cost associated with the policy of ordering quantities of that size. Annual demand = 20,000 units, ordering cost = Rs. 150 per order, and inventory carrying cost is 24% of average inventory value.

Solution: Given R = 20,000 units, A = Rs. 150/order, h = Rs. 0.24 ? unit/annum. Then

$$Q_0 = \sqrt{\frac{2AR}{h}} = 5000 \text{ units and } TC\,(Q_0) = \sqrt{2AhR} = \text{Rs. } 1{,}200.$$

EXAMPLE 11.2: An oil engine manufacturer purchases 42 lubricants pieces from a vendor. The requirement of these lubricants is 1,800 per year. What should be the order quantity per order, if the cost per placement of an order is Rs.16 and inventory carrying charge per rupee per year is 20 paise.

Solution: Given R = 1,800*42 = 75,600 units, A = Rs.16/order and h = 0.20 per unit/year. Then

$$Q_0 = \sqrt{\frac{2AR}{h}} = 34{,}776 \text{ units.}$$

Thus, the optimum inventory quantity of lubricant at the rate of Rs. 42 per lubricant = $Q_0/42$ = 83 lubricants.

EXAMPLE 11.3: A company uses rivets at a rate of 5,000 kg per year, rivets costing Rs. 2 per kg. It costs Rs. 20 to place an order and the carrying cost of inventory is 10% per annum. How frequently should order for rivets be placed and how much?

Solution: Given R = 5,000 kg/year, C = Rs 2/kg, A = Rs. 20/order and $h = Ci$ = 2 * 10 % per unit/year. Then $Q_0 = \sqrt{\dfrac{2AR}{Ci}}$ = 1,000 kg and $T_0 = \dfrac{Q_0}{R} = \dfrac{1}{5}$ years = 2.4 months.

EXAMPLE 11.4: A supplier ships 100-units of a product every Monday. The purchase cost of the product is Rs. 60 per unit. The cost of ordering and transportation from the supplier is Rs. 150 per order. The cost of carrying inventory is estimated at 15 % per year of the purchase cost. Find the lot-size that will minimize the cost of the system. Also, determine the optimum cost.

Solution: Given R = 100 units per week, A = Rs. 150/order, h = 15% of 60 = Rs. 9 per unit/year = Rs. 9/52 per unit/week. Then Q_0 = 416 units, and the optimum cost = $CR + \sqrt{2AhR}$ = Rs. 6,072.

EXAMPLE 11.5: A company plans to consume 760 pieces of a particular component. Past records indicate that the purchasing department spent Rs. 12,555 for placing 15,500 purchase orders. The average inventory was valued at Rs. 45,000 and the total storage cost was Rs. 7,650 which included wages, taxes, rent, insurance, etc. related to the store department. The company borrows capital at the rate of 10% per year. If the price of a component is Rs. 12 and the lot-size is 10, find the following:

1. Purchase price per year
2. Purchase expenses per year
3. Storage expenses per year
4. Capital cost per year
5. Total cost per year.

Solution: Given R = 760 pieces, volume = 15,500 purchase orders, storage cost = Rs. 7,650, ordering cost, A = Rs. 12,555/year, cost per order = 12555/15500 = Rs. 0.81 and average inventory = 45,000 units. Then

$$i = \text{Inventory carrying charge fraction} = \frac{\text{Storage cost}}{\text{Average inventory}} = \frac{7650}{45,000} = 0.17$$

1. Purchase price per year = 12 × 760 = Rs. 9,120.
2. Purchase expenses per year = 0.81 × 760 = Rs. 615.60.
3. Storage expenses per year = $(1/2)QCi$ = Rs. 10.20.
4. Capital cost per year = $(1/2)Q \times C \times 10$ % = Rs. 6.00.
5. Total cost per year = (1) + (2) + (3) + (4) = Rs. 9,751.80.

EXAMPLE 11.6: If in the model developed in Section 11.5, the set-up cost, A, is replaced by $A + bQ$ where b is the set-up cost per unit item produced, then show the optimum order quantity produced due to this change if the set-up cost remains unaffected.

Solution: With the new set-up cost, Eq. (11.4) in the form of T becomes

$$TC\,(T) = \frac{h}{2}RT + \frac{(A + bQ)}{T}$$

$$= \frac{h}{2}RT + \frac{(A + bRT)}{T}$$

$$= \frac{h}{2}RT + \frac{A}{T} + bR$$

For the optimum cost, $\frac{dTC(T)}{dT} = \frac{1}{2}hR - \frac{A}{T^2} = 0$ which gives $T_0 = \sqrt{\frac{2A}{hR}}$ and $Q_0 = \sqrt{\frac{2AR}{h}}$.

This is same as Eq. (11.5). Thus, there will be no change in the optimal order quantity due to change in the set-up cost.

EXAMPLE 11.7: Data relevant to component A used by Engineering India Private Limited in 20 different assemblies includes: purchase price = Rs. 15 per 100, annual usage = 1,00,000 units, cost of buying office (fixed) Rs. 15,575 per annum, set-up cost = Rs. 12 per order, rent of component = Rs. 3,000 per annum, interest = 25 % per annum, insurance = 0.05 % per annum based on total purchases, depreciation as 1 % per annum of all items purchase. Calculate

1. EOQ for component A
2. The percentage changes in total annual costs relating to component A if the annual usage was (a) = 1,25,000-units and (b) 75,000-units.

Solution: Given R = 1,00,000 units, A = Rs. 12/order

and $h = \frac{15}{100}(0.25 + 0.0005 + 0.01)$ = Rs. 0.039075 per unit per annum.

Then Q_0 = 7,837-units and $TC(Q_0)$ = Rs. 306.25

1. We have R_a = 1,25,000-units. Then Q_{a0} = 8,762-units and $TC_a\ (Q_{a0})$ = Rs. 342.31.
2. We have R_b = 75,000-units. Then Q_{b0} = 6,787-units and $TC_b\ (Q_{b0})$ = Rs. 265.20.

Therefore, the total annual cost increases by 12% when the annual demand is 1,25,000 units, whereas it decreases by 13% when the annual demand is 75,000-units.

11.7 EOQ MODEL WITH FINITE REPLENISHMENT RATE

In section 11.5, we assumed that the replenishment rate is infinite. We now discuss a system in which the replenishment rate, P is finite. Obviously, the replenishment rate P is larger than the demand rate R. The mathematical model in this section is derived under the same assumptions as those given in Section 11.5, except the following change in assumption (iv). We take it, as replenishment rate is finite at P units/time units with $P > R$. We describe and analyze one cycle as follows (Figure 11.3):

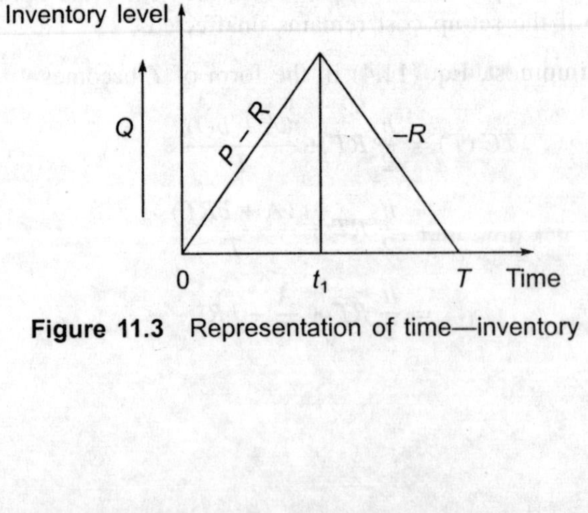

Figure 11.3 Representation of time—inventory level.

We start with zero inventory level. The production starts at this point of time at the rate of P-units per time unit and the demand occurring at the rate of R ($< P$)-units, are satisfied from the production. The production continues till $Q = RT$-units are produced. Thereafter, the demand is satisfied from accumulated inventory at the rate of R-units. The production again starts when on-hand inventory level reaches zero. In Figure 11.3, t_1 is time at which production stops and T is the cycle time at which the inventory level reaches zero.

Let $Q(t)$ denote the on-hand inventory at any instant of time t, $0 \le t \le T$. It is assumed that production of units continues in $(0, t_1)$ and during (t_1, T) demand is satisfied from accumulated inventory. Then the differential equation governing instantaneous state of inventory is given by

$$\frac{dQ(t)}{dt} = \begin{cases} P - R, & 0 \le t \le t_1 \\ -R, & t_1 \le t \le T \end{cases} \tag{11.12}$$

with initial condition $Q(0) = 0$ and boundary conditions $Q(t_1) = Q = RT$ and $Q(T) = 0$. The solution of Eq. (11.12) is

$$Q(t) = \begin{cases} (P - R)t, & 0 \le t \le t_1 \\ R(T - t), & t_1 \le t \le T \end{cases} \tag{11.13}$$

Note that $Q(t)$ is considered to be continuous function of time t. So we have $Q(t_1) = (P - R)\, t_1 = R\,(T - t_1)$, which give $t_1 = Q/P$. The average inventory in the system per time unit is

$$I_1(Q) = \frac{1}{T}\int_0^T Q(t)\, dt$$

$$= \frac{1}{T}\left[\int_0^{t_1} Q(t)\, dt + \int_{t_1}^{T} Q(t)\, dt\right] = \frac{1}{2}Q\left(1 - \frac{R}{P}\right)$$

Hence, the total cost of the system per time unit is

$$TC(Q) = IHC + 0C = hI_1(Q) + \frac{AR}{Q}$$

$$= \frac{1}{2}hQ\left(1 - \frac{R}{P}\right) + \frac{AR}{Q} \tag{11.14}$$

Setting $\dfrac{dTC(Q)}{dQ}$ 0 gives optimum value of lot-size,

$$Q = Q_0 = \sqrt{\frac{2AR}{h[1 - (R/P)]}} \tag{11.15}$$

Then the minimum total cost per time unit is

$$TC(Q_0) = \sqrt{2AhR\left(1 - \frac{R}{P}\right)} \tag{11.16}$$

because $\frac{d^2TC(Q)}{dQ^2} = \frac{2AR}{Q_0^3} > 0$ for all Q_0 and optimum cycle time $T = T_0$ is

$$T_0 = \sqrt{\frac{2A}{hR[1-(R/P)]}} \tag{11.17}$$

Note 1: If $P = R$, i.e. if the rate of replenishment is equal to the demand rate then replenishment will have to take place continuously. In this case, there will be neither carrying cost nor replenishment cost.

Note 2: If $P \to \infty$, i.e. replenishment rate is infinite, all equations derived here will be same as those derived in section 11.5.

EXAMPLE 11.8: A product is to be manufactured on a machine. The cost, production, demand, etc. are as follows:

Ordering cost per order = Rs. 30

Purchase cost per unit = Rs. 0.10

Inventory holding cost per unit per annum = Rs. 0.05

Production rate = 1,00,000 units per year

Demand rate = 10,000 units/year.

Determine the economic manufacturing quantity.

Solution: Given: A = Rs. 30 per order, C = Rs. 0.10 per unit, h = 0.05/unit/annum, P = 1,00,000 units per year and R = 10,000 units per year

$$\therefore \qquad Q_0 = \sqrt{\frac{2AR}{h[1-(R/P)]}} = 3{,}561 \text{ units}$$

EXAMPLE 11.9: A contractor has to supply 10,000 bearings per day to an automobile manufacturer. He finds that when he starts a production run, he can produce 25,000 bearings per day. The cost of holding a bearing in stock for one year is Rs. 2 and the set-up cost of a production run is Rs. 1,800. How frequently should production run be made?

Solution: Given: h = Rs. 2.00/bearing/year = Rs. 0.0055 / bearing/year, A = Rs. 1800/production run, R = 10,000 bearings/day, P = 25,000 bearings/day. Then

$$Q = \sqrt{\frac{2AR}{h[1-(R/P)]}} = 1{,}04{,}447 \text{ bearings.}$$

$$T = \frac{Q}{R} = 10.5 \text{ days.}$$

Length of production cycle = $t_1 = \frac{Q}{P} = 4$ days.

Thus, the production cycle starts at an interval of 10.5 days and the production continues for 4 days.

EXAMPLE 11.10: Find the most economic batch quantity of a product on a machine if the production rate of that item on the machine is 200 pieces per day and the demand is uniform at the rate of 100 pieces per day. The ordering cost is Rs. 200 per batch and the cost of holding one item in inventory is Rs. 0.81 per day. How will the batch quantity vary if the production rate is infinite?

Solution: Given: A = Rs. 200/order, h = Rs. 0.81/unit/day, R = 100 units/day, P = 200 units/day.

$$\therefore \qquad Q = \sqrt{\frac{2AR}{h[1 - (R/P)]}} = 317 \text{ units.}$$

Cycle time, $T = \dfrac{Q}{R} = 3.17$ days.

Length of production cycle, $t_1 = \dfrac{Q}{P} = 1.58$ days.

If the production rate is infinite, i.e. $P \to \infty$ then $Q = \sqrt{\dfrac{2AR}{h}} = 222$ units.

11.8 EOQ MODEL WITH SHORTAGES

The EOQ models derived in Sections 11.6 and 11.7 were based on the assumption that shortages are not allowed. However, allowing shortages increases the cycle time and reduces carrying costs. Also, back-log of units is advantageous when the time value of inventory is very high.

The assumption of Section 11.6 is relaxed here by allowing shortages for some period of time and shortage cost is π per unit short. Shortage cost is directly proportional to the average number of units short. This model is also known as ***Order Level System***.

In this model, the scheduling period T_P is prescribed constant, and so the lot-size $Q_P = RT_P$ raises the on-hand inventory at the beginning of each scheduling period to the order level S. Shortages are made up when the next procurement arrives. Order level, S is the decision variable. The time-inventory representation is exhibited in Figure 11.4.

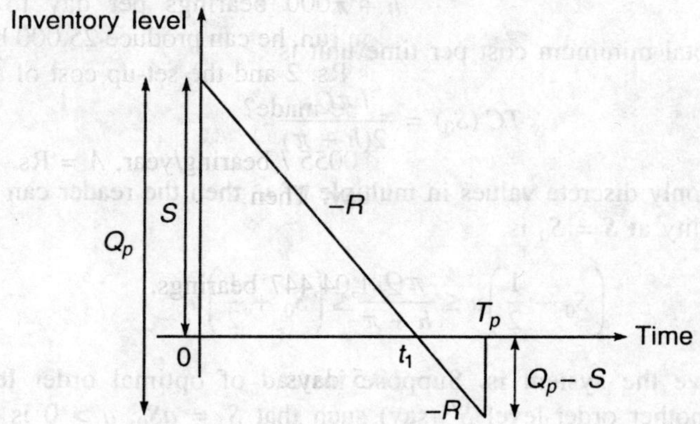

Figure 11.4 EOQ model with shortages.

Let $Q(t)$ denote the on-hand inventory at time t $(0 \le t \le T_P)$ of a cycle. Suppose that the system carries inventory during $(0, t_1)$ and runs with shortages during (t_1, T_P).

Then instantaneous state of $Q(t)$ is given by differential equation

$$\frac{dQ(t)}{dt} = \begin{cases} -R, & 0 \le t \le t_1 \\ -R, & t_1 \le t \le T_p \end{cases} \tag{11.18}$$

with initial condition $Q(0) = S$, $Q(t_1) = 0$ and $Q(T_P) = Q_P$.

Then the solution of Eq. (11.18) is given by

$$Q(t) = \begin{cases} S - Rt, & 0 \le t \le t_1 \\ R(T_p - t), & t_1 \le t \le T_p \end{cases} \tag{11.19}$$

Clearly, $Q(t_1) = 0$ gives $t_1 = S/R$. Hence, average inventory per time unit is

$$I_1(S) = \frac{1}{T_P} \int_0^{T_p} Q(t)\, dt = \frac{s^2}{2Q_P} \tag{11.20}$$

and average shortages per time unit is

$$I_2(S) = \frac{1}{T_P} \int_{t_1}^{T} -Q(t)\, dt = \frac{(Q_P - s)^2}{2Q_P} \tag{11.21}$$

Hence the total cost, $TC(S)$, of an inventory per time unit is

$$TC(S) = hI_1(S) + \pi I_2(S)$$

$$= \frac{hS^2}{2Q_P} + \frac{\pi(Q_P - S)^2}{2Q_P} \tag{11.22}$$

For the optimum value of $S = S_0$, we need to set $\dfrac{dTC(S)}{dS} = 0$, which gives

$$S_0 = \frac{\pi Q_P}{h + \pi} \tag{11.23}$$

and the corresponding total minimum cost per time unit is

$$TC\,(S_0) = \frac{h\pi Q_P}{2(h + \pi)} \tag{11.24}$$

If S is restricted to take only discrete values in multiple of u, then the reader can easily check that the condition for optimality at $S = S_0$ is

$$\left(S_0 - \frac{1}{2}\right)u \le \frac{\pi Q_P}{h + \pi} \le \left(S_0 + \frac{1}{2}\right)u \tag{11.25}$$

Let us see how sensitive the system is. Suppose instead of optimal order level S_0 given in Eq. (11.23), one uses another order-level S' (say) such that $S' = aS_0$, $a > 0$ is constant and the corresponding cost be $TC(S')$.

Then $$TC(S')^2 = \frac{hS'}{2Q_P} + \frac{\pi(Q_P - S')^2}{2Q_P}$$

$$= \frac{haS_0}{2Q_P} + \frac{\pi(Q_P - aS_0)^2}{2Q_P}$$

$$= TC\ (S_0) = (1-a)\frac{\pi}{h}\,TC(S_0), \quad 0 \le a \le \left(1 + \frac{h}{\pi}\right)$$

This gives $\frac{TC(S')}{TC(S_0)} = 1 + (1-a)\frac{\pi}{h}, \ 0 \le a \le \left(1 + \frac{h}{\pi}\right)$. Thus, the ratio $TC(S')/TC(S_0)$ depends on a, h and π.

Next, let us relax the assumption of placing an order at the prescribed cycle time. We discuss the mathematical model in which both lot-size and order level are decision variables.

11.9 ORDER-LEVEL, LOT-SIZE SYSTEM

In order-level, lot-size system, we need to balance the sum of carrying cost, shortage cost and ordering cost. The assumptions here are same as those in Section 11.8, with an addition that lot-size Q is a decision variable. The pictorial representation of order-level lot-size system is given in Figure 11.5.

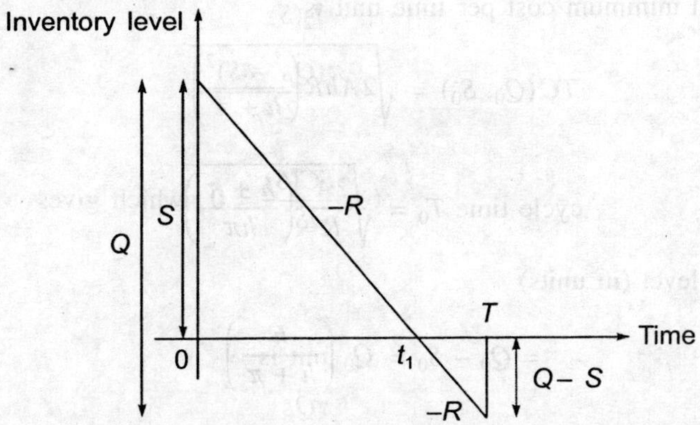

Figure 11.5 Order-level lot-size (OLLS) system.

We analyze one cycle. If T denotes cycle time, we obviously have $Q = RT$. Initially, we have order quantity Q. After clearing shortages of $(Q - S)$-units, the initial inventory level is S. Let $Q(t)$ denote the on-hand inventory at time t of a cycle, then clearly $Q(0) = S$. Suppose that the system carries inventory during $(0, t_1)$ and runs with shortages during (t_1, T). The differential equation that describes the instantaneous states of $Q(t)$, $0 \le t \le T$, is given by Eq. (11.18) and using $Q(0) = S$ and $Q(t_1) = 0$, the solution of differential Eq. (11.18) is

$$Q(t) = \begin{cases} S - Rt, & 0 \le t \le t_1 \\ R(t_1 - t), & t_1 \le t \le T \end{cases} \tag{11.26}$$

The condition $Q(t_1) = 0$ gives $t_1 = S/R$.

Let us calculate average inventory per time unit and average units shorts per time unit. Average inventory,

$$I_1(S, Q), \text{ per time unit} = \frac{1}{T}\int_0^{t_1} Q(t)\,dt = \frac{S^2}{2Q} \tag{11.27}$$

and average shortages

$$I_2(S, Q), \text{ per time unit} = \frac{1}{T}\int_{t_1}^{T} -Q(t)\,dt = \frac{(Q-S)^2}{2Q} \tag{11.28}$$

Hence, the total average cost, $TC(Q, S)$ per time unit is

$$TC(Q, S) = hI_1(S, Q) + \pi I_2(S, Q) + \frac{AR}{Q}$$

$$= \frac{hS^2}{2Q} + \frac{\pi(Q-S)^2}{2Q} + \frac{AR}{Q} \tag{11.29}$$

For optimum value of $Q = Q_0$ and $S = S_0$, we set $\frac{\partial TC(Q,S)}{\partial Q} = 0$ and $\frac{\partial TC(Q,S)}{\partial S} = 0$. It gives

$$S_0 = \sqrt{\frac{2AR}{h}\,\frac{\pi}{h+\pi}} \quad \text{and} \quad Q_0 = \sqrt{\frac{2AR}{h}\,\frac{(h+\pi)}{\pi}} \tag{11.30}$$

The corresponding total minimum cost per time unit is

$$TC(Q_0, S_0) = \sqrt{2AhR\left(\frac{\pi}{h+\pi}\right)} \tag{11.31}$$

$$\text{cycle time } T_0 = \sqrt{\frac{2A}{R}\cdot\left(\frac{h+\pi}{h\pi}\right)} \tag{11.32}$$

and optimum shortage level (in units)

$$= Q_0 - S_0 = Q_0\left(\frac{h}{h+\pi}\right) \tag{11.33}$$

EXAMPLE 11.11: The demand for a certain item is 16 units per period. Unsatisfied demand causes a shortage cost of Rs. 0.75 per unit per short period. The cost of initiating purchasing action is Rs. 15.00 per purchase and the holding cost is 15% of average inventory valuation per period. Item cost is Rs. 8.00 per unit. Find the minimum cost and purchase quantity.

Solution: Given $R = 16$ units, π = Rs. 0.75 per unit short, h = Rs. 8 × 15% = Rs. 1.20 and A = Rs. 15.00/order.

$$\therefore \quad Q = \sqrt{\frac{2AR}{h}\cdot\frac{h+\pi}{h}} = 32 \text{ units (appro.)}$$

$$TC = \sqrt{2AhR}\sqrt{\frac{\pi}{h+\pi}} = \text{Rs. } 14.88 \text{ (appro.)}$$

EXAMPLE 11.12: A television manufacturing company produces its own speakers, which are used in the production of its television sets. The television sets are assembled on a continuous production line at a rate of 8,000 per month. The company is interested in determining when and how much to procure, given the following information:

1. Each time a batch is produced, a set-up cost of Rs. 12,000 is incurred.
2. The cost of keeping a speaker in stock is Rs. 0.30 per month.
3. The production cost of a single speaker is Rs. 10.00 and can be assumed to be a unit cost.
4. Shortage of a speaker (if there exists) costs Rs. 1.10 per month.

Solution: Given R = 8,000 televisions per month, A = Rs. 12,000 per production run, h = Rs. 0.30 per unit per month, π = Rs. 1.10 per unit short per month.

Case (i): When shortages are not allowed

$$Q = \sqrt{\frac{2AR}{h}} = 25{,}298 \text{ speakers and } T = \frac{Q}{R} = 3.2 \text{ months.}$$

Thus, 25,298 speakers are to be produced every 3.2 months.

Case (ii): When shortages are permitted

$$Q = \sqrt{\frac{2AR}{h}}\sqrt{\frac{h+\pi}{\pi}} = 28{,}540 \text{ speakers and } T = \frac{Q}{R} = 3.6 \text{ months}$$

Hence, when shortages are permitted, 28,540 speakers are produced at every 3.6 months.

$$\text{Number of shortage of speakers} = \frac{\pi Q}{h+\pi} = 22{,}424 \text{ speakers.}$$

Thus, a shortage of 6,116 (= 28,540 – 22,424) speakers is permitted.

EXAMPLE 11.13: A dealer supplies you the following information with regard to a product dealt in by him: Annual demand = 5,000 units, ordering cost = Rs. 25.00 per order, inventory carrying cost is 30% per unit per year of purchase cost Rs. 100 per unit.

The dealer is considering the possibility of allowing some back-orders to occur for the product. He has estimated that the annual cost of back-ordering the product will be Rs. 10.00 per unit.

1. What should be the optimum number of units of the product he should buy in one lot?
2. What quantity of the product should he allow to be back-ordered?
3. How much additional cost will he have to incur on inventory if he does not permit back-ordering?

Solution: 1. Given R = 5,000 units, A = Rs. 250 per order, h = 100 * 0.30 = Rs. 30 per unit and π = Rs. 10.00 per unit.

$$\therefore \quad Q\sqrt{\frac{2AR}{h}}\sqrt{\frac{h+\pi}{\pi}} = 576 \text{ units and } S = \frac{\pi}{h+\pi}Q = 144 \text{ units.}$$

$\therefore$ The units to be back-ordered = $Q - S$ = 432 units.

$$2.\ TC = \sqrt{2AhR}\sqrt{\frac{\pi}{h+\pi}} = \text{Rs. } 4{,}330.$$

3. If back-ordered are not permitted, then the total cost of an inventory system per unit is $\sqrt{2AhR}$ = Rs. 8,660.

∴ Additional cost when back-orders are not permitted = 8,660 – 4,330 = Rs. 4,330.

EXAMPLE 11.14: The annual demand for a product is 3,600 units with an average of 12-units per day. The lead-time is 10 days. The ordering cost per order is Rs. 10 and the annual carrying cost is 25% of the value of the inventory. The price of the product per unit is Rs. 3.00.

1. What will be the EOQ?
2. Find the purchase cycle time.
3. Find the total inventory cost per year.
4. If the safety stock of 100-units is considered necessary, what will be the reorder level and the total annual cost of inventory which will be relevant to inventory decision?

Solution: 1. Given R = 3,600 units, A = Rs. 20 per order, h = Rs. 3 * 25% per unit per year and lead-time = 10 days. Since the demand is uniform at 12-units per day, the total number of working days in the year = 3,600/12 = 300.

$$\therefore \qquad Q = \sqrt{\frac{2AR}{h}} = 438 \text{ (appro.)}$$

2. Cycle time $= \dfrac{438}{12}$ = 36.5 days.

3. $TC = CR + \dfrac{AR}{Q} + \dfrac{hQ}{2}$ = Rs. 11,128.60.

4. Re-order level = Safety stock + Lead-time demand = 100 + 12 × 10 = 220 units.

$$\therefore \qquad \text{Average inventory} = \text{Safety stock} + \frac{Q}{2} = 319 \text{ units.}$$

$$\therefore \qquad TC = \frac{hQ}{2} + \frac{AR}{Q} = \text{Rs. } 164.38.$$

11.10 ORDER-LEVEL LOT-SIZE SYSTEM WITH FINITE REPLENISHMENT RATE

The order level, lot-size system with finite replenishment rate is based on the assumptions which are same as in the model developed in Section 11.9, except the assumption that "replenishment rate is finite". We analyze one cycle (Figure 11.6).

Let the maximum inventory level Q_1 (say) be reached at the end of time t_1. Then $Q_1 = (P - R)t_1$. After time t_1, the stock Q_1 is depleted during t_2. Then $Q_1 = Rt_2$. During time t_3, shortages accumulate at the rate of R. Thus, the maximum shortages (say) $Q_2 = Rt_3$. After time t_3, the production again starts and shortages are getting cleared at the rate of $(P - R)t_4$. Then $Q_2 = (P - R)t_4$.

$$\therefore \qquad \text{Average inventory} = \frac{1}{2}\frac{Q_1(t_1 + t_2)}{T}, \tag{11.34}$$

and

$$\text{average shortages} = \frac{1}{2}\frac{Q_2(t_3 + t_4)}{T} \tag{11.35}$$

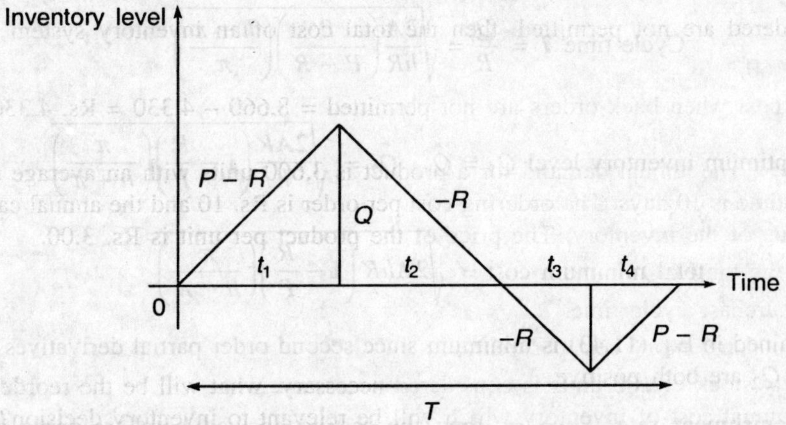

Figure 11.6 Order-level lot-size (OLLS) system with finite replenishment.

The cycle time, $T = t_1 + t_2 + t_3 + t_4$

$$= \frac{Q_1}{P-R} + \frac{Q_1}{R} + \frac{Q_2}{R} + \frac{Q_2}{P-R} = \frac{P(Q_1+Q_2)}{R(P-R)} \tag{11.36}$$

If Q is the lot-size then $Q_1 = Q - Q_2 - Rt_1 - Rt_4 = \left(\frac{P-R}{P}\right)Q - Q_2$.

or
$$Q_1 + Q_2 = \left(\frac{P-R}{P}\right)Q$$

Then, Eq. (11.36) becomes

$$T = \frac{Q}{R} \tag{11.37}$$

The total cost, TC, of an inventory system per time unit is

$$TC(Q_1, Q_2) = \frac{AR}{Q} + \frac{1}{2}\frac{Q_1(t_1+t_2)}{T}h + \frac{1}{2}\frac{Q_2(t_3+t_4)}{T}\pi$$

$$= \frac{AR}{Q} + \frac{1}{2Q}\left(\frac{P}{P-R}\right)\left[h\left(\frac{P-R}{P}Q - Q_2\right)^2 + Q_2^2\pi\right] \tag{11.38}$$

The optimum values of Q and Q_2 can be obtained by setting partial derivatives of $TC\ (Q_1, Q_2)$ with respect to Q and Q_2 equal to zero which gives

$$Q = \sqrt{\frac{2AR}{h}\left(\frac{P}{P-R}\right)\left(\frac{h+\pi}{\pi}\right)} \tag{11.39}$$

and
$$Q_2 = Q\left(1 - \frac{R}{P}\right)\frac{h}{h+\pi} \tag{11.40}$$

$$\therefore \qquad \text{Cycle time } T = \frac{Q}{R} = \sqrt{\frac{2A}{hR}\left(\frac{P}{P-R}\right)\left(\frac{h+\pi}{\pi}\right)} \tag{11.41}$$

$$\text{Optimum inventory level } Q_1 = Q - Q_2 = \sqrt{\frac{2AR}{h}\left(1-\frac{R}{P}\right)\left(\frac{\pi}{h+\pi}\right)} \tag{11.42}$$

and

$$\text{total minimum cost} = \sqrt{2AhR\left(1-\frac{R}{P}\right)\left(\frac{\pi}{h+\pi}\right)} \tag{11.43}$$

The cost obtained in Eq. (11.43) is minimum since second order partial derivatives of TC with respect to Q and Q_2 are both positive.

Note 1: If replenishment rate, $P \to \infty$, then the results derived here are same as those of Section 11.9.

Note 2: If $\pi \to \infty$, then the above derived results are same as the one in Section 11.7.

Note 3: If $P \to \infty$ and $\pi \to \infty$, then we get EOQ model derived in Section 11.5.

EXAMPLE 11.15: The demand for an item in a company is 18,000 units per year, and the company can produce the item at a rate of 3,000 per month. The cost of one set-up is Rs. 500 and the holding cost of one unit per month is Rs. 0.15. The shortage cost of one unit is Rs. 20.00 per month. Determine the optimum manufacturing quantity and the number of shortages. Also, determine the manufacturing time and the time between two set-up?

Solution: Given h = Rs. 0.15 per unit per month, π = Rs. 20.00 per unit short, A = Rs. 500 per order, P = 3,000 units per month and R = 18,000 unit per year = 1,500 units per month.

$$\therefore \qquad Q = \sqrt{\frac{2\pi(h+\pi)}{h\pi}\cdot\left(\frac{PR}{P-R}\right)} = 4{,}488 \text{ units (appro.)}$$

$$\text{Number of shortages} = \left(\frac{h}{h+\pi}\right)Q\left(1-\frac{R}{P}\right) = 17 \text{ units (appro.)}$$

$$\text{Manufacturing time} = \frac{Q}{P} = 0.1246 \text{ years and the time between two set-ups} = \frac{Q}{R} = 0.2493 \text{ years.}$$

11.11 SEVERAL ITEMS INVENTORY MODEL WITH CONSTRAINTS

Till now, we have discussed inventory models for an inventory system, which deals with single item. In general, the inventory system stocks several items. One can study each item individually as long as there is no interaction among the items. There can be many sorts of interactions among the items, viz. warehouse capacity may be limited and items are competing for floor space, or there may be an upper limit on the number of units to be purchased, or there may be an upper limit on the maximum investment in inventory. We now discuss cases with these constraints.

Suppose that there are N-items to be stored in an inventory system.

Let R_j = demand rate for jth-item.

A_j = replenishment cost for jth-item

C_j = purchase cost of jth-item

I_j = inventory carrying charge fraction per unit per annum for jth-item

Q_j = order quantity for jth-item (a decision variable)

$j = 1, 2, \ldots, N$.

Then the average annual cost per time unit for all the items is given by

$$TC = TC(Q_j, j = 1, 2, \ldots, N) = \sum_{j=1}^{N} \left[\frac{1}{2} C_j I_j Q_j + \frac{A_j R_j}{Q_j} \right] \tag{11.44}$$

Then, from Eqs. (11.5) and (11.6), we have optimum lot-size

$$Q_{j0} = \sqrt{\frac{2A_j R_j}{C_j I_j}}, \; j, 1, 2, \ldots, N \tag{11.45}$$

and the total minimum cost of an inventory system is

$$TC_0 = \sum_{j=1}^{N} \sqrt{2C_j I_j A_j R_j} \tag{11.46}$$

11.11.1 EOQ Model with Floor Space Constraint

Suppose that there is an upper limit (say) f of the square metres of warehouse floor space and that jth-item requires f_j square metres of floor space. So we must have

$$\sum_{j=1}^{N} f_j Q_j \le f \tag{11.47}$$

If the Q_{j0} ($j = 1, 2, \ldots, N$) given by Eq. (11.45) satisfies Eq. (11.47) then Q_{j0} ($j = 1, 2, \ldots, N$) are optimal and the total minimum cost can be obtained by Eq. (11.46). On the other hand, if $\sum_{j=1}^{N} f_j Q_j > f$ then the Q_{j0} ($j = 1, 2, \ldots, N$) given by Eq. (11.45) is not optimum. So we have to minimize the average annual cost per time unit for all N-items given in Eq. (11.44) subject to constraints Eq. (11.47) and $Q_j \ge 0$ for all j. We construct the non-negative Lagrangion function as

$$L(Q_j, \lambda) = TC + \lambda \left\{ \sum_{j=1}^{N} f_j Q_j - f \right\} \tag{11.48}$$

where λ is non-negative Lagrangion multiplier. λ indicates additional cost related to floor space used by each unit of the item. Then Kuhn-Tucker necessary conditions for L to be minimum are $\partial L/\partial Q_j = 0$ which gives

$$Q_j = \sqrt{\frac{2A_j R_j}{C_j I_j + 2\lambda f_j}} \tag{11.49}$$

and $$\frac{\partial L}{\partial \lambda} = 0 \text{ gives } \sum_{j=1}^{N} f_j Q_j = f \tag{11.50}$$

A trial and error method is to be used for the optimum value of λ.

EXAMPLE 11.16: Three machines are produced by a factory in lots. A factory has floor space of 600 square feet. The demand rate, purchase cost, ordering cost and floor space required are given in the following table:

Item	1	2	3
Demand rate (unit/year)	5,000	2,000	10,000
Purchase cost per unit (Rs.)	20	15	10
Ordering cost per order (Rs.)	100	150	200
Floor space required (sq. ft)	0.60	0.75	0.30

The factory uses an inventory carrying charge at 20% of average inventory per year. If no shortages are allowed, determine the optimal lot-size for each item under given floor constraints.

Solution: Start with $\lambda = 1$ and compute Q_1, Q_2, Q_3 using Eq. (11.49).

$$\therefore \quad Q_1 = \sqrt{\frac{2 \times 5000 \times 100}{0.20 \times 20 + 2 \times 1 \times 0.60}} \approx 438 \text{ units (appro.)}$$

$$Q_2 = \sqrt{\frac{2 \times 2000 \times 100}{0.20 \times 15 + 2 \times 1 \times 0.75}} \approx 298 \text{ units (appro.)}$$

$$Q_3 = \sqrt{\frac{2 \times 10000 \times 100}{0.20 \times 10 + 2 \times 1 \times 0.30}} \approx 877 \text{ units (appro.)}$$

The floor occupied is $$\sum_{j=1}^{3} f_j Q_j = 0.60 \times 438 + 0.75 \times 298 + 0.30 \times 877$$

$$= 749.4 \text{ (> 600 sq. ft. available floor space).}$$

So, we need some higher value of λ.

Consider $\lambda = 3$. Then we get $Q_1 \approx 362$ units, $Q_2 \approx 231$ units and $Q_3 \approx 725$ units and total floor space is 607.95 sq.ft., which is slightly more than the given floor area. Therefore, further computing Q_j, $j = 1, 2, 3$, for $\lambda = 3.2$, we get $Q_1 \approx 357$ units, $Q_2 \approx 226$ units and $Q_3 \approx 714$ units and the total floor space occupied is 597.90 sq. ft, which is very close to the available floor space.

11.11.2 EOQ Model with Average Inventory Level Constraint

We know that the average number of units in the inventory of jth-item is $Q_j/2$. Suppose that the total average number of units of N-items to be stocked in an inventory should not exceed (say) M. Thus, we must have

$$\frac{1}{2} \sum_{j=1}^{N} Q_j \le M \tag{11.51}$$

We need to minimize the cost given in Eq. (11.44) subject to the constraints Eq. (11.51) and $Q_j > 0$ for all j. Arguing as in Section 11.11.1, we have Lagrangian function

$$L(Q_j, \lambda) = TC + \lambda \left\{ \frac{1}{2} \sum_{j=1}^{N} Q_j - M \right\} \tag{11.52}$$

The necessary conditions for L to be minimum are

$$\frac{\partial L}{\partial Q_j} = 0 \text{ giving } Q_j = \sqrt{\frac{2A_j R_j}{C_j I_j + \lambda}} \tag{11.53}$$

and $$\frac{\partial L}{\partial \lambda} = 0 \text{ gives } \frac{1}{2} \sum_{j=1}^{N} Q_j = M$$

Use the above mentioned steps to find the value of λ which satisfies the total average inventory level.

11.11.3 EOQ Model with Investment Constraint

The firm always places an upper limit on the investment to be made for different items. Suppose the investor decides to invest Rs. D in inventory at a time, then we require that

$$\sum_{j=1}^{N} C_j Q_j \le D \tag{11.54}$$

We want to minimize the total cost of an inventory system given by Eq. (11.44), subject to the constraints Eq. (11.44) and $Q_j \ge 0$ for all j. Arguments given in sub-section 11.11.1 will give

$$Q_j = \sqrt{\frac{2A_j R_j}{C_j I_j + 2\lambda C_j}} \quad \text{and} \quad \sum_{j=1}^{N} C_j Q_j = D \tag{11.55}$$

EXAMPLE 11.17: A firm produces three items. The carrying costs per unit per year of these three items are Rs. 12, 20 and 15, respectively. The ordering costs per order are Rs. 30, 50 and 70 and unit purchase costs are Rs. 8, 9 and 10, respectively. The yearly demand of these items is of 8,000, 10,000 and 12,000 units. Determine optimum lot-sizes for three items subject to the condition that the maximum available capital is Rs. 4,000.

Solution: For $\lambda = 1$, Eq. (11.55) will give

$$Q_1 = \sqrt{\frac{2 \times 30 \times 8000}{12 + 2 \times 1 \times 8}} \approx 131 \text{ units}$$

$$Q_2 = \sqrt{\frac{2 \times 50 \times 10000}{20 + 2 \times 1 \times 9}} \approx 162 \text{ units}$$

$$Q_3 = \sqrt{\frac{2 \times 70 \times 12000}{15 + 2 \times 1 \times 10}} \approx 219 \text{ units}$$

Total investment = $\sum_{j=1}^{3} C_j Q_j$ = 1048 + 1458 + 2190 = 4696 > 4000 (available capital).

Let us compute Q_1, Q_2, Q_3 for $\lambda = 2$. $Q_1 \approx 104$, $Q_2 \approx 133$, $Q_3 \approx 174$ and the total investment = 3769, which is less than maximum investment. Next consider $\lambda = 1.7$. Then $Q_1 \approx 110$, $Q_2 \approx 140$ and $Q_3 \approx 185$. The total investment is $\sum C_j Q_j$ = 3990, which is nearer to the available maximum investment of Rs. 4000.

11.12 EOQ MODEL WITH QUANTITY DISCOUNTS

Till now, we have developed models by taking unit cost C to be known and constant during the cycle time. However, in practice, the retailer offers discount in purchase price to increase his sale (and consequently profit). Quantity discounts are offered in one of the following ways:

(i) All units discounts

(ii) Incremental quantity discounts.

The assumptions are same as those defined in Section 11.5, except the constant unit purchase cost. Since the purchase price of an inventory item is variable, it is to be included while finding the total cost of an inventory system.

In next section, we compute EOQ when price discounts are available by minimizing the total cost of an inventory system.

Suppose there are several price breaks say 0, b_1, b_2, …, b_n and the order quantity Q lies in the discount interval $b_{K-1} \le Q \le b_K$ and the corresponding unit cost for Q-units is C_K where $C_K < C_{K-1}$. Then the total annual cost in the discounted period is

$$TC_K = C_K R + \frac{AR}{Q} + \frac{C_K I Q}{2}, \quad b_{K-1} \le Q \le b_K.$$

Figure 11.7 shows that for each unit price, there is a different range. The broken curve indicates an infeasible solution.

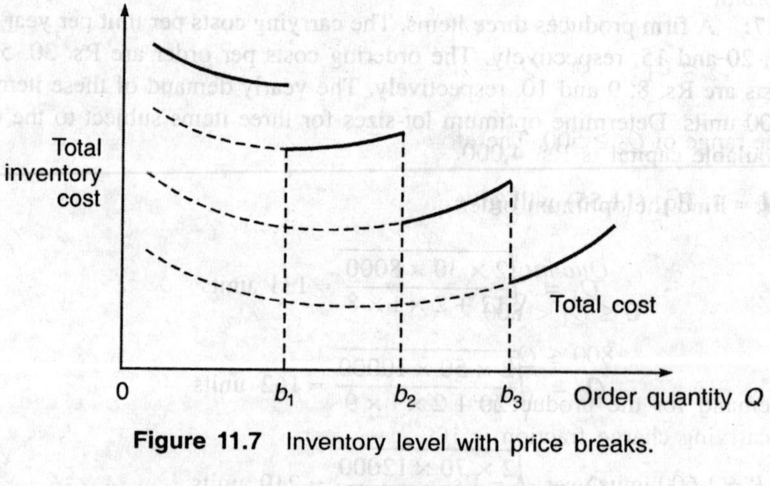

Figure 11.7 Inventory level with price breaks.

Since the total cost curve is not continuous, the calculus method fails. We need to move in each price break to find the optimum lot-size, which minimizes the total inventory cost. Let us discuss model with one-price break and two-price breaks in detail.

11.12.1 EOQ with One-Price Break

Suppose the retailer offers quantity discount at b_1, i.e.

Quantity	*Price/Unit*
$0 \le Q_1 < b_1$	C_1
$b_1 \le Q_2$	$C_2 (< C_1)$

We use the following algorithm to determine optimal purchase quantity.

Step 1: Consider the lowest price C_2 and compute Q_2 using the basic EOQ formula. If $b_1 \ge Q_2$ then Q_2 is the required lot-size to be procured and compute optimal cost associated with Q_2.

Step 2: If $Q_2 < b_1$ then compute Q_1 with price C_1 and the corresponding total cost $TC(Q_1)$. Compare $TC(b_1)$ and $TC(Q_1)$. If $TC(b_1) > TC(Q_1)$ then buy Q_1-units, otherwise purchase b_1-units.

EXAMPLE 11.18: Find the optimum order quantity for a product with price-breaks as under.

Quantity	*Unit cost* (Rs.)
$0 \le Q_1 < 500$	10.00
$500 \le Q_2$	9.25

The monthly demand for the product is 200-units, the holding cost is 2% of the unit cost and the cost of ordering is Rs. 350.00.

Solution: Given A = Rs. 350/order, R = 200 units/month, I = Rs. 0.20/unit/annum, C_1 = Rs. 10.00/unit and C_2 = Rs. 9.25/unit

Clearly, $C_2 < C_1 \quad \therefore \quad Q_2 = \sqrt{\dfrac{2AR}{C_2 I}} = 870 \text{ units} > 500\ (= b_1)$

i.e. Q_2 is within the range of $Q_2 \ge 500$. Therefore, the optimum purchase quantity is $Q_2 = 870$ units.

EXAMPLE 11.19: Find the optimum order quantity for a product for which the price breaks are as follows:

Quantity	*Unit cost* (in Rs.)
$0 \le Q_1 < 800$	Rs. 1.00
$800 \le Q_2$	Rs. 0.98

The yearly demand for the product is 1,600 units per year, the cost of placing an order is Rs. 5.00 and the carrying charge fraction is 10% per year.

Solution: Given R = 1,600 units/year, A = Rs. 5.00/order, I = Rs. 0.10 units/year, C_1 = Rs.1.00/unit, C_2 = Rs. 0.98/units. We have $C_2 < C_1$

$$\therefore \qquad Q_2 = \sqrt{\frac{2AR}{C_2 I}} = 404 \text{ units} < 800\ (= b_1), \text{ so go to step 2 of algorithm.}$$

$$Q_1 = \sqrt{\frac{2 \times 5 \times 1600}{0.10 \times 1.00}} = 400 \text{ units} < b_1$$

So we compute the total cost $TC(Q_1) = \sqrt{2 \times 5 \times 1600 \times 0.10} + 1600 = \text{Rs. } 1{,}640.$

and
$$TC(b_1) = C_2 R + \frac{AR}{b_1} + \frac{C_2 I b_1}{2} = \text{Rs. } 1{,}617.20.$$

Thus, $TC(b_1 = 800) < TC(400)$. Therefore, the optimum purchase quantity is 800-units.

11.12.2 EOQ with Two-Price Breaks

Suppose the price discount offer is as follows with two-price breaks (say) b_1 and b_2:

Quantity	*Price/unit* (In Rs.)
$0 < Q_1 < b_1$	C_1
$b_1 \leq Q_2 < b_2$	C_2
$b_2 \leq Q_3$	C_3

with $C_1 > C_2 > C_3$.

We follow steps as under to determine the optimal lot-size.

Step 1: Consider the lowest purchase price C_3. Compute Q_3 using EOQ formula. If $Q_3 \geq b_2$, then $(Q_3, TC(Q_3))$ is the optimal solution. If $Q_3 < b_2$, then go to step 2.

Step 2: Determine Q_2 with purchase cost C_2. If $b_1 \leq Q_2 < b_2$, then compare $TC(Q_2)$ and $TC(b_2)$. If $TC(Q_2) \geq TC(b_2)$, then $(b_2, TC(b_2))$ is the solution. Otherwise $(Q_2, TC(Q_2))$ is the optimal solution. If $Q_2 < b_1$ as well as b_2, then go to step 3.

Step 3: Find Q_1 with unit cost C_1. Compare $TC(b_1)$, $TC(b_2)$ and $TC(Q_1)$ to find optimum EOQ. The quantity with the lowest cost will be the optimum purchase quantity.

EXAMPLE 11.20: Find the optimal order quantity for a product for which the price breaks are as follows:

Quantity	*Unit cost* (In Rs.)
$0 \leq Q_1 < 500$	10.00
$500 \leq Q_2 < 750$	9.25
$750 \leq Q_3$	8.75

The monthly demand for the product is 200 units, the carrying charge fraction is 20 % of the unit cost, and the set-up cost is Rs. 350 per order.

Solution: We have A = Rs. 350/order, I = Rs. 0.20/unit/annum and R = 200 units/month. Then

$$Q_3 = \sqrt{\frac{2 \times 350 \times 200}{8.75 \times 0.20}} = 894 \text{ units} > 750\ (= b_2). \text{ Therefore, } Q_3 \text{ is the optimum purchase quantity.}$$

EXAMPLE 11.21: Find the optimal order quantity for a product for which the price breaks are as follows:

Quantity	*Unit cost* (Rs.)
$0 \le Q_1 < 50$	10.00
$50 \le Q_2 < 100$	9.00
$100 \le Q_3$	8.00

The monthly demand for the product is 200 units, the carrying charge fraction is 25% of the unit cost, and the replenishment cost is Rs. 20.00 per order.

Solution: We have R = 200 units/month, I = Rs. 0.25/unit/annum and A = Rs. 20.00/order.

$Q_3 = \sqrt{\dfrac{2 \times 2 \times 200}{8 \times 0.25}}$ = 63 units < b_2 (= 100). So we compute $Q_2 = \sqrt{\dfrac{2 \times 2 \times 200}{9 \times 0.25}}$ = 60 units. Since $Q_2 > b_1$ (= 50), to decide optimum purchase quantity we compare

$$TC(Q_2) = 200 \times 9 + 20 \times \frac{200}{60} + 9 \times 0.25 \times \frac{60}{2} = \text{Rs. } 1{,}934.16$$

and

$$TC(b_2) = 200 \times 8 + 20 \times \frac{200}{100} + 8 \times 0.25 \times \frac{100}{2} = \text{Rs. } 1{,}740.00.$$

then $TC(Q_2) > TC(b_2)$. Hence, b_2 = 100 units will be the optimum lot-size.

EXAMPLE 11.22: Find the optimum order quantity for a product with the following price-breaks:

Quantity	*Unit cost* (Rs)
$0 \le Q_1 < 100$	20
$100 \le Q_2 < 200$	18
$200 \le Q_3$	16

The monthly demand for the product is 400 units. The carrying charge fraction is 20 % of the unit cost of the product, and the cost of ordering is Rs. 25.00 per order.

Solution: We have R = 400, I = Rs. 0.20 and A = Rs. 25.00 (in proper units)

$$\therefore \quad Q_3 = \sqrt{\frac{2 \times 25 \times 400}{16 \times 0.20}} = 79 \text{ units.}$$

$$\therefore \quad Q_3 < b_2 \ (= 200). \text{ Then compute } Q_2.$$

$$Q_2 = \sqrt{\frac{2 \times 25 \times 400}{18 \times 0.20}} = 75 \text{ units.}$$

Again $Q_2 < b_1$ (= 100). So we need to compute Q_1.

$$Q_1 = \sqrt{\frac{2 \times 25 \times 400}{20 \times 0.20}} = 70 \text{ units.}$$

We have $Q_1 < b_1$. So we need to compare costs.

$$TC(Q_1) = 400 \times 20 + 25 \times \frac{400}{70} + 20 \times 0.20 \times \frac{70}{2} = \text{Rs. } 8{,}283$$

$$TC(b_1) = 400 \times 18 + 25 \times \frac{400}{100} + 18 \times 0.20 \times \frac{100}{2} = \text{Rs. } 7{,}480$$

$$TC(b_2) = 400 \times 16 + 25 \times \frac{400}{200} + 16 \times 0.20 \times \frac{200}{2} = \text{Rs. } 6{,}770$$

Since $TC(b_2) < TC(b_1) < TC(Q_1)$, the optimum purchase quantity is $b_1 = 100$ units.

In general, if there are n-price breaks, then use the following computational procedure for obtaining optimal purchase quantity:

Step 1: Compute Q_n. If $Q_n \geq b_{n-1}$, the optimum purchase quantity is decided.

Step 2: If $Q_n < b_{n-1}$, compute Q_{n-1}. If $Q_{n-1} \geq b_{n-1}$, proceed as in the case of one price break.

Step 3: If $Q_{n-1} < b_{n-2}$, compute Q_{n-2}. If $Q_{n-2} \geq b_{n-2}$, proceed as in the case of two-price breaks.

Step 4: If $Q_{n-2} < b_{n-2}$, compute Q_{n-3}. If $Q_{n-3} \geq b_{n-3}$, then compare $TC(Q_{n-3})$ with $TC(b_{n-3})$, $TC(b_{n-2})$ and $TC(b_{n-1})$.

Step 5: Continue the steps until $Q_{n-j} \geq b_{n-(j+1)}$ and then compare $TC(Q_{n-j})$ with $TC(b_{n-j-1})$, $TC(b_{n-j-2})$, ..., $TC(b_{n-1})$.

In the remaining part of the chapter, we discuss inventory systems in which the demand is not known with certainty, i.e. we discuss probabilistic scheduling-period systems. The scheduling period in all the system is constant. The scheduling period may be pre-specified or a decision variable.

11.13 PROBABILISTIC ORDER-LEVEL SYSTEM

We discuss the model with the assumption that the scheduling period T_P is pre-specified and the order-level S is the decision variable. The inventory levels of the probabilistic order-level system are shown in Figures 11.8 and 11.9 below.

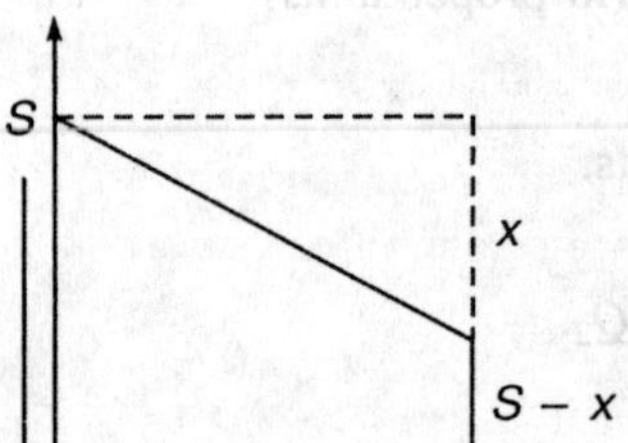

Figure 11.8 Case $x \leq S$.

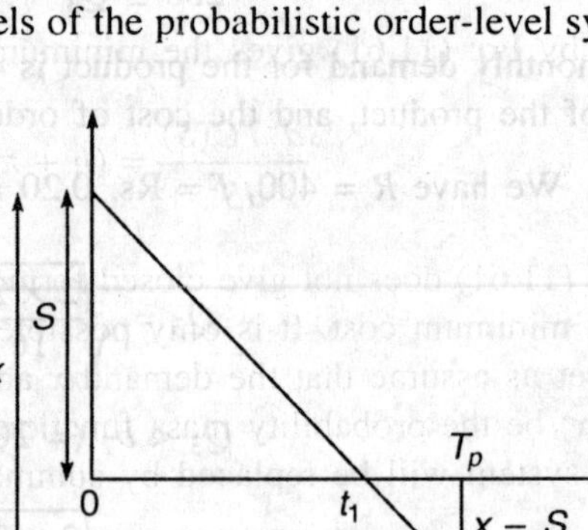

Figure 11.9 Case $x > S$.

Let $f(x)$ be the uniform probability density of demand x occurring during T_P. Let h be the inventory holding cost per unit per annum and π be the shortage cost per unit short. Two cases may arise, depending on the values of S and x.

Then average inventory $I_1(x)$ carried in the system is

$$I_1(x) = \begin{cases} S - (x/2), & x \le S \\ S^2/2x, & x > S \end{cases} \tag{11.56}$$

and average shortages, $I_2(x)$ is

$$I_2(x) = \begin{cases} 0, & x < S \\ (x - S)^2/2x, & x \ge S \end{cases} \tag{11.57}$$

The expected average amount of inventory and the expected shortages are

$$I_1(S) = \int_0^S \left(S - \frac{x}{2} \right) f(x)\,dx = \int_S^\infty \frac{S^2}{2x} f(x)\,dx \tag{11.58}$$

and

$$I_2(S) = \int_S^\infty \frac{(x - S)^2}{2x} f(x)\,dx \tag{11.59}$$

Hence, the expected total cost of the system is

$$TC(S) = hI_1(S) + \pi I_2(S) \tag{11.60}$$

To find the optimum order level S, we need to set differentiation of $TC(S)$ with respect to S equal to zero. Then we have

$$\frac{dTC(S)}{dS} = h\left[\int_0^S f(s)\,dx + \frac{S}{2} f(S) \right] + h\left[\int_S^\infty \frac{S}{x} f(x)\,dx - \frac{S}{2} f(S) \right] - \pi \int_S^\infty \frac{(x - S)}{x} f(x)\,dx = 0$$

i.e.

$$\int_0^S f(x)\,dx + \int_S^\infty \frac{S}{x} f(x)\,dx = \frac{\pi}{h + \pi} \tag{11.61}$$

S obtained by Eq. (11.61) gives the minimum total cost, because

$$\frac{d^2TC(S)}{dS^2} = (h + \pi) \int_S^\infty \frac{f(x)}{x}\,dx > 0 \text{ for all } S \tag{11.62}$$

As Eq. (11.61) does not give closed form of optimal order level S, it is not possible to evaluate the explicit minimum cost. It is only possible for some specific functional form of $f(x)$.

Next, let us assume that the demand x and order level S take discrete values say 0, u, $2u$, …, etc. and $P(x)$ be the probability mass function of the demand x. The integrals in the expected total cost of the system will be replaced by summations. Hence

$$TC(S) = h \sum_{x=0}^{S} \left(S - \frac{x}{2} \right) P(x) + h \sum_{x=S+u}^{\infty} \frac{S^2}{2x} P(x) + \pi \sum_{x=S+u}^{\infty} \frac{(x - S)^2}{2x} P(x) \tag{11.63}$$

Using the difference method, the necessary conditions for S to be optimal order level are

$$TC(S) \le TC(S + u) \tag{11.64}$$

$$TC(S) \le TC(S - u) \tag{11.65}$$

Using algebraic calculations, we get necessary condition for finding S as

$$M(S-u) \le \frac{\pi}{h+\pi} \le M(S) \tag{11.66}$$

where
$$M(S) = \sum_{x=0}^{S} P(x) + \left(S + \frac{u}{2}\right) \sum_{x=S+u}^{\infty} \frac{P(x)}{x} \tag{11.67}$$

EXAMPLE 11.23: The probability distribution of monthly sales of a certain item is as follows:

Monthly sales :	0	1	2	3	4	5	6
Probability :	0.02	0.05	0.30	0.27	0.20	0.10	0.06

The cost of carrying inventory is Rs. 10.00 per unit per month. The current policy is to maintain a stock of four items at the beginning of each month. Assuming that the cost of shortage is proportional to both time and quantity short, obtain the range of shortage cost of short unit.

Solution: Let π be the shortage cost per unit. Given $S = 4$ and h = Rs. 10/unit/month
Using Eq. (11.67), we have

$$\frac{\pi}{10+\pi} = P(0) + P(1) + P(2) + P(3) + \left(4 - \frac{1}{2}\right)\left[\frac{P(4)}{4} + \frac{P(5)}{5} + \frac{P(6)}{6}\right] = 0.92.$$

$$\therefore \qquad \pi = \text{Rs. } 115.$$

Similarly, the greatest value of π is given by

$$\frac{\pi}{h+\pi} = \sum_{x=0}^{4} P(x) + \left(S + \frac{1}{2}\right) \sum_{x=S+1}^{6} \frac{P(x)}{x}$$

i.e.
$$\frac{\pi}{10+\pi} = P(0) + P(1) + P(2) + P(3) + P(4) + \left(4 + \frac{1}{2}\right)\left[\frac{P(5)}{5} + \frac{P(6)}{6}\right] = 0.975$$

$$\therefore \qquad \pi = 390$$

Hence, the required range of shortage cost is Rs. 115 < π < Rs. 390.

11.14 PROBABILISTIC ORDER-LEVEL SYSTEM WITH INSTANTANEOUS DEMAND

In the previous section the probabilistic order-level system with uniform demand is discussed. Here we will deal with an instantaneous demand (see Figures 11.10 and 11.11).

Let $f(x)$ be the probability density function of demand x during T_P. It is assumed that this demand occurs at the beginning of each scheduling period immediately after the inventory level is raised to order level S. The inventory holding cost, h per unit per time unit and shortage cost, π per unit short are known during the review period.

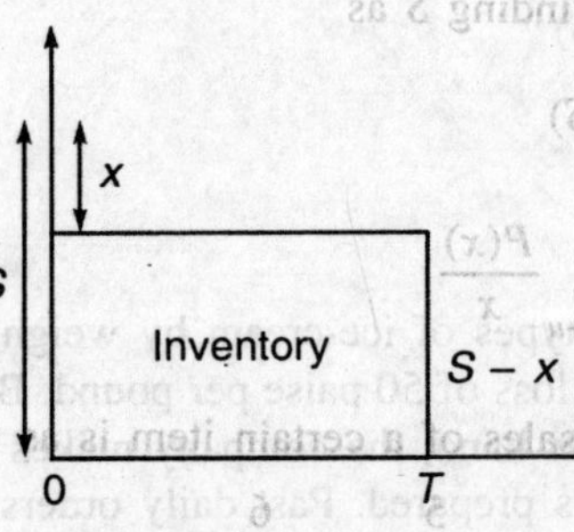

Figure 11.10 Case $x \le S$.

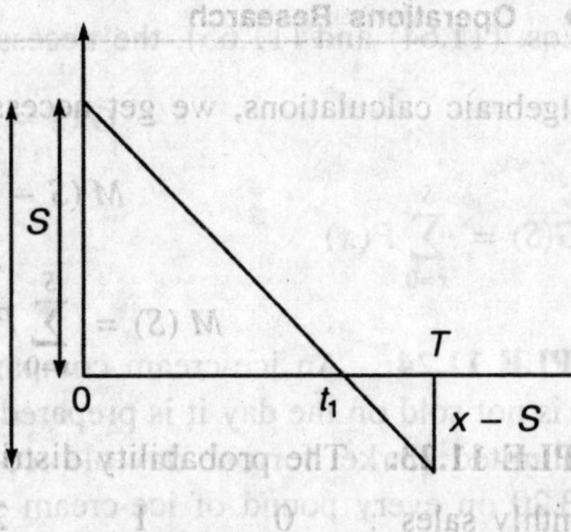

Figure 11.11 Case $x > S$.

The average inventory, $I_1(x)$ and average shortage, $I_2(x)$ for any demand x is given by

$$I_1(x) = \begin{cases} S - x, & x \le S \\ 0, & x > S \end{cases} \tag{11.68}$$

and

$$I_2(x) = \begin{cases} 0, & x \le S \\ x - S, & x > S \end{cases} \tag{11.69}$$

Therefore, the expected amount of inventory and the expected shortages are

$$I_1(S) = \int_0^S (S - x) f(x)\, dx \tag{11.70}$$

and

$$I_2(S) = \int_S^\infty (x - S) f(x)\, dx \tag{11.71}$$

Hence, the expected total cost of the system is

$$TC(S) = hI_1(S) + \pi I_2(S) \tag{11.72}$$

The optimum value of order level is the solution of

$$\frac{dTC(S)}{dS} = (h + \pi) \int_0^S f(x)\, dx - \pi = 0$$

i.e.

$$\int_0^S f(x)\, dx = \frac{\pi}{h + \pi} \tag{11.73}$$

Next, let us assume that demand x and the order level are restricted to take only discrete values (say) 0, u, $2u$, ..., etc. and $P(x)$ be the corresponding probability distribution of demand x. Then the expected total cost is given by

$$TC(S) = h \sum_{x=0}^{S} (S - x)\, dx + \pi \sum_{x=S+u}^{\infty} (x - S) P(x) \tag{11.74}$$

Using Eqs. (11.64) and (11.65), the necessary conditions for optimal order level S is

$$G(S-u) \le \frac{\pi}{h+\pi} \le G(S) \tag{11.75}$$

where $G(S) = \sum_{x=0}^{S} P(x)$.

EXAMPLE 11.24: An ice-cream company sells one of its types of ice-cream by weight. If the product is not sold on the day it is prepared, it can be sold at a loss of 50 paise per pound. But there is an unlimited market for one-day old ice-cream. On the other hand, the company makes a profit of Rs. 3.20 on every pound of ice-cream sold on the day it is prepared. Past daily orders form a distribution with $f(x) = 0.02 - 0.0002x$, $0 \le x \le 100$. How many pounds of ice-cream should the company prepare every day?

Solution: Given h = Rs. 0.50/pound and π = Rs. 3.20/unit short.

Let S be the quantity of ice-cream in pounds to be prepared daily. Then

$$\int_0^S f(x)\,dx = \frac{\pi}{h+\pi}$$

gives

$$\int_0^S (0.20 - 0.0002x)\,dx = \frac{3.20}{0.50 + 3.20}$$

i.e. $0.0002\,S^2 - 0.04\,S + 1.730 = 0 \Rightarrow S = 136.7$ or 63.3. $S = 136.7$ is not possible because $0 \le x \le 100$

$\therefore$ Required optimum $S = 63.3$ pounds.

EXAMPLE 11.25: The probability distribution of monthly sales of a certain item is as follows:

Monthly sales :	0	1	2	3	4	5	6
Probability :	0.01	0.06	0.25	0.35	0.20	0.03	0.10

The cost of carrying inventory is Rs. 30 per unit per month and the cost of unit short is Rs. 70 per month. Determine the optimum stock level which minimizes the total expected cost.

Solution: Given h = Rs. 30 per unit per month and π = Rs. 70 per month.

Then

$$\frac{h}{h+\pi} = \frac{70}{30+70} = 0.7$$

Monthly sales	*Probability*	*Cumulative probability*
0	0.01	0.01
1	0.06	0.07
2	0.25	0.32
3	0.35	0.67
		← 0.7
4	0.20	0.87
5	0.03	0.90
6	0.10	1.00

Clearly, $0.67 < 0.7 < 0.87$. So using Eq. (11.75), $S = 4$ is the optimum order level.

REVIEW EXERCISES

1. An aircraft company uses rivets at an approximate demand rate of 2,500 kg per year. Each unit costs Rs. 30 per kg and the company personnel estimate that it costs Rs. 130 to place an order, and that the carrying cost of inventory is 10% per year. How frequently should orders for rivets be placed? Also determine the optimum size of each order.

[**Ans:** $Q = 466$ units (appro.), $T = 0.18$ year, $n = 5$ orders/year]

2. The annual demand for an item is 3,200 units. The unit cost is Rs. 6 per unit and inventory carrying charges is 25% per annum. If the cost of one procurement is Rs. 150, determine (i) EOQ, (ii) number of orders per year, (iii) time between two consecutive orders, and (iv) the optimal cost.

[**Ans:** $Q = 800$ units, $n = 4$, $T = 3$ months, $TC =$ Rs. 20,400]

3. The annual requirements for a particular raw material are 2,000 units, costing Rs. 1.00 each to the manufacturer. The ordering cost is Rs. 10.00 per order and the carrying cost is 16% per annum of the average inventory value. Find the economic order quantity and the total cost of an inventory system.

[**Ans:** $Q = 500$ units, $TC =$ Rs. 80.00]

4. For an item, the production is instantaneous. The holding cost of one item is Rs. 1.00 per month and the set-up cost is Rs. 25 per run. If the demand is 200 units per month, find the optimum quantity to be produced per set-up and total cost of storage and set-up per month.

[**Ans:** $Q = 100$ units, Total cost of storage and set-up = Rs. 125]

5. A contract has a requirement for cement that amounts to 300 bags per day. No shortages are allowed. Cement costs Rs. 2.00 per bag, inventory carrying cost is 10% of the average inventory valuation per day and it costs Rs. 20 to purchase order. Find the minimum cost of purchase quantity.

[**Ans:** $Q = 100$ units, $TC =$ Rs. 120.00]

6. A manufacturer has to supply his customer 600 units of his product per year. Shortages are not allowed and the inventory holding cost is 60 paise per unit per year. The set-up cost per run is Rs. 80.00. Find (i) the economic order quantity, (ii) the minimum average yearly cost, (iii) the optimum number of order per year, (iv) the optimum period of supply per optimum order, and (v) the increase in the total cost associated with ordering (a) 20 % more and (b) 40 % less than EOQ.

[**Ans:** $Q = 400$ units, $TC =$ Rs. 240, $n = 3/2$, $T = 2/3$ yr., Rs. 4.00]

7. Amit manufactures 50,000 bottles of tomato ketch-up in a year. The factory cost per bottle is Rs. 5.00, the set-up cost per production run is estimated to be Rs. 90, and the carrying cost on finished goods inventory is 20% of the unit cost per annum. The production rate is 600 bottles per day and sales 150 bottles per day. What is the optimal production lot-size and the number of production runs?

8. The annual demand for a product is 1,00,000 units. The rate of production is 2,00,000 units per year. The set-up cost per production run is Rs. 5,000 and the variable production cost of each item is Rs. 10. The annual holding cost per unit is 20% of its value. Find the optimum production lot-size and the length of the production run.

[**Ans:** $Q = 31,600$ units, $T = 0.316$ yrs]

9. A contractor undertakes to supply diesel engines to a truck manufacturer at a rate of 25 per day. He finds that the cost of holding a completed engine in stock is Rs. 16 per month, and there is a clause in the contract penalizing him Rs. 10 per engine per day late for missing the scheduled delivery date. The production of engines is in batches, and each time a new batch is started, there are set-up costs of Rs. 10,000. How frequently should batches be started, and what should be the initial inventory level at the time each batch is completed?

[**Ans:** Q = 994 engines (approx.), T = 40 days (approx.)]

10. A commodity is to be supplied at a constant rate of 200 units per day. Supplies of any amounts can be had at any required time, but each ordering costs Rs. 50.00, cost of holding the commodity in inventory is Rs. 2.00 per unit per day, while the delay in the supply of the item induces a penalty of Rs. 10.00 per unit per delay of one day. Find the optimum order-level and reorder cycle time. What would be the best policy if the penalty cost becomes ∞?

[**Ans:** S = 109 units (approx.), T = 1/2 day, Q = 100 units]

11. The cost of parameters and other factors for a production inventory system of automobile pistons are given below. Find (i) optimum lot-size, (ii) number of shortages, and (iii) manufacturing time and time between two set-ups.

Demand per year = 6000 units	Unit cost = Rs. 40
Set-up cost = Rs. 500	Production rate per year = 36,000 units
Holding cost per year = Rs. 8	Shortage cost per unit per year = Rs. 20

[**Ans:** Q = 1,123 units, S = 267 units, t_1 = 0.03 yrs T = 0.19 yrs]

12. Consider a shop which produces three items. The items are produced in lots. The demand rate for each item is constant and deterministic. No shortages are allowed. The pertinent data for the items is given in the following table:

Item	1	2	3
Holding cost (Rs.)	20	20	20
Set-up cost (Rs.)	50	40	60
Cost per unit (Rs.)	6	7	5
Yearly demand rate	10,000	12,000	7,500

Determine approximately the economic order quantities when the total value of average inventory levels of three items is Rs. 1,000.

[**Ans:** Q_1 = 114, Q_2 = 105, Q_3 = 116, λ = 4.7]

13. A company, which produces three items, has a limited storage space of on an average 750 items of all types. Determine the optimal production quantities for each item separately, when the following information is given:

Product	1	2	3
Holding cost (Rs.)	0.05	0.02	0.04
Set-up cost (Rs.)	50	40	60
Demand rate per year	100	120	75

[**Ans:** Q_1 = 428 units, Q_2 = 628 units, Q_3 = 444 units, λ = 0.002]

14. A small shop produces three machines I, II and III in lots. The shop has only 650 sq./ft. storage space. The approximate data for the three items are presented in the following table:

Machine	I	II	III
Demand (units/year)	5,000	2,000	10,000
Set-up cost (Rs.)	100	200	70
Cost per unit (Rs.)	10	15	5
Floor space required (sq. ft/unit)	0.50	0.80	0.30

The shop uses an inventory carrying charge of 20% of average inventory valuation per annum. If no stock-outs are permitted, determine the optimal lot-size for such items.

15. In a central grain store, it takes about 15 days to get the stock after placing an order and daily 500 tons are dispatched to neighbouring markets. On an ad-hoc basis, safety stock is assumed to be 10 day's stock. Calculate reorder point.

[**Ans:** Reorder point = 12,500 tons.]

16. The annual demand of a product is 10,000 units. Each unit costs Rs. 100 if orders placed in quantities are below 200 units, but for orders of 200 or above, the unit price is Rs. 95. The annual inventory holding cost is 10% of the value of the item and the ordering cost is Rs. 5 per order. Find the economic lot-size.

[**Ans:** Q = 100 units]

17. Find the optimum order quantity for a product for which the price breaks are as follows:

Quantity (units)	*Price per unit* (Rs.)
$0 < Q_1 < 500$	10.00
$500 \le Q_2$	9.00

The monthly demand for the product is 200 units, the holding cost is 2% of the unit cost, and the cost of ordering is Rs. 350.00.

[**Ans:** $Q = b = 500$ units]

18. Find the optimum order quantity for a product for which the price breaks are as follows:

Quantity	*Purchase price* (Rs.)
$0 \le Q_1 < 100$	Rs. 20
$100 \le Q_2 < 200$	Rs. 18
$200 \le Q_3$	Rs. 16

The monthly demand for the product is 400 units. The holding cost is 20% of the unit cost, of the product, and the cost of ordering is Rs. 25.00 per month.

[**Ans:** $Q = b_1 = 100$ units]

19. (a) Minicomputer company purchases a component of which it has a steady usage of 1,000 units per year. The ordering cost is Rs. 50 per order. The estimated cost of money invested in inventory is 25% per year. The unit cost of the component is Rs. 40. Calculate the optimal ordering policy and the total cost of the inventory system, including purchase cost of the components.

[**Ans:** Q = 100 units, TC = Rs. 41,000]

(b) If in (a), the component supplier agrees to offer price discounts of minimum lot supplies as per the schedule given below, re-assess the decision on the optimal ordering policy and the total cost.

Lot-size (Units)	*Purchase price* (Rs.)
$0 \le Q_1 < 149$	40
$150 \le Q_2 < 499$	39
$Q_3 \le 500$	38

[Ans: Q = 150 units, TC = 40,064]

20. Find the optimal order quantity for a product where the annual demand for the product is 500 units, the cost of storage per unit per year is 10 % of the unit cost, and the ordering cost per order is Rs. 180. The unit costs are given below:

Quantity	*Unit cost* (Rs)
$0 \le Q_1 < 500$	25.00
$500 \le Q_2 < 1{,}500$	24.80
$1{,}500 \le Q_3 < 3{,}000$	24.60
$3{,}000 \le Q_4$	24.40

[Ans: Q_1 = 268 units]

21. A TV dealer finds that the cost of holding a television set in stock for a week is Rs. 20; customers who cannot obtain a new television set immediately tend to go to other dealers, and he estimates that for every customer who does not get immediate delivery, he loses on an average Rs. 200. For one particular model of television, the probabilities for a demand of 0, 1, 2, 3, 4, and 5 television sets in a week are 0.05, 0.10, 0.20, 0.30, 0.20 and 0.15, respectively. How many television sets per week should the dealer order? (Assume that there is no lead-time.)

[Ans: Q = 4 TV sets/week]

12 Queuing Theory

12.1 INTRODUCTION

The dictionary meaning of the word queue is a waiting line or the act of joining a line. In day-to-day life, we all come across situations where we have to line up in queues. For example, bank counter, ration shop, library, traffic signal, airport runways, telephone booth, video-on-demand system, production unit, income tax office, etc. Thus, waiting for a service has become an integral part of our day-to-day life. The objective is to formulate the system in such a manner that the average waiting time of the customers in queue is minimized and the utilization of the server is maximized.

In this chapter, we discuss a number of queuing models that account for a variety of service operations. The measures of performance of the system are derived. The models derived are the applications of the probability theory and stochastic processes.

12.2 QUEUING SYSTEM

A queuing system can be completely described by

- the input or arrival pattern (customers);
- the service mechanism (service pattern);
- the 'queue discipline'; and
- customer's behaviour.

The diagrammatic representation of the above components of queuing system is shown in Figure 12.1.

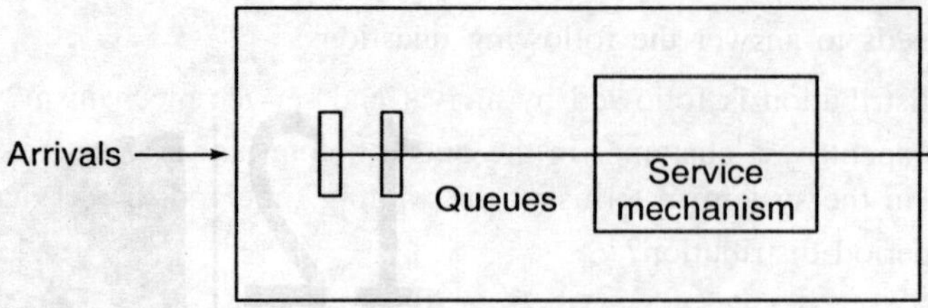

Figure 12.1 Queuing System.

The arrival pattern: Customers arriving to the system for a service will directly go to the service station without waiting in the queue if the server is free at that point of time. Otherwise, he will wait in the queue till the server becomes free. Generally, the customer's arrival is unpredictable. So the arrival pattern can be computed in terms of the probabilities and consequently, probability distribution for inter-arrival time (i.e. the time between two successive arrivals) must be defined. The present chapter deals with those queuing systems in which the customer arrivals follow the 'Poisson' distribution.

The service mechanism: This includes the distribution of the time to service a customer, the number of servers, and the arrangement of servers (in parallel or in series, etc.). If the number of servers is more that one, then this queue is an example of parallel counters for providing service. The system is said to be *queues in tandem* if the service is to be provided in multistage in sequential order. Service time is a random variable with the same distributions for all the arrivals or with a different service time distributions. In this chapter, service time follows 'negative exponential distribution' (Erlang or Gamma) probability distribution.

The queue discipline: This is the manner in which customers form a queue and the manner in which they are chosen for service. The simplest discipline is "first come, first served (FCFS)", according to which the customers are served in order of their arrivals. For example, such types of queue discipline are observed at reservation counters, at cinema ticket windows, at bank counters etc. If the last arrival gets served first, we have "last come, first served (LCFS)" queue discipline. This is observed in government offices, where the file which comes on table last gets cleared first, or in a big godown, where the items which come last are taken out first. The other queue disciplines observed are random selection or service at random order (SIRO) and priority selection (some customers are served before others regardless of their order of arrivals).

Customer's behaviour: Generally, it is assumed that the arrivals in the system are one by one. But, in practice, customers may arrive in groups. Such arrivals are called *bulk arrival*. This is observed when groups of ladies arrive at shopping malls during afternoon. The customers behave in the following ways:

- *Balking:* On arrival, a customer finds the queue length very long and he/she may not join the queue. This phenomenon is known as ***balking*** of customers.
- *Jockeying:* If there is more than one queue, the customer from one queue may shift to another queue because of its smaller size. This behaviour of the customer is known as ***queue jockeying***.
- *Reneging:* A customer who is already in the queue leaves the queue due to long waiting time. This kind of departure from the queue without receiving the service is known as ***reneging***.

Any queuing model needs to answer the following questions:

- What probability distribution is followed by arrival and service mechanism?
- How much time is spent by a customer in the queue before his service starts and the total time spent by him in the system in terms of the waiting time and the service time?
- What is the busy period distribution?

If the server is free when the customer arrives, the latter will be served immediately. During this time if some more customers arrive, then they will be served in their turn. This process will continue until no customer is left unserved and the server becomes free. This time is termed *busy period*. On the contrary, during *idle period*, no customer is present in the system. A *busy cycle* comprises a busy period and the idle period following it.

A system is said to be in '*transient state*' when its operating characteristics are dependent on time; otherwise, the system is said to be in the '*steady state*'. Let $P_n(t)$ denote the probability of having n-customers in the system at time t and $P'_n(t)$ be change in $P_n(t)$ with respect to time t. Then in steady state,

$$P_n(t) \to P_n \text{ as } t \to \infty \quad \text{and} \quad P'_n(t) \to 0 \text{ as } t \to \infty \qquad (12.1)$$

If the arrival rate of the system is greater than its service rate, a steady-state may not be reached regardless of long run-time. In this case, the queue length will increase with time. Such a state is called *explosive state.*

In this chapter, we will deal with only steady-state queuing systems. The mathematical models are developed by using the following notations:

N	Number of customers in the system
C	Number of servers in the system
$P_n(t)$	Probability of having n-customers in the system at time t
P_n	Steady state probability of having n-customers in the system
P_0	Probability of having no customer in the system
L_q	Average number of customers waiting in the queue
L_s	Average number of customers waiting in the system (in the queue and in the service unit)
W_q	Average waiting time of customers in the queue
W_s	Average waiting time of customers in the system (in the queue and in the service unit)
λ	Arrival rate of customers
μ	Service rate of the server
ρ	Utilization factor of the server (traffic intensity) defined as the ratio of λ and μ ($\lambda < \mu$)
M	Poisson arrival
N	Maximum number of customers allowed in the system
GD	General discipline for service

12.3 CLASSIFICATION OF QUEUING MODELS

Using Kendall's notation, the queuing model can be defined by

$$(a/b/c) : (d/e)$$

where

a = arrival rate distribution
b = service rate distribution
c = number of servers
d = capacity of the system
e = service discipline

For example, $(M/M/1)$: $(\infty/FCFS)$ means arrivals follow Poisson distribution, Poisson service rate, single server, system can accommodate infinite number of customers and service discipline is first come first served.

12.4 DISTRIBUTION OF ARRIVALS (THE POISSON PROCESS): PURE BIRTH PROCESS

Even though the arrival pattern of the customers varies from one system to another and it is random too, mathematically, we show that arrivals have a Poisson distribution. The model in which only arrivals are counted and no departure takes place is called *pure birth model*.

In order to derive the arrival distribution in queues, we have the following three axioms:

1. Assume that there are n-units in the system at time t, and the probability that exactly one arrival occur during small interval Δt be given by $\lambda\Delta t + O(\Delta t)$, where λ is the arrival rate independent of time t and $O(\Delta t)$ contains the terms of higher powers of Δt.
2. Under the assumption that Δt is very small, the probability of more than one arrival in time Δt is negligible.
3. The number of arrivals in non-overlapping intervals is mutually independent.

We wish to derive the probability of n-arrivals in time t. Denote it by $P_n(t)$, $(n \geq 0)$. The difference-differential equations governing the process in two different situations are as follows:

Case 1: For $n > 0$, there are two mutually exhaustive events of having n-units at time $(t + \Delta t)$ in the system.

- There are n-units in the system at time t and no arrival takes place during time interval Δt. So at time $(t + \Delta t)$, there will be n-units in the system.

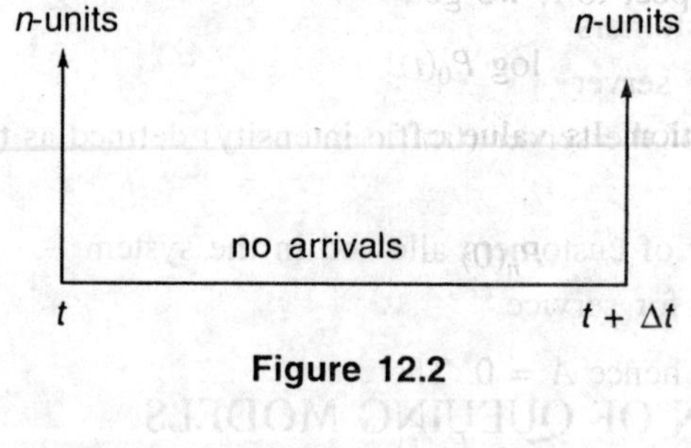

Figure 12.2

Therefore, the probability of these two combined events will be

= Probability of n-units at time t × Probability of no arrivals during Δt

$$= P_n(t)\ (1 - \lambda\Delta t) \tag{12.2}$$

- There are $(n - 1)$-units in the system at time t and one arrival takes place during time interval Δt. So at time $(t + \Delta t)$, there will be n-units in the system.

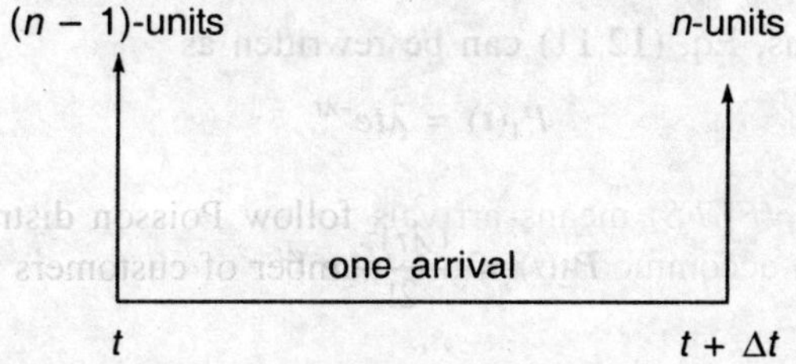

Figure 12.3

Therefore, the probability of these two combined events will be

$= $ Probability of $(n - 1)$-units at time $t \times$ Probability of one arrival during Δt

$$= P_{n-1}(t)\ \lambda\Delta t \tag{12.3}$$

Adding the above two probabilities, we get probability of n-arrivals at time $t + \Delta t$ as

$$P_n(t + \Delta t) = P_n(t)(1 - \lambda\Delta t) + P_{n-1}(t)\ \lambda\Delta t \tag{12.4}$$

Case 2: When $n = 0$, that is, there is no customer in the system. Then

$P_0(t + \Delta t) = $ Probability of no units at time $t \times$ Probability of no arrivals during Δt

$$= P_0(t)(1 - \lambda\Delta t) \tag{12.5}$$

Thus,

$$P_n(t + \Delta t) - P_n(t) = P_n(t)(1 - \lambda\Delta t) + P_{n-1}(t)\ \lambda\Delta t, \quad n > 0 \tag{12.6}$$

$$P_0(t + \Delta t) - P_0(t) = P_0(t)(1 - \lambda\Delta t), \quad n = 0 \tag{12.7}$$

The above two equations constitute the system of differential-difference equations. We need to solve these equations.

Equation (12.7) can be written as

$$\frac{P_0'(t)}{P_0(t)} = -\lambda$$

Integrating both sides with respect to t, we get,

$$\log P_0(t) = -\lambda t + A \tag{12.8}$$

where A is constant of integration. Its value can be computed using the boundary conditions

$$P_n(0) = \begin{cases} 1, & n = 0 \\ 0, & n > 0 \end{cases} \tag{12.9}$$

Then for $t = 0$, $P_0(0) = 1$ and hence $A = 0$. Therefore,

$$P_0(t) = e^{-\lambda t} \tag{12.10}$$

Putting $n = 1$ in Eq. (12.6), we get

$$P_1'(t) = -\lambda P_1(t) + \lambda P_0(t) = -\lambda P_1(t) + \lambda e^{-\lambda t}$$

which is linear differential equation of first order. Its solution is

$$e^{\lambda t}P_1(t) = \lambda t + B \tag{12.11}$$

Using Eq. (12.9), $B = 0$. Thus, Eq. (12.11) can be rewritten as

$$P_1(t) = \lambda t e^{-\lambda t}$$

Arguing as above, we get

$$P_2(t) = \frac{(\lambda t)^2}{2!} e^{-\lambda t}$$

$$\ldots$$

$$P_n(t) = \frac{(\lambda t)^n}{n!} e^{-\lambda t}$$

which is a Poisson distribution.

Alternative method of deriving $P_n(t)$ can be using the moment generating function (z-transform).

Define the moment generating function as

$$P(z, t) = \sum_{n=0}^{\infty} P_n(t)\, z^n$$

and

$$P'(z, t) = \sum_{n=0}^{\infty} P'_n(t)\, z^n$$

Multiply both sides of Eq. (12.6) by z^n and taking summation for $n = 1, 2, \ldots, \infty$, we get,

$$\sum_{n=1}^{\infty} z^n P'_n(t) = -\lambda \sum_{n=1}^{\infty} z^n P_n(t) + \lambda \sum_{n=1}^{\infty} z^n P_{n-1}(t)$$

To this, we add $P'_0(t) = -\lambda P_0(t)$. Then

$$\sum_{n=0}^{\infty} z^n P'_n(t) = -\lambda \sum_{n=0}^{\infty} z^n P_n(t) + \lambda \sum_{n=0}^{\infty} z^{n+1} P_n(t)$$

Equivalently,

$$P'(z, t) = -\lambda P(z, t) + \lambda z P(z, t),$$

i.e.

$$\frac{P'(z, t)}{P(z, t)} = \lambda(z - 1)$$

Integrating both sides,

$$\log P(z, t) = \lambda(z - 1)\, t + A$$

To find A, constant of integration, put $t = 0$. Then $\log P(z, 0) = A$. But

$$A = \log P(z, 0) = \log\left(\sum_{n=0}^{\infty} z^n P_n(0)\right) = \log\left(P_0(0) + \sum_{n=1}^{\infty} z^n P_n(0)\right)$$

$$= \log(1 + 0) = \log(1) = 0 \text{ by (Eq. 12.8)}$$

Hence, $P(z, t) = e^{\lambda(z-1)t}$

Now $P_n(t)$ can be defined as

$$P_n(t) = \frac{1}{n!}\left[\frac{d^n}{dz^n} P(z, t)\right] \text{ at } z = 0.$$

Then $P_0(t) = P(0, t) = e^{-\lambda t}$

$$P_1(t) = \frac{1}{1!}\left[\frac{d}{dz} P(z, t)\right] = \lambda t e^{-\lambda t}$$

$$P_2(t) = \frac{1}{2!}\left[\frac{d^2}{dz^2} P(z, t)\right] = \frac{(\lambda t)^2}{2!} e^{-\lambda t}$$

$$\ldots\ldots$$

$$P_n(t) = \frac{(\lambda t)^n}{n!} e^{-\lambda t}$$

Thus, the probability of n-arrivals in time t follows Poisson law.

12.5 DISTRIBUTION OF INTER-ARRIVAL TIME

The time T between two consecutive arrivals is called ***inter-arrival time***. Here, mathematical development is given to show that T (inter-arrival time) follows negative exponential law.

Let $f(T)$ be the probability density function of arrivals in time T. Then we show that

$$f(T) = \lambda e^{-\lambda T} \tag{12.12}$$

where λ is an arrival rate in time t.

Proof: Let t be the instant of an arrival. Since there is no arrival during $(t, t + T)$ and $(t + T, t + T + \Delta T)$, arrival be at $t + T + \Delta T$. Putting $n = 0$ and $t = T + \Delta T$ in Eq. (12.11)

$$P_0(T + \Delta T) = e^{-\lambda(T + \Delta T)} = e^{-\lambda T}[1 - \lambda\Delta T + O(\Delta T)]$$

But $P_0(T) = e^{-\lambda T}$.

So $$P_0(T + \Delta T) - P_0(T) = P_0(T)[-\lambda\Delta T + O(\Delta T)]$$

Dividing both sides by ΔT and taking limit $\Delta T \to 0$, we get

$$P_0'(T) = -\lambda P_0(T) \tag{12.13}$$

Clearly, LHS of Eq. (12.13) is probability density function of T, say $f(T)$. Therefore,

$$f(T) = \lambda e^{-\lambda T} \tag{12.14}$$

which is negative exponential law of probability for T.

The Markovian property of inter-arrival times states that at any instant of the time until the next arrival occurs is independent of the time that has elapsed since the occurrence of the last arrival, i.e. Prob. $(T \geq t_1/T \geq t_0)$ = Prob. $(0 \leq T \leq t_1 - t_0)$.

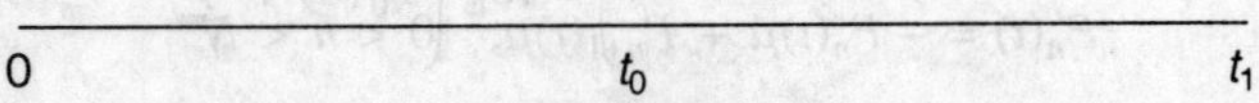

Figure 12.4

Proof: Using formula of conditional probability,

$$\text{Prob. } (T \geq t_1/T \geq t_0) = \frac{\text{Prob. } [(T \geq t_1) \text{ and } (T \geq t_0)]}{\text{Prob. } (T \geq t_0)}$$

$$= \frac{\int_{t_0}^{t_1} \lambda e^{-\lambda t} dt}{\int_{t_0}^{\infty} \lambda e^{-\lambda t} dt} = 1 - e^{-\lambda(t_1 - t_0)} = \text{Prob. } (0 \leq T \leq t_1 - t_0)$$

Hence, proved.

12.6 DISTRIBUTION OF DEPARTURES (PURE DEATH PROCESS)

The model in which only departures occur and no arrival takes place is called ***pure death process***. In this process, assume that there are N-customers in the system at time $t = 0$, no arrivals occur in the system, and departures occur at a rate μ per unit time. We will derive the distribution of departures from the system on the basis of the following three axioms:

1. The probability of exactly one departure during small interval Δt be given by $\mu\Delta t + O(\Delta t)$.
2. The term Δt is so small that the probability of more than one departure in time Δt is negligible.
3. The number of departures in non-overlapping intervals is mutually independent.

The following three cases arise:

Case 1: When $0 < n < N (1 \leq n \leq N - 1)$
The probability will be

$$P_n(t + \Delta t) = P_n(t)(1 - \mu\Delta t) + P_{n+1}(t)\, \mu\Delta t \tag{12.15}$$

Case 2: When $n = N$, that is, there are N-customers in the system. Then

$$P_N(t + \Delta t) = P_N(t)\, (1 - \mu\Delta t) \tag{12.16}$$

Case 3: When $n = 0$, that is, there is no customer in the system.

$$P_0(t + \Delta t) = P_0(t) + P_1(t)\, \mu\Delta t \tag{12.17}$$

Thus,

$$P_0(t + \Delta t) = P_0(t) + P_1(t)\, \mu\Delta t, \quad n = 0$$

$$P_n(t + \Delta t) = P_n(t)(1 - \mu\Delta t) + P_{n+1}(t)\, \mu\Delta t, \quad 0 < n < N$$

$$P_N(t + \Delta t) = P_N(t)(1 - \mu\Delta t), \quad n = N$$

Rearranging the above equations, dividing by Δt and taking limit $\Delta t \to 0$, we get

$$P'_0(t) = P_1(t)\mu, \quad n = 0 \tag{12.18}$$

$$P'_n(t) = -P_n(t)\mu + P_{n+1}(t)\mu, \quad 0 < n < N \tag{12.19}$$

$$P'_N(t) = -P_N(t)\mu, \quad n = N \tag{12.20}$$

Equations (12.18)–(12.20) are the required system of differential-difference equations for pure death process. The solution of Eq. (12.20) can be written as

$$\log P_N(t) = -\mu t + A$$

where A is constant of integration. Its value can be computed using the boundary conditions

$$P_n(0) = \begin{cases} 1, & n = N \neq 0 \\ 0, & n \neq N \end{cases}$$

gives $A = 0$. Therefore,

$$P_N(t) = e^{-\mu t} \tag{12.21}$$

Putting $n = N - 1$ in Eq. (12.19), we get

$$P'_{N-1}(t) + \mu P_{N-1}(t) = \mu e^{-\mu t}$$

which is linear differential equation of first order. Its solution is

$$P_{N-1}(t) = \mu t e^{-\mu t}$$

Putting $n = N - 2, N - 3, \ldots, N - n$, in Eq. (12.19), we get

$$P_{n-k}(t) = \frac{(\mu t)^k}{k!} e^{-\mu t}$$

In general,

$$P_n(t) = \frac{(\mu t)^{N-n}}{(N-n)!} e^{-\mu t}$$

which is a Poisson distribution.

12.7 DISTRIBUTION OF SERVICE TIME

Let T be the random variable denoting the service time and t be the possible value of T. Let $S(t)$ and $s(t)$ be the cumulative density function and the probability density function of T respectively. To find $s(t)$ for the Poisson departure case, it can be observed that the probability of no service during time $(0, t)$, which means the probability of having no departures during the same period. Thus,

Prob. (service time $T \geq t$) = Prob. (no departure during t) = $P_N(t)$

where there are N-units in the system and no arrival is allowed after N. Therefore, $P_N(t) = e^{-\mu t}$. So

$$S(t) = \text{Prob. (service time } T \leq t) = 1 - \text{Prob. (service time } T \geq t) = 1 - e^{-\mu t}$$

Differentiating both sides with respect to 't', we have

$$s(t) = \begin{cases} \mu e^{-\mu t}, & t \geq 0 \\ 0, & t < 0 \end{cases}$$

This shows that the service time distribution is exponential with mean service time $1/\mu$ and variance $1/\mu^2$.

12.8 SOLUTION OF QUEUING MODELS

The solution of queuing models defined in Section 12.3 consists of the following steps:

Step 1: To derive the system of steady-state equations governing the queue.

Step 2: To solve these equations for finding the probability distribution of the queue length.

Step 3: To obtain probability density function for waiting time distribution.

Step 4: To find busy period distribution.

Step 5: To derive formula for L_s, L_q, W_s, W_q, and var$\{n\}$ or $v\{n\}$.

Step 6: To obtain the probability of arrival during service time of any customer.

In the following sections, we discuss each model in detail.

12.9 MODEL 1 (M/M/1): (∞/FCFS): BIRTH AND DEATH MODEL

Birth and death model deals with a queuing system having a single server, Poisson arrival, exponential service and there is no limit on the system's capacity while the customers are served on a "first come, first served" basis.

Step 1: Formulation of difference-differential equations:

Let $P_n(t)$ denote the probability of n-customers in the system at time t. Then the probability that the system has n-customers at time $(t + \Delta t)$ may be expressed as the sum of the combined probability of following four mutually exclusive and exhaustive events:

$$\begin{aligned} P_n(t + \Delta t) = \; & P_n(t) \times P(\text{no arrival in } \Delta t) \times P(\text{no service completion in } \Delta t) \\ & + P_n(t) \times P(\text{one arrival in } \Delta t) \times P(\text{one service completion in } \Delta t) \\ & + P_{n+1}(t) \times P(\text{no arrival in } \Delta t) \times P(\text{one service completion in } \Delta t) \\ & + P_{n-1}(t) \times P(\text{one arrival in } \Delta t) \times P(\text{no service completion in } \Delta t) \\ = \; & P_n(t)(1 - \lambda\Delta t)(1 - \mu\Delta t) + P_n(t)\, \lambda\Delta t\, \mu\Delta t \\ & + P_{n+1}(t)(1 - \lambda\Delta t)\, \mu\Delta t + P_{n-1}(t)\, \lambda\Delta t\, (1 - \mu\Delta t) \end{aligned}$$

or
$$P_n(t + \Delta t) - P_n(t) = -(\lambda + \mu)\, P_n(t)\, \Delta t + P_{n+1}(t)\, \mu\Delta t + P_{n-1}(t)\, \lambda\Delta t$$

Dividing by Δt and taking limit $\Delta t \to 0$, we get

$$P_n'(t) = -(\lambda + \mu)\, P_n(t) + \mu P_{n+1}(t) + \lambda P_{n-1}(t),\ n \geq 1.$$

If there is no customer in the system at time $(t + \Delta t)$, there will be no service during Δt. Then for $n = 0$,

$$\begin{aligned} P_0(t + \Delta t) & = P_0(t) \times P(\text{no arrival in } \Delta t) \\ & \quad + P_1(t) \times P(\text{no arrival in } \Delta t) \times P(\text{one service completion in } \Delta t) \\ & = P_0(t)(1 - \lambda\Delta t) + P_1(t)(1 - \lambda\Delta t)\, \mu\Delta t \end{aligned}$$

or
$$P_0(t + \Delta t) - P_0(t) = -\lambda P_0(t)\, \Delta t + P_1(t)(1 - \lambda\Delta t)\, \mu\Delta t$$

Dividing by Δt and taking limit $\Delta t \to 0$, we get

$$P_0'(t) = -\lambda P_0(t) + \mu P_1(t),\ n = 0.$$

Thus, the required difference-differential equations are

$$P_n'(t) = -(\lambda + \mu)\, P_n(t) + P_{n+1}(t)\,\mu + P_{n-1}(t)\lambda, \quad n \geq 1 \tag{12.22}$$

$$P_0'(t) = -\lambda P_0(t) + \mu P_1(t), \quad n = 0 \tag{12.23}$$

Step 2: Deriving the steady-state difference-differential equations:
Using Eq. (12.1), the steady-state difference-differential equations are

$$0 = -(\lambda + \mu)P_n + \mu P_{n+1} + \lambda P_{n-1}, \quad n \geq 1 \tag{12.24}$$

$$0 = -\lambda P_0 + \mu P_1, \quad n = 0 \tag{12.25}$$

Step 3: To solve Eqs. (12.24) and (12. 25):
Take P_0. Then Eq. (12.25) gives $P_1 = (\lambda/\mu)\, P_0$.
For $n = 1$, Eq. (12.24) gives $P_2 = (\lambda/\mu)\, P_1 = (\lambda/\mu)^2\, P_0$.
In general, $P_n = (\lambda/\mu)^n\, P_0 = \rho^n P_0$.
To obtain the value of P_0, we proceed as follows:

$$1 = \sum_{n=0}^{\infty} P_n = \sum_{n=0}^{\infty} \rho^n P_0 = P_0 \sum_{n=0}^{\infty} \rho^n = \frac{P_0}{1-\rho}$$

or

$$P_0 = 1 - \rho \tag{12.26}$$

and

$$P_n = \rho^n(1 - \rho). \tag{12.27}$$

Step 4: Characteristics of Model:

1. Probability of queue size being greater than or equal to n

$$= \sum_{k=n}^{\infty} P_k = \sum_{k=n}^{\infty} (1-\rho)\,\rho^k = \rho^n \tag{12.28}$$

2. Average number of customers in the system

$$L_s = \sum_{n=0}^{\infty} nP_n = \sum_{n=0}^{\infty} n(1-\rho)\,\rho^n$$

$$= \rho(1-\rho) \sum_{n=1}^{\infty} n\rho^{n-1}$$

$$= \rho(1-\rho) \sum_{n=1}^{\infty} \frac{d}{d\rho}\rho^n$$

$$= \rho(1-\rho)\frac{d}{d\rho} \sum_{n=1}^{\infty} \rho^n = \rho(1-\rho)\frac{d}{d\rho}\left(\frac{1}{1-\rho}\right)$$

$$= \frac{\rho}{1-\rho} = \frac{\lambda}{\mu - \lambda} \tag{12.29}$$

3. Average queue length

$$L_q = \sum_{n=1}^{\infty}(n-1)P_n = \sum_{n=1}^{\infty} nP_n - \sum_{n=1}^{\infty} P_n$$

$$= \sum_{n=1}^{\infty} nP_n - \left(\sum_{n=0}^{\infty} P_n - P_0\right)$$

$$= \frac{\rho}{1-\rho} - [1-(1-\rho)] \quad \text{[using Eqs. (12.29) \& (12.26)]}$$

$$= \frac{\rho^2}{1-\rho} = \frac{\lambda^2}{\mu(\mu-\lambda)} \tag{12.30}$$

4. Average length of non-empty queue

$$= \frac{L_q}{P(n>1)}$$

$$P(n>1) = \sum_{n=0}^{\infty} P_n - P_0 - P_1 = 1 - P_0 - \rho P_0 = 1-(1+\rho)(1-\rho) = \rho^2$$

Therefore, the average length of the non-empty queue

$$= \frac{\rho^2}{1-\rho}\frac{1}{\rho^2} = \frac{1}{1-\rho} = \frac{\mu}{\mu-\lambda} \tag{12.31}$$

5. Variance of queue length

$$V\{n\} = \sum_{n=0}^{\infty} n^2 P_n - \left(\sum_{n=0}^{\infty} nP_n\right)^2$$

$$= \sum_{n=0}^{\infty} n^2(1-\rho)\rho^n - \left(\frac{\rho}{1-\rho}\right)^2$$

$$= (1-\rho)\sum_{n=0}^{\infty} n^2\rho^n - \left(\frac{\rho}{1-\rho}\right)^2$$

$$= (1-\rho)\,\rho X - \left(\frac{\rho}{1-\rho}\right)^2$$

where $X = \sum_{n=1}^{\infty} n^2\rho^{n-1}$. Integrating both sides by ρ,

$$\int_0^{\rho} X\, d\rho = \sum_{n=1}^{\infty}\frac{n^2\rho^n}{n} = \frac{\rho}{(1-\rho)^2}$$

Now differentiating both sides with respect to ρ, we get, $X = (1+\rho)/(1-\rho)^3$.

Therefore,

$$V\{n\} = \frac{\rho(1-\rho)(1+\rho)}{(1-\rho)^3} - \left(\frac{\rho}{1-\rho}\right)^2 = \frac{\rho}{(1-\rho)^2} \tag{12.32}$$

Waiting time distribution: The waiting time of a customer in a system is that time a customer entering for service immediately upon arrival. Let w be the time spent in the queue and $\psi_w(t)$ be its cumulative probability distribution. Then

$$\begin{aligned}\psi_n(0) &= P(w = 0) = P\text{ (no customer in the system upon arrival)}\\ &= P_0(1-\rho)\end{aligned} \tag{12.33}$$

We want to find $\psi_w(t)$. Let there be n-customers in the system upon arrival. Then for a customer, in order to go into service at a time between $(0, t)$, all n-customers must have been served by time t. Let $s_1, s_2, \ldots, s_n$ denote the service times of n-customers respectively. Then

$$w = \begin{cases} \sum_{i=1}^{n} s_i, & n \geq 1 \\ 0, & n = 0 \end{cases} \tag{12.34}$$

Then the probability distribution function of waiting time, w, for a customer who has to wait is given by

$$P(w \leq t) = P\left(\sum_{i=1}^{n} s_i \leq t\right), \quad n \geq 1 \tag{12.35}$$

Since the service time for each customer is independent, its probability distribution function is $\mu e^{-\mu t}(t > 0)$ where μ is the mean service rate.

$$\begin{aligned}\psi_w(t) &= \sum_{n=1}^{\infty} P_n \times P\,[(n-1)\text{-customers are served in time } t)\\ &\quad \times P\text{ (one customer is served in time } \Delta t)\\ &= \sum_{n=1}^{\infty} (1-\rho)\,\rho^n \frac{(\mu t)^{n-1}}{(n-1)!} e^{-\mu t}\,\mu \Delta t\end{aligned} \tag{12.36}$$

Hence, the waiting time of a customer who has to wait is given by

$$\psi(w) = \frac{d}{dt}\psi_w(t) = \rho(1-\rho)\,\mu e^{-\mu t(1-\rho)} = \lambda\left(\frac{1-\lambda}{\mu}\right)e^{-(\mu-\lambda)t} \tag{12.37}$$

Next, we define the characteristics of waiting time distribution.

1. Average waiting time of a customer in the queue

$$\begin{aligned}W_q &= \int_0^\infty t\psi(w)\,dt = \int_0^\infty t\rho(1-\rho)\,\mu e^{-\mu t(1-\rho)}\,dt\\ &= \frac{\rho}{\mu(1-\rho)} = \frac{\lambda}{\mu(\mu-\lambda)}\end{aligned} \tag{12.38}$$

2. Average waiting time of an arrival that has to wait in the system

$$W_s = \frac{L_q}{P(w > 0)}$$

Now $P(w > 0) = 1 - P(w = 0) = 1 - P_0 = 1 - (1 - \rho) = \rho$

Therefore, $$W_s = \frac{\rho}{\mu(1-\rho)\rho} = \frac{1}{\mu - \lambda} \quad (12.39)$$

3. The busy period distribution is

$$\psi(w/w > 0) = \frac{\psi(w)}{P(w > 0)} = (\mu - \lambda)\, e^{-(\mu - \lambda)t} \quad (12.40)$$

EXAMPLE 12.1: The arrival rate of a customer at a service window of a cinema hall follows a probability distribution with a mean rate of 45 per hour. The service rate of the clerk follows Poisson distribution with a mean of 60 per hour.

(a) What is the probability of having no customer in the system?
(b) What is the probability of having five customers in the system?
(c) Find L_s, L_q, W_s and W_q.

Solution: Given, arrival rate, $\lambda = 45$ per hour, service rate, $\mu = 60$ per hour. Then $\rho = \lambda/\mu = 0.75$.

(a) Probability of having no customer in the system $= P_0 = 1 - \rho = 1 - 0.75 = 0.25$.
(b) Probability of having five customers in the system $= P_5 = (1 - \rho)\,\rho^5 = 0.0593$.
(c) $L_s = \dfrac{\rho}{1-\rho} = 3$ customers. $\quad L_q = \dfrac{\rho^2}{1-\rho} = 2.25$ customers.

$W_s = \dfrac{1}{\mu - \lambda} = 0.067$ hour. $\quad W_q = \dfrac{\rho}{\mu - \lambda} = 0.05$ hour.

EXAMPLE 12.2: An arrival rate at a telephone booth is considered to be Poisson with an average time of 10 minutes and exponential call lengths averaging 3 minutes.

(a) Find the fraction of a day that the telephone will be busy.
(b) What is the probability that an arrival at the booth will have to wait?
(c) What is the probability that an arrival will have to wait more than 10 minutes before the phone is free?
(d) What is the probability that it will take him more than 10 minutes altogether to wait for phone and complete his call?

Solution: Given, arrival rate, $\lambda = 1/10$ per minute, service rate, $\mu = 1/3$ per minute.

(a) The fraction of the day that the phone will be busy, $\rho = \lambda/\mu = 0.3$.
(b) Probability that an arrival at the booth will have to wait $= 1 - P_0 = 1 - (1 - \rho) = \rho = 0.3$.
(c) Probability that an arrival will have to wait for more than 10 minutes before the phone is free $= \displaystyle\int_{10}^{\infty} \left(1 - \frac{\lambda}{\mu}\right) \lambda e^{-(\mu-\lambda)t}\, dt = 0.3e^{-2.3} = 0.03$.
(d) Probability of an arrival waiting in the system is greater than or equal to $10 = \displaystyle\int_{10}^{\infty} (\mu - \lambda)\, e^{-(\mu-\lambda)t}\, dt = e^{-2.3} = 0.1$.

EXAMPLE 12.3: Vehicles pass through a toll gate at a rate of 90 per hour. The average time to pass through the gate is 36 seconds. The arrival rate and the service rate follow Poisson distribution. There is a complaint that the vehicles wait for long duration. The authority is willing to install one more gate to reduce the average time to pass through the toll gate to 30 seconds if the idle time of the toll gate is less that 10% and the average queue length at the gate is more than 5 vehicles. Discuss whether the installation of the second gate is justified or not.

Solution: Given, arrival rate of vehicles at the toll gate, $\lambda = 90$ per hour, departure rate of vehicles through the gate, $\mu = 3{,}600/60 = 100$ vehicles per hour.
Then $\rho = \lambda/\mu = 0.9$.

(a) Waiting number of vehicles in the queue

$$L_q = \frac{\rho^2}{1-\rho} = 8.1 \text{ vehicles.}$$

(b) Expected time taken to pass through the gate = 30 seconds.

Then service rate, $\mu = 30$ seconds $= 3{,}600/30 = 120$ vehicles per hour.
So $\rho = \lambda/\mu = 0.75$.
Percent of the idle time of the gate $= 1 - \rho = 25\%$.

Thus, the average waiting number of vehicles in the queue is more than 5 but the idle time of the toll gate is not less than 10%. Hence, the installation of another gate is not justified.

EXAMPLE 12.4: At what average rate must a clerk at a super market work in order to ensure a probability of 0.90 that the customer will not wait longer than 12 minutes? It is assumed that there is only one counter, at which customers arrive in a Poisson fashion at an average rate of 15 per hour. The length of service by the clerk has an exponential distribution.

Solution: Given, arrival rate, $\lambda = 15/60 = 0.25$ customers per minute.
Let the departure rate of customers be μ.
Probability that the customer will not have to wait more than 12 minutes

$$= 1 - 0.9 = 0.1. \text{ Therefore, } 0.1 = \int_{12}^{\infty} \left(\frac{\lambda}{\mu}\right)(\mu - \lambda)\, e^{-(\mu-\lambda)t}\, dt$$

or
$$0.1 = \frac{\lambda}{\mu} e^{-12(\mu-\lambda)}$$

or
$$0.4\mu = e^{3-12\mu} \text{ gives } \frac{1}{\mu} = 2.48 \text{ minutes/customer.}$$

EXAMPLE 12.5: In a railway Marshall yard, goods trains arrive at a rate of 30 trains per day. Assuming that the inter-arrival time follows an exponential distribution and the service distribution is also an exponential with an average 36 minutes, calculate

(a) The mean size queue, and

(b) The probability that the queue size exceeds 10.

If the input of trains increases to an average 33 per day, what will be the changes in (a) and (b)?

Solution: Given, arrival rate, $\lambda = 30/(60 \times 24) = 1/48$ trains per minute, service rate, $\mu = 1/36$ trains per minute. Then $\rho = \lambda/\mu = 0.75$.

(a) The mean queue size, c. $L_s = \dfrac{\rho}{1-\rho} = 3$ trains.

(b) Probability (queue size $\geq$ 10 trains) $= \rho^{10} = 0.056$.

When the input increases to 33 trains per day
i.e. $\lambda = 33/(60 \times 24) = 11/480$ trains per minute, then $\rho = 0.83$. Here,

(a) The mean queue size, c. $L_s = \dfrac{\rho}{1-\rho} = 4.88 \approx 5$ trains.

(b) Probability (queue size $\geq$ 10 trains) $= \rho^{10} = 0.155$.

EXAMPLE 12.6: In a maintenance shop, the inter-arrival times at tool crib are exponential with an average time of 10 minutes. The length of the service (i.e. the amount of time taken by the tool crib operator to meet the needs of the maintenance man) time is assumed to be exponentially distributed with a mean 6 minutes. Find

(a) The probability that a person arriving at the booth will have to wait.
(b) The average length of the queue that forms and the average time that an operator spends in the queuing system.
(c) The probability that an arrival will have to wait for more than 12 minutes for service and to obtain his tools.
(d) The estimate of the fraction of the day that the tool crib operator will be idle.
(e) The probability that there will be six or more operators waiting for the service.
(f) The manager of the shop will install a second booth when an arrival would expect to wait 10 minutes or more for the service. By how much must the rate of arrival be increased in order to justify a second booth?

Solution: Given, arrival rate, $\lambda = 60/10 = 6$ per hour, departure rate, $\mu = 60/6 = 10$ per hour.

(a) Probability that the arrival will have to wait $= \rho = \lambda/\mu = 0.6$.

(b) Average number of arrivals waiting time in the queue, $L_q = \dfrac{\rho^2}{1-\rho} = 0.9$ and

Average waiting time in the system, $W_s = \dfrac{1}{\mu - \lambda} = 0.25$ hour.

(c) Probability that the arrival will have to wait more than 12 minutes

$$= \int_{12}^{\infty} \left(\frac{\lambda}{\mu}\right)(\mu - \lambda)\, e^{-(\mu-\lambda)t}\, dt = 0.6e^{-4/5} = 0.27.$$

(d) Probability of the tool crib operator to be idle $= P_0 = 1 - \rho = 0.4$.
Therefore, for 40% of the time the tool crib operator will remain free.

(e) Probability of six or more operators waiting for service $= \rho^6 = 0.05$.

(f) Average waiting time of a customer in the queue

$$W_q = \frac{\lambda}{\mu(\mu - \lambda)} = \frac{3}{20} \text{ hours} = 3 \times \frac{60}{20} = 9 \text{ minutes}.$$

The installation of the second booth will be justified if the arrival rate, λ' (say) is greater than the waiting time. Given W_q = 10 minutes = 1/6 hours. Then

$$\frac{1}{6} = \frac{\lambda'}{\mu(\mu - \lambda')} = \text{gives } \lambda' = 6.25$$

Therefore, if the arrival rate exceeds 6.25 per hour, the second booth will be justified.

12.10 MODEL 2 (M/M/1): (N/FCFS)

In Model 2 we assume that the capacity of the system is finite (say), N i.e. the system cannot accommodate more than N-arrivals in the system due to its own constraints. For example, a finite queue is observed in ICU-unit in a hospital. This model deals with a queuing system having a single server, Poisson arrival, exponential service and the customers are served on a "first come, first served" basis.

Step 1: Formulation of difference-differential equations:
The required probabilities equations derived in Model 1 will hold for this model for $n < N$. So

$$P_0(t + \Delta t) = P_0(t)\,(1 - \lambda\Delta t) + P_1(t)(1 - \lambda\Delta t)\,\mu\Delta t, \quad n = 0$$

$$P_n(t + \Delta t) = P_n(t)(1 - \lambda\Delta t)(1 - \mu\Delta t) + P_n(t)\lambda\Delta t\,\mu\Delta t$$
$$+ P_{n+1}(t)(1 - \lambda\Delta t)\,\mu\Delta t + P_{n-1}(t)\,\lambda\Delta t\,(1 - \mu\Delta t), \quad 1 \le n \le N$$

$$P_n(t + \Delta t) = P_n(t)(1 - \mu\Delta t) + P_{n-1}(t)\,\lambda\Delta t(1 - \mu\Delta t), \quad n = N$$

Then after simplification, the differential equations are

$$P_0'(t) = -\lambda P_0(t) + \mu P_1(t), \quad n = 0 \tag{12.41}$$

$$P_n'(t) = -(\lambda + \mu)\,P_n(t) + P_{n+1}(t)\,\mu + P_{n-1}(t)\lambda, \quad 1 \le n \le N \tag{12.42}$$

$$P_n'(t) = -\mu P_n(t) + \lambda P_{n-1}(t), \quad n = N \tag{12.43}$$

Step 2: Deriving the steady-state difference-differential equations:
Using Eq. (12.1), the steady-state difference-differential equations are

$$0 = -\lambda P_0 + \mu P_1, \quad n = 0$$

or
$$\lambda P_0 = \mu P_1, \quad n = 0 \tag{12.44}$$

$$0 = -(\lambda + \mu)\,P_n + \mu P_{n+1} + \lambda P_{n-1}, \quad 1 \le n \le N$$

or
$$\mu P_{n+1} = (\lambda + \mu)P_n - \lambda P_{n-1}, \quad 1 \le n \le N \tag{12.45}$$

$$0 = -\mu P_n + \lambda P_{n-1}, \quad n = N$$

or
$$\mu P_n = \lambda P_{n-1}, \quad n = N \tag{12.46}$$

Take P_0 and then Eq. (12.44) gives $P_1 = (\lambda/\mu)\,P_0$.
Solving Eqs. (12.44) and (12.45) iteratively gives $P_n = (\lambda/\mu)^n\,P_0$, $n \le (N - 1)$ and Eq. (12.46) gives $P_N = (\lambda/\mu)^N\,P_0$.

In general, $P_n = (\lambda/\mu)^n P_0 = \rho^n P_0$, for all n.
To obtain the value of P_0, we proceed as follows:

$$1 = \sum_{n=0}^{N} P_n = \sum_{n=0}^{N} \rho^n P_0 = P_0 \sum_{n=0}^{N} \rho^n = \begin{cases} \dfrac{P_0(1-\rho^{N+1})}{(1-\rho)}, & \rho \neq 1 \\ P_0(1+N), & \rho = 1 \end{cases}$$

or

$$P_0 = \begin{cases} \dfrac{1-\rho}{1-\rho^{N+1}}, & \rho \neq 1 \\ \dfrac{1}{N+1}, & \rho = 1 \end{cases} \tag{12.47}$$

and

$$P_n = \begin{cases} \dfrac{\rho^n(1-\rho)}{1-\rho^{N+1}}, & \rho \neq 1 \\ \dfrac{1}{N+1}, & \rho = 1 \end{cases} \tag{12.48}$$

The steady-state solution exists even if $\lambda > \mu$ because due to finite capacity of the system, arrival is controlled. If $\lambda < \mu$ and $N \to \infty$, we get Model 1.

Step 4: Characteristics of Model:

1. Average number of customers in the system

$$L_s = \sum_{n=0}^{N} nP_n = \sum_{n=0}^{N} nP_0\rho^n$$

$$= P_0\rho \sum_{n=0}^{N} n\rho^{n-1}$$

$$= P_0\rho \sum_{n=0}^{N} \frac{d}{d\rho}\rho^n$$

$$= P_0\rho \frac{d}{d\rho} \sum_{n=0}^{N} \rho^n = P_0\rho \frac{d}{d\rho}\left(\frac{1-\rho^{N+1}}{1-\rho}\right)$$

$$= \begin{cases} \dfrac{\rho}{1-\rho^{N+1}}\left[\dfrac{1-(N+1)\rho^N + N\rho^{N+1}}{1-\rho}\right], & \rho \neq 1 \\ \dfrac{N}{2}, & \rho = 1 \end{cases} \tag{12.49}$$

2. Fraction of time system is empty in $P_N = P_0\rho^N$
   Effective arrival rate $\lambda' = \lambda(1 - P_N)$
3. Expected number of customers waiting in the queue

$$L_q = L_s - \frac{\lambda'}{\mu} \tag{12.50}$$

4. Expected waiting time of a customer in the system

$$W_s = \frac{L_s}{\lambda'} \tag{12.51}$$

5. Expected waiting time of a customer in the queue

$$W_q = W_s - \frac{1}{\mu} \tag{12.52}$$

EXAMPLE 12.7: If for a period of two hours in the day (8.00 am to 10.00 am) trains arrive at the yard every 20 minutes, but the service time continues to remain 36 minutes, then calculate for this period

(a) the probability that the yard is empty,

(b) the average number of trains in the system, on the assumption that the yard capacity is limited to four trains only.

Solution: Given $N = 4$, arrival rate, $\lambda = 1/20$ trains per minute, service rate, $\mu = 1/36$ trains per minute then $\rho = \lambda/\mu = 1.8 > 1$.

(a) Probability that the yard is empty, $P_0 = \dfrac{1-\rho}{1-\rho^{N+1}} = 0.044$

(b) Average number of trains in the system

$$L_s = P_0 \sum_{n=0}^{4} n\rho^n = P_0(\rho + 2\rho^2 + 3\rho^3 + 4\rho^4) = 0.044 \times 67.77 = 2.98 \approx 3 \text{ trains.}$$

EXAMPLE 12.8: A petrol station has a single pump and space for not more than three cars (two waiting, one being served). A car arriving when the space is filled to its capacity goes elsewhere for petrol. Cars arrive according to a Poisson distribution at a mean rate of every 8 minutes. Their service time has an exponential distribution with a mean of 4 minutes.

The owner has the opportunity of renting an adjacent piece of land which would provide space for an individual car to wait. (He cannot build another pump.) The rent would be Rs. 10.00 per week. The expected net profit from each customer is Rs. 0.50 and the station is open for 10 hours every day. Would it be profitable to rent the additional space?

Solution: Given $N = 3$, arrival rate, $\lambda = 1/8$ cars per minute, service rate, $\mu = 1/4$ cars per minute then $\rho = \lambda/\mu = 0.5$.

Probability that there is no car in the system, $P_0 = \dfrac{1-\rho}{1-\rho^{N+1}} = 0.533.$

Probability of the system with utmost capacity, $P_3 = P_0\rho^3 = 0.067$.

So, the proportion of the lost customer = 0.067.

Under the new decision, $N = 4$ and $P_0 = 0.516$, $P_4 = 0.032$.

Thus, the proportion of the lost customer is 0.032.

Therefore, increase in cars served per hour $= \lambda\,(0.067 - 0.032) \times 60$

$= 0.262$ cars per hour.

Then increase in cars served per week $= 0.262 \times 10 \times 7 = 18.34$ cars per week

and profit per week $= 0.50 \times 18.34 =$ Rs. 9.17.

Since the rent for additional space would be Rs. 10.00 per week, it is not economical to go for the rented additional floor space.

12.11 MODEL 3 (M/M/c): (∞/FCFS)

Here the system has multiple servers in parallel equal to c. It is assumed that customers arrive at an average rate of λ following the Poisson fashion and are served according to "first come, first served"—queue discipline. These c-servers are identical, each serving customers according to an exponential distribution with an average rate of μ-customers. When there are n-customers in the system, the service rate of the server is obtained in the following two situations:

1. When the number of customers in the system is less than that of the servers (i.e. $n < c$), there will be no queue and $(c - n)$-servers will be idle. Hence, service rate $\mu_n = n\mu,\ n < c$.
2. When the number of customers in the system is more than or equal to the number of the servers (i.e. $n \geq c$), all servers will be busy and $(n - c)$-customers will form a queue. Then the service rate is $\mu_n = c\mu,\ n \geq c$.

Arguing as in Model 1, the steady-state difference-differential equations are

$$0 = -\lambda P_0 + \mu P_1, \quad n = 0 \tag{12.53}$$

$$0 = -(\lambda + n\mu)\, P_n + (n + 1)\, \mu P_{n+1} + \lambda P_{n-1}, \quad 1 \leq n < c \tag{12.54}$$

$$0 = -(\lambda + c\mu)\, P_n + c\mu P_{n+1} + \lambda P_{n-1}, \quad n \geq c \tag{12.55}$$

Then the probability of n-customers in the system is given by

$$P_n = \begin{cases} \dfrac{1}{n!}\rho^n P_0, & 1 \leq n \leq c \\[2mm] \dfrac{1}{c^{n-c}c!}\rho^n P_0, & n \geq c \end{cases} \tag{12.56}$$

To obtain the value of P_0, we proceed as follows:

$$1 = \sum_{n=0}^{\infty} P_n = \sum_{n=0}^{c-1} P_n + \sum_{n=c}^{\infty} P_n$$

$$= \sum_{n=0}^{c-1} \frac{1}{n!}\left(\frac{\lambda}{\mu}\right)^n P_0 + \sum_{n=c}^{\infty} \frac{1}{c!c^{n-c}}\left(\frac{\lambda}{\mu}\right)^n P_0$$

$$= P_0\left[\sum_{n=0}^{c-1} \frac{c^n}{n!}\left(\frac{\lambda}{c\mu}\right)^n + \sum_{n=c}^{\infty} \frac{c^n}{c!c^{n-c}}\left(\frac{\lambda}{c\mu}\right)^n\right]$$

$$= P_0\left[\sum_{n=0}^{c-1} \frac{(\rho c)^n}{n!} + \frac{c^c}{c!}\sum_{n=c}^{\infty} \rho^n\right]$$

$$= P_0\left[\sum_{n=0}^{c-1} \frac{(\rho c)^n}{n!} + \frac{c^c}{c!}\frac{\rho^c}{1-\rho}\right]$$

$$= P_0\left[\sum_{n=0}^{c-1} \frac{(\rho c)^n}{n!} + \frac{(\rho c)^c}{c!(1-\rho)}\right]$$

or $$P_0 = \left[\sum_{n=0}^{c-1} \frac{(\rho c)^n}{n!} + \frac{(\rho c)^c}{c!(1-\rho)}\right]^{-1} \tag{12.57}$$

Characteristics of the Model:

1. Probability that an arrival has to wait = Prob ($n \geq c$)

$$= \sum_{n=c}^{\infty} \frac{1}{c!c^{n-c}} \left(\frac{\lambda}{\mu}\right)^n P_0 \tag{12.58}$$

2. Probability that an arrival enters into the service without wait

$$= 1 - \text{Prob}\ (n \geq c)$$

$$= 1 - \sum_{n=c}^{\infty} \frac{1}{c!c^{n-c}} \left(\frac{\lambda}{\mu}\right)^n P_0 \tag{12.59}$$

3. Average queue length

$$L_q = \sum_{n=c}^{\infty} (n-c) P_n = \sum_{x=0}^{\infty} x P_{c+x} \quad \text{Put } n - c = x$$

$$= \sum_{x=0}^{\infty} x \frac{1}{c!c^x} \left(\frac{\lambda}{\mu}\right)^{c+x} P_0$$

$$= \frac{1}{c!} \left(\frac{\lambda}{\mu}\right)^c P_0 \sum_{x=0}^{\infty} x \left(\frac{\lambda}{c\mu}\right)^x$$

$$= \frac{1}{c!} \left(\frac{\lambda}{\mu}\right)^c P_0 \sum_{x=0}^{\infty} x y^x \quad \text{Put } y = \left(\frac{\lambda}{c\mu}\right)$$

$$= \frac{1}{c!} \left(\frac{\lambda}{\mu}\right)^c y P_0 \sum_{x=0}^{\infty} x y^{x-1}$$

$$= \frac{1}{c!} \left(\frac{\lambda}{\mu}\right)^c y P_0 \sum_{x=0}^{\infty} \frac{d}{dy} y^x$$

$$= \frac{1}{c!} \left(\frac{\lambda}{\mu}\right)^c y P_0 \frac{d}{dy} \sum_{x=0}^{\infty} y^x$$

$$= \frac{1}{c!} \left(\frac{\lambda}{\mu}\right)^c y P_0 \frac{d}{dy} \frac{1}{1-y}$$

$$= \frac{\lambda\mu (\lambda/\mu)^c}{(c-1)!(c\mu - \lambda)^2} P_0 \tag{12.60}$$

4. Average number of customers in the system

$$L_s = L_q + \left(\frac{\lambda}{\mu}\right) = \frac{\lambda\mu(\lambda/\mu)^c}{(c-1)!(c\mu-\lambda)^2} P_0 + \left(\frac{\lambda}{\mu}\right) \tag{12.61}$$

5. Average waiting time of a customer in the queue

$$W_q = \frac{L_q}{\lambda} \tag{12.62}$$

6. Average waiting time of a customer in the system

$$W_s = W_q + \frac{1}{\mu} \tag{12.63}$$

EXAMPLE 12.9: A tax consulting firm has four service stations (counters) in his office to receive people who have problems and complaints about their income, wealth and sales taxes. Arrivals follow a Poisson distribution and average 8 persons in 8 hours service day for six days. Each tax advisor spends an irregular amount of time servicing the arrivals which found to have an exponential distribution. The average service time is 20 minutes. Calculate the average number of customers in the system, the average number of customers waiting to be served, average time a customer spends in the system, and average waiting time for a customer in the queue.

Calculate how many hours a week a tax advisor spends performing his job. What is the probability that a customer has to wait before he gets service? What is the expected number of idle tax advisors at any specific time?

Solution: Given $c = 4$, arrival rate, $\lambda = 80/8 = 10$ clients per hour, service rate, $\mu = 60/20 = 3$ clients per hour.

Then
$$P_0 = \left[\sum_{n=0}^{c-1} \frac{(\rho c)^n}{n!} + \frac{(\rho c)^c}{c!(1-\rho)}\right]^{-1} = 0.021$$

$P_1 = 0.071$, $P_2 = 0.118$, $P_3 = 0.132$.

1. Average number of customers in a queue, $L_q = \dfrac{\lambda\mu(\lambda/\mu)^c}{(c-1)!\,(c\mu-\lambda)^2} P_0 = 3.3$

2. Average number of customers in a system, $L_s = L_q + \left(\dfrac{\lambda}{\mu}\right) = 3.3 + 3.3 = 6.6$

3. Average waiting time of a customer in the queue, $W_q = \dfrac{L_q}{\lambda} = 0.33$ hour

$= 20$ minutes

4. Average waiting time of a customer in the system, $W_s = W_q + \dfrac{1}{\mu} = 0.66$ hour

$= 40$ minutes

5. Probability that a customer has to wait before getting the service

$$= \frac{3(10/3)^4}{(4-1)!(12-10)} P_0 = 0.66$$

6. Expected number of idle tax advisors at any instant of time

$$= 4P_0 + 3P_1 + 2P_2 + 1P_3 = 0.67$$

Therefore, probability that any tax advisor is idle

$$= \frac{\text{Expected number of advisors}}{\text{Total number of advisors}}$$

$$= \frac{0.67}{4} = 0.17$$

So, probability that no tax advisor is idle = 1 – 0.17 = 0.83.
The expected weekly time a tax advisor spends in performing job

$$= 0.83 \times 48 = 48 \text{ hours}$$

EXAMPLE 12.10: A telephone exchange has two long distance operators. The telephone company finds that during the peak load, long distance calls arrive in a Poisson fashion at an average rate of 15 per hour. The length of service on these calls is approximately exponentially distributed with an average rate of 5 minutes.

1. What is the probability that a subscriber will have to wait for his long distance call during the peak hours of the day?
2. If the subscribers will wait and served in turn, what is the expected waiting time?

Solution: Given $c = 2$, arrival rate, $\lambda = 15/60$ calls per minute, service rate, $\mu = 1/5$ calls per minute.

Then
$$P_0 = \left[\sum_{n=0}^{c-1} \frac{(\rho c)^n}{n!} + \frac{(\rho c)^c}{c!(1-\rho)}\right]^{-1} = 0.23$$

1. Probability that a subscriber will have to wait

$$= \frac{(\lambda/\mu)^c}{c!(1-\rho)} P_0 = 0.48$$

2. Expected waiting time $= \dfrac{(\lambda/c\mu)(cP)^c}{c!(1-\rho)^2} P_0 \dfrac{1}{\lambda} = 3.2$ minutes.

12.12 MODEL 4 (M/M/c): (N/FCFS)

Model 4 is an extension of Model 3. Here the system under consideration has finite capacity. For example, the points near supermarkets once full to its capacity, new arrival vehicles are turned down. Here the vehicles are arrivals and the parking floor space is the server. Assume that customers arrive at an average rate of λ following Poisson fashion and are served according to "first come, first served"-queue discipline. Then

$$\lambda_n = \begin{cases} \lambda, & n \le N \\ 0 & n > N \end{cases} \quad \text{and} \quad \mu_n = \begin{cases} n\mu, & n < c \\ c\mu & c \le n \le N \end{cases}$$

Arguing as above, the probability of n-customers in the system in the steady-state condition is given by

$$P_n = \begin{cases} \dfrac{1}{n!}\rho^n P_0, & n \le c \\ \dfrac{1}{c^{n-c}\,c!}\rho^n P_0, & c < n \le N \\ 0, & n > N \end{cases} \tag{12.63}$$

To obtain the value of P_0, we proceed as follows:

$$1 = \sum_{n=0}^{N} P_n = \sum_{n=0}^{c-1} P_n + \sum_{n=c}^{N} P_n$$

$$= \sum_{n=0}^{c-1} \frac{1}{n!}\left(\frac{\lambda}{\mu}\right)^n P_0 + \sum_{n=c}^{N} \frac{1}{c!\,c^{n-c}}\left(\frac{\lambda}{\mu}\right)^n P_0$$

$$= P_0\left[\sum_{n=0}^{c-1} \frac{c^n}{n!}\left(\frac{\lambda}{c\mu}\right)^n + \sum_{n=c}^{N} \frac{c^n}{c!\,c^{n-c}}\left(\frac{\lambda}{c\mu}\right)^n\right]$$

Then

$$P_0 = \begin{cases} \left[\displaystyle\sum_{n=0}^{c-1} \frac{(c\rho)^n}{n!} + \frac{1}{c!}\left(\frac{\lambda}{\mu}\right)^c \frac{c\mu}{c\mu - \lambda}\left\{1 - \left(\frac{\lambda}{c\mu}\right)^{N-c+1}\right\}\right]^{-1}, & \rho \ne 1 \\ \left[\displaystyle\sum_{n=0}^{c-1} \frac{(c\rho)^n}{n!} + \frac{1}{c!}\left(\frac{\lambda}{\mu}\right)^c (N - c + 1)\right]^{-1}, & \rho = 1 \end{cases} \tag{12.64}$$

Clearly, for $N \to \infty$ and $\lambda/c\mu < 1$, the results are same as those of Model 3. If we take $c = 1$, we get Model 1.

1. Effective arrival rate $\qquad \lambda' = \lambda(1 - P_N) \qquad (12.65)$
2. Average queue length

$$L_q = \sum_{n=c}^{N} (n - c)\,P_n$$

$$= \frac{(c\rho)^c \rho P_0}{c!(1-\rho)^2}\left[1 - \rho^{N-c+1} - (1-\rho)(N-c+1)\rho^{N-c}\right] \tag{12.66}$$

4. Average number of customers in the system

$$L_s = L_q + \left(\frac{\lambda}{\mu}\right)(1 - P_N) \tag{12.67}$$

5. Average waiting time of a customer in the system

$$W_s = \frac{L_s}{\lambda}(1 - P_N) \tag{12.68}$$

6. Average waiting time of a customer in the queue

$$W_q = W_s - \frac{1}{\mu} \tag{12.69}$$

Remark: If the number of customers intended to join queue could not exceed c, then there is no queue and hence $L_q = W_q = 0$. Also

$$P_n = \frac{1}{n!}\left(\frac{\lambda}{\mu}\right)^n P_0 \quad \text{and} \quad P_0 = \left[\sum_{n=0}^{c} \frac{1}{n!}\left(\frac{\lambda}{\mu}\right)^n\right]^{-1}$$

Correspondingly, the performance characteristics for this special case are

1. Effective arrival rate, $\lambda' = \lambda(1 - P_c)$
2. Expected waiting time in the system $W_s = \dfrac{1}{\mu}$
3. Expected number of customers in the system $= \dfrac{\lambda}{\mu}$

EXAMPLE 12.11: A car servicing station has 3 stalls where service can be offered simultaneously. Due to space limitations, only four cars are allowed for servicing. The arrival pattern is Poisson with a mean of one car every minute during peak hours. The service time is exponential with mean 6 minutes. Find the average number of cars in the system during peak hours, the average waiting time of a car, and the average number of cars per hour that cannot enter the station because of full capacity.

Solution: Given, $c = 3$, $N = 4$, arrival rate, $\lambda = 1$ car per minute, service rate, $\mu = 1/6$ car per minute. Then $\rho = 6$.

$$P_0 = \left[\sum_{n=0}^{3-1} \frac{1}{n!}\left(\frac{\lambda}{\mu}\right)^n + \sum_{n=3}^{4} \frac{1}{3!3^{n-3}}\left(\frac{\lambda}{\mu}\right)^n\right]^{-1} = 0.00088$$

1. Expected number of cars in the queue

$$L_q = \frac{(c\rho)^c \rho P_0}{c!(1-\rho)^2}[1 - \rho^{N-c+1} - (1-\rho)(N-c+1)\rho^{N-c}] = 3.09 \text{ cars}$$

2. Expected number of cars in the system

$$L_s = L_q + \left(\frac{\lambda}{\mu}\right)(1 - P_N) = 6.06 \text{ cars}$$

3. Expected waiting time of a car in the system

$$W_s = \frac{L_s}{\lambda}(1 - P_N) = 12.3 \text{ minutes.}$$

4. Expected number of cars per hour that cannot enter the station

$$= 60 \times \lambda \times P_7 = 30.3 \text{ cars/hour.}$$

12.13 MODEL 5 (M/M/1): (R/GD) SINGLE SERVER, FINITE SOURCE OF ARRIVALS

Model 5 is similar to Model 1, except that the limited input sources of potential customers. Thus, additional arrivals are not allowed in the system when the system is in its full capacity. For example, if an airbus can accommodate 130 passengers, these 130 passengers are the customers and the airbus is the server.

When there are n-customers in the system, the system can accommodate $(R - n)$ more customers. Then the arrival rate of the customer in the system will be $\lambda (R - n)$. Thus,

$$\lambda_n = \begin{cases} \lambda(R-n), & n = 1, 2, \ldots, R \\ 0, & n > R \end{cases} \quad \text{and} \quad \mu_n = \mu,\ n = 1, 2, \ldots, R$$

Substituting values of λ_n and μ_n in the expression for P_n and P_0 in Model 3, we get

1. Probability that there is no customer in the system

$$P_0 = \left[\sum_{n=0}^{R} \frac{R!}{(R-n)!}\left(\frac{\lambda}{\mu}\right)^n\right]^{-1} \tag{12.70}$$

2. Probability that there are n-customers in the system

$$P_n = \frac{R!}{(R-n)!}\left(\frac{\lambda}{\mu}\right)^n P_0,\ n_1, 2, \ldots, R \tag{12.71}$$

3. Expected number of customers in the queue

$$L_q = \left[\sum_{n=1}^{R} (n-1)P_n = R - \left(\frac{\lambda+\mu}{\lambda}\right)(1 - P_0)\right] \tag{12.72}$$

4. Expected number of customers in the system

$$L_s = \sum_{n=0}^{R} nP_n = R - \left(\frac{\mu}{\lambda}\right)(1 - P_0) \tag{12.73}$$

5. Average waiting time of a customer in the queue

$$W_q = \frac{L_q}{\lambda}(R - L_s) \tag{12.74}$$

6. Average waiting time of a customer in the system

$$W_s = W_q + \frac{1}{\mu} \tag{12.75}$$

EXAMPLE 12.12: A mechanic repairs four machines. The mean time between service requirements is 5 hours for each machine and forms an exponential distribution. The mean repair time is one hour and follows an exponential distribution. Machine downtime costs Rs. 25 per hour and the mechanic costs Rs. 55 per day. Determine the following:

1. Probability that the service facility will be idle.
2. Expected number of machines waiting to be repaired, and being repaired.
3. Expected downtime cost per day.

Would it be economical to engage two mechanics, each repairing only two machines?

Solution: Given, $R = 4$ machines, arrival rate, $\lambda = 1/5 = 0.2$ machine per hour, service rate, $\mu = 1$ machine per hour. Then $\rho = 0.2$.

1. The probability that the service facility will be idle

$$P_0 = \left[\sum_{n=0}^{R} \frac{R!}{(R-n)!} \left(\frac{\lambda}{\mu} \right)^n \right]^{-1} = 0.4030$$

2. Expected number of machines to be out of order and being repaired

$$L_s = R - \left(\frac{\mu}{\lambda} \right) (1 - P_0) = 1.015 \text{ machines.}$$

3. Expected time a machine will wait in a queue for repairing

$$W_q = \frac{1}{\mu} \left[\frac{R}{1 - P_0} - \frac{\lambda + \mu}{\lambda} \right] = 0.7 \text{ hours} = 42 \text{ minutes}$$

Total cost with one mechanic = 55 + (8 × 25) = Rs. 255

If there are two mechanics, then $R = 2$ and $P_0 = 0.68$.

WLOG, it is assumed that each mechanic with his two machines forms two mutually exclusive systems. Then, the expected number of machines to be out of order and being repaired

$$L_s = R - \left(\frac{\mu}{\lambda} \right) (1 - P_0) = 0.4 \text{ machines.}$$

The expected downtime of the machine per day
= expected number of machines in the system × 8-hour day × number of mechanics
= 0.4 × 8 × 2 = 6.4 hours per day.

Total cost of hiring two mechanics
= two mechanic cost + machine downtime
= 2 × 55 + 6.4 × 25 = Rs. 270 per day

Cost analysis suggests that it is not economical to engage two mechanics.

12.14 MODEL 6 (M/M/c): (R/GD): MULTI SERVER–FINITE INPUT SOURCE

When the number of servers is $c (c > 1)$, the arrival rate and service rate are defined as follows:

$$\lambda_n = \begin{cases} \lambda(R-n), & 0 \le n < R \\ 0, & n \ge R \end{cases} \quad \text{and} \quad \mu_n = \begin{cases} n\mu, & 0 \le n < c \\ c\mu, & n \ge c \end{cases} \tag{12.76}$$

Then arguing as Model 4, we get

$$P_n = \begin{cases} \dfrac{R!}{n!(R-n)!} \left(\dfrac{\lambda}{\mu} \right)^n P_0, & 0 \le n \le c \\[2ex] \dfrac{R!}{n!(R-n)!\, c!\, c^{n-c}} \left(\dfrac{\lambda}{\mu} \right)^n P_0, & c < n \le R \end{cases} \tag{12.77}$$

and

$$P_0 = \left[\sum_{n=0}^{c-1} \frac{R!}{n!(R-n)!} \left(\frac{\lambda}{\mu}\right)^n + \sum_{n=c}^{R} \frac{R!}{n!(R-n)!\, c!c^{n-c}} \left(\frac{\lambda}{\mu}\right)^n \right]^{-1} \tag{12.78}$$

Characteristics:

1. Expected number of customers in the queue

$$L_q = \sum_{n=c+1}^{R} (n-c) P_n$$

$$= \sum_{n=0}^{R} nP_n - \sum_{n=0}^{c} nP_n - c\left\{ \sum_{n=0}^{R} P_n - \sum_{n=0}^{c} P_n \right\}$$

$$= \sum_{n=0}^{R} nP_n - \sum_{n=0}^{c} nP_n - c\left\{ 1 - \sum_{n=0}^{c} P_n \right\}$$

$$= L_s - c + \sum_{n=0}^{c} (c-n) P_n = L_s - (c - c') \tag{12.79}$$

where $c' = \sum_{n=0}^{c} (c-n) P_n$ = expected number of idle servers.

2. Expected number of customers in the system

$$L_s = L_q + (c - c') \tag{12.80}$$

Let λ_e represent the expected arrival rate $\lambda(R-n)$

$$\lambda_e = \sum_{n=0}^{R} \lambda(R-n) P_n = \lambda(R - L_s)$$

3. Average waiting time of a customer in the queue

$$W_q = \frac{L_q}{\lambda}(R - L_q) \tag{12.81}$$

6. Average waiting time of a customer in the system

$$W_s = \frac{L_s}{\lambda}(R - L_s) \tag{12.82}$$

EXAMPLE 12.13: There are 5 machines, each of which when running suffers breakdown at an average rate of 2 per hour. There are 2 servicemen and only one man can work on a machine at a time. If n machines are out of order when $n > 2$ then $(n-2)$ of them wait until the serviceman is free. Once a serviceman starts work on a machine, the time to complete the repair has an exponential distribution with 5 minutes. Find the distribution of number of machines out of action at a given time. Find also the average time an out-of-action machine has to spend waiting for the repairs to start.

Solution: Given, R = 5 machines, number of servicemen, c = 2 arrival rate, λ = 2 machines per hour, service rate, μ = 1/5 machines per minute = 60/5 = 12 machines per hour. Then

$$P_0 = \left[\sum_{n=0}^{c-1} \frac{R!}{n!(R-n)!}\left(\frac{\lambda}{\mu}\right)^n + \sum_{n=c}^{R} \frac{R!}{n!(R-n)!\,c!c^{n-c}}\left(\frac{\lambda}{\mu}\right)^n\right]^{-1}$$

$$= 0.3135$$

Expected number of customers in the queue

$$L_q = \sum_{n=c+1}^{R} (n-c)\,P_n = P_3 + 2P_4 + 3P_5 = 0.11 \text{ hours}$$

Now $$\lambda_e = \sum_{n=0}^{R} \lambda(R-n)\,P_n = \lambda\,[5P_0 + 4P_1 + 3P_2 + 2P_3 + P_4] = 7.976$$

Therefore, average waiting time = 0.11/7.976 = 0.013 hours.

12.15 MODEL 7 (M/E$_K$/1): (∞/FCFS) ERLANG SERVICE TIME DISTRIBUTION WITH k-PHASES

Let us discuss a model consisting of single service channel which has to pass through k-phases in series for services. See Figure 12.5.

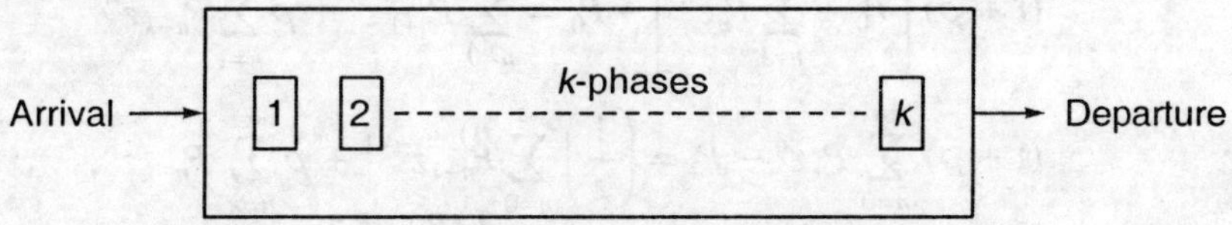

Figure 12.5 Queueing system with k-phases.

Let $P_n(t)$ = Probability that there are n-phases in the system at time t

n = Total number of phases in the system

k = Number of phases in series for services

$\lambda_n = \lambda$ = Phases arrive per unit time

μ = Number of units served per unit time

μk = Number of k-phases served per unit time

$1/\mu k$ = Average service time.

Arguing as Model 1, we have probability equations as

$$P_0(t+\Delta t) - P_0(t) = -\lambda P_0(t)\,\Delta t + P_1(t)\,k\mu\,\Delta t$$

$$P_n(t+\Delta t) - P_n(t) = -(\lambda + k\mu)\,P_n(t)\,\Delta t + P_{n+1}(t)k\mu\Delta t + P_{n-k}(t)\lambda\Delta t,\ n \geq 1$$

where $P_j(t) = 0$ for $j < 0$.

The required difference-differential equations are

$$P_0'(t) = -\lambda P_0(t) + k\mu P_1(t), \quad n = 0.$$

$$P_n'(t) = -(\lambda + k\mu)\, P_n(t) + P_{n+1}(t)\, k\mu + P_{n-k}(t)\lambda, \; n \geq 1.$$

Using Eq. (12.1), the steady-state difference-differential equations are

$$0 = -\lambda P_0 + k\mu P_1, \quad n = 0$$

$$0 = -(\lambda + k\mu)P_n + k\mu P_{n+1} + \lambda P_{n-k}, \quad n \geq 1$$

Therefore, $$P_1 = \rho P_0, \quad n = 0 \text{ where } \rho = \lambda/k\mu \tag{12.83}$$

$$(1 + \rho)P_n = P_{n+1} + \rho P_{n-k}, \; n \geq 1 \tag{12.84}$$

To solve the above equations, consider the generating function

$$P(z) = \sum_{n=0}^{\infty} P_n z^n \tag{12.85}$$

Multiply both sides of Eq. (12.84) by z^n and sum up from $n = 1$ to ∞.

$$(1+\rho)\sum_{n=1}^{\infty} P_n z^n = \sum_{n=1}^{\infty} P_{n+1} z^n + \rho \sum_{n=1}^{\infty} P_{n-k} z^n$$

or $$\rho P_0 + (1 + \rho) \sum_{n=1}^{\infty} P_n z^n = \rho P_0 \sum_{n=1}^{\infty} P_{n+1} z^n + \rho \sum_{n=1}^{\infty} P_{n-k} z^n$$

or $$(1 + \rho) \left[P_0 + \sum_{n=1}^{\infty} P_n z^n \right] - P_0 = \sum_{n=0}^{\infty} P_{n+1} z^n + \rho \sum_{n=1}^{\infty} P_{n-k} z^n$$

or $$(1 + \rho) \sum_{n=0}^{\infty} P_n z^n - P_0 = \left(\frac{1}{z}\right) \sum_{n=0}^{\infty} P_{n+1} z^{n+1} + \rho \sum_{n=k}^{\infty} P_{n-k} z^n$$

since $P_{n-k} = 0$ for $n - k < 0$

or $$(1 + \rho) \sum_{n=0}^{\infty} P_n z^n - P_0 = \left(\frac{1}{z}\right) \sum_{i1}^{\infty} P_i z^i + \rho \sum_{m=0}^{\infty} P_m z^{k+m}$$

or $$(1 + \rho)\, P(z) - P_0 = \left(\frac{1}{z}\right) \left[\sum_{i=0}^{\infty} P_i z^i - P_0 \right] + \rho z^k \sum_{m=0}^{\infty} P_m z^m$$

or $$(1 + \rho)\, P(z) - P_0 = \left(\frac{1}{z}\right) [P(z) - P_0] + \rho z^k P(z)$$

or $$P(z) = \frac{P_0(1 - z)}{(1 - z) - \rho z(1 - z^k)} = \frac{P_0}{1 - \rho z[(1 - z^k)/(1 - z)]}$$

$$= P_0 \left[1 - \rho z \left(\frac{1 - z^k}{1 - z} \right) \right]^{-1} = P_0 \sum_{n=0}^{\infty} (\rho z)^n \left(\frac{1 - z^k}{1 - z} \right)^n$$

$$= P_0 \sum_{n=0}^{\infty} (\rho z)^n [1 + z + z^2 + \cdots + z^{k-1}]^n$$

Put $z = 1$. Then $$P(1) = P_0 \sum_{n=0}^{\infty} (\rho k)^n = \frac{P_0}{1 - \rho k}$$

Also, Eq. (12.85) gives $$P(1) = \sum_{n=0}^{\infty} P_n = 1$$

Hence $$P_0 = 1 - \rho k \tag{12.86}$$

Again $$P(z) = (1 - \rho k) \sum_{n=0}^{\infty} (\rho z)^n (1 - z^k)^n (1 - z)^{-n}$$

or $$\sum_{n=0}^{\infty} P_n z^n = (1 - \rho k) \sum_{m=0}^{\infty} (\rho z)^m \sum_{i=0}^{m} (-1)^i \binom{m}{i} z^{ik} \sum_{j=0}^{\infty} \binom{m+j-1}{j} z^j$$

or $$\sum_{n=0}^{\infty} P_n z^n = (1 - \rho k) \sum_{m=0}^{\infty} \rho^m \sum_{j=0}^{\infty} \sum_{i=0}^{m} (-1)^i \binom{m}{i} \binom{m+j-1}{j} z^{m+ik+j}$$

Comparing coefficients of z^n from both sides gives

$$P_n = (1 - \rho k) \sum_{i,j,m} \rho^m (-1)^i \binom{m}{i} \binom{m+j-1}{j} \quad \text{where } m + ik + j = n \tag{12.87}$$

Characteristics of Model:

1. Expected number of phases (not units) in the system i.e.

$$L_s = \sum_{n=0}^{\infty} nP_n$$

Multiply both sides of Eq. (12.84) by n^2 and sum over 1 to ∞.

$$(1 + \rho) \sum_{n=1}^{\infty} n^2 P_n = \sum_{n=1}^{\infty} n^2 P_{n+1} + \rho \sum_{n=1}^{\infty} n^2 P_{n-k}$$

or $$(1 + \rho) \sum_{n=1}^{\infty} n^2 P_n = \sum_{n=1}^{\infty} n^2 P_{n+1} + \rho \sum_{n=k}^{\infty} n^2 P_{n-k}$$

or $$(1 + \rho) \sum_{n=1}^{\infty} n^2 P_n = \sum_{n=1}^{\infty} (n-1)^2 P_n + \rho \sum_{n=0}^{\infty} (n+k)^2 P_n$$

or $$(1 + \rho) \sum_{n=0}^{\infty} n^2 P_n = \sum_{n=0}^{\infty} (n-1)^2 P_n - P_0 + \rho \sum_{n=0}^{\infty} (n+k)^2 P_n$$

or $$(1 + \rho) \sum_{n=0}^{\infty} n^2 P_n = \sum_{n=0}^{\infty} [(n-1)^2 + \rho(n+k)^2] P_n - P_0$$

or $$(1 + \rho) \sum_{n=0}^{\infty} n^2 P_n = (1 + \rho) \sum_{n=0}^{\infty} n^2 P_n - 2(1 - k\rho) \sum_{n=0}^{\infty} nP_n + (1 + k^2\rho) \sum_{n=0}^{\infty} P_n - P_0$$

or $$2(1-k\rho)\sum_{n=0}^{\infty} nP_n = (1+k^2\rho)P_n - P_0$$

or $$L_s = \frac{\rho k(k+1)}{2(1-\rho k)} \tag{12.88}$$

The average number of phases of one unit in service = $(k + 1)/2$ with mean service rate = $1/\mu$. Then the time taken for service = $(k + 1)/2\mu$.

Now the expected number of units (not phases) in the queue

$$L_q = \frac{L_s - \text{Expected number of phases in the service}}{k}$$

$$= \frac{1}{k}\left[\frac{\rho k(k+1)}{2(1-\rho k)} - \frac{\lambda}{2\mu}(k+1)\right] \tag{12.89}$$

Hence, the expected number of phases arrived during time $(k + 1)/2\mu$ is equal to $(k + 1)l/2\mu$. Therefore,

2. $$L_q = \frac{k(k+1)}{2}\,\frac{\lambda^2}{\mu(\mu-\lambda)} = \frac{k(k+1)}{2}\,\frac{\rho^2}{1-\rho k} \tag{12.90}$$

3. $$W_q = \frac{L_q}{\lambda} = \frac{k(k+1)}{2}\,\frac{\lambda}{\mu(\mu-\lambda)} \tag{12.91}$$

4. $$L_s = L_q + \frac{\lambda}{\mu} = \frac{k(k+1)}{2}\,\frac{\lambda^2}{\mu(\mu-\lambda)} + \frac{\lambda}{\mu} \tag{12.92}$$

5. $$W_s = \frac{(k+1)}{2k}\,\frac{\lambda}{\mu(\mu-\lambda)} + \frac{1}{\mu} \tag{12.93}$$

Special case: If there is no queue and only one customer in the system, we get steady-state difference equations as

$$0 = -\lambda P_0 + k\mu P_1, \quad n = 0$$

$$0 = -k\mu P_n + k\mu P_{n+1}, \quad 1 \le n \le k$$

$$0 = -k\mu P_n + \lambda P_0, \quad n = k.$$

So, $P_n = (\lambda/k\mu)\, P_0$ for all $n = 1, 2, \ldots, k$.

Now $$\sum_{n=0}^{k} P_n = 1 \text{ implies } P_0 + \sum_{n=1}^{k} P_n = 1$$

or $$P_0 + \sum_{n=1}^{k} \frac{\lambda}{k\mu} P_0 = 1$$

or $$P_0 = \left[1 + \frac{\lambda}{\mu}\sum_{n=1}^{k}\frac{1}{k}\right]^{-1} = \frac{\mu}{\lambda+\mu}$$

Hence, $P_n = \dfrac{1}{k}\,\dfrac{\lambda}{\lambda+\mu}$

EXAMPLE 12.14: A hospital clinic has a doctor examining every patient brought in for a general check-up. The doctor spends 4 minutes on each phase of check-up, although the distribution of time spent on each phase is approximately exponential. If each patient goes through 4 phases in the check-up and if arrivals of the patients to the doctor's clinic is approximately Poisson at the average rate of 3 per hour,

1. What is the average time spent by a patient waiting in the doctor's clinic?
2. What is the average time spent in the check-up?
3. What is the most probable time spent in the examination?

Solution: Given $k = 4$ phases, arrival rate, $\lambda = 3$ patients per hour, service rate per phase $= 1/4\mu$ = 4 patients per minute.
so, $\mu = 1/16$ patients per minute = 60/16 = 4 patients per hour.

1. Average time spent by a patient in the doctor's clinic

$$L_q = \frac{k(k+1)}{2} \cdot \frac{\lambda^2}{\mu(\mu+\lambda)} = \frac{10}{15} \text{ hour} = 40 \text{ minutes.}$$

2. Average time spent in the check-up $= 1/\mu = 16$ minutes.

3. Most probable time spent in the examination $= \dfrac{k-1}{k\mu} = 12$ minutes.

EXAMPLE 12.15 Repairing a certain type of machine, which breaks down in a given factory, consists of five basic steps that should be performed in a particular sequence. The time taken to perform each of the five steps is found to have an exponential distribution with a mean of 5 minutes and is independent of the other steps. If these machines break down in a Poisson fashion at an average rate of two per hour, and if there is only one repairman, what is the average idle time for each machine that has broken down?

Solution: Given $k = 5$ phases, average arrival rate, $\lambda = 1/30$ machines per minute, average service rate, $\mu = 1/25$ machines per minute.

Therefore, the expected idle time of the machine

= average time an arrival spends in the system

$$= \frac{(k+1)}{2k} \cdot \frac{\lambda}{\mu(\mu-\lambda)} + \frac{1}{\mu} = 100 \text{ minutes.}$$

REVIEW EXERCISES

1. A TV repairman finds that the time spent on his jobs has an exponential distribution with mean 30 minutes. If he repairs sets in the order in which they come in, and if the arrival of sets is approximately Poisson with an average rate of 10 per 8-hour day, what is the repairman's idle time each day? How many jobs are ahead of the average set just brought in?

[Ans. 3 hours, 5/3 jobs]

2. At a man barber shop, customers arrive according to the Poisson distribution with a mean arrival rate of 5 per hour and his hair cutting time was exponentially distributed with an average hair cut taking 10 minutes. It is assumed that because of his expertise customers were always willing to wait. Calculate the following:

1. Average number of customers in the shop and the average number of customers waiting for a hair cut.
2. The percent of time an arrival can walk right in without having to wait.
3. The percentage of customers who have to wait prior to getting into the barber's chair?

[**Ans.** 4.8 customers, 4 customers, 16.7%, 83.3%]

3. A drive-in bank window has a mean service time of 2 minutes, while the customers arrive at a rate of 20 per hour. Assuming that these rates represent Poisson distribution, determine

1. The proportion the teller will be idle?
2. How long a customer will wait before reaching the server?
3. What fraction of the customers will have to wait in the line?
4. The probability that a customer has to wait?

[**Ans.** 33% of time, 6 min, 4/3 customers, 2/3 customers]

4. On an average, 96 patients per 24-hour day require the service of an emergency clinic. Also, on an average, a patient requires 10 minutes of active attention. Assume that the facility can handle only one emergency at a time. Suppose that it costs the clinic Rs. 100 per patient treated to obtain an average servicing time of 10 minutes, and that each minute of decrease in this average time would cost Rs. 10 per patient treated. How much would have to be budgeted by the clinic to decrease the average size of the queue from one and one-third patients to half a patient?

[**Ans.** Rs. 125 per patient]

5. A refinery distributes its products by trucks, loaded at the loading dock. Both company trucks and independent distributors' trucks are loaded. The independent firms complained that sometimes they have to wait in line and thus lose money paying for a truck and a driver that are only waiting. They requested the refinery either to put in second loading dock or to discount prices equivalent to the waiting time. Extra loading dock costs Rs. 100 per day whereas the waiting time for the independent firms costs Rs. 25 per hour. The following data have been collected. The average arrival rate of all trucks is 2 per hour and average service rate is 3 per hour. Thirty percent of all trucks are independent. Assuming that these rates are random according to the Poisson distribution, determine

1. The probability that a truck has to wait.
2. The waiting time of a truck that waits.
3. The expected cost of waiting time of independent trucks per day.

Is it advantageous to decide in favour of a second loading dock to ward off the complaints?

[**Ans.** 0.66, 1 hour, Rs. 80]

6. Consider the self-service store with one cashier. Assume Poisson arrivals and exponential service times. Suppose that nine customers arrive on an average every 5 minutes and the cashier can serve 10 in 5 minutes. Find

1. The average number of customers' queuing for the service.
2. The probability of having more than 10 customers in the system.
3. The probability that a customer has to wait for more than 2 minutes.

If the service can be speeded up to 12 in 5 minutes using a different cash register, what will be the changes in the (1)–(3)?

[Ans. 3, $(0.9)^{10}$, 0.67 : 3, $(0.75)^{10}$, 0.30]

7. A departmental store has a single cashier. During the rush hours, customers arrive at a rate of 20 customers per hour. The average number of customers that can be processed by the cashier is 24 per hour. Assume that the conditions for the use of the single channel queuing model apply.

1. What is the probability that the cashier is idle?
2. What is the average number of customers in the queuing system?
3. What is the average time a customer spends in the system?
4. What is the average number of customers in the queue?
5. What is the average time a customer spends in the queue waiting for service?

[Ans. 0.17, 5 customers, 0.25, 4.17 customers, 0.21 hour]

8. Assume that the goods trains are coming in a yard at the rate of 30 trains per day and suppose that the inter-arrival times follow an exponential distribution. The service time for each train is assumed to be exponential with an average of 36 minutes. If the yard can admit 9 trains at a time (there being 10 lines, one of which is reserved for shunting purpose), calculate the probability that the yard is empty and find the average queue length.

[Ans. 0.28, 1.55 trains]

9. A stenographer has 5 persons with whom she performs stenographic work. The arrival rate is Poisson and service times are exponential. The average arrival rate is 4 per hour with an average service time of 10 minutes. Cost of waiting is Rs. 8.00 per hour while the cost of servicing is Rs. 2.50 each. Calculate the average waiting time of an arrival, the average length of the waiting line, and the average time which an arrival spends in the system.

[Ans. 12.4 minutes, 0.79 customers, 22.4 minutes]

10. A shipping company has a single unloading berth with ships arriving in a Poisson fashion at an average rate of three per day. The unloading time distribution for a ship with n-unloading crews is found to be exponential with average unloading time $1/2n$ days. The company has a large labour supply without regular working hours, and to avoid long waiting lines the company has a policy of using as many unloading crews on a ship as there are ships waiting in line or being unloaded. Under these conditions, what will be the average number of unloading crews working at any time? What is the probability that more than 4 crews will be needed?

[Ans. 1.5 crews, 0.019]

11. Problems arrive at a computing center in Poisson fashion at an average rate of 5 per day. The rules of the computer center are such that any man waiting to get his problem solved must aid the man whose problem is being solved. If the time to solve a problem with one man has an exponential distribution with mean time of 1/3 day, and if the average solving time is inversely proportional to the number of people working on the problem, approximate the expected time in the center for a person entering the center.

[**Ans.** 1.67, 8 hours]

12. Four counters are being run on the frontier of a country to check the passports and necessary papers of the tourists. The tourists choose a counter at random. If the arrivals at the frontier are Poisson at the rate λ and the service time is exponential with parameter $\lambda/2$, what is the steady-state average queue at each counter?

[**Ans.** 4/23]

13. A supermarket has two girls running up sales at the counters. If the service time for each customer is exponential with mean 4 minutes, and if people arrive in a Poisson fashion at the rate of 10 per hour.

1. What is the probability of customers having to wait for the service?
2. What is the expected percentage of idle time for each girl?
3. If a customer has to wait, what is the expected length of his waiting time?

[**Ans.** 0.167, 67%, 3 minutes]

14. A bank has two tellers working on saving accounts. The first teller handles withdrawals only. The second teller handles depositors only. It has been found that the service time distribution for both deposits and withdrawals is exponential with mean service time 3 minutes per customer. Depositors and withdrawals are found to arrive in Poisson fashion throughout the day, with mean arrival rate of 16 and 14 per hour respectively. What would be the effect on the average waiting line for depositors and withdrawers if each teller could handle both withdrawals and depositors? What would be the effect if this could only be accomplished by increasing the service time to 3.5 minutes?

[**Ans.** 1.93, 5.97, 0.199 hours]

15. A general insurance company has three claim adjusters in its branch office. People with claim against the company are found to arrive in Poisson fashion, at an average rate of 20 per 8-hour day. The amount of time that an adjuster spends with a claimant is found to have a negative exponential distribution, with mean service time 40 minutes. Claimants are processed in the order of their appearance.

1. How many hours a week can an adjuster expect to spend with the claimants?
2. How much time, on an average, does a claimant spend in the branch office?

[**Ans.** 22.2 hours, 49 minutes]

16. A group of engineers has two terminals available to aid their calculations. The average computing job requires 20 minutes of terminal time, and each engineer requires some computation about once every 0.5 hours, i.e. the mean time between a call for service is 0.5 hours. Assume these are distributed according to an exponential distribution. If there are six engineers in the group, find

1. The expected number of engineers waiting to use one of the terminals.
2. The total lost time per day.

[**Ans.** 1.4 engineers, 11.2 hours/day]

17. At a certain airport it takes exactly 5 minutes to land an airplane, once it is given the signal to land. Although incoming planes have scheduled arrival times, the wide variability in arrivals produces an effect which makes the incoming planes appear to arrive in a Poisson fashion at an average rate of 6 per hour. This produces occasional stack-ups at the airport which can be dangerous and costly. Under these circumstances, how much time will a pilot expect to spend circulating the field waiting to land?

[**Ans.** 2.5 minutes]

18. A colliery working one shift per day uses a large number of locomotives which break down at random intervals, on an average one fails per 8-hour shift. The fitter carries out a standard maintenance schedule on each faulty locomotive. Each of the five main parts of this schedule takes on an average 1/2 hour, but the time varies widely. How much time will the fitter have for the other tasks and what is the average time a locomotive is out of the service?

[**Ans.** 5.5 hours, 3.18 hours]

13

Replacement Models

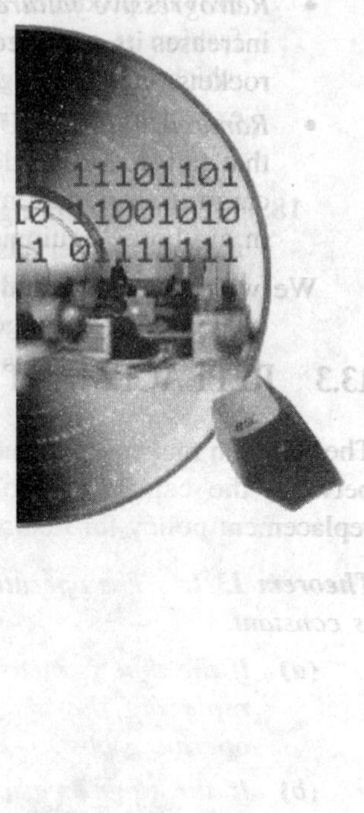

13.1 INTRODUCTION

The replacement problems deal with replacing items due to decrease in efficiency, failure or breakdown. These problems arise because of various reasons, viz. some items require maintenance which turns out to be expensive with time, some items fail due to sudden physical stock, accidental death, new version of machinery is available in the market, etc. Due to the above mentioned reasons, efficiency goes on decreasing with the age and as a result, there is an increase in the operating cost, and decrease in the scrap value. So we need to decide best policy to determine an age, when the replacement is most economical.

13.2 FAILURE OF ITEMS

In a broader sense, 'failure' means decrease in efficiency. There are two types of failure.

1. *Gradual failure:* Gradual failure occurs progressively. Here efficiency decreases with time. Consequently,

- There is increase in expenditure in terms of operating costs,
- Productivity of the item decreases, and
- Resale value of the item decreases.

For example, automobile tyres, ball bearings etc.

2. *Sudden failure:* The failure which occurs all of a sudden after using equipment for some time is termed as *sudden failure*. The period between installation and failure is uncertain but can be estimated by some frequency distributions, which may be progressive, retrogressive or random in nature.

- *Progressive failure:* Here the probability of failure increases with increase in the life of an item. For example, electric light tubes, automobile tyres, medicines, etc.
- *Retrogressive failure:* When the ability of the item to survive in the initial stage of life increases its expected life, it is termed as *retrogressive failure*. For example, aircraft engines, rockets, etc.
- *Random failure:* Under this failure, constant probability failure is associated with items that fail due to random causes like physical shocks, mishandling during loading/unloading cargo, transportation, not related to age. For example, clay items, glass ware, vacuum tube in air–borne equipment, fruits and vegetable, etc.

We will discuss the following situations of the replacement.

13.3 REPLACEMENT OF ITEMS THAT DETERIORATE

The decision maker has a question: "When the replacement is optimal?" He needs to get equilibrium between the capital cost of an item, the running costs and scrap value. Let us first discuss replacement policy for items whose operating cost increases with time and money value is constant.

Theorem 13.1: *The operating cost of a machine is increasing function of time and its scrap value is constant.*

(a) If the time is measured continuously, then the average annual cost will be minimized by replacing the machine when the average cost to date becomes equal to the current operating cost.

(b) If the time measured is discrete, then the average annual cost will be minimized by replacing the machine when the next period's operating cost is greater than the current average annual cost.

Proof: Let

C = The purchase cost of a machine
S = The scrap value of a machine
$R(t)$ = The operating cost at time t.

(a) Let t be a continuous variable. The total operating cost of a machine for n-years $= \int_0^n R(t)\,dt$.

Hence, the total cost incurred on the machine for n-years is

$$TC(n) = C - S + \int_0^n R(t)\,dt \tag{13.1}$$

and the average total cost is

$$ATC(n) = \frac{TC(n)}{n} \tag{13.2}$$

For obtaining time n for which $ATC(n)$ is minimum, set differentiation of $ATC(n)$ with respect to n equal to zero, i.e.

$$\frac{dATC(n)}{dn} - \frac{1}{n^2}(C - S) + \frac{1}{n}R(n) - \frac{1}{n^2}\int_0^n R(t)\,dt = 0$$

i.e. $$R(n) = \frac{C-S}{n} + \frac{1}{n}\int_0^n R(t)\,dt = ATC(n) \quad [\because \text{ of Eq. (13.2)}] \tag{13.3}$$

Thus, the optimum time n is when the operating cost for n-years is equal to average cost in n-years.

(b) When time 't' is a discrete variable.

Here Eq. (13.2) can be written as

$$ATC(n) = \frac{C-S}{n} + \sum_{t=1}^{n} R(t) \tag{13.4}$$

By using finite differences, $ATC(n)$ will be minimum if

$$\Delta ATC(n-1) < 0 < \Delta ATC(n) \tag{13.5}$$

where $\Delta ATC(n) = ATC(n+1) - ATC(n)$.

Let us compute $\Delta ATC(n) = ATC(n+1) - ATC(n)$

$$= \frac{C-S}{n+1} + \sum_{t=1}^{n+1} R(t) - \frac{C-S}{n} - \sum_{t=1}^{n} R(t)$$

$$= \frac{R(n+1)}{n+1} - \sum_{t=1}^{n} \frac{R(t)}{n(n+1)} - \frac{C-S}{n(n+1)}$$

Since $\Delta ATC(n) > 0$ for minimum $ATC(n)$, we have

$$\frac{R(n+1)}{n+1} > \sum_{t=1}^{n} \frac{R(t)}{n(n+1)} + \frac{C-S}{n(n+1)}$$

i.e. $$R(n+1) \geq \sum_{t=1}^{n} \frac{R(t)}{n} + \frac{C-S}{n} = ATC(n) \tag{13.6}$$

Similarly, $\Delta ATC(n-1) < 0$ implies $R(n) < ATC(n)$ (13.7)

From Eqs. (13.6) and (13.7), the optimal policy is

$$R(n) < ATC(n) < R(n+1) \tag{13.8}$$

EXAMPLE 13.1: A firm is considering replacement of a machine whose cost price is Rs. 12,200 and the scrap value is only Rs. 200. The operating costs (in rupees) are found from experience as follows:

Year :	1	2	3	4	5	6	7	8
Operating cost :	200	500	800	1,200	1,800	2,500	3,200	4,000

When should the machine be replaced?

Solution: Given C = Rs. 12,200 and S = Rs. 200.

The average cost per year can be computed as given in Table 13.1.

Table 13.1

Year (*n*) (1)	*R*(*n*) (2)	$\sum R(n)$ (3)	*C* – *S* (4)	*TC* (*n*) (5) = (3) + (4)	*ATC* (*n*) (5)/(1)
1	200	200	12,000	12,200	12,200
2	500	700	12,000	12,700	6,350
3	800	1,500	12,000	13,500	4,500
4	1,200	2,700	12,000	14,700	3,675
5	1,800	4,500	12,000	16,500	3,300
6	**2,500**	**7,000**	**12,000**	**19,000**	**3,167***
7	3,200	10,200	12,000	22,200	3,171
8	4,000	14,200	12,000	26,200	3,275

* denotes the optimum solution.

The above table shows that the value *ATC* (6) during the sixth year is minimum. Hence, the machine should be replaced after every 6 year.

EXAMPLE 13.2: A firm is using a machine whose purchase price is Rs. 13,000. The installation charges amount to Rs. 3,600 and the machine has a scrap value of only Rs. 1,600. The maintenance cost in different years is as follows:

Year	:	1	2	3	4	5	6	7
Operating cost	:	250	750	1,000	1,500	2,100	2,900	4,000

The firm wants to determine after how many years the machine should be replaced on economic grounds, assuming that the machine replacement can be done only at the end of the year.

Solution: Given purchase cost = Rs. 13,000 and installation charges = Rs. 3,600. Then C = Rs. 13,000 + 3,600 = 16,600 and S = Rs. 1,600.

The optimum replacement period is determined as follows:

Table 13.2

Year (*n*) (1)	*R*(*n*) (2)	$\sum R(n)$ (3)	*C* – *S* (4)	*TC* (*n*) (5) = (3) + (4)	*ATC* (*n*) (5)/(1)
1	250	250	15,000	15,250	15,250
2	750	1,000	15,000	16,000	8,000
3	1,000	2,000	15,000	17,000	5,607
4	1,500	3,500	15,000	18,500	4,625
5	2,100	5,600	15,000	20,600	4,120
6	**2,900**	**8,500**	**15,000**	**23,500**	**3,917***
7	4,000	12,500	15,000	27,500	3,929

* denotes the optimum solution.

Table 13.2 shows that the value *ATC* (6) during the sixth year is minimum. Hence, the machine should be replaced after every 6 year.

EXAMPLE 13.3: A truck owner finds from his past records that the maintenance costs per year of a truck whose purchase price is Rs. 8,000 are given as:

Year	:	1	2	3	4	5	6	7	8
Maintenance cost (Rs.)	:	1,000	1,300	1,700	2,200	2,900	3,800	4,800	6,000
Resale price (Rs.)	:	4,000	2,000	1,200	600	500	400	400	400

Determine at which time it is profitable to replace the truck.

Solution: Given C = Rs. 8,000 and the maintenance cost $R(n)$ and the resale value (say) $S(n)$. The values of $ATC(n)$ for each year are computed in Table 13.3.

Table 13.3

Year (n) (1)	$R(n)$ (2)	$\sum R(n)$ (3)	$S(n)$ (4)	$C - S(n)$ (5)	$TC(n)$ (6) = (3) + (5)	$ATC(n)$ (6)/(1)
1	1,000	1,000	4,000	4,000	5,000	5,000
2	1,300	2,300	2,000	6,000	8,300	4,150
3	1,700	4,000	1,200	6,800	10,800	3,600
4	2,200	6,200	600	7,400	13,600	3,400
5	**2,900**	**9,100**	**500**	**7,500**	**16,600**	**3,320***
6	3,800	12,900	400	7,600	20,500	3,417
7	4,800	17,700	400	7,600	25,300	3,614
8	6,000	23,700	400	7,600	31,300	3,913

* denotes the optimum solution.

The $ATC(5)$ is minimum. Hence, the truck should be replaced every 5 year.

EXAMPLE 13.4: Fleet cars have increased their costs as they continue in service due to increased direct operating cost (gas and oil) and increased maintenance costs. The initial cost is Rs. 3,500 and the trade-in value drops as the time passes until it reaches a constant value of Rs. 500.

Given the cost of operating, maintenance and the trade-in value, determine the proper length of service before cars should be replaced.

Year of service	:	1	2	3	4	5
Year end trade-in value (Rs.)	:	1,900	1,050	600	500	500
Annual operating cost (Rs.)	:	1,500	1,800	2,100	2,400	2,700
Maintenance cost (Rs.)	:	300	400	600	800	1,000

Solution: Given C = Rs. 3,500, $S(n)$ = year end trade-in value and $R(n)$ = operating cost + maintenance cost.

The optimum replacement period is determined in Table 13.4 below.

Table 13.4

Year (n) (1)	$R(n)$ (2)	$\sum R(n)$ (3)	$C - S(n)$ (4)	$TC(n)$ (5) = (3) + (4)	$ATC(n)$ (5)/(1)
1	1,800	1,800	1,600	3,400	3,400
2	2,200	4,000	2,450	6,450	3,225
3	**2,700**	**6,700**	**2,900**	**9,600**	**3,200***
4	3,200	9,900	3,000	12,900	3,225
5	3,700	13,600	3,000	16,600	3,320

* denotes the optimum solution.

The table indicates that $ATC(3)$ is minimum. Hence, the car should be replaced every third year.

EXAMPLE 13.5: A machine shop has a press which is to be replaced as it wears out. A new press is to be installed now. Further, an optimum replacement plan is to be found for next 7 years after which the press is no longer required. The following data is given:

Year	:	1	2	3	4	5	6	7
Installation cost at the beginning of the year (Rs.)	:	200	210	220	240	260	290	320
Solving value at the end of the year (Rs.)	:	100	50	30	20	15	10	0
Operating cost during the year (Rs.)	:	60	80	100	120	150	180	230

Find an optimum replacement policy and the corresponding minimum cost.

Solution: With the given data, the minimum average annual cost of the press is computed in Table 13.5.

Table 13.5

Year (n)	$R(n)$	$\sum R(n)$	$C - S(n)$	$TC(n)$	$ATC(n)$
(1)	(2)	(3)	(4)	(5) = (3) + (4)	(5)/(1)
1	60	60	200 – 100 = 100	160	160
2	80	140	210 – 50 = 160	300	150
3	**100**	**240**	**220 – 30 = 190**	**430**	**143***
4	120	360	240 – 20 = 220	580	145
5	150	510	260 – 15 = 245	755	151
6	180	690	290 – 10 = 280	970	162
7	230	920	320 – 0 = 320	1,240	178

* denotes the optimal solution.

From the table, the minimum average annual cost is ATC (3) = Rs. 143.
The machine should be replaced every third year.

EXAMPLE 13.6: (a) Machine A costs Rs. 9,000. Annual operating costs are Rs. 200 for the first year and then increase by Rs. 2,000 every year. Determine the best age at which to replace the machine. If the optimum replacement policy is followed, what will be the average yearly cost of owning and operating the machine?

(b) Machine B costs Rs. 10,000. Annual operating costs are Rs. 400 for the first year, and then increase by Rs. 800 every year. You now have machine A, which is one year old. Should you replace it with B? If so, when?

Assume that resale values for both the machines are negligible.

Solution: (a) First, let us compute the average total annual cost $ATC_A(n)$ for machine A. We have C = Rs. 9,000 and S = 0.

Table 13.6(a)

Year (n)	$R(n)$	$\sum R(n)$	$C - S$	$TC_A(n)$	$ATC_A(n)$
(1)	(2)	(3)	(4)	(5) = (3) + (4)	(5)/(1)
1	200	200	9,000	9,200	9,200
2	2,200	2,400	9,000	11,400	5,700
3	**4,200**	**6,600**	**9,000**	**15,600**	**5,200***
4	6,200	12,800	9,000	21,800	5,450
5	8,200	21,000	9,000	30,000	6,000

* denotes the optimal solution.

Table 13.6(a) suggests that machine *A* should be replaced after 3 years and the corresponding average annual cost of owning and operating is Rs. 5,200.

(b) Now we compute the optimal policy for machine *B* [Table 13.6(b)].
Given C = Rs. 10,000 and $S = 0$

Table 13.6(b)

Year (n) (1)	$R(n)$ (2)	$\sum R(n)$ (3)	$C - S$ (4)	$TC_A(n)$ (5) = (3) + (4)	$ATC_A(n)$ (5)/(1)
1	400	400	10,000	10,400	10,400
2	1,200	1,600	10,000	11,600	5,800
3	2,000	3,600	10,000	13,600	4,533
4	2,800	6,400	10,000	16,400	4,100
5	**3,600**	**10,000**	**10,000**	**20,000**	**4,000***
6	4,400	14,400	10,000	24,400	4,066

* denotes the optimal solution.

The minimum average annual cost for machine *B* is Rs. 4,000, which is lower than that for machine *A*. Machine *B* should be replaced by machine *A*.

We need to decide the time of replacement. Since the salvage value is negligible, we need to consider only the maintenance cost. We would keep machine *A* so long as the annual maintenance cost is lower than Rs. 4,000 and replace it as soon as it exceeds Rs. 4,000.

On the one-year old machine *A*, the maintenance cost for 2nd year is Rs. 2,200 and for the 3rd year, it is Rs. 4,200. So we need to replace machine *A* for one-year and replace it thereafter.

EXAMPLE 13.7: (a) A transport manager finds from his past records that the costs per year of running a truck whose purchase price is Rs. 6,000 are as given below:

Year	:	1	2	3	4	5	6	7	8
Operating cost (Rs.)	:	1,000	1,200	1,400	1,800	2,300	2,800	3,400	4,000
Resale value	:	3,000	1,500	750	375	200	200	200	200

Determine at what age is replacement due?

(b) Let the owner of a fleet have three trucks, two of which are two years old and the third one is one year old. The cost price, running cost and resale value of these trucks are same as given in (a). Now, he is considering a new type of truck with 50% more capacity than one of the old ones at a unit price of Rs. 8,000. He estimates that the running costs and resale price for the truck will be as follows:

Year	:	1	2	3	4	5	6	7	8
Running cost (Rs.)	:	1,200	1,500	1,800	2,400	3,100	4,000	5,000	6,100
Resale price (Rs.)	:	4,000	2,000	1,000	500	300	300	300	300

Assuming that the loss of flexibility due to fewer trucks is of no importance and that he will continue to have sufficient work for three of the old trucks, what should his policy be?

Solution: (a) Given C = Rs. 6,000. The computation of the optimum age of replacement is exhibited in Table 13.7(a).

Table 13.7(a)

Year (n) (1)	$R(n)$ (2)	$\sum R(n)$ (3)	$S(n)$ (4)	$C - S(n)$ (5)	$TC(n)$ (6) = (3) + (5)	$ATC(n)$ (6)/(1)
1	1,000	1,000	3,000	3,000	4,000	4,000
2	1,200	2,200	1,500	4,500	6,700	3,350
3	1,400	3,600	750	6,250	8,850	2,950
4	**1,800**	**5,400**	**375**	**5,625**	**11,025**	**2,700***
5	2,300	7,700	200	5,800	13,500	2,717
6	2,800	10,500	200	5,800	16,300	2,814
7	3,400	13,900	200	5,800	19,700	2,814
8	4,000	17,900	200	5,800	23,700	2,962

* denotes the optimal solution.

From the table, the average annual cost per year is minimum for the 5th year. So, the machine should be replaced after 5th year.

(b) Let us compute the optimal policy for the new truck (Table 13.7(b)). Given C = Rs. 8,000.

Table 13.7(b)

Year (n) (1)	$R(n)$ (2)	$\sum R(n)$ (3)	$S(n)$ (4)	$C - S(n)$ (5)	$TC(n)$ (6) = (3) + (5)	$ATC(n)$ (6)/(1)
1	1,200	1,200	4,000	4,000	5,200	5,200
2	1,500	2,700	2,000	6,000	8,700	4,350
3	1,800	4,500	1,000	7,000	11,500	3,833
4	2,400	6,900	500	7,500	14,400	3,600
5	**3,100**	**10,000**	**300**	**7,700**	**17,700**	**3,540***
6	4,000	14,000	300	7,700	21,700	3,616
7	5,000	19,000	300	7,700	26,700	3,814
8	6,000	25,000	300	7,700	32,800	4,100

* denotes the optimal solution.

From the table, it is observed that the new truck should be replaced after every 5th year and the corresponding average annual cost is Rs. 3,540.

Given that the capacity of the new truck is 50% more than that of the old truck, therefore the capacity of the two new trucks is equivalent to three smaller trucks. So, the minimum average annual cost for the new truck will be Rs. 3,540 * 2/3 = Rs. 2,360 for one of the old trucks. Hence, the old smaller truck should be replaced by a new truck. Now we need to decide, "When to purchase the new trucks?" For uniformity, let us assume that the replacement will involve two new trucks and all three old trucks. The new trucks should be purchased to replace three old trucks when the running cost for the next year of the three old trucks exceeds the average annual cost for two new trucks. Let us compute the total cost of the old trucks in the subsequent years.

Year of service	*Annual total cost of old trucks (Rs.)*
1	4,000
2	6,700 – 4,000 = 2,700
3	8,850 – 6,700 = 2,150
4	11,025 – 8,850 = 2,175
5	13,500 – 11,025 = 2,475

The average cost for two new trucks is equal to Rs. 7,080 (=2 * 3,540). Also, we are given that two trucks are 2 years old and one is one year old. The computations of the average annual cost for the older ones in subsequent years are as follows:

Year	*Annual annual cost (Rs.)*
1	2 * 2,150 + 2,700 = 7,000
2	2 * 2,175 + 2,150 = 6,500
3	2 * 2,475 + 2,175 = 7,125
4	2 * 2,800 + 2,475 = 8,075

From these calculations, we conclude that the total cost of three old trucks up to 2nd year is Rs. 6,500 which is less than the total average cost (Rs. 7,080) for new trucks. Hence, all the three old trucks should be replaced after two years of service without waiting for their optimal replacement age of 5 years.

13.4 REPLACEMENT OF ITEMS WITH INCREASING RUNNING COST

Let us try to understand the term "the value of money". For example, if the interest rate on Rs. 100 is 8% per year, then the value of money of Rs. 100 to be spent after one year will be Rs. 108. This is called the *value of money.* The value of money that decreases with constant rate is known as its *depreciation ratio* or *discounted factor*. Thus, the discounted value is the amount of the money required at the time of the policy decision to make up funds at compound interest large enough to pay the required cost when due. For example, if the interest rate on Rs. 100 is r% per annum, then the present value (or worth) of Rs. 100 to be spent after n-years will be

$$d = \frac{100}{(100 + r)^n}$$

where d is the discount rate. Here, the objective will be to minimize the total equivalent cost, to determine the age at which the machine should be replaced.

EXAMPLE 13.8: The cost pattern for two machines A and B, when money value is not considered, is given below:

Year	*Cost at the beginning of the year in Rs.*	
	Machine A	*Machine B*
1	900	1,400
2	600	100
3	700	700

Find the cost pattern for each machine, when money is worth 10% per year. Also find which machine is less costly.

Solution: When the money value is not taken into account, the total cost of both the machines is Rs. 2,200 and hence suggests that both are equally good.

When the money worth is 10% per annum, the present value of the money to be spent over in a period of one year is

$$d = \frac{100}{100 + 10} = 0.9091$$

Now let us compute discounted cost for the data.

Year	*Discounted cost at 10% rate in Rs.*	
	Machine A	*Machine B*
1	900.00	1,400.00
2	$600d$ = 545.45	$100d$ = 90.91
3	$700d^2$ = 578.52	$700d^2$ = 578.82
Total	2023.98	2069.73

Clearly, the total cost for machine *A* is less than that for machine *B* for the same period. Thus, machine *A* is cheaper than machine *B*.

EXAMPLE 13.9: A manual stamper currently valued at Rs. 1,000 is expected to last 2 years and costs Rs. 4,000 per year to operate. An automatic stamper whose cost price is Rs. 3,000 will last 4 years and can be operated at an annual cost of Rs. 3,000. If the money carries the interest rate of 10% per annum, determine which stamper should be purchased.

Solution: We have $d = \frac{100}{100 + 10} = 0.9091$

The stampers have different expected life span. So, we shall consider a length of four years during which we have to purchase either two manual stampers or one automatic stamper.

The present value of investments on the two manual stampers used in 4 years is

$$= 1{,}000\,(1 + d^2) + 4{,}000\,(1 + d + d^2 + d^3) \approx \text{Rs. } 15{,}773$$

Now, the present value of investments on the one automatic stamper for the next four years is

$$= 3{,}000 + 3{,}000\,(1 + d + d^2 + d^3) \approx \text{Rs. } 13{,}460$$

Since the present value of future costs for the automatic stamper is less than that of the manual stamper, one should go for the purchase of an automatic stamper.

EXAMPLE 13.10: A machine is due for repairs. It will cost Rs. 8,000 and last for 3 years. On the other hand, a new machine can be purchased at a cost of Rs. 25,000 and lasts for 1 year. Assuming the rate of interest to be 10% and negligible salvage value, decide which alternative is profitable.

Solution: Consider two types of machines for infinite replacement periods of 10 years for the new machine and 3 years for the existing machine.

The present value factor is given by

$$d = \frac{100}{100 + 10} = 0.9091$$

Let $$DC(n) = c + cd^n + cd^{2n} + \cdots = \frac{C}{1 - d^n}$$

For the existing machine C = Rs. 8,000, d = 0.9091 and n = 3 years.

Then $$DC(3) = \frac{8,000}{1 - 0.9091^3} \approx \text{Rs. } 32,172$$

and for new machine with C = Rs. 25,000, d = 0.9091 and n = 10 years

$$DC(10) = \frac{25,000}{1 - 0.9091^{10}} \approx \text{Rs. } 40,688$$

Since $DC(3) < DC(10)$, the existing machine should be repaired.

The above discussed example suggests that the money value can be visualized in two different ways. Accordingly, the following two methods

(i) The operating cost increased with time and the money value with a given rate, i.e. discounted value is constant.

(ii) The amount to be spent is loaned at a given (constant) rate of interest under the condition of repaying it in pre-decided number of installments.

To decide the optimal replacement policy, we have the following theorem.

Theorem 13.2: *Given that the operating cost increases with time and the money value decreases with constant rate. Then the replacement policy will be*

(a) *Replace if the next period's cost is more than the weighted average of previous costs.*

(b) *Otherwise, do not replace.*

Proof: Let C be the purchase price of an item to be replaced.

$R(n)$ be the operating cost incurred at the beginning of the n-th year.

r be the annual interest rate.

d be the discounted value per unit of money during a year ($d = (1 + r)^{-1}$).

$PV(n)$ be the present value of all future discounted costs associated with the replacement of the item at the end of every n year.

Let us assume that the item is replaced after every n year of service and has no resale value. The replacement policy can be formulated by computing the total amount of money for purchase and operating the item for n years. We need to find best optimal time at which the sum of the above mentioned costs is minimum.

The present value $PV(n)$ of all future costs of purchasing and operating the items with the assumption of replacement of the item after every n year is given by

$$\begin{aligned} PV(n) &= \{C + R(1) + R(2)\, d + R(3)\, d^2 + \cdots R(n)^{n-1}\} \quad \text{(for } 1 + n \text{ years)} \\ &\quad + \{(C + R1)\, d^n + R(2)\, d^{n+1} + \cdots + r(n) d^{2n-1}\} \quad \text{(for } n + 1 \text{ to } 2n \text{ years)} \\ &= [C + R(1) + R(2)\, d + \cdots + R(n)\, d^{n-1}][1 + d^n + d^{2n} + \cdots] \\ &= \left[C + \sum_{i=1}^{n} d^{i-1} R(i)\right]\left[\frac{1}{1 - d^n}\right] \quad \text{(sum of infinite } GP,\ d < 1) \\ &= \frac{F(n)}{1 - d^n} \end{aligned} \tag{13.9}$$

where $$F(n) = C + \sum_{i=1}^{n} d^{i-1} R(i)$$

The value of $PV(n)$ in Eq. (13.9) is the total money required for the machine with a replacement policy of every n year. Since n takes only discrete values, for obtaining minimum value of $PV(n)$, the necessary condition is

$$PV(n + 1) > PV(n) < PV(n - 1) \tag{13.10}$$

i.e. $$PV(n + 1) - PV(n) > 0 \text{ and } PV(n) - PV(n - 1) < 0.$$

From Eq. (13.9), we have

$$PV(n + 1) - PV(n) = \frac{F(n + 1)}{1 - d^{n+1}} \frac{PV(n)}{1 - d^n}$$

$$= \frac{F(n + 1) - F(n) + d^{n+1} F(n) - d^n F(n + 1)}{(1 - d^n)(1 - d^{n+1})}$$

$$= \frac{d^n R(n + 1) + d^{n+1} F(n) - d^n \{F(n) - d^n R(n + 1)\}}{(1 - d^n)(1 - d^{n+1})}$$

$$= \frac{d^n (1 - d^n) R(n + 1) - d^n (1 - d) F(n)}{(1 - d^n)(1 - d^{n+1})}$$

$$= \frac{d^n (1 - d)}{(1 - d^n)(1 - d^{n+1})} \left[\frac{1 - d^n}{1 - d} R(n + 1) - F(n) \right] \tag{13.11}$$

Since $0 < d < 1$ and so $1 - d^n > 0$. Therefore $PV(n + 1) - PV(n)$ is always positive. Replacing n by $n - 1$ in Eq. (13.11), we have

$$PV(n) - PV(n - 1) = \frac{d^{n-1} (1 - d)}{(1 - d^{n-1})(1 - d^n)} \left[\frac{1 - d^{n-1}}{1 - d} R(n) - f(n - 1) \right]$$

$$= \frac{d^{n-1} (1 - d)}{(1 - d^{n-1})(1 - d^n)} \left[\frac{1 - d^{n-1}}{1 - d} R(n) - \{f(n) - R(n)\, d^{n-1}\} \right]$$

$$= \frac{d^{n-1} (1 - d)}{(1 - d^{n-1})(1 - d^n)} \left[\frac{1 - d^n}{1 - d} R(n) - F(n) \right] \tag{13.12}$$

Using Eqs. (13.11) and (13.12) in Eq. (13.10), we get

$$\frac{1 - d^n}{1 - d} R(n) - F(n) < 0 < \frac{1 - d^n}{1 - d} R(n + 1) - F(n)$$

or $$\frac{1 - d^n}{1 - d} R(n) < F(n) < \frac{1 - d^n}{1 - d} R(n + 1)$$

or $$R(n) < \frac{C + R(1) + dR(2) + d^2 R(3) + \cdots + d^{n-1} R(n)}{1 + d + d^2 + \cdots + d^{n-1}} < R(n + 1) \tag{13.13}$$

The expression between $R(n)$ and $R(n + 1)$ in Eq. (13.13) represents the weighted average of all costs up to the $(n - 1)$–periods with weights $1, d, d^2, \ldots, d^{n-1}$ respectively. These weights $W(n)$ for n-year are actually the discounted factors of the costs in the previous costs. Equation (13.13) determines the age n for replacing the given machine.

EXAMPLE 13.11: Assuming $d = 0.9$ and the purchase price Rs. 5,000, what would be the optimum replacement age when the running cost varies as follows:

Year :	1	2	3	4	5	6	7
Running cost (Rs.) :	400	500	700	1,000	1,300	1,700	2,100

Solution: Based on the given information, the computation of optimum replacement age is exhibited in Table 13.8.

Table 13.8

Year (n)	$R(n)$	d^{n-1}	$R(n)\,d^{n-1}$	$C + \sum_k R(k)\,d^{k-1}$	$\sum d^{k-1}$	$W(n)$
(1)	(2)	(3)	(4)	(5)	(6)	(5)/(6)
1	400	1.000	400	5,400	1.000	5,400
2	500	0.900	450	5,850	1.900	3,079
3	700	0.810	567	6,417	2.710	2,368
4	1,000	0.729	729	7,146	3.439	2,038
5	1,300	0.656	853	7,999	4.095	1,953
6	**1,700**	**0.599**	**1,016**	**9,015**	**4.694**	**1,921***
7	2,100	0.540	1,134	10,149	5.234	1,939

* denotes the optimal solution.

Since $W(6) = 1{,}921 < R(7) = 2{,}100$, optimum replacement is under 6 years.

EXAMPLE 13.12 The cost of a new machine is Rs. 5,000. The maintenance cost of nth year is given by $R(n) = 500\,(n - 1)$; $n = 1, 2, \ldots$. Suppose that the discount rate per year is 0.05. After how many years it will be economic to replace the machine by a new one?

Solution: Given C = Rs. 5,000 and the discount rate of money per year, $r = 0.05$. Then the present value of the money to be spent over a period of one year is $d = (1 + 0.05) = 0.9523$. The optimum replacement time is determined in Table 13.9.

Table 13.9

Year (n)	$R(n)$	d^{n-1}	$R(n)\,d^{n-1}$	$C + \sum_k R(k)\,d^{k-1}$	$\sum d^{k-1}$	$W(n)$
(1)	(2)	(3)	(4)	(5)	(6)	(5)/(6)
1	0	1.0000	0	5,000	1.0000	5,000
2	500	0.9523	476	6,476	1.9523	2,805
3	1,000	0.9070	907	6,383	2.8593	2,232
4	1,500	0.8638	1,296	7,679	3.7231	2,063
5	**2,000**	**0.8227**	**1,645**	**9,324**	**4.5458**	**2,051***
6	2,500	0.7835	1,959	11,283	5.3293	2,117

* denotes the optimal solution.

It is observed from the table that $W(5)$ is minimum and $R(4) = 1{,}500 < W(5) > R(6) = 2{,}500$. So, it is economical to replace the machine by a new one at the end of five years.

EXAMPLE 13.13: A manufacturer is offered two machines *A* and *B*. *A* is priced at Rs. 5,000 and the running costs are estimated to be Rs. 800 for each of the first five years, increasing by Rs. 200 per year in the sixth and subsequent years. Machine *B*, which has the same capacity as *A*, costs Rs. 2,500 but will have running costs Rs. 1,200 per year for six years, increasing by Rs. 200 per year thereafter.

If the money is worth 10% per year, which machine should be purchased? (Assume that the machine will eventually be sold for scrap of a negligible price.)

Solution: The present value of the money to be spent over a period of one year is $d = (1 + 0.10) = 0.9091$. Let us compute (Tables 13.10(a) and (b)) for machines *A* and *B* respectively, by using the present value of money of one rupee to be spent in *n*-years from now onwards. For machine *A*, C = Rs. 5,000.

Table 13.10(a)

Year (n)	R(n)	d^{n-1}	$R(n)\, d^{n-1}$	$C + \sum_k R(k)\, d^{k-1}$	$\sum d^{k-1}$	W(n)
(1)	(2)	(3)	(4)	(5)	(6)	(5)/(6)
1	800	1.0000	800	5,800	1.0000	5,800
2	800	0.9091	727	6,527	1.9091	3,418
3	800	0.8264	661	7,188	2.7355	2,627
4	800	0.7513	601	7,789	3.4868	2,233
5	800	0.6830	546	8,335	4.1698	1,998
6	1,000	0.6209	621	8,956	4.7907	1,896
7	1,200	0.5645	677	9,633	5.3552	1,798
8	1,400	0.5132	718	10,351	5.8684	1,763
9	**1,600**	**0.4665**	**746**	**11,097**	**6.3349**	**1,751***
10	1,800	0.4241	763	11,860	6.7590	1,754

* denotes the optimal solution.

Then $R(10) = 1{,}800 > W(9) = 1{,}751$. So the machine should be replaced after every nine years.

For machine *B*, C = Rs. 2,500

Table 13.10(b)

Year (n)	R(n)	d^{n-1}	$R(n)\, d^{n-1}$	$C + \sum_k R(k)\, d^{k-1}$	$\sum d^{k-1}$	W(n)
(1)	(2)	(3)	(4)	(5)	(6)	(5)/(6)
1	1,200	1.0000	1,200	3,700	1.0000	3,700
2	1,200	0.9091	1,091	4,791	1.9091	2,509
3	1,200	0.8264	991	5,782	2.7355	2,114
4	1,200	0.7513	901	6,683	3.4868	1,917
5	1,200	0.6830	820	7,503	4.1698	1,799
6	1,200	0.6209	745	8,248	4.7907	1,722
7	1,400	0.5645	789	9,037	5.3552	1,687
8	**1,600**	**0.5132**	**821**	**9,858**	**5.8684**	**1,679***
9	1,800	0.4665	839	10,697	6.3349	1,688
10	2,000	0.4241	848	11,545	6.7590	1,709

* denotes the optimal solution.

For machine B, $R(9) = 1,800 > W(8) = 1,679$. So, machine B should be replaced after every 8 years. Also, as the weighted average annual cost for machine B is less, it is advisable to purchase machine B.

13.5 REPLACEMENT OF ITEMS THAT FAIL COMPLETELY

It is very uncertain to predict that a particular piece of equipment will fail at a particular time. This failure uncertainty can be calculated using mortality concept as given below.

Let $M(t)$ be the number of the survivor at any time t

$M(t-1)$ be the number of the survivor at any time $t-1$

N be the initial number of components in a piece of equipment.

Then $P(t) = \dfrac{M(t-1) - M(t)}{N}$ is the probability of failure during time t and $P_c(t) = \dfrac{M(t-1) - M(t)}{M(t-1)}$ is conditional probability of failure (the probability that a component has survived to an age $(t-1)$, and will fail during the interval $(t-1, t)$). $P_s(t) = \dfrac{M(t)}{N}$ is the probability of survival to an age t.

The problem of deaths and survivals can be exhibited in the following theorem.

Theorem 13.3 (Mortality theorem): *A large population is subject to a given mortality law for a very long period of time. All deaths are immediately replaced by the births and there are no other entries or exits. Show that the age distribution ultimately becomes stable and the number of deaths per unit time becomes constant and is equal to the size of the total population divided by the mean age at death.*

Proof: Let us assume that the death (or failure) occurs just before some time $t = k$, where k is an integer, and that no member of the population remains alive more than $(k+1)$–time units. Let $f(t)$ be the number of births (replacements) at time t and $P(x)$ be the probability of death (failure) just before the age $x + 1$, equivalently at the age x and $\sum_{x=0}^{k} P(x) = 1$. Then $f(t - x)$ denotes the number of births at time $(t - x)$, $t = k, k + 1, k + 2, \ldots$. Hence, the expected number of deaths from survivors at time t is $P(x)\, f(t - x)$. Therefore, the total number of deaths at time t will be

$$\sum_{x=0}^{k} P(x)\, f(t-x), \quad t = k, k+1, k+2, \ldots$$

Also, the total number of births at time $(t + 1)$ is $f(t + 1)$. Given that all deaths at time t are immediately replaced by births at time $(t + 1)$. Therefore

$$f(t+1) = \sum_{x=0}^{k} P(x)\, f(t-x), \quad t = k, k+1, k+2, \ldots \tag{13.14}$$

Equation (13.14) in t can be solved by substituting $f(t) = Aw^t$. Then Eq. (13.14) becomes

$$Aw^{t+1} = A \sum_{x=0}^{k} P(x)\, w^{t-x}, \quad t = k, k+1, k+2, \ldots$$

Divide both sides by Aw^{t-k},

$$w^{k+1} = \sum_{x=0}^{k} P(x)\, w^{k-x} = w^k \sum_{x=0}^{k} P(x)\, w^{-x} = w^k\{P(0) + P(1)\, w^{-1} + \ldots\}$$

$$w^{k+1} - \{P(0)\, w^k + P(1)\, w^{k-1} + \cdots + P(k)\} = 0 \tag{13.15}$$

Since $$\sum_{x=0}^{k} P(x) = 1 \text{ or } 1 - \{P(0) + P(1) + \cdots + P(k)\} = 0 \tag{13.16}$$

Comparing Eqs. (13.15) and (13.16), the one root (say) of Eq. (13.15) is w_0 (say) = 1. Now, the polynomial Eq. (13.15) must have exactly $(k + 1)$ roots by fundamental theorem of algebra. Denote the remaining roots by $w_1, w_2, \ldots, \alpha_k$.

Equation (13.15) can be written as

$$f(t) = A_0 + A_1 w_1^t + \cdots + A_k w_k^t \tag{13.17}$$

where $A_0, A_1, \ldots, A_k$ are constants and can be determined using age distribution at some given point of time. Further, using the theory of equations, the absolute value of all the remaining roots is less than unity, i.e. $|w_i| < 1$, $i = 1, 2, \ldots, k$. Therefore, the value of these roots tends to zero as $t \to \infty$. Consequently, Eq. (13.17) gives $f(t) = A_0$ (constant), which is the number of deaths per time unit (also the number of births).

Next, it remains to be proved that the age distribution ultimately becomes stable.

Now to determine A_0.

Let $g(x)$ = probability of survival for more than x-years
= 1 – prob. (survivor will die before age x)
= $1 - \{P(0) + P(1) + \cdots + P(x - 1)\}$

Assume that $g(0) = 1$.

Since the number of births as well as deaths is at a constant rate A_0, the expected number of survivors of age x is also stable and given by $A_0 * g(x)$. Also, since the number of births is always equal to the number of deaths, the size N of the total population is constant, i.e.

$$N = A_0 \sum_{x=0}^{k} g(x) \tag{13.18}$$

or, $$A_0 = \frac{N}{\sum_{x=0}^{k} g(x)} \tag{13.19}$$

From Eq. (13.18), the number of survivors A_0, $A_0P(1)$, $A_0P(2)$ ... aged at 0, 1, 2, ..., can be computed. To prove that the age distribution tends to stability, we need to establish that $\sum_{x=0}^{k} P(x)$ is the mean age at death.

Consider $$\sum_{x=0}^{k} P(x)\, 1 = \sum_{x=0}^{k} P(x)\, [(x + 1) - x] = \sum_{x=0}^{k} P(x)\, \Delta x$$

$$= \left[P(x)\, x\right]_0^{k+1} - \sum_{x=0}^{k} (x - 1)\, \Delta P(x)$$

$$= P(k + 1)(k + 1) - \sum_{x=0}^{k} (x + 1)\, \Delta P(x) \tag{13.20}$$

We have $P(k+1) = 1 - \{P(0) + P(1) + \cdots + P(k)\}$ and $\Delta P(x) = P(x+1) - P(x)$, Eq. (13.20) becomes

$$\sum_{x=0}^{k} P(x) = \sum_{x=0}^{k} (x+1)\, P(x) = \sum_{y=0}^{k+1} yP(y-1) \quad (\text{set } x+1=y)$$

$$= \sum_{y=0}^{k+1} y \text{ Prob. (that age at death is } y) = \text{Mean age at death.}$$

13.6 GROUP REPLACEMENT POLICY

A heavy loss is incurred when a system completely fails and immediate replacement of the item(s) may not be possible. In such a situation, the decision favours group replacement policy. Under this policy, items are replaced: (i) individually as and when they fail during a specified time, (ii) in groups at some point of time without waiting for their failure. Here, we need to study (i) the rate of individual replacement during the given time period, and (ii) the total cost incurred for individual as well as group replacement during the given time period. To calculate the optimal time period for replacement, the decision maker needs to know (i) probability of failure, (ii) loss incurred due to these failures, (iii) cost of individual replacement, and (iv) cost of group replacement. The decision for group replacement is based on the following theorem.

Theorem 13.4 (Group replacement policy): *(a) Group replacement should be made at the end of the period t, if the cost of individual replacement for the period t is greater than the average cost per time through the end of period t.*

(b) Group replacement is not advisable at the end of the period t if the cost of individual replacement at the end of period (t – 1) is less than the average cost per period through the end of period t.

Proof: Let n = total number of items in the system

$f(t)$ = number of items failing during time t

$C(t)$ = total cost of group replacement until the end of period t

$C_1(t)$ = unit cost of replacement in a group

$C_2(t)$ = unit cost of individual replacement after failure

L = maximum life of any item

$P(t)$ = probability of failure of any item at age t

Under the above notations:

The number of failures at any time t is

$$f(t) = \begin{cases} nP(t) + \sum_{x=1}^{t-1} P(x)\, f(t-x), & t \le L \\ \sum_{x=1}^{L} P(x)\, f(t-x), & t > L \end{cases} \tag{13.21}$$

And the cost of group replacement after time period t is

$$C(t) = nC_1 + C_2 \sum_{x=1}^{t-1} f(x) \tag{13.22}$$

where nC_1 is the cost of replacing the items as a group and $C_2 \sum_{x=1}^{t-1} f(x)$ is the cost of replacing the individual failures at the end of each $(t - 1)$ periods before the group is replaced. The average cost per time unit is

$$\frac{C(t)}{t} = \frac{nC_1}{t} + \left(\frac{C_2}{t}\right) \sum_{x=1}^{t-1} f(x) \tag{13.23}$$

Here, time t takes discrete values so the condition for minimum average cost is

$$\Delta\left\{\frac{C(t-1)}{t-1}\right\} < 0 < \Delta\left\{\frac{C(t)}{t}\right\}$$

Now for $\Delta\left\{\frac{C(t)}{t}\right\} > 0$ implies $\frac{C(t+1)}{t+1} - \frac{C(t)}{t} > 0$

i.e.
$$C_2 f(t) > \frac{nC_1 + C_2 \sum_{x=1}^{t-1} f(x)}{t} \tag{13.24}$$

Similarly, $\Delta\left(\frac{C(t)}{t}\right) > 0$ implies $\frac{C(t-1)}{t-1} - \frac{C(t)}{t} > 0$

i.e.
$$C_2 f(t-1) > \frac{nC_1 + C_2 \sum_{x=1}^{t-2} f(x)}{t-1} \tag{13.25}$$

Inequalities (13.24) and (13.25) define the necessary condition for optimal group replacement at the end of period t.

EXAMPLE 13.14: There are 1,000 bulbs in the system. Survival rate is given below:

Week	:	0	1	2	3	4
Bulb in operation at the end of the week	:	1,000	850	500	200	00

The group replacement of 1,000 bulbs costs Rs. 0.10 and individual replacement is 0.50 per bulb. Discuss suitable replacement policy.

Solution: From the given data of survival rate, we compute probability $P(n)$ of failure during the week n as follows:

Week	:	1	2	3	4
Probability of survival	:	0.85	0.50	0.20	0.00
Probability of failure $P(n)$	:	0.15	0.35	0.30	0.20

The expected life of each bulb is $\sum_{n=1}^{4} nP(n) = 1P(1) + 2P(2) + 3P(3) + 4P(4) = 2.55$ weeks.

Therefore, the average number of failures per week is 1,000/2.55 = 392.16.

Let N_n denote the number of replacement at the end of nth week. Given N_0 = 1,000. Then

$$N_1 = N_0P_1 = 1{,}000 * 0.15 = 150$$

$$N_2 = N_0P_2 + N_1P_1 = 1{,}000 * 0.35 + 150 * 0.15 = 373$$

$$N_3 = N_0P_3 + N_1P_2 + N_2P_1 = 409$$

$$N_4 = N_0P_4 + N_1P_3 + N_2P_2 + N_3P_1 = 437$$

On the basis of the mean life of 2.55 weeks, the individual replacement cost is (1,000 * 0.50)/2.55 = Rs. 196.20.

It is given that the replacement of all bulbs simultaneously costs Rs. 0.10 per bulb and the replacement of an individual bulb on failure costs Rs. 0.50. We compute the average cost for different group replacement policies as under:

End of week	*Individual replacement*	*Total cost = Individual + Group Rs.*	*Average cost Rs.*
1	**150**	**75.00 + 100 = 175.00**	**175.00**
2	523	261.50 + 100 = 361.50	180.75
3	932	466.00 + 100 = 566.00	188.86
4	1,369	684.50 + 100 = 784.50	196.12

It is observed from the above table that the average cost Rs. 175.00 for week 1 is minimum for group replacement, and it is lower than Rs. 196.20 for individual replacement. So, the group replacement policy is better.

EXAMPLE 13.15: There are 10,000 light bulbs, all of which must be kept in working order. If a bulb fails in service, it costs Rs. 1.00 to replace it, but if all the bulbs are replaced in the same operation, it costs only Rs. 0.35 per bulb. If the proportion of bulbs failing in successive time intervals is known, decide the best replacement policy. Following mortality rates for the light bulbs have been observed:

Week	:	1	2	3	4	5	6
Probability of failure $P(t)$	:	0.09	0.16	0.24	0.36	0.12	0.03

Solution: Let N_n denote the number of replacement at the end of nth week. Given N_0 = 10,000. Then

$$N_1 = N_0P_1 = 900$$

$$N_2 = N_0P_2 + N_1P_1 = 1{,}681$$

$$N_3 = N_0P_3 + N_1P_2 + N_2P_1 = 2{,}695$$

$$N_4 = N_0P_4 + N_1P_3 + N_2P_2 + N_3P_1 = 4{,}324$$

$$N_5 = N_0P_5 + N_1P_4 + N_2P_3 + N_3P_2 + N_4P_1 = 2{,}747$$

$$N_6 = N_0P_6 + N_1P_5 + N_2P_4 + N_3P_3 + N_4P_2 + N_5P_1 = 2{,}599$$

Expected life $= \sum_{i=1}^{6} x_iP(x_i)$

$= 1(0.09) + 2(0.16) + 3(0.14) + 4(0.36) + 5(0.12) + 6(0.03)$

$=$ 3.35 weeks.

The average number of failures per week is = N/mean age = 10,000/3.35 = 2,985 bulbs. Hence, the total cost of individual replacement @ Rs. 1.00 per bulb is Rs. 2,985 * 1.00 = 2,985.

Since the replacement of all the 10,000 bulbs simultaneously costs Rs. 0.35 per bulb, the average cost for different group replacement policies is given below.

End of week	*Total cost of group replacement*	*Average cost/week*
1	900(1) + 10,000(0.35) = 4,400	4,400
2	2,581(1) + 10,000(0.35) = 6,081	3,041
3	**5,276(1) + 10,000(0.35) = 8,776**	**2,925***
4	9,550(1) + 10,000(0.35) = 13,050	3,263
5	12,297(1) + 10,000(0.35) = 15,797	3,159
6	14,896(1) + 10,000(0.35) = 18,396	3,066

* denotes the optimal solution.

The average cost is lowest in the third week, so it is optimal to have group replacement after every third week. Further, the average cost Rs. 2,925 for group replacement is lower than that of the individual replacement which is Rs. 2,985. Hence, the policy of group replacement is better.

EXAMPLE 13.16: (a) At time zero, all items in a system are new. Each item has a probability p of failing immediately before the end of the first month of life and a probability $q = 1 - p$ of failing immediately before the end of the second month. If all items are replaced as they fail, then show that the expected number of failures $f(x)$ at the end of the month x is given by $f(x) = \frac{N}{1+q}[1-(-q)^{x+1}]$ where N is the number of items in the system.

(b) If the cost per item of individual replacement is C_1 and the cost per item of group replacement is C_2, find the condition under which (i) a group replacement policy at the end of each month is most profitable; (ii) no group replacement policy is better than that of pure individual replacement.

Solution: (a) Let N_i be the expected number of items to fail at the end of the ith month. Then

N_0 = number of items in the system in the beginning (=N)

$N_1 = N_0 p$ = number of failures at the end of the first month = $N(1 - q)$

N_2 = expected number of failures at the end of second month

$= N_0 q + N_1 p = Nq + N_1(1-q) = Nq + N(1-q)^2 = N(1 - q + q^2)$

$N_3 = N(1 - q + q^2 - q^3)$

$N_k = N[1 - q + q^2 - q^3 + \cdots + (-q)^k]$

$N_{k+1} = N_{k-1}q + N_k p = N[1 - q + q^2 - q^3 + \cdots + (-q)^{k+1}]$

By mathematical induction, the expected number of failures, $f(x)$ at the end of the month x is given by $f(x) = N[1 - q + q^2 - q^3 + \cdots + (-q)^x] = \frac{N}{1+q}\{1-(-q)^{x+1}\}$.

(b) In the steady-state, the expected number of failures tends to $f(x) \to N/(1 + q)$ as $x \to \infty$, $q < 1$. Here $1 + q$ denotes the mean age at failure. Then, the average cost per month for an individual replacement policy @ C_1 per item will be $NC_1/(1 + q)$ and that for group replacement policy at the end of every month is $NC_2 + NC_1 p = NC_2 + NC_1(1 - q)$.

(i) A group replacement policy at the end of each month is the most profitable when $NC_2 + NC_1(1 - q) < NC_2$ and $NC_1/(1 + q) > NC_2$.

(ii) No group replacement policy is better than a policy of pure individual replacement, when $NC_2 > NC_1/(1 + q)$ and $NC_2 + NC_1(1 - q) > NC_2$.

13.7 RECRUITMENT AND PROMOTIONAL PROBLEMS

The principle of replacement problems can also be applicable to the problems of staffing. The problem of staffing involves fixed total staff, fixed size of staff groups, the proportion of the staff in each group due for promotion.

EXAMPLE 13.17: (a) An airline requires 200 assistant hostesses, 300 hostesses and 50 supervisors. Girls are recruited at age 21, and are still in service, retire at the age of 60. Given life table

Age	21	22	23	24	25	26	27	28
No. in service	1,000	600	480	384	307	261	228	206
Age	29	30	31	32	33	34	35	36
No. in service	190	181	173	167	161	155	150	146
Age	37	38	39	40	41	42	43	44
No. in service	141	136	131	125	119	113	106	99
Age	45	46	47	48	49	50	51	52
No. in service	93	87	80	73	66	59	53	46
Age	53	54	55	56	57	58	59	
No. in service	39	33	27	22	18	14	11	

Determine (i) How many girls should be recruited each year? (ii) At what age should promotion take place?

(b) For the above data, an airline has staff whose ages are distributed in the following table. It is estimated that for the next two years, staff requirement will increase by 10% per year. If girls are to be recruited at the age of 21, how many should be recruited for the next year and at what age will promotion take place?

Assistants

Age	21	22	23	24	25	
Number	90	50	30	20	10	Total = 200

Hostesses

Age	26	27	28	29	30	31	32	33	34
Number	40	35	35	30	28	26	20	18	16
Age	35	36	37	38	39	40	41		
Number	12	10	8	–	8	8	6	Total = 300	

Supervisors

Age	42	43	44	45	46	47	48	49	50	51
Number	5	4	5	3	3	3	6	2	–	–
Age	52	53	54	55	56	57	58	59		
Number	4	3	5	–	3	2	–	2	Total = 50	

Solution: The total number of girls recruited at age 21 and those serving up to the age of 59 will be equal to 6,480 whereas the airline requires 550 (=200 + 300 + 50) girls in all. The recruitment every year is 1,000 when the total number of girls is 6,480 after 59 years. Therefore, in order to maintain a requirement of 550 hostesses, we should recruit (550 * 1,000)/6,480 H ≈ 85 girls every year.

If we want to promote the assistant hostesses at the age x, then up to the age $(x - 1)$, we need 200 assistant hostesses. Among 550, there are 200 assistant hostesses. Therefore, out of total 1,000, there will be (200 * 1,000)/550 ≈ 364 assistant hostesses, and from the life table, this number is available up to the age of 24 years. Hence, the promotion of assistant hostesses will be due in 25th year.

Also, out of 550 recruitments, we need only 300 hostesses. Therefore, if we recruit 1,000 then we shall require (300 * 1,000)/550 ≈ 545 hostesses.

Hence, the number of hostesses and assistant hostesses in a recruitment of 1,000 will be 909 (=364 + 545). So, we need only 1,000 – 909 = 91 supervisors, whereas at the age of 46 only 86 will survive. Hence, the promotion of hostesses to supervisors will be due in 46th year.

(b) First we compute the expected number of survivals from supervisors for one year, using life table. The probability of being in service at 42 = $\dfrac{\text{Number in service at 42}}{\text{Number in service at 41}}$ and so on.

Present age (1)	*No. of supervisors* (2)	*Prob. of being in service for one year hence* (3)	*Expected survivals after one year* (4) = (2) * (3)	*New age* (5)
42	5	0.947	4.735	43
43	4	0.942	3.768	44
44	5	0.936	4.680	45
45	3	0.923	2.769	46
46	3	0.915	2.745	47
47	3	0.906	2.718	48
48	6	0.906	5.436	49
49	2	0.896	1.792	50
50	0	0.885	0	51
51	0	0.873	0	52
52	4	0.860	3.440	53
53	3	0.846	2.538	54
54	5	0.831	4.155	55
55	0	0.815	0	56
56	3	0.798	2.394	57
57	2	0.780	1.560	58
58	0	0.761	0	59
59	2	0.741	1.482	
Total	50		43	

From the above table, we observe that after one year only 43 supervisors will be in the service. Also, there is 10% increase in the posts, i.e. there will be 55 posts of supervisors after one year and only 43 remain in the service. Hence, 12 hostesses are to be promoted on the basis of the age.

Now, there are 6 hostesses of age 41. Their probability of survival for one year is 0.952. Therefore, the expected number of hostesses aged 41 who will be in the service for one year more i.e. up to 42 years of age is 5.712 (=6 * 0.952).

Similarly, there are 8 hostesses of age 40 years with probability of survival for one year being 0.957, 8 * 0.957 = 7.656 hostesses will be in service for one more year, i.e. up to 41 years of age.

Thus, after one year from the present age (5.712 + 7.656) = 13.3, senior most hostesses will be of age 42 and 41 years and we want to promote 12 out of them. Hence, all hostesses of age 41 and 42 and one of age 43 will be promoted as supervisors after one year.

EXAMPLE 13.18: A research team is planned to raise a strength of 50 chemists and then to remain at that level. The wastage of recruits, depending on their length of service, is as follows:

Year	1	2	3	4	5	6	7	8	9	10
Total % who have left at the end of the year	5	36	56	63	68	73	79	87	97	100

What is the recruitment per year necessary to maintain the required strength? There are 8 senior posts for which the length of service is the main criterion. What is the average length of service after which the new entrant expects promotion to one of the posts?

Solution: The computation of probability of a person being in service at the end of the year is exhibited in the following table.

Year n	*No. of persons who left at the end of the year*	*No. of persons in service at the end of the year*	*Probability of leaving at the end of the year*	*Probability of persons in service at the end of the year P(n)*
0	0	100	0.00	1.00
1	5	95	0.05	0.95
2	36	64	0.36	0.64
3	56	44	0.56	0.44
4	63	37	0.63	0.37
5	68	32	0.68	0.32
6	73	27	0.73	0.27
7	79	21	0.79	0.21
8	87	13	0.87	0.13
9	97	3	0.97	0.03
10	100	0	1.00	0.00
		436		

Thus, if 100 chemists are appointed each year then the total number of chemists serving in the laboratory would have been 436. Thus, in order to maintain a strength of 50 chemists, we must recruit (100 * 50)/436 = 12 chemists every year.

If $P(n)$ denotes the probability of a person to be in the service at the end of the nth year, then out of 12 recruits, the total number of survivals at the end of year n will be 12 * $P(n)$. The following table is for the number of chemists in the service at the end of each year.

Year (n)	0	1	2	3	4	5	6	7	8	9	10
$P(n)$	1.00	0.95	0.64	0.44	0.37	0.32	0.27	0.21	0.13	0.03	0.00
No. of chemists = 12 * $P(n)$	12	11	8	5	4	4	3	2	2	0	0

Given that there are 8 senior posts for which the length of service is the main criterion. From the above table, it can be observed that there are 3 persons in service during the 6th year, 2 persons in 7th year, and 2 persons in 8th year, i.e. in all 7 persons are there in service from 6th year to 8th year which is less than the total number of senior posts. Hence, the promotion of the new entrant will start by the end of the 5th year.

13.8 EQUIPMENT RENEWAL PROBLEM

The term 'renewal' means either to install new equipment in place of the old one or to repair the old equipment so that the probability density function (pdf) of its future life time is that of the new one. The probability that a renewal occurs during the small time interval Δt is called the renewal rate at time t, where t is measured from the instant the first machine was started. This probability is called ***the renewal density function*** and is denoted by $h(t)\, dt$.

Theorem 13.5: *The renewal rate of a machine is asymptotically reciprocal of the mean life of the machine.*

Proof: Let $f(x)$ be the pdf of failure time of a machine. If X_i $(i = 1, 2, 3, \ldots)$ is life span for ith machine then each $X_1, X_2, \ldots$ has the pdf of $f(x)$. Let the machine fail $(n - 1)$-times during period t, and as soon as the machine fails, it is immediately replaced by a similar type of a machine. Suppose nth machine is in the service at the end of this period. Then $X_1 + X_2 + \cdots + X_{n-1} < t$ and $X_1 + X_2 + \cdots + X_{n-1} + X_n > t$. Denote $P\left\{t \le \sum_{i=1}^{r} X_i \le t + \Delta t\right\} = f_r(t)dt$. As rth machine can fail during interval $(t, t + \Delta t)$, we have $h(t) = \sum_{r=1}^{\infty} f_r(t)$.

Therefore, if N machines are used at a time, the expected number of replacements at the end of the tth period is equal to $N \int_0^t h(y)\, dy$.

[*Note:* It is not necessary that $\int_0^\infty h(t)\, dt$, but the function $h(t)$ possesses the additive property, $h(t_2 - t_1) = h(t_2) - h(t_1)$ for $t_2 > t_1$.]

The Laplace–Stieljes transform of functions $h(t)$ and $f(t)$ are defined as

$$H(z) = \int_0^\infty e^{-zt} h(t)\, dt \quad \text{and} \quad F(z) = \int_0^\infty e^{-zt} f(t)\, dt$$

Thus

$$H(z) = \int_0^\infty e^{-zt}\left[\sum_{r=1}^{\infty} f_r(t)\right] = \sum_{r=1}^{\infty}\left[\int_0^\infty e^{-zt} f_r(t)\right] = \sum_{r=1}^{\infty} [F(z)]^r = \frac{F(z)}{1 - F(z)}$$

If the mean life of the machine is given by $\lambda = \int_0^\infty x f(x)\, dx$ then $H(z) \to 1/(\lambda z)$ (neglecting higher powers of z). Taking inverse Laplace transform of both sides $h(t) \to (1/\lambda)$.

EXAMPLE 13.19: Suppose that the life X of electric bulb follows the gamma distribution $P(x \le X < x + \Delta x) = \dfrac{a^p}{\Gamma(rp)} e^{-ax} x^{rp-1}\, dx,\ (a > 0,\ 0 \le x < \infty)$. Determine the renewal rate for one point at the end of time period $(0, t)$.

Solution: Using the additive property of gamma distribution, we have

$$f_r(x)\, dx = P\left\{t \le \sum_{i=1}^{r} X_i \le t + \Delta t\right\} = \frac{a^{rp}}{\Gamma(rp)} e^{-ax} x^{rp-1}\, dx$$

Therefore, by definition of renewal rate

$$h(t) = e^{-ax} \sum_{r=1}^{\infty} \frac{a^{rp}}{\Gamma(rp)} x^{rp-1} \to \sum_{r=1}^{\infty} \frac{a^{rp}}{\Gamma(rp)} x^{rp-1} \text{ as } t \to \infty$$

EXAMPLE 13.20: A certain piece of equipment is extremely difficult to adjust. During a period when no adjustment is made, the running cost increases linearly with time at a rate b rupees each hour. The running cost immediately after an adjustment is not known precisely until the adjustment has been made. Before the adjustment, running cost x is deemed to be random variable with probability density function $f(x)$. If each adjustment cost is k rupees, when should the replacement be made?

Solution: The running cost x after adjustment is a random variable with probability density function $f(x)$. Let X be the maximum value of x, such that $0 \le x < X$. Now if the adjustment is made when the running cost is equal to z, there may arise two possibilities: (a) $z > X$ and (b) $z < X$.

Case (a): Let the initial cost at time $t = 0$ be Rs. X and suppose that the adjustment is made after time t hours. Then, the running cost at time t will be equal to Rs. $(x + bt)$ and hence, $t = (z - x)/b$. If $C(z)$ denotes the total cost during the period of one adjustment to another then

$$C(z) = \text{Cost of adjustment} + \text{total running cost}$$

$$= k + \int_0^t (x + bt)\, dt = k + \frac{(z^2 - x^2)}{2b}$$

$$\text{Average cost per hour} = \frac{C(z)}{t} = \frac{kb}{(z - x)} + \frac{(z + x)}{2}$$

Therefore, the expected cost per hour is

$$E[C(z)] = E\left(\frac{C(z)}{t}\right) = \int_0^x \left(\frac{kb}{z - x} + \frac{z + x}{2}\right) f(x)\, dx$$

For minimum value of $E[C(z)]$, we need to set $\dfrac{d}{dz} E[C(z)] = 0$ and $\dfrac{d^2}{dz^2} E[C(z)] > 0$.

$$\text{Now} \quad \frac{d}{dz} E[C(z)] = \frac{d}{dz} \int_0^x \left(\frac{kb}{z - x} + \frac{z + x}{2}\right) f(x)\, dx = \int_0^x \frac{d}{dz}\left(\frac{kb}{z - x} + \frac{z + x}{2}\right) f(x)\, dx$$

$$= \int_0^x \left(\frac{-kb}{(z - x)^2} + \frac{1}{2}\right) f(x)\, dx = 0 \text{ implies } \int_0^x \frac{1}{(z - x)^2} f(x)\, dx = \frac{1}{2kb}.$$

When the functional form of $f(x)$ is known, the value of z can be easily determined from the above relation.

In case (b), when $z < x$, it is left for the reader to show that the minimum of z does not occur. Hence, the minimum value of z can be determined only in the first case.

EXAMPLE 13.21: A piece of equipment can fail completely, so that it has to be scrapped (no salvage value), or may suffer a minor defect which can be repaired. The probability that it will not be scrapes before age t is $f(t)$. The conditional probability that it will need a repair in the time interval $(t, t + dt)$, knowing that it was in running order at age t, is $r(t)\,dt$. The probability of a repair or complete failure is dependent only on the age of the equipment, and not on the previous repair history. Each repair costs Rs. C and completes replacement costs Rs. K. For some considerable time, the policy has been to replace only on failure.

(a) Derive a formula for the expected cost per unit time of the present policy of replacing only on failure.

(b) It has been suggested that it might be cheaper to scrape equipment at some fixed age T, thus avoiding the higher risk of repairs with advancing age. Show that the expected cost per unit of time of such policy is $\dfrac{k + C\int_0^T f(u)\,r(u)\,du}{\int_0^T f(u)\,du}$

Solution: The probability that the equipment is not scrapped before age t is $f(t)$. As the equipment will evidently fail at some time, we must have $\int_0^x f(t)\,dt = 1$. Also, when it is known that the equipment was running at age t, the probability that the equipment requires repair in time interval $(t, t + dt)$ is given by $r(t)\,dt$.

(a) Now the probability that the equipment requires repairs between the age $(u, u + du)$ is $f(u)\ r(u)\ du$.

Therefore, the expected cost of repair is $C\int_0^x f(u)\,r(u)\,du$ and the total expected cost is

$$\frac{k + C\int_0^x f(u)\,r(u)\,du}{\int_0^\infty f(u)\,du} = k + C\int_0^x f(u)\,r(u)\,du \text{ since } \int_0^\infty f(u)\,du = 1$$

(b) If we have a policy of scrapping at age T, the total expected cost of repair is $C\int_0^T f(u)\,r(u)\,du$ and the total expected cost up to age T is $\left(k + C\int_0^T f(u)\,r(u)\,du\right)$. Hence, the expected cost per unit of time will be $\dfrac{k + C\int_0^T f(u)\,r(u)\,du}{\int_0^T f(u)\,du}$.

REVIEW EXERCISES

1. The costs per year of running a truck whose purchase price is Rs. 30,000 are as follows:

Year	1	2	3	4	5	6	7
Running cost (Rs.)	5,000	6,000	7,000	9,000	11,500	14,000	17,000
Resale cost (Rs.)	15,000	7,500	3,750	1,875	1,000	1,000	1,000

Determine when is the replacement due.

[**Ans.** End of 5th year]

2. A firm is considering replacement of a machine whose cost price is Rs. 12,200 and the scrape value is Rs. 200. The operating costs found from experience are as follows:

Year	1	2	3	4	5	6	7	8
Operating cost (Rs.)	200	500	800	1,200	1,800	2,500	3,200	4,000

When should the machine be replaced?

[**Ans.** End of 6th year]

3. A truck owner finds from his past records that the operating costs per year of a truck whose purchase price is Rs. 8,000, are as follows:

Year	1	2	3	4	5	6	7	8
Running cost (Rs.)	1,000	1,300	1,700	2,200	2,900	3,800	4,800	6,000
Resale cost (Rs.)	4,000	2,000	1,200	600	500	400	400	400

Determine at what time it is profitable to replace the truck.

[**Ans.** End of 5th year]

4. A new tempo costs Rs. 8,000 and may be sold at the end of any year at the following prices:

Year	1	2	3	4	5	6
Running cost (Rs.)	1,000	1,200	1,500	2,000	3,000	5,000
Resale cost (Rs.)	5,000	3,300	2,000	1,100	600	100

It is not only possible to sell tempo after use but also to buy a second hand tempo. It may be cheaper to do so than to replace with a new tempo.

Year	0	1	2	3	4	5
Purchase cost (Rs.)	8,000	5,800	4,000	2,600	1,600	1,000

What is the age to buy and sell the tempo to minimize the average annual cost?

[**Ans.** End of 5th year]

5. Machine *A* costs Rs. 3,600. Annual operating costs are Rs. 400 for the first year and then increase by Rs. 360 every year. Assuming that machine *A* has no resale value, determine the best replacement age. Another machine *B*, which is similar to machine *A*, costs Rs. 4,000. Annual operating costs are Rs. 200 for the first year and then increase by Rs. 200 every year. It has resale value of Rs. 1,500 for the first year, Rs. 1,000 for the second year, and Rs. 500 for the third year. It has no resale value during fourth year and onwards. Which machine would you prefer to purchase?

[**Ans.** Replace machine *A* at the end of 5th year and *B* at the end of 6th year; machine *B* should be purchased]

6. The data on the operating costs per year and resale price of equipment *A* whose purchase price is Rs. 10,000 is given below:

Year	1	2	3	4	5	6	7
Running cost (Rs.)	1,500	1,900	2,300	2,900	3,600	4,500	5,500
Resale cost (Rs.)	5,000	2,500	1,250	600	400	400	400

(i) What is the optimum period for replacement?

(ii) When equipment *A* is 2 years old, equipment *B* which is a new model for the same usage, is available. The optimum period for replacement is 4 years with an average cost of Rs. 3,600. Should we replace equipment *A* with *B*? If so, when?

[**Ans.** Replace equipment *A* at the end of 5th year and replace equipment *A* by *B* when it is 4 years old]

7. A truck is priced at Rs. 60,000 and the running costs are estimated at Rs. 6,000 for each of the first four years, increasing by Rs. 2,000 per year in the fifth and subsequent years. If the money is worth 10% per year, when should the truck be replaced? Assume that the truck will eventually be sold at a negligible price.

[**Ans.** Replace at the end of 9th year]

8. An engineering company is offered two types of material handling equipment *A* and *B*. *A* is priced at Rs. 60,000 including cost of installation, and the costs of operation and maintenance are estimated to be Rs. 10,000 for each of the first five years, increasing by Rs. 3,000 per year in the sixth and subsequent years. Equipment *B* with a related capacity same as *A*, requires an initial investment of Rs. 30,000 but in terms of operation and maintenance it costs more than *A*. These costs for *B* are estimated to be Rs. 13,000 per year for the first six years, increasing by Rs. 4,000 per year for each year thereafter. The company expects a return of 10% on all its investments. Neglecting the scrape value of the equipment at the end of its economic life, determine which equipment should the company buy?

[**Ans.** Purchase B, replace it after 7 years]

9. The following failure rates have been observed for certain items:

End of month	1	2	3	4	5
Probability of failure of date	0.10	0.30	0.55	0.85	1.00

The cost of replacing an individual item is Rs. 1.25. The decision is made to replace all items simultaneously at fixed intervals and also to replace individual items as they fail. If the cost of group replacement is Rs. 0.50, what is the best interval of group replacement? At what group replacement price per item would a policy of strictly individual replacement become preferable to the adopted policy?

[**Ans.** Group replacement at the end of 3rd month, at Rs. 391.25 for individual replacement]

10. The following failure rates have been observed for a certain type of light bulbs:

Week	1	2	3	4	5
% of failure by the end of the week	10	25	50	80	100

There are 1,000 bulbs in use, and it costs Rs. 2.00 to replace an individual bulb which has burnt out. If all the bulbs were replaced simultaneously, it would cost Rs. 0.50 per bulb. It is proposed to replace all bulbs at fixed intervals, whether or not they have burnt out, and to continue replacing burnt out bulbs as they fail. At what intervals should all the bulbs be replaced?

[**Ans.** Group replacement at the end of second week]

11. A computer contains 10,000 resistors. When any resistor fails, it is replaced. The cost of replacing a resistor individually is Rs. 1.00. If all the resistors are replaced at the same time, the cost per resistor would be reduced to Rs. 0.35. The percentage of surviving resistors, $S(t)$ at the end of month t and $P(t)$, the probability of failure during the month t, are

t	0	1	2	3	4	5	6
$S(t)$	100	97	90	70	30	15	0
$P(t)$	–	0.03	0.07	0.20	0.40	0.15	0.15

What is the optimum replacement plan?

[**Ans.** Group replacement at the end of three months]

12. A large TV manufacturer has to provide "service after sales" on an annual contract basis. The company has now 600 TV sets and has to decide on service policy. The service is restricted to replacement of minor parts. The failure pattern of these minor parts is as under:

Month	1	2	3	4	5	6	7
Number of failure after month of service	10	20	60	130	160	180	40

It costs Rs. 50 to replace minor parts as and when they fail. It costs Rs. 20 to replace minor parts on a planned service basis, when parts are replaced even before failure. Find the optimal replacement policy?

[**Ans.** Group replacement at the end of fourth month]

13. Calculate the probability of staff resignation in each year from the following survival table:

Year	0	1	2	3	4	5	6	7	8	9	10
No. of original staff in service at the end of the year	1,000	940	820	580	400	280	190	130	70	30	0

14. Automobile batteries are manufactured by a firm at a factory cost of Rs. 20 each. The mortality table for the battery life is given below. The batteries are covered under a guarantee policy such that if a battery fails during the first month after purchase, full price of the new battery is refunded; a failure in the second month carries a refund of 19/20 of the full price, in the third month 18/20, and so on till the 20th month, during which a failure carries a refund of 1/20 of the full price. What should be the break-even selling price of the batteries?

Year	*Probability of failure in next month*	*Year*	*Probability of failure in next month*
1	0.05	11	0.01
2	0.00	12	0.01
3	0.00	13	0.01
4	0.00	14	0.01
5	0.00	15	0.015
6	0.00	16	0.020
7	0.00	17	0.025
8	0.00	18	0.030
9	0.00	19	0.035
10	0.00	≥ 20	0.785
		Total	1.000

[**Ans.** Break-even price Rs. 23 (approx.)]

14

Dynamic Programming

14.1 INTRODUCTION

Certain problems require decisions to bė made at a number of stages for a component or for sub-system and/or for a system in some particular sequence. Such problems are known as ***sequentially decision problems*** or ***multistage decision problems.*** Richard Bellman, in the early 1950s, gave a mathematical technique for the optimization of sequentially decision problems. This mathematical technique is termed as ***dynamic programming*** (DP).

In DP, the multistage decision problem is decomposed into a series of single decision problems so that the output of the one stage is the input of the succeeding stage, i.e. a N-variable problem is represented in a series of N-single variable problems which are to be solved successively. These N-single variable problems are considered as sub-programs and comparatively easier to solve than the original ones. The decomposition to N sub-problems is done in such a way that the optimal solution of the given N-variables problem can be obtained from the optimal solutions of the N sub-programs.

14.2 COMPONENTS OF DYNAMIC PROGRAMMING

In previous section, we studied that the DP problem is to be decomposed into a series of smaller sub-programs. These sub-programs are called ***stages***. At each stage, a single variable is optimized by selecting the most appropriate alternative. Stages vary according to the type of the problem, for example, for a salesman travelling different cities, city is a stage; for a replacement problem, each year is a stage; for capital budgeting, each plan represents a stage, etc.

Each stage in a DP has various conditions on the decision process. These conditions are referred as ***states***. The variables which specify the relevant information for the future course of action because of the current solution are called ***state variables***. At any stage of the decision-making process, there could be a finite or infinite number of states. For example, for a salesman travelling different cities, the shortest route is the state.

Using the state variables in a particular stage, a recursive function called ***return function*** is constructed. This return function is used to arrive at an optimal solution in a stage under consideration, which will affect the state of the system at the next stage.

For a multistage decision process, the functional relationship among state, stage and decision variables is as follows:

Let n be the stage number,

s_n be the state input to stage n from stage $(n + 1)$,

d_n be the decision variable at stage n (independent of previous stages).

It represents the alternative to be selected while making decision at stage n.

$f_n\ [=r_n(s_n, d_n)]$ be the return function for stage n.

These n-stages are interconnected by the relation (called ***transition relation***):

$$s_{n-1} = s_n * d_n$$

i.e. Output at stage $(n - 1)$ = (input to stage n) * (decision at stage n)

where * represents any mathematical operation depending on the problem.

14.3 COMPUTATIONAL ALGORITHM

The DP-problem can be solved using the following steps.

Step 1: Identify the decision variables and specify objective function to be optimized (under limitations, if any).

Step 2: Decompose the given problem into a number of smaller sub-programs (called stages). Identify the state variables at each stage and formulate the transformation function constituting the state variable and decision variable at the next stage.

Step 3: Construct a recursive relation for computing the optimal policy. Solve the problem.

Step 4: Tabulate the required values of the return function at each stage.

Step 5: Determine the overall optimal policy.

The optimal policy is based on the Bellman's principle of optimality which states that "*the optimality policy must be one such that, regardless of how a particular state is reached, all later decisions proceeding from that state must be optimal.*"

The solution of the problem (step 3) can be obtained by any of the following procedure:

(i) **Backward induction procedure:** Here, the problem is solved by solving the problem in the last stage and moving backward to the first stage, making optimal decisions at each stage of the problem.

(ii) **Forward induction procedure:** Here, the optimal decision is to be made by solving in the first stage and moving towards the last stage, to solve N-stage sub-programs.

14.4 SHORTEST ROUTE PROBLEM

EXAMPLE 14.1: Find the shortest route from city A to city B along arcs, joining various cities lying between A and B as shown in the following figure. Distances between each city are given.

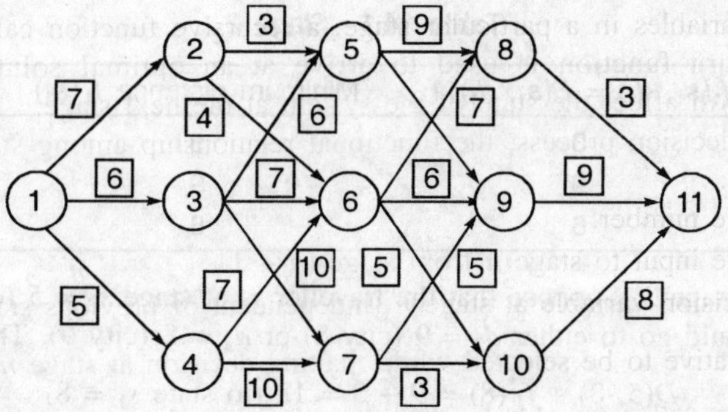

Solution: Let us divide the problem into 5 stages. Let d_n be the decision variable that defines the immediate decision when there are n (n = 1, 2, 3, 4, 5)-stages to go.

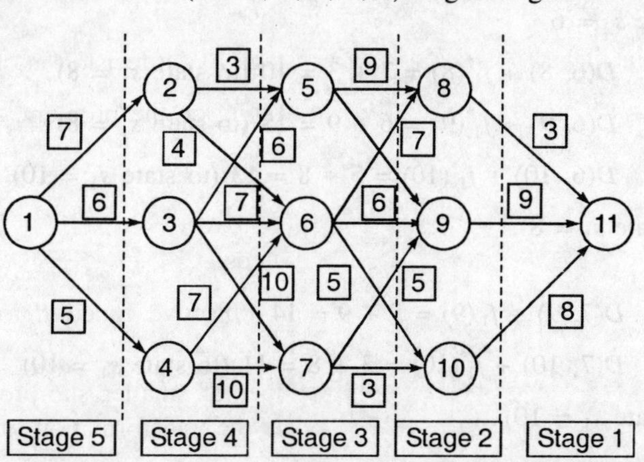

s_n be the state variables describing a specific city at any stage. $D(s_n, d_n)$ be the distance associated with the state variable s_n, and the decision variable, d_n for the nth stage. $f_n(s_n, d_n)$ be the minimum distance for the last n-stages, given that the traveller is in state s_n and selects d_n as the immediate destination. $f_n^*(s_n)$ be the optimal path (minimum distance) when the traveller is in state s_n with n more stages to go for reaching the destination.

We shall use the backward induction procedure. Start from destination city 11 and move backward to be at stage 1. The recursive function is defined as

$$f_n^*(s_n) = \text{mini } \{D(s_n, d_n) + f_{n-1}^*(d_n)\}; \qquad n = 1, 2, 3, 4.$$

where the minimum is to be taken over d_n and $f_{n-1}^*(d_n)$ is the minimum distance for the previous stages.

In stage 1, from state s_1 = 3 (city 8), s_1 = 9 (city 9) and s_1 = 8 (city 10), we have $D(8, 11)$ = 3, $D(9, 11)$ = 9 and $D(10, 11)$ = 8 respectively. Therefore, the optimal value of $f_1^*(s_1)$ = 3 is minimum. Let us tabulate these values in Table 14.1.

Table 14.1 Stage 2

Decision d_1 →		$f_1(s_1, d_1) = D(s_1, d_1)11$	Minimum distance $f_1^*(s_1)$	Optimal decision
State s_1	8	3	3	11
	9	9	9	11
	10	8	8	11

Now, let us move to stage 3. Suppose that the traveller is at stage $s_2 = 5$ (city 5). Now he has to decide whether he should go to either $d_2 = 9$ (city 8) or $d_2 = 8$ (city 9). Then

$$D(5, 8) + f_1^*(8) = 9 + 3 = 12 \text{ (to state } s_1 = 8)$$

or

$$D(5, 9) + f_1^*(9) = 8 + 9 = 17 \text{ (to state } s_1 = 9)$$

Then $f_2(s_2) = \text{mini}\{12, 17\} = 12$ (to state $s_1 = 8$) is the distance function from state $s_2 = 5$.

Similarly, for state $s_2 = 6$

$$D(6, 8) + f_1^*(8) = 7 + 3 = 10 \text{ (to state } s_1 = 8)$$

or

$$D(6, 9) + f_1^*(9) = 6 + 9 = 15 \text{ (to state } s_1 = 8)$$

$$D(6, 10) + f_1^*(10) = 5 + 8 = 13 \text{ (to state } s_1 = 10)$$

Then $f_2(6) = 10$ (to state $s_1 = 8$).

For state, $s_2 = 7$

$$D(7, 9) + f_1^*(9) = 5 + 9 = 14$$

$$D(7, 10) + f_1^*(10) = 3 + 8 = 11 \text{ (to state } s_1 = 10)$$

Then $f_2(7) = 11$ (to state $s_1 = 10$).

Table 14.2 Stage 3

Decision d_2 →		$f_2(s_2, d_2) = D(s_2, d_2) + f_1^*(d_2)$			Minimum distance $f_2^*(s_2)$	Optimal decision
		8	9	10		
State s_2	5	12	17	–	12	8
	6	10	15	13	10	8
	7	–	14	11	11	10

Similarly, move backward to stage 4. Suppose the traveller is at stage $s_3 = 2$ (city 2). He needs to decide whether to go to stage 5 or 6 or 7. Then,

$$D(2, 5) + f_2^*(5) = 3 + 12 = 15$$

$$D(2, 6) + f_2^*(6) = 4 + 10 = 14 \text{ (to state } s_2 = 6)$$

Then $f_2(2) = 14$ (to state $s_2 = 6$).

$$D(3, 5) + f_2^*(5) = 6 + 12 = 18$$

$$D(3, 6) + f_2^*(6) = 7 + 10 = 17 \text{ (to state } s_2 = 6)$$

$$D(3, 7) + f_2^*(7) = 7 + 11 = 18$$

Then $f_2(3) = 17$ (to state $s_2 = 6$).

$$D(4, 6) + f_2^*(6) = 10 + 10 = 20 \text{ (to state } s_2 = 6).$$

$$D(4, 7) + f_2^*(7) = 10 + 11 = 21$$

Then $f_2(4) = 20$ (to state $s_2 = 6$).

Table 14.3 Stage 4

Decision d_3	→	$f_3(s_3, d_3) = D(s_3, d_3) + f_2^*(d_3)$			Minimum distance $f_3^*(s_3)$	Optimal decision
		5	6	7		
State s_3	2	15	14	–	14	6
	3	18	17	18	17	6
	4	–	20	21	20	6

Table 14.4 Stage 5

Decision d_4	→	$f_4(s_4, d_4) = D(s_4, d_4) + f_3^*(d_4)$			Minimum distance $f_4^*(s_4)$	Optimal decision
		2	3	4		
State s_4	1	21	23	25	21	2

Then optimal results at various stages are as follows:

	Entering states (city)				
Sequence	11	8	5	2	1
	11	8	6	2	1

and both have minimum distance of 21 kilometers.

14.5 SINGLE ADDITIVE CONSTRAINT, MULTIPLICATIVE SEPARABLE RETURN FUNCTION

The general form of the problem is

$$\text{Maximize } z = f_1(d_1)\, f_2(d_2) \cdots f_n(d_n)$$

subject to the constraints

$$a_1d_1 + a_2d_2 + \cdots + a_nd_n = b,\ d_j,\ a_j,\ b \geq 0 \text{ for } j = 1, 2, \ldots, n$$

where j = jth number of stage.

d_j = decision variable at jth stage; a_j = constant.

Define state variables as

$$s_n = b$$
$$s_{n-1} = s_n - a_nd_n.$$
$$\vdots$$
$$s_{j-1} = s_j - a_jd_j.$$
$$\vdots$$
$$s_1 = s_2 - a_2d_2.$$

i.e. $s_{j-1} = t_j(s_j, d_j)$, $j = 1, 2, \ldots, n$ is the state transition function.

At the nth stage, the maximum value of $z = f_n^*(s_n)$ is given by

$$f_n^*(s_n) = \text{maxi } \{f_1(d_1)\, f_2(d_2)\, \ldots\, f_n(d_n)\}$$

subject to the constraint $s_n = b$

Clearly, for a fixed value of d_n, the maximum value of z will be given by

$$f_n(s_n) = \text{maxi } \{f_1(d_1)\, f_2(d_2) \ldots f_{n-1}(d_{n-1})\} = f_n(d_n) * f_{n-1}^*(s_{n-1})$$

The maximum value of $f_{n-1}^*(s_{n-1})$ of z because of decision variables d_j ($j = 1, 2, \ldots, n-1$) depends upon the state variable $s_{n-1} = t_n(s_n, d_n)$. Hence, we get the general recursive relation for maximum z for any feasible value of all decision variables as

$$f_j^*(d_j) = \text{maxi } \{f_j(d_j) * f_{j-1}^*(s_{j-1})\}, \quad j = n, n-1, \ldots, 2$$

and
$$f_1(s_1) = f_1(d_1)$$

where $s_{j-1} = t_j(s_j, d_j)$.

EXAMPLE 14.2: Divide a positive quantity c into n-parts so as to maximize their product.

Solution: Maxi $Z = y_1 y_2 \ldots y_n$

subject to the constraints $y_1 + y_2 + \cdots + y_n = c$ and $y_j \geq 0$, $j = 1, 2, \ldots, n$

Let $f_n(c)$ denote the maximum product. Here n denotes the number of stages. The recurrence relation is

$$f_n(c) = \text{maxi } \{x f_{n-1}(c - x)\}, \quad 0 < x \leq c.$$

For stage 1, $f_1(c) = \text{maxi } \{y_1\} = c$.

For stage 2, divide c into two parts (say) x and $c - x$.

$$f_2(c) = \text{maxi } \{y_1 y_2\} = \text{maxi } \{x(c - x)\} = \text{maxi. } \{x\, f_1(c - x)\},\ 0 < x \leq c.$$

For stage 3, we need to divide c into three parts, given the initial values of x which leaves $c - x$ to be further divided into two parts. Denote the maximum product for $c - x$ into two parts by $f_2(c - x)$.

Therefore,
$$f_3(c) = \text{maxi } \{x f_2(c - x)\},\ 0 < x \leq c$$

Continuing in a similar manner, we get $f_n(c) = \text{maxi } \{x f_{n-1}(c - x)\}, 0 < x \leq c$.

For $n = 2$, the function $x(c - x)$ attains its maximum value at $x = c/2$ and $f_2(c) = (c/2)^2$.

For $n = 3$, $f_3(c) = \text{maxi } \{x\,[(c - x)/2]^2\}$. This function attains its maximum value at $x = c/3$ and $f_3(c) = (c/3)^3$.

In general, for n-stage problem, we assume that optimal policy is $(c/n, c/n, \ldots, c/n)$ and $f_n(c) = (c/n)^n$ for $n = 1, 2, \ldots, m$.

Now for $n = m + 1$, the recursive equation is $f_{m+1}(c)$

$$= \text{maxi } \{x f_m(c - x)\}$$

$$= \text{maxi } \left\{ x \left(\frac{c - x}{m} \right)^m \right\},\ 0 < x \leq c$$

$$= \left(\frac{c}{m + 1} \right)^{1/(m+1)}$$

as the maximum value of $x\,[(c - x)/m)^m$ which is attained at $x = c/(m + 1)$. Hence, the result holds for $n = m + 1$. Therefore, by mathematical induction, the optimal policy is $(c/n, c/n, \ldots, c/n)$ and $f_n(c) = (c/n)^n$.

EXAMPLE 14.3: Use DP to maximize $Z = y_1 y_2 y_3$, subject to the constraints $y_1 + y_2 + y_3 = 5$ and $y_j \geq 0$, $j = 1, 2, 3$.

Solution: Let $f_3(5) = \text{maxi}\ \{y_1 y_2 y_3\}$.

Then $$f_1(5) = \text{maxi}\ \{y_1\} = 5 \text{ (stage 1)}$$

For two stage problem, divide 5 into two parts (say) $y_1 = x$ and $y_2 = 5 - x$. Then

$$f_2(5) = \text{maxi}\ \{y_1 y_2\} = \text{maxi}\ \{x\,(5 - x)\}$$

Using differential calculus, $f_2(5)$ is maximum for $x = 5/2$ and $f_2(5) = (5/2)^2$.

Similarly, for three stage problem, (using example 14.2), we have

$$f_3(5) = \text{maxi}\ \{x f_2(5 - x)\} = \text{maxi}\left\{x\left(\frac{5-x}{2}\right)^2\right\} = \left(\frac{5}{3}\right)^3$$

It is left for the readers to verify that the function $x\,[(5 - x)/2)^2]$ attains its maximum value at $x = 5/3$. Hence, the required optimal policy is $(5/3, 5/3, 5/3)$ with maxi $Z = (5/3)^3$.

EXAMPLE 14.4: A government space project is conducting research on a certain engineering problem that must be solved before the man can fly to the moon safely.

Three research teams are currently trying three different approaches for solving this problem. The estimate has been made that under the present circumstances, the probability that the respective teams (say) A, B and C will not succeed are 0.40, 0.60 and 0.80, respectively. Thus, the current probability that all three teams will fail is 0.192 (= 0.40 * 0.60 * 0.80). Since the objective is to minimize this probability, the decision has been made to assign two or more top scientists among the three teams in order to lower it as much as possible.

The following table gives the estimated probability that the respective teams will fail when 0, 1 or 2 additional scientists are added to that team:

		Team		
		A	*B*	*C*
Number of new scientist(s)	0	0.40	0.60	0.80
	1	0.20	0.40	0.50
	2	0.15	0.20	0.30

How should the additional scientists be allocated to the team?

Solution: Here, the stages correspond to the research teams and the state s denotes the number of new scientists still available for assignment at that stage. The decision variable x_j ($j = 1, 2, 3$) are the number of additional scientists allocated to stage j. Let $p_j(x_j)$ be the probability of failure for team j if it is assigned x_j additional scientists.

The problem is, minimize $Z = p_1(x_1)\, p_2(x_2)\, p_3(x_3)$ subject to the constraints $x_1 + x_2 + x_3 = 2$, $x_1, x_2, x_3 \geq 0$ are integers.

Define $f_j(x_j)$ to be the value of the optimal allocation for team 1 through j, i.e. for $j = 1$, $f_1(s, x_1) = \{p_1(x_1)\}$. Let $f_j(s, x_j)$ be the probability associated with the optimum solution $f_j^*(s)$,

$j = 1, 2, 3$. Then $f_j(s, x_j) = p_j(x_j) * \text{mini}\left\{\prod_{i=j+1}^{3} pi(x_i)\right\}$ such that $\sum_{i=j}^{3} x_i = s$.

The recursive equations are

$$f_1^*(s) = \text{mini } f_1(s_1, x_1),\ x_1 \le s \quad \text{and} \quad f_j(s, x_j) = p_j(x_j) * f_{j+1}^*(s - x_j)$$

where $f_j^*(s) = \text{mini }\{p_j(x_j) * f_{j+1}^*(s - x_j)\}$; $j = 1, 2, 3$, $x_j \le s$ and for $n = 3$,

$$f_3^*(s) = \text{mini }\{p_3(x_3)\},\quad x_3 \le s.$$

We will use backward induction, i.e. start with $f_3(s)$ and obtain $f_1^*(s)$.
For $j = 3$, the computations for one stage problem are as follows:

s	$f_3^*(s)$	x_3^*
0	0.80	0
1	0.50	1
2	0.30	2

For $j = 2$ (two stage problem), we have $f_2(s, x_2) = p_2(x_2)\, f_3^*(s - x_2)$

	x_2	0	1	2	$f_2^*(s)$	x_2^*
s	0	0.60 * 0.80			0.48	0
	1	0.60 * 0.50	0.40 * 0.80		0.30	0
	2	0.60 * 0.30	0.40 * 0.50	0.20 * 0.80	0.16	2

For $j = 1$, we have $f_1(s, x_1) = p_1(x_1)\, f_2^*(s - x_1)$

	x_1	0	1	2	$f_1^*(s)$	x_1^*
s	0	0.40 * 0.80			0.192	0
	1	0.40 * 0.30	0.20 * 0.48		0.096	1
	2	0.40 * 0.16	0.20 * 0.30	0.15 * 0.48	0.072	1

The optimal solution is $x_1^* = 1$ which makes $s = 1$ at stage 2, so that $x_2^* = 0$ which makes $s = 1$ at stage 3, so that $x_3^* = 1$. Hence, the teams 1 and 3 should each receive one additional scientist. The new probability that all three teams will fail would be 0.60.

14.6 SINGLE ADDITIVE CONSTRAINT, ADDITIVE SEPARABLE RETURN FUNCTION

The general form of the problem is

$$\text{Minimize } z = f_1(d_1) + f_2(d_2) + \cdots + f_n(d_n)$$

subject to the constraints

$$a_1d_1 + a_2d_2 + \cdots + a_nd_n \geq b,\ d_j,\ a_j,\ b \geq 0 \text{ for } j = 1, 2, \ldots, n$$

Define state variables as

$$s_n = a_1d_1 + a_2d_2 + \cdots + a_nd_n \geq b$$

$$s_{n-1} = s_n - a_nd_n.$$

$$\vdots$$

$$s_{j-1} = s_j - a_jd_j.$$

$$\vdots$$

$$s_1 = s_2 - a_2d_2.$$

i.e. $s_{j-1} = t_j(s_j, d_j)$, $j = 1, 2, \ldots, n$ is the state transition function.
At the nth stage, the minimum value of $z = f_n^*(s_n)$ is given by

$$f_n^*(s_n) = \text{mini}\ \{f_1(d_1) + f_2(d_2) + \cdots + f_n(d_n)\}, \text{ subject to the constraint } s_n \geq b.$$

The general recursive relation for minimizing z for all decision variables is

$$f_j^*(d_j) = \text{mini}\ \{f_j(d_j) + f_{j-1}^*(s_{j-1})\},\quad j = 1, 2, \ldots, n \text{ and } f_1^*(s_1) = f_1(d_1)$$

where $s_{j-1} = t_j(s_j, d_j)$.

EXAMPLE 14.5: Find the maximum value of $z = b_1x_1 + b_2x_2 + \cdots + b_nx_n$, subject to the constraints $x_1 + x_2 + \cdots + x_n = c$, $x_j \geq 0$, $j = 1, 2, \ldots, n$.

Solution: Let $f_n(c)$ be maximum value of $b_1x_1 + b_2x_2 + \cdots + b_nx_n$.
For $n = 1$ (stage 1), we have $f_1(c) = b_1c$.
For stage 2, divide c into two parts x_1 and x_2 such that $x_1 + x_2 = c$. Then

$$\begin{aligned} f_2(c) &= \text{maxi}\ \{b_2y + f_1(c - y)\},\quad 0 < y \leq c \\ &= \text{maxi}\ \{b_2y + b_1(c - y)\}, \text{ since } f_1(c) = b_1c. \\ &= \text{maxi}\ \{(b_2 - b_1)\ y + b_1c\} \end{aligned}$$

If $(b_2 - b_1) > 0$, then $f_2(c) = b_2c$ is maximum value for $y = c$.
Similarly, for stage 3,

$$\begin{aligned} f_3(c) &= \text{maxi}\ \{b_3y + f_2(c - y)\},\quad 0 < y \leq c \\ &= \text{maxi}\ \{b_3y + b_2(c - y)\} \\ &= \text{maxi}\ \{(b_3 - b_2)\ y + b_2c\} \\ &= b_3c \text{ is maximum value for } y = c. \end{aligned}$$

In general, for n-stage problem, $f_n(c) = b_nc$. It is left for the reader to check that the above statement holds for all $n \in N$ by mathematical induction. Hence, the required optimal policy is $x_1 = x_2 = \ldots x_{n-1} = 0$, $x_n = c$ and $f_n(c) = b_nc$.

EXAMPLE 14.6: A member of a certain political party is making plans for an upcoming presidential election. He has received the services of six volunteer workers for precinct work and he wishes to assign them to three precincts in such a way as to maximize their effectiveness. He feels that it would be inefficient to assign a worker to more than one precinct, but he is willing to assign no workers to anyone of the precincts if they can accomplish more in other precincts.

The following table gives the estimated increase in the plurality of the party's candidate if it were allocated various number of workers:

Number of workers	Precincts 1	2	3
0	0	0	0
1	25	20	33
2	42	38	43
3	55	54	47
4	63	65	50
5	69	73	52
6	74	80	53

How many of the workers should be assigned to each of the three precincts in order to maximize total estimated increase in the plurality of the party's candidate?

Solution: Here, stages are precincts. Since there are three precincts, we will divide the problem into three stages. Let decision variables x_j $(j = 1, 2, 3)$ be the number of workers at the jth stage from previous one and $p_j(x_j)$ be the expected plurality for the assignment of x_j workers to precinct j. Thus, the problem formulation is

$$\text{Maximize } z = p_1(x_1) + p_2(x_2) + p_3(x_3)$$

subject to the constraints: $x_1 + x_2 + x_3 = 6,\ x_1, x_2, x_3 \geq 0$

Let s be the number of available workers for remaining j–precincts. Define $f_j(x_j)$ be the value of the optimal assignment for precinct 1 through 3. Then for stage 1, $f_1(s, x_1) = \{p_1(x_1)\}$. Let $f_j(s, x_j)$ be the profit associated with the optimum $f_j^*(s)$, $j = 1, 2, 3$. Then $f_1^*(s) = \text{maxi } \{p_1(x_1)\}$, $0 \leq x_1 < s$.

Thus, recurrence relation is

$$f_j(s, x_j) = p_j(x_j) + f_{j+1}^*(s - x_j); \quad j = 1, 2, 3$$

and

$$f_j^*(s) = \text{maxi } \{f_j(s, x_j)\}, \quad 0 \leq x_j \leq s.$$

We will use backward induction. The optimal policy is denoted by x_j^*, $j = 1, 2, 3$.

The computations for one stage problem are as follows:

s	$f_3^*(s)$	x_3^*
0	0	0
1	33	1
2	43	2
3	47	3
4	50	4
5	52	5
6	53	6

For $j = 2$ (two stage problem), we have $f_2(s, x_2) = p_2(x_2) + f_3^*(s - x_2)$

$x_2 s$	0	1	2	3	4	5	6	$f_2^*(s)$	x_2^*
0	0 + 0							0	0
1	0 + 33	20 + 0						33	0
2	0 + 43	20 + 33	38 + 0					53	1
3	0 + 47	20 + 43	38 + 33	54 + 0				71	2
4	0 + 50	20 + 47	38 + 43	54 + 33	65 + 0			87	3
5	0 + 52	20 + 50	38 + 47	54 + 43	65 + 33	73 + 0		98	4
6	0 + 53	20 + 52	38 + 50	54 + 47	65 + 43	73 + 33	80 + 0	108	4

For $j = 3$ (three stage problem), we have $f_1(s, x_1) = p_1(x_1) + f_2^*(s - x_1)$

$x_1 s$	0	1	2	3	4	5	6	$f_1^*(s)$	x_1^*
6	0 + 108	25 + 98	42 + 87	55 + 71	63 + 53	69 + 33	74 + 0	129	2

The above computations suggest that the maximum increase in plurality is 129 for $x_1^* = 2$. Then $s = 6 - 2 = 4$ for two stage problem which gives $x_2^* = 3$. Then $s = 4 - 3 = 1$ gives $x_3^* = 1$. Hence the optimal solution is $x_1^* = 2$, $x_2^* = 3$, $x_3^* = 1$ and the maximum increase in plurality is 129.

EXAMPLE 14.7: Minimize $z = x_1^2 + x_2^2 + x_3^2$

subject to the constraints $x_1 + x_2 + x_3 \geq 15$ and $x_1, x_2, x_3 \geq 0$.

Solution: The three stages can be defined as follows:

$$s_3 = x_1 + x_2 + x_3 \geq 15$$

$$s_2 = x_1 + x_2 = s_3 - x_3$$

$$s_1 = x_1 = s_2 - x_2$$

Therefore, the recurrence relation is

$$f_1(s_1) = \text{mini } \{x_1^2\} = (s_2 - x_2)^2, \quad 0 \leq x_1 \leq s_1.$$

$$f_2(s_2) = \text{mini } \{x_1^2 + x_2^2\} = \text{mini } \{x_2^2 + (s_2 - x_2)^2\} = \text{mini } \{x_2^2 + f_1(s_1)\}, \quad 0 \leq x_2 \leq s_2.$$

$$f_3(s_3) = \text{mini } \{x_1^2 + x_2^2 + x_3^2\} = \text{mini } \{x_3^2 + f_2(s_2)\}, \quad 0 \leq x_3 \leq s_3.$$

It is left for the reader to check that the function $x_2^2 + (s_2 - x_2)^2$ attains the minimum value at $x_2 = s_2/2$ and $f_2(s_2) = s_2^2/2$.

Again, $f_3(s_3) = \text{mini } \{x_3^2 + f_2(s_2)\} = \text{mini } \{x_3^2 + (s_3 - x_3)^2/2\} = \text{mini } \{x_3^2 + (15 - x_3)^2/2\}$. The minimum value of the function $x_3^2 + (15 - x_3)^2/2$ is attained at $x_3 = 5$ and $f_3(15) = 75$. Thus, $s_3 = 15 \Rightarrow x_3 = 5$; $s_2 = s_3 - x_3 = 15 - 5 = 10 \Rightarrow x_2 = s_2/2 = 5$ and $s_1 = s_2 - x_2 = 10 - 5 = 5 \Rightarrow x_1 = 5$. Hence, the optimal policy is attained at $(x_1, x_2, x_3) = (5, 5, 5)$ and minimum value is 75.

EXAMPLE 14.8: Maximum $z = x_1^2 + 2x_2^2 + 4x_3$, subject to the constraints $x_1 + 2x_2 + x_3 \leq 8$ and $x_1, x_2, x_3 \geq 0$.

Solution: The three stages can be defined as follows:

$$s_3 = x_1 + 2x_2 + x_3 \leq 8$$

$$s_2 = x_1 + 2x_2 = s_3 - x_3$$

$$s_1 = x_1 = s_2 - 2x_2$$

Therefore, the recurrence relation is

$$f_1(s_1) = \text{maxi } \{x_1^2\} = (s_2 - 2x_2)^2, \quad 0 \le x_1 \le s_1$$

$$f_2(s_2) = \text{maxi } \{x_1^2 + 2x_2^2\} = \text{maxi } \{2x_2^2 + (s_2 - 2x_2)^2\}, \quad 0 \le x_2 \le \frac{s_2}{2}$$

$$f_3(s_3) = \text{maxi } \{x_1^2 + 2x_2^2 + 4x_3\} = \text{maxi } \{4x_3 + (s_3 - x_3)^2\} = \text{maxi } \{x_3^2 - 12x_3 + 64\}, \quad 0 \le x_3 \le 8.$$

It is left for the reader to check that the function $2x_2^2 + (s_2 - 2x_2)^2$ attains the maximum value at $x_2 = 0$ or at $x_2 = s_2/2$. At $x_2 = 0$, $f_2(s_2) = s_2^2$ and at $x_2 = s_2/2$, $f_2(s_2) = s_2^2/2$. We will take maximum value of $f_2(s_2) = s_2^2$. It is easy to verify that the maximum value of $f_3(8)$ occurs at $x = 6$. Since this value of $f_3(8)$ is within the range of 0 and 8, maximum value occurs either at $x_3 = 0$ or $x_3 = 8$. At $x_3 = 0$, $f_3(8) = 64$ and at $x_3 = 8$, $f_3(8) = 32$. We need to choose maximum value. So, $x_3 = 0$.

Now, $s_3 = 8 \Rightarrow x_3 = 0$; $s_2 = s_3 - x_3 = 8 - 0 = 8 \Rightarrow x_2 = 0$ and $s_1 = s_2 - 2x_2 = 8 - 0 = 8 \Rightarrow x_1 = 8$. Hence, the optimal policy is attained at $(x_1, x_2, x_3) = (8, 0, 0)$ and maximum value is 64.

EXAMPLE 14.9: Seven units of the capital can be invested in four activities with return from each activity given in the following table. Find the allocation of the capital to each activity that will maximize the total return.

Q	$R_1(Q)$	$R_2(Q)$	$R_3(Q)$	$R_4(Q)$
0	0	0	0	0
1	2	3	2	1
2	4	5	3	3
3	6	7	4	5
4	7	9	5	6
5	8	10	5	7
6	9	11	5	8
7	9	12	5	8

Solution: Consider activity as a stage. So we are with four stage problem. Let x_j $(j = 1, 2, 3, 4)$ be the number of units to be invested at the jth stage, $p_j(x_j)$ be the expected return from allocation of x_j units to activity j and s be the units available for j-remaining activities.

The DP formulation is

$$\text{Maximize } z = p_1(x_1) + p_2(x_2) + p_3(x_3) + p_4(x_4)$$

subject to the constraints $x_1 + x_2 + x_3 + x_4 = 7$ and $x_j \ge 0$, $j = 1, 2, 3, 4$.

The recurrence relation is

$$f_1(s, x_1) = \{p_1(x_1)\} \quad \text{i.e. } f_1^*(s) = \text{maxi } \{p_1(x_1)\}, \quad 0 \le x_1 \le s.$$

and $$f_j^*(s) = \text{maxi } \{p_j(x_j) + f_j^*(s - x_j)\}, \quad 0 \le x_j \le s, j = 1, 2, 3, 4.$$

We start with $f_4^*(s)$ and end at $f_1^*(s)$.

Stage 1 computations:

s	0	1	2	3	4	5	6	7
$f_4^*(s)$	0	1	3	5	6	7	8	8
x_4^*	0	1	2	3	4	5	6	6 or 7

Stage 2 computations:

$s \backslash x_3$	0	1	2	3	4	5	6	7	$f_3^*(s)$	x_3^*
0	0 + 0								0	0
1	0 + 1	2 + 0							2	1
2	0 + 3	2 + 1	3 + 0						3	0,1,2
3	0 + 5	2 + 3	3 + 1	4 + 0					5	0,1
4	0 + 6	2 + 5	3 + 3	4 + 1	5 + 0				7	1
5	0 + 7	2 + 6	3 + 5	4 + 3	5 + 1	5 + 0			8	1,2
6	0 + 8	2 + 7	3 + 6	4 + 5	5 + 3	5 + 1	5 + 0		9	1,2,3
7	0 + 8	2 + 8	3 + 7	4 + 6	5 + 5	5 + 3	5 + 1	5 + 0	10	1,2,3,4

Stage 3 computations:

$s \backslash x_2$	0	1	2	3	4	5	6	7	$f_2^*(s)$	x_2^*
0	0 + 0								0	0
1	0 + 2	3 + 0							3	1
2	0 + 3	3 + 2	5 + 0						5	1,2
3	0 + 5	3 + 3	5 + 2	7 + 0					7	2,3
4	0 + 7	3 + 5	5 + 3	7 + 2	9 + 0				9	3,4
5	0 + 8	3 + 7	5 + 5	7 + 3	9 + 2	10 + 0			11	4
6	0 + 9	3 + 8	5 + 7	7 + 5	9 + 3	10 + 2	11 + 0		12	2,3,4,5
7	0 + 10	3 + 9	5 + 8	7 + 7	9 + 5	10 + 3	11 + 2	12 + 0	14	3,4

Stage 4 computations:

$s \backslash x_1$	0	1	2	3	4	5	6	7	$f_1^*(s)$	x_1^*
7	0 + 14	2 + 12	4 + 11	6 + 9	7 + 7	8 + 5	9 + 3	9 + 0	15	2,3

Thus, the maximum profit is 15. The optimal solution is $x_1 = 2$ or 3 which makes $s = 7 - 2 = 5$ or $s = 7 - 3 = 4$ for three stage problem. Therefore, $x_2 = 4$ when $x_1 = 2$ and $x_2 = 3$ or 4 when $x_1 = 3$. Now $x_2 = 4$ makes $s = 5 - 4 = 1$, which gives $x_3 = 1$; $x_2 = 3$ makes $s = 4 - 3 = 1$, which gives $x_3 = 1$ and $x_2 = 4$ makes $s = 1 - 1 = 0$ which gives $x_4 = 0$ and $x_3 = 0$ makes $s = 0 - 0 = 0$, which gives $x_4 = 0$. Hence, there are three alternative solutions:

$R_1(Q)$	$R_2(Q)$	$R_3(Q)$	$R_4(Q)$
2	4	1	0
3	3	1	0
3	4	0	0

EXAMPLE 14.10 A company has five salesmen, who have to be allocated to three marketing zones. The profit from each zone depends upon the number of salesmen working at that zone. The expected profits for different number of salesmen in different zones, as estimated from the past records, are given in the table. Determine the optimal allocation policy.

Number of salesman	Marketing zones		
	1	2	3
0	45	30	35
1	58	45	45
2	70	60	52
3	82	70	64
4	93	79	72
5	101	90	82

Solution: Define three marketing zones to be stages and the number of salesmen allocated to a particular zone to be state variables. Let s denote the total number of salesmen available, x_j (j = 1, 2, 3) be the number of salesmen allocated to marketing zone (j = 1, 2, 3) and $p_j(x_j)$ be the profit from zone j when x_j–salesmen are allocated.
The DP formulation is

$$\text{Maximize } z = p_1(x_1) + p_2(x_2) + p_3(x_3) + p_4(x_4)$$

subject to the constraints $x_1 + x_2 + x_3 + x_4 \leq 5$ and $x_j \geq 0$ (j = 1, 2, 3) are integers.
The recurrence relation

$$f_j(s) = \text{maxi } \{p_j(x_j) + f_{j+1}^*(s - x_j)\}, \quad 0 \leq x_j \leq s, \quad j = 1, 2, 3$$

represent the optimal allocation of the salesmen to marketing zone j and x_j is the initial allocation to marketing zone. Let us solve three stage problem using backward induction.

Stage 1 computations:

s	0	1	2	3	4	5
$f_3^*(s)$	35	45	52	64	72	82
x_3	0	1	2	3	4	5

Stage 2 computations:

$s \backslash x_2$	0	1	2	3	4	5	$f_2^*(s)$	x_2
0	65						65	0
1	75	80					80	1
2	82	90	95				95	2
3	94	97	105	105			105	2,3
4	102	109	112	115	114		115	3
5	112	117	124	122	124	125	125	5

Stage 3 computations:

$s \backslash x_1$	0	1	2	3	4	5	$f_1^*(s)$	x_1^*
5	170	173	175	177	173	166	177	3

Thus, the maximum profit is 177 corresponding to x_1 = 3 salesmen which gives s = 5 – 3 = 2 salesmen for stage 2. For s = 2, we have x_2 = 2 which gives s = 2 – 2 = 0, i.e. no salesmen for marketing zone 3 (stage 1). Hence, the optimal solution is three salesmen from zone 1, two salesmen from zone 2, and no salesmen from zone 3.

14.7 SINGLE MULTIPLICATIVE CONSTRAINT, ADDITIVE SEPARABLE RETURN FUNCTION

Consider the problem.

$$\text{Minimize } z = f_1(d_1) + f_2(d_2) + \cdots + f_n(d_n)$$

subject to the constraints $d_1 . d_2 . \ldots d_n \ge b$, d_j, $b \ge 0$ for $j = 1, 2, \ldots, n$

Define state variables as

$$s_n = d_1 . d_2 \ldots . \ d_n \ge b$$

$$s_{n-1} = \frac{s_n}{d_n}.$$

$$\vdots$$

$$s_{j-1} = \frac{s_j}{d_j}.$$

$$\vdots$$

$$s_1 = \frac{s_2}{d_2}.$$

Arguing as in Section 14.6, the recurrence relation for minimum value of z for all decision variables and for any feasible value of decision variables will be given by $f_j(s_j) = \text{mini } \{f_j(d_j) + f^*_{j-1}(s_{j-1})\}$, $j = 1, 2, \ldots, n$ and $f_1(s_1) = f_1(d_1)$, where $s_{j-1} = t_j(s_j, d_j)$.

EXAMPLE 14.11: Minimize $z = y_1^2 + y_2^2 + \cdots + y_n^2$ subject to the constraints $y_1 . y_2 \ldots y_n = c$; $y_j \ge 0$, $j = 1, 2, \ldots, n$ and $c \ne 0$.

Solution: Let $f_n(c)$ be the minimum value of c when c is divided into n factors. For $n = 1$, we have $y_1 = c$. Therefore, $f_1(c) = \text{mini } \{y_1^2\} = c^2$, $y_1 = c$. For $n = 2$, let $y_1 = x$ and $y_2 = c/x$. Then, $f_2(c) = \text{mini } \{y_1^2 + y_2^2\} = \text{mini } \{x^2 + (c/x)^2\}$, $0 < x \le c$.

It is left for the reader to check that the function $x^2 + (c/x)^2$ attains the minimum value at $x = c^{1/2}$ and minimum value is $2c^{1/2}$.

For $n = 3$, let $y_1 = x$ and $y_2 y_3 = c/x$. Then, $f_3(c) = \text{mini } \{y_1^2 + y_2^2 + y_3^2\} = \text{mini } \{x^2 + f_2(c/x)\}$, $0 < x \le c$.

Here, $f_2(c/x) = 2c/x$. $f_3(c)$ attains minimum value $3c^{1/3}$ at $\{c^{1/3}, c^{1/3}, c^{1/3}\}$.

Using the principle of mathematical induction, the recursive relation $f_n(c) = \text{mini } \{x^2 + f_{n-1}(c/x)\}$ attains minimum value $nc^{1/n}$ at $\{c^{1/n}, c^{1/n}, c^{1/n}\}$.

14.8 SOLUTION OF LINEAR PROGRAMMING PROBLEM

Let us consider a general LPP.

$$\text{Maximize } z = \sum_{j=1}^{n} c_j x_j$$

subject to $\quad \sum_{i=1}^{m} a_{ij} x_j \le b_i$, $i = 1, 2, \ldots, m$ and $x_j \ge 0, j = 1, 2, \ldots, n$.

The amount of available resource for allocation to the current stage j ($j = 1, 2, \ldots, n$) and the succeeding stages will be considered as the state variables. Let $a_{1j}, a_{2j}, \ldots, a_{mj}$ be the amount of resources i ($i = 1, 2, \ldots, m$) respectively allocated to an activity c_j at the jth stage, and $f_j(a_{1j}, a_{2j}, \ldots, a_{mj})$ be the optimum value of the objective function of LPP for stages $j, j+1, \ldots, n$ and for stages $a_{1j}, a_{2j}, \ldots, a_{mj}$. Thus, the LPP is a sequence of functions given by $f_n(a_{1n}, a_{2n}, \ldots, a_{mn}) =$ maxi $\sum_{j=1}^{n} c_j x_j$ over the decision variable x_j subject to $\sum_{i=1}^{m} a_{ij} x_j \le b_i,\ x_j \ge 0$.

The recursive relations for optimization are

$$f_n(a_{1n}, a_{2n}, \ldots, a_{mn}) = f_n(b_1, b_2, \ldots, b_m)$$

$$= \text{maxi } \{c_n x_n + f_{n-1}(b_1 - a_{1n}x_n,\ b_2 - a_{2n}x_n,\ \ldots,\ b_m - a_{mn}x_n)\}$$

and the maximum value of b that a variable x_n can assume is mini $\{b_1/a_{1n}, b_2/a_{2n}, \ldots, b_m/a_{mn}\}$.

EXAMPLE 14.12: Solve the LPP.

Maxi $z = x_1 + 9x_2$, subject to the constraints $2x_1 + x_2 \le 25$, $x_2 \le 11$, $x_1, x_2 \ge 0$.

Solution: Here, we have two resources and two decision variables. So, this is a two stage problem (say) a_{1j} and a_{2j} for $j = 1, 2$.

Then for $f_2(a_{12}, a_{22})$ = maxi $\{9x_2\}$, where the maximum is taken over $0 \le x_2 \le 25$ and $0 \le x_2 \le 11$. Therefore, $f_2(a_{12}, a_{22}) = 9 *$ maxi $\{25, 11\}$. Since the maximum of x_2 satisfying the constraints $x_2 \le 25$ and $x_2 \le 11$ is the minimum of $\{25, 11\}$ then $x_2 = 11$.

Now, $f_1(a_{11}, a_{21})$ = maxi $\{x_1 + f_2(a_{11} - 2x_1, a_{21} - 0)\}$, $0 \le x_1 \le 25/2$.

Therefore, $f_1(25, 11)$ = maxi $\{x_1 + 9 *$ mini $(25 - 2x_1, 11)\}$

$$\text{mini } (25 - 2x_1, 11) = \begin{cases} 11, & 0 \le x_1 \le 7 \\ 22 - 2x_1, & 7 \le x_1 \le 25/2 \end{cases}$$

Therefore,
$$x_1 + 9 * \text{mini } (25 - 2x_1, 11) = \begin{cases} x_1 + 99, & 0 \le x_1 \le 7 \\ 225 - 17x_1, & 7 \le x_1 \le 25/2 \end{cases}$$

Since the maximum of both $x_1 + 99$ and $225 - 17x_1$ occurs at $x_1 = 7$, we have $f_1(25, 11) = 7 + 9 *$ mini $\{11, 11\} = 106$. Therefore, x_2 = mini $\{25 - 2x_1, 11\}$ = mini $\{11, 11\} = 11$. Hence, the optimal solution is $x_1 = 7$, $x_2 = 11$, and maxi $z = 106$.

EXAMPLE 14.13: Solve the LPP.

Maxi $z = 50x_1 + 100x_2$, subject to the constraints $10x_1 + 5x_2 \le 2{,}500$, $4x_1 + 10x_2 \le 2{,}000x_1 + 3x_2/2 \le 450$, $x_1, x_2 \ge 0$.

Solution: The problem has three resources and two decision variables. So this is a three stage problem (say) a_{1j}, a_{2j} and a_{3j} for $j = 1, 2$.

Thus, $f_1(a_{11}, a_{21}, a_{31})$ = maxi $\{50x_1\}$, where maximum is taken over $0 \le x_1 \le 2{,}500$, $0 \le 4x_1 \le 2{,}000$ and $0 \le x_2 \le 450$.

Therefore, $f_1(a_{11}, a_{21}, a_{31}) = 50 *$ mini $\{(2{,}500 - 5x_2)/10,\ (2{,}000 - 10x_2)/4,\ 450 - 3x_2/2\}$.

The second stage problem is to find the value of $f_2(2{,}500, 2{,}000, 450)$.

Therefore, $f_2(a_{12}, a_{22}, a_{32})$ = maxi $\{100x_2 + 50$ *mini $\{(2{,}500 - 5x_2)/10,\ (2{,}000 - 10x_2)/4,\ 450 - 3x_2/2\}$.

Now, the maximum value of x_2 (satisfying all the constraints) is mini {2,500/10, 2,000/10, 450/(3/2)} = 200.

Therefore, mini $\{(2{,}500 - 5x_2)/10,\ (2{,}000 - 10x_2)/4,\ 450 - 3x_2/2\}$

$$= \begin{cases} \dfrac{2{,}500 - 5x_2}{10}, & 0 \le x_2 \le 125 \\ \dfrac{2{,}000 - 10x_2}{4}, & 125 \le x_2 \le 200 \end{cases}$$

$$\text{Therefore,}\quad f_2(a_{12}, a_{22}, a_{32}) = \text{maxi} \begin{cases} 100x_2 + 50\left(\dfrac{2{,}500 - 5x_2}{10}\right), & 0 \le x_2 \le 125 \\ 100x_2 + 50\left(\dfrac{2{,}000 - 10x_2}{4}\right), & 125 \le x_2 \le 200 \end{cases}$$

$$= \text{maxi} \begin{cases} 75x_2 + 12{,}500, & 0 \le x_2 \le 125 \\ 25{,}000 - 25x_2, & 125 \le x_2 \le 200 \end{cases} = 21{,}875 \text{ at } x_2 = 125.$$

Therefore, $f_2(2{,}500, 2{,}000, 450) = 21{,}875$ at $x_2 = 125$.

Therefore, $x_1 = \text{mini}\ \{(2{,}500 - 5x_2)/10,\ (2{,}000 - 10x_2)/4,\ 450 - 3x_2/2\}$

$= \text{mini}\ \{187.5, 187.5, 262.5\} = 187.5.$

Hence, the optimal solution is $x_1 = 187.5$, $x_2 = 125$ and maxi $z = 21{,}875$.

14.9 SOME APPLICATIONS

EXAMPLE 14.14: A man is engaged in buying and selling identical items. He operates from a warehouse that can store 500 items. Each month, he can sell any quantity that he chooses up to the stock at the beginning of the month. Each month, he can buy as much as he wishes for delivery at the end of the month so long as his stock does not exceed 500 items. For the next four months, he has the following error free forecasts of costs and sales prices:

Month (i)	:	1	2	3	4
Cost C_i	:	27	24	26	28
Sales price P_i	:	28	25	25	27

If he currently has a stock of 200 units, what quantities should he sell and buy in the next four months?

Solution: Here, the month will be considered the stage, so we have a four stage problem. Let x_i be the units to be sold during the month i, y_i be the units to be ordered during the month i, P_i be the sale price of the unit in the month i, c_i be the purchase price in the month i and W be the warehouse capacity.

Let $f_n(b_n)$ be the maximum possible return when there are n months to proceed and the initial stock is b_n.

The recursive relation for the problem is given by

$$f_1(b_n) = \text{maxi } \{P_1x_n - c_1y_n\},\ b_n \geq x_n \text{ and } b_n - x_n + y_n \leq W$$

$$f_n(b_n) = \text{maxi } \{P_nx_n - c_ny_n + f_{n-1}(b_n - x_n + y_n)\}$$

For $n = 1$, we have $f_1(b_1) = \text{maxi } \{P_1x_1 - c_1y_1\}$
Initially, $y_1 = 0$ and $x_1 = b_1$. Therefore, $f_1(b_1) = P_1b_1 = 27b_1$. But $b_1 = b_2 - x_2 + y_2$.
Therefore, for $n = 2$, we have $f_2(b_2) = \text{maxi } \{P_2x_2 - c_2y_2 + f_1(b_2 - x_2 + y_2)\}$ where $y_2 \leq W - b_2 + x_2$ or $y_2 \leq 500 - b_2 + x_2$.
Therefore, $f_2(b_2) = \text{maxi } \{26b_2 - x_2 + 500\} = 26b_2 + 500$ (taking $x_2 = 0$ for maximum)
But $b_2 = b_3 - x_3 + y_3$.
Therefore, for $n = 3$, we have

$$\begin{aligned}
f_3(b_3) &= \text{maxi } \{P_3x_3 - c_3y_3 + f_2(b_3 - x_3 + y_3)\} \\
&= \text{maxi } \{25x_3 - 24y_3 + 26(b_3 - x_3 + y_3) + 500\} \text{ where } y_3 \leq 500 - b_3 + x_3. \\
&= \text{maxi } \{26b_3 - x_3 + 2y_3 + 500\} \\
&= \text{maxi } \{26b_3 - x_3 + 2(500 - b_3 + x_3) + 500\} \\
&= \text{maxi } \{24b_3 + x_3 + 1{,}500\} = 25b_3 + 1{,}500 \ (\because\ b_3 \geq x_3,\ b_3 = x_3 \text{ for maximum})
\end{aligned}$$

But $b_3 = b_4 - x_4 + y_4$.
Therefore, for $n = 4$, we have

$$\begin{aligned}
f_4(b_4) &= \text{maxi } \{P_4x_4 - c_4y_4 + f_3(b_4 - x_4 + y_4)\} \\
&= \text{maxi } \{28x_4 - 27y_4 + 25(b_4 - x_4 + y_4) + 500\} \text{ where } y_4 \leq 500 - b_4 + x_4. \\
&= \text{maxi } \{25b_4 + 3x_4 - 2y_4 + 1{,}500\} \\
&= \text{maxi } \{25b_4 + 3x_4 + 1{,}500\} = 28b_4 + 1{,}500 \ (\because\ y_4 = 0,\ b_4 = x_4 \text{ for maximum } x)
\end{aligned}$$

But, we have

	$b_4 = 0$	then $x_4 = 200$	and $y_4 = 0$
Therefore,	$b_3 = 200 - 200 + 0$	then $x_3 = 0$	and $y_3 = 500$
	$b_2 = 0 - 0 + 500$	then $x_2 = 0$	and $y_2 = 0$
	$b_1 = 500 - 0 + 0$	then $x_1 = 500$	and $y_1 = 0$

Therefore, the required optimal policy in each month for purchase and sale is as follows:

Month	1	2	3	4
Purchase	0	500	0	0
Sale	200	0	0	500

and the maximum profit = 28 * 200 + 1,500 = Rs. 7,100.

EXAMPLE 14.15 (Production allocation problem): The owner of a chain of four grocery stores has purchased six crates of fresh strawberries. The estimated probability distribution of potential sales of the strawberries before spoilage differs among the four stores. The following table gives the estimated total expected profit at each store, when it is allocated various number of crates:

Number of crates	Store 1	2	3	4
0	0	0	0	0
1	4	2	6	2
2	6	4	8	3
3	7	6	8	4
4	7	8	8	4
5	7	9	8	4

For administrative reasons, the owner does not wish to split crates between stores. However, he is willing to distribute zero crates to any of his stores. Find the allocation of six crates to four stores as to maximize the expected profit.

Solution: Consider four stores as four stages. Let x_j be the number of crates allocated at the jth stage, $j = 1, 2, 3, 4$ and $P_j(x_j)$ be the expected profit from allocation of x_j crates to store j. The objective is

$$\text{Maxi } z = P_1(x_1) + P_2(x_2) + P_3(x_3) + P_4(x_4)$$

subject to the constraints $x_1 + x_2 + x_3 + x_4 = 6$ and $x_i \geq 0$, $i = 1, 2, 3, 4$

Let there be s crates left for the remaining j-stores and x_j be the initial allocation. Define $f_j(x_j)$ as the value of the optimal allocations for stores 1 to 4.

Therefore, $$f_1(s, x_1) = \{P_1(x_1)\}$$

If $f_j(s, x_j)$ denotes the profit associated with the optimum solution $f_j(s)$, $j = 1, 2, 3, 4$, then

$$f_1(s) = \text{maxi } \{P_1(x_1)\}, \quad 0 \leq x_1 \leq s.$$

Therefore, the recurrence relation is given by

$$f_j(s, x_j) = P_j(x_j) + f_{j+1}(s - x_j) \text{ and } f_j(s) = \text{maxi } \{P_j(x_j) + f_{j+1}(s - x_j)\}, \quad 0 \leq x_j \leq s.$$

Let us solve the given problem by backward induction.

Stage 1 computations:

s	0	1	2	3	4	5	6
$f_4(s)$	0	2	3	4	4	4	4
x_4	0	1	2	3	3, 4	3, 4, 5	3, 4, 5, 6

Stage 2 computations:

$$f_3(s, x_3) = P_3(x_3) + f_4(s - x_3)$$

$s \backslash x_3$	0	1	2	3	4	5	6	$f_3(s)$	x_3
0	0 + 0							0	0
1	0 + 2	6 + 0						6	1
2	0 + 2	6 + 2	8 + 0					8	1, 2
3	0 + 4	6 + 3	8 + 2	8 + 0				10	2
4	0 + 4	6 + 4	8 + 3	8 + 2	8 + 0			11	2
5	0 + 4	6 + 4	8 + 4	8 + 3	8 + 2	8 + 0		12	2
6	0 + 4	6 + 4	8 + 4	8 + 4	8 + 3	8 + 2	8 + 0	12	2, 3

Stage 3 computations:

$$f_2(s, x_2) = P_2(x_2) + f_3(s - x_2)$$

$s \backslash x_2$	0	1	2	3	4	5	6	$f_2(s)$	x_2
0	0 + 0							0	0
1	0 + 6	2 + 0						6	1
2	0 + 8	2 + 6	4 + 0					8	0, 1
3	0 + 10	2 + 8	4 + 6	6 + 0				10	0, 1, 2
4	0 + 11	2 + 10	4 + 8	6 + 6	8 + 0			12	1, 2, 3
5	0 + 12	2 + 11	4 + 10	6 + 8	8 + 6	9 + 0		14	2, 3, 4
6	0 + 12	2 + 12	4 + 11	6 + 10	8 + 8	9 + 6	10 + 0	16	3, 4

Stage 4 computations:

$$f_1(s, x_1) = P_1(x_1) + f_2(s - x_1)$$

$s \backslash x_1$	0	1	2	3	4	5	6	$f_2(s)$	x_2
6	0 + 16	4 + 14	6 + 12	7 + 10	7 + 8	7 + 6	7 + 0	18	1, 2

The maximum profit is Rs. 18 and the optimum allocation of crates to the four stores is as follows:

Store 1 x_1	*Store* 2 x_2	*Store* 3 x_3	*Store* 4 x_4
1	2	2	1
1	3	1	1
1	3	2	0
1	4	1	0
2	1	2	1
2	2	1	1
2	2	2	0
2	3	1	0

REVIEW EXERCISES

1. Use DP to maximize $z = y_1 y_2 y_3$, subject to the constraints $y_1 + y_2 + y_3 = 5$ and $y_1, y_2, y_3 \geq 0$.

   [**Ans.** (5/3, 5/3, 5/3) and $z = 125/27$]

2. Use DP to maximize $z = y_1^2 + y_2^2 + y_3^2$ subject to the constraints $y_1 y_2 y_3 = 6$ and $y_1, y_2, y_3 \geq 0$.

   [**Ans.** (1, 6, 1) or (1, 1, 6) or (6, 1, 1) and $z = 38$]

3. Use DP to maximize $z = (x_1 - 2/3)^2 - (x_2 - 1)^2$, subject to the constraints $x_1 + x_2 \leq 2$, $2x_1 + x_2 \leq 3$ and $x_1, x_2 \geq 0$.

   [**Ans.** (1, 1) and $z = 1/9$]

4. Solve the following LPP using backward induction:
Maxi $z = 2x_1 + 4x_2$, subject to the constraints $2x_1 + 3x_2 \leq 48$, $x_1 + 3x_2 \leq 42$, $x_1 + x_2 \leq 21$, $x_1, x_2 \geq 0$.

[**Ans.** (6, 12) and $z = 60$]

5. A company has 6 salesmen and three market areas (say) *A*, *B*, *C*. It is desired to determine the number of salesmen to be allocated to each market to maximize the profit. The following table gives the profit from each market area as a function of the number of salesmen allocated:

Area	*Salesmen*						
	0	1	2	3	4	5	6
A	38	41	48	58	66	72	83
B	40	42	50	60	66	75	82
C	60	64	68	78	90	102	109

Use DP technique to solve the problem.

[**Ans.** (6, 0, 0) or (1, 0, 5) and profit = 183]

6. A machine deteriorates with age. The operating cost, $c(n)$ of a machine n-years old at the beginning of the year; trade in value, $t(n)$ received when such a machine is traded for a new machine at the start of the year and salvage value, $s(n)$ received for a machine that is n-years old at the end of 5 years are given below:

n	0	1	2	3	4	5
$c(n)$	10	13	20	40	70	100
$t(n)$	–	32	21	11	5	0
$s(n)$	–	25	17	8	0	0

If a new machine costs Rs. 50 and we have now a machine which is two years old, what is the optimum policy of replacement? Solve the problem by dynamic programming.

7. The chemical manufacturer uses cupric chloride as the basic material for the production of copper complex. For a smooth functioning of its production schedule, the company may have enough stock every month of its basic material. The purchase price $p(n)$ and the demand $d(n)$ forecast for the next six months by the management are given below:

Month n	1	2	3	4	5	6
$p(n)$	11	18	13	17	20	10
$d(n)$	8	5	3	2	7	4

Due to limited space, the warehouse cannot carry more than 9 units of the basic material. The basic material is bought at the beginning of each month. When the initial stock is 2 units and the final stock is required to be zero, the company wishes to find an ordering policy for the next 6 months so as to minimize the total purchase cost.

[**Ans.** The quantity to be purchased at the beginning of the month (7, 4, 9, 3, 0, 4) and the minimum cost = Rs. 357]

8. A shoe store sells rubber shoes for a particular season which lasts from December 1 through February 29. The sales division has forecast the following demands for the next year.

Month	December	January	February
Demand	30	40	30

All shoes sold by the store are purchased from outside sources. The following information is known about this particular shoe.

(a) The unit purchase cost is Rs. 100 per pair, however, the supplier will only sell in lots of 10, 20, 30 or 40 pairs. Any orders for more than 50 or less than 10 will not be entertained.

(b) The following quantity discounts apply on lot size orders:

Lot size	10	20	30	40
Discount (%)	5	5	10	20

(c) For each order placed, the store incurs a fixed cost of Rs. 20. In addition, the supplier charges an average amount of Rs. 50 per order to cover transportation costs, insurance, packaging, and so on, irrespective of the amount ordered.

(d) Due to large in-process inventories, the store will carry no more than 40 pairs of shoes in inventory at the end of any month. Carrying charges are Rs. 5 per pair per month, based on the end of the month inventory. It is desirable to have both incoming and outgoing seasonal inventory at zero.

Find an ordering policy which will minimize the total seasonal costs.

[**Ans.** If $Q(n)$ stands for the quantity ordered at the nth period then $Q(1) = 0$, $Q(2) = 40$, $Q(3) = 40$ and mini cost = Rs. 8,560]

9. The World Health Council is devoted to improving health care in the under-developed countries of the world. It has now five medical teams available to allocate among three such countries to improve their medical care, health, education and training programs. Therefore, the council needs to determine how many teams (if any) to allocate to each of these countries to maximize the total effectiveness of the five teams. The measure of effectiveness being used is additional man-years of life. (For a particular country, this measure equals the country's increased life expectancy in year's times.) The following table gives the estimated additional man-years of life (in multiple of 1,000) for each country for each possible allocation of medical teams:

No. of medical team(s)	*Thousands of additional man-years of life for each country*		
	1	2	3
0	0	0	0
1	45	20	50
2	70	45	70
3	90	75	80
4	105	110	100
5	120	150	130

Determine how many teams should be allocated to each country for maximum effectiveness.

[**Ans.** (1, 3, 1)-medical teams to be allocated to the countries (1, 2, 3) and maximum effectiveness is 170]

10. A ship is to be loaded with a stock of three items. Each unit of item n has a weight $w(n)$ and the value $v(n)$. The maximum cargo weight the ship can take is five and the details of the three items are as follows:

Item (n)	*Weight w(n)*	*Value v(n)*
1	2	7
2	3	10
3	1	3

Find the most valuable cargo load without exceeding the maximum cargo weight by using DP technique.

[**Ans.** (1, 1, 0) or (2, 0, 1), maximum value of load is 17]

15

Project Management

15.1 INTRODUCTION

At one point or another almost every organization will take on a large and complex project. A construction company putting up an office building or laying a highway must complete thousands of costly activities. A shipyard requires tens of thousands of steps in constructing an ocean-going tugboat. An oil refinery about to be shut down for a major maintenance project faces astronomical expenses if this difficult task is unduly delayed for any reason. Almost every industry worries about how to manage similar large-scale, complicated projects effectively.

Large, often one-time, projects are difficult challenges to operations managers. The stakes are high. Millions in cost overruns have been wasted due to poor planning on projects. Unnecessary delays have occurred due to poor scheduling. And companies have gone bankrupt due to poor controls.

Special projects that take months or years to complete are usually developed outside the normal production system. Project organizations within the firm are set up to handle such jobs and are often disbanded when the project is complete. The management of large projects involves three phases.

1. Planning
2. Scheduling
3. Control

Project planning	*Tools*
• Setting goals	Time and cost estimates
• Defining the project	Budgets
• Tying needs into timed project activities	Cash flow charts
• Organizing the term	Material availability details
	Personnel data charts
	Engineering diagrams

Project scheduling	Tools
• Typing resources (people, money supplies) to specific activities • Relating activities to each other • Updating and revising on regular basis	CPM and PERT Milestone charts Cash flow schedules Gantt charts
Project controlling	*Tools*
• Monitoring resources, costs, quality budgets • Revising and changing plans • Shifting resources to meet time, cost, and' quality demands	PERT charts Reports describing • budgets by department • delayed activities • slack activities • quality of work completed

15.1.1 Project Planning

Projects can usually be defined as a series of related tasks directed towards a major output. A new organization form, developed to make sure existing programs continue to run smoothly on a day-to-day basis while new projects are successfully completed, is called ***project organization***.

A project organization is an effective way of pooling the people and physical resources needed for a limited time to complete a specific project or goal. It is basically a temporary organization structure designed to achieve results by using specialists from throughout the firm.

The project organization works best when

- the work can be defined with a specific goal and deadline,
- the job is unique or somewhat unfamiliar to the existing organization,
- the work contains complex interrelated tasks requiring specialized skills,
- the project is temporary but critical to the organization.

15.1.2 Project Scheduling

Project scheduling is determining the project's activities in the time sequence in which they have to be performed. Materials and people needed at each stage of production are computed in this phase, and the time each activity will take is also set. Separate schedules for personnel need by type of skill (management, engineering) are charted. Charts can also be developed for scheduling materials. One popular project scheduling approach is the Gantt chart (named after Henry Gantt).

Whatever the approach taken by a project manager, project scheduling serves several purposes.

- It shows the relationship of each activity to others and to the whole project.
- It identifies the precedence relationships among activities.
- It encourages the setting of realistic time and cost estimates for each activity.
- It helps make better use of people, money, and material resources by identifying critical bottlenecks in the project.

15.1.3 Project Controlling

The control of large projects, like the control of any management system, involves close monitoring of resources, costs, quality and budgets. Control also means using a feedback loop to revise the project plan and having the ability to shift resources to where they are needed most.

The management of big projects that consist of a large number of activities poses complex problems in *planning, scheduling and control*, especially when the project activities have to be performed in a specified technological sequence. With the help of PERT (Program Evaluation and Review Technique), and CPM (Critical Path Method), the project manager can

1. plan the project ahead of time and foresee possible sources of troubles and delays in completion,
2. schedule the project activities at the appropriate times to conform with proper job sequence so that the project is completed as soon as possible,
3. coordinate and control the projects activities so as to stay on schedule in completing the project.

Thus, both PERT and CPM are aids to efficient project management. They differ in their approach to the problem and the solution technique. The nature of the project generally dictates the proper technique to be used.

15.2 ORIGIN AND USE OF PERT

PERT was developed in the US Navy during the late 1950s to accelerate the development of the Polaris Fleet Ballistic Missile. The development of this weapon involved the coordination of the work of thousands of private contractors and other government agencies. The coordination by PERT was so successful that the entire project was completed 2 years ahead of the schedule. Nowadays, it is extensively used in industries and other service organizations as well.

The time required to complete the various activities in a research and development project is generally not known *a priori*. Thus, PERT incorporates uncertainties in activity times in its analysis. It determines the probabilities of completing various stages of the project by specified deadlines. It also calculates the expected time to complete the project. An important and extremely useful by-product of PERT analysis is its identification of various "bottlenecks" in a project. In other words, it identifies the activities that have high potential for causing delays in completing the project on schedule. Thus, even before the project has started, the project manager knows where he or she can expect delays. The manager can then take the necessary preventive measures to reduce possible delays so that the project schedule is maintained.

Because of its ability to handle uncertainties in job times, PERT is mostly used in research and development projects.

15.3 ORIGIN AND USE OF CPM

Critical path method closely resembles PERT in many aspects but was developed independently by E.I. du Pont de Nemours Company. Actually, both techniques, PERT and CPM, were developed almost simultaneously. It was developed to have a better planning in controlling the overhaul and maintenance of chemical plants. The major difference between the two techniques is that CPM does not incorporate uncertainties in job times. Instead, it assumes that activity times are proportional to the amount of resources allocated to them, and by changing the level of resources the activity times and the project completion time can be varied. Thus, CPM assumes prior experience with similar projects from which the relationships between resources and job times are available. CPM then evaluates the trade-off between project costs and project completion time.

CPM is mostly used in construction projects where there is prior experience in handling similar projects.

15.4 APPLICATIONS OF PERT AND CPM

A partial list of applications of PERT and CPM techniques in project management is as follows:

- Construction projects (e.g. buildings, highways, houses, and bridges)
- Preparation of bids and proposals for large projects
- Maintenance planning of oil refineries, ship repairs, and other large operations
- Development of new weapons systems and new manufactured products
- Manufacture and assembly of large items such as airplanes, ships, and computers
- Simple projects

15.5 FRAMEWORK OF PERT AND CPM

Six steps are common to both PERT and CPM. The procedure is as follows:

1. Define the projects and all of its significant activities or tasks.
2. Develop the relationships among the activities. Decide which activities must precede and which must follow others.
3. Draw the network connecting all of the activities.
4. Assign time and/or cost estimates to each activity.
5. Compute the longest time path through the network; this is called the ***critical path.***
6. Use the network to help plan, schedule, monitor and control the project.

Step 5, finding the critical path, is a major part of controlling a project. The activities on the critical path represent the tasks that will delay the entire project if they are delayed. Managers derive flexibility by identifying noncritical activities and replanning, rescheduling, and reallocating resources such as labour and finances.

Although PERT and CPM differ to some extent in terminology and in the construction of the network, their objectives are the same. Furthermore, the analysis used in both techniques is very similar. The major difference is that PERT employs three time estimates for each activity. Each estimate has an associated probability of occurrence, which, in turn, is used in computing the expected values and standard deviations for the activity times. CPM makes the assumption that activity times are known with certainty, and hence only one time factor is given for each activity.

PERT and CPM are important because they can help answer questions such as the following about projects with thousands of activities.

- When will the entire project be completed?
- What are the critical activities or tasks in the project, that is, the ones that will delay the entire project if they are late?

- Which are the noncritical activities, that is, the ones that can run late without delaying the whole project's completion?
- What is the probability that the project will be completed by a specific date?
- On any particular date, is the project on schedule, behind the schedule, or ahead of the schedule?
- On any given date, is the money spent equal to, less than, or greater than the budgeted amount?
- Are there enough resources available to finish the project on time?
- If the project is to be finished in a shorter amount of time, what is the best way to accomplish this at the least costs?

15.6 CONSTRUCTING THE PROJECT NETWORK

The analysis by PERT/CPM techniques uses the network formulation to represent the project activities and their ordering relations. The construction of a project network is done as follows:

- Arcs in the network represent individual jobs or activities in the project.
- Nodes represent specific points in time which mark the completion of one or more jobs in the project.
- Direction on the arc is used to represent the job sequence. It is assumed that any job directed towards a node must be completed before any job directed away from that node can begin. We illustrate the construction of project networks with a few examples.

EXAMPLE 15.1: Given the following information, develop a network.

Activity	*Immediate predecessor (S)*
A	—
B	—
C	*A*
D	*B*

You will note that we assigned each event a number. As you will see later, it is possible to identify each activity with a beginning and ending event or node. For example, activity *A* in Figure 15.1 is the activity that starts with event 1 and ends at node, or event 2. In general, we number node from left to right. The beginning node, or event, of the entire project is number 1, while the last node, or event, in the entire project bears the largest number. The last node shows the number 4.

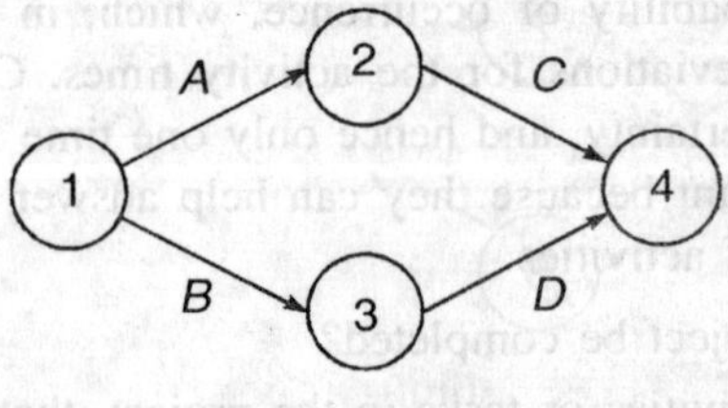

Figure 15.1

EXAMPLE 15.2: Consider seven jobs *A, B, C, D, E, F* and *G* with the following job sequence:

Job *A* precedes *B* and *C*
Job *C* and *D* precede *E*
Job *B* precedes *D*
Job *E* and *F* precede *G*

In the network (Figure 15.2), every arc (*i, j*) represents a specific job in the project. Node 1 represents the start of the project, whereas node 6 denotes the project's completion time. The intermediate nodes represent the completion of various stages of the project. The nodes of the project network are generally called ***events***.

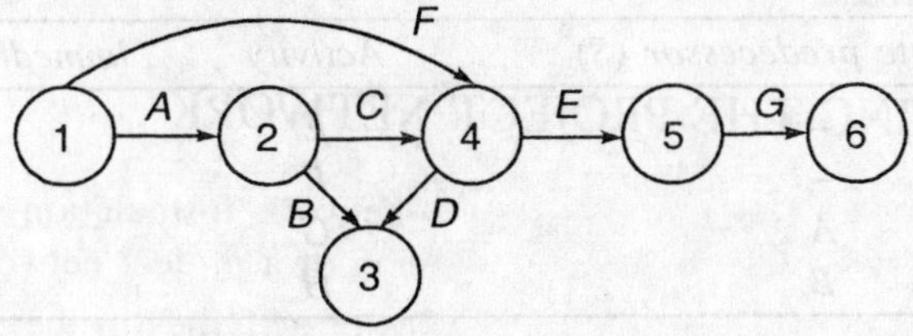

Figure 15.2

An ***event*** is a specific point in time that marks the completion of one or more activities, well recognizable in the project.

We can also specify the network by events and the activities that occur between events. The following example shows how to develop a network based on this type of specification scheme.

EXAMPLE 15.3: Given the following table, develop a network.

Beginning event	*Ending event*	*Activity*
1	2	1–2
1	3	1–3
2	4	2–4
3	4	3–4
3	5	3–5
4	6	4–6
5	6	5–6

Beginning with the activity that starts at event 1 and ends at event 2, we can construct the following network (Figure 15.3).

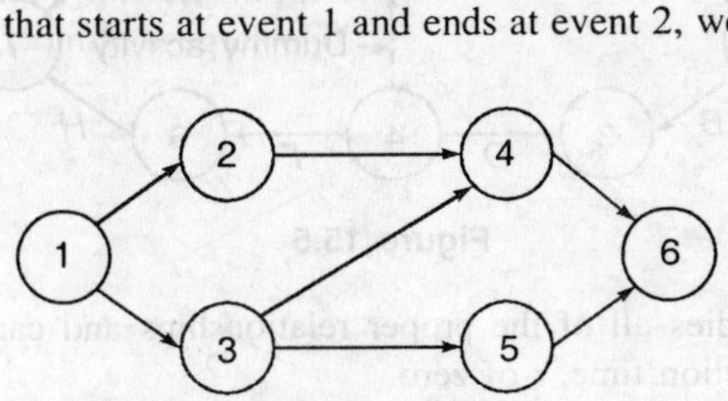

Figure 15.3

All that is required to construct a network is the starting and ending events for each activity.

15.7 DUMMY ACTIVITIES AND EVENTS

You may encounter a network that has two activities with identical starting and ending events. Dummy activities and events can be inserted into the network to deal with this problem. The use of dummy activities and events is especially important when computer programs are to be employed in determining the critical path, project completion time, project variance, and so on. Dummy activities and events can also ensure that the network properly reflects the project under consideration. The following example illustrates the procedure.

EXAMPLE 15.4: Develop a network based on the following information.

Activity	*Immediate predecessor (S)*	*Activity*	*Immediate predecessor (S)*
A	—	*E*	*C, D*
B	—	*F*	*D*
C	*A*	*G*	*E*
D	*B*	*H*	*F*

Given these data, you might develop the following network (Figure 15.4).

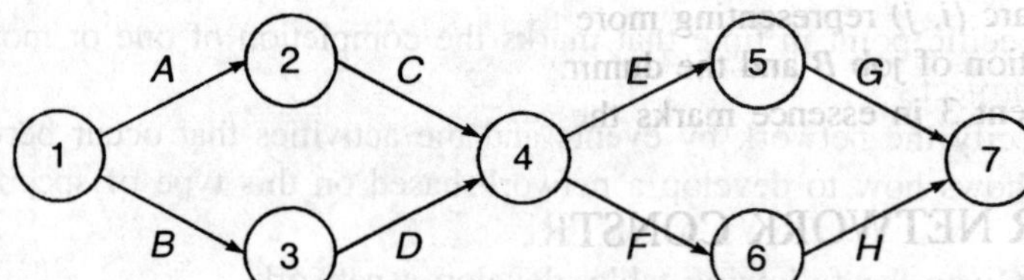

Figure 15.4

Look at activity *F*. According to the network, both activities *C* and *D* must be completed before we can start *F*, but in reality, only activity *D* must be completed (see the table). Thus, the network is not correct. The addition of a dummy activity and a dummy event can overcome this problem, as shown in Figure 15.5.

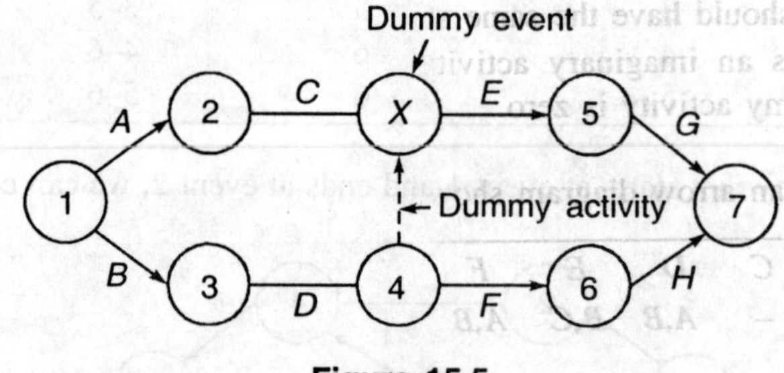

Figure 15.5

Now, the network embodies all of the proper relationships and can be analyzed as usual. A dummy activity has a completion time, *t* of zero.

EXAMPLE 15.5: Consider a project with five jobs *A*, *B*, *C*, *D* and *E* with the following job sequence:

Job *A* precedes *C* and *D*
Job *B* precedes *D*
Job *C* and *D* precede *E*.

The completion times for *A*, *B*, *C*, *D* and *E* are 3, 1, 4, 2, 5 days, respectively.

The project network is shown in Figure 15.6.

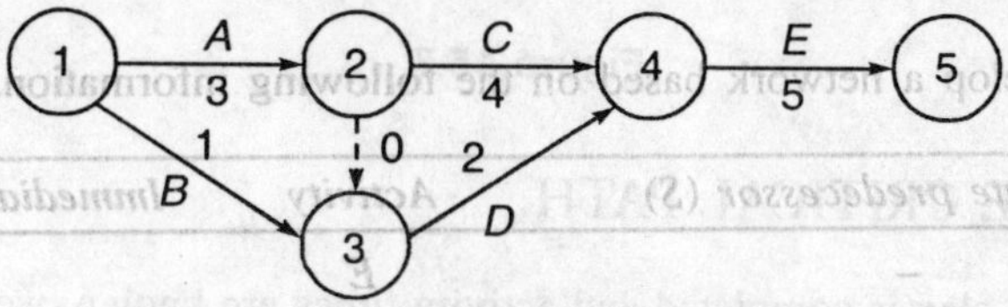

Figure 15.6

Arc (2, 3) (dotted line in the figure) represents a dummy job that does not exist in reality in the project. The dummy activity is necessary so as to avoid ambiguity in the job sequence. The completion time of the dummy job is always zero, and it is added in the project network whenever we want to avoid an arc *(i, j)* representing more than one job in the project. In the figure, event 3 represents the completion of job *B* and the dummy job. Since the dummy job is completed as soon as *A* is completed, event 3 in essence marks the completion of jobs *A* and *B*.

15.8 RULES FOR NETWORK CONSTRUCTION

The following are the primary rules for constructing AOA (Activity on Arrow) diagram.

- The starting event and the ending event of an activity are called ***tail event*** and ***head event***, respectively.
- The network should have a unique starting node (tail event).
- The network should have a unique completion node (head event).
- No activity should be represented by more than one arc in the network.
- No two activities should have the same starting node and the same ending node.
- Dummy activity is an imaginary activity indicating precedence relationship only. The duration of a dummy activity is zero.

EXAMPLE 15.6: Draw an arrow diagram showing the following relationships.

Activity	*A*	*B*	*C*	*D*	*E*	*F*	*G*	*H*	*I*	*J*	*K*	*L*	*M*	*N*
Immediate predecessor	–	–	–	*A,B*	*B,C*	*A,B*	*C*	*D,E,F*	*D*	*G*	*G*	*H,J*	*K*	*I,L*

The use of the dummy 2–5 is very important here (Figure 15.7). It is necessary here because if it is eliminated, node 5 becomes the ending node of activity *B* and the initial node of activity *E*, implying that *D* and *F* require all *A*, *B* and *C* to be completed before their start, which is not the case. The inclusion of this activity thus enables us to present the precedence relationships in a correct manner.

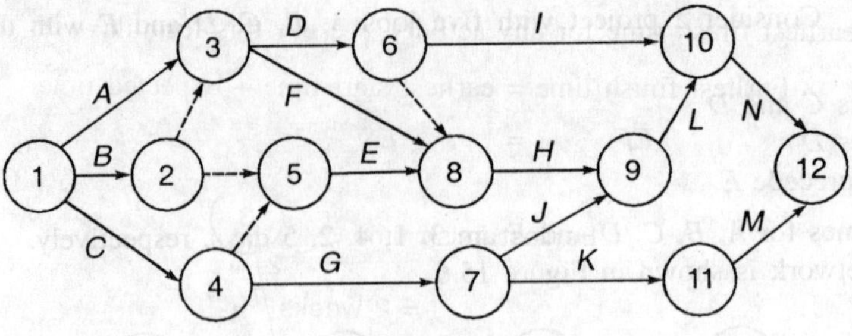

Figure 15.7

15.9 FINDING THE CRITICAL PATH

After the project network plan is completed and activity times are known, we consider the questions how long the project would take to complete and when the activities may be scheduled. This can be answered by finding out the critical path of the network. For this, we require an arrow diagram and the time duration of the various activities. These computations involve a *forward* and a *backward* pass through the network. The forward pass calculations yield the *earliest start* and *the earliest finish times* for each activity, while the backward pass calculations render the *latest allowable start* and *the latest finish times* for each activity. We shall demonstrate the calculation of earliest start, earliest finish, latest start and latest finish times of various activities of a project with the help of the following examples.

EXAMPLE 15.7: Consider the following information on the activities required for a project.

Activity:	*A*	*B*	*C*	*D*	*E*	*F*	*G*	*H*	*I*	*J*	*K*	*L*
Immediate predecessors:	–	–	–	*A*	*A*	*E*	*B*	*B*	*D,F*	*C*	*H,J*	*G,I,K*
Duration:	2	2	2	3	4	0	7	6	4	10	3	4

Finding the critical path: To estimate how long the project will require, we will have to determine the critical path of this network. Since the work described by all the paths must be done before the project is considered complete, we must find that path that requires most work, the longest path through the network; this is called the ***critical path***. If we want to reduce the time for the project, we will have to shorten the critical path; that is, we will have to reduce the time of one or more activities on that path—but first we have to find it.

When the network is larger, it is very tedious, often impossible, to find the critical path by listing all the paths and picking the longest one. We need a more organized method. For this purpose, to begin with, a value of 0 (zero) is assigned to the initial event of the project. Thus, each of the activities initiated from the starting node of the network is assumed to start at time 0 (the beginning of the day 1, say). The earliest finish time for each activity is obtained by adding the time duration of the activity to its earliest start time.

We start at node 1 with a starting time we define as zero; we then compute an earliest start time and an earliest finish time for each activity in the network. Look at activity *A* with an expected time of 2 weeks.

To find the earliest finish time for any activity, we use this formula:

$$\text{Earliest finish time} = \text{earliest start time} + \text{expected time}$$

$$EF \quad = \quad ES \quad + \quad t$$

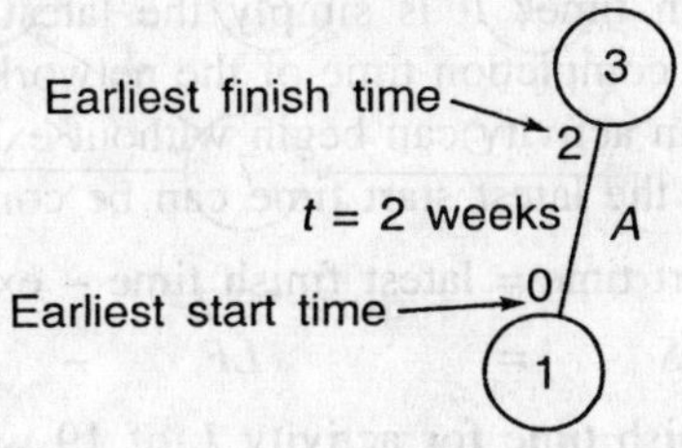

Now we must find the *ES* time and the *EF* time for all the activities in the network.

According to the earliest-start-time rule, ***"since no activity can begin until all its predecessor activities are complete, the earliest start time for an activity leaving any node is equal to the largest earliest finish time of all activities entering that same node."***

Look at the first few activities in the network.

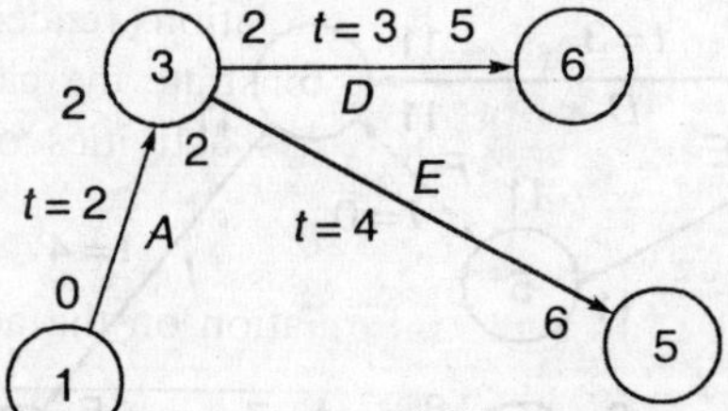

In this instance, the earliest start time for activities *D* and *E* is 2, the earliest finish time for activity *A*. Using this procedure we make what is called a ***Forward pass*** through the network to get all the *ES* and *EF* times as shown in Figure 15.8. We can see right away from the earliest finish time for activity *L* that it is going to take 19 weeks to finish this project, and that is only if all the activities run on schedule.

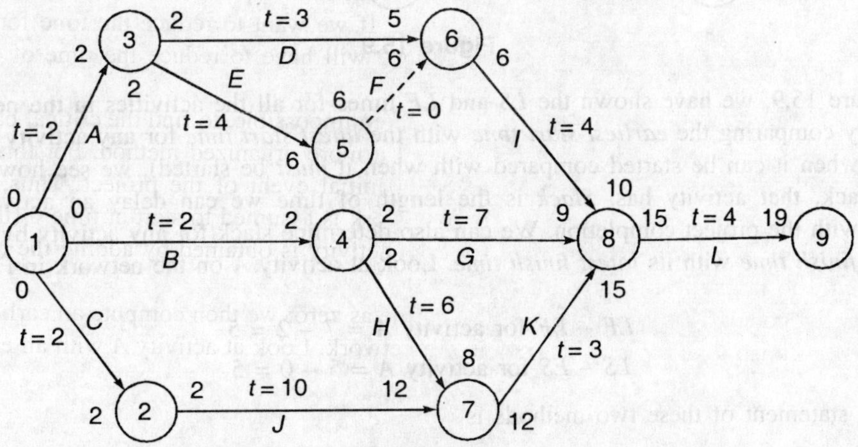

Figure 15.8

The second step in finding the critical path is to compute a latest start time and latest finish time for each activity. This is done by using what is called a ***Backward Pass***; that is, we begin at the completion point, node 9, and—using a latest finish time of 19 weeks for that activity (which we found in our forward pass method)—compute the latest finish time and latest start time for every activity. What is the latest finish time? It is simply the latest time at which an activity can be completed without extending the completion time of the network. In the same sense, the latest start time is the latest time at which an activity can begin without extending the completion time on the project. In a more formal sense, the latest start time can be computed with

$$\text{Latest start time} = \text{latest finish time} - \text{expected time}$$

$$LS = LF - t$$

For example, given the latest finish time for activity L of 19 weeks, then

$$LS \text{ (for activity } L) = 19 - 4 = 15$$

According to the latest-finish-time rule, ***"the latest finish time for an activity entering any node is equal to the smallest latest start time for all activities leaving that same node."***

Look at node 4 in Figure 15.9. The latest finish time for activity B entering that node is 6, the smallest start time for the two activities leaving node 4.

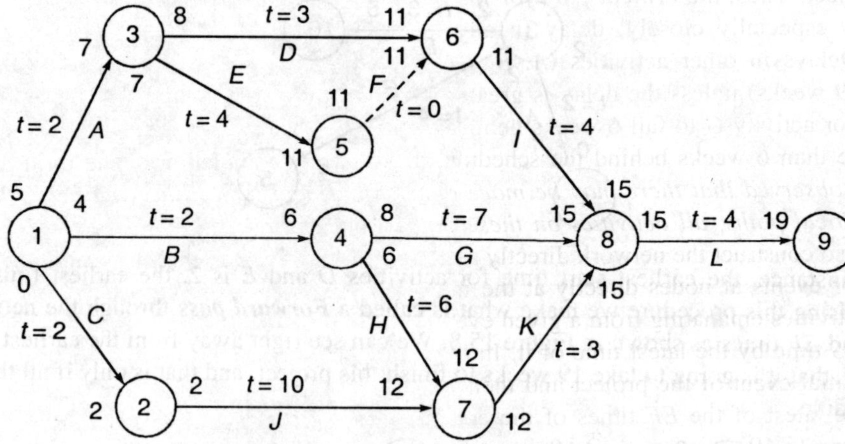

Figure 15.9

In Figure 15.9, we have shown the LS and LF times for all the activities in the network.

Now by comparing the *earliest start time* with the *latest start time* for any activity (that is, by looking at when it can be started compared with when it *must* be started), we see how much free time, or slack, that activity has. *Slack* is the length of time we can delay an activity without interfering with the project completion. We can also determine slack for any activity by comparing its *earliest finish time* with its *latest finish time.* Look at activity A on the network in Figures 15.8 and 15.9.

$$LF - EF \text{ for activity } A = 7 - 2 = 5$$

$$LS - ES \text{ for activity } A = 5 - 0 = 5$$

The formal statement of these two methods is

$$\text{Slack} = LF - EF \text{ or } LS - ES$$

In the following table, we have shown *LF*, *EF*, *LS*, *ES*, and slack for all the activities in the network.

Activity	*Earliest start (ES)*	*Latest start (LS)*	*Earliest finish (EF)*	*Latest finish (LF)*	*Slack (LS–ES) or (LF–EF)*	*Activity on critical path*
A	0	5	2	7	5	
B	0	4	2	6	4	
C	0	0	2	2	0	YES
D	2	8	5	11	6	
E	2	7	6	11	5	
F			Dummy activity			
G	2	8	9	15	6	
H	2	6	8	12	4	
I	6	11	10	15	5	
J	2	2	12	12	0	YES
K	12	12	15	15	0	YES
L	15	15	19	19	0	YES

Those activities without any slack are *C*, *J*, *K*, and *L*. None of these can be delayed without delaying the whole project. Thus, *the critical path for the project is C–J–K–L.* We will have to watch these four activities especially closely; delay in any one of them will cause a delay in the project completion. Delays in other activities (*A*, *B*, *D*, *E*, *G*, *H* and *I*) will not affect on-time project completion (19 weeks) unless the delay is greater than the slack time an activity has. For example, it is all right for activity *G* to fall 6 weeks behind the schedule because it has 6 weeks of slack; but if it falls more than 6 weeks behind the schedule, it will delay completion of the project.

It can be observed that there may be more than one critical path in a given network. In case of multiple critical paths, all activities on these paths would be critical.

We can also construct the network directly as follows involving only the early start and late start calculations for events at nodes directly at the node [*ES*, *LS*] will be written at the node.

For the activities emanating from a given event, the *ES* time would be given by the earliest time of it and the *LS* time by the latest time of it. In the forward pass, a 0 would be taken as the earliest time for the initial event of the project and then for each subsequent event, the earliest time would be taken as the latest of the *EF* times of the activities concluding on that event. See the [*ES*, *LS*] entries in Figure 15.10.

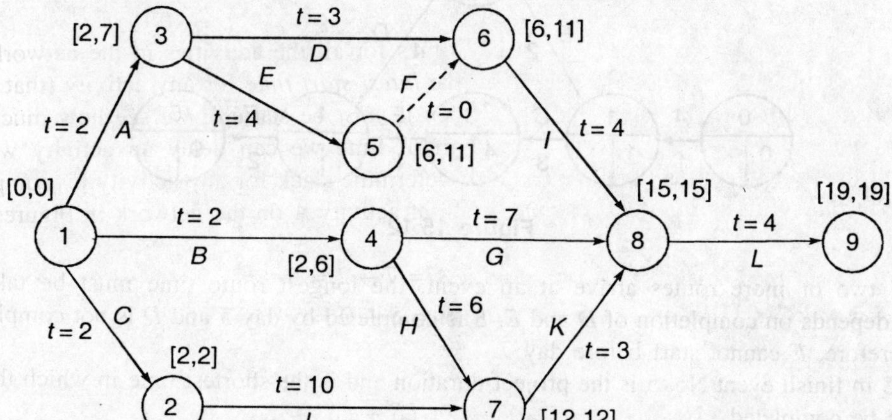

Figure 15.10

Similarly, the terminal event of the project would be assigned the latest time equal to its earliest time (or other time if it is given and desired). Then, rolling back, the events are assigned the latest times. If only one activity starts from the node representing a given event, then the latest time for the event is taken to be the difference between the latest time of the head event of this activity and the activity duration time. In case, however, more than one activity starts from this node, then the minimum of such differences, as mentioned above, would be taken as the latest time for the event. See the [*ES*, *LS*] entries in the following figure.

This method is to facilitate us in finding the critical path by calculating the slack at a node by directly computing *LS minus ES*.

An alternative to depict the earliest and the latest timings for each of the activities is shown in the following example. Notice that each circle representing an event is divided into three parts: containing the event number, its earliest start time and its latest start time, as shown in the index.

EXAMPLE 15.8: Assume the following network (Figure 15.11) has been drawn and the activity times estimated in days.

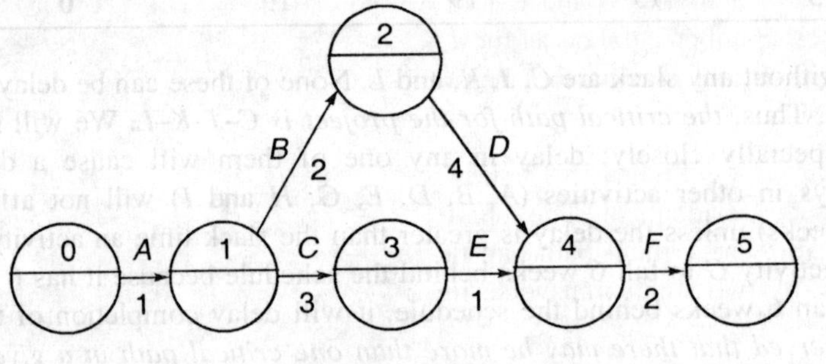

Figure 15.11

The ES times for the activities can be inserted as follows.

The *ES* of a head event is obtained by adding onto the *ES* of the tail event the linking activity duration starting from event 0, time 0 and working forward through the network. See Figure 15.12.

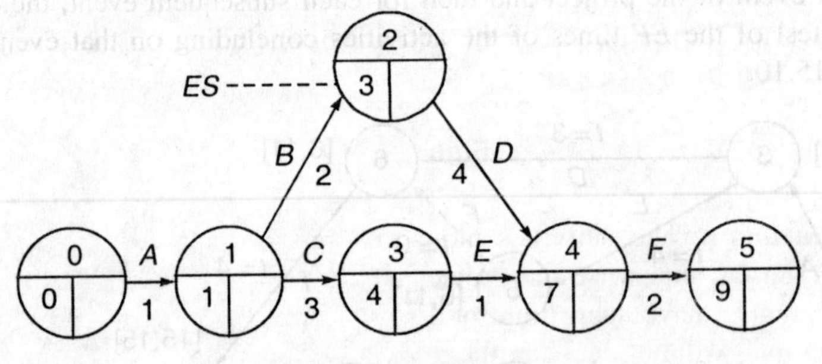

Figure 15.12

Where two or more routes arrive at an event, the longest route time must be taken, e.g. Activity *F* depends on completion of *D* and *E*. *E* is completed by day 5 and *D* is not complete until day 7. Therefore, *F* cannot start before day 7.

The *ES* in finish event No. 5 is the project duration and is the shortest time in which the whole project can be completed.

The LS times are inserted as follows in Figure 15.13.

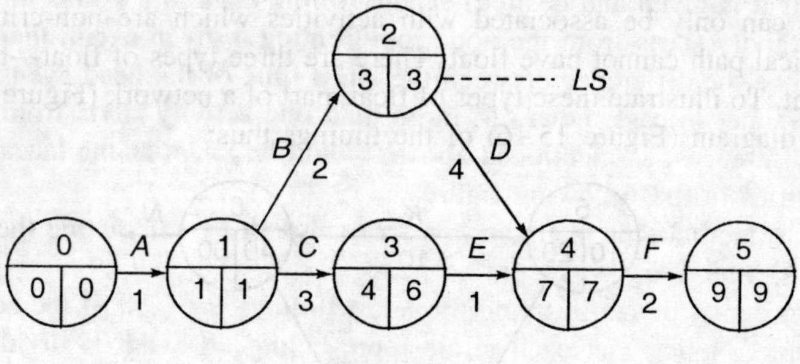

Figure 15.13

Starting at the finish event No. 5, insert the *LS* (i.e. day 9) and work backwards through the network, deducting each activity duration from the previously calculated *LS*.

Where the tails of activities *B* and *C* join event No. 1, the *LS* for *C* is day 3 and the *LS* for *B* is day 1. The lowest number is taken as the *LS* for event No. 1 because if event No. 1 occurred at day 3 then activities *B* and *D* could not be completed by day 7 as required and the project would be delayed.

Finding the critical path: Figure 15.13 shows that one path through the network (*A*, *B*, *D*, *F*) has *ES*'s and *LS*'s which are identical. This chain of activities, which has the longest duration, is the required critical path. The critical path can be indicated on the network either by a heavy line or different colour or by two small transverse lines across the arrows along the path thus:

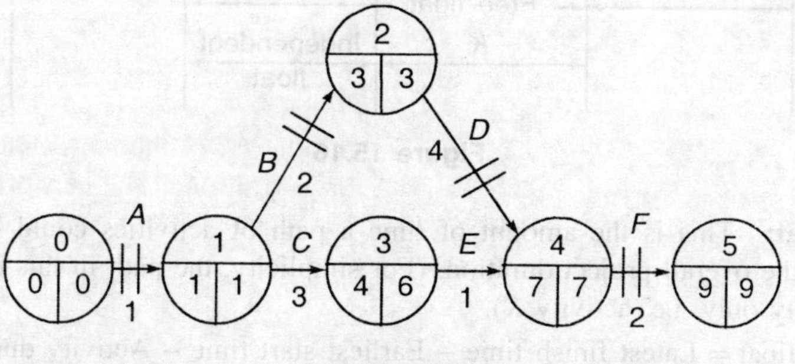

Figure 15.14

Critical path implications: The activities along the critical path are vital ones which must be completed by their *ES*/*LS*, otherwise the project will be delayed. The noncritical activities (in the example above, *C* and *E*) have spare time or float available, i.e. *C* and/or *E* could take up to an additional 2 days in total without delaying the project duration. If it is required to reduce the overall project duration, then the time of one or more of the activities on the critical path must be reduced perhaps by using more labour, or more or better equipment or some other method of reducing job times.

15.9.1 Floats

Float or spare time can only be associated with activities which are non-critical. By definition, activities on the critical path cannot have float. There are three types of float—total float, free float and independent float. To illustrate these types of float, part of a network (Figure 15.15) will be used together with a bar diagram (Figure 15.16) of the timings thus:

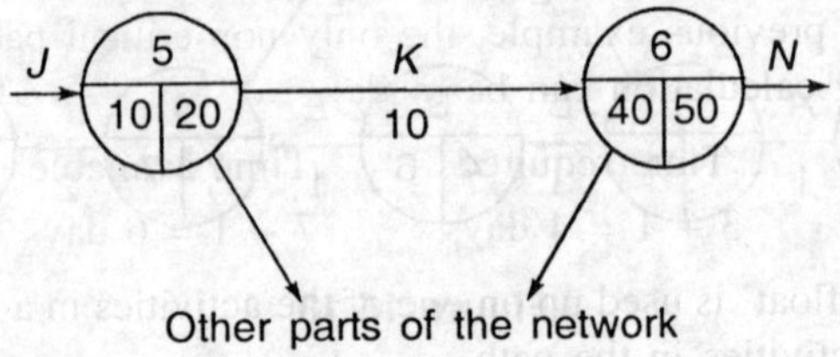

Figure 15.15

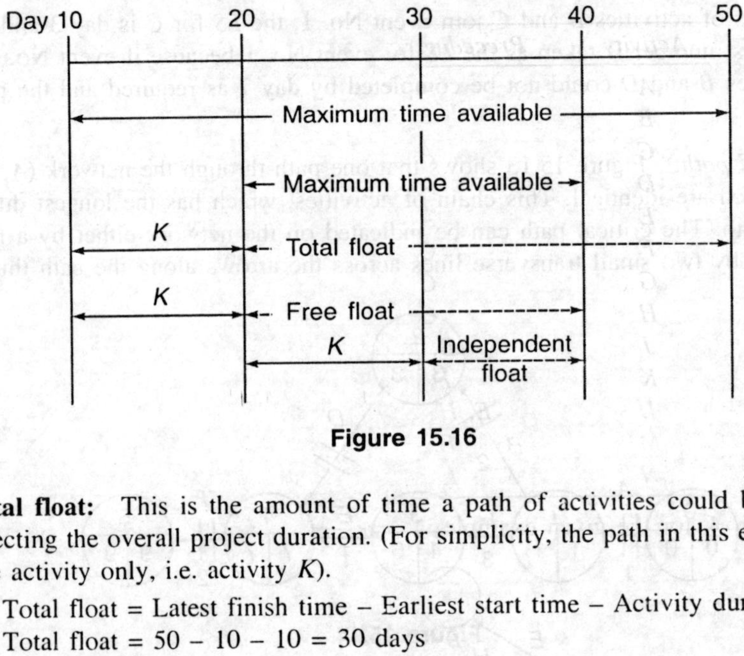

Figure 15.16

(a) **Total float:** This is the amount of time a path of activities could be delayed without affecting the overall project duration. (For simplicity, the path in this example consists of one activity only, i.e. activity *K*).

Total float = Latest finish time – Earliest start time – Activity duration

Total float = 50 – 10 – 10 = 30 days

(b) **Free float:** This is the amount of time an activity can be delayed without affecting the commencement of a subsequent activity at its earliest start time, but may affect float of a previous activity.

Free float = Earliest finish time – Earliest start time – Activity duration

Free float = 40 – 10 – 10 = 20 days

(c) **Independent float:** This is the amount of time an activity can be delayed when all preceding activities are completed as late as possible and all succeeding activities completed as early as possible. Independent float, therefore, does not affect the float of either preceding or subsequent activities.

Independent float = Earliest finish time – Latest start time – Activity duration

Independent float = 40 – 20 – 10 = 10 days

Notes:

(a) The most important type of float is total float because it is involved with the overall project duration. On occasions, the term 'float' is used without qualification. In such cases assume that total float is required.

(b) Total float can be calculated separately for each activity, but it is often useful to find the total float over paths of non-critical activities between critical events. For example, in Figure 15.16 of the previous example, the only non-critical path of activities is *C*, *E* for which the following calculation can be made:

Non-critical path	Time required	Time available	Total float over path
C, *E*	3 + 1 = 4 days	7 − 1 = 6 days	= 2 days

If some of the 'path float' is used up on one of the activities in a path, it reduces the leeway available to other activities in the path.

EXAMPLE 15.9: A simple network example is given.

Activity	*Preceding activity*	*Duration*
A	–	9
B	–	3
C	*A*	8
D	*A*	2
E	*A*	3
F	*C*	2
G	*C*	6
H	*C*	1
J	*B*, *D*	4
K	*F*, *J*	1
L	*E*, *H*, *G*, *K*	2
M	*E*, *H*	3
N	*L*, *M*	4

Solution: The network for the given example is shown in Figure 15.17.

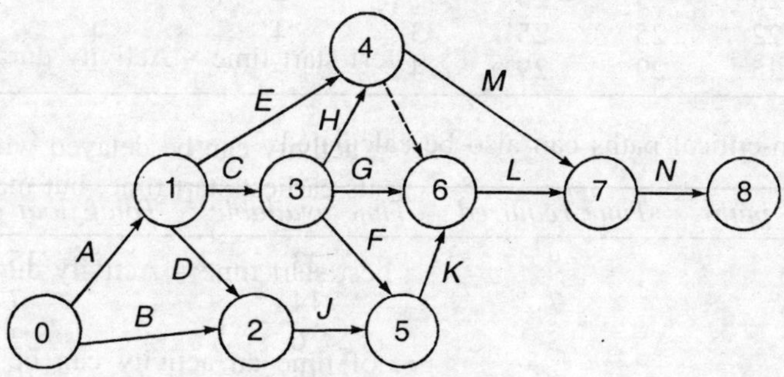

Figure 15.17

A dummy (4–6) was necessary because of the preceding activity requirements of activity *L*. If activities *E*, *H* had not been specified as preceding activity *L*, the dummy would not have been necessary.

The network is shown in the normal manner in the following figure (Figure 15.18) from which it will be seen that the critical path is: *A–C–G–L–N* with a duration of 29 days.

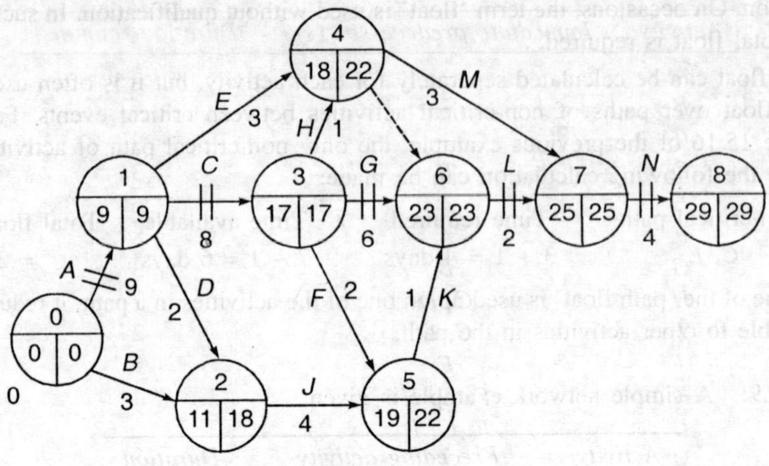

Figure 15.18

The float calculations:

Activity	*ES*	*LS*	*EF*	*LF*	*D*	*Total float (LF–ES--D)*	*Free float (EF–ES–D)*	*Independent float (EF–LS–D)*
A	0	0	9	9	9	–	–	–
B	0	0	11	18	3	15	8	8
C	9	9	17	17	8	–	–	–
D	9	9	11	18	2	7	–	–
E	9	9	18	22	3	10	6	6
F	17	17	19	22	2	3	–	–
G	17	17	23	23	6	–	–	–
H	17	17	18	22	1	4	–	–
J	11	18	19	22	4	7	4	–
K	19	22	23	23	1	3	1	–
L	23	23	25	25	2	–	–	–
M	18	22	25	25	3	4	4	–
N	25	25	29	29	4	–	–	–

Total float on the non-critical paths can also be calculated:

Non-critical path	*Time required*	*Time available*	*Total float over path*
B, J, K	8	23	15
D, J, K	7	14	7
F, K	3	6	3
E, M	6	16	10
H, M	4	8	4
E, dummy	3	14	9
H, dummy	1	6	5

Now, we see one more method for calculating the critical path and the floats.

EXAMPLE 15.10: Consider the table summarizing the details of a project involving 14 activities.

Activity	*Immediate predecessor (s)*	*Duration (months)*
A	–	2
B	–	6
C	–	4
D	*B*	3
E	*A*	6
F	*A*	8
G	*B*	3
H	*C, D*	7
I	*C, D*	2
J	*E*	5
K	*F, G, H*	4
L	*F, G, H*	3
M	*I*	13
N	*J, K*	7

Solution: The network is shown in Figure 15.19.

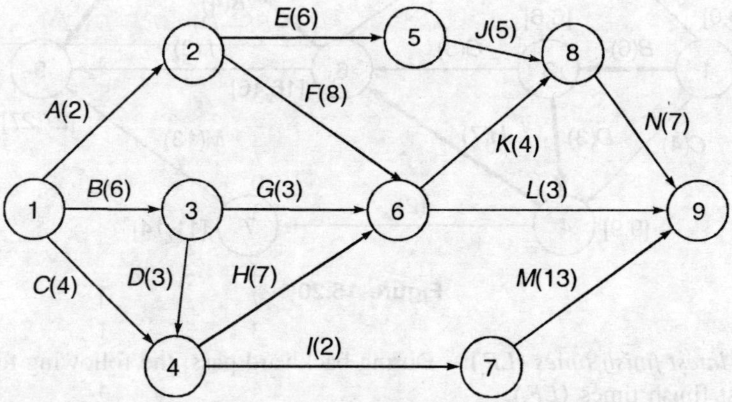

Figure 15.19

Let D_{ij} be the duration of the activity (i, j). ES_j be the earliest start times of all the activities which are emanating from node j. Lf_j be the latest finish times of all the activities which are ending at node j.

Determination of earliest start times (ES_j): During forward pass, use the following formula to compute earliest start times for all nodes:

$$ES_j = \max_i (ES_i + D_{ij})$$

The calculations of ES_j are summarized below.

Node 1: For Node 1, $ES_1 = 0$

Node 2: $ES_2 = ES_1 + D_{1,2} = 0 + 2 = 2$

Node 3: $ES_3 = ES_1 + D_{1,3} = 0 + 6 = 6$

Node 4: $ES_4 = \max_{i=1,3} (ES_i + D_{i,4})$

$= \max (ES_1 + D_{1,4}, ES_3 + D_{3,4})$

$= \max (0 + 4, 6 + 3) = 9$

Node 5: $ES_5 = ES_2 + D_{2,5} = 2 + 6 = 8$

Node 6: $ES_6 = \max_{i=2,3,4} (ES_i + D_{i,6})$

$= \max (ES_2 + D_{2,6}, ES_3 + D_{3,6}, ES_4 + D_{4,6})$

$= \max (2 + 8, 6 + 3, 9 + 7)$

$= \max (10, 9, 16)$

$= 16$

Similarly, the ES_j values for all other nodes are computed and summarized in Figure 15.20 and written in the format [*ES*, *LS*].

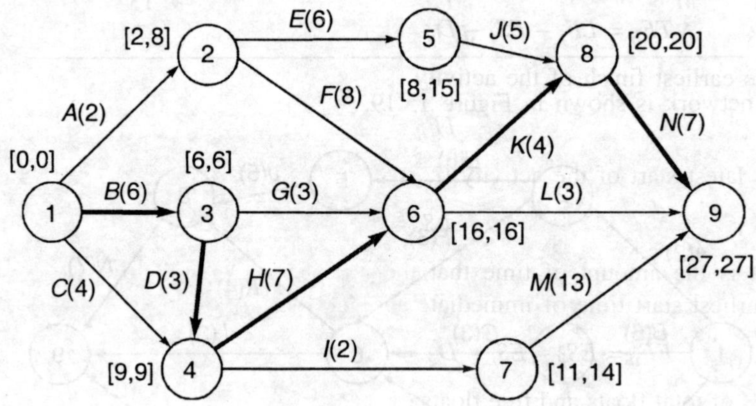

Figure 15.20

Determination of latest finish times (LF_i): During backward pass, the following formula is used to compute the latest finish times (LF_i):

$$LF_i = \min_j (LF_i - D_{ij})$$

Node 9: $LF_9 = ES_9 = 27$

Node 8: $LF_8 = LF_9 - D_{8,9} = 27 - 7 = 20$

Node 7: $LF_7 = LF_9 - D_{7,9} = 27 - 13 = 14$

Node 6: $LF_6 = \min_{j=8,9} (LF_j - D_{6,j})$

$= \min (LF_8 - D_{6,8}, LF_9 - D_{6,9})$

$= \min (20 - 4, 27 - 3)$

$= 16$

Node 5: $LF_5 = LF_8 - D_{5,8} = 20 - 5 = 15$

Node 4: $$LF_4 = \min_{j=6,7} (LF_j - D_{4,j})$$
$$= \min (LF_6 - D_{4,6}, LF_7 - D_{4,7})$$
$$= \min (16 - 7, 14 - 2)$$
$$= 9$$

Similarly, the LF_i values for all other nodes are summarized in the above figure, besides the *ES* values.

An activity (i, j) is said to be critical if all the following conditions are satisfied.

$$ES_i = LF_i, \quad ES_j = LF_j, \quad ES_j - ES_i = LF_j - LF_i = D_{ij}$$

By applying the above conditions to the activities in Figure 15.20, the critical activities are identified and are shown in the same figure with thick lines on them. The corresponding critical path is 1–3–4–6–8–9 (B–D–H–K–N). The project completion time is 27 months.

Total float: It is the amount of time that the completion time of an activity can be delayed without affecting the project completion time. Therefore,

$$TF_{ij} = LF_j - ES_i - D_{ij} = LF_j - (ES_i + D_{ij}) = LF_j - EF_{ij}$$

where, EF_{ij}, the earliest finish of the activity (i, j).

Also, $$TF_{ij} = LS_{ij} - ES_i$$

where LS_{ij}, the latest start of the activity (i, j) is

$$LS_{ij} = LF_j - D_{ij}$$

Free float: It is the amount of time that the activity completion time can be delayed without affecting the earliest start time of immediate successor activities in the network.

$$FF_{ij} = ES_j - ES_i - D_{ij} = ES_j - (ES_i + D_{ij}) = ES_j - EF_{ij}$$

The calculations of total floats and free floats of the activities are summarized in the following table.

Activity (i, j)	*Duration* (D_{ij})	*Total float* (TF_{ij})	*Free float* (FF_{ij})
1–2	2	6	0
1–3	6	0	0
1–4	4	5	5
2–5	6	7	0
2–6	8	6	6
3–4	3	0	0
3–6	3	7	7
4–6	7	0	0
4–7	2	3	0
5–8	5	7	7
6–8	4	0	0
6–9	3	8	8
7–9	13	3	3
8–9	7	0	0

Any critical activity will have zero total float and zero free float. Based on this property also, one can determine the critical activities. From the above table one can check that the total floats and free floats for the activities (1, 3), (3, 4), (4, 6), (6, 8) and (8, 9) are zero. Hence, they are critical activities. The corresponding critical path is 1–3–4–6–8–9 (B–D–H–K–N).

15.10 PROJECT EVALUATION AND REVIEW TECHNIQUE (PERT)

So far, in our analysis the probability considerations in the management of a project were not included. CPM assumed that the job times are known but can be varied by changing the level of resources. However, in all the research and development projects, many activities are performed only once. Hence, no prior experience with similar activities is available. The management of such projects is done by PERT, which takes into account uncertainties in the completion times of the various activities.

For each activity in the project network, PERT assumes three times estimates on its completion time. They include (i) a most probable time denoted by m, (ii) an optimistic time denoted by a, and (iii) a pessimistic time denoted by b.

The most probable time is the time required to complete the activity under the normal conditions. To include uncertainties, a range of variation in job time is provided by the optimistic and pessimistic times. The optimistic estimate is a good guess on the minimum time required when everything goes according to the plan, whereas the pessimistic estimate is a guess on the maximum time required under adverse conditions such as mechanical breakdowns, minor labour troubles, or shortage of or delays in delivery of material. It should be remarked here that the pessimistic estimate does not take into consideration unusual and prolonged delays or other catastrophes. Because both these estimates are only qualified guesses, the actual time for an activity could lie outside this range. (From a probabilistic view point, we can only say that the probability of a job time falling outside this range is very small.)

Most PERT analysis assumes a Beta distribution for the job times as shown in Figure 15.21 where μ represents the average length of the job duration. The value of μ depends on how close the values of a and b are relative to m.

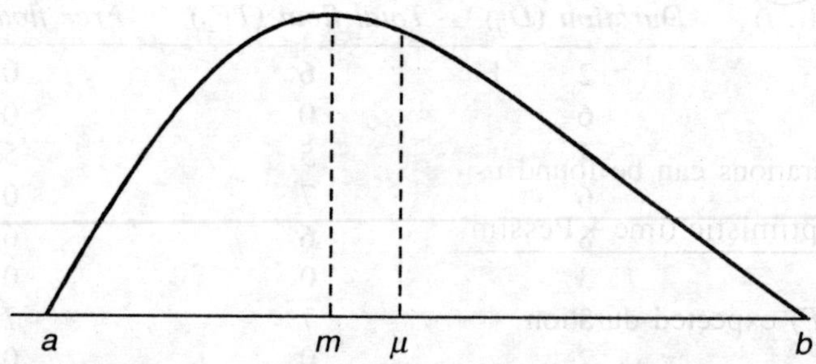

Figure 15.21 Beta distribution for job time.

The expected time to complete an activity is approximated as

$$\mu = \frac{a + 4m + b}{6} \qquad \text{(i)}$$

Since the actual time may vary from its mean value, we need the variance of the job time. For most unimodal distributions (with single peak values), the end values lie within three standard deviations from the mean value. Thus, the spread of the distribution is equal to six times the standard deviation value (σ).

Thus, $$6\sigma = b - a \quad \text{or} \quad \sigma = \frac{b-a}{6}$$

The variance of the job time equals.

$$\sigma^2 = \left(\frac{b-a}{6}\right)^2 \tag{ii}$$

With the three time estimates on all the jobs, PERT calculates the average time and the variance of each job using Eqs. (i) and (ii). Treating the average times as the actual job times, the critical path is found. The duration of the project (T) is given by the sum of all the job times in the critical path. But the job times are random variables. Hence, the project duration T is also a random variable, and we can talk of the average length of the project and its variance.

The expected length of the project is the sum of all the average times of the jobs in the critical path. Similarly, the variance of the project duration is the sum of all the variances of the jobs in the critical path, assuming that all the job times are independent.

EXAMPLE 15.11: Assume that a simple project has the network shown in the Figure 15.22. The activity times are in weeks and three estimates have been given for each activity in the order *a*, *m*, *b*. The scheduled date for completion is week 19.

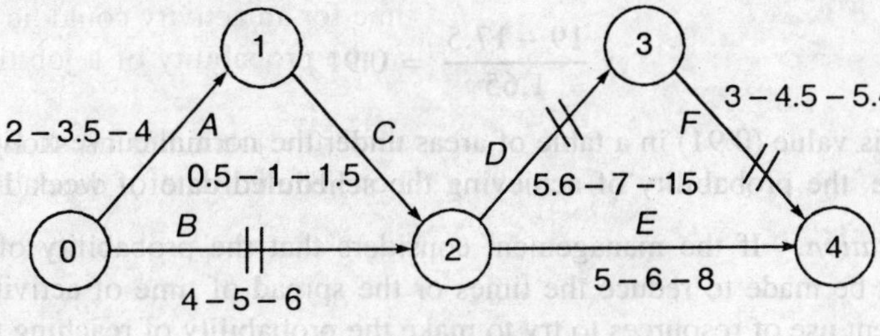

Figure 15.22

The expected durations can be found using what is known as the PERT formula:

$$\frac{\text{Optimistic time} + \text{Pessimistic time} + 4 \times \text{Most likely time}}{6}$$

Critical path (B, D, F) expected duration

$$B = \frac{4 + 6 + 4(5)}{6} = 5 \text{ weeks}$$

$$D = \frac{5.6 + 15 + 4(7)}{6} = 8.1 \text{ weeks}$$

$$F = \frac{3 + 5.4 + 4(4.5)}{6} = \underline{4.4}$$

$$17.5$$

If the critical activities were to occur at their optimistic times, event 4 would be reached in 12.6 weeks, but if the critical activities occurred at their pessimistic times, event 4 would be reached in 26.4 weeks. As these durations span the scheduled date of week 19, some estimate of the probability of achieving the schedule date must be calculated, as follows.

(a) Make an estimate of the standard deviation for each of the critical activities using

$$\frac{\text{Pessimistic time} - \text{Optimistic time}}{6}$$

i.e., standard deviation of Activity $B = \dfrac{6-4}{6} = 0.33$

Activity $D = \dfrac{15-5.6}{6} = 1.57$

Activity $F = \dfrac{5.4-3}{6} = 0.4$

(b) Find the standard deviation of event 4 by calculating the statistical sum (the square root of the sum of the squares) of the standard deviations of all activities on the critical path.

i.e., standard deviation of event 4 $= \sqrt{0.33^2 + 1.57^2 + 0.4^2}$

$= 1.65$ weeks

(c) Find the number of event standard deviations that the scheduled date is away from the expected duration.

i.e. $\dfrac{19-17.5}{1.65} = 0.91$

(d) Look up this value (0.91) in a table of areas under the normal curve to find the probability. In this case, the probability of achieving the scheduled date of week 19 is 82%.

Probability interpretation. If the management considers that the probability of 82% is not high enough, efforts must be made to reduce the times or the spread of time of activities on the critical path. It is an inefficient use of resources to try to make the probability of reaching the scheduled date 100% or very close to 100%. In this case, the management may well accept the 18% chance of not achieving the scheduled date as realistic.

Notes:

(a) The methods of calculating the expected duration and standard deviation as shown above cannot be taken as strictly mathematically valid but are probably accurate enough for most purposes. It is considered by some experts that the standard deviation, as calculated above, underestimates the 'true' standard deviation.

(b) When activity times have variations, the critical path will often change as the variations occur.

EXAMPLE 15.12: Consider a project consisting of nine jobs (*A*, *B*, ..., *I*) with the following precedence relations and time estimates.

Activity	*Predecessors*	*Optimistic time (a)*	*Most probable time (m)*	*Pessimistic time (b)*
A	–	2	5	8
B	*A*	6	9	12
C	*A*	6	7	8
D	*B, C*	1	4	7
E	*A*	8	8	8
F	*D, E*	5	14	17
G	*C*	3	12	21
H	*F, G*	3	6	9
I	*H*	5	8	11

First we compute the average time and the variance for each job. They are tabulated as follows:

Activity	*Average time*	*Standard deviation*	*Variance*
A	5	1	1
B	9	1	1
C	7	1/3	1/9
D	4	1	1
E	8	0	0
F	13	2	4
G	12	3	9
H	6	1	1
I	8	1	1

Figure 15.23 gives the project network, where the numbers on the arcs indicate the average job times. Using the average job times, the earliest and latest times of each event are calculated. The critical path is found as 1→2→4→5→6→7→8. The critical jobs are *A*, *B*, *D*, *F*, *H* and *I*.

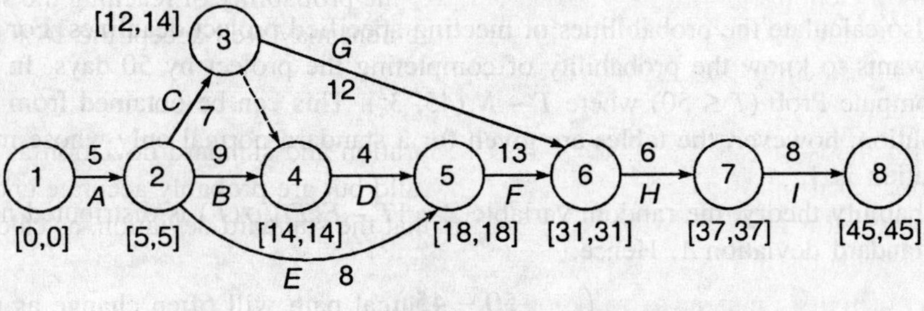

Figure 15.23

Let *T* denote the project duration. Then the expected length of the project is

$E(T)$ = Sum of the expected times of jobs *A*, *B*, *D*, *F*, *H* and *I*

$= 5 + 9 + 4 + 13 + 6 + 8 = 45$ days

The variance of the project duration is

$V(T)$ = Sum of the variance of jobs A, B, D, F, H and I

$= 1 + 1 + 1 + 4 + 1 + 1 = 9$

The standard deviation of the project duration is

$$\sigma(T) = \sqrt{V(T)} = 3$$

Probabilities of completing the project

The project length T is the sum of all job times in the critical path. PERT assumes that all the job times are independent, and are identically distributed. Hence, by the *central limit theorem*, T has a normal distribution with mean $E(T)$, and variance $V(T)$. The following figure (Figure 15.24) exhibits a normal distribution with mean μ and variance σ^2.

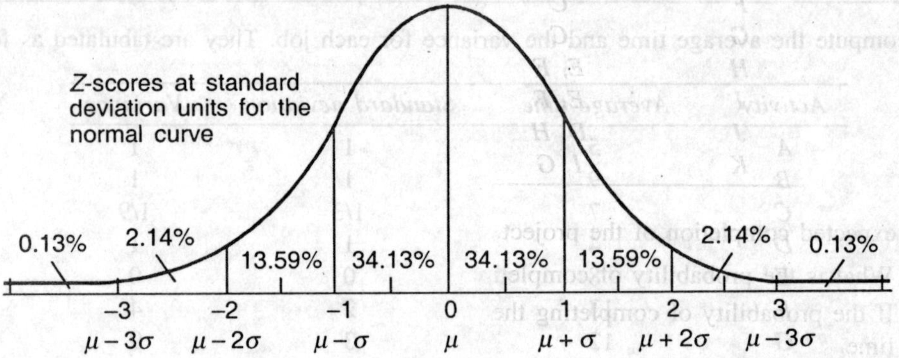

Figure 15.24

In our example, T is distributed normal with mean 45 and standard deviation 3. For any normal distribution, the probability that the random variable lies within one standard deviation from the mean is 0.68. Hence, there is a 68% chance that the project duration will be between 42 and 48 days. Similarly, there is a 99.7% chance that T will lie within three standard deviations (i.e. between 36 and 54).

We can also calculate the probabilities of meeting specified project deadlines. For example, the management wants to know the probability of completing the project by 50 days. In other words, we have to compute Prob ($T \le 50$) where $T \sim N(45, 3^2)$. This can be obtained from the tables of normal distribution; however, the tables are given for a standard normal only whose mean is 0 and standard deviation is 1.

From probability theory, the random variable $Z = [T - E(T)]/\sigma(T)$ is distributed normally with mean 0 and standard deviation 1. Hence,

$$\text{Prob } (T \le 50) = \text{Prob }\left(Z \le \frac{50 - 45}{3}\right) = \text{Prob } (Z \le 1.67) = 0.95$$

Thus, there is a 95% chance that the project will be completed within 50 days.

Suppose we want to know the probability of completing the project 4 days sooner than expected. This means we have to compute

$$\text{Prob } (T \le 41) = \text{Prob }\left(Z \le \frac{41 - 45}{3}\right) = \text{Prob } (Z \le -1.33) = 0.09$$

Hence, there is only a small 9% chance that the project will be completed in 41 days.

Note: When multiple critical paths exist, the variance of each critical path may be different, even though the expected values are the same. In such a circumstance, it is recommended that the largest variance of T be used for probability estimates.

EXAMPLE 15.13: Consider the details of a project involving 11 activities.

Activity	*Predecessor (s)*	*Duration (weeks)*		
		a	*M*	*B*
A	–	6	7	8
B	–	1	2	9
C	–	1	4	7
D	*A*	1	2	3
E	*A, B*	1	2	9
F	*C*	1	5	9
G	*C*	2	2	8
H	*E, F*	4	4	4
I	*E, F*	4	4	10
J	*D, H*	2	5	14
K	*I, G*	2	2	8

Find the expected completion of the project.

(a) What is the probability of completing the project on or before 25 weeks?

(b) If the probability of completing the project is 0.84, find the expected project completion time.

Solution: The expected duration and variance of each activity is shown in the table. The project network is shown in the figure (Figure 15.25). The calculations of critical path based on expected durations are summarized in Figure 15.25. The critical path is *A*-Dummy-*E*–*H*–*J* and the corresponding project completion time is 20 weeks.

Activity	*Duration (weeks)*			*Mean duration*	*Variance*
	a	*m*	*b*		
A	6	7	8	7	0.11
B	1	2	9	3	1.78
C	1	4	7	4	1.00
D	1	2	3	2	0.11
E	1	2	9	3	1.78
F	1	5	9	5	1.78
G	2	2	8	3	1.00
H	4	4	4	4	0.00
I	4	4	10	5	1.00
J	2	5	14	6	4.00
K	2	2	8	3	1.00

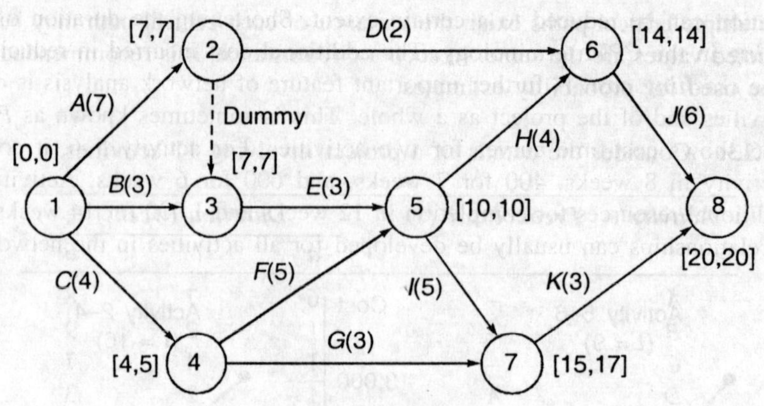

Figure 15.25

(a) The sum of the variances of all the activities on the critical path is:

$$0.11 + 1.78 + 0.00 + 4.00 = 5.89 \text{ weeks}$$

Therefore, $\sigma = \sqrt{5.89} = 2.43$ weeks.

Also, $$P(x \le 25) = P\left(\frac{x-\mu}{\sigma} \le \frac{25-20}{2.43}\right)$$

$$= P(z \le 2.06) = 0.9803$$

This value is obtained from standard normal table. Therefore, the probability of completing the project on or before 25 weeks is 0.9803.

(b) We also have $P(x \le C) = 0.84$.

Therefore, $$P\left(\frac{x\ \mu}{\sigma} \le \frac{C-\mu}{\sigma}\right) = 0.84$$

$$P\left(Z \le \frac{C-20}{2.43}\right) = 0.84$$

From the standard normal table, the value of z is 0.99, when the cumulative probability is 0.84.

Therefore,

$$\frac{C-20}{2.43} = 0.99 \text{ or } C = 22.4 \text{ weeks}$$

The project will be completed in 22.41 weeks (approximately 23 weeks) if the probability of completing the project is 0.84.

15.11 PERT/COST ANALYSIS

The basic assumption in CPM is that the activity times are proportional to the level of resources allocated to them. By assigning additional resources (capital, people, materials, and machines) to an activity, its duration can be reduced to a certain extent. Shortening the duration of an activity is known as ***crashing*** in the CPM terminology. The additional cost incurred in reducing the activity time is called the ***crashing cost***. A further important feature of network analysis is concerned with the costs of activities and of the project as a whole. This is sometimes known as *PERT/COST*.

Figure 15.26 shows cost-time curves for two activities. For activity 5–6, it costs Rs. 300 to complete the activity in 8 weeks, 400 for 7 weeks, and 600 for 6 weeks. Activity 2–4 requires Rs. 3,000 of additional resources for completion in 12 weeks and 1,000 for 14 weeks. Similar cost-time curves or relationships can usually be developed for all activities in the network.

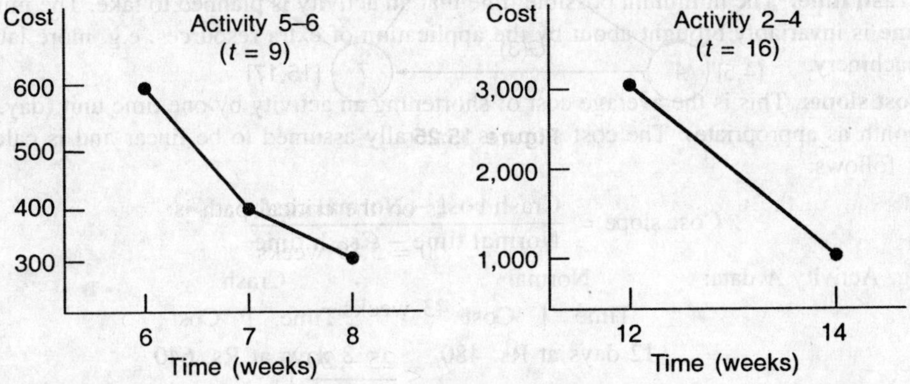

Figure 15.26

We learned earlier that the duration of the critical activities determines the project completion time. Thus, by crashing the critical jobs, the project duration can be reduced. Of course, crashing the critical activities increases the total direct cost of the project, but the reduction in project duration may result in other advantages or returns that may offset this increased cost. These may include indirect costs such as equipment rental, supervisory personnel, supplies, and other costs that are directly proportional to the project duration. There may be other economic benefits in completing the project ahead of schedule. For instance, a new product may capture a larger share of the market if it is introduced before its competitor's.

Penalties and bonuses: A common feature of many projects is a penalty clause for delayed completion. Network costs analysis is often combined with a penalty and/or bonus situation with the general aim of calculating whether it is worthwhile paying extra to reduce the project time so as to save a penalty.

Thus, the total cost of the project is the sum of the direct costs (proportional to the activity times) and the indirect costs (proportional to the project duration). The critical path method essentially studies the trade-off between the total cost of the project and its completion time.

For the critical path analysis, it is assumed that every job has a *normal completion time* (maximum time) if no additional resources were assigned, and a *crash completion time* (minimum time) with the maximum amount of resources. In addition, a cost versus time relationship is available for every job in the project. The project management problem is to determine the amount by which the various jobs are to be crashed that will minimize the total cost of the project (direct and indirect).

15.12 COST AND NETWORKS—BASIC DEFINITIONS

(a) **Normal cost:** The costs associated with a normal time estimate for an activity. Often, the 'normal' time estimate is set at the point where resources (men, machines, etc.) are used in the most efficient manner.

(b) **Crash cost:** The costs associated with the minimum possible time for an activity. Crash costs, because of extra wages, overtime premiums, extra facility costs, are always higher than the normal costs.

(c) **Crash time:** The minimum possible time that an activity is planned to take. The minimum time is invariably brought about by the application of extra resources, e.g. more labour or machinery.

(d) **Cost slope:** This is the average cost of shortening an activity by one time unit (day, week, month as appropriate). The cost slope is generally assumed to be linear and is calculated as follows:

$$\text{Cost slope} = \frac{\text{Crash cost} - \text{Normal cost}}{\text{Normal time} - \text{Crash time}}$$

e.g. Activity *A* data:

Normal		Crash	
Time	Cost	Time	Cost
12 days at	Rs. 480	8 days at	Rs. 640

$$\text{Cost slope} = \frac{640 - 480}{12 - 8}$$

$$= \text{Rs. } 40/\text{day}$$

(e) **Least cost scheduling or 'crashing':** The process which finds the least cost method of reducing the overall project duration, time period by time period.

15.13 LEAST COST SCHEDULING RULES

The basic rule of least cost scheduling is simply stated. Reduce the time of the activity on the critical path with the lowest cost slope and progressively repeat this process until the desired reduction in time is achieved. Complications occur when time reductions cause several paths to become critical simultaneously, thus necessitating several activities to be reduced at the same time. These complications are explained below as they occur.

Method I: For each activity, there will exist a reduction in activity time and the cost incurred for that time reduction. Let

M_i = Maximum reduction of time for activity *i*

C_i = Additional cost associated with reducing activity time for activity *i*

K_i = Cost of reducing activity time by one time unit for activity *i*

$$K_i = \frac{C_i}{M_i}$$

It is clear that this K_i is the cost slope.

With this information, it is possible to determine the least cost of reducing the project completion date.

EXAMPLE 15.14: Given the following information, determine the least cost of reducing the project completion time by one week.

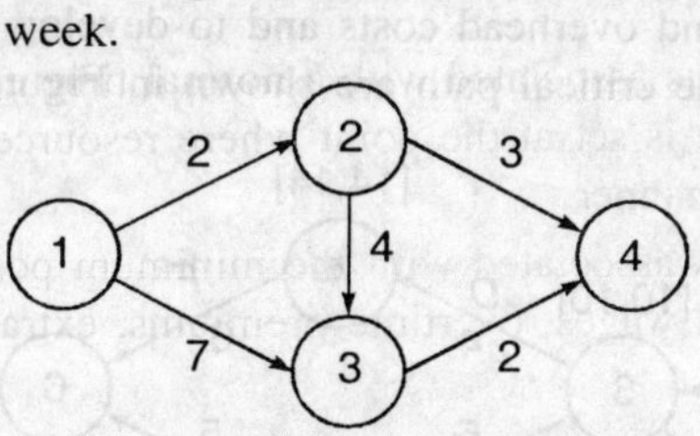

Activity	*t (Weeks)*	*M (Weeks)*	*C*	*Activity*	*ES*	*EF*	*LS*	*LF*	*S*
1–2	2	1	300	1–2	0	2	1	3	1
1–3	7	4	2,000	1–3	0	7	0	7	0
2–3	4	2	2,000	2–3	2	6	3	7	1
2–4	3	2	4,000	2–4	2	5	6	9	4
3–4	2	1	2,000	3–4	7	9	7	9	0

Solution: The first step is to compute *K* for each activity:

Activity	*M*	*C*	*K*	*On critical path*
1–2	1	300	300	No
1–3	4	2,000	500	Yes
2–3	2	2,000	1,000	No
2–4	2	4,000	2,000	No
3–4	1	2,000	2,000	Yes

The second step is to locate that activity on the critical path with the smallest value of K_i. The critical path consists of activities 1–3 and 3–4. Since activity 1–3 has a lower value of K_i, we can reduce the project completion time by one week, to eight weeks, by incurring an additional cost of Rs. 500.

We must be very careful in using this procedure. Any further reduction in activity time along the critical path would cause the critical path also to include activities 1–2, 2–3 and 3–4. In other words, there would be two critical paths and activities on both would need to be "crashed" to reduce the project completion time.

Method II:

EXAMPLE 15.15: Consider a project consisting of eight jobs (*A, B, C, D, E, F, G, H*). About each job, we know the following:

Job	*Predecessors*	*Normal time (days)*	*Crash time (days)*	*Cost of crashing per day*
A	–	10	7	4
B	–	5	4	2
C	*B*	3	2	2
D	*A, C*	4	3	3
E	*A, C*	5	3	3
F	*D*	6	3	5
G	*E*	5	2	1
H	*F, G*	5	4	4

Giving the overhead costs as Rs. 5 per day, we want to determine the optimal duration of the project in terms of both the crashing and overhead costs and to develop an optimal project schedule.

The project network and the critical path are shown in Figure 15.27.

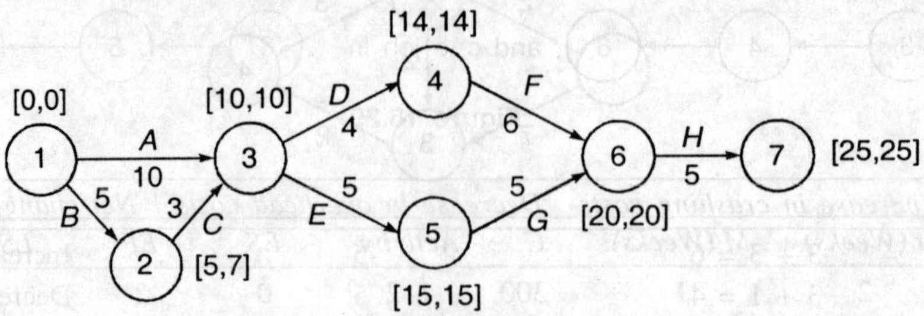

Figure 15.27

If all the jobs are done at their normal times, the project duration (length of the longest path) is 25 days. Hence, under a "no crashing" schedule,

$$\text{Total cost} = \text{Overhead costs} + \text{Crashing costs} = 5(25) + 0 = 125$$

If all the jobs were crashed to their minimum time, then the project duration is 17 days. Under this schedule, the total cost = 5(17) + 47 = 132. The project management problem is to determine the optimal duration of jobs that will minimize the total cost.

The project completion time is 25 days, and the project network has two critical paths as shown below in Figure 15.28.

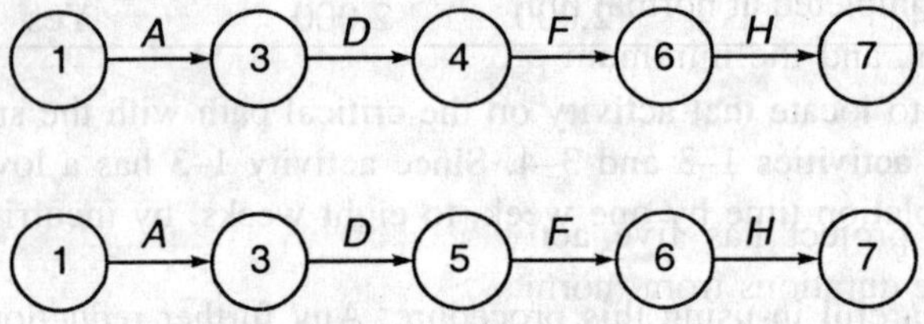

Figure 15.28

Between the nodes 3 and 6 we have *parallel critical paths*. The critical activities are jobs *A*, *D*, *E*, *F*, *G* and *H*. The total cost of the project under normal time is Rs. 125.

To reduce the project duration, it is necessary to reduce the duration of the critical jobs. Consider the critical job *H*, which can be crashed by 1 day at a cost of Rs. 4. This reduces the project duration by 1 day at a savings of Rs. 5 in the overhead costs. Hence, job *H* is crashed to its lowest limit of 4 days and the total cost is reduced to Rs. 124.

Consider the crashing of job *A* now. This also results in a net savings of Re. 1 in the total cost for each day of crashing. But job *A* cannot be crashed to its minimum value of 7 days because when *A* is crashed to 8 days, jobs *B* and *C* also become critical. This results in parallel critical paths between nodes 1 and 3, and any reduction in *A* alone will not reduce the project duration. Hence, job *A* is crashed only to 8 days, and the total cost is reduced to 122.

To reduce the project duration by one more day, we must crash job *A* by 1 day and either job *B* or *C* by 1 day. The total cost of crashing *A* and *B* is Rs. 6, which is more than the savings in the overhead costs. Similarly, crashing *A* and *C* is also not economical.

Now consider the critical jobs *D*, *E*, *F* and *G*. Since we have parallel critical paths between nodes 3 and 6, we have to crash one job in the path to reduce the project length. This means we must try four different combinations as shown in Figure 15.29.

, and one job in

Figure 15.29

Jobs	*Increase in crashing costs*	*Decrease in overhead costs*	*Net change in total cost*
D and *E*	3 + 3 = 6	5	Increases by 1
D and *G*	3 + 1 = 4	5	Decreases by 1
F and *E*	5 + 3 = 8	5	Increases by 3
F and *G*	5 + 1 = 6	5	Increases by 1

From the above table, we find that the combination *D* and *G* alone is economical, and when we crash both jobs *D* and *G* by one day, the total cost reduces to Rs. 121. No further crashing is economical. Hence, the optimal project schedule is

Crash job *A* to 8 days
Crash job *D* to 3 days
Crash job *G* to 4 days
Crash job *H* to 4 days

Jobs *B*, *C*, *E* and *F* are completed at normal times 5, 3, 5 and 6 days, respectively. The optimal length of the project is 21 days, and the minimum project cost is Rs. 121.

Method III:

EXAMPLE 15.16: A project has five activities and it is required to prepare the least cost schedules for all possible durations from 'normal time'—'normal cost' to 'crash time'—'crash cost'. The cost slope has been calculated from the data given and inserted in the last column (Figure 15.30).

	Preceding	*Time (days)*		*Costs (Rs.)*		*Cost slope*
Activity	*activity*	*Normal*	*Crash*	*Normal*	*Crash*	
A	–	4	3	360	420	60
B	–	8	5	300	510	70
C	*A*	5	3	170	270	50
D	*A*	9	7	220	300	40
E	*B*, *C*	5	3	200	360	80

Project durations and costs

(a) Normal durations, 14 days
Critical path, *A*, *C*, *E*
Project cost (i.e. cost of all activities at normal time) = Rs. 1,250
(i.e. 360 + 300 + 170 + 220 + 200)

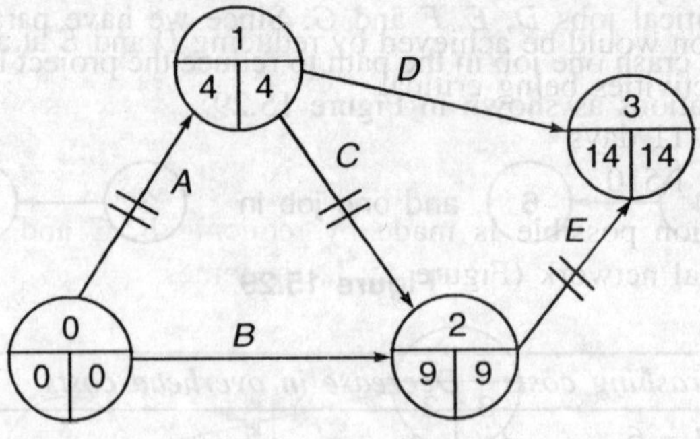

Figure 15.30

(b) Reduce by 1 day the activity on the critical path with the lowest cost slope
Reduce activity *C* at an extra cost of Rs. 50
Project duration, 13 days
Project cost, Rs. 1,300
Note: All activities are now critical.

(c) Several alternative ways are possible to reduce the project time by a further 1 day but note 2 or 3 activities need to be shortened because there are several critical paths.

Possibilities available

Reduce by 1 day	*Extra costs*	*Activities critical*
A and *B*	60 + 70 = 130	All
D and *E*	40 + 80 = 120	All
B, *C* and *D*	70 + 50 + 40 = 160	All
A and *E*	60 + 80 = 140	*A*, *D*, *B*, *E*

An indication of the total extra costs apparently indicates that the second alternative (i.e. *D* and *E* reduced) is the cheapest. However, a closer examination of the last alternative (i.e. *A* and *E* reduced) reveals that activity *C* is non-critical and with 1 day float. It may be recalled that activity *C* was reduced by 1 day previously at an extra cost of Rs. 50. If in conjunction with *A* and *E* reduction, activity *C* is **increased** by 1 day, Rs. 50 is saved and all activities become critical. The net cost, therefore, for the 12 day duration is 1,300 + (140 – 50) = Rs. 1,390. The network is now as in Figure 15.31.

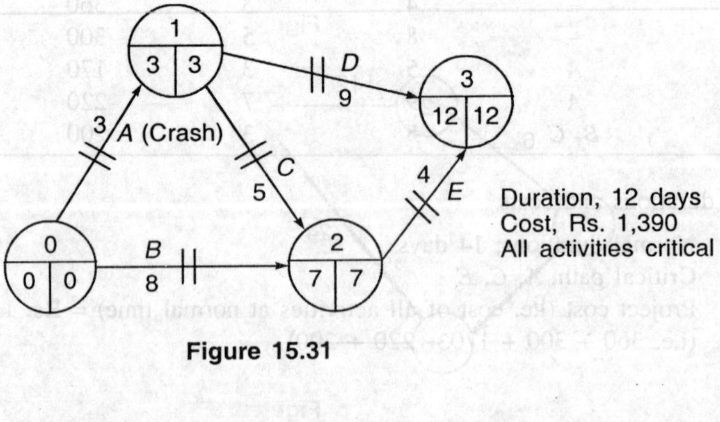

Figure 15.31

(d) The next reduction would be achieved by reducing D and E at an increase of Rs. 120 with once again all activities being critical.

Project duration, 11 days
Project cost, Rs. 1,510

(e) The final reduction possible is made by reducing B, C and D at an increased cost of Rs. 160. The final network (Figure 15.32) becomes:

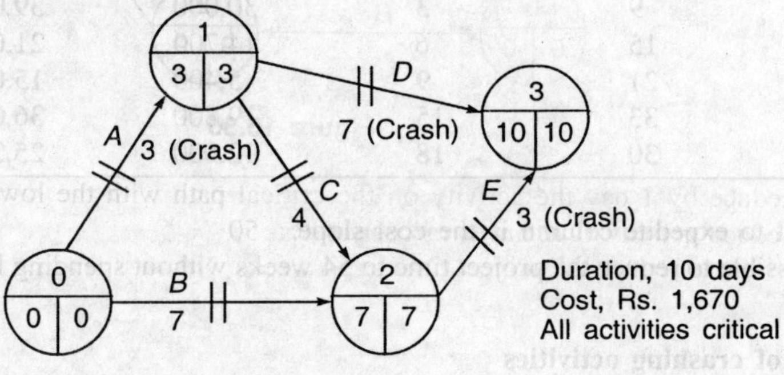

Figure 15.32

EXAMPLE 15.17: Consider two networks, developed on the basis of the data given in the table using all normal times for the activities and the other using all crash times (see Figures 15.33 and 15.34). The critical path in the figures is shown by a heavy line. If the project is completed on a normal basis, the completion time is 99 weeks and the project cost is Rs. 1,38,300. If all activities are crashed, the project completion time reduces to 54 weeks with a completion cost of Rs. 2,35,200.

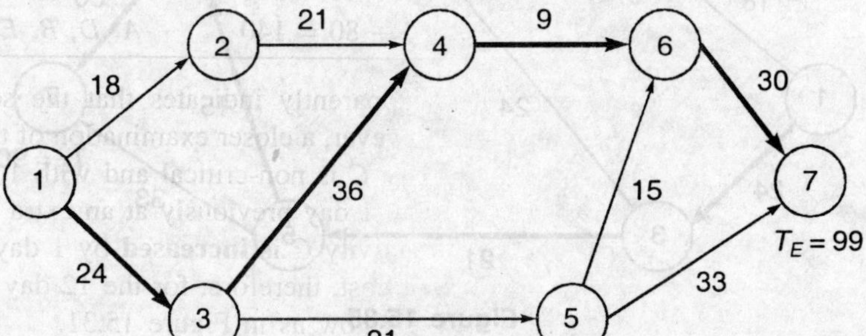

Figure 15.33

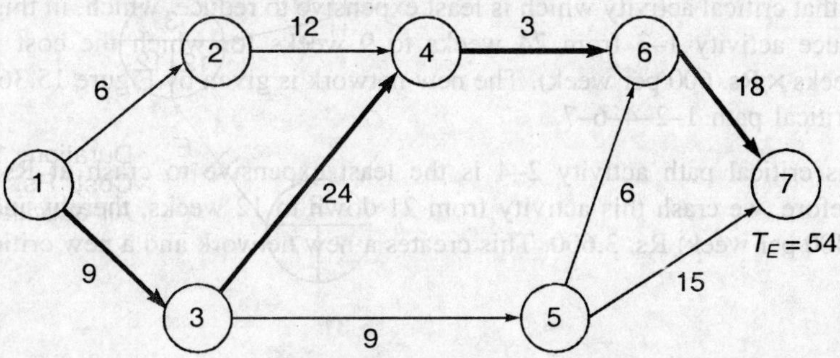

Figure 15.34

Activity	Normal time (Weeks)	Crash time (Weeks)	Normal cost (Rs.)	Crash cost (Rs.)	Cost to expedite (Rs./Week)
1–2	18	6	12,000	36,000	2,000
1–3	24	9	9,000	18,000	600
2–4	21	12	8,400	12,000	400
3–4	36	24	27,000	33,000	500
4–6	9	3	30,000	39,000	1,500
5–6	15	6	14,700	21,000	700
3–5	21	9	5,400	15,000	800
5–7	33	15	19,800	36,000	900
6–7	30	18	12,000	25,200	1,100

Note: Cost to expedite column is the cost slope.

Is it possible to reduce the project time to 54 weeks without spending Rs. 2,35,200 as direct total costs?

1. Process of crashing activities

Step 1: Let us first mark the critical path in Figure 15.34. It is 1–3–4–6–7. Find out which is the least expensive critical activity. In our example, it is activity 3–4 (Rs. 500 per week). We crash this activity to its minimum time of 24 weeks at a total cost for this action of (12 weeks × 500 per week) Rs. 6,000. When we crash this activity, it creates a new critical path which is shown in Figure 15.35 by a heavy line.

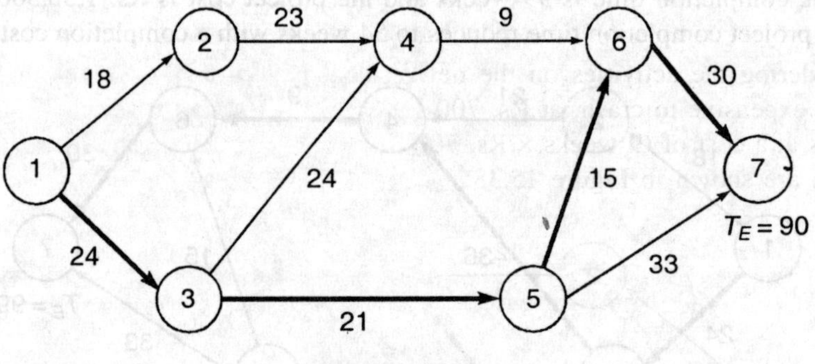

Figure 15.35

Step 2: The new critical path is 1–3–5–6–7 with a total completion time of 90 weeks. As in step 1, we crash that critical activity which is least expensive to reduce, which, in this case, is activity 1–3. Let us reduce activity 1–3 from 24 weeks to 9 weeks for which the cost incurred will be Rs. 9,000 (15 weeks × Rs. 600 per week). The new network is given by Figure 15.36. In this network we get a new critical path 1–2–4–6–7.

Step 3: On this critical path activity 2–4 is the least expensive to crash at Rs. 400 per week. Proceeding as before, we crash this activity from 21 down to 12 weeks, thereby incurring a cost of (9 weeks × Rs. 400 per week) Rs. 3,600. This creates a new network and a new critical path as given in Figure 15.37.

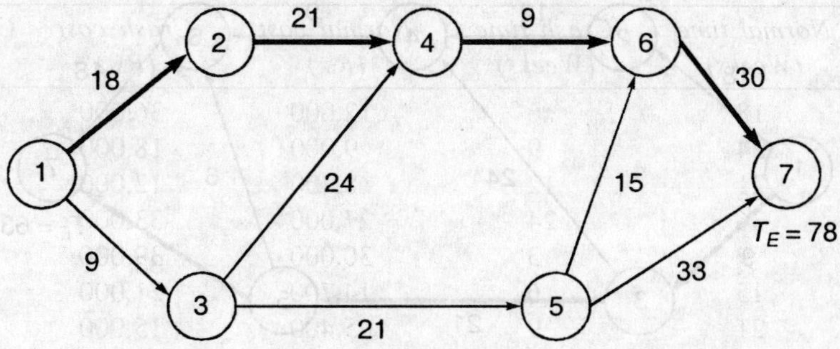

Figure 15.36

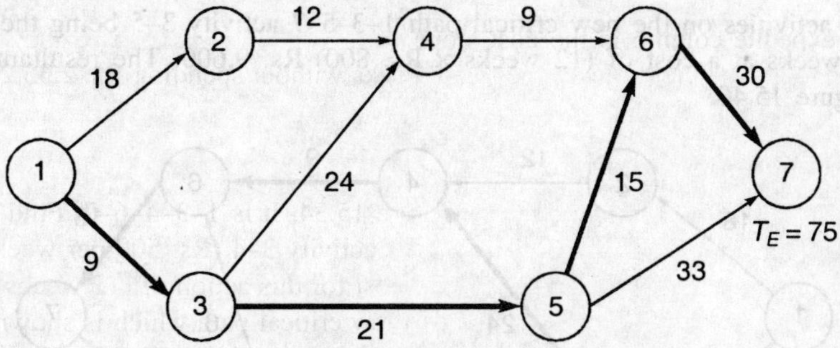

Figure 15.37

Step 4: Considering the activities on the new critical path 1–3–5–6–7, we observe that activity 5–6 is the least expensive to crash, at Rs. 700 per week. Let us crash activity 5–6 to its minimum time of 6 weeks at a cost of (9 weeks × Rs. 700 per week) Rs. 6,300. The consequent network and the critical path are shown in Figure 15.38.

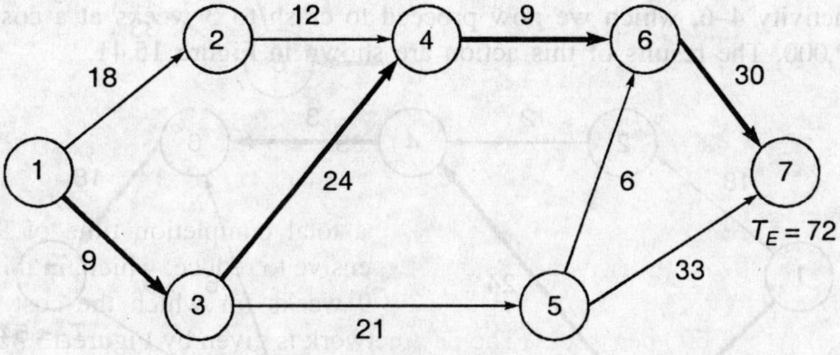

Figure 15.38

Step 5: Out of the activities on the new critical path 1–3–4–6–7, activity 6–7 is the least expensive to crash at this point and can be crashed to 18 weeks, at a cost of (12 weeks × Rs. 1,100) Rs. 13,200. As a result, we get the new network and the critical path as shown in Figure 15.39.

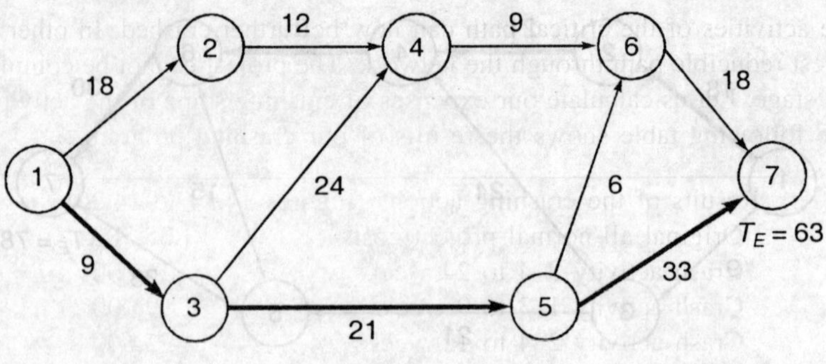

Figure 15.39

Step 6: Of the activities on the new critical path 1–3–5–7 activity 3–5 being the least expensive is crashed to 9 weeks at a cost of (12 weeks × Rs. 800) Rs. 9,600. The resultant critical path is illustrated in Figure 15.40.

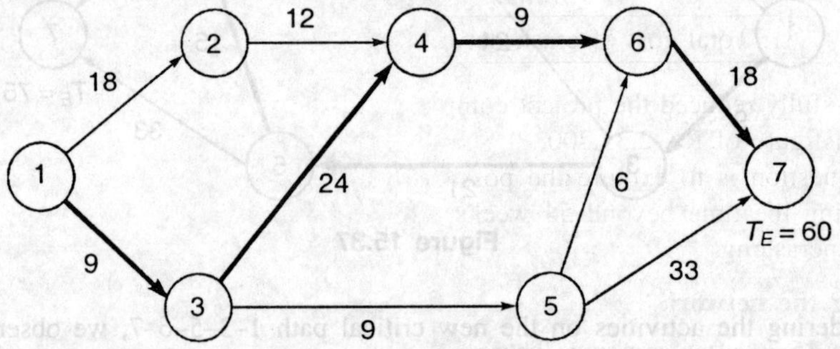

Figure 15.40

Step 7: While examining the new critical path 1–3–4–6–7, we notice that all activities have been crashed except activity 4–6, which we now proceed to crash to 3 weeks at a cost of (6 weeks × Rs. 1,500) Rs. 9,000. The results of this action are shown in Figure 15.41.

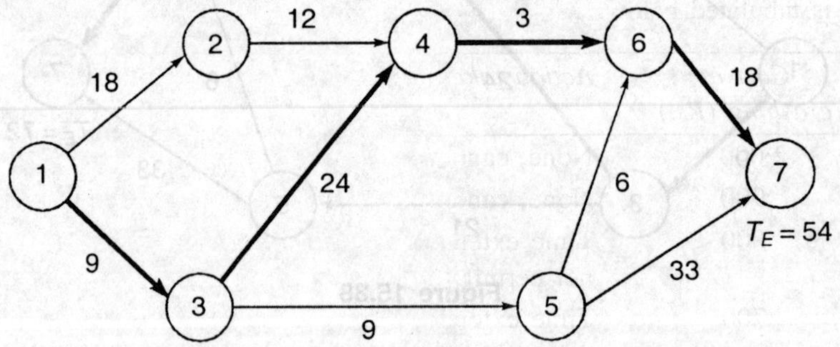

Figure 15.41

None of the activities of the critical path can now be further crashed. In other words, we have defined the longest reducible path through the network. The project cannot be completed in less than 54 weeks at this stage. Let us calculate our expenses of crashing some of the activities commencing with step 1. The following table shows the results of our crashing program.

Results of the crashing actions (Figures 14.14 to 14.20)	
Original all-normal project costs	1,38,300
Crash activity 3–4 to 24 weeks	6,000
Crash activity 1–3 to 9 weeks	9,000
Crash activity 2–4 to 12 weeks	3,600
Crash activity 5–6 to 6 weeks	6,300
Crash activity 6–7 to 18 weeks	13,200
Crash activity 3–5 to 9 weeks	9,600
Crash activity 4–6 to 3 weeks	9,000
	56,700
Normal cost	1,38,000
Total cost of crash network	1,95,000

We have successfully reduced the project completion time of 54 weeks without increasing the cost to the old crash figure of Rs. 2,35,200.

The next question is to explore the possibility of reducing the project cost even further but without increasing the time beyond 54 weeks. In order to do this, we shall learn the concept of decrashing or uncrashing.

2. Uncrashing the network

Consider Figure 15.36 after crashing. There are only four activities on the critical path. We can attempt, therefore, the uncrashing of the non-critical activities (in other words, we can increase the time of the non-critical activities) which amounts to reducing the project cost further.

First consider the most expensive activity that has been crashed. It is activity 1–2 at Rs. 2,000 per week. We can reduce the project cost more if we uncrash it. Later, we proceed to the next most expensive activity to uncrash it, and continue till we reach a point where no further uncrashing is possible. In other words, this stage gives us the least project cost with the time period of 54 weeks. The uncrashing is tabulated below.

Non-critical activity	*Cost of crashing (Rs.)*	*Action taken*	*Net gain obtain (Rs.)*
1–2	2,000	None, cannot be uncrashed further	0
5–7	900	None, cannot be uncrashed further	0
3–5	800	Time extended to 12 weeks, path 1–3–5–7 will not permit further extension	2,400
5–6	700	Time extended to 15 weeks is the normal for this activity	6,300
2–4	400	Time extended to 15 weeks path 1–2–4–6–7 will not permit further extension	1,200
		Total gains from uncrashing non-critical activities	9,900

We can see this is the minimum project cost, with 54 weeks as project completion time. The resulting network is shown in Figure 15.42.

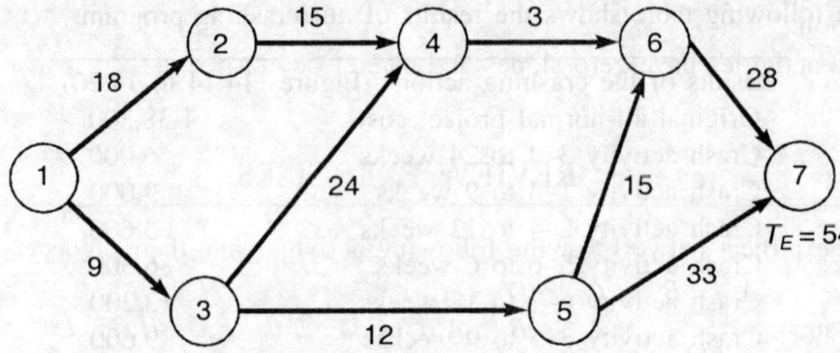

Figure 15.42

The project cost for the crashed network is Rs. 1,95,000 from which we can subtract Rs. 9,900, being the total gains of uncrashing, to give us a minimum project cost of Rs. 1,85,100. Please note that all the paths in Figure 15.42 are critical paths.

To sum up:

- Locate the critical path of the normal network.
- Crash the least expensive activity on the critical path to get a new critical path with its least expensive activity to crash. Proceed in the manner till we get a critical path on which all activities are at their crash time (non-reducible critical path).
- Reverse the procedure by considering the non-critical activities and begin uncrashing by choosing the most expensive activity and proceeding to the least expensive activity, allowing uncrashing to the extent of critical path or to their normal times, whichever is shorter.

3. Important points for crashing networks

- Only critical activities affect the project duration, so take care not to crash non-critical activities.
- The minimum possible project duration is not necessarily the most profitable option. It may be cost-effective to pay some penalties to avoid highest crash costs.
- If there are several independent critical paths then several activities will need to be crashed simultaneously. If there are several critical paths which are not separate, i.e. they share an activity or activities, then it may be cost-effective to crash the shared activities, even though they may not have the lowest cost slopes.
- Always look for the possibility of increasing the duration of a previously crashed activity when subsequent crashing renders it non-critical, i.e. it has float.
- Cost analysis of networks seeks the cheapest ways of reducing project times.
- The crash cost is the cost associated with the minimum possible time for an activity, which is known as the ***crash time***.
- The average cost of shortening an activity by one time period (day, weeks, etc.) is known as the ***cost slope***.
- Least cost scheduling finds the cheapest method of reducing the overall project time by reducing the time of the activity on the critical path with the lowest cost slope.

- The total project cost includes all activity costs not just those on the critical path.
- The usual assumption is that the cost slope is linear. This need not be so and care should be taken not to make the linearity assumption when circumstances point to some other conclusion.
- Dummy activities have zero slopes and cannot be crashed.

REVIEW EXERCISES

1. Draw the project network for the following activities and their predecessors.

Activity	*A*	*B*	*C*	*D*	*E*	*F*	*G*	*H*	*I*	*J*	*K*	*L*	*M*
Immediate predecessor	–	–	*A*	*B*	*A,B*	*C,D*	*F,B*	*E,G*	*H,G*	*I,F*	*J,L*	*A*	*K*

2. Consider the following project activities and their duration.

Activity	*A*	*B*	*C*	*D*	*E*	*F*	*G*	*H*	*I*	*J*	*K*	*L*	*M*	*N*	*O*	*P*	*Q*
Imm. Pred	–	–	–	*A*	*A*	*B*	*B*	*C*	*C*	*D*	*E*	*F*	*G*	*H*	*I*	*J,K,L*	*M,N,O*
Duration (months)	4	8	5	4	5	7	4	8	3	6	5	4	12	7	10	5	8

(a) Construct the CPM network.
(b) Determine the critical path.
(c) Compute total floats and free floats for non-critical activities.

3. Draw a network for the following activities and their predecessors.

Activity	*Immediate predecessor*	*Activity*	*Immediate predecessors*
A	–	*L*	*K*
B	*A*	*M*	*J*
C	*B*	*N*	*G*
D	*C*	*O*	*I, L*
E	*D*	*P*	*F*
F	*E*	*Q*	*O*
G	*F*	*R*	*P, Q*
H	*F*	*S*	*H, I*
I	*F*	*T*	*O, S*
J	*B*	*U*	*R, T*
K	*J*		

4. Draw the network for a project consisting of 16 jobs *A*, *B*, *C*, ..., *M*, *N*, *O*, *P* with the following job sequence.

$$A, B, C, D \rightarrow E, F, G$$
$$E, F, G \rightarrow H$$
$$H \rightarrow I$$
$$I \rightarrow J, K, L, M, N$$
$$J, K, L, M, N \rightarrow O$$
$$G, O \rightarrow P$$

5. The department of Mathematics of the University is holding a faculty development programme. It has planned the following activities. Prepare a network diagram showing the interrelationships of various activities.

Activity	*Description*	*Predecessors*
A	Design conference meetings and theme	–
B	Design the front cover of the conference proceedings	*A*
C	Prepare the brochure and send request for papers	*A*
D	Complete the list of distinguished speakers/guests	*A*
E	Finalize the brochure and print it	*C,D*
F	Make travel arrangements for distinguished speakers/guests	*D*
G	Dispatch brochurres	*E*
H	Receive papers for the conference	*G*
I	Edit papers and assemble proceedings	*F, H*
J	Print the proceedings	*B, I*

6. Given the following information on a small project, draw a network based on this information.

Activity	*A*	*B*	*C*	*D*	*E*	*F*	*G*	*H*
Immediate predecessor	–	*A*	*A*	*B,C*	*C*	*D*	*E*	*F,G*

7. Consider the following project activities and their predecessors and time estimates.

Activity	*A*	*B*	*C*	*D*	*E*	*F*	*G*	*H*	*I*
Predecessor	–	–	*A, B*	*A, B*	*B*	*D, E*	*C, F*	*D, E*	*G, H*
Duration (days)	15	10	10	10	5	5	20	10	15

Determine the earliest completion time of the project, and identify the critical path.

8. Draw a network.

Activity	*Immediate predecessor*	*Activity*	*Immediate predecessors*
A	–	*H*	*F*
B	–	*I*	*C, D, G,* H
C	–	*J*	*I*
D	–	*K*	*I*
E	*A*	*L*	*J, K*
F	*B*	*M*	*J, K*
G	*E*	*N*	*M*

9. For a small project of 12 activities, the details are given below. Draw the network and compute earliest occurrence time, latest occurrence time, critical activities and project completion time.

Activity	*A*	*B*	*C*	*D*	*E*	*F*	*G*	*H*	*I*	*J*	*K*	*L*
Imm. Prede	–	–	–	*B,C*	*A*	*C*	*E*	*E*	*D,F,H*	*E*	*I,J*	*G*
Duration (days)	9	4	7	8	7	5	10	8	6	9	10	2

10. The activities involved in a garment manufacturing company are listed with their time estimates as in the following table. Draw the network and carry out the critical path calculations.

Activity	*Description*	*Immediate predecessors*	*Duration (days)*
A	Forecast sales volume	–	10
B	Study competitive market	–	7
C	Design item and facilities	*A*	5
D	Prepare production plan	*C*	3
E	Estimate cost of production	*D*	2
F	Set sales price	*B,E*	1
G	Prepare budget	*F*	14

11. The information about various activities of a project and the precedence relationships are given below. Draw a network using as few dummies as possible.

Activity	*Immediate predecessors*	*Activity*	*Immediate predecessors*
A	–	*I*	*F,G,N*
B	–	*J*	*O,E,N*
C	–	*K*	*B,C,D*
D	–	*L*	*K*
E	*B,C,D*	*M*	*B,C,D*
F	*A,B,C,D*	*N*	*B,C,D*
G	*A,B,C,D*	*O*	*A,B,C,D*
H	*A,B,C,D*	*P*	*I,J,M,L*

12. Consider the following data regarding a project.

Activity	*Predecessors*	*Duration*		
		Optimistic (a)	*Most likely (m)*	*Pessimistic (b)*
A	–	3	5	8
B	–	6	7	9
C	*A*	4	5	9
D	*B*	3	5	8
E	*A*	4	6	9
F	*C,D*	5	8	11
G	*C,D,E*	3	6	9
H	*F*	1	2	9

(a) Construct the project network.
(b) Find the expected duration and the variance of the activity.
(c) Find the critical path and the expected project completion time.
(d) What is the probability of completing the project on or before 30 weeks?
(e) If the probability of completing the project is 0.9, find the expected project completion time.

13. Consider the project network given below.

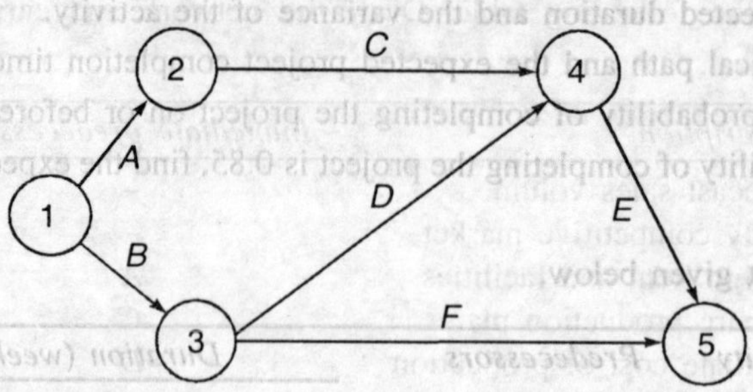

The project executive has made estimates of the optimistic, most likely, and pessimistic time (in days) for completion of the various activities as follows.

Activity	*Duration*		
	Optimistic (a)	*Most likely (m)*	*Pessimistic (b)*
A	2	5	14
B	9	12	15
C	5	14	17
D	2	5	8
E	6	9	12
F	8	17	20

(a) Find the critical path.
(b) Determine the expected project completion time and its variance.
(c) What is the probability that the project will be completed in 30 days?

14. Consider the following data regarding a project.

Activity	*Predecessors*	*Duration (weeks)*		
		(a)	*(m)*	*(b)*
A	–	4	4	10
B	–	1	2	9
C	–	2	5	14
D	*A*	1	4	7
E	*A*	1	2	3
F	*A*	1	5	9
G	*B,C*	1	2	9
H	*C*	4	4	4
I	*D*	2	2	8
J	*E,G*	6	7	8
K	*F,H*	2	2	8
L	*F,H*	5	5	5
M	*I,J,K*	1	2	9
N	*L*	6	7	8

(a) Construct the project network.
(b) Find the expected duration and the variance of the activity.
(c) Find the critical path and the expected project completion time.
(d) What is the probability of completing the project on or before 35 weeks?
(e) If the probability of completing the project is 0.85, find the expected project completion time.

15. Consider a project given below.

Activity	*Predecessors*	*Duration (weeks)*		
		(*a*)	(*m*)	(*b*)
A	–	2	5	8
B	*A*	6	9	12
C	*A*	5	14	17
D	*B*	5	8	11
E	*C,D*	3	6	9
F	–	3	12	21
G	*E,F*	1	4	7

(a) Construct the project network.
(b) Find the expected duration and the variance of the activity.
(c) What is the expected length of the project and its variance?
(d) What is the probability of completing the project
 (i) 3 days earlier than expected?
 (ii) no more than 5 days later than expected?

16. Consider the following data regarding a project.

Activity	*Predecessors*	*Duration (weeks)*		
		(*a*)	(*m*)	(*b*)
A	–	4	5	12
B	–	1	1.5	5
C	*A*	2	3	4
D	*A*	3	4	11
E	*A*	2	3	4
F	*C*	1.5	2	2.5
G	*D*	1.5	3	4.5
H	*B,E*	2.5	3.5	7.5
I	*H*	1.5	2	2.5
J	*F,G,I*	1	2	3

(a) Construct the project network.
(b) Find the expected duration and the variance of the activity.
(c) Find the critical path and the expected project completion time.
(d) What is the probability of completing the project
 (i) in 20 weeks?
 (ii) in 15 weeks?

17. Find the total and the free slack associated with each of the activities of the project.

Activity	*A*	*B*	*C*	*D*	*E*	*F*	*G*	*H*	*I*	*J*
Imm. prede	–	–	–	*A,B*	*A,B*	*C*	*C*	*F,G*	*D*	*E,I*
Duration (days)	11	8	6	3	7	7	4	16	5	9

18. A project consists of the following activities.

Activity	*A*	*B*	*C*	*D*	*E*	*F*	*G*
Imm. prede	–	–	*A*	*B,C*	*B,C*	*D*	*E,F*
Duration (weeks)	6	9	9	3	12	6	3

(a) Draw a network.
(b) Compute *ES*, *EF*, *LS* and *LF* for each activity.
(c) What is the project completion time? Which of the activities must be completed in time so that the project may be completed in time?
(d) If, for activity *E*, the immediate predecessors are not *B* and *C*, but instead *D*, how would, if at all, it affect the project duration?

19. The data regarding a project is given below.

Activity	*Predecessors*	*Duration (weeks)*		
		(a)	*(m)*	*(b)*
A	–	2	2	2
B	–	1	3	7
C	*A*	4	7	8
D	*A*	3	5	7
E	*B*	2	6	9
F	*B*	5	9	11
G	*C,D*	3	6	8
H	*E*	2	6	9
I	*C,D*	3	5	8
J	*G,H*	1	3	4
K	*F*	4	8	11
L	*J,K*	2	5	7

Draw the PERT Network. Indicate the expected total slack for each activity and hence indicate the average critical path. Within how many days would you expect the project to be completed with a 99% chance?

20. Consider the data of a project as shown in the following table.

Activity	*Normal time (weeks)*	*Normal cost (Rs.)*	*Crash time (weeks)*	*Crash cost (Rs.)*
1–2	8	800	5	950
1–3	5	500	3	700
1–4	9	600	6	1050
2–5	1	900	8	1300
3–5	5	700	3	1100
3–6	6	1200	5	1500
4–6	7	1300	5	1400
5–7	2	400	1	500
6–7	4	500	2	900

If the indirect cost per week is Rs. 300, find the optimal crashed project completion time.

21. Consider the project network given below.

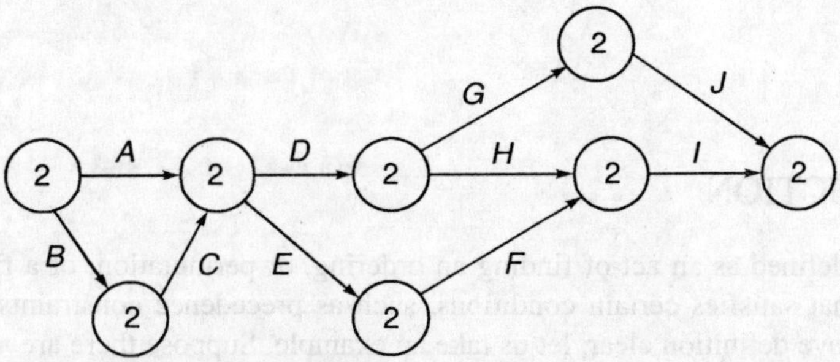

The data for normal times, crash times, and crashing costs are given below.

Activity	*Normal time (days)*	*Crash time (days)*	*Cost of crashing per day (Rs.)*
A	10	7	4
B	5	4	2
C	3	2	2
D	4	3	3
E	5	3	3
F	6	3	5
G	5	2	1
H	6	4	4
I	6	4	3
J	4	3	3

Let T represent the earliest completion time of the project. Determine the maximum and the minimum value of T.

16

Sequencing

16.1 INTRODUCTION

Sequencing can be defined as an act of finding an ordering, or permutation, of a finite collection of objects, like jobs, that satisfies certain conditions, such as precedence constraints.

To make the above definition clear, let us take an example. Suppose there are *n*-jobs (1, 2, 3…*n*) and *m* machines (*A*, *B*, *C*,…). The order of processing each job through each machine is given. The jobs are required to be processed one by one but parallely on the available machines. The total number of ways in which these jobs can be performed in a sequence is $(n!)\, m$. The problem now is to find out a sequence for processing the given jobs on the given machines such that the total elapsed time for all the jobs is minimum.

16.2 NOTATIONS AND TERMINOLOGIES

The following notations and terminologies will be used throughout this chapter.

16.2.1 Notations

t_{ij} = Processing time for job *I* on machine *j*.

I_{ij} = Idle time on machine *j* from the end of job $(i - 1)$ to the start of job *i*.

T = Total elapsed time for processing all jobs on given machines including idle time, if any.

16.2.2 Terminologies

1. ***Number of machines:*** The total number of available service facilities through which a job has to pass before it finishes.

2. ***Processing order:*** The order or the sequence in which the machines are required to complete the job.
3. ***Processing time:*** The time required by a job on a single machine.
4. ***Idle time on a machine:*** The time for which the machine has no job to process, i.e. when it is not giving service to a machine from the end of job $(i - 1)$ to the start of job i.
5. ***Total elapsed time:*** The time interval between starting the very first job and completing the last job performed in order of their machines, including the idle time for the machines.

The no passing rule: The rule says that the order in which jobs are performed on the machines should be maintained. If n jobs are to be processed on three machines M_1, M_2 and M_3 in order $M_2M_1M_3$, then each job should first reach machine M_2, should finish its processing on M_2, then to M_1, and should go to machine M_3 only when the processing on M_1 is over. The jobs will be processed only when the machines are not processing any other job, otherwise it starts a waiting line or joins a waiting line if it already exists. The waiting jobs will be processed as soon as the machines become idle.

16.3 PRINCIPAL ASSUMPTIONS

1. No machine can process more than one operation (job) at a time.
2. Each operation once started must be performed till completion.
3. Each operation must be completed before the next operation is started.
4. Time intervals for processing are independent of the order in which operations are performed.
5. A job is processed as soon as possible subject to the ordering requirements.
6. All jobs are known in advance and are ready to be processed.
7. The time required to transfer jobs between machines is negligible.

16.4 SEQUENCING RULES

(a) ***Highest customer priority:*** Sometimes the operations are sequenced with respect to the importance of customers. Sequencing works by customer priority. It may mean that high volume customers may receive high level of service, but many times it deteriorates the service given to other customers. This method is generally deployed at vendors' places where the customers are given services based on their ratings or priorities.

(b) ***First come, first serve:*** Many times the operations are given service in the order of their arrival to a particular resource or a service provider or a machine. This method of treatment is called *first come, first serve rule*. It appears fair and reasonable to humans who demand services from some resources such as at post offices or financial institutions like banks.

(c) ***Last come, first serve:*** If the jobs are stacked in order of their arrival at a machine, it may be easier to process the job that arrived latest first as it is on the top of the stack. This method of providing service is referred to as *last come, first serve sequencing*. Unloading an elevator is most efficient and convenient using this method, if there is only one door.

(d) ***Shortest operation time:*** When the operations are scheduled in increasing order of their processing time, including their set-up time, the first operation to be processed will be the one having the shortest time. This method is also known as ***shortest processing time*** as set-up time is neglected in many cases.

(e) ***Longest operation time:*** When the operations are scheduled in decreasing order of their processing time, including their set-up time, the first operation to be processed will be the one having the longest time. This method is also known as ***longest processing time*** as set-up time is not considered in many cases.

(f) ***Earliest due date:*** The jobs are prioritized based on their due dates. The earlier is the due date, the more is the priority. Earliest due dates usually improve the delivery reliability. The number of operations and the sum of operations times are neglected.

(g) ***Initial slack time (IST):*** In this method, before the processing for any operation starts, the total slack time for every operation is computed. The operation with the smallest slack time gets the priority. Hence,

IST = Due date – Sum of operation times – Current date

(h) ***Dynamic slack time (DST):*** In this method, before the processing for any operation starts, the total slack time for every operation is computed. The operation with the smallest slack time gets the priority. Hence,

DST = Due date – Sum of remaining operation times – Current date

(i) ***Dynamic slack time per operation (DST/O):*** For each job the dynamic slack time remaining per operation is computed. The operation with the smallest slack time per operation takes the priority.

DST/O = Due date – Sum of remaining operation times – Current date/Number of remaining operations

(j) ***Dynamic slack time ratio (DSTR):*** For each job the dynamic slack time ratio is computed. The operation with the smallest slack time ratio takes the priority.

DSTR = Due date – Current date/Number of remaining operations

16.5 SEQUENCING JOBS THROUGH ONE PROCESS

Before we move on to explanation of processing multiple jobs on multiple machines, let us first consider the process of sequencing *n* number of jobs on one machine. Following are the terms used in the sequencing rules.

Completion time: Time for a job to flow through the system. It is also termed *flowtime.*

Makespan: Time between the moment you start the first job till the time you end the last job.

Tardiness: Difference between a late job's due date and its completion time.

Here we illustrate a few simple sequencing rules with the help of an example. Consider the following scenario in which five jobs are to be performed on a single machine with the processing time for each job and its expected due date.

Job	*Processing time*	*Due date*
A	5	10
B	10	15
C	2	5
D	8	12
E	6	8

1. ***First come, first serve:***

FCFS	*Start sequence*	*Processing time*	*Completion time*	*Due date*	*Tardiness*
A	0	5	5	10	0
B	5	10	15	15	0
C	15	2	17	5	12
D	17	8	25	12	13
E	25	6	31	8	23

2. ***Earliest due date:***

Due date sequence	*Start sequence*	*Processing time*	*Completion time*	*Due date*	*Tardiness*
C	0	2	2	5	0
E	2	6	8	8	0
A	8	5	13	10	3
D	13	8	21	12	9
B	21	10	31	15	16

3. ***Initial slack time:***

Slack sequence	*Start sequence*	*Processing time*	*Completion time*	*Due date*	*Tardiness*
E	0	6	6	8	0
C	6	2	8	5	3
D	8	8	16	12	4
A	16	5	21	10	11
B	21	10	31	15	16

Slack calculation:

$A\ (10 - 0) - 5 = 5$

$B\ (15 - 0) - 10 = 5$

$C\ (5 - 0) - 2 = 3$

$D\ (12 - 0) - 8 = 4$

$E\ (8 - 0) - 6 = 2$

4. ***Shortest processing time:***

Slack sequence	*Start sequence*	*Processing time*	*Completion time*	*Due date*	*Tardiness*
C	0	2	2	5	0
A	2	5	7	10	0
E	7	6	13	8	5
D	13	8	21	12	9
B	21	10	31	15	6

All the above sequencing rules can be compared on the basis of their tardiness as follows.

Rule	*Average completion time*	*Average tardiness*	*No. of jobs tardy*	*Maximum tardiness*
FCFS	18.60	9.6	3	23
DDATE	15.00	5.6	3	16
IST	16.40	6.8	4	16
SPT	14.80	6.0	3	16

The following guidelines can be followed while selecting a sequencing rule.

1. SPT most useful when the shop is highly congested.
2. Use IST for periods of normal activity.
3. Use DDATE when only small tardiness values can be tolerated.
4. Use LPT if subcontracting is anticipated.
5. Use FCFS when operating at low-capacity levels.
6. Do not use SPT to sequence jobs that have to be assembled with other jobs at a later date.

16.6 SEQUENCING JOBS THROUGH TWO SERIAL PROCESS

The mathematics is much more difficult as soon as we start the process of sequencing n number of jobs on two machines. We start with the following system:

There are three jobs, J_1, J_2, and J_3. Each needs to be processed first on machine M_1, then on machine M_2. The processing times are as follows:

Machines	*Jobs*		
	J_1	J_2	J_3
M_1	8	5	10
M_2	6	6	6

We could have 6 possible sequences for the jobs: 1–2–3, 1–3–2, 2–1–3, 2–3–1, 3–1–2, and 3–2–1. For any sequence, machine M_1 will start working at $T = 0$, and work till $T = 8 + 5 + 10 = 23$. However, the utilization of M_2 needs more attention due to the following reasons.

1. It will not work at the initial period when M_1 is doing its first scheduled job. This hints that we should try to do the shortest job on M_1 first!
2. What happens if the second operation (operation on M_2) for a job is very short? In this case, M_2 will finish this job, while M_1 is still working on the first operation of the next job. This will make M_2 idle for some time. This hints that we should try to place jobs that have long second operations in the beginning.

In order to make it easy to identify the optimal sequence, we deliberately choose all equal processing time on machine M_2. Note that whatever sequence we use, it is clear that machine M_1 will begin at $T = 0$, and be fully utilized for the duration = sum of operation 1 durations for all jobs.

Now let us look at this more carefully, using the Gantt charts (Figure 16.1).

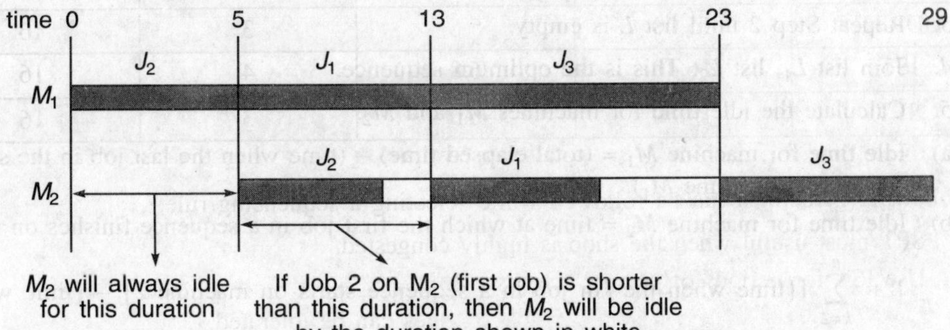

Figure 16.1

Therefore, all scheduling of jobs we perform must concentrate on trying to make the Gantt chart for machine 2 as compact as possible. Clearly, we cannot do much better than this (since machine 1 must operate till $T = 23$, and thereafter, Machine 2 still needs 6 units of time to complete the last job on Machine 1).

It appears to make sense to always put the shortest job of Machine 1 at the beginning, for this will minimize the initial idle time of M_2.

Also, since Machine 2 must work on the second operation of the final job after all work on Machine 1 is finished, it also makes sense to always put the shortest operation of the second machine at the end of the sequence.

Now the question is, "What can we say about the jobs in between?" Mainly, we would like to minimize the white portions as much as we can. How can we do this? Johnson noticed that this could be done if

1. We perform the shortest machine 1 operations as early as we can. In the above Gantt chart, if operation 1 of J_1 becomes shorter, the first white strip becomes slimmer.
2. At the same time, we would like to perform jobs with the longest operation 2 as early as we can. In the Gantt chart, as the length of operation 2 of J_2 increases, it also eats up more of the first white strip.

16.7 JOHNSON'S ALGORITHM

Job J_i (i = 1, 2, ..., n) has two operations, of duration t_{i1}, t_{i2}, to be done on machine M_1, M_2 in that sequence.

Step 1: List $L = \{1, 2, \ldots, n\}$, list $L_1 = \{\}$, list $L_2 = \{\}$.

Step 2: From all available operation durations, pick the minimum. If the minimum belongs to J_{k1}, remove K from list L; Add K to end of list L_1. If minimum belongs to J_{k2}, remove K from list A; Add K to beginning of list L_2.

If there is a tie in selecting the minimum processing times, then there may be three situations.

(i) If they are on different machines, we can randomly pick either.

(ii) If both choices are on machine 1, pick the one with the longer operation 2 first.

(iii) If both are on machine 2, pick the one with the longer operation 1 first.

Step 3: Repeat Step 2 until list L is empty.

Step 4: Join list L_1, list L_2. This is the optimum sequence.

Step 5: Calculate the idle time for machines M_1 and M_2.

(a) Idle time for machine M_1 = (total elapsed time) – (time when the last job in the sequence finishes on machine M_1).

(b) Idle time for machine M_2 = time at which the first job in a sequence finishes on machine $1 + \sum_{k=2}^{n}$ [{time when the kth job in a sequence starts on machine 2} – {time when the $(k-1)$th job in a sequence starts on machine 2}]

Let us see this with the help of another example.

Machine	*Jobs*					
	J_1	J_2	J_3	J_4	J_5	J_6
M_1	1	5	8	7	3	3
M_2	5	6	5	2	2	10

Step 1: $L = \{1, 2, 3, 4, 5, 6\}$, $L_1 = \{\}$, $L_2 = \{\}$.

Step 2.1: Shortest job is J_{11}; remove job 1 from list A, and add job 1 to the end of list L_1.

$$L = \{2, 3, 4, 5, 6\}, L_1 = \{1\}, L_2 = \{\}$$

Step 2.2: Now, there are two shortest remaining jobs: t_{42}, t_{52}.
Since both are on machine 2, pick the one with the longer operation 1 first.
We select job 4. Remove job 4 from list A, add job 4 to the beginning of list L_2.

$$L = \{2, 3, 5, 6\}, L_1 = \{1\}, L_2 = \{4\}$$

Step 2.3: Shortest remaining operation is t_{52}, so we remove job 5 from list A, and add it to the beginning of list L_2.

$$L = \{2, 3, 6\}, L_1 = \{1\}, L_2 = \{5, 4\}$$

Step 2.4: Shortest remaining operation is t_{61}, so we remove job 6 from list A, and add it to the end of list L_1.

$$L = \{2, 3\}, L_1 = \{1, 6\}, L_2 = \{5, 4\}$$

Step 2.5: Now, there are two shortest remaining operations: t_{21}, t_{32}. Since they are on different machines, we can randomly pick either. We select (randomly) job 2. Remove job 2 from list L, add job 2 to the end of list L_1.

$$L = \{3\}, L_1 = \{1, 6, 2\}, L_2 = \{5, 4\}$$

Step 2.6: Shortest remaining operation is t_{32}. Remove job 3 from A, add to the beginning of L_2.

$$L = \{\}, L_1 = \{1, 6, 2\}, L_2 = \{3, 5, 4\}$$

Step 3: List L is exhausted. Join L_1 and L_2, to get the optimum sequence.

$$\{1, 6, 2, 3, 5, 4\}$$

Step 4: The minimum elapsed time can now be computed as follows.

Job	*Machine 1*		*Machine 2*		*Idle time for machine 2*
	Time in	*Time out*	*Time in*	*Time out*	
J_1	0	1	1	6	1
J_6	1	4	6	16	0
J_2	4	9	16	22	0
J_3	9	17	22	27	0
J_5	17	20	27	29	0
J_4	20	27	29	31	0

From the above table, it is obvious that the minimum total time to finish all the 6 jobs is 31 units of time and idle time for machine 1 is 4 units of time (31 – 27) and for machine 2, 1 unit of time.

EXAMPLE 16.1: XYZ manufacturing company processes 6 different jobs on two machines A and B. The number of units of each job and its processing times on A and B are given in the following table. Find the optimum sequence, the total minimum elapsed time and idle time for each machine.

Job number	*No. of units of each job*	*Processing time*	
		Machine A (in minute)	*Machine B (in minute)*
1	3	5	8
2	4	16	7
3	2	6	11
4	5	3	5
5	2	9	7.5
6	3	6	14

Solution: According to Johnson's algorithm, we can get the optimum sequence:

$$\{4, 1, 3, 6, 5, 2, 3\}$$

Determining total elapsed time

Job number	*Number of units of job*	*Machine A*		*Machine B*	
		In (in minute)	*Out (in minute)*	*In (in minute)*	*Out (in minute)*
4	Ist	0	3	3	8
	IInd	3	6	8	12
	IIIrd	6	9	13	18
	IVth	9	12	18	23
	Vth	12	15	23	28
1	Ist	15	20	28	36
	IInd	20	25	36	44
	IIIrd	25	30	44	52
3	Ist	30	36	52	63
	IInd	36	42	63	74
6	Ist	42	48	74	88
	IInd	48	54	88	102
	IIIrd	54	60	102	116
5	Ist	60	69	116	123.5
	IInd	69	78	123.5	131
2	Ist	78	94	131	138
	IInd	94	110	138	145
	IIIrd	110	126	145	152
	IVth	126	142	152	159

Therefore, the total elapsed time for all the jobs including the number of units is 159 minutes. However, machine A lingers for 17 (159 – 142) minutes and machine B lingers for 3 minutes.

16.8 PROCESSING *n* JOBS THROUGH THREE MACHINES

Johnson's method only works optimally for two machines. However, since it is optimal and easy to compute, some researchers have tried to adopt it for m machines, ($m > 2$). First, we will discuss the case $m = 3$. The problem can be described as: (i) only three machines M_1, M_2, and M_3 are drawn in, (ii) each job is processed in the prescribed order M_1 M_2 M_3, (iii) transfer of job is not permitted, and (iv) expected processing times are given in following table.

Job	*Machine* M_1	*Machine* M_2	*Machine* M_3
1	t_{11}	t_{12}	t_{13}
2	t_{21}	t_{22}	t_{23}
.	.	.	.
.	.	.	.
n	t_{n1}	t_{n2}	t_{n3}

The iterative procedure of obtaining an optimal sequence is as follows.

Step 1: Check whether either one or both of the following hold:

(i) The minimum time on machine $M_1 \geq$ the maximum time on machine M_2.

(ii) The minimum time on machine $M_3 \geq$ the maximum time on machine M_2.

Step 2: If the inequalities of step 1 are not satisfied, the method fails. Otherwise go to step 3.

Step 3: Convert the three machine problem into two machine problem by introducing two imaginary machines G and H, such that

$$t_{iG} = t_{i1} + t_{i2} \quad \text{and} \quad t_{iH} = t_{i2} + t_{i3},\ i = 1, 2, \ldots, n.$$

Step 4: Apply the Johnson's rule discussed earlier for obtaining the optimal sequence of performance of the jobs on G and H. The resulting sequence will also be optimal for the original problem.

EXAMPLE 16.2: Six jobs have to be processed at three machines A, B and C in the order ABC. The time taken by each job on each machine is indicated below. Each machine can process only one job at a time.

	Job	J_1	J_2	J_3	J_4	J_5	J_6
Processing time in minutes on machines	A	12	8	7	11	10	5
	B	3	4	2	5	1.5	4
	C	7	10	9	6	10	4

Determine the sequence for the jobs so as to minimize the processing time.

Solution: Here,

$$\min A_k = 5,\ \max B_k = 5,\ \min C_k = 4;\ k = 1, 2, \ldots, 6$$

Since one of two conditions is satisfied by $\min A_k = \max B_k$, so the given problem can be converted into a six jobs and two machines problems by considering G and H as the imaginary machines, such that

$$G_k = A_k + B_k \quad \text{and} \quad H_k = B_k + C_k;\quad k = 1, 2, \ldots, 6$$

We proceed to make the consolidation table as shown below.

Jobs	*Processing times*	
	$G_k\ (= t_{kA} + t_{kB})$	$H_k\ (= t_{kB} + t_{kC})$
J_1	15	10
J_2	12	14
J_3	9	11
J_4	16	11
J_5	11.5	11.5
J_6	9	8

Using the optimum sequence algorithm, the following optimum sequences are easily obtained.

$$\{J_3, J_2, J_5, J_4, J_1, J_6\} \quad \text{or} \quad \{J_3, J_5, J_2, J_4, J_1, J_6\}$$

The total elapsed time can now be obtained as shown in the table below.

Jobs	Machine A		Machine B			Machine C		
	In	Out	In	Out	Idle time	In	Out	Idle time
J_3	0	7	7	9	7	9	18	9
J_2	7	15	15	19	6	19	29	1
J_5	15	25	25	26.5	6	29	39	0
J_4	25	36	36	41	9.5	41	47	2
J_1	36	48	48	51	7	51	58	4
J_6	48	53	53	57	2	58	62	0

The above table indicates that the minimum total elapsed time is 62 minutes.

Idle time for machine A is 9 minutes (62 – 53), for C 16 minutes.

Idle time on machine B = (62 – 57) + 37.5 = 42.5 minutes.

16.9 PROCESSING n JOBS THROUGH m MACHINES

Let there be n jobs to be processed on m machines, $M_1, M_2, \ldots, M_m$ in the order $M_1, M_2, \ldots, M_m$, and t_{ij} denote the time taken by the jth machine to complete the ith job. The iterative procedure of obtaining an optimal sequence is as follows.

Step 1: Find (i) $\min\limits_{1 \le i \le n} (t_{i1})$, (ii) $\min\limits_{1 \le i \le n} (t_{im})$, and (iii) $\max\limits_{1 \le i \le n} (t_{ij})$ $j = 2, 3, \ldots, m - 1$.

Step 2: Check whether

(i) $\min\limits_{1 \le i \le n} (t_{i1}) \ge \max\limits_{1 \le i \le n} (t_{ij})$ $j = 2, 3, \ldots, m - 1$.

or

(ii) $\min\limits_{1 \le i \le n} (t_{im}) \ge \max\limits_{1 \le i \le n} (t_{ij})$ $j = 2, 3, \ldots, m - 1$.

Step 3: If the inequalities of step 1 are not satisfied, the method fails. Otherwise go to step 3.

Step 4: Convert the m machine problem into two machine problem by introducing two imaginary machines G and H, such that

$$t_{iG} = t_{i1} + t_{i2} + \cdots + t_{i(m-1)} \quad \text{for } i = 1, 2, \ldots, n \text{ and}$$

$$t_{iH} = t_{i2} + t_{i3} + \cdots + t_{im} \quad \text{for } i = 1, 2, \ldots, n.$$

Step 5: Apply the Johnson's rule discussed earlier for obtaining the optimal sequence of performance of the jobs on G and H. The resulting sequence will also be optimal for the original problem.

Note: In addition to the conditions given in step 4,

1. If $t_{i1} + t_{i2} + \cdots + t_{i(m-1)}$ = constant say K for all $i = 1, 2, \ldots, n$, then generate optimal sequence for n jobs and two machines M_1 and M_m in the order M_1M_m by using optimal sequence algorithm.
2. If $t_{i1} = t_{im}$ and $t_{iG} = t_{iH}$ for $i = 1, 2, \ldots, n$, then $n!$ number of the optimal sequence will exist.

EXAMPLE 16.3: Solve the following sequencing problem giving an optimal solution when passing is not allowed.

Machines	*Jobs*			
	J_1	J_2	J_3	J_4
M_1	5	7	10	9
M_2	1	2	3	4
M_3	5	4	3	2
M_4	8	9	12	6

Solution: Here,

$$\min_{1 \le i \le 4} (t_{i1}) = 5 \quad \text{and} \quad \min_{1 \le i \le 4} (t_{i4}) = 6$$

$$\max_{1 \le i \le 4} (t_{i2}) = 4 \quad \text{and} \quad \max_{1 \le i \le 4} (t_{i3}) = 5$$

Since the conditions

$$\min_{1 \le i \le 4} (t_{i1}) \ge \max_{1 \le i \le 4} (t_{ij}) = 5 j = 2, 3$$

and

$$\min_{1 \le i \le 4} (t_{i4}) \ge \max_{1 \le i \le 4} (t_{ij}) = 5 j = 2, 3$$

are satisfied, convert this problem into four jobs and two machines problem.

Also, $t_{i2} + t_{i3} = 6$ for all $i = 1, 2, 3, 4$, therefore the problem will reduce to an optimal sequence for four jobs and machines M_1 and M_4 in the order M_1M_4. It means M_2 and M_3 have no effect on optimality of the sequences.

Following the usual optimal sequence algorithm, the optimal sequence is: {1, 3, 2, 4}

The total elapsed time may be calculated as given in the following table.

Minimum elapsed time

Job sequence	*Machine*				
	M_1	M_2	M_3	M_4	M_5
J_1	0–7	7–12	12–14	14–17	17–27
J_3	7–12	12–16	16–21	21–27	27–36
J_2	12–18	18–24	24–28	28–33	36–47
J_4	18–26	26–29	29–32	33–35	47–54

The above table shows that the minimum total elapsed time is 54 hours. The idle time for machine M_1, M_2, M_3, M_4, and M_5 is 28, 36, 40, 38 and 17 hrs., respectively.

16.10 SCOPE OF SEQUENCING

You may have noticed that Johnson's method only works when each part has the same set of machines to visit, in the same sequence. Clearly, this is an important restriction. In practical conditions, Johnson's method is most useful in scheduling operations for a family of parts within a group (since most parts of a family require similar processing)—and hence its use in Group Technology.

16.10.1 What is Scheduling?

A schedule for a sequence of jobs, say $j_1, ..., j_n$, is a specification of start times, say $t_1, ..., t_n$, such that certain constraints are met. A schedule is sought that minimizes cost and/or some measure of time, like the overall project *completion time*, i.e. when the last job is finished or the *tardy time,* i.e. the amount by which the completion time exceeds a given deadline. There are precedence constraints, such as in the construction industry, where a wall cannot be erected until the foundation is laid.

There is a variety of scheduling heuristics. Two of these for scheduling jobs on machines are *list heuristics:* the *shortest processing time* and the *longest processing time*. These rules put jobs on the list in non-decreasing and non-increasing order of processing time, respectively.

- Last stage of planning before the production occurs.
- Specifies when labour, equipment, facilities are needed to produce a product or provide a service.

The objectives of scheduling are as follows:

- Meet customer due dates
- Minimize job lateness
- Minimize response time
- Minimize completion time
- Minimize time in the system
- Minimize overtime
- Maximize machine or labour utilization
- Minimize idle time
- Minimize work-in-process inventory.

REVIEW EXERCISES

1. A company has jobs on hand from *A* to *F*. All the jobs have to go through two machines M_1 and M_2. The time required, in hours, on each machine is given below:

	A	*B*	*C*	*D*	*E*	*F*
M_1	3	12	18	9	15	6
M_2	9	18	24	24	3	15

Suggest an optimal sequence of processing the above jobs on two machines.

2. Five jobs are to be processed through two machines *A* and *B* in the order *AB*, with their processing time, in hours, listed as follows.

	1	2	3	4	5
A	10	2	18	6	20
B	4	12	14	16	8

Determine a sequence for the jobs that will minimize the elapsed time *T*.

3. A refrigeration company has six plants located in different parts of a city. Every year it is necessary for each plant to be completely serviced. The servicing is done by two groups of workers. The second group of workers performs the final overhauling of the refrigerators. So, they cannot start the work until the first group have completed.

Plant	P_1	P_2	P_3	P_4	P_5	P_6
Group 1	6	6	4	6	5	8
Group 2	4	2	10	5	3	6

(a) Determine the optimum sequence of servicing the plants.
(b) Calculate the total elapsed time.

4. Six jobs are to be processed on six different machines *A*, *B* and *C* in the order *ACB*. The time taken by each job on the three machines is given below. Processing of one job at a time is allowed on each machine. Based on the given data, determine the optimum sequence of jobs and the total elapsed time.

Processing time in minutes on machines

Jobs	*Machine A*	*Machine B*	*Machine C*
1	50	40	30
2	80	80	40
3	90	70	20
4	70	60	10
5	60	20	50
6	75	45	35

5. A textile company has to process its raw materials through three stages of processing before they are sent to the shopkeepers for selling. The time taken by each of the three stages for processing the raw materials is given below.

Processing time in hours on machines

Item	*Machine A*	*Machine B*	*Machine C*
1	5	2	10
2	7	6	12
3	3	7	11
4	4	5	13
5	5	9	12
6	7	5	10
7	12	8	11

Find an orderly sequence of steps in which the items should be processed so as to minimize the time taken to process all items through three stages.

6. Find a sequence that minimizes the total elapsed time required to complete the following tasks on three machines in the order *ABC*.

Tasks	*Machine A*	*Machine B*	*Machine C*
1	12	7	3
2	6	8	4
3	5	9	1
4	11	4	5
5	5	7	2
6	7	8	3
7	6	3	4

7. A machine operator has to perform three operations: turning, threading and knurling on a number of different jobs. The time required to perform these operations (in minutes) for each job is known. Determine the order in which the jobs should be processed in order to minimize the total elapsed time to finish all the jobs on all the machines one by one.

Jobs	*Time for turning*	*Time for threading*	*Time for knurling*
1	6	16	26
2	24	12	28
3	10	8	18
4	4	12	24
5	18	6	16
6	22	2	26

8. A manufacturing firm works 80 hours a week and has a capacity of overtime work to the extent of 40 hours in a week. It has received seven orders to be processed on three machines M_1, M_2, and M_3 in order M_1, M_2, M_3 to be delivered in a week's time from now. The process times (in hours) are recorded in the table given below:

	M_1	M_2	M_3
1	14	4	12
2	16	4	10
3	12	2	8
4	12	6	8
5	14	6	4
6	16	4	2
7	10	8	10

The manager, who, in fairness, insists on performing the jobs in the sequence in which they are received, is refusing to accept an eighth order, which requires 14, 4 and 10 hours respectively on M_1, M_2, and M_3 machines, because, according to him, the eighth job would require a total of 122 hours for processing, which exceeds the firm's capacity. Advise him.

9. XYZ Pvt. Ltd. has three levels of managers to perform activities on the projects assigned to them. The higher level managers cannot perform their activities until the middle level managers have done their activities. Similarly, the middle level managers cannot proceed until the lower level people have performed their activities. The time taken in days for six activities for all three levels of managers is given in the following table. Suggest the order in which the activities should be performed so as to minimize the total time for completing the project.

Activities	*Higher level managers*	*Middle level managers*	*Lower level managers*
1	24	12	14
2	20	10	12
3	18	12	12
4	28	8	10
5	14	4	8
6	18	8	8

17

Simulation

17.1 INTRODUCTION

The stepping stone of deep behind 5,000 years to China war games, called ***Weich`i*** and continues through 1780, when the Persians used the games to test military strategies under simulated environment. This inspired the great mathematician John Van Neumann to develop a quantitative technique called **Monte-Carlo simulation**. Nowadays, simulation is one of the most widely used quantitative analysis technique in almost all management problems. To simulate is to replicate the features, appearance, and characteristics of a real system, i.e. to model a real world situation mathematically and then to study its properties and operating characteristics to make the optimal decision based on the results of the simulation. In the next section, we study the various steps involved in the simulation process of a problem.

17.2 STEPS INVOLVED IN SIMULATION

Figure 17.1 presents the various steps involved in designing or analyzing a complex system by simulation.

Step 1: Identify the problem by defining decision variables, objective and decision rules.

Step 2: Formulate a numerical model to be analyzed on the computer.

Step 3: To ensure the validity of the system being analyzed and reliability of the results.

Step 4: Design the experiments with the simulation by assigning specific values to the decision variables to be tested at each trial.

Step 5: Run the model and get the operating characteristics.

Step 6: Analyze the results of the problem in terms of reliability and correctness. If results are as per the requirement/planning, then select the best alternative, otherwise make desired changes in the model decision variables, parameter or modelling and go to step 2.

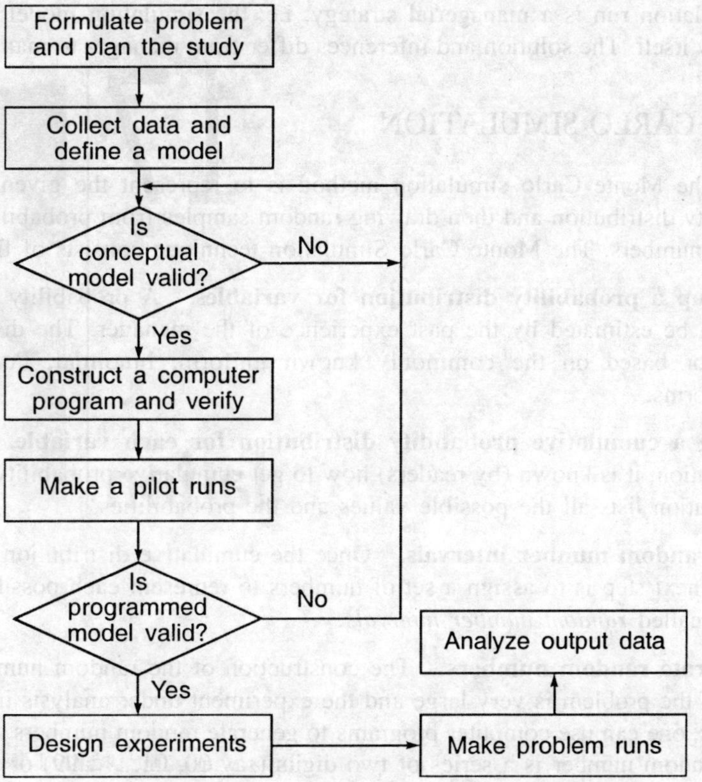

Figure 17.1 Flow of simulation study.

17.3 ADVANTAGES AND DISADVANTAGES OF SIMULATION

Simulation is widely used by managers, researchers, etc. for the following reasons.

- It is flexible and relatively straightforward.
- Simulation allows us to study interdependence of variables and to sort out the most important one. Also (sometimes), it is time saving and also cost saving, in the sense, it may not be possible to build and solve a mathematical model of a complex real-world situation that incorporates important economic, finance, environment factors. With the help of software, simulation is used to model mega cities, hospitals, educational institutes, stock markets, and many more.
- Simulation is used to experiment on a model of a real situation without incurring the costs of operating on the system, i.e. simulation can be considered a reliability test to formulate new policies and decision rules for operating a system before investing in the real system.

The disadvantages of simulation are:

- Simulation may be expensive for modelling complex situations. Sometimes, it is a time-consuming complex process.
- It is a trial and error approach producing different results in the repeated runs, and, as a result, the decision maker may end up with a sub-optimal solution.

- Each simulation run is a managerial strategy, i.e. the simulation model does not produce answers by itself. The solution and inferences differ from manager to manager, firm to firm.

17.4 MONTE CARLO SIMULATION

The idea behind the Monte Carlo simulation method is to represent the given system by some observed probability distribution and then drawing random samples from probability distribution by means of random numbers. The Monte Carlo Simulation technique consists of five steps.

Step 1: **Setting up a probability distribution for variables.** A probability distribution for a given variable can be estimated by the past experience of the manager. The distributions can be either empirical or based on the commonly known uniform, binomial, Poisson, normal or exponential, etc. forms.

Step 2: **Building a cumulative probability distribution for each variable.** From the given probability distribution, it is known (by readers) how to get cumulative probability distribution. The cumulative distribution lists all the possible values and the probabilities.

Step 3: **Setting random number intervals.** Once the cumulative distribution for each variable is established, the next step is to assign a set of numbers to represent each possible outcome. This set of numbers is called *random number intervals*.

Step 4: **To generate random numbers.** The construction of the random numbers can be done in several ways. If the problem is very large and the experiment under analysis involves thousands of simulation trials, one can use computer programs to generate random numbers. Depending on the experiment, the random number is a series of two digits (say 00, 01, …, 99) or three digits or so.

Step 5: **Simulate the experiment by means of random sampling.** Repeat the process until the required number of simulation runs has been generated.

In the next section, we will see applications of the simulation technique in varieties of problems.

17.5 APPLICATIONS OF SIMULATION

EXAMPLE 17.1: A retailer deals in perishable items, the daily demand and supply of which are random variables. The past 500 days data show the following.

Supply		*Demand*	
Available (kg)	*Number of days*	*Available* (kg)	*Number of days*
10	40	10	50
20	50	20	110
30	190	30	200
40	150	40	100
50	70	50	40

The retailer buys the item at Rs. 20 per kg and sells at Rs. 30 per kg. If any of the commodity remains at the end of the day, it has no salable value and is a dead loss. Moreover, the loss on any unsatisfied demand is Rs. 8 per kg.

Given the following random numbers: 31, 18, 63, 84, 15, 79, 07, 32, 43, 75, 81, and 27. Use the random numbers alternately to simulate supply and demand for six days sales.

Solution: The probability distributions for demand and supply, allotted random numbers (RN) to each level of supply and demand in the proportions are as in the following table.

Supply	*Probability*	*RNI*	*Demand*	*Probability*	*RNI*
10	0.08	00–07	10	0.10	00–09
20	0.10	08–17	20	0.22	10–31
30	0.38	18–55	30	0.40	32–71
40	0.30	56–85	40	0.20	72–91
50	0.14	86–99	50	0.08	92–99

Using given random numbers, we simulate for six days sales.

Day	*RN*	*Supply* (kg)	*RN*	*Demand* (kg)	*Cost* (Rs.)	*Revenue* (Rs.)	*Loss* (Rs.)	*Profit* (Rs.)
1	31	30	18	20	600	600	–	
2	63	40	84	40	800	1,200	–	400
3	15	20	79	40	400	600	160	40
4	07	10	32	30	200	300	160	–60
5	43	30	75	40	600	900	80	220
6	81	40	27	20	800	600	–	–200

From the last column of the table, it is observed that the retailer makes a net profit of Rs. 400.

EXAMPLE 17.2: The output of a production line is checked by an inspector for three different types of defects (say) *A*, *B* and *C*. If defect *A* occurs, the item is scrapped. If defect *B* or *C* occurs, the item must be reworked. The time required to rework a *B* defect is 15 minutes and the time required to rework a *C* defect is 30 minutes. The probabilities of *A*, *B* and *C* defects are 0.15, 0.20 and 0.10, respectively. For 10 items coming off the assembly line, determine the number of items without any defects, the number scrapped and the total minutes of rework time. Use the following random numbers:

RN for defect *A*	48	55	91	40	93	01	83	63	47	52
RN for defect *B*	47	36	57	04	79	55	10	13	57	09
RN for defect *C*	82	96	18	96	20	84	56	11	52	03

Solution: Let us compute random number intervals (RNI) from the probabilities of defects of three types *A*, *B* and *C*.

Defect A		*Defect B*		*Defect C*	
RNI	*Yes/No*	*RNI*	*Yes/No*	*RNI*	*Yes/No*
00–14	Yes	00–19	Yes	00–09	Yes
15–99	No	20–99	No	10–99	No

Next we compute for ten items coming off the assembly without any defects and total time for rework.

Item No.	*RN (A)*	*RN (B)*	*RN (C)*	*Defects*	*Rework time (min.)*
1	48	47	82	None	–
2	55	36	95	None	–
3	91	57	18	None	–
4	40	04	96	*B*	15
5	93	79	20	None	–
6	01	55	84	*A*	Scrap
7	83	10	56	*B*	15
8	63	13	11	*B*	15
9	47	57	52	None	–
10	52	09	03	*B, C*	45
					90

Thus, out of ten items, five are defect free, one is to be scrapped, and four require rework time 90 minutes.

EXAMPLE 17.3: A book store wishes to carry a particular book in the stock. The demand is probabilistic and the replenishment of stock takes 2 days. The probabilities of demand are given below:

Daily demand	0	1	2	3	4
Probability	0.05	0.10	0.30	0.45	0.10

Each time an order is placed, the store incurs an ordering cost of Rs. 10 per order. The store also incurs a carrying cost of 0.05 per book per day. The inventory holding cost is calculated on the basis of the stock at the end of each day. The manager of the book-store wishes to compare two options for his inventory decision.

I: Order 5 books when the inventory at the beginning of the day plus orders outstanding is less than 8 books.

II: Order 8 books when the inventory at the beginning of the day plus orders outstanding is less than 8 books.

Initially, (beginning of the first day) the store has a stock of 8 books plus 6 books ordered two days ago and expected to arrive next day. Use simulation for 10 cycles. Recommend which option the manager should choose using following random numbers: 89, 34, 78, 63, 61, 81, 39, 16, 13, 73.

Solution: Using the given data of the daily demand and probability, we obtain random number intervals in the following table:

Daily demand	*Probability*	*Cumu. prob.*	*RNI*
0	0.05	0.05	00–04
1	0.10	0.15	05–14
2	0.30	0.45	15–44
3	0.45	0.90	45–89
4	0.10	1.00	90–99

Option I: Given that the stock in hand is 8 books and the stock on order is 5 books (expected next day).

RN	*Daily demand*	*Closing stock in hand*	*Received*	*Opening stock*	*Stock on order*	*Order quantity*	*Closing stock*
89	3	8	–	8 – 3 = 5	6	–	6
34	2	5	6	6 + 5 – 2 = 9	–	–	–
78	3	9	–	9 – 3 = 6	–	5	5
63	3	6	–	6 – 3 = 3	5	–	5
61	3	3	–	3 – 3 = 0	5	5	10
81	3	0	5	5 – 3 = 2	5	5	10
39	2	2	–	2 – 2 = 0	10	–	10
16	2	0	5	5 – 2 = 3	5	–	5
13	1	3	5	5 + 3 – 1 = 7	0	5	5
73	3	7	–	7 – 3 = 4	5	–	5
				39			

The above table suggests that during a cycle, order is kept four times. Therefore, the total ordering cost = Rs. 10 * 4 = Rs. 40. The closing stock of 10 days is 39 books resulting inventory cost = Rs. 0.50 * 39 = Rs. 19.50.
Therefore, the total cost for 10 days = Rs. 40 + 19.50 = Rs. 59.50.
Now let us consider *Option II* and find the total cost for 10 days.

RN	*Daily demand*	*Closing stock in hand*	*Received*	*Opening stock*	*Stock on order*	*Order quantity*	*Closing stock*
89	3	8	–	8 – 3 = 5	6	–	6
34	2	5	6	6 + 5 – 2 = 9	–	–	–
78	3	9	–	9 – 3 = 6	–	8	8
63	3	6	–	6 – 3 = 3	8	–	8
61	3	3	–	3 – 3 = 0	8	–	8
81	3	0	8	8 + 0 – 3 = 5	–	8	8
39	2	5	–	5 – 2 = 3	8	–	8
16	2	3	–	3 – 2 = 1	8	–	8
13	1	1	8	8 + 1 – 1 = 8	–	–	–
73	3	8	–	8 – 3 = 5	–	8	8
				45			

From the above table, it is observed that order of 8 books is kept three times. Therefore, the total ordering cost is Rs. 10 * 3 = Rs. 30. During 10 days cycle, the storekeeper keeps the stock of 45 books, then the holding cost is Rs. 0.50 * 45 = Rs. 22.50.
Therefore, the total cost for 10 days = Rs. 30 + 22.50 = Rs. 52.50.
Since option II has lower total cost than option I , the manager should choose option II.

EXAMPLE 17.4: A company manufactures around 200 mopeds. Depending upon the availability of raw materials and other conditions, the daily production has been varying from 196 mopeds to 204 mopeds, whose probability distribution is as given below.

Production/day	196	197	198	199	200	201	202	203	204
Probability	0.05	0.09	0.12	0.14	0.20	0.15	0.11	0.08	0.06

The finished mopeds are transported in a specially designed three storied lorry that can accommodate only 200 mopeds. Use 15 random numbers: 82, 89, 78, 24, 53, 61, 18, 45, 04, 23, 50, 77, 27, 54, 10 to simulate the process and find out:

(i) What will be the average number of mopeds waiting in the factory?

(ii) What will be the average number of empty spaces on the lorry?

Solution: The random number intervals are exhibited in the following table:

Production/day	*Probability*	*Cumu. prob.*	*RNI*
196	0.05	0.05	00–04
197	0.09	0.14	05–13
198	0.12	0.26	14–25
199	0.14	0.40	26–39
200	0.20	0.60	40–59
201	0.15	0.75	60–74
202	0.11	0.86	75–85
203	0.08	0.94	86–93
204	0.06	1.00	94–99

Using given 15 random numbers, we simulate the production per day as follows:

Day	*RN*	*Production/day*	*No. of mopeds waiting*	*No. of empty spaces in lorry*
1	82	202	2	–
2	89	203	3	–
3	78	202	2	–
4	24	198	–	2
5	53	200	0	–
6	61	201	1	–
7	18	198	–	2
8	45	200	0	–
9	04	196	–	4
10	23	198	–	2
11	50	200	0	–
12	77	202	2	–
13	27	199	–	1
14	54	200	0	–
15	10	197	–	3
			10	14

Therefore, the average number of mopeds waiting in the factory = 10/15 = 0.67/day and the average number of empty spaces on the lorry = 14/15 = 0.93/day.

EXAMPLE 17.5: Observations of the past data show the following patterns in respect of inter-arrival time and service time in a single channel queuing system. Using the random numbers given below, simulate the queue behaviour for a period of 60 minutes and estimate the probability of the service being idle and the mean time spent by a customer waiting in for the service.

Inter-arrival time		*Service time*	
Minutes	*Probability*	*Minutes*	*Probability*
2	0.15	1	0.10
4	0.23	3	0.22
6	0.35	5	0.35
8	0.17	7	0.23
10	0.10	9	0.10

Random numbers are 93, 14, 72, 10, 21, 81, 87, 90, 38, 10, 29, 17, 11, 68, 99, 51, 40, 30, 52 and 71.

Solution: First, let us compute random number intervals for the arrival time.

Inter-arrival time			
Minutes	*Probability*	*Cumulative frequency*	*RNI*
2	0.15	0.15	00–14
4	0.23	0.38	15–37
6	0.35	0.73	38–72
8	0.17	0.90	73–89
10	0.10	1.00	90–99

In the next table, we exhibit random number intervals for the service time.

Service time			
Minutes	*Probability*	*Cumulative frequency*	*RNI*
1	0.10	0.10	00–09
3	0.22	0.32	10–31
5	0.35	0.67	32–66
7	0.23	0.90	67–89
9	0.10	1.00	90–99

The simulation runs are given in the following table:

RN	Inter-arrival time	Arrival time	Service starts	RN	Service time	Service ends	Waiting time attendent	Customer	Line length
93	10	9.10	9.10	71	7	9.17	10	–	–
14	2	9.12	9.17	63	5	9.22	–	5	1
72	6	9.18	9.22	14	3	9.25	–	4	1
10	2	9.20	9.25	53	5	9.30	–	5	1
21	4	9.24	9.30	64	5	9.35	–	6	1
81	8	9.32	9.35	42	5	9.40	–	3	1
87	8	9.40	9.40	07	1	9.41	–	–	–
90	10	9.50	9.50	54	5	9.55	9	–	–
38	6	9.56	9.56	66	5	10.01	1	–	–
	56				41		20	23	5

Then, average queue length = 5/9 ≈ 1 customer

average waiting time of the customer before service = 23/9 = 2.56 min.

average service idle time = 20/9 = 2.22 min.

average service time = 41/9 = 4.56 min.

time that a customer spends in the system = 4.56 + 2.56 = 7.12 min.

% of service idle time = 20/(20 + 41) = 33%.

EXAMPLE 17.6: The management of ABC company is considering the question of marketing a new product. The fixed cost required in the project is Rs. 4,000. Three factors, viz. the selling price, variable cost and the annual sales volume are uncertain. The product has a life of only one year. The management has the data for these three factors as under:

Selling price (Rs.)	*Probability*	*Variable cost (Rs.)*	*Probability*	*Sales volume (units)*	*Probability*
3	0.2	1	0.3	2,000	0.3
4	0.5	2	0.6	3,000	0.3
5	0.3	3	0.1	5,000	0.4

Consider the following sequence of thirty numbers : 81, 32, 60, 04, 46, 31, 67, 25, 24, 10, 40, 02, 39, 68, 08, 59, 66, 90, 12, 64, 79, 31, 86, 68, 82, 89, 25, 11, 98, 16. Using the sequence (first three random numbers for the first trial, etc.), simulate the average profit for the above project on the basis of the 10 trials.

Solution: First we compute random number intervals for the selling price, variable cost and sales volume using respective probabilities:

Selling price (Rs.)	*Probability*	*Cumulative probability*	*RNI*
3	0.2	0.2	00–19
4	0.7	0.7	20–69
5	0.3	1.0	70–99
Variable cost (Rs.)			
1	0.3	0.3	00–29
2	0.6	0.9	30–89
3	0.1	1.0	90–99
Sales volume (units)			
2,000	0.3	0.3	00–29
3,000	0.3	0.6	30–59
5,000	0.4	1.0	60–99

Next is simulation table to find the average profit.

S.No.	*RN*	*Selling price (Rs.)* (1)	*RN*	*Variable cost (Rs.)* (2)	*RN*	*Sales volume* (3)	*Profit (Rs.)* ((1) – (2))*(3) – 4,000
1	81	5	32	2	60	5,000	11,000
2	04	3	46	2	31	3,000	–1,000
3	67	4	25	1	24	2,000	2,000
4	10	3	40	2	02	2,000	–2,000
5	39	4	68	2	08	2,000	0
6	59	4	66	2	90	5,000	6,000
7	12	3	64	2	79	5,000	1,000
8	31	4	86	2	68	5,000	6,000
9	82	5	89	2	25	2,000	2,000
10	11	3	98	3	16	2,000	–4,000
							21,000

Therefore, the average profit = Rs. 21,000/10 = Rs. 2,100.

EXAMPLE 17.7 The director of finance for a farm co-operative is concerned about the yields per acre. She can expect from this year's corn crop. The probability distribution of the yields for the current weather condition is given below.

Yield in kg/acre	120	140	160	180
Probability	0.18	0.26	0.44	0.12

She would like to see a simulation of the yields. She might expect 10 years for weather conditions similar to those she is now experiencing.

(i) Simulate the average yield she might expect per acre using the random numbers 20, 72, 34, 54, 30, 22, 48, 74, 76, 02. She is also interested in the effect of market price fluctuations on the cooperative's farm revenue. She makes this estimate of selling prices per kg for corn.

Price/kg	2.00	2.10	2.20	2.30	2.40	2.50
Probability	0.05	0.15	0.30	0.25	0.15	0.10

(ii) Simulate the price she might expect to observe over the next 10 years using the following random numbers: 82, 95, 18, 96, 20, 84, 56, 11, 52, 03.

(iii) Assuming that the prices of yields combine these two into the revenue per acre and also find out the average revenue per acre she might expect every year.

Solution: (i) The probability distribution of yield is as follows:

Yield in (kg/acre.)	*Probability*	*Cumulative probability*	*RNI*
120	0.18	0.18	00–17
140	0.26	0.44	18–43
160	0.44	0.88	44–87
180	0.12	1.00	88–99

Next, we have simulation of the yield for the next 10 years using the given random numbers:

Year	*RN*	*Simulated yield*
1	20	140
2	72	160
3	34	140
4	54	160
5	30	140
6	22	140
7	48	160
8	74	160
9	76	160
10	02	120
		1,480

Therefore, the average yield is 1,480/10 = 148 kg/acre.

(ii) We now simulate the price she expects in the next 10 years based on the given random numbers:

Price (Rs.)	*Probability*	*Cumulative probability*	*RNI*
2.00	0.05	0.05	00–04
2.10	0.15	0.20	05–19
2.20	0.30	0.50	20–49
2.30	0.25	0.75	50–74
2.40	0.15	0.90	75–89
2.50	0.10	1.00	90–99

Simulation for prices for the next 10 years is

Year	*RN*	*Price* (1)	*Simulated yield* (2)	*Revenue/acre* (1) * (2)
1	20		140	336
2	72		160	400
3	34		140	294
4	54		160	400
5	30		140	308
6	22		140	336
7	48		160	368
8	74		160	336
9	76		160	368
10	02		120	240
				3,386

(iii) Average revenue per acre is Rs. 3,386/10 = Rs. 338.60.

EXAMPLE 17.8: After studying the weekly receipts and payments over the past 200 weeks, a retailer has gathered the following information:

Weekly receipts (Rs.)	*Probability*	*Weekly payments (Rs.)*	*Probability*
3,000	0.20	4,000	0.30
5,000	0.30	6,000	0.40
7,000	0.40	8,000	0.20
12,000	0.10	10,000	0.10

Simulate the weekly pattern of receipts and payments for 12 weeks of the next quarter, assuming a beginning bank balance is Rs. 8,000. What is the estimated balance at the end of the 12 weeks, the highest weekly balance during the quarter, and the average weekly balance for the quarter? Use the following random numbers:

For receipts:	03,	91,	38,	55,	17,	46,	32,	43,	69,	72,	24,	22
For payments:	61,	96,	30,	32,	03,	88,	48,	28,	88,	18,	71,	99

Solution: First, we compute random number intervals for both the receipts and the payments using given data:

Receipts	*Probability*	*Cumu. Prob.*	*RNI*	*Payments*	*Probability*	*Cumu. Prob.*	*RNI*
3,000	0.20	0.20	00–19	4,000	0.30	0.30	00–29
5,000	0.30	0.50	20–49	6,000	0.40	0.70	30–69
7,000	0.40	0.90	50–89	8,000	0.20	0.90	70–89
12,000	0.10	1.00	90–99	10,000	0.10	1.00	90–99

Using the random numbers for the receipts and payments, let us simulate balance for next 12 weeks:

	Receipts		Payments		
Week	*RN*	*Amount (Rs.)*	*RN*	*Amount (Rs.)*	*Balance (Rs.)*
0					8,000
1	03	3,000	61	6,000	5,000
2	91	12,000	96	10,000	7,000
3	38	5,000	30	6,000	6,000
4	55	7,000	32	6,000	7,000
5	17	3,000	03	4,000	6,000
6	46	5,000	88	8,000	3,000
7	32	5,000	48	6,000	2,000
8	43	5,000	28	4,000	3,000
9	69	7,000	88	8,000	5,000
10	72	7,000	18	4,000	5,000
11	24	5,000	71	8,000	2,000
12	22	5,000	99	10,000	–3,000

From the above table, it is observed that at the end of 12 weeks, the retailer faces a deficit of Rs. 3,000. The maximum weekly balance is Rs. 7,000 and the average balance is Rs. 3,750.

EXAMPLE 17.9: A job has to be processed over two machines (say) M_1 and M_2 in that order. The distribution of inter-arrival time of the job at the first machine is as follows:

Time (min.)	1	2	3	4
Probability	0.2	0.2	0.2	0.4

The processing times at the two machines are as follows:

Machine M_1		Machine M_2	
Time (min.)	*Probability*	*Time (min.)*	*Probability*
1	0.1	4	0.2
2	0.2	5	0.3
3	0.3	6	0.4
4	0.3	7	0.1
5	0.1	–	–

On the basis of 10 simulation runs, find out the queue length before machine M_1 and the average queue length before machine M_2.

Solution: The algorithm for simulation is as follows:

1. Simulate the inter-arrival time of the *i*th (i = 1, 2, ...) job on machine M_1 with the help of random numbers.

2. Arrival time of ith job = arrival time of $(i - 1)$th job $(i = 2, 3, \ldots)$ plus inter-arrival time of the ith job. (Note that the arrival time of the first job is equal to the inter-arrival time of the first job.)
3. Simulate the processing time on machine M_1.
4. Departure time on machine M_1 = Arrival time for processing on machine M_2 = Maxi. (Arrival time of ith job, processing completion time of $(i - 1)$th job on machine M_1) plus processing time of ith job on machine M_1.
5. If the arrival time of ith job is less than the process completion time of $(i - 1)$th job, then ith arrival has to wait. If the arrival time of ith job is less than the process completion of $(i - 2)$th job, both ith and $(i - 1)$th arrivals will wait.
6. Simulate the processing time on machine M_2.
7. Process completion by machine M_2 of ith job is equal to Maxi. (Arrival time of ith job, process completion time of $(i - 1)$th job) plus process time by machine M_2.
8. If the arrival time of ith job is less than the process completion time of $(i - 1)$th job, the ith arrival will wait. If the arrival time of ith job is less than the process completion time of $(i - 2)$th, then both ith and $(i - 1)$th arrivals wait, and so on.

Using algorithm, let us compute simulation of processing times on machines M_1 and M_2 for 10 days.

Run	*RN*	*Inter-arrival time*	*Arrival time on M_1*	*RN*	*Process time on M_1*	*Exit time on M_1*	*RN*	*Process time on M_2*	*Exit time on M_2*	*Queue size M_1*	*M_2*
1	8	4	4	0	1	5	3	5	10	–	–
2	7	4	8	6	4	12	0	4	16	–	–
3	8	4	12	9	5	17	0	4	21	–	–
4	9	4	16	3	3	20	0	4	25	1	1
5	4	3	19	7	4	24	0	4	29	1	1
6	4	3	22	0	1	25	2	5	34	1	1
7	0	1	23	0	1	26	4	5	39	2	2
8	6	4	27	5	3	30	5	6	45	–	2
9	8	4	31	6	4	35	1	4	49	–	2
10	7	4	35	4	3	38	2	5	54	–	3
										5	12

Thus, the average queue size before machine M_1 is 0.5 and that before machine M_2 is 1.2.

EXAMPLE 17.10: A project consists of seven activities. The time for performance of each of the activities is a random variable with the respective probabilities given as:

Activity	Immediate processor	Time (in days) and its probabilities				
A	–	3 0.20	4 0.60	5 0.20		
B	–	4 0.10	5 0.30	6 0.30	7 0.20	8 0.10
C	A	1 0.15	3 0.75	5 0.10		
D	B, C	4 0.80	5 0.20			
E	D	3 0.10	4 0.30	5 0.30	6 0.30	
F	D	5 0.20	7 0.80			
G	E, F	2 0.50	3 0.50			

(a) Draw the network diagram and identify the critical path using the expected activity times.

(b) Simulate the project using random numbers: (68, 99, 57, 57, 77), (13, 93, 33, 12, 37), (09, 18, 49, 31, 34), (20, 24, 65, 96, 11), (73, 22, 92, 86, 27), (07, 07, 98, 92, 10) and (92, 29, 00, 91, 59) respectively for the activities *A*, *B*, *C*, *D*, *E*, *F*, and *G*. Find the critical path and projection duration.

(c) Repeat the simulation for four times. Is the same path critical in all the simulation runs?

Solution: (a) Using the given data of activities, the network is

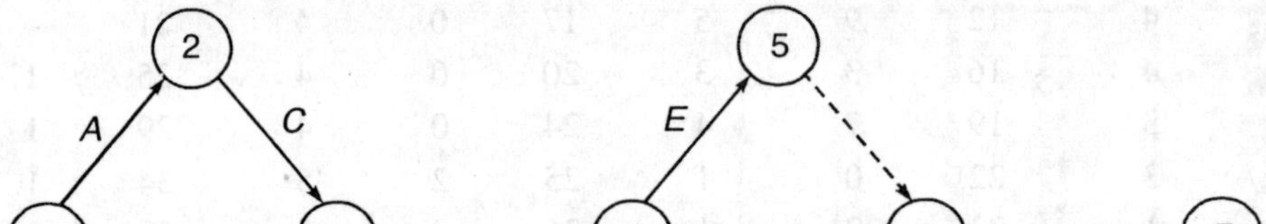

Then the critical path of the project is 1 → 2 → 3 → 4 → 6 → 7, with an expected duration of 20.2 days.

(b) and (c): Using probabilities and times for each activity, we compute random number intervals as below:

Activity	Time	Probability	Cumu. Prob.	RNI
A	3	0.20	0.20	00–19
	4	0.60	0.80	20–79
	5	0.20	1.00	80–99

Activity	*Time*	*Probability*	*Cumu. Prob.*	*RNI*
B	4	0.10	0.10	00–09
	5	0.30	0.40	10–39
	6	0.30	0.70	40–69
	7	0.20	0.90	70–89
	8	0.10	1.00	90–99
C	1	0.15	0.15	00–14
	3	0.75	0.90	15–89
	5	0.10	1.00	90–99
D	4	0.80	0.80	00–79
	5	0.20	1.00	80–99
E	3	0.10	0.10	00–09
	4	0.30	0.40	10–39
	5	0.30	0.70	40–69
	6	0.30	1.00	70–99
F	5	0.20	0.20	00–19
	7	0.80	1.00	20–99
G	2	0.50	0.50	00–49
	3	0.50	1.00	50–99

Simulation of activity:

Run	*A*		*B*		*C*		*D*		*E*		*F*		*G*	
	RN	*D*	*RN*	*D*	*RN*	*D*	*RN*	*D*	*RN*	*D*	*RN*	*D*	*RN*	*Days*
1	68	4	13	5	09	1	20	4	73	6	07	5	92	3
2	99	5	93	8	18	3	24	4	22	4	07	5	29	2
3	57	4	33	5	49	3	65	4	65	4	98	7	00	2
4	57	4	12	5	31	3	96	5	96	5	92	7	91	3
5	77	4	37	5	34	3	11	4	27	4	10	5	59	3

Simulation run	*Project duration (Days)*	*Critical path (s)*
1	18	$1 \rightarrow 2 \rightarrow 3 \rightarrow 4 \rightarrow 5 \rightarrow 6 \rightarrow 7$
		$1 \rightarrow 3 \rightarrow 4 \rightarrow 5 \rightarrow 6 \rightarrow 7$
2	19	$1 \rightarrow 2 \rightarrow 3 \rightarrow 4 \rightarrow 6 \rightarrow 7$
		$1 \rightarrow 3 \rightarrow 4 \rightarrow 6 \rightarrow 7$
3	20	$1 \rightarrow 2 \rightarrow 3 \rightarrow 4 \rightarrow 6 \rightarrow 7$
4	22	$1 \rightarrow 2 \rightarrow 3 \rightarrow 4 \rightarrow 6 \rightarrow 7$
5	19	$1 \rightarrow 2 \rightarrow 3 \rightarrow 4 \rightarrow 6 \rightarrow 7$

It is observed that the critical path is not unique.

EXAMPLE 17.11: The occurrence of a rain in a city on a day is dependent upon whether or not it rained on the previous day. If it rained on the previous day, the rain distribution is:

Event	No rain	1 cm rain	2 cm rain	3 cm rain	4 cm rain	5 cm rain
Probability	0.50	0.25	0.15	0.05	0.03	0.02

If it did not rain the previous day, the rain distribution is

Event	No rain	1 cm rain	2 cm rain	3 cm rain
Probability	0.75	0.15	0.06	0.04

Simulate the city's weather for 10 days and determine by simulation the total days without rain as well as the total rainfall during the period. Use the random numbers 67, 63, 39, 55, 29, 78, 70, 06, 78 and 76 for simulation. Assume that for the first day of simulation, it had not rained the day before.

Solution: Computation of random number intervals if there was a rain on the previous day:

Event	*Probability*	*Cumu. Prob.*	*RNI*
No rain	0.50	0.50	00–49
1 cm rain	0.25	0.75	50–74
2 cm rain	0.15	0.90	75–89
3 cm rain	0.05	0.95	90–94
4 cm rain	0.03	0.98	95–97
5 cm rain	0.02	1.00	98–99

Computation of random number intervals if there was no rain on the previous day:

Event	*Probability*	*Cumu. Prob.*	*RNI*
No rain	0.75	0.75	00–74
1 cm rain	0.15	0.90	75–89
2 cm rain	0.06	0.96	90–95
3 cm rain	0.04	1.00	96–99

Let us simulate rain weather for 10 days using the given random numbers:

Day	*RN*	*Event*
1	67	No rain
2	63	No rain
3	39	No rain
4	55	No rain
5	29	No rain
6	78	1 cm rain
7	70	1 cm rain
8	06	No rain
9	78	1 cm rain
10	76	2 cm rain

It is observed that out of 10 days, the city has not experienced rain for 6 days and during 4 days, the total rainfall is of 5 cm.

REVIEW EXERCISES

1. A confectioner sells confectionary items. The data of demand per week (in hundred kg) with frequency is given below:

Demand/week	0	5	10	15	20	25
Frequency	2	11	8	21	5	3

Using the following sequence of random numbers, generate the demand for the next 15 weeks. 35, 52, 90, 13, 23, 73, 34, 57, 35, 83, 94, 56, 67, 66, 60. Also find the average demand per week.

2. A manager of a warehouse is interested in designing an inventory control system for one of the product in stock. The demand for the product comes from various retail outlets and orders arrive on a weekly basis. The warehouse receives its stock from the factory but the lead-time is not constant. The manager wants to determine the best time to release orders to the factory so that stock-outs are minimized, yet inventory holding costs are at acceptable levels. Any order from retailers not supplied on a given day constitutes lost demand. Based on a sampling study, the following data is available:

Demand/week (in thousands)	*Probability*	*Lead-time*	*Probability*
0	0.20	2	0.30
1	0.40	3	0.40
2	0.30	4	0.30
3	0.10		

The manager of the warehouse has determined the ordering cost as Rs. 50/order, inventory holding cost as Rs. 2/thousand units/week and shortage cost as Rs. 10/thousand units.

The objective of inventory analysis is to determine the optimal size of an order and the best time to place an order. The policy is, "Whenever the inventory level becomes less than or equal to 2,000 units (reorder level), an order equal to the difference between the current inventory balance and the specified maximum replenishment level is equal to 4,000 units is placed."

Simulate the policy for 10 weeks assuming that (i) the beginning inventory is 3,000 units, (ii) no backorders are permitted, (iii) each reorder is placed at the beginning of the week as soon as the inventory level is less than or equal to the reorder level, and (iv) the replenishment orders are received at the beginning of the week. Use random numbers: 31, 70, 53, 86, 32, 78, 26, 64, 45, 12.

3. A firm has single channel service station with the following arrival and service time probability distribution:

Arrival time (min.)	*Probability*	*Service time (min.)*	*Probability*
1.0	0.35	1.0	0.20
2.0	0.25	1.5	0.35
3.0	0.20	2.0	0.25
4.0	0.12	2.5	0.15
5.0	0.08	3.0	0.05

The customer's arrival at the service station is random and the time between the arrivals varies from one minute to five minutes. The service time varies from one minute to three minutes. The queuing process begins at 10.00 am and proceeds nearly for one hour. An arrival goes to the service facility immediately, if it is free. Otherwise, he will wait in a queue. The queue discipline is FIFS.

If the attendant's wages are Rs. 8 per hour and the customer waiting time costs Rs. 9 per hour, then would it be economical to engage a second attendant? Use the following random numbers for simulation:

Arrival time: 23, 46, 73, 05, 14, 86, 92, 10, 37, 56, 61, 00.

Service time: 08, 12, 69, 82, 76, 54, 26, 39, 43, 04, 14, 86, 47, 59, 23, 47, 90, 61, 22, 41.

4. A process involves the production of a particular component which is then installed into an end product. The average production time for the component is 4 minutes and the following probability distribution has been derived from the past observation:

Production time (min.)	2	3	4	5	6	7
Probability	0.10	0.25	0.40	0.10	0.10	0.05

The time taken to install a component is 3 minutes on an average with the following probability distribution:

Installation time (min.)	2	3	4	5
Probability	0.30	0.45	0.15	0.10

The system uses one operator for installation but the company is considering to employ another operator for the installation process.

Simulate 10 arrivals on the current system, using the following random numbers: 20, 74, 81, 22, 93, 45, 44, 16, 04, 32, 03, 62, 61, 89, 01, 27, 49, 50, 90, 98.

5. An investment company wants to study the investment projects based on market demand, profit and investment required, which are independent of each other. Following probability distributions are estimated for each of these three factors:

Annual demand (units in thousand)	25	30	35	40	45	50	55
Probability	0.05	0.10	0.20	0.30	0.20	0.10	0.05

Profit/unit	3.00	5.00	7.00	9.00	10.00
Probability	0.10	0.20	0.40	0.20	0.10

Investment required (in thousands of Rs.)	2,750	3,000	3,500
Probability	0.25	0.50	0.25

Using simulation process, repeat the trial 10 times. Compute the investment on each trial taking these factors into trial. What is the most likely return? Use the following random numbers: (30, 12, 16), (59, 09, 69), (63, 94, 26), (27, 08, 74), (64, 60, 61), (28, 28, 72), (31, 23, 57), (54, 85, 20), (64, 68, 18), (32, 31, 87). In the bracket, the first random number is for annual demand, the second one is for profit and the third one is for the investment required.

18 Game Theory

18.1 INTRODUCTION

In many practical problems, it is required to take decision in a situation where there are two (or more) opposite parties with conflicting interests, and the action of one depends upon the action which the opponent takes. The outcome of the situation is controlled by the decisions of all the parties involved. Such a situation is termed a *competitive situation*. Such problems occur frequently in all sorts of activities, in games, sports, business, economic, political, social, and military fields. The generic term used to characterize these situations is games, that is, general situations of conflict over time.

In games, the participants are competitors; the success of one is usually at the expense of the other. Each participant selects and executes those strategies which he believes will result in his "winning the game". In games, the participants make use of deductive and inductive logic in determining a strategy for winning. The mathematics of the theory of games is of interest to us for this reason.

The theory of games started in the 20th century. But the mathematical treatment of games began in 1944 when John Von Neumann and Morgenstern published their well-known "theory of games and economic behaviour". The Von Neumann's approach utilizes the *minimax* principle which involves the fundamental idea of the minimization of maximum loss. Many of the competitive problems can be handled by this game theory.

A competitive situation is called a ***game*** if it has the following four properties:

1. There are a finite number of competitors, called ***players***. A game involving n persons is called a ***n person game***. In a game, interests of only two parties may be in conflict. Such a game is termed a ***two person game***.
2. A list of finite or infinite number of possible ***courses of action***, each called a ***strategy***, is available to each player. The list need not be the same for each player.

The strategy of a player is the pre-determined rule by which a player decides his course of action from his own list during the game. To make the decision, regarding the choice of strategy, neither player needs the definite information about the opponent's strategy.

Generally two types of strategies are employed by the players in a game. A ***pure strategy*** is that in which one knows in advance all strategies, out of which he always selects only one particular strategy. This choice is made irrespective of the strategy others may choose. A ***mixed strategy*** is that in which a player decides in advance his courses of action in accordance with some fixed probability distribution. Thus, in case of mixed strategy, we associate probability to each course of action. Mathematically, a mixed strategy to any player is an ordered set of non-negative real numbers (probabilities) which add up to 1.

The advantage of the mixed strategy over the pure strategy is that a player has only finite choices of pure strategies (those available to him) but he has infinite number of mixed strategies.

3. A ***play*** is played when each player chooses one of his courses of action. The choices are assumed to be made simultaneously, so that no player knows his opponent's choice until he has decided his own course of action.
4. Every play, i.e. a combination of courses of action is associated with an outcome, known as ***pay-off***, which determines a set of gains, one to each player. Here a loss is considered a negative gain. Thus, after each play of the game, one player pays to others an amount determined by the courses of action chosen. In short, a pay-off matrix is a table which shows how payments should be made at the end of a play or the game.

Before moving on to concrete concepts, let us understand a few games.

EXAMPLE 18.1: Look at the following two person game.

		Player B	
		Strategy B_1	*Strategy* B_2
Player A	*Strategy* A_1	Player A wins 2	Player A wins 3
	Strategy A_2	Player B wins 1	Player B wins 2

The players A and B are equal in intelligence and ability. Each has a choice of two strategies. Each knows the outcomes for every possible combination of strategies. Note that the play is biased against player B, but since he is required to play, he will do his best. This is analogous to the business situation in which short-run loss is inevitable; these losses must be minimized by good strategy.

We can now look at the pay-off matrix as follows:

		Player B	
		B_1	B_2
Player A	A_1	2	3
	A_2	–1	–2

The solution to this simple game is easily obtained by analyzing the possible strategies of each player:

1. A wins the game only by playing his strategy A_1; thus he plays A_1 all the time.
2. B realizes that A will play strategy A_1 all the time and, in an effort to minimize A's gains, plays his strategy B_1.

3. The solution to the game is thus A_1, B_1.
4. A wins 2 points (B loses 2 points) each time the game is played; thus the value of the game to A is 2; the value of the game to B is –2.

The term value of the game used in this sense is the average winnings per play over a long series of plays. Though player B loses this game, he is still playing his optimum strategy; that is, he is minimizing his losses. If he had used strategy B_2, his losses would have been 3 per play. We can see that in this game, the gains of player A are equal to the absolute value of the losses of player B.

A game in which the gains of one player are the losses of the other players, is called a ***zero-sum game***, i.e. in a zero-sum game the algebraic sum of gains to all players after a play is bound to be zero.

18.2 TWO PERSON ZERO-SUM GAMES

As mentioned earlier, a game with two players in which the gain of one player is equal to the loss of the other is called a ***two person zero-sum game***.

Each combination of the alternatives of the players in a two person zero-sum game is associated with an outcome a_{ij} in the form of a pay-off matrix. If a_{ij} is positive, it represents a gain to player A, and a loss to player B. If it is negative, it represents a loss to A and a gain to B. We generally write the pay-off matrix in favour of the player whose strategies are written in rows. A sample pay-off matrix in favour of player A is as shown in the following table.

		Player *B*				
		B_1	B_2	B_3	$\cdots$	B_n
Player A	A_1	a_{11}	a_{12}	a_{13}	$\cdots$	a_{1n}
	A_2	a_{21}	a_{22}	a_{23}	$\cdots$	a_{2n}
	A_3	a_{31}	a_{32}	a_{33}	$\cdots$	a_{3n}
	A_m	a_{m1}	a_{m2}	a_{m3}	$\cdots$	a_{mn}

The players in the game thrive for ***optimal strategies***. An optimal strategy provides the best situation in the game in the sense that it provides maximal pay-off to the players. The expected outcome per play when the players follow their optimal strategy is called the ***value of the game***. It is generally denoted by *V*. A game, whose value is zero, is called a ***fair*** game. By *solving* a game, we mean to find the best strategies for both the players and the value of the game.

Let us understand the above mentioned terminology by the following example.

EXAMPLE 18.2:

		Player B	
		B_1	B_2
Player A	A_1	2	4
	A_2	1	–3

B sees that his only chance to win, –3, occurs if A plays A_2, which will never happen. If A plays A_1, B must play B_1 to reduce his average loss to 2 instead of 4. The final strategies are A_1, B_1 and the value of the game is 2.

EXAMPLE 18.3:

		Player B		
		B_1	B_2	B_3
Player A	A_1	2	0	4
	A_2	1	–3	2

A observes that B's only chance to win, 3 from A (entry –3 in the matrix), occurs if A plays A_2, hence A plays A_1 all the time. To minimize his losses, B then plays B_2. Neither player wins. Strategies are A_1, B_1 and $V = 0$. This is a *fair* game.

EXAMPLE 18.4:

		Player B		
		B_1	B_2	B_3
Player A	A_1	3	2	–2
	A_2	1	–3	–4
	A_3	0	1	–3

B sees that A cannot win if B plays B_3, he therefore plays B_3 all the time. To minimize his losses, then A must play A_1. Strategies A_1, B_3 and $V = -2$.

18.3 MAXIMIN AND MINIMAX PRINCIPLES

In game theory, we determine the best strategies for each player on the basis of *maximin* and *minimax* criterion of optimality. It is as follows:

"A player lists his worst possible outcomes and then he chooses that strategy which corresponds to the best of these worst outcomes."

EXAMPLE 18.5: Consider the following pay-off matrix for a two person zero-sum game.

		Player B			
		B_1	B_2	B_3	B_4
Player A	A_1	8	–2	9	–3
	A_2	6	5	6	8
	A_3	–2	4	–9	5

The solution of the game is based on securing the best of the worst for each player. If A selects strategy A_1, then regardless of what B does, the worst that can happen is that A would lose 3 units to B. Similarly, strategy A_2 worst outcome is for A to gain 5 units from B, and strategy A_3 worst outcome is for A to lose 9 units to B. These results form the "row minima" column as follows. To achieve the best of the worst, A chooses the strategy A_2 because it corresponds to the *maximum of all row minima values.*

		Player B					
		B_1	B_2	B_3	B_4	*Row minima*	
	A_1	8	–2	9	–3	–3	
Player A	A_2	6	5	6	8	**5**	Maximin value
	A_3	–2	4	–9	5	–9	
Column maxima		8	**5**	9	8		
			Minimax value				

Next, consider B's strategy. Because the given pay-off matrix is for player A, B's best of the worst criteria requires determining the minimax value. It is shown in the row of column maxima. B now has to choose strategy B_2 in order to *minimize his maximum losses.*

The optimal solution of the game calls for selecting strategies A_2 and B_2. Here the strategies A_2 and B_2 are the optimal strategies. The pay-off will be in favour of player A because he will gain 5 units from B. In this case we say the value of the game is 5, i.e. $V = 5$, and that A and B are using a *saddle-point* situation.

The saddle-point situation guarantees that neither of the players is tempted to select a better strategy. If B moves to another strategy (B_1, B_3 or B_4), player A can stay with strategy A_2, which ensures that B will lose a worse amount 6 or 8. In a similar way, A does not want to use a different strategy because if A moves to strategy A_3, B can move to B_3 and realize a gain of 9 units. A similar conclusion is realized if A moves to A_1.

Consider the standard pay-off matrix given in Section 18.2. If player A chooses his *i*th strategy, then he gains at least the pay-off min a_{ij}, which is the minimum of the *i*th row elements. Since his objective is to maximize his pay-off, he can choose i so as to make this minimum pay-off as large as possible. Hence,

$$\text{pay-off to A} \geq \max_i \min_j a_{ij}$$

Similarly, if player B can choose *j*th column strategy, then he looses at the most pay-off a_{ij}, which is the maximum of the *j*th column elements. Since his objective is to minimize his losses, he can choose j so as to make this maximum pay-off as small as possible. Hence,

$$\text{pay-off to } B \leq \min_j \max_i a_{ij}$$

If the maximin value for a player is equal to the minimax value for another player, that is,

$$\max_i \min_j a_{ij} = \min_j \max_i a_{ij}$$

then the game is said to have a saddle point and the corresponding strategies are the optimal strategies. The amount of pay-off at the saddle point is the value of the game V.

It is evident that

$$\max_i \min_j a_{ij} = \min_j \max_i a_{ij} = V$$

A saddle point can be recognized because it corresponds to *both* the *smallest* numerical value in its row and the *largest* numerical value in its column. Consider for a moment the significance of this. Player B would rather have as a pay-off the smallest numerical value in any row. Player A would rather have as a pay-off the largest numerical value in any column. Naturally, when one numerical value satisfies both these conditions (a saddle point), both players will be playing optimally if each chooses that value.

If a game has a saddle point, then the pure strategies corresponding to the saddle point are the optimal strategies and the number at that point is the value of the game.

Of course, not all two person games have a saddle point. An examination of the game will reveal whether one is present.

Following are some examples of pay-off matrices for games without saddle points.

		Player B	
		B_1	B_2
Player A	A_1	1	0
	A_2	–4	3

		Player B		
		B_1	B_2	B_3
Player A	A_1	4	–2	3
	A_2	0	5	6

		Player B	
		B_1	B_2
	A_1	1	2
Player A	A_2	3	4
	A_3	5	6

The optimal saddle-point solution of a game need not be characterized by pure strategies. Instead, the solution may require mixing two or more strategies randomly.

EXAMPLE 18.6: Consider the following pay-off matrix for a two person zero-sum game.

		Player B			
		B_1	B_2	*Row minima*	
Player A	A_1	1	0	**0**	Maximin value
	A_2	–4	3	–4	
Column maxima		**1**	3		
		Minimax value			

Here the maximin and the minimax values of the game are 0 and 1, respectively. Because the two values are not equal, the game does not have a pure strategy solution. In particular, if A_1 is used by player A, player B will select B_2 so that he does not lose anything. If A_2 is used by player A, player B will select B_1 to gain 4 units from A. This continuous temptation by either player to switch to another strategy shows that a pure strategy solution is not acceptable. Instead, both players must use proper random mixes of their respective strategies. In this case, the optimal value of the game will occur somewhere between the maximin and the minimax values of the game, that is

$$\text{Maximin (lower) value} \leq \text{value of the game} \leq \text{Minimax (upper) value}$$

For games with mixed strategy (with no saddle point), we have

$$\underline{v} \leq v \leq \overline{v}$$

A game is said to be a *fair* game if the maximin and the minimax values of the game are equal and both equal zero, i.e. $\underline{v} = 0 = \overline{v}$

A game is said to be strictly determinable if the maximin and minimax values of the game are equal and both equal the value of the game, i.e. $\underline{v} = v = \overline{v}$

18.4 MIXED STRATEGIES, EXPECTED PAY-OFF

For games with saddle points, the best strategies were the pure strategies. As a matter of fact, every pure strategy is a special case of a mixed strategy in which all strategies except the one are selected with probability zero and the given one with unit probability. For games which do not involve saddle points, the best strategies are the mixed strategies. Therefore, our problem becomes one of determining the probabilities with which each strategy should be selected.

The optimal strategy mixture for each player may be determined by assigning to each strategy its probability of being chosen. The strategies so determined are called ***mixed strategies*** because they are probabilistic combination of available choices of strategy. The value of the game obtained by the use of mixed strategies represents the least player A can *expect* to gain and the least the player B can *expect* to lose.

Let (a_{ij}) be an arbitrary pay-off matrix of order $m \times n$. Consider the following pay-off matrix (Figure 18.1).

		Player B						
		q_1	q_2	.	q^*	.	q_n	*Row minima*
Player A	p_1	$E(p_1, q_1)$	$E(p_2, q_2)$	.	$E(p_1, q^*)$	.	$E(p_1, q_n)$	$\min_q E(p_1, q)$
	p_2	$E(p_2, q_1)$	$E(p_2, q_2)$	.	$E(p_2, q^*)$	.	$E(p_2, q_n)$	$\min_q E(p_2, q)$
	.							
	p^*	$E(p^*, q_1)$	$E(p^*, q_2)$		$E(p^*, q^*)$		$E(p^*, q_n)$	$\min_q E(p^*, q)$
	.							
	p_m	$E(p_m, q_1)$	$E(p_m, q_2)$	.	$E(p_m, q^*)$	.	$E(p_m, q_n)$	$\min_q E(p_m, q)$
Column maxima (Maximum in each column)		$\max_p E(p, q_1)$	$\max_p E(p, q_2)$	.	$\max_p E(p, q^*)$		$\max_p E(p, q_n)$	

Figure 18.1

Then the expected pay-off to player A in a game is given by

$$E(p, q) = \sum_{i=1}^{m} \sum_{j=1}^{m} p_i \, a_{ij} \, q_j \; = P^T AQ \text{ (matrix notation)}$$

where $P = [p_1, p_2, \ldots, p_m]$, $Q = [q_1, q_2, \ldots, q_n]$ and p_i, q_j are probabilities of choosing the strategies by players A and B respectively. For $E(p, q)$, $p \in R_m$, $q \in R_n$, if p is kept fixed at some value (say p^* in figure) and q is varied (i.e. we move along row corresponding to p^*), then $E(p, q)$ will be minimum for some value of q. Let this minimum value be ϕ.

Then $\phi = \min_q E(p^*, q)$. Thus by changing p's, a set of values of ϕ is obtained. This set will also have a maximum. (Look at row minima column.)

Call $\underline{v} = \max_p \min_q E(p, q)$. Similarly, we can interpret $\overline{v} = \min_q \max_p E(p, q)$.

In fact, player A wants to maximize his minimum gains. So $\underline{v} = \max_p \min_q E(p, q)$ and player B wants to minimize his maximum losses, so $\overline{v} = \min_q \max_p E(p, q)$.

For games with mixed strategy (with no saddle point), we have, $\underline{v} \le v \le \overline{v}$. We prove this result now. This result is a general result for any game (pure or mixed strategy).

Theorem 18.1: *Let $E(p, q)$ be such that both $\min_q \max_p E(p, q)$ and $\max_p \min_q E(p, q)$ exist, then $\max_p \min_q E(p, q) \le \min_q \max_p E(p, q)$.*

Proof: Consider the following pay-off matrix shown before.

Let p^* and q^* be the arbitrarily chosen mixed strategies for players A and B.

For fix q^* and for every p, $\max_p E(p, q^*) \ge E(p^*, q^*)$ (1)

(because $\max_p E(p, q^*)$ is the maximum value in that column.)

For fix p^* and for every q, $\min_q E(p^*, q) \le E(p^*, q^*)$ (2)

(because $\min_q E(p^*, q)$ is the minimum value in that row.)

From (1) and (2), $\min_q E(p^*, q) \le \max_p E(p, q^*)$ (3)

is true for all p and q because p^* and q^* are arbitrarily chosen. Hence (3) is also true for that strategy for which $\max_p E(p, q)$ has the minimum value; i.e. the entry $\min_q E(p^*, q)$ will be less than or equal to any entry which is the minimum of all $\max_p E(p, q)$.

Therefore, $\min_q E(p^*, q) \le \min_q \max_p E(p, q)$ is true for all p and q. (4)

Again, if the above result (4) is true for all p and q, it will also be true for a strategy p for which $\min_q E(p, q)$ has the maximum value; i.e. $\min_q \max_p E(p, q) \le \min_q \max_p E(p, q)$.

Note: The above result can also be stated as follows:

1. Let $f(x, y)$ be a real valued function for $\overline{x} \in R_m$, $\overline{y} \in R_n$ such that both $\max_x \min_y f(x, y)$ and $\min_y \max_x f(x, y)$ exist. Then

$$\max_x \min_y f(x, y) = \min_y \max_x f(x, y)$$

2. Let (a_{ij}) be a $m \times n$ pay-off matrix for a two person zero-sum game. Then

$$\max_i \min_j a_{ij} = \min_j \max_i a_{ij}$$

We now look at the mathematical definitions of saddle point explained earlier and the necessary and sufficient condition for its existence. Of course, *saddle points exist for only pure strategy games*.

1. Let $f(x, y)$ be a real valued function of two variables. A point (x_0, y_0) is said to be a saddle point of $f(x, y)$ if

$$f(x, y_0) \le f(x_0, y_0) = f(x_0, y)$$

2. Let $E(p, q)$ be a function of $p \in R_m$, $q \in R_n$. The function $E(p, q)$ is said to have a saddle point at (p^*, q^*) if

$$E(p, q^*) \le E(p^*, q^*) \le E(p^*, q)$$

Theorem 18.2: *Necessary and sufficient condition for the existence of a saddle point:*

Let $E(p, q)$ be such that both $\min_q \max_p E(p, q)$ and $\max_p \min_q E(p, q)$ exist. Then the necessary and sufficient condition for the existence of a saddle point (p^*, q^*) of $E(p, q)$ is that $E(p^*, q^*)$ $= \min_q \max_p E(p, q) = \max_p \min_q E(p, q)$.

Proof: *Necessary condition:* Suppose (p^*, q^*) is a saddle point of $E(p, q)$. Then the inequality

$$E(p, q^*) \le E(p^*, q^*) \le E(p^*, q) \text{ holds for all } p \text{ and } q \tag{1}$$

From (1), as $E(p, q^*) \le E(p^*, q^*)$ holds for all p and q, we get

$$\max_p E(p, q^*) \le E(p^*, q^*) \text{ holds for all } p \tag{2}$$

Now,
$$\min_q \max_p E(p, q) \le \max_p E(p, q^*) \tag{3}$$

From (2) and (3),
$$\min_q \max_p E(p, q) \le E(p^*, q^*) \tag{4}$$

[Interpretation from Figure 18.1, (p^*, q^*) being a saddle point, it is the biggest in that column. So $E(p^*, q^*) \ge \max_p E(p, q^*)$. So $E(p^*, q^*)$ is the maximum even if we take $\min_q \max_p E(p, q)$].

Again, from (1), $E(p^*, q^*) \le E(p^*, q)$ holds for all p and q.

Therefore, $E(p^*, q^*) \le \min_q E(p^*, q)$ holds for all q. (5)

Now,
$$\min_q E(p^*, q) \le \max_p \min_q E(p, q) \tag{6}$$

From (5) and (6),
$$E(p^*, q^*) \le \max_p \min_q E(p, q) \tag{7}$$

From (4) and (7),
$$\min_q \max_p E(p, q) \le \max_p \min_q E(p, q) \tag{8}$$

But we know that in general from Theorem 18.1, we have

$$\max_p \min_q E(p, q) \le \min_q \max_p E(p, q) \tag{9}$$

From (8) and (9),

$$E(p^*, q^*) = \max_p \min_q E(p, q) = \min_q \max_p E(p, q)$$

Sufficient condition: Let us assume that the point (p^*, q^*) satisfies the equality.

$$E(p^*, q^*) = \max_p \min_q E(p, q) = \min_q \max_p E(p, q) \tag{1}$$

Let the maximum of $\min_q E(p, q)$ occur at p^* and the minimum of $\max_p E(p, q)$ occur at q^*

i.e.
$$\max_p \min_q E(p, q) = \min_q E(p^*, q) \tag{2}$$

and
$$\min_q \max_p E(p, q) = \max_p E(p, q^*) \tag{3}$$

Using (1), (2) and (3), $\min_q E(p^*, q) = \max_p E(p, q^*) = E(p^*, q^*)$

Now, $\min_q E(p^*, q) = E(p^*, q^*)$ means $E(p^*, q^*)$ is the minimum of all $E(p^*, q)$ over q.

Therefore,
$$E(p^*, q^*) \le E(p^*, q) \tag{4}$$

and $\max_p E(p, q^*) = E(p^*, q^*)$ means $E(p^*, q^*)$ is the maximum of all $E(p, q^*)$ over p.

Therefore,
$$E(p, q^*) \le E(p^*, q^*) \tag{5}$$

Using (4) and (5), $E(p, q^*) \le E(p^*, q^*) \le E(p^*, q)$. Hence, (p^*, q^*) is the saddle point of $E(p, q)$.

Note: The above result can be stated as follows:

3. Let $f(x, y)$ be a real valued function for $\overline{x} \in R_m$, $\overline{y} \in R_n$ such that both $\max_x \min_y f(x, y)$ and $\min_y \max_x f(x, y)$ exists. Then (x_0, y_0) is a saddle point of $f(x, y)$ if and only if

$$f(x_0, y_0) = \max_x \min_y f(x, y) = \min_y \max_x f(x, y)$$

4. Let (a_{ij}) be a $m \times n$ pay-off matrix for a two person zero-sum game. Then a necessary and sufficient condition for (a_{ij}) to have a saddle point for $i = r$ and $j = s$ is that

$$a_{rs} = \max_i \min_j a_{ij} = \min_j \max_i a_{ij}$$

In Example 18.5 we saw a pure strategy game and a unique saddle point. Now we see an example where we have more than one saddle points. The value of the game remains the same for all the points.

EXAMPLE 18.7:

		Player B		
		B_1	B_2	B_3
Player A	A_1	–2	15	–2
	A_2	–5	–6	–4
	A_3	5	0	–8

Let us find the maximin and the minimax values for the game.

		Player B			
		B_1	B_2	B_3	*Row minima*
Player A	A_1	–2	15	–2	**–2** Maximin value
	A_2	–5	–6	–4	–6
	A_3	–5	20	–8	–8
Column maxima		**–2**	20	**–2**	
		Minimax value		Minimax value	

In reply to A's strategy A_1, B could employ either of his strategies B_1 or B_3.

Since the pay-off corresponding to A's maximin and B's minimax values are the same, we have two saddle points here — (A_1, B_1) and (A_1, B_3). The value of the game is the same at both the points. It is –6 which indicates a loss of 6 to A and a gain of 6 to B.

The fundamental theorem of game theory (minimax theorem—John von Neumann) is every matrix game can be solved in terms of mixed strategies, i.e. if mixed strategies are adopted, there always exists a value of the game, i.e. $\underline{v} = v = \overline{v}$.

18.5 SOLUTION OF 2 × 2 MIXED STRATEGY GAME

Now we will derive the formula for finding out the probabilities to be assigned to the strategies of both the players in case of a 2 × 2 mixed strategy game (i.e. games without saddle point). We have two equally efficient methods to be discussed here.

Method 1. It is in the form of the following theorem.

Method 2. Method of oddments discussed in Section 18.6.

Theorem 18.3: For any two person zero-sum game whose optimal strategies are not pure strategies, and whose pay-off matrix in favour of player A is

		Player B	
		B_1	B_2
Player A	A_1	a_{11}	a_{12}
	A_2	a_{21}	a_{22}

and (p_1, p_2), $p_1 + p_2 = 1$ and (q_1, q_2), $q_1 + q_2 = 1$, are the probabilities of choosing the respective strategies for players A and B respectively. Then

$$\frac{p_1}{p_2} = \frac{a_{22} - a_{21}}{a_{11} - a_{12}} \quad \text{and} \quad \frac{q_1}{q_2} = \frac{a_{22} - a_{12}}{a_{11} - a_{21}}$$

and the value of the game V is

$$V = \frac{a_{11}a_{22} - a_{12}a_{21}}{(a_{11} + a_{22}) - (a_{12} + a_{21})}$$

Proof: The expected gains to A are

E_1: $a_{11} p_1 + a_{21} p_2$ for B's move B_1

E_2: $a_{12} p_1 + a_{22} p_2$ for B's move B_2 where $p_1 + p_2 = 1$.

The expected losses to B are

E_3: $a_{11}q_1 + a_{12}q_2$ for A's move A_1

E_4: $a_{21}q_1 + a_{22}q_2$ for A's move A_2 where $q_1 + q_2 = 1$.

The fundamental theorem of game theory tells us that each rectangular game has a solution. So suppose V is the value of the game, then since A expects to get at least V, we have

$$E_1 \geq V, \quad E_2 \geq V \tag{1}$$

Again, since B expects to lose at most V, we have

$$E_3 \leq V, \quad E_4 \leq V \tag{2}$$

Assuming all the constraints of (1) and (2) as strict equalities, we get from (1),

$$E_1 = V = E_2$$

or

$$\frac{p_1}{p_2} = \frac{a_{22} - a_{21}}{a_{11} - a_{12}} \tag{3}$$

Similarly, from (2), we get

$$\frac{q_1}{q_2} = \frac{a_{22} - a_{12}}{a_{11} - a_{21}} \tag{4}$$

Individual values of p_1, p_2, q_1 and q_2 can be obtained by using (3) and (4) with $p_1 + p_2 = 1$ and $q_1 + q_2 = 1$. They are

$$p_1 = \frac{a_{22} - a_{21}}{(a_{11} + a_{22}) - (a_{12} + a_{21})} \qquad p_2 = \frac{a_{11} - a_{12}}{(a_{11} + a_{22}) - (a_{12} + a_{21})}$$

$$q_1 = \frac{a_{22} - a_{12}}{(a_{11} + a_{22}) - (a_{12} + a_{21})} \qquad q_2 = \frac{a_{11} - a_{21}}{(a_{11} + a_{22}) - (a_{12} + a_{21})}$$

and use this p_1, p_2 in either of relations in (1) to get the value of the game

$$V = \frac{a_{11}a_{22} - a_{12}a_{21}}{(a_{11} + a_{22}) - (a_{12} + a_{21})}$$

EXAMPLE 18.8:

		Player B	
		B_1	B_2
Player A	A_1	6	9
	A_2	8	4

Here we can see that the game does not have a saddle point. So suppose A and B play their strategies with probabilities (p_1, p_2), $p_1 + p_2 = 1$ and (q_1, q_2), $q_1 + q_2 = 1$.

The entries are $a_{11} = 6$, $a_{12} = 9$, $a_{21} = 8$, $a_{22} = 4$.
Using the above formula from the theorem directly, we get

$$\frac{p_1}{p_2} = \frac{a_{22} - a_{21}}{a_{11} - a_{12}} = \frac{4-8}{6-9} = \frac{4}{3}$$

Using it with $p_1 + p_2 = 1$, we get

$$p_1 = \frac{4}{7} \text{ and } p_2 = \frac{3}{7}$$

Similarly, $\dfrac{q_1}{q_2} = \dfrac{a_{22} - a_{12}}{a_{11} - a_{21}} = \dfrac{4-9}{6-8} = \dfrac{5}{2}$. Using it with $q_1 + q_2 = 1$, we get

$$q_1 = \frac{5}{7} \quad \text{and} \quad q_2 = \frac{2}{7}$$

Value of the game $\quad V = \dfrac{a_{11}a_{22} - a_{12}a_{21}}{(a_{11} + a_{22}) - (a_{12} + a_{21})}$

$$= \frac{(6 \times 4) - (9 \times 8)}{(6 + 4) - (9 + 8)}$$

$$= \frac{24 - 72}{10 - 17}$$

$$= \frac{48}{7}$$

18.6 SOLUTION OF 2 × 2 MIXED STRATEGY GAME BY THE METHOD OF ODDMENTS

Let us understand this easy procedure for finding out the solution of 2 × 2 games without saddle point by the method of oddments.

Consider the following pay-off matrix for a mixed strategy game.

		Player B	
		B_1	B_2
Player A	A_1	a	b
	A_2	c	d

Step 1: Find the absolute difference of the two numbers written in the first column and write this number below the second column. (See the following resultant pay-off matrix.)

Step 2: Find the absolute difference of the two numbers written in the second column and write this number below the first column.

Step 3: Perform this operation with the rows.

The values calculated are called the *oddments* of the various pure strategies and indicate their frequencies in the optimal strategies of the players. The sum of the oddments of the rows and columns must be the same.

		Player B		
		B_1	B_2	*oddments*
Player A	A_1	a	b	$c \sim d$
	A_2	c	d	$a \sim b$
Oddments		$b \sim d$	$a \sim c$	

Compute the probabilities p_1 and p_2 of player A and q_1 and q_2 of player B as follows:

$$p_1 = \frac{c \sim d}{a \sim b + c \sim d}, \quad p_2 = \frac{a \sim b}{a \sim b + c \sim d}$$

$$q_1 = \frac{b \sim d}{a \sim c + b \sim d}, \quad q_2 = \frac{a \sim c}{a \sim c + b \sim d}$$

i.e. each probability = its respective oddment divided by the sum of the oddments of rows (or columns, both have the same sum).

The value of the game V is computed by any of the formulae given below.

$$V = \frac{a(c \sim d) + c(a \sim b)}{a \sim b + c \sim d} \text{ or}$$

$$V = \frac{b(c \sim d) + d(a \sim b)}{a \sim b + c \sim d} \text{ or}$$

$$V = \frac{a(b \sim d) + b(a \sim c)}{a \sim c + b \sim d} \text{ or}$$

$$V = \frac{c(b \sim d) + d(a \sim c)}{a \sim c + b \sim d}$$

EXAMPLE 18.9:

		Player B	
		B_1	B_2
Player A	A_1	5	1
	A_2	3	4

The pay-off matrix with oddments is given below.

		Player B		
		B_1	B_2	
Player A	A_1	5	1	**1**
	A_2	3	4	**4**
		3	**2**	

The sum of the oddments of the rows and columns is the same, here 5. Hence the optimal strategies of the two players are (use formula given above): A(1/5,4/5), B(3/5,2/5).

And the value of the game $V = (5 \times 1 + 3 \times 4)/(1 + 4) = 17/5$.

Also, $V = (1 \times 1 + 4 \times 4)/5$ or $(5 \times 3 + 1 \times 2)/5$ or $(3 \times 3 + 4 \times 2)/5$.

18.7 DOMINANCE PRINCIPLE

The dominance principles are used to reduce the size of the pay-off matrix for two person zero-sum games without saddle point. By doing so if we can obtain a 2×2 game, we can solve it with the help of the formula derived in Section 18.5 or 18.6.

Often, it is possible to find an entire row (or column) which one player will avoid when there is another row (or column), which is always better for him or her to play. In that case, we say that the avoided row (or column) is dominated by another row (or column).

Rules:

1. If all the elements of a column (say ith column) are greater than or equal to the corresponding elements of any other column (say jth column), then ith column is dominated by the jth column. The ith column is hence removed from the pay-off table.
2. If all the elements of a row (say ith row) are greater than or equal to the corresponding elements of any other row (say jth row), then ith row dominates the jth row. The jth row is hence removed from the pay-off table.
3. A pure strategy of a player may also be dominated if it is inferior to some convex combination of two or more pure strategies in particular, inferior to the average of two or more pure strategies. In that case we delete that pure strategy.
4. It is also possible that a particular row (column) dominates the average of two other rows (columns). In that case, we will delete any one row (column), which was involved in finding the average.

The rows and columns once deleted will never be used for determining the optimum strategy for both the players.

It is always advisable to apply the rules of dominance to a game before evaluating it, so that the size of the game can be reduced.

Note: Dominance principles discussed above are used when the pay-off matrix is a profit matrix for the player whose strategies are listed in rows and a loss matrix for the player whose strategies are listed in columns. Otherwise the principles get reversed.

EXAMPLE 18.10: Reduce the following game as far as possible and then solve it.

		Player B			
		B_1	B_2	B_3	B_4
	A_1	–1	2	3	0
Player A	A_2	–4	–1	–1	0
	A_3	–1	1	1	–4
	A_4	4	–1	2	–7

We search for the saddle point if it is there at all. For that, we find the minimax and the maximin values.

		Player B				
		B_1	B_2	B_3	B_4	*Row minima*
	A_1	–1	2	3	0	–1
Player A	A_2	–4	–1	–1	0	–4
	A_3	–1	1	1	–4	–1 Maximin
	A_4	4	–1	2	–7	–7
Column maxima		4	2	3	0 Minimax	

Clearly, we can see that there is no saddle point. So, the solution of the game V has to be such that $-1 \le V \le 0$.

We now see if we can reduce the size of the game to facilitate solving the game by mixed strategy formulas discussed earlier.

All the elements of a first row are greater than or equal to the corresponding elements of the third row. So A_1 dominates A_3. So we remove A_3 from the matrix.

	B_1	B_2	B_3	B_4
A_1	–1	2	3	0
A_2	–4	–1	–1	0
A_4	4	–1	2	–7

All the elements of a third column are greater than or equal to the corresponding elements of the second column. So B_2 dominates B_3. So we remove B_3 from the matrix.

	B_1	B_2	B_4
A_1	–1	2	0
A_2	–4	–1	0
A_4	4	–1	–7

All the elements of a first row are greater than or equal to the corresponding elements of the second row. So A_1 dominates A_2. So we remove A_2 from the matrix.

	B_1	B_2	B_4
A_1	–1	2	0
A_4	4	–1	–7

All the elements of a second column are greater than or equal to the corresponding elements of the third column. So B_4 dominates B_2. So we remove B_2 from the matrix.

	B_1	B_4
A_1	–1	0
A_4	4	–7

Now we see that the game cannot be reduced any further. We can solve this resultant game by any of the mixed strategy methods mentioned above.

The pay-off matrix with oddments is given below.

		Player B		
		B_1	B_2	
Player A	A_1	–1	0	**11**
	A_2	4	–7	**1**
		7	**5**	

The sum of the oddments of the rows and columns is the same, here 12.

Hence, the optimal strategies of the two players are (use formula given above): A(11/12,1/12), B(7/12,5/12) and the value of the game $V = \dfrac{-1 \times 11 + 4 \times 1}{1 + 11} = \dfrac{-7}{12}$

EXAMPLE 18.11:

		Player B		
		B_1	B_2	B_3
Player A	A_1	3	–2	4
	A_2	–1	4	2
	A_3	2	2	6

We search for the saddle point if it is there at all. For that, we find the minimax and the maximin values.

		Player B				
		B_1	B_2	B_3	*Row minima*	
Player A	A_1	3	–2	4	–2	
	A_2	–1	4	2	–1	
	A_3	2	2	6	**2**	Maximin
Column maxima		**3**	4	6		
		Minimax				

Clearly, we can see that there is no saddle point. So, the solution of the game V has to be such that $2 \le V \le 3$.

We now see if we can reduce the size of the game to facilitate solving the game by mixed strategy formulas discussed earlier.

All the elements of a third column are greater than or equal to the corresponding elements of the first column. So B_1 dominates B_3. So we remove B_3 from the matrix.

	B_1	B_2
A_1	3	–2
A_2	–1	4
A_3	2	2

The average of the first and the second rows gives (1, 1). We see that this average is dominated by the third row. So, we can delete either of the first two rows. Deleting the first row gives

	B_1	B_2
A_2	–1	4
A_3	2	2

We now see that here we find a saddle point (A_3, B_1) for the game and $V = 2$.

If we would have deleted the second row instead of the first, we would have obtained

	B_1	B_2
A_1	3	–2
A_3	2	2

In this case also, we would have obtained a saddle point (A_3, B_2) and $V = 2$.

EXAMPLE 18.12: Show that dominance occurs in the pay-off matrix of a 2×2 game if and only if there is a saddle point.

Consider the game whose pay-off matrix is

		Player B	
		B_1	B_2
Player A	A_1	a	b
	A_2	c	d

Suppose A_1 is dominated by A_2. Then, $a \le c$ and $b \le d$ (in fact, at both these places there cannot be = sign, otherwise the two strategies will coincide).

Now, if we consider the column maximum, then both the elements c and d are the largest elements in their respective columns. Now, if in the second row, the minimum is c, then there is a saddle point or if d is minimum, then also there is a saddle point.

Similarly, we can show that if A_2 is dominated by A_1, then there is a saddle point in the first row.

Similarly, we can prove the existence of a saddle point in case of column dominance.

Conversely, suppose there is a saddle point in the matrix at the element d.

Then this is the least in the second row and the greatest in the second column.

$$b \le d \le c$$

Now, if in the first row, minimum is b, then B_2 dominates B_1. Suppose in the first row the minimum is a, i.e.

$$a \le b$$

Now, if in the first column, maximum is a, i.e.

$$c \le a$$

Combining all,

$$a \le b \le d \le c \le a$$

It shows that

$$a = b = d = c$$

Thus, in this case dominance occurs.

Now if in the first column, maximum is c, then $a \le c$. Thus in this case A_2 dominates A_1 and hence the result.

Similarly, we can show the occurrence of dominance taking the saddle point at other places of the matrix.

18.8 SOLUTION OF GAME BY MATRIX METHOD

The optimal strategy mixture and the value of a mixed strategy game with square pay-off matrices can be obtained by the matrix method. Consider a standard square pay-off matrix for a mixed strategy game.

Step 1: Compute the adjoint matrix *Adj* of the given pay-off matrix.

Step 2: Compute the cofactor matrix *Cof.*

Step 3: Compute the matrix $D = (1\ 1)\ (Adj)\ (1\ 1)$

Step 4: Optimal strategy for player A = [(1 1) (Adj)]/D

Step 5: Optimal strategy for player B = [(1 1) (*Cof*)]/*D*

Step 6: Value of the game = Row matrix of A's optimal strategies × Pay-off matrix × Column matrix of B's optimal strategies

For games with sizes greater than 2 × 2, sometimes this method gives a solution with negative probabilities. It is advisable to solve the game by this method after reducing it to a 2 × 2 matrix.

EXAMPLE 18.13:

		Player B	
		B_1	B_2
Player A	A_1	8	18
	A_2	16	9

First we calculate $Adj = \begin{matrix} 9 & -18 \\ -16 & 8 \end{matrix}$

and $\quad Cof = \begin{matrix} 9 & -16 \\ -18 & 8 \end{matrix}$

Now,
$$D = (1\ 1)\begin{pmatrix} 9 & -18 \\ -16 & 8 \end{pmatrix}(1\ 1)$$
$$= -17$$

Optimal strategy for player
$$A = \frac{(1\ 1)(Adj)}{D}$$
$$= \frac{(-7 - 10)}{-17}$$
$$= \begin{pmatrix} \frac{7}{17} & \frac{10}{17} \end{pmatrix}$$

i.e. $p_1 = 7/17$ and $p_2 = 10/17$

Optimal strategy for player
$$B = \frac{(1\ 1)(Cof)}{D}$$
$$= \frac{(-9 - 18)}{-17}$$
$$= \begin{pmatrix} \frac{9}{17} & \frac{8}{17} \end{pmatrix}$$

i.e. $q_1 = 9/17$ and $q_2 = 8/17$

Value of the game = Row matrix of A's optimal strategies × Pay-off matrix × Column matrix of B's optimal strategies

$$= \begin{pmatrix} \frac{7}{17} & \frac{10}{17} \end{pmatrix}\begin{pmatrix} 8 & 16 \\ 16 & 9 \end{pmatrix}\begin{pmatrix} \frac{9}{17} \\ \frac{8}{17} \end{pmatrix}$$

$$= \frac{216}{17}$$

18.9 SOLUTION OF A TWO PERSON ZERO-SUM 2 × *n* GAME

Now we shall consider the solution of games where either of the players has only two strategies available. When player A, for example, has only two strategies to choose from and player B has n, the game shall be of the order $2 \times n$, whereas in case B has only two strategies available to him and A has m strategies, the game shall be a $m \times 2$. If a game has a saddle point or it is reducible to a 2×2 game by dominance, then it can be solved easily. But if neither of the things happen, then it can be shown that there exists for the player with more than two courses of action, a combination of just two out of his actions, which gives his best strategy. Thus, there will be a 2×2 sub game within the given $2 \times n$ game which provides the solution of the given $2 \times n$ game. Therefore, before solving the game, we need to identify this 2×2 sub game. For this we write all 2×2 sub games and determine the value of each 2×2 sub game in turn.

EXAMPLE 18.14:

		Player B		
		B_1	B_2	B_3
Player A	A_1	–4	3	–1
	A_2	6	–4	–2

The saddle point does not exist and the dominance principles also cannot help.
We consider all 2×2 sub games as follows:

Sub game (1)

		B	
		B_1	B_2
A	A_1	–4	3
	A_2	6	–4

No saddle point exists. The value of the game using the mixed strategy formula is 2/17.

Sub game (2)

		B	
		B_1	B_2
A	A_1	–4	–1
	A_2	6	–2

No saddle point exists. The value of the game using the mixed strategy formula is –14/11.

Sub game (3)

		B	
		B_1	B_2
A	A_1	3	–1
	A_2	–4	–2

The saddle point exists and the value of the game turns out to be –1.

Now, since it is player B who has to decide about his courses of action, he will select that pair of strategies corresponding to the 2 × 2 sub game whose value is least out of all possible values. Thus, by using B_1 and B_3, B can prevent A to gain more than (–14/11). Hence sub game (2) provides the solution to the given original 2 × 3 game.

Solving the sub game completely gives A(8/11,3/11), B(1/11,0,10/11) and V = (–14/11).

The above method is equally good for the game in which player A has more than two courses of action. However, in that case A will select that pair of courses of actions corresponding to the 2 × 2 sub game whose value is greatest out of all the values.

18.10 GRAPHICAL METHOD FOR SOLVING A 2 × N OR M × 2 GAME

Now we shall consider the solution of games where either of the players has only two strategies available. When player A, for example, has only two strategies to choose from and player B has n, the game shall be of the order 2 × n, whereas in case B has only two strategies available to him and A has m strategies, the game shall be a m × 2.

Optimal strategies for both the players assign non-zero probabilities to the same number of pure strategies. Therefore, if one player has only two strategies, the other will also use the same number of strategies. Hence, this method is useful in finding out which of the two strategies can be used. Consider the following 2 × n pay-off matrix of a game without saddle point.

		Player B					Prob. for A
		B_1	B_2	B_3	…	B_n	
Player A	A_1	a_{11}	a_{12}	a_{13}	…	a_{1n}	p_1
	A_2	a_{21}	a_{22}	a_{23}	…	a_{2n}	p_2 (= 1 – p_1)
Prob. for B		q_1	q_2	q_3	…	q_n	

Player A has two strategies A_1 and A_2 with the chance of choice of both being p_1 and p_2 such that $p_1 + p_2 = 1$, and $p_1, p_2 \geq 0$.

For each move taken by B, the expected pay-off for A can be computed as follows.

Strategy adopted by B	*Expected pay-off for A*
B_1	$E_1(p_1) = a_{11}p_1 + a_{21}p_2$
B_2	$E_2(p_1) = a_{12}p_1 + a_{22}p_2$
⋮	⋮
B_n	$E_n(p_1) = a_{1n}p_1 + a_{2n}p_2$

The objective of player A is to select p_1 and p_2 in such a way that his expected pay-off is the maximum of all his minimum expected pay-offs.

This is done by plotting the lines $E_1, E_2, \ldots, E_n$ after simplifying them in terms of p_1 by using the relation $p_2 = 1 - p_1$.

To plot this line, we draw two parallel axes one unit distance apart and mark a scale on each. The two lines represent two strategies of A. The distance between these lines is taken as unity because the value of probability p_1 cannot be more than 1. Also $p_1 = 0$ is taken at the point O on A's strategy A_1, which is the vertical standing line on the left and p_1 increases as we move from left to right. $p_1 = 1$ on the line to the right.

We now pick up the line E_1, and plot the points obtained by putting $p_1 = 0$ or 1, on the two lines. We now join these points. Likewise, we plot all the lines.

Now A chooses a suitable value of p_1 to maximize his guaranteed gain. To identify this point that maximizes the minimum expected gain to A, we bound the figure so formed from below. The highest point on the lower boundary of these lines will give the maximum expected pay-off among the minimum expected pay-offs on the lower boundary and the optimum value of probability p_1 and hence of p_2.

The intersecting lines at the obtained point will correspond to the course of action taken by B. Likewise, we end up getting the probabilities with which A plays his strategies and the optimal strategies that B chooses. We thereby obtain a reduced 2 × 2 game which can be solved by the analytic method discussed earlier.

This method is equally good when player B has only 2 and A has more than two courses of action, i.e. when the matrix is $m \times 2$. However, in that case we plot the graph of B's loss or A's gain against the value of q_1 and q_2, and bound the figure from above (Minimizing B's maximum losses). The lowest point on this boundary shows the two courses of action which A should use and the probability values of q_1 and hence q_2.

EXAMPLE 18.15: Solve the following game graphically.

		Player B		
		B_1	B_2	B_3
Player A	A_1	–4	3	–1
	A_2	6	–4	–2

We search for the saddle point if it is there at all. For that we find the minimax and the maximin values.

		Player B			
		B_1	B_2	B_3	*Row minima*
Player A	A_1	–4	3	–1	–4 Maximin
	A_2	6	–4	–2	–4 Maximin
column maxima		6	3	–1	
				Minimax	

Clearly, we can see that there is no saddle point. So, the solution of the game V has to be such that $-4 \le V \le -1$.

Player A has two strategies A_1 and A_2 with the chance of choice of both being p_1 and p_2 such that $p_1 + p_2 = 1$, and $p_1, p_2 \ge 0$.

For each move taken by B, the expected pay-off for A can be computed as follows.

Strategy adopted by B	*Expected pay-off for A*
B_1	$E_1(p_1) = (-4)p_1 + 6p_2$
B_2	$E_2(p_1) = 3p_1 + (-4)p_2$
B_3	$E_3(p_1) = (-1)p_1 + (-2)p_2$

Using $p_1 + p_2 = 1$, i.e. $p_2 = 1 - p_1$ in the above equations we get

Strategy adopted by B	*Expected pay-off for A*
B_1	$E_1(p_1) = 6 - 10p_1$
B_2	$E_2(p_1) = -4 + 7p_1$
B_3	$E_3(p_1) = -2 + p_1$

Now, we plot these lines and obtain the following graph.

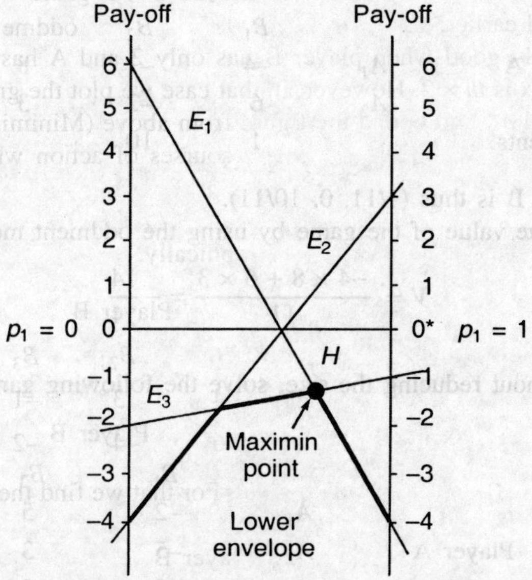

We have drawn the expected pay-off lines for A, the maximin player. Since A is a maximin player, he tries to maximize his minimum gains shown by the lower envelope formed by his expected pay-off lines drawn. The highest point in the lower envelope is formed by the intersection of the lines $E_1(p_1)$ and $E_3(p_1)$. So the two moves that B needs to use are B_1 and B_3. The probabilities can be found out by equating the two equations of these lines as shown below.

$$E_1(p_1) = E_3(p_1)$$

$$6 - 10p_1 = -2 + p_1$$

$$11p_1 = 8$$

$$p_1 = 8/11$$

and hence $p_2 = 3/11$.

The value of the game can be found by putting the value of p_1 in either $E_1(p_1)$ or $E_5(p_1)$. Thus the value of the game is

$$V = E_1\left(\frac{8}{11}\right) = 6 - 10\left(\frac{8}{11}\right) = -\frac{14}{11}$$

Now to find the optimal strategies of player B, we take the two moves obtained for B from the graph, i.e. B_1 and B_3 and form the 2 × 2 pay-off matrix as follows and solve it by the mixed strategy formulas discussed earlier. This is shown below.

		Player B	
		B_1	B_3
Player A	A_1	–4	–1
	A_2	6	–2

		Player B		
		B_1	B_2	oddments
Player A	A_1	–4	–1	8
	A_2	6	–2	3
oddments		1	10	

The optimum strategy for B is thus (1/11, 0, 10/11).

We can also verify the value of the game by using the oddment method formula

$$V = \frac{-4 \times 8 + 6 \times 3}{11} = -\frac{14}{11}$$

EXAMPLE 18.16: Without reducing the size, solve the following game graphically.

		Player B	
		B_1	B_2
	A_1	–2	5
Player A	A_2	–5	3
	A_3	0	–2
	A_4	–3	0
	A_5	1	–4

Clearly, we can see that the game does not have a saddle point.

Player B has two strategies B_1 and B_2 with the chance of choice of both being q_1 and q_2 such that $q_1 + q_2 = 1$, and $q_1, q_2 \geq 0$.

For each move taken by A, the expected pay-off for B can be computed as follows.

Strategy adopted by A	*Expected pay-off for B*
A_1	$E_1(p_1) = -2q_1 + 5q_2$
A_2	$E_2(p_1) = -5q_1 + 3q_2$
A_3	$E_3(p_1) = 0q_1 + -2q_2$
A_4	$E_4(p_1) = -3q_1 + 0q_2$
A_5	$E_5(p_1) = 1q_1 + -4q_2$

Using $q_1 + q_2 = 1$, i.e. $q_2 = 1 - q_1$ in the above equations we get,

Strategy adopted by A	*Expected pay-off for B*
A_1	$E_1(q_1) = 5 - 7q_1$
A_2	$E_2(q_1) = 3 - 8q_1$
A_3	$E_3(q_1) = -2 + 2q_1$
A_4	$E_4(q_1) = -3q_1$
A_5	$E_5(q_1) = -4 + 5q_1$

Now, we plot these lines and obtain the following graph.

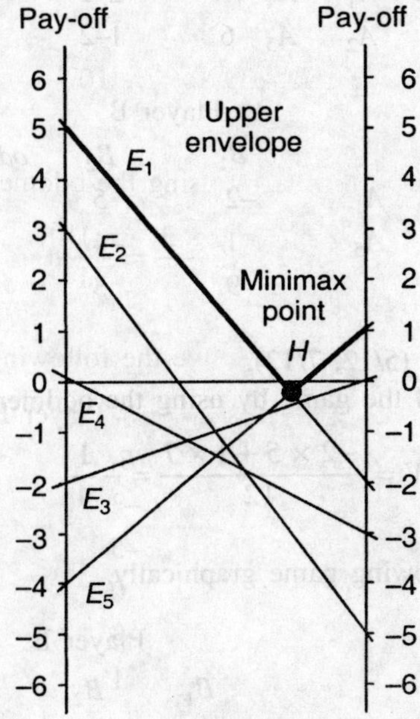

We have drawn the expected pay-off lines for B, the minimax player. Since B is a minimax player, he tries to minimize his maximum losses shown by the upper envelope formed by his expected pay-off lines drawn. The lowest point in the upper envelope is formed by the intersection of the lines $E_1(q_1)$ and $E_5(q_1)$. So, these are the two moves that A needs to use. The probabilities can be found out by equating the two equations of these lines as shown below.

$$E_1(q_1) = E_5(q_1)$$

$$5 - 7q_1 = -4 + 5q_1$$

$$12q_1 = 9$$

$$q_1 = 3/4$$

and hence $q_2 = 1/4$.

The value of the game can be found by putting the value of q_1 in either $E_1(q_1)$ or $E_5(q_1)$. Thus the value of the game is

$$V = E_1\left(\frac{3}{4}\right) = 5 - 7\left(\frac{3}{4}\right) = -\frac{1}{4}$$

Now to find the optimal strategies of player A, we take the two moves obtained for A from the graph, i.e. A_1 and A_5 and form the 2 × 2 pay-off matrix as follows and solve it by the mixed strategy formulas discussed earlier. This is shown below:

		Player B	
		B_1	B_2
Player A	A_1	–2	5
	A_5	1	–4

		Player B		
		B_1	B_2	*oddments*
Player A	A_1	–2	5	5
	A_5	1	–4	7
oddments		9	3	

The optimum strategy for A is thus (5/12, 7/12).

We can also verify the value of the game by using the oddment method formula

$$V = \frac{-2 \times 5 + 1 \times 7}{12} = -\frac{1}{4}$$

EXAMPLE 18.17: Solve the following game graphically.

		Player B		
		B_1	B_2	B_3
Player A	A_1	6	4	3
	A_2	2	4	8

We search for the saddle point if it is there at all. For that we find the minimax and the maximin values.

		Player B				
		B_1	B_2	B_3	*Row minima*	
Player A	A_1	6	4	3	**3**	Maximin
	A_2	2	4	8	2	
column maxima		6	**4**	8		
			Minimax			

Clearly, we can see that there is no saddle point. So, the solution of the game V has to be such that $3 \le V \le 4$.

Player A has two strategies A_1 and A_2 with the chance of choice of both being p_1 and p_2 such that $p_1 + p_2 = 1$, and $p_1, p_2 \geq 0$.

For each move taken by B, the expected pay-off for A can be computed as follows.

Strategy adopted by B	*Expected pay-off for A*
B_1	$E_1(p_1) = 6p_1 + 2p_2$
B_2	$E_2(p_1) = 4p_1 + 4p_2$
B_3	$E_3(p_1) = 3p_1 + 8p_2$

Using $p_1 + p_2 = 1$, i.e. $p_2 = 1 - p_1$ in the above equations we get

Strategy adopted by B	*Expected pay-off for A*
B_1	$E_1(p_1) = 2 + 4p_1$
B_2	$E_2(p_1) = 4$
B_3	$E_3(p_1) = 8 - 5p_1$

Now, we plot these lines and obtain the following graph.

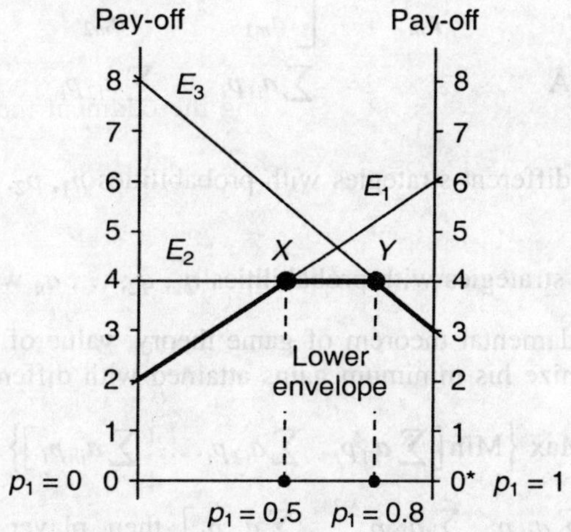

The shaded region in the graph shows the lines drawn for the expected pay-off for A. Since we require the highest point in the lower envelope, we observe that there is no highest point here. Instead, we get a portion *XY* of the lower envelope, which is a linear segment which corresponds to the value 4. Hence, 4 is the value of the game. The optimal value of the probabilities associated with the choice of strategies of A lies on the probability axis and corresponds to this linear segment *XY* obtained on the lower envelope. To get these points, we equate E_1, E_2 and then equate E_2, E_3. We get the points 0.5 and 0.8. So, any pair $(p_1, 1 - p_1)$, where $0.5 \leq p_1 \leq 0.8$, is an optimal strategy for A. Thus, A has infinite number of mixed optimal strategies.

By solving 2×2 sub-games formed by two different pairs of B's strategies, it can be shown that for B, his optimal strategy is his pure strategy B_2.

It is clear, then, that the optimal strategy for B would be (0,1,0). Thus, we have $A\ (p, 1-p)$, $0.5 \leq p \leq 0.8$ and B (0,1,0) and $V = 4$.

18.11 LINEAR PROGRAMMING METHOD FOR THE SOLUTIONS OF GAME

It is difficult to solve a game problem with a $m \times n$ matrix having neither a saddle point nor any dominant row or column. Also, the graphical method can be applied only if m or n is 2. We need to determine:

- m probabilities p_i (i = 1, 2, ..., m) for player A, with which he must mix his m-pure strategies to get his mixed strategy.
- n probabilities q_j (j = 1, 2, ..., n) for player B, with which he must mix his n-pure strategies to get his mixed strategy.
- Optimum value of the game.

The two person zero-sum game can be solved by linear programming.
Consider the following pay-off matrix:

$$\begin{array}{llcccc} & & & & \text{Player B} & \\ & & q_1 & q_2 & \cdots & q_n \\ \text{Player A} & \begin{array}{c} p_1 \\ p_2 \\ \vdots \\ p_m \end{array} & \multicolumn{4}{c}{\left[\begin{array}{cccc} a_{11} & a_{12} & \cdots & a_{1n} \\ a_{21} & a_{22} & \cdots & a_{2n} \\ \vdots & & & \\ a_{m1} & a_{m2} & \cdots & a_{mn} \end{array}\right]} \\ \text{Expected gain to A} & & \sum a_{i1} p_i & \sum a_{i2} p_i & \cdots & \sum a_{in} p_i \end{array}$$

Let player A play with different strategies with probabilities $p_1, p_2, \ldots, p_m$ with $\sum_{i=1}^{m} p_i = 1$ and player B play with different strategies with probabilities $q_1, q_2, \ldots, q_n$ with $\sum_{i=1}^{n} q_j = 1$. Let V be the value of the game. (By fundamental theorem of game theory, value of the game exists.)

Player A tries to maximize his minimum gains attained with different moves of B,

i.e. $$\text{Max}\left\{\text{Min}\left[\sum a_{i1} p_i,\ \sum a_{i2} p_i, \ldots, \sum a_{in} p_i\right]\right\}.$$

If we take $V = \text{Min}\left[\sum a_{i1} p_i,\ \sum a_{i2} p_i, \ldots, \sum a_{in} p_i\right]$ then, player A wants to select a set of $p_i(i = 1, 2, \ldots, m)$ such that he can maximize V. Now to obtain the values of p_i, the value of the game to player A for all strategies by player B must be at least equal to V. Hence, we have a set of $(n + 1)$–constraints as follows:

$$\sum a_{i1} p_i \geq v,$$

$$\sum a_{i2} p_i \geq v$$

$$\vdots$$

$$\sum a_{in} p_i \geq v$$

with $\sum_{i=1}^{m} p_i = 1$ and $p_i \geq 0$, i = 1, 2, ..., m.

Writing the problem from A's point of view, we have not yet formed a standard LPP, because V need not be non-negative. To overcome this difficulty, we assume that V is positive. For $V > o$, it is enough that all the elements of the pay-off matrix are positive.
(*Note:* If there is a negative entry in the pay-off table, a constant M, which is equal to one more than the absolute value of the maximum of the negative values of the pay-off matrix, is added to each of the entries in the pay-off matrix. After solving the problem, the true value of the game is obtained by subtracting M from the value of the game.)

Now let us divide the above inequalities by V (positive) and formulate the LPP from A's point of view:

Maximize V

subject to the constraints:

$$\frac{\sum a_{i1} p_i}{V} \geq 1,$$

$$\frac{\sum a_{i2} p_i}{V} \geq 1$$

$$\vdots$$

$$\frac{\sum a_{in} p_i}{V} \geq 1$$

with $\sum_{i=1}^{m} \frac{p_i}{V} = \frac{1}{V}$ and $(p_i/V) \geq 0$, $i = 1, 2, \ldots, m$.

Now suppose $p_i/V = x_i$, $i = 1, 2, \ldots, m$.

Also $$\text{Max } V = \text{Min}\left(\frac{1}{V}\right)$$

$$= \text{Min}\left(\frac{p_1}{V} + \frac{p_2}{V} + \cdots + \frac{p_m}{V}\right)$$

Thus, we can write the above LPP as:

$$\text{Minimize } Z_A = x_1 + x_2 + \cdots + x_m$$

subject to

$$\sum a_{i1} x_i \geq 1,$$

$$\sum a_{i2} x_i \geq 1$$

$$\vdots$$

$$\sum a_{in} x_i \geq 1$$

with $x_i \geq 0$, $i = 1, 2, \ldots, m$.

The values of p_i and V are obtained using the relation, $V = 1/Z_A$ and $p_i = Vx_i$, $i = 1, 2, \ldots, m$. The problem from B's point of view is written as follows.

We know that every LPP has its dual problem associated with it. If we write the dual of the above LPP, it will be in the favour of player B. As a matter of fact, it is always advisable to write the problem in favour of player B because in that case it becomes a standard LPP with maximization and all constraints with ≤ sign.

$$\text{Max. } Z_B = y_1 + y_2 + \cdots + y_n$$

subject to

$$\sum a_{1j}y_j \le 1,$$
$$\sum a_{2j}y_j \le 1$$
$$\vdots$$
$$\sum a_{mj}y_j \le 1$$

with $y_i = 0, j = 1, 2, \ldots, n$ where $y_j = q_j/V$, $\sum q_j = 1$, V is positive and the values of q_j and V are obtained using the relation, $V = 1/Z_B$ and $q_j = Vy_j, j = 1, 2, \ldots, n$.

Algorithm to solve the game by converting it to a LPP: The following steps should be performed.

Step 1: For the game, find the maximin value $\underline{v}$.

Step 2: For the game, find the minimax value $\overline{v}$.

Step 3: If $\underline{v} = \overline{v}$ then the game has a saddle point, otherwise the value of the game v is such that $\underline{v} \le v \le \overline{v}$.

Step 4: If $\underline{v} < 0$, then add a constant equal to one more than the absolute value of the maximum of the negative values of the pay-off matrix, to all entries of the matrix.

Step 5: Write the LPP from the point of view of player B. (One whose strategies are given in columns.) So it is maximization LPP with all constraints of ≤ sign.

Step 6: Apply the simplex algorithm on the LPP

$$\text{Max. } Z_B = y_1 + y_2 + \cdots + y_n = (1/v)$$

subject to $AY \le 1$ with $Y \ge 0$ where A is pay-off matrix and $Y = [y_1, y_2, \ldots, y_n]^T$

Step 7: (i) Find v by using $v = 1/Z_B$.

(ii) Find q_j by using $q_j = vy_j, j = 1, 2, \ldots, n$

(iii) If you have added a constant to the pay-off matrix's entries earlier then modify v by using

value of original game = (value of modified game) – (constant)

EXAMPLE 18.18: Solve the following game.

Player B

Player A		B_1	B_2	B_3
	A_1	2	–2	3
	A_2	–3	5	–1

Step 1 and *Step 2:* First of all let us check for the saddle point.

Player B

		B_1	B_2	B_3	*Row minima*
Player A	A_1	2	–2	3	**–2** Maximin
	A_2	–3	5	–1	–3
Column maxima		**2**	5	3	
		Minimax			

Clearly, the game does not have a saddle point.

Step 3: The value of the game V will be such that $-2 \le V \le 2$.

Step 4: Since $\underline{v} < 0$, i.e. there are negative entries in the table, we add a constant equal to one more than the absolute value of the most negative entry, here –3.

So we add a constant 4 to all the entries and the resultant game matrix becomes

		Player B		
		B_1	B_2	B_3
Player A	A_1	6	2	7
	A_2	1	9	3

Step 5: Now we formulate the LPP with respect to player B.

Let q_1, q_2, and q_3 be the probabilities with which player B plays his strategies.

And let $x_i = q_i/V$, $i = 1, 2, 3$

$$\text{Maximize } Z_B = x_1 + x_2 + x_3$$

Subject to

$$6x_1 + 2x_2 + 7x_3 \le 1$$

$$x_1 + 9x_2 + 3x_3 \le 1$$

with $x_1, x_2, x_3 \ge 0$.

Adding the necessary slack variables we have,

$$\text{Maximize } Z_B = x_1 + x_2 + x_3 + 0s_1 + 0s_2$$

Subject to

$$6x_1 + 2x_2 + 7x_3 + s_1 = 1$$

$$x_1 + 9x_2 + 3x_3 + s_2 = 1$$

with $x_1, x_2, x_3, s_1, s_2, s_3 \ge 0$.

Step 6: Solution by the simplex algorithm.

		c_j	1	1	1	0	0	
c_B	B	x_B	x_1	x_2	x_3	s_1	s_2	RR
0	s_1	1	6	2	7	1	0	1/2
0	s_2	1	1	9	3	0	1	1/9 →
z	0	$c_j - z_j$	1	1 ↑	1	0	0	
0	s_1	7/9	52/9	0	19/3	1	–2/9	7/52 →
1	x_2	1/9	1/9	1	1/3	0	1/9	1
z	1/9	$c_j - z_j$	8/9 ↑	0	2/3	0	–1/9	
1	x_1	7/52	1	0	57/52	9/52	–2/52	
1	x_2	5/52	0	1	11/52	–1/52	3/26	
z	12/52	$c_j - z_j$	0	0	–4/13	–2/13	–1/13	

Step 7: The optimal solution is: $x_1 = 7/52$, $x_2 = 5/52$, $x_3 = 0$ and $Z_B = 12/52 = 1/V$

hence $$V = \frac{1}{Z_B}$$

$$= \frac{52}{12}$$

Thus, the probabilities $$q_1 = V \times x_1 = \frac{7}{12}$$

$$q_2 = V \times x_2 = \frac{5}{12}$$

$$q_3 = V \times x_3 = V \times 0 = 0$$

Now, at last the value of the original game is obtained by subtracting the constant 4 that we added initially to all the entries of the game matrix.

Thus, the value of the original game = $\left(\frac{52}{12}\right) - 4$

$$\text{original } V = \frac{1}{3}$$

The optimal strategy values for player A can be found out directly from the simplex table. They are the absolute values of the values corresponding to s_1, s_2 in the last simplex table. They are:

$$y_1 = |s_1| = \frac{2}{13}, \quad y_2 = |s_2| = \frac{1}{13}$$

and hence the probabilities associated with the choice of the strategies for A are:

$p_1 = V \times y_1 = (52/12)\ (2/13) = 2/3$ (Please use the value of the game obtained from the simplex table and not that we modified.)

$$p_2 = V \times y_2 = (52/12)\ (1/13) = 1/3$$

Thus, A(2/3, 1/3), B(7/12, 5/12, 0) and $V = 1/3$.

Note: This value of the game is for player B. For player A it is –1/3.

EXAMPLE 18.19: Solve the following game.

		Player B		
		B_1	B_2	B_3
Player A	A_1	1	–1	–1
	A_2	–1	–1	3
	A_3	–1	2	–1

Step 1 and *Step 2:* First of all let us check for the saddle point.

		Player B			
		B_1	B_2	B_3	*Row minima*
Player A	A_1	1	–1	–1	**–1** Maximin
	A_2	–1	–1	3	**–1** Maximin
	A_3	–1	2	–1	**–1** Maximin
Column maxima		**1** Minimax	2	3	

Clearly, the game does not have a saddle point.

Step 3: The value of the game V will be such that $-1 \le V \le 1$.

Step 4: Since $\underline{v} < 0$, i.e. there are negative entries in the table we add a constant equal to one more than the absolute value of the most negative entry, here –1.

So we add a constant 2 to all the entries and the resultant game matrix becomes

		Player B		
		B_1	B_2	B_3
Player A	A_1	3	1	1
	A_2	1	1	5
	A_3	1	4	1

Step 5: Now we formulate the LPP with respect to player B.
Let q_1, q_2, and q_3 be the probabilities with which player B plays his strategies.
And let $x_i = q_i/V$.

Maximize $Z_B = x_1 + x_2 + x_3$

subject to

$$3x_1 + x_2 + x_3 \le 1$$
$$x_1 + x_2 + 5x_3 \le 1$$
$$x_1 + 4x_2 + x_3 \le 1$$

with $x_1, x_2, x_3 \ge 0$.

Adding the necessary slack variables we have,

Maximize $Z_B = x_1 + x_2 + x_3 + 0s_1 + 0s_2 + 0s_3$

Subject to

$$3x_1 + x_2 + x_3 + s_1 = 1$$
$$x_1 + x_2 + 5x_3 + s_2 = 1$$
$$x_1 + 4x_2 + x_3 + s_3 = 1$$

with $x_1, x_2, x_3, s_1, s_2, s_3 \ge 0$.

Step 6: Solution by the simplex algorithm.

		c_j	1	1	1	0	0	0	
c_B	B	x_B	x_1	x_2	x_3	s_1	s_2	s_3	RR
0	s_1	1	3	1	1	1	0	0	1/3 →
0	s_2	1	1	1	5	0	1	0	1
0	s_3	1	1	4	1	0	0	1	1
z	0	$c_j - z_j$	1 ↑	1	1	0	0	0	
1	x_1	1/3	1	1/3	1/3	1/3	0	0	1
0	s_2	2/3	0	2/3	14/3	–1/3	1	0	1
0	s_3	2/3	0	11/3	2/3	–1/3	0	1	2/11 →
z	1/3	$c_j - z_j$	0	2/3 ↑	2/3	–1/3	0	0	
1	x_1	3/11	1	0	3/11	4/11	0	–1/11	1
0	s_2	6/11	0	0	50/11	–3/11	1	–2/11	3/25 →
1	x_2	2/11	0	1	2/11	–1/11	0	3/11	1
z	5/11	$c_j - z_j$	0	0	6/11 ↑	–3/11	0	–2/11	
1	x_1	6/25	1	0	0	19/50	–3/50	–2/25	
1	x_3	3/25	0	1	0	–3/50	11/50	–1/25	
1	x_2	4/25	0	0	1	–2/25	–1/25	7/25	
z	13/25	$c_j - z_j$	0	0	0	–6/25	–3/25	–4/25	

Step 7: The optimal solution is: $x_1 = 6/25$, $x_2 = 4/25$, $x_3 = 3/25$ and $Z_B = 13/25 = 1/V$

hence
$$V = \frac{1}{Z_B}$$
$$= \frac{25}{13}$$

Thus, the probabilities
$$q_1 = V \times x_1 = \frac{6}{13}$$
$$q_2 = V \times x_2 = \frac{4}{13}$$
$$q_3 = V \times x_3 = \frac{3}{13}$$

Now, at last the value of the original game is obtained by subtracting the constant 2 that we added initially to all the entries of the game matrix.

$$\text{Thus, the value of the original game } = \frac{25}{13} - 2$$

$$\text{original } V = -\frac{1}{13}$$

The optimal strategy values for player A can be found out directly from the simplex table. They are the absolute values of the values corresponding to s_1, s_2, s_3 in the last simplex table. They are:

$$y_1 = |s_1| = \frac{6}{25},\ y_2 = |s_2| = \frac{3}{25},\ y_3 = |s_3| = \frac{4}{25}$$

and hence the probabilities associated with the choice of the strategies for A are:

$p_1 = V \times y_1 = (25/13)\ (6/25) = 6/13$ (Please use the value of the game obtained from the simplex table and not that we modified.)

$$p_2 = V \times y_2 = \left(\frac{25}{13}\right)\left(\frac{3}{25}\right) = \frac{3}{13}$$

$$p_1 = V \times y_3 = \left(\frac{25}{13}\right)\left(\frac{4}{25}\right) = \frac{4}{13}$$

Thus, A(6/13, 3/13, 4/13), B(6/13, 4/13, 3/13) and $V = -(1/13)$

Note: This value of the game is for player B. For player A it is 1/13.

18.12 ALGEBRAIC METHOD FOR SOLVING A GAME

The algebraic method for solving games is quite a lengthy one. Consider the standard pay-off matrix (a_{ij}), $i = 1, 2, \ldots, m$ and $j = 1, 2, \ldots, n$. Let player A play with different strategies with probabilities $p_1, p_2, \ldots, p_m$ with $\sum_{i=1}^{m} p_i = 1$ and player B play with different strategies with probabilities $q_1, q_2, \ldots,$ q_n with $\sum_{j=1}^{n} q_j = 1$. Let V be the value of the game. (By fundamental theorem of game theory, value of the game exists.)

Player A's expected gains when B uses his strategies $j = 1, 2, \ldots, n$ are

$$\sum a_{i1} p_i,\ \sum a_{i2} p_i,\ \ldots,\ \sum a_{in} p_i, \quad i = 1, 2, \ldots, m$$

Since A expects at least V, we have

$$\sum_{i=1}^{m} a_{ij} p_i \geq V,\ j = 1, 2, \ldots, n \qquad (1)$$

Similarly, by considering the losses to B when A uses his strategies $i = 1, 2, \ldots, m$, B expects the loss of at the most V. So we have

$$\sum_{j=1}^{n} a_{ij} q_j \leq V,\ i = 1, 2, \ldots, m \qquad (2)$$

Also we have,

$$\sum_{i=1}^{m} p_i = 1 \text{ and } \sum_{j=1}^{n} q_j = 1 \text{ and } p_i \geq 0 \text{ and } q_j \geq 0 \text{ for all } i \text{ and } j. \quad (3)$$

Thus, the problem is to find the values of $p_1, p_2, \ldots, p_m$ and $q_1, q_2, \ldots, q_n$ and V which satisfy (1), (2) and (3).

First of all, we treat all the inequalities of (1) and (2) as equations and then try to solve this system of equations with (3). If we get a solution satisfying (1), (2) and (3) simultaneously, then the problem is over. (2 × 2 games are always solvable in this way. But in higher order pay-off matrices, the system of equations may not be consistent). If the system of equations is inconsistent, then we conclude that at least one of the inequalities is a strict inequality. Now, we go on trying with one or more strict inequalities and remaining equations, to get a solution until we get the required solution. This calls for a trial and error method approach.

EXAMPLE 18.20:

		Player B		
		B_1	B_2	B_3
Player A	A_1	–1	2	1
	A_2	1	–2	2
	A_3	3	4	–3

We have the following inequalities after taking the probabilities for A and B as p_1, p_2, p_3 and q_1, q_2, q_3 and V as the value of the game.

$$-1p_1 + 1p_2 + 3p_3 \geq V \quad (1)$$

$$2p_1 - 2p_2 + 4p_3 \geq V \quad (2)$$

$$1p_1 + 2p_2 - 3p_3 \geq V \quad (3)$$

$$-1q_1 + 2q_2 + 1q_3 \leq V \quad (4)$$

$$1q_1 - 2q_2 + 2q_3 \leq V \quad (5)$$

$$3q_1 + 4q_2 - 3q_3 \leq V \quad (6)$$

$$p_1 + p_2 + p_3 = 1 \quad (7)$$

$$q_1 + q_2 + q_3 = 1 \quad (8)$$

$$p_1, p_2, p_3, q_1, q_2, q_3 \geq 0 \quad (9)$$

Firstly, we consider all the first six inequalities as equations. We have

$$-1p_1 + 1p_2 + 3p_3 = V \quad (10)$$

$$2p_1 - 2p_2 + 4p_3 = V \quad (11)$$

$$1p_1 + 2p_2 - 3p_3 = V \quad (12)$$

$$-1q_1 + 2q_2 + 1q_3 = V \quad (13)$$

$$1q_1 - 2q_2 + 2q_3 = V \quad (14)$$

$$3q_1 + 4q_2 - 3q_3 = V \quad (15)$$

$$p_1 + p_2 + p_3 = 1 \quad (16)$$

$$q_1 + q_2 + q_3 = 1 \quad (17)$$

Adding (10) and (12), we have $p_2 = (2/3)V$ and again adding 2 times of (10) in (11), we get $p_3 = (3/10)V$. Putting these values in any of the (10), (11), (12), we get $p_1 = (17/30)V$. Substituting all these in (16), we get $V = 15/23$. So, $p_1 = 17/46$, $p_2 = 10/23$, and $p_3 = 9/46$.

Now, putting this value of V in (13), (14), (15) and solving them, we get $q_1 = 7/23$, $q_2 = 6/23$, $q_3 = 10/23$. These values of q_1, q_2, q_3 also satisfy (17). Thus we have obtained a solution of this system of equations. The solution also satisfies (9).

EXAMPLE 18.21:

		Player B		
		B_1	B_2	B_3
Player A	A_1	1	–1	–1
	A_2	–1	–1	3
	A_3	–1	2	–1

We have the following inequalities after taking the probabilities for A and B as p_1, p_2, p_3 and q_1, q_2, q_3 and V as the value of the game.

$$1p_1 - 1p_2 - 1p_3 \geq V \tag{1}$$

$$-1p_1 - 1p_2 + 2p_3 \geq V \tag{2}$$

$$-1p_1 + 3p_2 - 1p_3 \geq V \tag{3}$$

$$1q_1 - 1q_2 - 1q_3 \leq V \tag{4}$$

$$-1q_1 - 1q_2 + 3q_3 \leq V \tag{5}$$

$$-1q_1 + 2q_2 - 1q_3 \leq V \tag{6}$$

$$p_1 + p_2 + p_3 = 1 \tag{7}$$

$$q_1 + q_2 + q_3 = 1 \tag{8}$$

$$p_1, p_2, p_3, q_1, q_2, q_3 \geq 0 \tag{9}$$

Firstly, we consider all the first six inequalities as equations. We have

$$1p_1 - 1p_2 - 1p_3 = V \tag{9}$$

$$-1p_1 - 1p_2 + 2p_3 = V \tag{10}$$

$$-1p_1 + 3p_2 - 1p_3 = V \tag{11}$$

$$1q_1 - 1q_2 - 1q_3 = V \tag{12}$$

$$-1q_1 - 1q_2 + 3q_3 = V \tag{13}$$

$$-1q_1 + 2q_2 - 1q_3 = V \tag{14}$$

Adding (9), (10) and (9), (11)

$$-2p_1 + p_3 = 2V \quad \text{and} \quad 2p_2 - 2p_3 = 2V \tag{15}$$

Again adding these, $-p_3 = 4$ V, i.e. $p_3 = -4V$. Using (15) and (9), we get $p_2 = -3V$ and hence $p_1 = -6V$. Putting these in (7), we get $-6V - 3V - 4V = 1$ or $V = -(1/13)$. Hence, we get $p_1 = 6/13$, $p_2 = 3/13$, $p_3 = 4/13$.

Putting $V = -(1/13)$ in (12), (13), (14) and then solving them in accordance with (8), we obtain $q_1 = 6/13$, $q_2 = 4/13$, $q_3 = 3/13$ and value of the game $V = 1/13$.

18.13 SOLUTION OF 3 × 3 GAMES WITH MIXED STRATEGY BY THE METHOD OF ODDMENTS

The game does not have a saddle point nor can it be reduced by dominance. We understand the procedure with the help of an example.

EXAMPLE 18.22:

		Player B		
		B_1	B_2	B_3
Player A	A_1	3	1	1
	A_2	1	1	5
	A_3	1	4	1

Step 1: Subtract each row from the row above, i.e. $A_1 - A_2$ and $A_2 - A_3$ and write the differences in the form of two successive rows below the rows of the pay-off matrix.

Step 2: Subtract each column from the column to its left, i.e. $B_1 - B_2$ and $B_2 - B_3$ and write the differences in the form of two successive columns to the right of the pay-off matrix.

	B_1	B_2	B_3	$B_1 - B_2$	$B_2 - B_3$
A_1	3	1	1	2	0
A_2	1	1	5	0	–4
A_3	1	4	1	–3	3
$A_1 - A_2$	2	0	–4		
$A_2 - A_3$	0	–3	4		

Step 3: Now calculate the oddments for the strategies as follows:

$$\text{Oddment for } A_1 = \text{determinant} \begin{vmatrix} 0 & -4 \\ -3 & 3 \end{vmatrix} = 12$$

$$\text{Oddment for } A_2 = \text{determinant} \begin{vmatrix} 2 & 0 \\ -3 & 3 \end{vmatrix} = 6$$

$$\text{Oddment for } A_3 = \text{determinant} \begin{vmatrix} 2 & 0 \\ 0 & -4 \end{vmatrix} = -8$$

$$\text{Oddment for } B_1 = \text{determinant} \begin{vmatrix} 0 & -4 \\ -3 & 4 \end{vmatrix} = 12$$

$$\text{Oddment for } B_2 = \text{determinant} \begin{vmatrix} 2 & -4 \\ 0 & 4 \end{vmatrix} = 8$$

$$\text{Oddment for } B_3 = \text{determinant} \begin{vmatrix} 2 & 0 \\ 0 & -3 \end{vmatrix} = -6$$

Step 4: Write the oddments neglecting the signs as shown below:

		B_1	B_2	B_3	*oddments*
Player A	A_1	3	1	1	12
	A_2	1	1	5	6
	A_3	1	4	1	8
Oddments		12	8	6	**26**

Step 5: Check that the sum of the oddments of both the players is the same. Here it is 26. This is a very important condition that needs to be satisfied if the game has to be solved by this method. It means that both the players are using up all their pure strategies.

If the two sums of the oddments happen to be different, then it means that the players are not using one of their pure strategies, i.e. either of p_i or q_j is zero in the final assignment of probabilities.

Step 6: We now calculate the probabilities in a manner similar to the oddment method for 2 × 2 mixed strategy games.

Each probability = Its respective oddment divided by the sum of the oddments of rows (or columns, both have the same sum)

Hence we get A (12/26, 6/26, 8/26) = (6/13, 3/13, 4/13)

B (12/26, 8/26, 6/26) = (6/13, 4/13, 3/13)

and the value of the game $V = [(3 \times 12) + (1 \times 6) + (1 \times 8)]/26 = 25/13$

Note: For a solution of 3 × 3 games with the mixed strategy by the method of oddments, none of the probability values turn out to be zero.

18.14 ITERATIVE METHOD FOR APPROXIMATE SOLUTION

In many practical problems, there is no need of determining an exact optimal solution of a game; it is sufficient to determine an approximate solution which gives an average gain close enough to the value of the game. One of the methods for determining approximate solution is the method of iteration. It is based on the following principle:

The two players are supposed to play the plays of the game iteratively and at each play the players choose a strategy which is best to himself or say worst to the opponent, in view of what the opponent has done up to that iteration.

Suppose player A (whose strategies are listed in rows) starts the game by selecting arbitrarily his strategy A_i.

Then player B selects that strategy B_j which is best for him or most unfavourable to A. To do this, B selects that strategy which corresponds to the least element in A's strategy A_i.

Now A selects that strategy which maximizes his average gain. To do this, A selects that strategy which corresponds to the largest element in B's strategy.

Now B responds to the pair of two strategies by A, by his strategy B_r which minimizes the average loss to him. To do this, B adds both the strategies of A and then selects that strategy out of his, which corresponds to the least element.

Again, A adds both the strategies of B and selects that strategy which corresponds to the greatest element in B's strategy.

In this way A and B play a series of plays. Finally, at any iteration for any player, a mixed strategy can be obtained by dividing the number of times the respective pure strategies are used, by the total number of iterations up to that stage. The method is very slow and requires many iterations. But it is useful for large games.

EXAMPLE 18.23:

		Player B		
		B_1	B_2	B_3
Player A	A_1	−1	2	1
	A_2	1	−2	2
	A_3	3	4	−3

We write the strategy of A below the matrix and circle the smallest element indicating the B's next strategy to be selected. Similarly, the strategy of B is written on the right of the matrix. Of B's strategy, the greatest element is circled indicating A's next strategy. In case of tie in selecting the strategy of any player, we will select the strategy different than previously used strategy.

		B													
		B_1	B_2	B_3											
	A_1	−1	2	1	1	2	(4)	(5)	4	(6)	5	6	7	(9)	4/10
A	A_2	1	−2	2	(2)	(4)	2	4	(5)	3	4	(6)	(8)	6	5/10
	A_3	3	4	−3	−3	−6	−2	−5	−2	2	(5)	2	−1	3	1/10
		3	4	(−3)											
		4	2	(−1)											
		5	(0)	1											
		4	2	(2)											
		(3)	4	3											
		4	(2)	5											
		(3)	4	6											
		6	8	(3)											
		7	6	(5)											
		8	(4)	7											
		2/10	3/10	5/10											

Probability of any strategy = No. of times it is used/Total no. of iterations

Ten iterations are showed here. A's best strategy based on these ten iterations is (4/10, 5/10, 1/10) and B's best strategy is (2/10, 3/10, 5/10)

Now,

The lower value of the game = (Min. element of the lowest row/Total no. of iterations)

$$= \frac{4}{10}$$

The upper value of the game = (Largest element in 10th column/Total no. of iterations)

$$= \frac{9}{10}$$

Thus, if V is the value of the game, then

$$\frac{4}{10} \le V \le \frac{9}{10}$$

The optimal solution to this particular problem is given elsewhere in this chapter (algebraic method). Note that, the strategies determined above are not too far from the optimal strategies. They can be made more and more closer to optimal strategies by increasing the number of iterations.

EXAMPLE 18.24:

		Player B			
		B_1	B_2	B_3	B_4
	A_1	2	3	–1	0
Player A	A_2	5	4	2	–2
	A_3	1	3	8	2

We arbitrarily start with strategy A_3 for A and go up to 10 iterations.

		B														
		B_1	B_2	B_3	B_4											
	A_1	8	–2	9	–3	2	2	2	2	2	2	2	4	6	8	0
A	A_2	6	5	6	8	(5)	3	1	–1	–3	–5	–7	–2	3	8	1/10
	A_3	–2	4	–9	5	1	(3)	(5)	(7)	(9)	(11)	(13)	(14)	(15)	(16)	9/10
		(1)	3	8	2											
		6	7	10	(3)											
		7	10	18	(2)											
		8	13	26	(4)											
		9	16	34	(6)											
		10	19	42	(8)											
		11	22	50	(10)											
		(12)	25	58	12											
		(13)	23	66	14											
		(14)	31	74	16											
		4/10	0	0	6/10											

Ten iterations are showed here. A's best strategy based on these ten iterations is (4/10, 0, 0, 6/10) and B's best strategy is (0, 1/10, 9/10).

Now,

The lower value of the game = (Min. element of the lowest row/Total no. of iterations)

$$= \frac{14}{10}$$

The upper value of the game = (Largest element in 10th column/Total no. of iterations)

$$= \frac{16}{10}$$

Thus, if V is the value of the game, then

$$\frac{14}{10} \leq V \leq \frac{16}{10}$$

Note: Game theory does not insist on how a game should be played, but only tells the procedure and principles by which the action should be selected. Thus, it is a decision theory useful in competitive situations. Further, the fundamental theorem of game theory assures us that there always exists a solution and the value of a rectangular game in terms of mixed strategies.

The solution of the game has the following property:

If one of the players adheres to his optimal strategy and the other one deviates from his optimal strategy, the deviating player can only decrease and cannot, in any case, increase his yield.

18.15 SUMMARY OF THE PROCEDURE TO SOLVE A GAME

1. Search for the saddle point.
2. If not, try to reduce the size of the game by the dominance principles.
3. For 2 × 2 game, use the mixed strategy formula or method of oddments.
4. For 2 × n or m × 2 games, use the graphical method, or the sub game method.
5. If games are bigger than 2 × 2, use the linear programming method.
6. For approximate solutions use the iterative method.

EXAMPLE 18.25: Solve the following game.

		Player B			
		B_1	B_2	B_3	B_4
	A_1	3	2	4	0
Player A	A_2	3	4	2	4
	A_3	4	2	4	0
	A_4	0	4	0	8

We search for the saddle point if it is there at all. For that, we find the minimax and the maximin values.

	B_1	B_2	B_3	B_4	Row minima
A_1	3	2	4	0	0
A_2	3	4	2	4	**2** Maximin
A_3	4	2	4	0	0
A_4	0	4	0	8	0
Column maxima	**4**	**4**	**4**	8	

Minimax

Clearly, we can see that there is no saddle point. So the solution of the game V has to be such that $2 \le V \le 4$.

We now see if we can reduce the size of the game to facilitate solving the game by mixed strategy formulas discussed earlier.

All the elements of the third row are greater than or equal to the corresponding elements of the first row. So A_1 is dominated by A_3. So we remove A_1 from the matrix.

	B_1	B_2	B_3	B_4
A_2	3	4	2	4
A_3	4	2	4	0
A_4	0	4	0	8

All the elements of the first column are greater than or equal to the corresponding elements of the third column. So B_1 is dominated by B_3. So we remove B_1 from the matrix.

	B_2	B_3	B_4
A_2	4	2	4
A_3	2	4	0
A_4	4	0	8

Now, the average of the second and the third columns gives (3 2 4). We see that if we compare this with the first column, then all the entries of the first column are greater than or equal to the corresponding elements of this average column. So, the average column dominates the first column. So, we remove B_2 from the matrix.

	B_3	B_4
A_2	2	4
A_3	4	0
A_4	0	8

Now, the average of the second and the third rows gives (2 4). We see that if we compare this with the first row, then all the entries of the first row are equal to the corresponding elements of this average row. So we can neglect the first row. So we remove A_2 from the matrix.

	B_3	B_4
A_3	4	0
A_4	0	8

Now we see that the game cannot be reduced any further. We can solve this resultant game by any of the mixed strategy methods mentioned above.

We solve it by the method of oddments.

	B_3	B_4	*oddments*
A_3	4	0	**8**
A_4	0	8	**4**
oddments	**8**	**4**	

The sum of the oddments is 12.

Probability of selection of the strategy = Corresponding oddment/Sum of oddments

The probability with which the player plays his strategy $A_3 = 8/(8 + 4) = 2/3$

The probability with which the player plays his strategy $A_4 = 4/12 = 1/3$

The probability with which the player plays his strategy $B_3 = 8/12 = 2/3$

The probability with which the player plays his strategy $B_4 = 4/12 = 1/3$

And the value of the game $= [(4 \times 8) + (0 \times 4)]/12 = 32/12 = 8/3$.

Thus, the optimal solution is A(0, 0, 2/3, 1/3), B(0, 0, 2/3, 1/3) and $V = 8/3$.

REVIEW EXERCISES

1. Find the range of values for p and q which will render the entry (2, 2) a saddle point in the game with the following pay-off matrix.

$$\begin{matrix} 1 & q & 3 \\ P & 5 & 10 \\ 6 & 2 & 3 \end{matrix}$$

[**Ans.** $p \geq 5, q \leq 5$]

2. Solve the following game using the dominance principle.

	a	b	c	d
p	3	2	4	0
q	3	4	2	4
r	4	2	4	0
s	0	4	0	8

[**Ans.** A's strategy (0, 0, 2/3, 1/3), B's strategy (0, 0, 2/3, 1/3), $V = 8/3$]

3. If the pay-off matrix for the first player in a game is

$$\begin{matrix} d & c & c \\ a & f & e \\ b & d & c \end{matrix}$$

such that $0 < a < b < c < d < e < f$, the vectors (x_1, x_2, x_3) and (y_1, y_2, y_3) are optimal strategies for the first and the second player and V is the value of the game then prove that

(i) $x_3 = y_2 = 0$

(ii) $x_1 > (1/2)$

(iii) $c < V < d$

4. Solve the game whose pay-off matrix is given by

$$\begin{matrix} 1 & 7 & 2 \\ 6 & 2 & 7 \\ 5 & 1 & 6 \end{matrix}$$

[**Ans.** A's strategy (2/5, 3/5, 0), B's strategy (1/2, 1/2, 0), $V = 4$]

5. A and B each take out one or two matches and guess how many matches the opponent has taken. If one of the players guesses correctly then the opponent has to pay him as many rupees as the sum of the number of matches had by both the players, otherwise the pay-out is zero. Write down the pay-off matrix and obtain the optimal strategies for both the players.

[**Ans.** 2 0
0 4; V = 4/3, A(2/3, 1/3), B(2/3, 1/3)]

6. Two players A and B, without showing each other, put on a table a coin with heads or tails up. If the coin shows the same side (both heads or both tails up), player A takes both the coins, otherwise B gets them. Construct the matrix of the game and solve it.

[**Ans.** 1 –1
–1 1; V = 4/3, A(1/2, 1/2), B(1/2, 1/2)]

7. In a game of matching coins with two players, suppose A wins one unit of value when there are two heads: wins nothing when there are two tails and loses 1/2 unit of value when there is one heads and one tails. Determine the pay-off matrix, the optimal strategies for both the players.

[**Ans.** 1 –(1/2)
–(1/2) 0, V = –(1/8), A(1/4, 3/4), B(1/4, 3/4)]

8. Consider the matching coins game. The matching player is paid Rs. 8 if the two coins are both heads and Re. 1 if both are tails. The non-matching player is paid Rs. 3 when coins do not match. Given the choice of being the matching or the non-matching player, which would you choose and what would be your strategy?

[**Ans.** 8 –3
–3 1, V = –(1/5) and the optimal strategy for each player is (4/15, 11/15).]

As the non-matching player is always expecting to gain by using optimal strategy, we would like to be the non-matching player.)

9. Solve the following games.

(a)

		Player B				
		I	II	III	IV	V
	I	4	0	1	7	–1
Player A	II	0	–3	–5	–7	5
	III	3	2	3	4	3
	IV	–6	1	–1	0	5
	V	0	0	6	0	0

[**Ans.** V = 2]

(b)

		Player B		
		I	II	III
	I	–2	15	–2
Player A	II	–5	–6	–4
	III	–5	20	–8

[**Ans.** V = –2, A: I, B: I or III]

(c)

		Player B		
		I	II	III
	I	2	–1	3
Player A	II	2	–1	2
	III	–1	0	0
	IV	2	0	4

[**Ans.** A: IV, B: II, $V = 0$]

(d)

		Player B				
		I	II	III	IV	V
	I	3	5	4	9	6
Player A	II	5	6	3	7	8
	III	8	7	9	8	7
	IV	4	2	8	5	3

[**Ans.** A: III, B: II, $V = 7$]

(e)

		Player B		
		I	II	III
	I	–5	–1	–1
Player A	II	4	0	2
	III	–5	2	0

[**Ans.** A(0, 7/11, 4/11), B(2/11, 9/11, 0), $V = 8/11$]

(f) Solve graphically: Pay-off matrix in favour of player A

		Player B				
		I	II	III	IV	V
	I	2	–1	5	–2	6
Player A	II	–2	4	–3	1	0

[**Ans.** A(3/7, 4/7), B(3/7, 0, 0, 4/7, 0), $V = -(2/7)$]

(g) Solve graphically: Pay-off matrix in favour of player A

		Player B	
		I	II
	I	2	5
Player A	II	3	1
	III	0	3

[**Ans.** A(2/5, 3/5), B(4/5, 1/5), $V = 13/15$]

(h) Solve graphically: Pay-off matrix in favour of player A

		Player B	
		I	II
	I	1	6
Player A	II	4	5
	III	5	3

[**Ans.** A(0, 2/3, 1/3), B(2/3, 1/3), $V = 13/3$]

(i)

		Player B			
		I	II	III	IV
	I	6	2	4	8
Player A	II	2	–1	1	12
	III	2	3	3	9
	IV	5	2	6	10

[**Ans.** A: (1/5, 0, 4/5, 0), B(1/5, 4/5, 0, 0), $V = 14/5$]

(j)

		Player B				
		I	II	III	IV	V
	I	2	5	10	7	2
Player A	II	3	3	6	6	4
	III	4	4	8	12	1

[**Ans.** A: (0, 3/4, 1/4), B(3/4, 0, 0, 0, 1/4), $V = 13/4$]

(k) Solve graphically: Pay-off matrix in favour of player A

		Player B	
		I	II
	I	1	3
Player A	II	3	1
	III	5	–1
	IV	6	–6

[**Ans.** A (3/4, 0, 1/4), B (1/2, 1/2), $V = 2$]

(l)

		Player B					
		I	II	III	IV	V	VI
	I	4	2	0	2	1	1
Player A	II	4	3	1	3	2	2
	III	4	3	7	–5	1	2
	IV	4	3	4	–1	2	2
	V	4	3	3	–2	2	3

[**Ans.** A (0, 6/7, 1/7, 0, 0), B(0, 0, 4/7, 3/7, 0, 0), $V = 13/7$]

10. Show that if the 2×2 game

$$\begin{matrix} a & a \\ c & d \end{matrix}$$

is strictly determined, i.e. if two elements in a row are equal, then the game has a saddle point, similarly for columns.

11. Show that if the 2×2 game

$$\begin{matrix} a & b \\ c & d \end{matrix}$$

is non strictly determined if either: $a < b$, $a < c$, $d < b$ and $d < c$ or $a > b$, $a > c$, $d > b$ and $d > c$.

12. If the pay-off matrix in a two person zero-sum game is skew-symmetric, then show that the value of the game is zero.

13. Show that a strictly determined game is fair if and only if there is a zero entry in its pay-off matrix such that all the entries in its row and column are non-negative and non-positive respectively.

14. A and B play a game as follows: They simultaneously and independently write one of three numbers 1, 2, 3. If the sum of the numbers written is even, B pays to A this sum in rupees. If it is odd, A pays the sum to B in rupees. Form the matrix of the game for A and solve it.

[**Ans.**

2	–3	4
–3	4	–5
4	–5	6

$V = 0$, A(1/4, 1/2, 1/4), B(1/4, 1/2, 1/4)]

15. The following matrix represents the pay-offs to player A in a rectangular game between two persons A and B.

		Player B			
		I	II	III	IV
	I	19	15	–5	–2
Player A	II	19	15	17	16
	III	0	20	15	5

By the notion of dominance, show that the game is equivalent to one represented by a 2 × 4 matrix which is a sub-matrix of the above. Then obtain a solution of the game graphically.

[**Ans.** A(0, 15/16, 1/16), B(0, 11/16, 0, 5/16), V = 245/16]

16. Solve the following games by formulating them as a LPP.

(a)

		Player B		
		I	II	III
	I	1	–1	3
Player A	II	3	5	–3
	III	6	2	–2

[**Ans.** A(2/3, 1/3, 0), B(0, 1/2, 1/2), V = 1]

(b)

		Player B		
		I	II	III
	I	6	0	3
Player A	II	8	–2	3
	III	4	6	5

[**Ans.** A(0, 1/6, 5/6), B(2/3, 1/3, 0) or B(1/3, 0, 2/3), V = 143/3]

(c)

		Player B		
		I	II	III
	I	1	–1	–1
Player A	II	–1	–1	3
	III	–1	2	–1

[**Ans.** A(6/13, 3/13, 4/13), B(6/13, 4/13, 3/13), $V = -(1/13)$]

(d)

		Player B		
		I	II	III
	I	2	3	–4
Player A	II	5	–2	6
	III	2	6	3

[**Ans.** A(0, 0.36, 0.64), B(0.728, 0.272, 0), $V = 3.09877$]

17. Players A and B play a game in which each player has three coins –20 paise, 25 paise and 50 paise. Each of them selects a coin without the knowledge of the other person. If the sum of the values of the coins is an even number, A wins B's coins. If that sum is an odd number, B wins A's coins.

(a) Develop a pay-off matrix with respect to player A.

(b) Find the optimal strategies for the players.

[**Ans.** A(5/9, 4/9, 0), B(1/2, 1/2, 0) and $V = 0$]

18. Prove that a symmetric game has the value zero and the two optimal strategies are identical.

19. Prove that if we add (or subtract) a fixed number M to (from) each element of the pay-off matrix, then the optimal strategies remain unchanged while the value of the game increases (or decreases) by M.

20. Prove that if we multiply the pay-off matrix by a fixed number M, then the optimal strategies remain unchanged while the value of the game becomes M times the value of the original game.

21. Consider the game "Two Finger Morra". Two players A and B both simultaneously show either one or two fingers. If the number of fingers of one coincides with the number of fingers of the other, then player A wins and gets 1 point from B. If they do not coincide, then B wins and takes 1 point from A. Construct the pay-off matrix and solve the game.

$$\left[\textbf{Ans.}\quad \begin{pmatrix} 1 & -1 \\ -1 & 1 \end{pmatrix}\right]$$

22. Player A has two ammunition stores, one of which is twice as valuable as the other. Player B is an attacker who can destroy an undefended store but he can only attack one of them. A knows that B is about to attack one of the stores but does not know which. What should he do? Note that A can successfully defend only one store at a time.

Appendix

Statistical Tables

Table A1 Values of e^x and e^{-x}

x	e^x	e^{-x}	x	e^x	e^{-x}
0.00	1.000	1.000	3.00	20.086	0.050
0.10	1.105	0.905	3.10	22.198	0.045
0.20	1.221	0.819	3.20	24.533	0.041
0.30	1.350	0.741	3.30	27.113	0.037
0.40	1.492	0.670	3.40	29.964	0.033
0.50	1.649	0.607	3.50	33.115	0.030
0.60	1.822	0.549	3.60	36.598	0.027
0.70	2.014	0.497	3.70	40.447	0.025
0.80	2.226	0.449	3.80	44.701	0.022
0.90	2.460	0.407	3.90	49.402	0.020
1.00	2.718	0.368	4.00	54.598	0.018
1.10	3.004	0.333	4.10	60.340	0.017
1.20	3.320	0.301	4.20	66.686	0.015
1.30	3.669	0.273	4.30	73.700	0.014
1.40	4.055	0.247	4.40	81.457	0.012
1.50	4.482	0.223	4.50	90.017	0.011
1.60	4.943	0.202	4.60	99.484	0.010
1.70	5.474	0.183	4.70	109.95	0.009
1.80	6.050	0.165	4.80	121.51	0.008
1.90	6.686	0.150	4.90	134.29	0.007
2.00	7.389	0.135	5.00	148.41	0.007
2.10	8.166	0.122	5.10	164.02	0.006
2.20	9.025	0.111	5.20	181.27	0.006
2.30	9.974	0.100	5.30	200.34	0.005
2.40	11.023	0.091	5.40	221.41	0.005
2.50	12.182	0.082	5.50	244.69	0.004
2.60	13.464	0.074	5.60	270.43	0.004
2.70	14.880	0.067	5.70	298.87	0.003
2.80	16.445	0.061	5.80	330.30	0.003
2.90	18.174	0.055	5.90	365.04	0.003
3.00	20.086	0.050	6.00	403.43	0.002

Table A2 Area under Standard Normal Curve

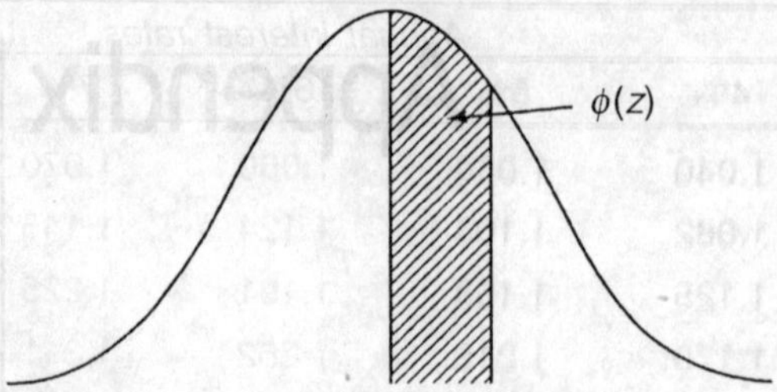

z	0.00	0.01	0.02	0.03	0.04	0.05	0.06	0.07	0.08	0.09
0.0	0.0000	0.0040	0.0080	0.0120	0.0160	0.0199	0.0239	0.0279	0.0319	0.0359
0.1	0.0398	0.0438	0.0478	0.0517	0.0557	0.0596	0.0636	0.0675	0.0714	0.0753
0.2	0.0793	0.0832	0.0871	0.0910	0.0948	0.0987	0.1026	0.1064	0.1103	0.1141
0.3	0.1179	0.1218	0.1255	0.1293	0.1331	0.1368	0.1406	0.1443	0.1480	0.1517
0.4	0.1554	0.1591	0.1628	0.1664	0.1700	0.1736	0.1772	0.1808	0.1844	0.1879
0.5	0.1915	0.1950	0.1985	0.2019	0.2054	0.2088	0.2123	0.2157	0.2190	0.2224
0.6	0.2257	0.2291	0.2324	0.2357	0.2389	0.2422	0.2454	0.2486	0.2517	0.2549
0.7	0.2580	0.2611	0.2642	0.2673	0.2703	0.2734	0.2764	0.2794	0.2823	0.2852
0.8	0.2881	0.2910	0.2939	0.2967	0.2995	0.3023	0.3051	0.3078	0.3106	0.3133
0.9	0.3159	0.3181	0.3212	0.3238	0.3264	0.3289	0.3315	0.3340	0.3365	0.3389
1.0	0.3413	0.3438	0.3461	0.3485	0.3508	0.3531	0.3554	0.3577	0.3599	0.3621
1.1	0.3643	0.3665	0.3686	0.3708	0.3729	0.3749	0.3770	0.3790	0.3810	0.3830
1.2	0.3849	0.3869	0.3888	0.3907	0.3925	0.3944	0.3962	0.3980	0.3997	0.4015
1.3	0.4032	0.4049	0.4066	0.4082	0.4099	0.4115	0.4131	0.4147	0.4162	0.4177
1.4	0.4192	0.4207	0.4222	0.4236	0.4251	0.4265	0.4279	0.4292	0.4306	0.4319
1.5	0.4332	0.4345	0.4357	0.4370	0.4302	0.4394	0.4406	0.4418	0.4429	0.4441
1.6	0.4452	0.4463	0.4474	0.4484	0.4405	0.4505	0.4515	0.4525	0.4535	0.4545
1.7	0.4554	0.4564	0.4573	0.4582	0.4591	0.4599	0.4608	0.4616	0.4625	0.4633
1.8	0.4641	0.4649	0.4656	0.4664	0.4671	0.4678	0.4686	0.4693	0.4699	0.4706
1.9	0.4713	0.4719	0.4726	0.4732	0.4738	0.4744	0.4750	0.4756	0.4761	0.4767
2.0	0.4772	0.4778	0.4783	0.4788	0.4793	0.4798	0.4803	0.4808	0.4812	0.4817
2.1	0.4821	0.4826	0.4830	0.4834	0.4838	0.4842	0.4846	0.4850	0.4852	0.4857
2.2	0.4861	0.4864	0.4868	0.4871	0.4875	0.4878	0.4881	0.4884	0.4887	0.4890
2.3	0.4893	0.4896	0.4898	0.4901	0.4904	0.4906	0.4909	0.4911	0.4913	0.4916
2.4	0.4918	0.4920	0.4922	0.4925	0.4927	0.4926	0.4931	0.4932	0.4934	0.4936
2.5	0.4938	0.4940	0.4941	0.4943	0.4945	0.4946	0.4948	0.4949	0.4951	0.4952
2.6	0.4953	0.4955	0.4956	0.4957	0.4959	0.4960	0.4961	0.4962	0.4963	0.4964
2.7	0.4965	0.4966	0.4967	0.4968	0.4969	0.4970	0.4971	0.4972	0.4973	0.4974
2.8	0.4974	0.4975	0.4976	0.4977	0.4977	0.4978	0.4979	0.4979	0.4980	0.4981
2.9	0.4981	0.4982	0.4982	0.4983	0.4984	0.4985	0.4985	0.4985	0.4986	0.4986
3.0	0.4987	0.4987	0.4987	0.4988	0.4988	0.4989	0.4989	0.4989	0.4990	0.4990

An entry in the table is the proportion under the entire curve which is between $z = 0$ and a positive value of z. Areas for negative values of z are obtained by symmetry:

$$P(z \leq 1.35) = 0.5 + \phi(1.35) = 0.5 + 0.4115 = 0.9115$$

$$P(z \leq -1.35) = 0.5 - \phi(1.35) = 0.5 - 0.4115 = 0.0885$$

Table A3 Single-payment Compound Amount Factor (CAF)

Number of years (n)	*Annual interest rates*						
	3%	4%	5%	6%	7%	8%	10%
1	1.030	1.040	1.050	1.060	1.070	1.080	1.100
2	1.061	1.082	1.103	1.124	1.145	1.166	1.210
3	1.093	1.125	1.158	1.191	1.225	1.260	1.331
4	1.126	1.170	1.216	1.262	1.311	1.360	1.464
5	1.159	1.216	1.276	1.338	1.403	1.469	1.661
6	1.194	1.265	1.340	1.419	1.501	1.587	1.774
7	1.230	1.316	1.407	1.504	1.606	1.714	1.949
8	1.267	1.369	1.477	1.594	1.718	1.858	2.144
9	1.305	1.423	1.551	1.689	1.838	1.999	2.358
10	1.344	1.480	1.629	1.791	1.967	2.159	2.694
11	1.384	1.539	1.710	1.898	2.105	2.332	2.853
12	1.426	1.601	1.796	2.012	2.252	2.518	3.138
13	1.469	1.665	1.886	2.133	2.410	2.720	3.452
14	1.513	1.732	1.980	2.261	2.579	2.937	3.797
15	1.558	1.801	2.079	2.397	2.759	3.172	4.177
16	1.605	1.874	2.183	2.540	2.952	3.426	4.595
17	1.653	1.948	2.292	2.693	3.159	3.700	5.054
18	1.702	2.026	2.407	2.854	3.380	3.996	5.500
19	1.754	2.107	2.527	3.026	3.617	4.316	6.116
20	1.806	2.191	2.653	3.207	3.870	4.661	6.727
21	1.860	2.279	2.786	3.400	4.141	5.034	7.400
22	1.916	2.370	2.925	3.604	4.430	5.437	8.140
23	1.974	2.465	3.072	3.820	4.741	5.871	8.594
24	2.033	2.563	3.225	4.049	5.072	6.341	9.850
25	2.094	2.666	3.386	4.292	5.427	6.348	10.835

Table A4 Single-payment Present Worth Factor (PWF)

Number of years (n)	*Annual interest rates*						
	3%	4%	5%	6%	7%	8%	10%
1	0.9709	0.9615	0.9524	0.9434	0.9346	0.9259	0.9090
2	0.9420	0.9246	0.9070	0.8900	0.8734	0.8573	0.8264
3	0.9151	0.8890	0.8638	0.8396	0.8163	0.7938	0.7513
4	0.8885	0.8548	0.8227	0.7921	0.7629	0.7350	0.6830
5	0.8626	0.8219	0.7835	0.7473	0.7130	0.6806	0.6209
6	0.8375	0.7903	0.7462	0.7050	0.6663	0.6302	0.5645
7	0.8131	0.7599	0.7107	0.6651	0.6227	0.5834	0.5132
8	0.7894	0.7307	0.6768	0.6274	0.5820	0.5403	0.4665
9	0.7664	0.7026	0.6446	0.5919	0.5439	0.5002	0.4241
10	0.7441	0.6756	0.6139	0.5584	0.5083	0.4632	0.3855
11	0.7224	0.6496	0.5847	0.5268	0.4751	0.4289	0.3505
12	0.7016	0.6246	0.5568	0.4970	0.4440	0.3971	0.3186
13	0.6810	0.6006	0.5303	0.4688	0.4149	0.3677	0.2897
14	0.6611	0.5775	0.5051	0.4423	0.3878	0.3405	0.2633
15	0.6419	0.5553	0.4810	0.4173	0.3624	0.3152	0.2394
16	0.6232	0.5339	0.4581	0.3936	0.3387	0.2919	0.2176
17	0.6050	0.5133	0.4363	0.3714	0.3166	0.2703	0.1978
18	0.5874	0.4936	0.4155	0.3503	0.2959	0.2502	0.1799
19	0.5703	0.4746	0.3957	0.3305	0.2765	0.2317	0.1635
20	0.5537	0.4564	0.3769	0.3118	0.2584	0.2145	0.1486
21	0.5375	0.4388	0.3589	0.2942	0.2515	0.1987	0.1351
22	0.5219	0.4220	0.3418	0.2775	0.2257	0.1839	0.1228
23	0.5067	0.4057	0.3256	0.2618	0.2109	0.1703	0.1117
24	0.4919	0.3901	0.3101	0.2470	0.1971	0.1577	0.1015
25	0.4776	0.3751	0.2953	0.2330	0.1842	0.1460	0.0923

Table A5 Random Numbers

27767	43584	85301	88977	29490	69714	64015	64874	32444	48277
13025	14338	54066	15243	47724	66733	74108	88222	88570	74015
80217	36292	98525	24335	24432	24896	62880	87873	95160	59221
10875	62004	93391	61105	67411	06368	11784	12102	80580	41867
54127	57326	26629	19087	24472	88779	17944	05600	60478	03343
60311	42824	37301	42678	45990	43242	66067	42792	95043	52680
49739	71484	92003	98086	76668	73209	54244	91030	45547	70818
78626	51584	16453	94614	39014	97066	30945	57589	31732	57260
66692	13986	99837	05582	81232	44987	69170	37403	86995	90307
44071	28091	07362	97703	76447	42537	08345	88975	35840	85771
59820	96163	78851	16499	87064	13075	73035	41207	74699	09310
25704	91035	26313	77463	5538	72681	47431	43905	31048	56699
23304	90314	78438	66276	18396	73538	43277	58874	11466	16082
25852	58905	55018	56374	35824	71708	30540	27886	61732	75454
46780	56487	75211	10271	36633	68424	17374	52003	70707	70214
69849	96169	87195	46092	26787	60939	59202	11973	02902	33250
47670	07654	30342	40277	11049	72049	83012	09832	25571	77628
94304	71803	73465	0981	58869	35220	09504	96412	90193	79568
09105	59987	21437	36786	49226	77837	98524	97831	65704	09514
64281	61826	18555	64937	64654	25843	41145	42820	14924	39650
66847	70495	32350	02985	01755	14750	48968	38603	70312	05682
72461	33230	21529	53424	72877	17334	39283	04149	09850	64618
21032	91050	13058	16218	06554	07850	73950	79552	24781	89683
95362	67011	06651	16136	57216	39618	49856	99326	40902	05069
49712	97380	10404	55452	09971	59481	37006	22186	72682	07385
58275	61764	97586	54716	61459	21647	87417	17198	21443	41080
89514	11788	68224	23417	46376	25366	94746	49580	01176	28838
15472	50669	48139	36732	26825	05511	12459	91314	80482	71944
12120	86124	51247	44302	87112	21476	14713	71181	13177	55292
95294	00556	70481	06905	21785	41101	49386	5440	23604	23554
66986	34099	74474	20740	47458	64809	06312	88940	15995	69321
80620	51790	11436	38072	40405	68032	60942	00307	11897	92674
55411	85667	77535	9992	71209	92061	92329	98932	78284	46347
95083	06783	28102	57816	85561	29671	77936	6374	31384	51924
90726	57166	98884	08583	95889	57067	38101	77756	11657	13897
68984	83620	89747	98882	92613	89719	39641	69457	91339	22502
36421	16489	18059	51061	67667	60631	8404	40455	99396	63680
92638	40333	67054	16067	24700	71594	47468	03577	57649	63266
21036	82808	77501	97427	76479	68562	43321	31370	28977	23896
13173	33365	41468	85149	49554	17994	91178	10174	29420	90438
86716	38746	94559	37559	49678	53119	98189	81851	29651	84215
92581	02262	41615	70360	64114	58660	96717	54244	10701	41393
12470	56500	50273	93113	41794	86861	39448	93136	25722	08564
01016	00857	41396	80504	90670	08289	58137	17829	22751	36518
30030	60726	25807	24260	71529	78920	47648	13885	70669	93406
50259	46345	06170	97965	88302	98041	11947	56203	19324	20504
73659	76145	60808	5444	74412	8105	69181	96845	38525	11600
46874	37088	80940	44893	10408	36222	14004	2313	69249	05747
60883	52109	19516	90120	46759	71643	62342	07589	08899	05895

Index